THE GREY ZONE

The high civilian death toll in modern, protracted conflicts such as those in Syria or Iraq indicates the limits of international law in offering protections to civilians at risk. A recent conference of states convened by the International Committee of the Red Cross referred to 'an institutional vacuum in the area of international humanitarian law implementation'. Yet both international humanitarian law and the law of human rights establish a series of rights intended to protect civilians. But which law or laws apply in a particular situation, and what are the obstacles to their implementation? How can the law offer greater protections to civilians caught up in new methods of warfare, such as drone strikes, or targeted by new forms of military organisation, such as transnational armed groups? Can the implementation gap be filled by the growing use of human rights courts to remedy violations of the laws of armed conflict, or are new instruments or mechanisms of civilian legal protection needed?

This volume brings together contributions from leading academic authorities and legal practitioners on the situation of civilians in the grey zone between human rights and the laws of war. The chapters in Part 1 address key contested or boundary issues in defining the rights of civilians or non-combatants in today's conflicts. Those in Part 2 examine remedies and current mechanisms for redress both at the international and national level, and those in Part 3 assess prospects for the development of new mechanisms for addressing violations. As military intervention to protect civilians remains contested, this volume looks at the potential for developing alternative approaches to the protection of civilians and their rights.

The Grey Zone

Civilian Protection Between Human Rights and the Laws of War

Edited by

Mark Lattimer and Philippe Sands

·HART·

OXFORD · LONDON · NEW YORK · NEW DELHI · SYDNEY

HART PUBLISHING

Bloomsbury Publishing Plc

Kemp House, Chawley Park, Cumnor Hill, Oxford, OX2 9PH, UK

HART PUBLISHING, the Hart/Stag logo, BLOOMSBURY and the Diana logo are
trademarks of Bloomsbury Publishing Plc

First published in Great Britain 2018

A catalogue record for this book is available from the British Library.

Library of Congress Cataloging-in-Publication data

Names: Lattimer, Mark, editor. | Sands, Philippe, 1960- editor.

Title: The grey zone : civilian protection between human rights and the laws of war /
edited by Mark Lattimer and Philippe Sands.

Description: Oxford [UK] ; New York, NY : Hart Publishing, [2018] |
Includes bibliographical references and index.

Identifiers: LCCN 2018010513 (print) | LCCN 2018012288 (ebook) |
ISBN 9781509908653 (Epub) | ISBN 9781509908639 (hardback : alk. paper)

Subjects: LCSH: War—Protection of civilians. | Combatants and noncombatants
(International law) | War (International law) | Civilians in war. |
Civilian war casualties. | War victims—Legal status, laws, etc. |
War victims—Civil rights. | Humanitarian law.

Classification: LCC KZ6515 (ebook) | LCC KZ6515 .G74 2018 (print) |
DDC 341.6/7—dc23

LC record available at https://lccn.loc.gov/2018010513

ISBN: HB: 978-1-50990-863-9
       ePDF: 978-1-50990-864-6
       ePub: 978-1-50990-865-3

Typeset by Compuscript Ltd, Shannon
Printed and bound in Great Britain by TJ International Ltd, Padstow, Cornwall

To find out more about our authors and books visit www.hartpublishing.co.uk.
Here you will find extracts, author information, details of forthcoming events
and the option to sign up for our newsletters.

Preface

The high and apparently growing civilian death toll in protracted contemporary conflicts reflects the limits on the ability of international rules, and the legal order of which they form a part, to protect civilians at risk. A recent conference of states convened by the International Committee of the Red Cross described 'an institutional vacuum in the area of international humanitarian law implementation'. Such understatement is coupled with the absence of political will—by states and international organisations—to act.

Since 1945 a body of international humanitarian and human rights laws has been adopted to establish a series of rights—for individuals and groups—that should, in theory at least, protect civilians. But which law or laws apply in a given situation, and what are the real obstacles to their implementation, their application and enforcement? How can the law assist civilians injured by new methods and means of warfare, such as drone strikes, or targeted by new forms of military organisation, such as transnational armed groups? Can the implementation gap be filled by the growing but sometimes controversial use of human rights courts to remedy violations committed in armed conflict, or by proposals for new instruments or mechanisms of civilian legal protection?

This volume brings together contributions from leading scholars and legal practitioners to assess the situation of civilians in the grey zone, under humanitarian law and human rights law, two areas that have emerged separately and are subject to their own communities of practice (the terms 'international humanitarian law' (IHL) and 'law of armed conflict' are used interchangeably in the volume, depending on the preference of the individual contributor or the relevant context). In Part I, each chapter considers a key contested or boundary issue in defining the rights of civilians or non-combatants in today's conflicts. Part II examines remedies and current mechanisms for redress both at the international and national level. Part III assesses the development of new or potential mechanisms for addressing violations.

The practical importance of these legal questions for the protection of civilians has been impressed on both of us over the years as we worked, separately, on many cases of atrocity, including in the former Yugoslavia, the Democratic Republic of Congo, and Iraq. We are grateful to the many colleagues with whom we have worked and shared ideas and whose names are too numerous to list here. Particular thanks go to Lorenza Cocco and

Déborah San Nicolás Del Amo for their excellent legal research assistance. At Hart Publishing we would like to thank Sinead Moloney and Emily Braggins. Thanks too to Piers Feltham, Ziyad Marar, Maggie Murphy and the trustees of the Ceasefire Centre for Civilian Rights.

The understanding of the inter-relationship between IHL and human rights law has advanced markedly in recent years, as reflected in the contributions to this book. It continues to be a swiftly-changing field, in response not just to developments in warfare and growing public concern at the erosion of basic humanitarian norms, but also to legal innovation as practitioners seek new avenues for obtaining effective redress and an end to mass impunity. We hope that this volume might offer a contribution to the potential for developing a more effective practice of civilian rights protection, and to the protection of the individuals and groups who constitute civilian populations.

Mark Lattimer
Philippe Sands
September 2017

Contents

Part III: Developments

List of Contributors

Bill Bowring is Professor of Law at Birkbeck College, University of London. He is also currently a Fellow of the Human Rights Centre at the University of Essex, a Senior Research Fellow at the Institute of Advanced Legal Studies, and a Visiting Professor at the University of Northampton. A practising barrister at Field Court Chambers, Gray's Inn, he has extensive professional practice representing applicants and appearing in the European Court of Human Rights, and he has published widely on international law, human rights, and the law of Russia and other former Soviet Union countries.

Stuart Casey-Maslen is Honorary Professor at the University of Pretoria, specialising in the use of force under international law. He holds a doctorate in the law of armed conflict, and master's degrees in international human rights law and forensic ballistics. He is co-author of *The Arms Trade Treaty: A Commentary* (Oxford, Oxford University Press, 2016) and editor of *Weapons under International Human Rights Law* (Cambridge, Cambridge University Press, 2014).

Christine Chinkin is Emeritus Professor of International Law and Director of the Centre on Women, Peace and Security at the London School of Economics and Political Science. She is a barrister and a member of Matrix Chambers, and William C Cook Global Law Professor at the University of Michigan Law School. She has held visiting appointments in Australia, the United States, Singapore and the People's Republic of China and was Scientific Advisor to the Council of Europe's Committee for the drafting of the Convention on Preventing and Combating Violence against Women and Domestic Violence.

Amichai Cohen is a Professor of International law at the Ono Academic College, Faculty of Law, Israel, and a Senior Fellow at the Israel Democracy Institute. He holds an LLB from the Hebrew University in Jerusalem, and an LLM and JSD from Yale Law School. His research focuses on international humanitarian law, Israeli national security law and the application of international law in Israeli law.

Emily Crawford is Senior Lecturer at the Sydney Law School at the University of Sydney, and an affiliate of the Sydney Centre for International Law. She is the author of *The Treatment of Combatants and Insurgents under the Law of Armed Conflict* (Oxford, Oxford University Press, 2010), *Identifying the Enemy: Civilian Participation in Armed Conflict* (Oxford, Oxford University Press, 2015) and co-author of *International Humanitarian Law* (Cambridge, Cambridge University Press, 2015).

Carla Ferstman is the Director of REDRESS, a human rights organisation that helps torture survivors obtain justice and reparation. Formerly, she has practised as a criminal law barrister in Canada, has worked with the UN High Commissioner for Human Rights in post-genocide Rwanda, with Amnesty International as a legal researcher on trials in Central Africa and as Executive Legal Advisor to Bosnia and Herzegovina's Commission for Real Property Claims of Displaced Persons and Refugees (CRPC).

Gloria Gaggioli is Assistant Professor and Grant Holder of Excellence at the University of Geneva as well as Lecturer at the Geneva Academy of International Humanitarian Law and Human Rights and at the University of Neuchâtel (Switzerland). She formerly worked as Legal Adviser at the International Committee of the Red Cross (Legal Division, Geneva). She has researched and/or taught in several universities in Denmark, Sweden, France and the United States.

Blinne Ní Ghrálaigh is a barrister at Matrix Chambers in London, where she specialises in international law, human rights and public law. She advises and represents states, non-governmental organisations, and other bodies and individuals before domestic, regional and international courts and tribunals. Her chapter in this volume was drafted during the course of her Visiting Fellowship at Harvard Law School's Human Rights Programme.

Françoise Hampson is Emeritus Professor of Law at the University of Essex. She was an independent expert member of the UN Sub-Commission on the Promotion and Protection of Human Rights from 1998 to 2007, is a member of the UN Commission of Inquiry on Burundi, and has successfully litigated many cases before the European Court of Human Rights in Strasbourg. She has acted as a consultant on humanitarian law to the International Committee of the Red Cross and taught at Staff Colleges or equivalents in the United Kingdom, the United States, Canada and Ghana.

Pavle Kilibarda is a PhD candidate at the Faculty of Law of the University of Geneva and a teaching assistant at the Geneva Academy of International Humanitarian Law and Human Rights. He has formerly worked as a legal training associate for the International Committee of the Red Cross, as well as a researcher at the Belgrade Centre for Human Rights. He has written in the areas of public international law, refugee and human rights law.

Mark Lattimer is Executive Director of the Ceasefire Centre for Civilian Rights. Formerly with Amnesty International, he has also been since 2001 Executive Director of Minority Rights Group International, where he established a strategic litigation programme that has won leading cases before the European Court of Human Rights and the African Court of Human and Peoples' Rights. His previous books include (also with Philippe Sands) *Justice for Crimes Against Humanity* (Oxford, Hart Publishing, 2003).

Carrie McDougall PhD is the Legal Adviser at Australia's Permanent Mission to the United Nations in New York. Previously she served as Assistant Director of the International Law Section of the Australian Department of Foreign Affairs and Trade and before this was a lecturer and research fellow at Melbourne Law School. She is the author of *The Crime of Aggression under the Rome Statute of the International Criminal Court* (Cambridge, Cambridge University Press, 2013).

Lois Moore practised for many years as a lawyer in Freshfields Brockhaus Derringer and Shearman & Sterling. She has an LLM in human rights law from the London School of Economics, specialising in the topic of sexual violence in armed conflict, and from 2015 to 2016 was a Visiting Fellow in the Centre for Women, Peace and Security.

Cedric Ryngaert (PhD Leuven University 2007) is Professor of Public International Law at Utrecht University. Among other publications, he authored *Jurisdiction in International Law* (2nd edn, Oxford, Oxford University Press, 2015), and *Unilateral Jurisdiction and Global Values* (The Hague, Eleven, 2015), coauthored *International Law from a European Perspective* (London, Bloomsbury, 2018), and coedited *The International Prosecutor* (Oxford, Oxford University Press, 2012), and *Judicial Decisions of the Law of International Organizations* (Oxford, Oxford University Press, 2016).

Leila Nadya Sadat is James Carr Professor of International Criminal Law at Washington University School of Law and Director of the Whitney R Harris World Law Institute. She is also Special Adviser on Crimes Against Humanity to the Prosecutor of the International Criminal Court. In 2008, Sadat launched the Crimes Against Humanity Initiative, an international effort to study the problem of crimes against humanity and draft a global treaty addressing their punishment and prevention. She has published more than 100 books, articles and essays in leading journals, academic presses and media outlets throughout the world, including (as editor) *Forging a Convention for Crimes Against Humanity* (2nd edn, Cambridge, Cambridge Cambridge University Press, 2013).

Philippe Sands QC is Professor of Law at University College London, Director of the Centre on International Courts and Tribunals and a practising barrister at Matrix Chambers. He is a regular commentator on the BBC and CNN, writes frequently for leading newspapers, and has extensive experience litigating cases before the International Court of Justice, the International Tribunal for the Law of the Sea, the International Center for the Settlement of Investment Disputes, and the European Court of Justice. His books include *Lawless World* (London, Allen Lane, 2006) and *Torture Team* (London, Allen Lane, 2008). His latest book *East West Street: On the Origins of Genocide and Crimes Against Humanity* (London, Weidenfeld & Nicolson, 2016) won the Baillie Gifford Prize for Non-Fiction.

François Voeffray was until 2016 Ambassador-at-Large for International Humanitarian Law at the Swiss Federal Department of Foreign Affairs. He is currently Minister and Deputy Head of the Embassy of Switzerland to the United Kingdom. His book *L'actio popularis ou la défense de l'intérêt collectif devant les juridictions internationales* (Geneva, Graduate Institute, 2004) was awarded the Prix Paul Guggenheim in 2004.

Sharon Weill PhD is a senior lecturer and associate researcher at Sciences-Po Paris. Since 2017 she is member of the French National Consultative Commission on Human Rights (CNCRDH) and is currently conducting empirical research on criminal trials of foreign fighters in French courts for the French Ministry of Justice. She is the author of *The Role of National Courts in Applying International Humanitarian Law* (Oxford, Oxford University Press, 2014) and coeditor (with K Carston and K Seelinger) of *The Hissene Habré Trial—New Model for Prosecuting International Crimes?* (Oxford University Press, forthcoming).

Jennifer M Welsh is Professor and Chair in International Relations at the European University Institute and a Senior Research Fellow at Somerville College, University of Oxford. She was previously a Professor in International Relations at the University of Oxford, and co-director of the Oxford Institute for Ethics, Law and Armed Conflict. Between 2013 and 2016 she served as UN Special Adviser to the Secretary-General on the Responsibility to Protect. Her recent publications include *The Responsibility to Prevent: Overcoming the Challenges of Atrocity Prevention* (coedited with Serena K Sharma) (Oxford, Oxford University Press, 2015).

Liesbeth Zegveld is head of the international law and human rights department at Prakken d'Oliviera human rights lawyers in the Netherlands, and Professor of War Reparations and Director of the War Reparations Centre at the University of Amsterdam. Specialising in liability for human rights violations, she has worked on numerous high-profile cases focusing on the victims of war. In 2011 she set up the Nuhanović Foundation, aimed at facilitating access to justice for war victims. In the same year she received the Clara Meijer-Wichmann medal in recognition of her commitment to defending human rights and in 2016 she was voted 'Most Valued Lawyer' of the year in the Netherlands.

Valentin Zellweger is Permanent Representative of Switzerland to the United Nations and other international organisations in Geneva. Until 2016 he was the Legal Adviser and Director of the Directorate of International Law at the Swiss Federal Department of Foreign Affairs. From 2003 to 2007 he was the head of office of the first serving president of the International Criminal Court.

Table of Cases

European Court of Human Rights

Inter-American Court of Human Rights

International Criminal Court

International Court of Justice

International Criminal Tribunal for Rwanda

International Criminal Tribunal for the former Yugoslavia

Permanent Court of International Justice

Special Court for Sierra Leone

UN Human Rights Committee

UN Committee on the Elimination of Discrimination against Women

UN Committee Against Torture

National Courts

Australia

Belgium

Bosnia-Herzegovina

Canada

Chile

Democratic Republic of Congo

Table of Treaties and Other International Acts

Abbreviations

ACHPR	African Charter on Human and Peoples' Rights
ACHR	American Convention on Human Rights
AP	Additional Protocol to the Geneva Convention
ARS	Articles on the Responsibility of States
ASP	Assembly of States Parties
ATT	Arms Trade Treaty
CAT	Convention against Torture
CCF	continuous combat function
CRC	Convention on the Rights of the Child
DARIO	Draft Articles on the Responsibility of International Organisations
DPH	direct participation in hostilities
ECHR	European Convention on Human Rights
ECtHR	European Court of Human Rights
GC	Geneva Convention
HRC	Human Rights Committee
HRL	human rights law
IAC	international armed conflict
ICC	International Criminal Court
ICCPR	International Covenant on Civil and Political Rights
ICESCR	International Covenant on Economic, Social and Cultural Rights
ICJ	International Court of Justice
ICL	international criminal law
ICRC	International Committee of the Red Cross
ICTR	International Criminal Tribunal for Rwanda
ICTY	International Criminal Tribunal for the former Yugoslavia
IDF	Israeli Defense Forces
IHL	international humanitarian law
IHRL	international human rights law
ILC	International Law Commission
LOAC	law of armed conflict
NIAC	non-international armed conflict
NSAG	non-state armed group
POW	prisoner of war
R2P	Responsibility to Protect
SWGCA	Special Working Group on the Crime of Aggression

UNCAT	United Nations Convention against Torture and Other Cruel, Inhuman or Degrading Treatment or Punishment
UNCED	United Nations Convention on Enforced Disappearances
UNCLOS	UN Convention on the Law of the Sea
UNMO	Military Observer for the United Nations
VCLT	Vienna Convention on the Law of Treaties

Introduction

MARK LATTIMER

T HE INTERNATIONAL LAW of armed conflict developed over centuries primarily to regulate the conduct of war between polities or states; the law of human rights was developed mainly to place limits on how a given state could treat its own population. The contemporary face of war, however, is dominated by non-international armed conflicts (NIACs) fought between government forces and armed opposition groups—albeit often with extensive foreign support for either side—in a context where the national government is unable or unwilling to protect its own population. What happens to the civilian population caught in this grey zone between the traditional fields of application of human rights and the laws of war?

There is a rapidly growing number of cases where international courts and treaty-monitoring bodies are considering rules of the law of armed conflict or international humanitarian law (IHL)[1] side by side with rules of international human rights law (IHRL).[2] The assumption is that state obligations under both sets of laws may apply concurrently. In addition, there is increased acceptance that human rights obligations may also be held by non-state actors including, in the case of armed conflict, by armed opposition groups and by peacekeeping forces and officials of international and regional organisations.[3]

After 2001 these developments were further driven by the burgeoning jurisprudence in reaction to the policies and practices of the United States and its allies in the so-called 'War on Terror'—including the targeted killing

---

[1] The terms 'law of armed conflict' and 'international humanitarian law' (IHL) are used interchangeably in this volume to denote the *jus in bello*, the law governing the conduct of hostilities and the protection of civilians and those no longer participating in hostilities. IHL does not govern the recourse to war (*jus ad bellum*), which is considered in chapter 16.

[2] Classic instances include International Court of Justice: *Legality of the Threat or Use of Nuclear Weapons* (Advisory Opinion) [1996] ICJ Rep 226; *Legal Consequences of the Construction of a Wall in the Occupied Palestinian Territory* (Advisory Opinion) [2004] ICJ Rep 136; *Armed Activities on the Territory of the Congo (Democratic Republic of the Congo v Uganda)* [2005] ICJ Rep 168; and *Bamaca Velásquez v Guatemala* (Judgment) Inter-American Court of Human Rights Series C No 70 (25 November 2000). See below for illustrative cases before the European Court of Human Rights. See also United Nations Convention on the Rights of the Child (adopted 20 November 1989, entered into force 2 September 1990) 1577 UNTS 3 (CRC) Art 38.

[3] For a summary, see A Clapham, *Human Rights Obligations of Non-State Actors* (Oxford, Oxford University Press, 2006) 271–317.

of presumed terrorists and the indefinite detention of foreign fighters. But they also reflect broader developments in warfare. With the decline in the number and intensity of inter-state conflicts, intra-state or civil conflicts now present the predominant face of modern war. The shift of legal focus from inter-state relations to the domestic sphere has moved the conduct of war onto a terrain that is at once the traditional domain of the law of human rights and one where the rules of IHL have historically been less elaborated and the obligations less certain. At the same time, human rights campaigners confronted by states of emergency where the capacity or will of the state to ensure respect for human rights is lacking may look to applicable IHL rules to secure fundamental protections.

But in any given situation, which body of law will apply? If both are applicable, which set of rules holds precedence? Are there gaps in protection, where neither human rights law nor IHL appear to apply, or where states or other parties to conflict attempt to avoid obligations by looking for the least onerous law? In seeking answers to these questions this volume will focus on the effective protections, including legal remedies, available to the individual victim of violations. But it will also consider whether, despite the existence of overlapping bodies of law, structural obstacles exist which impede the development of an effective system of civilian rights protection in situations of armed conflict.

I. SCOPE OF APPLICATION

IHRL and IHL have developed separately, with their own sources in both customary and conventional international law. (A description of their evolution is outside the scope of this introduction, but it should be noted that the law of armed conflict is far older, dating back 2,500 years to Sun Tzu's *Art of War*.) Until the 1970s it was widely considered that IHRL and IHL were, if not mutually exclusive, then separate for practical purposes in that they generally applied to different subjects at different times.[4] IHL is now codified in the four 1949 Geneva Conventions and their 1977 Additional Protocols[5] as well as other multilateral instruments, providing binding

---

[4] See eg K Suter, 'An Enquiry Into the Meaning of the Phrase "Human Rights in Armed Conflicts"' (1976) 15 *Revue de Droit Penal Militaire et de Droit de la Guerre* 393.

[5] Geneva Convention I for the Amelioration of the Condition of the Wounded and Sick in Armed Forces in the Field (adopted 12 August 1949, entered into force 21 October 1950) 75 UNTS 31 (GC I); Geneva Convention II for the Amelioration of the Condition of Wounded, Sick and Shipwrecked Members of Armed Forces at Sea (adopted 12 August 1949, entered into force 21 October 1950) 75 UNTS 85 (GC II); Geneva Convention III Relative to the Treatment of Prisoners of War (adopted 12 August 1949, entered into force 21 October 1950) 75 UNTS 135 (GCIII); Geneva Convention IV Relative to the Protection of Civilian Persons in Time of War (adopted 12 August 1949, entered into force 21 October 1950) 75 UNTS 287 (GC IV);

standards for the treatment of prisoners-of-war, the wounded, sick and others placed *hors de combat* as well as civilian populations in both international armed conflicts (IACs) and, in more limited respects, in NIACs. IHL does not apply outside of situations of armed conflict or occupation. On the other hand, human rights law, as laid out in numerous UN-sponsored treaties that followed on from the 1948 Universal Declaration of Human Rights, provides standards for protecting the rights of a state's own population and others within its jurisdiction, primarily in peacetime. An inner core of non-derogable rights does continue to apply in time of armed conflict, but at no time does the state owe human rights obligations to those outside its jurisdiction.

In practice, however, the situation is significantly more complex than that suggested above. A considerable literature already exists on the extraterritorial application of human rights in armed conflict situations,[6] but this is hardly the only area of contention in the mutual scope of application of IHRL and IHL. A more systematic listing of some of the main grey areas might attempt to cover questions not just over the territorial scope of application of the relevant branch of law, but also the personal and material scope of application. Questions regarding the territorial scope of application should include the application of human rights to territories/persons under effective control, and the application of human rights law and/or law of NIAC to cross-border rebels ('exported' civil conflicts) or to transnational armed groups. Regarding the personal scope of application, there arise questions over the extent of the obligations under IHL and human rights law of armed opposition groups, including national rebel groups, transnational armed groups, and peoples seeking self-determination; of third party states or foreign sponsors involved in a NIAC; and of peacekeeping forces and international or regional organisations. Finally, there are further questions regarding the threshold of violence triggering application of IHL and/or application of derogation powers under IHRL, and regarding the effect on IHL/human rights obligations of the qualification of conflicts as international or non-international, and the 'internationalisation' of internal conflicts through the involvement of foreign states.

Protocol I Additional to the Geneva Conventions of 12 August 1949 and relating to the Protection of Victims of International Armed Conflicts (adopted 8 June 1977, entered into force 7 December 1978) 1125 UNTS 3 (Protocol I or AP I); Protocol II Additional to the Geneva Conventions of 12 August 1949 and relating to the Protection of Victims of Non-International Armed Conflicts (adopted 8 June 1977, entered into force 7 December 1978) 1125 UNTS 609 (Protocol II or AP II).

[6] This is the only applicability issue covered in any detail in the UN Sub-Commission's working paper on the relationship between IHRL and IHL; F Hampson and I Salama, 'Working Paper on the Relationship Between Human Rights Law and International Humanitarian Law' (21 June 2005) UN Doc E/CN.4/Sub.2/2005/14. See also M Milanovic, *Extraterritorial Application of Human Rights Treaties* (Oxford, Oxford University Press, 2011).

This is hardly an exhaustive list. A number of issues are grey areas in one body of law which have been commented on, sometimes extensively, by scholars in the relevant discipline, but where the implications for the mutual application of both disciplines are yet to be fully explored. For example, the application of the Geneva Conventions is only triggered once armed violence has reached a certain level of intensity and organisation, beyond 'internal disturbances' and 'sporadic acts of violence'.[7] But what is the relationship of either the violence threshold in common Article 3, or the higher threshold in Additional Protocol II, to provisions in human rights treaties which empower states to derogate from certain of their obligations in times of public emergency? The advantages of linking the thresholds and ensuring a continuity of some form of protection across the two branches of law should be obvious. In practice, however, states are generally reluctant to acknowledge the existence of an armed conflict on their territory (partly to avoid appearing to confer any form of legitimacy on rebel fighters), whereas they are often much quicker to invoke emergency powers.

All the issues listed above remain controversial. For example, while a number of states, including the USA,[8] reject the extra-territorial applicability of human rights, the European Court of Human Rights (ECtHR) has recognised its extra-territorial application in situations of occupation or 'effective control' over territory,[9] where persons are detained,[10] and where a level of control is combined with exercise of public powers,[11] although not in a case of aerial bombing.[12] The Inter-American Commission on Human Rights, on the other hand, has recognised an extra-territorial claim from the victims of aerial bombing even before effective control was established on the ground.[13]

II. RELATIONSHIP BETWEEN NORMS

Although they were designed to deal with very different situations, the core of IHRL and IHL both tend towards the same aim: protection of the fundamental integrity of the human person. To what extent, then, does it matter

---

[7] AP II, Art 1(2).

[8] See eg 'USA, Follow-Up Response to the Human Rights Committee by State Party' (2008) UN Doc CCPR/C/USA/CO/3/Rev.1/Add.1, 2–3.

[9] eg *Loizidou and Cyprus (intervening) v Turkey* (1997) 23 EHRR 513.

[10] eg *Issa and ors v Turkey* (2004) 41 EHRR 567; *Öcalan v Turkey* (App no 46221/99) ECHR 12 May 2005; *Al-Jedda v the United Kingdom* (App no 27021/08) ECHR 7 July 2011.

[11] *Al-Skeini and ors, Bar Human Rights Committee (intervening) and ors (intervening) v United Kingdom* (2011) 53 EHRR 18.

[12] *Banković and ors v Belgium and ors* (2007) 44 EHRR SE5.

[13] *Disabled Peoples' International v USA* (1987) Inter-American Commission on Human Rights Case No 9213.

which of the two applies to a particular situation, or that in an increasing number of situations both branches of law are recognised to apply?

For example, the Geneva Conventions' common Article 3, often described as a treaty in miniature, establishes minimum standards in non-international conflicts for the treatment of 'persons taking no active part in the hostilities', including the prohibition of violence to life and person, the prohibition of torture and cruel treatment, the prohibition of hostage-taking, the prohibition of discrimination, and fair trial guarantees. The list is similar to that provided in most human rights instruments for those personal integrity rights that cannot be derogated from in a state of emergency.

Marco Sassòli and Laura Olson thus conclude that where there is overlap between IHL and IHRL, 'both branches mostly lead to the same results'.[14] They go on, however, to draw attention to two crucial questions where 'not only is the relationship between the two branches unclear, but also the answer of humanitarian law alone': admissible killing and the internment of fighters.[15] Sassoli and Olson's focus is on non-international conflicts, where practical problems are most likely to arise, but consideration of these two issues generally in IHRL and IHL shows not just a lack of clarity but the existence of a conflict in the application of norms.

Although in human rights law the right to life is not absolute, the use of deadly force by law enforcement officers is strictly circumscribed. The force used must be 'no more than absolutely necessary', it must be directed towards a legitimate aim such as to defend others from unlawful violence or to effect a lawful arrest, and it must be proportionate to that aim.[16] In contrast, 'the starting point of ... IHL is the soldier's right to kill'.[17] Whereas human rights standards generally require a clear warning to be given of the intention to use firearms,[18] it is perfectly legal under IHL for combatants to be bombed in their beds.

If we compare the human rights standards governing detention of criminal suspects with the security detention of combatants in IAC, the differences in approach are similarly stark. Under IHRL the detention of suspects needs to be subject to judicial review and any sentence of imprisonment imposed by a properly constituted court. Under IHL prisoners of war can be

---

[14] M Sassòli and LM Olson, 'The Relationship Between International Humanitarian Law and Human Rights Law Where It Matters: Admissible Killing and Internment of Fighters in Non-International Armed Conflicts' (2008) 90 *International Review of the Red Cross* 871, 600.

[15] ibid, 601.

[16] European Convention for the Protection of Human Rights and Fundamental Freedoms (as amended by Protocols Nos 11 and 14, 4 November 1950) ETS 5 (ECHR), Art 2(2).

[17] Hampson and Salama (n 6) 13.

[18] United Nations Basic Principles on the Use of Force and Firearms by Law Enforcement Officials (adopted by the Eighth UN Congress on the Prevention of Crime and the Treatment of Offenders, Havana, Cuba, 27 August–7 September 1990) para 10.

interned indefinitely (ie without recourse to a judge), but need to be released (and repatriated) without delay once active hostilities have ceased.[19]

In fact, admissible killing and the detention of suspects/fighters are such central questions for both IHL and IHRL that the differences in approach give rise to a whole set of further spiralling issues. In NIACs, should members of rebel armed groups benefit from human rights protections limiting killing when they are not actively or directly participating in hostilities?[20] If rebel fighters in non-international conflicts are subject to attack under IHL rules, should civilians in their vicinity also be protected under IHL rules prohibiting indiscriminate or disproportionate attacks or under IHRL rules governing the proportionate use of force? (ie which proportionality test is applicable?) Should every killing involving the use of force by state agents warrant an investigation (as required by IHRL) or only where a possible IHL violation has occurred?

To decide which body of law should be determinative when both are in play, the International Court of Justice (ICJ) has referred to the doctrine of *lex specialis*, first in the *Nuclear Weapons* Advisory Opinion and then in the *Wall* Advisory Opinion, where it stated that: '[T]he Court will have to take into consideration both these branches of international law, namely human rights law and, as *lex specialis*, international humanitarian law.'[21]

The maxim *lex specialis derogat legi generali* provides that a more specialised law, specifically addressing the subject matter at hand, takes precedence over more general laws. Exactly how the ICJ intended this maxim to apply was not explained in the judgments and has been the subject of some scholarly debate. It is clear from the context, however, that the ICJ did not envisage IHL, as the *lex specialis*, displacing IHRL as a whole during armed conflict. Rather it suggests that the general rules of human rights, applicable at all times, would need to be interpreted at times of armed conflict in light of the more specialised rules of IHL specific to that context. The prohibition on arbitrary killing under IHRL, for example, would continue to apply, but the assessment of what was meant by 'arbitrary' in the context of armed conflict would be interpreted in the light of IHL principles on distinction, military necessity and proportionality.

---

[19] GCIII, Arts 118–19.

[20] For the notion of direct participation in hostilities, see N Melzer, 'Interpretive Guidance on the Notion of Direct Participation in Hostilities under International Humanitarian Law' (2008) 90 *International Review of the Red Cross* 991. But see also K Watkin, 'Opportunity Lost: Organized Armed Groups and the ICRC "Direct Participation in Hostilities" Interpretive Guidance' (2010) 42 *New York University Journal of International Law and Politics* 3.

[21] *Legal Consequences of the Construction of a Wall in the Occupied Palestinian Territory* (n 2) para 106.

UN human rights bodies, for their part, have noted the application of *lex specialis* while seeking to emphasise 'that human rights and humanitarian law are complementary and mutually reinforcing'.[22] Both IHRL and IHL practitioners have subsequently promoted a range of approaches which seek to articulate both branches on a case-by-case or rule-by-rule basis, filling perceived gaps or resolving uncertainties in one branch by recourse to a more detailed or specialised rule in the other branch. Crucially this appears to recognise that, in some cases, human rights law may constitute the *lex specialis*. Thus Louise Doswald-Beck (giving the human right to life as an example):

> [W]here there is any kind of doubt, or where the [IHL] rules are too general to provide all the answers, then human rights law will fill the gap, provided that this law is not incompatible with the overall fundamental aim and purpose of IHL.[23]

In her view, 'any law needs to be interpreted in the light of the aim and purpose of that law'.[24] Sassòli and Olson similarly remark that 'when formal standards do not indicate a clear result, the teleological criterion must weigh in, even though it allows for personal preferences'.[25]

Although such approaches may be attractive from a humanitarian point of view, they nonetheless give rise to problems of consistency, not least because other parties' views of the aims and purposes of international law may differ. Why, for example, should human rights advocates be able to pick and choose from provisions of IHL and IHRL, when they criticise the USA for its own selective or hybrid approach in targeting foreign fighters/terrorists and detaining them in Guantánamo without according them the corresponding protections under international law?

But perhaps the more fundamental problem arises from the fact that IHL in particular depends for its implementation on the need to provide combatants in advance with clear instructions as to what is and is not permissible. Any approach which depends on the post-hoc interpretation of complex and overlapping bodies of law by international lawyers may be workable for controlling violations caused by decisions of administrative bodies, but is unlikely to result in clear rules of engagement for combatants that will withstand the stress of battle.

---

[22] UN Commission on Human Rights Res 2005/63 (20 April 2005) UN Doc E/CN.4/RES/2005/63. See also UN Human Rights Committee, 'General Comment 31: Nature of the General Legal Obligation on States Parties to the Covenant'(26 May 2004) UN Doc CCPR/C/21/Rev.1/Add.13, para 11.

[23] L Doswald-Beck, 'The Right to Life in Armed Conflict: Does International Humanitarian Law Provide All the Answers?' (2006) 864 *International Review of the Red Cross*, 903.

[24] ibid.

[25] Sassòli and Olson (n 14) 604.

III. IMPLEMENTATION AND AVAILABILITY OF REMEDIES

It has become commonplace to remark on the relative weakness of the enforcement regime for IHL compared to IHRL (although such statements sometimes overestimate the effectiveness of the latter). But it is important to recognise that the system of implementation or enforcement of each is very different.

Human rights law is mainly implemented through civil law (including public law) remedies at the national level, overseen by a range of international intergovernmental mechanisms, including human rights courts and monitoring bodies. IHL is also designed to be implemented mainly at the national level, but through the criminal law, whether courts martial or the ordinary criminal law of the state concerned. But here, as Timothy McCormack points out, 'the disparity between perpetration and prosecution is staggering'.[26] Even leaving aside technical questions such as the higher burden of proof in criminal cases and, in IACs, the extra-territorial collection of evidence, states have shown a great reluctance to prosecute members of their own armed forces.

In practice, then, where IHL binds it has mostly been through self-restraint. Adherence to IHL is clearly encouraged by the international law principle of reciprocity, but does not depend on it.[27] (Note in addition that, under the four Geneva Conventions and Additional Protocol I, most forms of belligerent reprisal are now outlawed.)

The most significant international contribution to the enforcement of IHL in recent decades has been the establishment of international criminal tribunals. International criminal law draws on both IHL and IHRL, with some particular sources of its own, including the London Charter of the International Military Tribunal at Nuremberg.[28] The detailed codification of war crimes in non-international conflicts, describing conduct which if carried out by government forces would also constitute gross human rights violations, has gone some way to addressing the problems noted above.[29] The Rome Statute of the International Criminal Court (ICC) also introduced a number of important innovations with regard to victims' rights. Victims of crimes cannot refer a matter directly to the Court, but they and/ or NGOs can communicate information to the Prosecutor who can initiate

---

[26] T McCormack, 'Their Atrocities and Our Misdemeanours: the Reticence of States to Try their Own Nationals for International Crimes' in M Lattimer and P Sands (eds), *Justice for Crimes Against Humanity* (Oxford, Hart Publishing, 2003) 108.

[27] *Legal Consequences for States of the Continued Presence of South Africa in Namibia (South West Africa) notwithstanding Security Resolution 276 (1970)* (Advisory Opinion) [1971] ICJ Rep 16, para 231.

[28] For a summary, see Lattimer and Sands (n 26) 3–5.

[29] See Rome Statute of the International Criminal Court (adopted 17 July 1998, entered into force 1 July 2002) UN Doc A/CONF 183/9 (ICC Statute), Art 8(c)–(e).

an investigation on the basis of information received.[30] Victims can also be represented at trials and have the right to seek reparations. But it is perhaps still too early to assess the impact of international criminal justice, and the length and expense of international trials mean that only a small number of cases will ever be heard at the ICC.

Meanwhile, the wider availability of IHRL mechanisms at both UN and regional level and the growth of rights of individual petition have led to an expansion of human rights approaches and remedies in armed conflict situations. Of particular note are the large number of cases, including those dealing with conflicts in Chechnya, Turkey and Iraq, decided by the ECtHR. The Court does not directly apply IHL but rather has developed an approach to applying the law of the European Convention on Human Rights to armed conflict situations that in respect of civilians is not inconsistent with IHL.[31]

In terms of the mutual implementation of IHL and IHRL, then, one could describe a similar effect to that which we saw in terms of norms above, with a gap or vacuum in one branch drawing in remedies from the other branch. Two further initiatives should be mentioned in this context. In a major study the International Committee of the Red Cross identified at least 136 rules of customary humanitarian law that applied to NIAC. In many cases the state practice cited showed states applying rules of international conflict to civil conflicts by analogy, although notably decisions of human rights bodies were also cited.[32]

The other initiative is the process to draw up a UN declaration of 'fundamental standards of humanity'. This arose out of the 1990 Turku Declaration on Minimum Humanitarian Standards, itself an attempt to address the perceived gap in protection identified above in situations of 'internal disturbances' or low-intensity violence.[33] But the UN process has stalled, meeting both a lukewarm response from states and a distinct lack of enthusiasm from human rights campaigners and IHL practitioners, who variously feared the watering down of existing standards or compromising the separate integrity of IHL and IHRL, with their distinct aims.[34]

The argument could be made that even to speak of *gaps* in protection is potentially dangerous, because it can lead states to believe that certain constraints on their action do not exist, when in fact such constraints could

---

[30] ibid, Art 15.

[31] See eg *Isayeva v Russia* (App no 57950/00) ECHR 24 February 2005. See also W Abresh, 'A Human Rights Law of Internal Armed Conflict: The European Court of Human Rights in Chechnya' (2005) Center for Human Rights and Global Justice Working Paper No 4.

[32] See JM Henckaerts and L Doswald-Beck, *Customary International Humanitarian Law*, Vol I: *Rules* (Cambridge, Cambridge University Press, 2006).

[33] Declaration of Minimum Humanitarian Standards (3 March 1995) UN Doc E/CN.4/1995/116 (Declaration of Turku).

[34] See E Crawford, 'Road to Nowhere? The Future for a Declaration on Fundamental Standards of Humanity' (January 2012) Legal Studies Research Paper No 12/02.

be found in one or other branch of law. The need to focus on implementation rather than additional standards-setting is no more obvious than in the current Syrian conflict, where the overwhelming issue is not identifying the applicable law but rather that both IHL and IHRL are being blatantly flouted with, up to now, almost complete impunity.

But many of the controversies outlined above show no signs of abating and the grey areas seem only to be expanding. This is partly because of innovations in warfare, whether technical (eg the use of unmanned combat air vehicles—drones—to carry out targeting killings), organisational (eg the growth of transnational non-state armed groups such as al-Qaeda and ISIS), or legal (eg the classification by the United States of its adversaries as 'unlawful enemy combatants'). Meanwhile an effective system of accessible remedies, including for civilian victims, remains ever elusive.

IV. RIGHTS, REMEDIES AND DEVELOPMENTS

This introduction has sought to outline a range of boundary issues in IHRL and IHL covering competing norms, mutual scopes of application and implementation, and availability of remedies. The chapters in this volume look critically at such boundary issues and at areas of uncertainty in the application of IHL and/or the law of human rights in order to bring new perspectives to the rights of civilians, and to the remedies available for violations, and to assess emerging legal developments with a potential impact on civilian protection.

The principle of distinction—the obligation to distinguish at all times between civilians, or civilian objects, and military objectives, and to direct attacks only against the latter—is both the bedrock of IHL and the starting point for understanding civilian rights. It requires, naturally, a clear appreciation of who is, and is not, a civilian. But in certain crucial respects this understanding is not settled, as Emily Crawford explains in the first chapter. To the practical challenges presented by irregular armed forces often merging with the civilian population are joined a number of legal questions. If civilians lose their immunity from attack when directly participating in hostilities, how is direct participation defined and how long does it last? What of the driver, the cook or the fund-raiser (or, for that matter, the lawyer) and members of armed opposition groups who do not engage in combat? Crawford critically reviews the extant treaty law, state practice and some recent attempts to provide authoritative guidance, including the introduction by the International Committee of the Red Cross (ICRC) of the notion of 'continuous combat function' to delimit those members of opposition groups in a NIAC who become targetable on account of their membership. However, the continuing uncertainty around membership of armed opposition groups in particular, as well as the scope of direct participation in hostilities, benefits neither state parties to conflict nor civilians, and Crawford ends with a plea for greater clarity.

Few practices have a greater tendency to undermine the application of IHL than the refusal to investigate or even acknowledge civilian casualties. In chapter 2, Mark Lattimer considers the wide-ranging positive duties in international law to investigate civilian deaths. In locating many such duties in the law of the Geneva Conventions and in customary IHL, he argues that the obligation to investigate does not depend on the availability of a human rights jurisdiction, and is binding on both state parties and non-state parties to conflict. An important section of the duty to investigate is governed by one of the few civilian protections in IHL explicitly formulated in terms of rights, namely 'the right of families to know the fate of their relatives'.[35]

After the principle of distinction, the principle of proportionality is essential to an understanding of the legal limits on military action. If the law of armed conflict is fundamentally concerned with the balance between military necessity and humanitarian considerations, then the principle of proportionality provides a description of the calibration point. As Amichai Cohen notes in chapter 3, however, an agreed measure for calculating what is proportionate and what is disproportionate has yet to be found—and is unlikely ever to be found. Looking in particular at the way in which the principle of proportionality is interpreted in the context of targeted killing operations, he instead suggests that it is the prominence accorded to procedures—legal, bureaucratic—in the application of the principle which has modified the interpretation of proportionality in the practice of leading states in modern asymmetrical conflicts.

The evolution of weapons systems has both led to frequent claims that 'surgical' attacks are now possible which enable better adherence to the IHL principles of distinction and proportionality and at the same time given rise to new concerns over compatibility with international law. Perhaps no development has occasioned more controversy than the deployment of 'unmanned combat aerial vehicles' or armed drones. First put into operation by the USA under President George W Bush, their use was significantly expanded during the Obama administration and has now spread more widely (even ISIS has experimented with armed drones in Iraq). Stuary Casey-Maslen raises general concerns over the development of both unmanned and autonomous weapons systems but identifies the area of greatest current legal concern as the use of armed drones to attack targets outside the area of active hostilities. He argues that any such attacks should conform to the applicable legal regime governing law enforcement, rather than the law governing the conduct of hostilities. Targeted killings outside the conduct of hostilities which then ignore law enforcement rules might be more properly characterised as assassinations.

[35] AP I, Art 32.

The increase in the transnational use of force against non-state armed groups has led to claims of the existence of a transnational or even global NIAC. This concept and related conflict classification issues are placed under critical scrutiny by Pavle Kilibarda and Gloria Gaggioli in the context of a typology of NIACs. While recognising that a NIAC may take place on the territory of more than one state, they point out that the contemporary practice of distinguishing between international and non-international conflicts solely on the basis of the state or non-state identity of the parties can produce unfortunate outcomes, not least for civilian protection. They argue in favour of the limited revival of a territorial criterion in defining the scope of application of NIAC rules in order to avoid the application of rules of armed conflict in peacetime situations for which they were not designed and for which other legal protection regimes are better suited.

Civilians suspected of directly participating in hostilities or otherwise deemed to pose a threat are detained without charge or trial in NIACs across the world. But under what authority? Françoise Hampson begins by considering the justification for a system of administrative detention or internment in NIAC—and the potential consequences if one is not available. While the authority to intern may be available to the territorial state by virtue of domestic law—within the limits stipulated by human rights standards—such authority is less certain under international law, placing in question the practice of detention by foreign states involved in NIACs, including those operating under a multinational mandate. Reviewing recent jurisprudence from the English courts and the ECtHR, she suggests ways forward for states to clarify customary IHL on detention in NIACs, including the need for a detention review mechanism and procedural guarantees.

The existence not just of overlapping branches of law but also both military and ordinary (civilian) criminal justice systems further complicates the protection of civilians (and the rights of both victims and the accused). This is particularly the case with regard to rape and sexual violence, as Lois Moore and Christine Chinkin explain. While courts martial remain the appropriate forum for trying offences of military discipline, since the operation of the international military tribunals at Nuremberg and Tokyo there has been a move away from applying military justice systems to crimes under international law, including those committed in armed conflict. In general, military tribunals have been slow to prosecute personnel for IHL breaches, particularly senior officers, despite recognising the concept of command responsibility. This undermines the incentives on superior officers to ensure compliance, detracting from IHL's ability to protect civilians from sexual violence. Moore and Chinkin conclude that while there are real advantages in national as well as international prosecutions for sexual violence being made for war crimes and crimes against humanity rather than 'ordinary' domestic crimes—not least the increased stigma that a conviction may attract—primary responsibility for prosecution should rest with the ordinary civilian criminal justice system. They finish with a number of

recommendations to improve state compliance with international obligations to suppress sexual violence in armed conflict.

Part II of this book considers the availability of remedies for civilians
whose rights have been violated. From its various origins in damages payments made by a defeated party after an armed conflict and in the human
rights law right to a remedy, the notion of a right to reparation for victims
of armed conflict has progressively become accepted as a matter of international law, as Carla Ferstman notes. She discusses both the procedural
component of the right, the access to a remedy and the substantive component, which may entail any combination of restitution, compensation, rehabilitation, satisfaction and guarantees of non-repetition. While the required
standard, as first articulated by the Permanent Court of International Justice, is 'full' reparation—wiping out the consequences of the violation and
re-establishing as far as possible the situation before the breach—the practice of states when confronted by widespread loss and destruction is piecemeal, leaving victims struggling to assert their rights.

On the procedural side, Ferstman notes that whereas there is an obligation to afford reparations, there is no independent IHL right for victims to
claim reparations. So how do national courts deal with claims from victims of alleged violations of IHL? The question is particularly significant
given the weakness of IHL implementation mechanisms at the international
level, including the absence of an individual complaint mechanism. Sharon
Weill constructs a typology of roles to characterise the response of national
courts to the challenge of adjudicating such claims, ranging from the role of
apologist for the national state to a utopian role seeking to implement international law norms against the grain of national legislation. Citing jurisprudence from Israel, the USA, the UK and Spain, she describes how courts
may also avoid jurisdiction, or defer to the executive branch, but suggests
that performing a limiting or normative role enables national courts to fulfil
most closely the function of the judicial branch in upholding the rule of law.

Given the lack of mechanisms for obtaining individual remedies under
IHL, it is the regional human rights mechanisms that have developed most
of the international jurisprudence concerning the protection of the rights
of civilians in armed conflict. Since the dictum of the ICJ in the *Nuclear
Weapons* case describing IHL as *lex specialis*, the human rights courts have
had two decades to chew over the relationship between IHL and IHRL.
Noting the very different origins of the two branches of law, Bill Bowring
reviews cases before the Inter-American Commission and Court of Human
Rights, the ECtHR, and the recommendations of the African Commission
on Human and Peoples' Rights, and finds IHL being used as an interpretive
tool or as a test for arbitrariness, but always in a role subsidiary to the purpose of establishing whether or not a violation of the relevant human rights
convention has occurred. He asks whether the *lex specialis* rule has, in this
context, finally been laid to rest. He quotes the African Commission statement that '[a]ny violation of IHL resulting in death, including war crimes,

will be an arbitrary deprivation of life', and finds that this approach will strengthen the enforcement of victims' rights for both IHL and human rights violations in armed conflict.

As regional human rights courts underscore the continued application of human rights obligations during armed conflict, few legal issues have proved more contentious than the extra-territorial application of those obligations. The ECtHR, in particular, has struggled to find a satisfactory formulation for when human rights law applies extra-territorially since its problematic decision in 2011 in *Banković*. Cedric Ryngaert undertakes a critique of the main existing approaches to the extra-territorial application of human rights, including those that make such application dependent on a state exercising effective control (either over territory or persons). Instead, he proposes approximating extra-territorial human rights obligations with the notion of state responsibility under general international law.

The expansion of UN and other intergovernmental peacekeeping operations around the world has led to numerous situations where international peacekeeping forces become the first line of protection for threatened civilians. How effective that protection is in practice may depend on a range of factors, including the terms of the relevant mandate and the conditions on the ground, as well as whether the job is done well. But what duties do peacekeepers owe civilians? To answer this question, Liesbeth Zegveld draws on her extensive experience before the Dutch court litigating the *Nuhanović* case, which concerned the acts and omissions of a Dutch battalion of UN peacekeepers in the 'safe area' at Srebrenica during the Bosnian war. Given the very wide immunity enjoyed by the UN, a central issue in the case was whether the Netherlands could be held liable for Dutchbat's decision to send Hasan Nuhanović's family away from the UN compound (effectively to their deaths). In finding that it could, and raising the possibility of dual attribution of responsibility between the UN and the troop-contributing state, the case enhanced the access of victims to reparation.

Although the development of remote, autonomous and other new weapons technologies is a focus of the recent IHL literature on weapons, the vast majority of violent civilian deaths in contemporary conflicts are the result of attacks using conventional weapons. The entry into force of the Arms Trade Treaty in 2014 offered new hope to limit the human suffering caused by the $70 billion annual international trade in conventional weapons. But what protections does the Treaty offer in practice to civilians in conflict zones and what enforcement mechanisms does it provide to secure those protections and to hold states to account for their undertakings in relation to arms control? Blinne Ní Ghrálaigh analyses in detail the new state obligations contained at the heart of the Treaty in Articles 6 and 7. She concludes that measures to enforce national laws and regulations implementing the Treaty's provisions, including the scrutiny of national courts, are key to the effectiveness of the Treaty in practice, and considers how its protections have fared in the first litigation under the Treaty, a case before the English court concerning weapons exported from the UK to Saudi Arabia that were used to commit violations of international law in the war in Yemen.

In Part III we turn to the development of new mechanisms or international legislation to secure the implementation of IHL and human rights law in armed conflicts. Valentin Zellweger and François Voeffray describe first the deficiencies in the existing implementation mechanisms established under the IHL treaties, before describing the diplomatic process facilitated by the ICRC and the government of Switzerland to promote implementation by establishing a dedicated intergovernmental forum for IHL. Compliance mechanisms integrated into the 1949 Geneva Conventions, including the institution of protecting powers and the conciliation and enquiry procedures, as well as the International Humanitarian Fact-Finding Commission established under Additional Protocol I, have rarely if ever been used in recent decades. This is due to a number of factors, including the requirement to obtain the consent of the parties to the conflict and the fact that they were not designed for the complexity and proliferation of actors that characterise contemporary NIACs in particular. The need to anchor compliance in a broader institutional structure is what has driven the ongoing diplomatic process to create a forum of states to enhance IHL implementation.

In chapter 15, Jennifer Welsh explains that the 'responsibility to protect' (R2P) establishes a series of international political commitments to protect populations from atrocity besides the legal mechanisms for civilian protection explored elsewhere in this book. However, the R2P norms, as encapsulated in the outcome document from the 2005 UN World Summit,[36] arguably follow a state-centric model of atrocity prevention, whereas civilians are increasingly at risk from non-state armed groups (NSAGs). Professor Welsh, until recently the UN Special Adviser to the Secretary-General on the Responsibility to Protect, analyses the concept of R2P in relation to the threat posed by such groups, noting that the category covers a wide array of actors from those pushing for governmental reform to those seeking the creation of a new territorial or political order. She seeks to clarify some of the legal dilemmas around international support for NSAGs and the states fighting them, concluding that the role and function of R2P should and can extend to the threat posed by NSAG perpetrators of atrocity crimes.

The last two chapters consider innovations in international criminal law that have the potential to strengthen civilian protection. Quite apart from the active implementation of human rights and the *jus in bello*, it is the prohibition and prevention of armed conflict itself which perhaps holds the greatest promise for preventing harm to civilians. Carrie McDougall looks at the most serious forms of the illegal use of inter-state force: the crime of aggression. She critically reviews the main objections—including those of

---

[36] UNGA, '2005 World Summit Outcome' (24 October 2005) UN Doc A/RES/60/1, paras 138–39.

the five permanent members of the UN Security Council—to current developments bringing the crime within the jurisdiction of the ICC. These include concerns over the definition of the crime and the provisions for engaging jurisdiction, as well as wider questions over the impact on international peace and security. Given that the aggression amendments to the ICC Statute provide states parties to the Statute with the opportunity to lodge an 'opt-out' declaration, she concludes that the concerns are overblown and that the effective criminalisation of aggression has the potential to deter the most serious forms of the illegal use of force and thereby to prevent the deaths of countless victims.

The protection of civilians from attack is central not only to IHL but also to the international law on crimes against humanity and genocide (crimes which, it should be recalled, can also be committed outside of an armed conflict). Leila Nadya Sadat sketches the legal development of crimes against humanity from their early codification at Nuremberg to their definition in the ICC Statute as murder or other specific acts committed as part of a 'widespread or systematic attack directed against any civilian population, with knowledge of the attack'. Unlike the crime of genocide, however, crimes against humanity are not covered by a standalone convention aimed at their prevention and punishment. Professor Sadat describes the work of the Crimes Against Humanity Initiative and, more recently, that of the International Law Commission to draft such a convention, arguing that it could close significant gaps in the legal suppression of these egregious crimes against civilian populations.

* * *

From these varied contributions, coming from both the IHL and human rights traditions, can we discern the beginnings of a practice of civilian rights? It is notable that today's conflicts evidence not just the failure to implement basic humanitarian norms but also deliberate attempts by states and other parties to conflict to avoid legal interdictions through such strategies as the widespread use of proxy militias, lack of transparency concerning the investigation and recording of civilian casualties, and the over-application of certain IHL concepts or rules to situations they were never designed to address. Contending with these trends, however, there is a new confidence by human rights bodies and mechanisms to assert their competence in situations of armed conflict and a growing legal activism seeking reparation for IHL violations at the suit of civilian victims. If, forty years after the conclusion of the Additional Protocols to the Geneva Conventions, we still seem far from the operation of an effective system of civilian protection, there is nonetheless a widening realisation that the failure to spare the civilian population in armed conflict has legal consequences and that what begins in the command centre may well end up in court.

Part I

Rights

1

Who Is a Civilian? Membership of Opposition Groups and Direct Participation in Hostilities

EMILY CRAWFORD

I. INTRODUCTION

THE LAW OF armed conflict (also known as international humanitarian law, or IHL)[1] provides comprehensive protections for civilians in times of armed conflict. Enshrined in treaty and customary law applicable in both IACs[2] and NIACs[3] are prohibitions on directly targeting civilian objects and installations, and objects essential to the survival of the civilian population,[4] obligations on parties to the conflict to ensure that civilians and civilian installations or property are protected from the direct effects of military operations,[5] and rules regarding how civilians in the hands of an adverse party are to be treated.[6] Primary among these rules protecting civilians in armed conflict is the fundamental obligation on parties to the conflict to distinguish between civilians (and civilian objects) and military objectives, and to direct attacks only against military objectives.[7]

---

[1] The terms 'law of armed conflict' and 'international humanitarian law' will be used interchangeably in this chapter.

[2] The substantive treaty law regarding the protection of civilians in IACs can be found in the four Geneva Conventions of 1949, and Protocol I Additional to the Geneva Conventions (Protocol I or AP I).

[3] The substantive treaty law relating to NIACs comprises Article 3 to the Geneva Conventions (known as Common Article 3) and Protocol II Additional to the Geneva Conventions (Protocol II or AP II).

[4] AP I, Art 54.

[5] These include rules on proportionality in attack (contained in Art 51(5) AP I), prohibitions on indiscriminate attacks (Art 51(4) AP I), and obligations on parties to take precautions in attack (Art 57 AP I) and in defence (Art 58 AP I).

[6] Contained in Geneva Convention IV, regarding the treatment of civilians under belligerent occupation.

[7] Art 48 of AP I provides that: '[I]n order to ensure respect for and protection of the civilian population and civilian objects, the parties to an armed conflict shall at all times distinguish

This is known as the principle of distinction, an elementary principle of the law of armed conflict that has been affirmed as one of the 'fundamental and intransgressible principle[s]'[8] of IHL.

The principle of distinction, considered to be customary international law,[9] is given practical effect through provisions such as Article 51(2) of Additional Protocol I of the Geneva Conventions, which provides that 'the civilian population as such, as well as individual civilians, shall not be the object of attack'. Civilians are immune from being directly targeted in situations of armed conflict. Combatants—persons entitled to directly participate in hostilities—are not afforded such immunity from targeting, and may be intentionally targeted by an adverse party for their participation in the armed conflict. However, civilian immunity is not absolute: the immunity from targeting afforded to civilians is contingent on civilians refraining from directly participating in hostilities. As outlined in Article 51(3) of Additional Protocol I, civilians are not to be made the object of attack 'unless and for such time as they take a direct part in hostilities'.

Acting in compliance with the principle of distinction is thus contingent on being able to answer a specific question: who is a civilian? Being able to answer this question accurately can mean the difference between an act being a lawful attack under IHL and that same act being a war crime. However, the question of who is a civilian is by no means easy to answer and the question of when a civilian is considered to be taking a direct part in hostilities is even more contested. The situation is complicated because the treaty law of IHL does not provide detailed rules regarding how and when a civilian will lose his or her immunity due to their direct participation in hostilities—neither the Geneva Conventions nor Additional Protocols provide instruction as to what particular acts amount to direct participation in hostilities.

With this background in mind, this chapter will examine the questions raised by the notion of the civilian under IHL, and the concept of civilian loss of protection against targeting due to direct participation in hostilities. To that end, this chapter will examine both the treaty and customary law relating to civilians and to direct participation, and will explore some of the most notable attempts in recent years, by states and non-state entities alike, to define the concept of direct participation in hostilities. In doing so,

---

between the civilian population and combatants and between civilian objects and military objectives. Accordingly, they shall direct their operations only against military objectives.'

[8] *Legality of the Threat or Use of Nuclear Weapons* (Advisory Opinion) [1996] ICJ Rep 226.

[9] See JM Henckaerts and L Doswald-Beck (eds), *Customary International Humanitarian Law* (Cambridge, Cambridge University Press, 2005) r 1, which states that the principle of distinction, as outlined in Art 48 of AP I, is considered customary international law.

this chapter will attempt to discern if there is a common accepted understanding of the notion of the civilian and civilian direct participation under current IHL.

II. THE CIVILIAN IN INTERNATIONAL HUMANITARIAN LAW

As noted above, one of the fundamental principles of the law of armed conflict is the principle of distinction—the dyad of targetable military objectives and non-targetable civilians and civilian objects. However, while the treaty and customary law of IHL goes into some detail in outlining how one might determine whether a particular objective is military,[10] none of the extant treaty law of IHL contains a stand-alone definition of a civilian. This is the case in the law relating to both IACs and NIACs.

A. The Definition of Civilian in the Law of International Armed Conflicts

Civilians are defined in the negative in relation to combatants in the treaty law of IACs.[11] Thus, in Article 50(1)–(2) of Additional Protocol I:

> A civilian is any person who does not belong to one of the categories of persons referred to in Article 4 A (1), (2), (3) and (6) of the Third Convention and in Article 43 of this Protocol. In case of doubt whether a person is a civilian, that person shall be considered to be a civilian.

> The civilian population comprises all persons who are civilians.

All persons who do not fall into the categories outlined in Article 4A(1)–(3) and (6) of Geneva Convention III and Article 43 of Protocol I are considered civilians in IHL. Thus, in order to understand who IHL considers a civilian, one must look at how IHL categorises non-civilians—the persons referred to in Article 4A(1)–(3) and (6) of Geneva Convention III, and Article 43 of Protocol I. Such persons are known as combatants, and they include:

(1) Members of the armed forces of a Party to the conflict as well as members of militias or volunteer corps forming part of such armed forces.

(2) Members of other militias and members of other volunteer corps, including those of organized resistance movements, belonging to a Party to the conflict and operating in or outside their own territory, even if this territory

---

[10] AP I, Art 52(2).

[11] Dinstein notes that a benefit of this negative definitional approach is that 'there is no undistributed middle between the categories of combatants/military objectives and civilians/civilian objects'. See Y Dinstein, *The Conduct of Hostilities under the Law of International Armed Conflict*, 3rd edn (Cambridge, Cambridge University Press, 2016) 142.

is occupied, provided that such militias or volunteer corps, including such organized resistance movements, fulfil the following conditions:

    (a)   that of being commanded by a person responsible for his subordinates;
    (b)   that of having a fixed distinctive sign recognizable at a distance;
    (c)   that of carrying arms openly;
    (d)   that of conducting their operations in accordance with the laws and customs of war.

(3)   Members of regular armed forces who profess allegiance to a government or an authority not recognized by the Detaining Power.

…

(6)   Inhabitants of a non-occupied territory, who on the approach of the enemy spontaneously take up arms to resist the invading forces, without having had time to form themselves into regular armed units, provided they carry arms openly and respect the laws and customs of war.[12]

This is the definition of civilian in the treaties relating to IAC, and the formula for determining civilian status—ie, a civilian is a person who is not a combatant—is replicated consistently in state practice. Numerous military manuals affirm that, in IACs, a civilian is any person not belonging to the armed forces (or a participant in a *levée en masse*—the situation described in Article 4A(6) of Geneva Convention III),[13] while some military manuals include reference to civilians being persons who are not combatants and who do not take part in hostilities.[14] National legislation[15] and national case law[16] have repeated this formulation.

---

[12] Geneva Convention III, Art 4a(1)–(3), (6). Art 43 AP I adds guerrilla and national liberation fighters to the categories of combatant, and amends the requirements of open carriage of arms and the wearing of a fixed distinctive emblem visible at a distance.

[13] See, for example, the military manuals of Argentina, Australia, Benin, Burundi, Cameroon, Canada, the Central African Republic, Chad, Colombia, Côte d'Ivoire, Croatia, Ecuador, France, Hungary, Ireland, Israel, Italy, Kenya, Madagascar, Mexico, the Netherlands, Peru, the Philippines, Poland, Russia, Sierra Leone, South Africa, Spain, Sweden, Togo, Ukraine, the UK and the USA—the relevant sections of these manuals is duplicated in Henckaerts and Doswald-Beck (n 9) r 5.

[14] See the manuals of Côte d'Ivoire, the Dominican Republic, Ecuador, France, Indonesia, Israel, the Netherlands, Peru, Russia, Sierra Leone and the USA (reprinted in the practice for Henckaerts and Doswald-Beck (n 9) r 5).

[15] See, for example, the Australian Criminal Code Act (1995) (Cth); Azerbaijan's Law Concerning the Protection of Civilian Persons and the Rights of Prisoners of War (1995 as amended to Law 430-IIIQD 9 October 2007); and Spain's Penal Code (1995), which criminalise attacks on the 'civilian population as such or individual civilians not taking direct part in hostilities' (Criminal Code Act (1995) s 268.35), or protected persons defined as 'the civilian population and individual civilians protected by the Fourth Geneva Convention of 12 August 1949 or Additional Protocol I of 8 June 1977' (Penal Code (1995) Art 608(3)); or otherwise define civilians as 'persons not belonging to the armed forces of the party to the conflict' (Law Concerning Protection of Civilians Persons (1995) Art 3).

[16] For example, in the investigation into the bombing of fuel tankers in Kunduz by a colonel of the German armed forces, the German Federal Prosecutor General stated that for the purposes of the *Völkerstrafgesetzbuch* (the German Code of Crimes against International Law

B. The Definition of Civilian in the Law of Non-International Armed Conflicts

Determining who is a civilian in a *non-international* armed conflict is a harder prospect—in part because there is no combatant status in NIAC against which a civilian can be measured. Neither Common Article 3 nor Additional Protocol II define the term 'civilian', even though the term is used a number of times in Protocol II.[17] As such, determining who is a civilian in a NIAC relies in large part on inference.

At this point, it is necessary to make a distinction between different kinds of participation in NIAC, as it potentially influences how a person in a NIAC is classified, and what kinds of protection and treatment under the law such a person can expect. It is generally accepted that in a NIAC, members of the armed forces of a state who are entitled to take direct part in hostilities are not considered civilians, and do not enjoy any of the protections specifically provided for civilians. Much of the practice on this issue,[18] including the commentaries to Additional Protocol II,[19] supports this reading. However, there are persons *not* part of the state armed forces who directly participate in hostilities in NIACs. Are they civilians, or do they occupy a different category? If one were to apply a strict reading to the Protocol, would the word 'civilian' carry 'its usual meaning, a person not associated with the military'?[20] Would all persons who are involved in a NIAC who are *not* members of a state armed force therefore be considered 'civilians', thus rendering any direct attack against such persons unlawful under IHL?

This interpretation does not seem supportable from a purposive reading of Additional Protocol II, which makes reference to the Protocol applying to armed conflicts involving a state's 'armed forces and dissident armed forces or other organized armed groups which, under responsible command, exercise such control over a part of its territory as to enable them to

---

(2002) (VStGB)), a civilian is any person 'who does not belong to one of the categories of persons referred to in Art 4 paragraph A sub-paragraphs (1), (2), (3), and (6) of the Convention III and in Article 43' of AP I (*Decision of the Prosecutor General* (2010) German Federal Court of Justice, www.generalbundesanwalt.de/docs/einstellungsvermerk20100416offen.pdf, 47). The same formulation for 'civilian' was used in *The Public Committee Against Torture in Israel v The Government of Israel* HCJ 769/02 (2006) (*Targeted Killings* case) para 26.

[17] For example, in Part IV, which details protections for the civilian population in situations of NIAC.

[18] See Henckaerts and Doswald-Beck (n 9) r 5.

[19] Y Sandoz, C Swinarski and B Zimmerman (eds), *Commentary on the Additional Protocols of 8 June 1977 to the Geneva Conventions of 12 August 1949* (Geneva, ICRC, 1987) 1453, para 4789; and M Bothe, KJ Partsch and W Solf (eds), *New Rules for Victims of Armed Conflicts: Commentary on the Two 1977 Protocols Additional to the Geneva Conventions of 1949*, 2nd edn (The Hague, Martinus Nijhoff, 2013) 773–74.

[20] G Solis, *The Law of Armed Conflict: International Humanitarian Law in War* 2nd edition (Cambridge, Cambridge University Press, 2016) 217.

carry out sustained and concerted military operations and to implement this Protocol'.[21] As Protocol II is intended to apply to armed conflicts involving a state's armed forces engaged against dissident armed forces or other organised armed groups, it would suggest that the Protocol does not consider such members of dissident or organised armed groups as being civilians, but rather as analogous to enemy armed forces, and thus liable for targeting. This interpretation is supported by the Commentary to Additional Protocol II,[22] which states that the reference to dissident armed forces and other organised armed groups 'inferentially recognised the essential conditions of armed forces, as they apply in IAC, and that it follows that civilians are all persons who are not members of such forces of groups'.[23] Indeed, the case law and relevant state practice, discussed below, affirm the notion that persons who are considered members of dissident armed forces or other organised armed groups are not to be considered civilians, and may be targeted for their direct participation in hostilities. How this determination is reached will be discussed in more detail below.

However, the law of armed conflict also acknowledges that there may be instances of persons who are *not* members of *either* the armed forces of a state *or* of a dissident or organised armed group who take part in hostilities (either in IAC or NIAC). This is known as 'direct participation in hostilities' and also results in liability for direct attack in armed conflict. This principle is enshrined in Article 51(3) of Additional Protocol I and Article 13(3) of Additional Protocol II—that civilians are protected from direct attack 'unless and for such time as they take a direct part in hostilities.'

Such direct participation does not, generally speaking, always transform a civilian into a combatant. The wording of Article 51(3) and Article 13(3)— 'for such time'—makes it clear that the loss of protection for direct participation is intended to be temporary. Civilians who take direct or active part in hostilities remain civilians while they take such part—they simply lose their protection from attack, and are targetable for the duration of that participation. But even when that civilian directly participates, they remain a civilian. Their direct participation, for so long as it occurs, does not, generally speaking, cause them to permanently, irrevocably lose their civilian status.

As such, it is possible to see that IHL broadly (and informally) categorises its participants under three umbrellas: members of a state's armed forces, members of dissident or organised armed forces, and civilians taking direct part in hostilities. Common to all these three categories is the underlying notion that it is the *actual participation* in armed conflict that renders a

---

[21] AP II, Art 1.
[22] See Bothe, Partsch and Solf (n 19) 773.
[23] Henckaerts and Doswald-Beck (n 9) r 5.

person targetable. This is broadly true for civilians who take direct part in hostilities—their hostile acts against an adversary are what render them targetable in armed conflict. However, members of a state's armed forces are targetable even when they pose no active or immediate threat (eg if they are asleep in barracks).[24] Members of a state's armed forces are targetable at all times during armed conflict because of their status as members of a state's armed forces. Therefore, participants in armed conflicts can also be divided into two sub-categories: those that are targetable at all times due to status, and those that are targetable at certain times due to their behaviour. Targeting of persons can be lawfully carried out under IHL either because the targeted person is a threat because of their status as a participant or because they are a threat due to their activities as a participant.[25]

The upshot of this complex situation is that a definition of civilian in NIAC can only be reached by defining two concepts: the criteria for membership in an armed group and the concept of 'direct participation in hostilities'. Indeed, the relevant case law, discussed below, demonstrates how the term 'civilian' in NIAC is deeply enmeshed with the idea of direct participation and membership in armed groups. However, the case law often presents differing and contradictory approaches to defining civilian direct participation. For example, in the International Criminal Tribunal for the former Yugoslavia (ICTY), the Trial Chamber in *Tadić* held that a person 'cannot be considered a traditional "non-combatant" because he is actively involved in the conduct of hostilities by membership in some form of resistance group',[26] which seems to take a 'membership approach' to defining the notions of civilian, direct participation, and membership in an armed group,[27] while the ICTY Trial Chamber in *Blagojevic and Jokic* held that the term civilians refers to 'persons not taking part in hostilities',[28] which

---

[24] Solis (n 20) 202.

[25] Kleffner calls this division the 'membership' approach and the 'specific acts' approach. See J Kleffner, 'From "Belligerents" to "Fighters" and Civilians Directly Participating in Hostilities—On the Principle of Distinction in Non-International Armed Conflicts One Hundred Years After the Second Hague Peace Conference' (2007) LIV *Netherlands International Law Review* 315, 327.

[26] *Prosecutor v Tadić* (Judgment) ICTY-94-1-T (7 May 1997) para 639.

[27] A position seemingly followed by the ICTY in *Prosecutor v Blaškić* (Judgment) ICTY-95-14 (3 March 2000) para 180, where the Trial Chamber referred to civilians as persons 'who are not, or no longer, members of the armed forces', and *Prosecutor v Galić* (Judgment) ICTY-98-29 (5 December 2003) para 47, which stated that a civilian is 'defined negatively as anyone who is not a member of the armed forces or of an organised military group belonging to a party to the conflict'. However, see Kleffner (n 25) 327, who sees the ICTY decision in *Blaškić* as a 'membership' approach to direct participation, and the *Tadić* decision as a 'specific acts' approach to direct participation.

[28] *Prosecutor v Blagojević and Jokić* (Judgment) ICTY-02-60 (17 January 2005) para 544. This formulation was followed by the ICTY Trial Chamber in *Prosecutor v Strugar* (Judgment) ICTY-01-42 (31 January 2005) para 282, which defined civilians as 'people who are not taking any active part in the hostilities'.

suggests a 'specific acts' approach to defining a civilian, direct participation, and membership in an armed group.

Neither the criteria for membership in an armed group, nor what acts amount to direct participation in hostilities, is settled in current thinking in IHL. A number of questions thus remain, which make the process of defining a civilian in NIAC notably difficult. When can a civilian be considered as taking a direct part due to their actions? When is one considered a member of a dissident or organised armed force? Put another way, does repeated and persistent direct participation by a civilian change the nature of their direct participation? Does such regular direct participation change a civilian to a member of an organised armed force, such that they permanently lose their civilian status?

The term 'direct participation in hostilities' is remarkably opaque—the treaties do not define what amounts to 'participation', let alone 'direct' participation, nor is there any explanation of the associated elements of what amounts to 'hostilities' and 'for such time'. The practice in relation to direct participation both before and since its express codification in 1977 has also been singularly unhelpful in contributing to a better understanding of the concept. Indeed, when the ICRC released its study into the customary status of international humanitarian law in 2005, it stated that 'a precise definition of the term "direct participation in hostilities" does not exist'.[29] It is these questions that will be the focus of the reminder of this chapter—what is meant by the term 'direct participation in hostilities'? When do acts by a civilian render them as taking direct part? And when and how often must one take direct part in order to lose one's civilian status and become instead a member of an armed opposition group?

III. DIRECT PARTICIPATION IN HOSTILITIES IN IHL—DEFINING THE TERM IN TREATIES AND STATE PRACTICE

As noted above, the idea of direct participation in hostilities, or DPH, was first expressly codified in the Additional Protocols in 1977. In Protocol I, DPH is outlined in Article 51(3) providing that 'civilians shall enjoy the protection afforded by this Section, unless and for such time as they take a direct part in hostilities'. DPH is also outlined in Article 13(3) of Protocol II, and is worded similarly to Article 51(3) of Protocol I. Neither provision makes explicit what DPH actually comprises, as, during the drafting of Article 51(3), states chose not to provide a precise definition of what was meant by the phrase.[30]

---

[29] Henckaerts and Doswald-Beck (n 9) r 6.
[30] See 'Official Records of the Diplomatic Conference on the Reaffirmation and Development of International Humanitarian Law Applicable in Armed Conflicts' (Geneva, 1974–77)

Subsequent commentaries on the Protocols attempted to engage with the scope of DPH. The 1987 ICRC Commentary to the Additional Protocols did not provide much additional insight into the concept, stating only that civilians were entitled to immunity from targeting but that

> the immunity afforded individual civilians is subject to an overriding condition, namely, on their abstaining from all hostile acts. Hostile acts should be understood to be acts which by their nature and purpose are intended to cause actual harm to the personnel and equipment of the armed forces.[31]

The 1982 Commentary on the Protocols went further than the ICRC:

> [I]t is clear that civilians who personally try to kill, injure or capture enemy persons or to damage material are directly participating in hostilities. This is also the case of a person acting as a member of a weapons crew, or one providing target information for weapons systems intended for immediate use against the enemy such as artillery spotters or members of ground observer teams.[32]

Also included in DPH, as far as Bothe et al were concerned, was 'preparation for combat … [for example] direct logistic support for units engaged directly in battle such as the delivery of ammunition to a firing position'.[33] However, both the ICRC and Bothe Commentaries affirmed that DPH did not include 'civilians providing only indirect support to the armed forces, such as workers in defence plants or those engaged in distribution or storage of military supplies in rear areas',[34] as such persons 'do not pose an immediate threat to the adversary'.[35]

State practice on the question of the scope and content of DPH also provided little clarification. In the few relevant instruments or documents where reference to DPH was made, it was frequently done without actually

---

vol XV, CDDH/III/224, 330; see also Sandoz, Swinarski and Zimmerman (n 19) 618–19, paras 1942–45; and Bothe, Partsch and Solf (n 19) 301–04.

[31] Sandoz, Swinarski and Zimmerman (n 19) 618, para 1942. The commentary on the DPH provision in Art 13(3) AP II is essentially identical to that of Art 51(3) AP I—based on the notion of 'acts of war that by their nature or purpose struck at the personnel and *matériel* of enemy armed forces', and would likely include preparation for and return from combat activities. See Sandoz, Swinarski and Zimmerman (n 19) 1453, para 4788; and Bothe, Partsch and Solf (n 19) 678. Thus, reference will be made to the commentary to Art 51, as is it the more detailed of the two commentaries, even though this section is examining DPH in NIACs. Indeed, the ICRC commentary to Art 13 affirms that 'both as regards substance and structure, this article corresponds to the first three paragraphs of art 51 of Protocol I … and reference may also be made to the commentary thereon' (Sandoz, Swinarski and Zimmerman (n 19) 1448). Similar sentiments are contained in the Art 13 commentary in Bothe, Partsch and Solf (n 19) 778–81.

[32] Bothe, Partsch and Solf (n 19) 303.

[33] ibid.

[34] ibid.

[35] ibid.

explaining what amounted to DPH.[36] Only a few sources, such as the US Field Manual of 1956, set out specific criteria for what might amount to DPH.[37] The adoption of the Additional Protocols, while finally codifying DPH, prompted some states to attempt to define DPH,[38] with varying degrees of specificity and broadness of scope.[39] Definitions of DPH ranged from the active commission of hostile acts, to more broad conceptualisations of 'posing a threat'.[40]

National and international judicial and quasi-judicial bodies have also attempted to define what amounts to DPH. The Inter-American Commission on Human Rights examined the question of DPH in 1999 in a report on human rights in Colombia, dividing DPH into direct or active participation in hostilities, and indirect participation, and defined 'direct participation in hostilities' as acts which, by their nature or purpose, are intended to cause actual harm to enemy personnel and material. Importantly for the process of defining DPH, the Commission put forward a test of causation,

---

[36] For instance, in the Operational Code of Conduct for the Nigerian Army (1967) issued in relation to the Biafran Civil War, it states that 'youths and school children must not be attacked unless they are engaged in open hostilities against Federal Government Forces' (Art 3(c)); see reprinted version in AHM Kirk-Greene, *Crisis and Conflict in Nigeria, A Documentary Sourcebook*, vol 1 (Cambridge, Cambridge University Press, 1966–69) 455–57. The UK Manual on the Law of Armed Conflict also references DPH without further clarification; see Manual on the Law of Armed Conflict (2004) JSP 383, 626. Similar non-definition of DPH can be found in national legislation and national military manuals of Ghana (Armed Forces Act (1962) Art 98); India (Army Act (1950) s 3(x)); Malaysia (Armed Forces Act (1972)); and Pakistan (Army Act (1952) ch 1, s 8(8)). See also 'Report on Practice on Rule 6' in Henckaerts and Doswald-Beck (n 9).

[37] DPH is defined in the US Field Manual as acts by 'persons who are not members of the armed forces ... who bear arms or engage in other conduct hostile to the enemy thereby deprive themselves of many of the privileges attaching to the members of the civilian population ... [such hostile acts include] sabotage, destruction of communications facilities, intentional misleading of troops by guides [and] liberation of prisoners of war' (see 'The Law of Land Warfare' (18 July 1956, modified by Change no 1, 15 July 1976) Field Manual 27-10, para 60).

[38] Including Australia, Belgium, Benin, Burundi, Canada, Chad, Colombia, Côte d'Ivoire, Croatia, the Dominican Republic, Ecuador, El Salvador, Ethiopia, France, Germany, India, Indonesia, Italy, Kenya, Madagascar, the Netherlands, New Zealand, Nigeria, the Russian Federation, Sierra Leone, South Africa, Spain, Sweden, Togo, the UK and the USA. See 'Report on Practice on Rule 6' in Henckaerts and Doswald-Beck (n 9).

[39] The military manual of the Netherlands suggested that DPH would include 'firing on hostile troops, throwing Molotov cocktails or blowing up a bridge over which enemy materiel is transported, and transporting equipment to battle positions' but excluded 'actions such as manufacturing and transporting military materiel in the rear area' (see Humanitair Oorlogsrecht: Handleiding, Voorschift No 27-412, Koninklijke Landmacht (2005) para 0520). The naval manual of Ecuador includes 'serving as guards, intelligence agents or lookouts on behalf of military forces' as acts of DPH (see Aspectos Importantes del Derecho Internacional Maritimo que Deben Tener Presente los Comandantes de los Buques (1989) para 11.3).

[40] In the Canadian Forces Code of Conduct, it is stated that 'force used during operations must be directed against opposing forces and military objectives ... civilians not taking part in hostilities must not be targeted'. However, the Code of Conduct defines 'opposing force' very broadly as 'any individual or group of individuals who pose a threat to you or your mission' (see Code of Conduct for Canadian Forces Personnel (2005) r 1, paras 3–5).

stressing that before a civilian could be considered as taking direct part in hostilities, there needed to be a direct causal relationship between the activity engaged in and harm done to the enemy at the time and place where the activity occurs:

> Civilians whose activities merely support the adverse party's war or military effort or otherwise only indirectly participate in hostilities cannot on these grounds alone be considered combatants. This is because indirect participation, such as selling goods to one or more of the armed parties, expressing sympathy for the cause of one of the parties or, even more clearly, failing to act to prevent an incursion by one of the armed parties, does not involve acts of violence which pose an immediate threat of actual harm to the adverse party.[41]

In the last twenty-five years, defining direct participation in hostilities has become a key area of concern for judicial bodies, with a notable proliferation of cases relating to DPH. Tribunals for the Former Yugoslavia and Rwanda, the Special Court of Sierra Leone, and the ICC have all had cases requiring careful analysis of the concept of DPH.[42] Their rulings have contributed greatly to understanding what acts might amount to DPH, with examples of DPH deemed to include

> bearing, using or taking up arms, taking part in military or hostile acts, activities, conduct or operations, armed fighting or combat, participating in attacks against enemy personnel, property or equipment, transmitting military information for the immediate use of a belligerent, transporting weapons in proximity to combat operations.[43]

Such activities are to be distinguished from indirect participation in hostilities, which includes

> participating in activities in support of the war or military effort of one of the parties to the conflict, selling goods to one of the parties to the conflict, expressing sympathy for the cause of one of the parties to the conflict, accompanying and

---

[41] 'Third Report on the Human Rights Situation in Colombia' (26 February 1999) OEA/Ser.L/V/II.102 Doc 9 rev 1, ch IV, 53, 56.

[42] In the ICTY, these included *Prosecutor v Simić et al* (Judgment) ICTY-95-9-T (17 October 2003) para 659; *Prosecutor v Milošević* (Judgment) ICTY-98-29/1-T (12 December 2007) para 947; *Prosecutor v Strugar* (Appeals Judgment) ICTY-01-42-A (17 July 2008) paras 172–78; *Prosecutor v Kordić and Čerkez* (Appeals Judgment) ICTY-95-14/2-A (7 December 2004) para 51; *Prosecutor v Galić*, para 48. In the ICTR, cases looking at DPH included *Prosecutor v Bagilishema* (Judgment) ICTR-95-1A-T (7 June 2001) para 104. In the Special Court for Sierra Leone, the cases of *Prosecutor v Fofana and Kondewa* (Judgment) SCSL-04-14-T (2 August 2007) paras 134–35 and *Prosecutor v Sesay et al* (Judgment) SCSL-04-15-T (2 March 2009) paras 1720, 1723–24. For the ICC, these cases include *Prosecutor v Thomas Lubanga Dyilo* (Decision on the Confirmation of Charges) ICC-01/04-01/06 (14 May 2007) paras 261–63; *Prosecutor v Bahar Idriss Abu Garda* (Decision on the Confirmation of Charges) ICC-02/05-02/09 (8 February 2010) paras 78–82; and *Prosecutor v Mbarushimana* (Decision on the Confirmation of Charges) ICC-01/04-01/10-465-Red (16 December 2011) para 340.

[43] *Prosecutor v Strugar* (n 42) para 177, affirmed in *Prosecutor v Bahar Idriss Abu Garda* (n 42) para 81.

supplying food to one of the parties to the conflict, gathering and transmitting military information, transporting arms and munitions, and providing supplies, and providing specialist advice regarding the selection of military personnel, their training or the correct maintenance of weapons.[44]

However, it has not just been international judicial and quasi-judicial bodies that have contributed to clarification on DPH; state domestic courts and tribunals have also contributed. Perhaps most notable of these was the Israeli Supreme Court in 2006, in the *Public Committee Against Torture in Israel v The Government of Israel*, also known as the *Targeted Killings* case. The Court was asked to determine the legality of the Israeli policy of targeted killing of terrorists—in effect, Israel had to account for its understanding of what constituted direct participation in hostilities so as to render a civilian targetable under IHL. The Court was faced with, among other things, determining whether the concept of direct participation in hostilities should be defined narrowly or broadly. After affirming the customary status of all parts of Article 51(3),[45] the Court set about examining the scope of the term 'direct part in hostilities', identifying certain categories of persons who could be considered as taking direct part in hostilities, including persons collecting intelligence on the armed forces; persons transporting unlawful combatants[46] to or from the place where hostilities are occurring; and persons who operate weapons that unlawful combatants use, or supervise their operation, or provide service to them.[47] The Court also considered that civilians involved in transporting ammunition to places for use in hostilities, as well as persons acting as voluntary human shields should be considered as taking direct part in hostilities.[48] In coming to this reasoning, the Court explained that:

> [The] direct character of the part taken should not be narrowed merely to the person committing the physical act of attack, those who have sent him, as well, take 'a direct part'. The same goes for the person who decided upon the act, and the person who planned it. It is not to be said about them that they are taking an indirect part in hostilities.[49]

---

[44] *Prosecutor v Strugar* (n 42) para 177.

[45] *Targeted Killings* case (n 16) paras 23, 29–30.

[46] The term 'unlawful combatants' was used by the Court in an essentially descriptive manner; at para 27 in the judgment, the Court noted that the respondents had requested the Court to recognise a 'third category' of persons under IHL, in line with Israel's own law regarding unlawful combatants (Detention of Unlawful Combatants Law (2002), 1834 *Sefer Hahukim* 192). However, the Court declined to take a 'stance regarding the question whether it is desirable to recognise this third category. The question before us is not one of desirable law, rather one of existing law. In our opinion, as far as existing law goes, the data before us are not sufficient to recognise this third category' (para 28).

[47] *Targeted Killings* case (n 16) para 35.

[48] ibid, paras 35, 36.

[49] ibid, para 37.

Excluded, however, from the scope of DPH were certain persons and acts, including selling food and medicine to unlawful combatants; providing general strategic analysis, logistical and other general support, including monetary aid; and distributing propaganda.[50]

In addition to the *Targeted Killings* case, additional domestic court examination of DPH has come in the US cases of *Al-Marri*[51] and *Hamdan*.[52] In *Al-Marri*, DPH was defined as

> immediate and actual action on the battlefield likely to cause harm to the enemy because there is a direct causal relationship between the activity engaged in and the harm done to the enemy. The phrase 'direct participation in hostilities' does not mean indirect participation in hostilities, such as gathering and transmitting military information, transporting weapons, munitions and other supplies, or forward deployment.[53]

This position on DPH was affirmed in the US Military Commission ruling *United States of America v Salim Ahmed Hamdan*, where it was held that delivery of munitions did amount to direct participation in hostilities.[54]

The question of what acts amount to DPH was also examined by the German Federal Prosecutor General in 2010, in the so-called *Fuel Tankers* case. In that instance, the Prosecutor General was tasked with investigating the bombing of two fuel tankers by the German Commander of the International Security Assistance Force (ISAF) Provincial Reconstruction Team (PRT) at Kunduz, Afghanistan. The tankers had been stolen by the Taliban, but had become stuck in a sandbank on the Kunduz River. Concerned that the tankers and the fuel they carried would ultimately be used in an attack on the PRT or against Afghan police stations, the German Commander ordered an airstrike on the tankers.[55] At the time of the strike, numerous civilians were attempting to siphon fuel from the tankers, and were killed.[56]

---

[50] ibid, para 35.

[51] *Ali Saleh Kahlah Al-Marri v Commander John Pucciarelli* 534 F.3d 213, 216 (2008).

[52] *United States of America v Salim Ahmed Hamdan* (On Reconsideration Ruling on Motion to Dismiss for Lack of Jurisdiction) (2007). See also the US case *Hamlily v Obama* 616 F Supp 2d 63 (2009) where the Court affirmed that the scope of DPH includes the hostile act, as well as preparation for and return from the hostile act (paras 20–21); and the case of *Gherebi v Obama* 609 F Supp 2d 43 (2009), which also looked at the concept of DPH, but did not go into detail regarding specific examples of DPH.

[53] 'Message from the President of the United States Transmitting Two Optional Protocols to the Convention on the Rights of the Child', S Treaty Doc No 106-37 (2000) VII.

[54] *United States of America v Salim Ahmed Hamdan* (n 52) para 6.

[55] See Deutscher Bundestag, 'Report of the German Parliamentary Investigation Committee' (25 October 2011) 17 Wahlperiode Drucksache 17/7400, http://dip21.bundestag.de/dip21/btd/17/074/1707400.pdf.

[56] See United Nations Assistance Mission in Afghanistan (UNAMA) 'Annual Report on Protection of Civilians in Armed Conflict, 2009' (January 2010) unama.unmissions.org/sites/default/files/protection_of_civilian_2009_report_english_1.pdf.

The question at issue for the Prosecutor was therefore whether the targeting of the tankers was lawful, given the presence of civilians in the vicinity of the tankers. While the Prosecutor ultimately dismissed the case, he did comment on the scope of DPH, stating that hostilities are to be understood not just

> in the narrow sense as armed acts of destroying personnel and equipment of the adverse forces. ... Rather, the term also comprises all acts which negatively affect the military capacities and operations of a party to the conflict, with a direct causal link between the act and the disadvantage caused and an objective link (belligerent nexus) between the damage caused to the adversary and the advantage for the opposing party being required. ... Consequently, acts of sabotage, the disruption of the enemy's logistics and communications are covered ... whereas the general disruption of the civilian infrastructure of the country in which the armed conflict is taking place, even if negatively affecting the enemy forces, is not.[57]

IV. DEFINING DIRECT PARTICIPATION IN OTHER INSTRUMENTS

Note should also be made with regards to other attempts to define the concept of direct participation in hostilities made by other organisations and institutions. Most notable, and controversial, of these has been the ICRC's Interpretive Guidance on Direct Participation in Hostilities, which was established to address three questions: who is a civilian for the purposes of the principle of distinction? What conduct amounts to direct participation in hostilities? And what modalities govern the loss of protection against direct attack?[58] The Guidance defines civilians in an IAC as 'all persons who are neither members of the armed forces of a party to the conflict nor participants in a *levée en masse*'.[59] Such persons are 'entitled to protection against direct attack unless and for such time as they take a direct part in hostilities'.[60]

In NIACs, the definition of civilians is as follows:

> All persons who are not members of State armed forces or organised armed groups of a party to the conflict are civilians and, therefore, entitled to protection against direct attack unless and for such time as they take a direct part in hostilities. In non-international armed conflict, armed groups constitute the armed forces of a non-State party to the conflict and consist only of individuals whose continuous function is to take a direct part in hostilities ('continuous combat function').[61]

---

[57] *Fuel Tankers case* (Decision) Germany Federal Court of Justice 3 BJs 6/10-4 (2010) 59–63.

[58] N Melzer, 'Interpretive Guidance on the Notion of Direct Participation in Hostilities under International Humanitarian Law' (2008) 90 *International Review of the Red Cross* 991, 994.

[59] ibid, 995. The Guidance thus defines 'armed forces', as 'all armed actors showing a sufficient degree of military organisation and belonging to a party to the conflict'.

[60] ibid, 997.

[61] ibid, 1002.

In a NIAC, armed forces are thus to include state armed forces and organised armed groups. 'Organised armed groups' is interpreted to include the Additional Protocol II categories of 'dissident armed forces' and 'other organised armed groups'.[62] The term 'dissident armed forces' is interpreted as members of state armed forces who have turned against the government; the term 'organised armed groups' is taken as civilians who have joined an armed group of sufficient military organisation to conduct hostilities against another party to the conflict. Generally speaking, 'organised armed group' is meant to refer to the armed or military wing of a non-state party: 'its armed forces in a functional sense',[63] and not to the political, social or humanitarian segments of a rebel or insurgent organisation.

The ICRC eschewed the approach taken by other bodies of listing certain activities as amounting to direct participation in hostilities, instead devising a formula to be applied to any kind of act to determine whether it amounted to DPH. The Interpretive Guidance thus states that, in order to qualify as direct participation:

> A specific act must meet the following cumulative criteria: (1) the act must be likely to adversely affect the military operations of military capacity of a party to an armed conflict or alternatively to inflict death, injury, or destruction on persons or objects protected against direct attack (threshold of harm); (2) there must be a direct causal link between the act and the harm likely to result from that act, or from a coordinated military operation of which that act constitutes an integral part (direct causation); and (3) the act must be specifically designed to directly cause the required threshold of harm in support of a party to the conflict and to the detriment of another (belligerent nexus).[64]

The three-step formula for DPH as envisaged by the ICRC requires an assessment of the threshold of harm—that it 'must be likely to adversely affect the military operations or military capacity of a party to an armed conflict or, alternatively, to inflict death, injury or destruction on persons or objects protected against direct attack';[65] of direct causation—that 'there must be a direct causal link between the specific act and the harm likely to result either from that act, or from a coordinated military operation of which that act constitutes an integral part';[66] and a belligerent nexus—that the act of violence must be specifically undertaken 'in support of a party to an armed conflict and to the detriment of another'.[67] By combining these

---

[62] AP II, Art 1(1).
[63] Melzer (n 58) 1006.
[64] ibid, 1016.
[65] ibid.
[66] ibid, 1019.
[67] ibid, 1026.

three elements—threshold of harm, direct causation and belligerent nexus—the Guidance aims to

> permit a reliable distinction between activities amounting to direct participation in hostilities and activities which, although occurring in the context of an armed conflict, are not part of the conduct of hostilities and, therefore, do not entail loss of protection against direct attack.[68]

DPH was also examined in other non-binding manuals of instruction on armed conflict, namely the 2006 San Remo Manual on the Law of Non-International Armed Conflict,[69] the 2009 Manual on International Law Applicable to Air and Missile Warfare,[70] and the 2013 Tallinn Manual on the International Law Applicable to Cyber Warfare.[71] The San Remo Manual outlines DPH in section 1.1.2, where direct participation is defined as acts where there is 'sufficient causal relation between the active participation and its immediate consequences',[72] and gives examples of DPH as including sabotaging enemy installations, operating or assisting in the operation of weapons systems, delivering ammunition, and gathering military intelligence.[73] The Harvard Manual addresses the question of DPH in Article 28, where it restates that 'civilians lose their protection from attack if and for such time as they take a direct part in hostilities'.[74] Article 29 then illustrates what kinds of conduct amount to DPH, including (but not limited to) defending military objectives from attack, operating or controlling weapons systems, and employing military communications networks in support of specific combat operations.[75] The Tallinn Manual also examined DPH, affirming the three-step test outlined by the ICRC DPH Guidance.[76]

V. DURATION OF DIRECT PARTICIPATION IN HOSTILITIES—WHEN DOES DPH TERMINATE AND WHEN DOES LOSS OF IMMUNITY DUE TO DIRECT PARTICIPATION CEASE TO BE TEMPORARY?

The examples discussed above—the court cases and soft law instruments—all share a commonality in that they attempt to outline what kinds of acts

---

[68] ibid, 1031.

[69] M Schmitt, C Garraway and Y Dinstein (eds), *The San Remo Manual on the Law of Non-International Armed Conflict* (San Remo, 2006) 4–5.

[70] *HPCR Manual on International Law Applicable to Air and Missile Warfare* (Harvard, Cambridge University Press, 2009).

[71] M Schmitt (ed), *The Tallinn Manual on the International Law Applicable to Cyber Warfare* (New York, Cambridge University Press, 2013).

[72] Schmitt, Garraway and Dinstein (n 69) ss 1.1.2, 4.

[73] ibid.

[74] *HPCR Manual on International Law* (n 70) Art 28.

[75] ibid, Art 29.

[76] Schmitt (n 71) 119.

amount to direct participation in hostilities, ie acts which result in the loss of immunity from attack for such persons committing the acts in question. However, only a few of the above-mentioned examples examine the other part of DPH—its cessation. Much of the discussion of DPH focuses on what acts trigger DPH, but there has been comparatively little examination of when and if cessation of DPH results in a civilian regaining his or her immunity from targeting, whether repeated acts of DPH result in the permanent loss of civilian immunity (and therefore, the permanent loss of civilian status), and, if indeed one can lose one's civilian status, how such a loss occurs (that is to say, how is membership in an armed group determined).

Article 51(3) and Article 13(3) both make it clear that loss of protection from targeting is temporary—the terminology 'for such time' indicates that loss of immunity endures only for as long as the direct participation is taking place. So how is this determined? And are there certain activities that result in irrevocable loss of civilian immunity and even civilian status?

A. Civilians and Loss/Reacquisition of Immunity from Attacks

The Israeli Supreme Court noted that a person who has ceased taking a direct part in hostilities regains his or her protection from targeting.[77] This was affirmed by the ICRC Guidance, which states that civilians directing participating will regain their immunity from direct attack upon cessation of direct participation.[78] For the ICRC Interpretive Guidance, the Article 51(3) element of 'for such time' includes measures preparatory to the execution of the specific act of participation, including both the deployment to and return from the location of the execution of the act of DPH.[79] Any activities prior to or following an act of DPH that are 'of a specifically military nature and so closely linked to the subsequent execution of a specific hostile act that they already constitute an integral part of that act'[80] are thus also considered DPH. This approach to the duration of DPH is seen also in the Tallinn Manual.[81]

This has come to be known as the 'revolving door'[82] of civilian protection—that civilians do not lose their status *as civilians* while engaging in DPH, but that their protection against direct attack is suspended for the time that they take direct part in hostilities. Once they cease taking direct

---

[77] *Targeted Killings* case (n 16) para 39.
[78] See also Schmitt (n 71) 120–21.
[79] Melzer (n 58) 1031.
[80] ibid, 1031–32.
[81] Schmitt (n 71) 121, which states that DPH includes actions 'immediately preceding or subsequent to' the act of DPH.
[82] Melzer (n 58) 1035.

part, they regain their civilian immunity from attack.[83] However, if such an approach were strictly applied to all persons directly participating in armed conflict—both those persons sporadically participating, and those persons who were routinely taking part in hostilities as the member of a non-state armed group—it would, as the ICRC has pointed out, seem

> to create an imbalance between such [armed] groups and governmental armed forces. Application of this rule would imply that an attack on members of armed opposition groups is only lawful for 'such time as they take a direct part in hostilities' while an attack on members of governmental armed forces would be lawful at any time.[84]

However, practice to date does not support such an approach. The Israeli Supreme Court specifically drew the distinction between a person who may take sporadic part and those persons who have actively joined a 'terrorist organisation' and, while within that organisation, commit a chain of hostile acts, even if there are short 'rest' periods between such acts.[85] The Court noted that for a member of an organisation, such rest intervals did not constitute a cessation of active participation, but rather a brief interlude preparatory to the commission of and/or participation in the next hostile act.[86] The ICRC likewise has affirmed this approach, stating that members of armed opposition groups can, by virtue of their membership in such a group, be 'either considered to be continuously taking a direct part in hostilities or not considered to be civilians'.[87] How such membership is determined is difficult to ascertain. Few attempts have been made to devise a formulation for membership of an armed group—indeed, the Israeli Supreme Court did not, in the *Targeted Killings* case, provide a definition of what constituted membership of an armed group.

However, the ICRC, in its Interpretive Guidance, *did* examine the membership criteria. For the ICRC, membership of an armed opposition group in a NIAC is connected to the idea of 'continuous combat function' (CCF). Membership in a dissident armed group—ie former members of a state's armed force who have turned against their government—is to be determined by the status of the person at the time the armed group became a dissident armed force. That is to say, a person who was a member of a state's armed forces remains a member of the armed forces if and when that armed force opposes its government, so long as they 'remain organised under the

---

[83] ibid.

[84] See 'Commentary to Rule 6' in Henckaerts and Doswald-Beck (n 9).

[85] *Targeted Killings* case (n 16) paras 39–40.

[86] ibid, paras 39–40. See also the ICTY in *Blaškić*, where the Appeals Chamber noted that if a person 'is a member of an armed organisation, the fact that he is not armed or in combat at the time of the commission of crimes, does not accord him civilian status' (*Prosecutor v Blaškić* (Appeals Judgment) ICTY-95-14-A (29 July 2004) para 47).

[87] See 'Commentary to Rule 6' in Henckaerts and Doswald-Beck (n 9).

structures of the State armed forces to which they formerly belonged'.[88] For other organised armed groups, the ICRC takes a functional approach, noting that membership of such a group will depend on whether the person undertakes a CCF—ie there is evidence of ongoing high-level involvement in the planning and execution of hostilities. Such a test of CCF 'distinguishes members of the organised fighting forces of a non-State party from civilians who directly participate in hostilities on a merely spontaneous, sporadic, or unorganised basis, or who assume exclusively political, administrative or other non-combat functions'.[89] The idea of CCF ensures that certain persons are excluded from the definition of DPH, including any civilians who take on support functions, such as

> recruiters, trainers, financiers and propagandists [who] may continuously contribute to the general war effort of a non-State party, but ... are not members of an organised armed group belonging to that party unless their function additionally includes activities amounting to direct participation in hostilities.[90]

Also excluded from CCF are persons who sole function is the acquisition, manufacture, and maintenance of weapons and other equipment outside active military operations, and persons engaged in intelligence collection of a general, rather than tactical, nature.[91]

The Guidance states that determining CCF may be achieved a number of ways. Visual markers, such as the open carriage of arms, or the wearing of a uniform or other distinctive sign or emblem associated with parties to the armed conflict can assist with such a determination. Other grounds for such an assessment include what the Guidance calls 'conclusive behaviour':

> [F]or example, where a person has repeatedly directly participated in hostilities in support of an organised armed group in circumstances indicating that such conduct constitutes a continuous function rather than a spontaneous, sporadic, or temporary role assumed for the duration of a particular operation.[92]

For members of organised groups, there is no 'revolving door' of protection/ loss of protection. As long as such persons are deemed to be assuming a CCF, they will remain targets.[93] This correlates with the position in Article 13(3) of Additional Protocol II relating to DPH, where the Commentary makes it clear that persons who belong to the armed forces or to armed groups 'may be attacked at any time'.[94]

---

[88] Melzer (n 58) 1006.
[89] ibid, 1007.
[90] ibid, 1008.
[91] ibid.
[92] ibid.
[93] ibid, 1035.
[94] Sandoz, Swinarski and Zimmerman (n 19) 1453, para 4789.

However, the ICRC position—whereby only persons with a CCF would be considered members of an armed group—has come in for criticism by some academics and practitioners, who feel that such an approach unfairly privileges armed non-state actors; that for regular armed forces, 'the cook, the cleaner, the lawyer and others without a combat function'[95] remain targetable by virtue of their status as members of the armed forces, but that the holders of equivalent positions in an armed group would not be targetable unless they also maintained a CCF.[96] As such, an imbalance is created between state armed forces and non-state groups, which would seem contrary to one of the aims of IHL—namely, the equality of belligerents.[97]

VI. WHO IS A CIVILIAN? MAKING SENSE OF DPH AND MEMBERSHIP IN ARMED GROUPS

Given these differing and diverse approaches to defining civilian DPH and memberships in an armed group, is there a common ground on the issues, a set of minima that have been universally agreed on? The definition of DPH and of membership in an armed opposition group is, as demonstrated above, something that has been largely undefined in the treaty law of armed conflict. As such, it has been to customary law that states and other stakeholders have looked in order to help define those concepts. However, also as demonstrated above, customary law in respect of both DPH and membership of armed opposition groups has been notably sparse. This is problematic because the treatment one is accorded under the law of armed conflict varies greatly depending on whether one is a civilian taking no part in hostilities, a civilian taking direct if sporadic part in hostilities, and a person who is considered a member of an armed opposition group taking continuous part in hostilities. Of these groups, the civilian taking no part may not be directly targeted, the civilian taking direct but intermittent part in hostilities can be targeted only while taking direct part, and the member of the armed group may always be lawfully targeted because of his or her membership. Accurately assessing who falls into which category thus has implications for both the person being assessed for targeting, and the person undertaking the targeting. Given the limited amount of detailed practice we have on

---

[95] D Akande, 'Clearing the Fog of War? The ICRC's Interpretive Guidance on Direct Participation in Hostilities' (2010) 59 *ICLQ* 180, 187.

[96] Y Dinstein, *Non-International Armed Conflicts in International Law* (Cambridge, Cambridge University Press, 2014) 62.

[97] See generally V Koutroulis, 'And Yet It Exists: In Defence of the "Equality of Belligerents" Principle' (2013) 26 *Leiden Journal of International Law* 449; A Roberts, 'The Equal Application of the Laws of War: A Principle Under Pressure' (2008) 90 *International Review of the Red Cross* 931.

the scope of DPH and membership in armed groups, what can be said, at a minimum, are the accepted minimum criteria for DPH and membership?

For DPH, it seems that the minimum consensus is broadly similar to that enunciated by the ICTY in *Strugar*, which excludes basic support activities such as the supply of food and provisions but includes activities such as transmitting military information for the immediate use of a belligerent, and transporting weapons in proximity to combat operations,[98] in addition to more obvious acts of DPH, such as bearing, using or taking up arms, as well as actual armed fighting or combat.[99] This seems largely congruent with DPH tests outlined by domestic and international courts, in manuals such as the San Remo, Tallinn and Harvard Manuals, and by the ICRC, as outlined above. Thus, mindful of the presumption of civilian immunity,[100] if in light of circumstances ruling at the time, a person appears to be taking a direct part in hostilities, and that their actions are more than indirect (ie political support, provision of basic sustenance such as food or water) but are likely to cause actual harm to an enemy, one could feasibly maintain a charge of DPH.

Determining membership of an armed group is a harder prospect, and can only conceivably be done on a case-by-case basis, in light of any relevant intelligence gathered on the person or persons in question.[101] The visual indicia of DPH will be the same whether the person is taking intermittent DPH, or whether the person is a high-level member of an armed group, and, as Dinstein has noted, armed opposition groups are 'not likely to issue membership cards'.[102] As such, additional information acquired through intelligence-gathering will remain the best measure for determining someone's status.

VII. CONCLUDING THOUGHTS

Civilians are deserving of and indeed entitled to protection under the law of armed conflict applicable in both IACs and NIACs. However, it is

---

[98] See Schmitt, Garraway and Dinstein (n 69) 4–5.

[99] *Prosecutor v Strugar* (n 42) para 177.

[100] As outlined in Art 50(1) AP I, and affirmed in *Prosecutor v Đorđević* (Judgment) ICTY-05-87/1 (23 February 2011) para 2066. As noted in that judgment, Art 13 AP II does not contain a similarly worded provision; however, ICRC Commentary to Art 13 notes that 'in case of doubt regarding the status of an individual, he is presumed to be a civilian' (see Sandoz, Swinarski and Zimmerman (n 19) para 4789). The Study on Customary International Humanitarian Law did not state that the presumption of civilian immunity was customary in NIACs in 2005 (see 'Commentary to Rule 6' in Henckaerts and Doswald-Beck (n 9)), though it has stated that the same approach to a presumption of civilian immunity in IACs would be justified in NIACs. A case could thus be made that the principle is crystallising as custom in 2016.

[101] See Dinstein (n 96) 62.

[102] ibid.

commonplace for civilians to be unduly impacted, either negligently or deliberately, when armed conflict erupts. The laws designed to protect civilians in times of armed conflict are comprehensive, but their application depends on being able to determine who is a civilian. Moreover, those protections for civilians—specifically the protection from direct targeting—can be suspended and even entirely lost when the civilian takes a direct part in hostilities. Determining precisely when, how and for how long a civilian loses his or her protection from targeting is by no means settled. The uncertainties of the scope of DPH in all its potential permutations have ramification for both civilians and non-civilians alike, as the lack of clarity on DPH and the associate issue of membership in armed groups makes respecting the law difficult for parties to an armed conflict, and makes life for civilians in war zones more dangerous. As such, all parties with a stake in the law of armed conflict must endeavour to bring further clarity to the question of DPH, in the interests of protecting all persons affected by armed conflict.

2

The Duty in International Law to Investigate Civilian Deaths in Armed Conflict

MARK LATTIMER

I. INTRODUCTION

IT IS WIDELY recognised that civilians constitute the majority of the victims of today's armed conflicts, but the precise extent of loss of civilian life and injury to civilians in any given conflict often remains unestablished. In a number of recent conflicts, authoritative estimates of the civilian death toll have either proved unobtainable or have displayed huge ranges.

In the absence of an explicit obligation to investigate civilian damage on the face of the Geneva Conventions, belligerents have often appeared reluctant to inquire into the circumstances of civilian deaths, including those for which they might be responsible. Following the US-led invasions of Afghanistan in 2001 and Iraq in 2003, there was increasing public criticism of the US position on recording deaths, a position encapsulated in a quote frequently ascribed to General Tommy Franks: 'We don't do body counts.'[1]

The obstacles to obtaining an accurate account of both the number and circumstances of deaths are numerous. They include: the sheer scale of the total killing in recent conflicts as well as the large number of separate incidents; the proliferation of armed actors, including forces not regularly constituted; difficulties in distinguishing civilians from combatants or fighters, particularly in NIACs; the publication of claims and counter-claims of atrocities, including the deliberate spreading of misinformation; rapidly shifting patterns of control over territory; inadequate security on the ground for the purposes of conducting investigations and collecting material evidence; and dysfunctional or compromised judicial and law enforcement systems.

---

[1] See NC Crawford, *Accountability for Killing: Moral Responsibility for Collateral Damage in America's Post-9/11 Wars* (Oxford, Oxford University Press, 2013) 88.

However, establishing the facts behind reports of civilian deaths in general, and allegations of violations in particular, is essential for providing reparation to victims; securing accountability of belligerents, and suppressing and deterring violations; establishing the record for post-conflict transitional justice; and also guiding the humanitarian, security and reconstruction policies of national as well as international actors.

Within this policy context, this chapter asks whether international law imposes a positive duty on parties to a conflict to investigate civilian deaths. Under IHL the killing of civilians is not always unlawful, but is assessed according to a balance between military necessity and humanitarian requirements; for example, civilian deaths that are caused in the course of an attack on a legitimate military target will be lawful if they were not expected to be excessive in relation to the concrete and direct military advantage anticipated. It will be argued, however, that IHL places obligations on parties to an armed conflict to account for the dead irrespective of the legality of an attack and imposes further obligations where the killing of civilians is potentially unlawful.

While it is settled in international law that an investigation is required in cases where a war crime is suspected, the obligation to investigate certain other cases of civilian deaths is disputed, both by some states and in the academic literature.[2] It is often believed that such a wider obligation depends on the applicability of human rights standards and therefore may not arise when a human rights jurisdiction cannot be established. This chapter will, however, consider to what extent such investigatory obligations arise in all situations of armed conflict by virtue of IHL.

The chapter first considers the general obligations on parties to conflict to account for the missing and the dead, particularly after any engagement, to perform examinations, and to mark and register grave sites. Second, it turns to specific obligations on parties where a suspected violation of IHL has occurred. The need to take precautions in attack, which itself is derived from the fundamental IHL principles of distinction and proportionality, arguably gives rise to specific investigatory obligations. The small but growing literature on the requirements of post-attack reviews and other assessments of collateral damage is discussed, including the findings of the Turkel Commission, a public commission established by the Government of Israel following the *Mavi Marmara* incident during the Gaza blockade.[3] Third, the paper considers briefly additional investigatory obligations that apply in the case of a suspected war crime or other violation of international criminal

---

[2] See section III below.

[3] The Public Commission to Examine the Maritime Incident of 31 May 2010 (Turkel Commission), 2nd Report, 'Israel's Mechanisms for Examining and Investigating Complaints and Claims of Violations of the Laws of Armed Conflict According to International Law' (February 2013).

law, including the liability regarding failures to investigate that arises under the doctrine of command responsibility.

The approach will be to analyse first the relevant provisions of treaty law, particularly the four Geneva Conventions for the protection of war victims of 1949 and the two Additional Protocols of 1977 relating to the protection of victims of IACs (I) and NIACs (II).[4] We then consider how the question of obligations to investigate is treated under customary IHL, drawing in particular on the extensive study of customary IHL published by the International Committee of the Red Cross in 2005.[5] However, given that the ICRC study has some noteworthy detractors, an attempt will be made to supplement this with examples of practice from 'specially affected' states, including those who are not party to the Additional Protocols.[6] In the case of an investigation of a suspected war crime, sources of international criminal law will also be discussed, including the Rome Statute establishing the ICC.

The duty to investigate is the subject of a growing jurisprudence in international human rights courts, such as the ECtHR and the Inter-American Commission and Court of Human Rights, including in cases involving the right to life.[7] A full discussion of the substantive human rights law on the

---

[4] Geneva Convention I for the Amelioration of the Condition of the Wounded and Sick in Armed Forces in the Field (adopted 12 August 1949, entered into force 21 October 1950) 75 UNTS 31 (GC I); Geneva Convention II for the Amelioration of the Condition of Wounded, Sick and Shipwrecked Members of Armed Forces at Sea (adopted 12 August 1949, entered into force 21 October 1950) 75 UNTS 85 (GC II); Geneva Convention III Relative to the Treatment of Prisoners of War (adopted 12 August 1949, entered into force 21 October 1950) 75 UNTS 135 (GC III); Geneva Convention IV Relative to the Protection of Civilian Persons in Time of War (adopted 12 August 1949, entered into force 21 October 1950) 75 UNTS 287 (GC IV); Protocol I Additional to the Geneva Conventions of 12 August 1949 and relating to the Protection of Victims of International Armed Conflicts (adopted 8 June 1977, entered into force 7 December 1978) 1125 UNTS 3 (AP I); Protocol II Additional to the Geneva Conventions of 12 August 1949 and relating to the Protection of Victims of Non-International Armed Conflicts (adopted 8 June 1977, entered into force 7 December 1978) 1125 UNTS 609 (AP II). While the Geneva Conventions enjoy universal ratification, a number of states are not party to the Additional Protocols.

[5] JM Henckaerts and L Doswald-Beck, *Customary International Humanitarian Law* (Cambridge, Cambridge University Press, 2005).

[6] See eg US Department of State, 'Initial Response of US to ICRC Study on Customary International Humanitarian Law with Illustrative Comments' (3 November 2006) www.state. gov/s/1/2006/98860.htm. The US criticisms included that the state practice cited in the ICRC Study was 'insufficiently dense' and that it failed to pay due regard to the practice of 'specially-affected states' which had a greater extent and depth of experience of participation in armed conflict.

[7] eg *McCann and ors v UK* (App no 18984/91) ECHR 27 September 1995; *Isayeva v Russia, Yusupova v Russia, Bazayeva v Russia* (Apps no 57947/00, 57948/00, 57949/00) ECHR 24 February 2005; *Al-Skeini and ors, Bar Human Rights Committee (intervening) and ors (intervening) v United Kingdom* (2011) 53 EHRR 18; *Bamaca Velásquez v Guatemala* (Judgment) Inter-American Court of Human Rights Series C No 70 (25 November 2000). See section III below.

obligation to investigate is beyond the scope of this chapter, although reference will be made to cases where international courts have ruled on state obligations in respect of civilian killings in armed conflict, including the elaboration of specific investigatory standards.

The terms 'investigate' and 'investigation' are used here in their ordinary sense in English, which is potentially wider than the sense of the terms in criminal law (where the latter sense is intended, the term 'criminal investigation' will be used if it is not otherwise clear from the context). As such, an investigation refers to a careful examination of facts in order to establish the truth, and it may consist of some of a number of components, including the search for bodies, medical examination, recording the fact of death, identification, registration, examination of information on circumstances of death, collection and analysis of statistical data, and communication of information, as well as the specific collection of evidence for the purposes of establishing criminal responsibility. (Specific investigative practices may also be referred to by a range of terms, including 'fact-finding', 'inquiry', 'casualty tracking/recording', 'monitoring, documentation and/or reporting', etc.) To some extent, the methodological content of any particular investigation, and the standards by which it is governed, may depend not just on the mandate of the investigating body and on whether a crime is suspected, but also on factors such as the legal status of the conflict or that of the parties, which may themselves be the subject of legal controversy.[8]

In conclusion, the chapter seeks to define the parameters of the positive duty in international law on parties to an armed conflict to investigate civilian deaths. In particular, it attempts to clarify whether an investigation is required only in cases of a suspected war crime, more broadly in cases involving any possible violation of international humanitarian law, or in all cases involving civilian deaths. Finally, in identifying a positive duty on parties to a conflict to investigate civilian deaths, the chapter asks whether the duty places an unmanageable burden on belligerents that will prove inoperable in practice.

II. GENERAL OBLIGATIONS ON PARTIES TO ACCOUNT FOR THE DEAD

This section identifies those obligations in IHL that amount to a general duty on parties to an armed conflict to account for the dead. Such a duty

---

[8] For example, recent debates over the legality of civilian deaths in US airstrikes against suspected members of transnational armed groups in Pakistan, Yemen, Syria and other jurisdictions have included consideration of whether the conflict(s) were international or non-international, or indeed whether they constituted an armed conflict at all; and on the status of irregular fighters or civilians directly participating in hostilities.

stems, as shall be seen, from the fundamental principle of humanity, but is further linked in IHL with the right of families to know the fate of their relatives, a rationale that has significant implications for the transparency of investigations. This general duty to account for the dead, binding on all parties—and, arguably, universally—underpins the further specific obligations, considered in sections III and IV, on parties responsible for attacks in which civilians are killed.

A. The Principle of Humanity and the Treatment of the Dead

The principle of humanity, universally recognised as one of the basic principles of IHL, informs not just the treatment of the living but also that of the dead. This goes beyond a prohibition on the defilement of corpses to recognition of positive obligations to account for and bury the dead with respect.

Formal recognition of the need to respect human remains and to return them for proper burial is a recurrent theme in the historical and philosophical sources of IHL from at least the time of antiquity. The need to honour and protect the bodies of the fallen is mentioned repeatedly in Homer's *Iliad* and sometimes drives the action, most famously over the treatment of Hector's body after he is slain by Achilles.[9] In Antigone, the action centres on King Creon's refusal to accord proper burial rites to Polynices, a decision for which he suffers terrible retribution. The proper treatment of the dead here is seen to derive not just from divine law but also from family ties, as in Antigone's 'He has no right to keep me from my own.'[10]

Respect for the bodies of the dead is also a common theme in Shakespeare's histories, reflecting interpretations in his historical sources of the medieval chivalric code. In *Henry V*, for example, after the battle of Agincourt the French herald Montjoy comes to ask for licence:

That we may wonder o'er this bloody field

To book our dead and then to bury them.[11]

In a response that anticipates modern IHL, Henry orders his own heralds to accompany Montjoy to bring him 'just notice of the numbers dead/ On both our parts'.[12]

In more recent conflicts, authorities have consistently linked treatment of the dead with considerations of humanity. During the Vietnam war, General

---

[9] Homer, *The Iliad*, 22: 253–66, 338–43; 24: 35–52.
[10] Sophocles, *Antigone*, line 56.
[11] *Henry V*, IV, vii, 69–71. For a discussion of the treatment of bodies in Shakespeare and his sources, see T Meron, *Bloody Constraint: War and Chivalry in Shakespeare* (New York, Oxford University Press, 2001) 75–80.
[12] ibid, 122–24. See eg GC I, Arts 15–16; AP I, Art 33(4).

Westmoreland wrote to all commanders to end the practice of US soldiers collecting ears or fingers of the dead as trophies, describing it as 'subhuman' and 'contrary to all policy and below the minimum standards of human decency'.[13] Outrages against the dignity of the dead now constitute a war crime.[14] Positive obligations regarding the dead have also been recognised to derive from humanity. In the *Jenin (Mortal Remains)* case, Israel's High Court of Justice described the task of identifying the dead as a 'highly important humanitarian need', stemming from 'respect for every dead'.[15]

B. Components of the Duty to Account for the Dead

Most of the examples given above relate to treatment of the bodies of combatants, partly reflecting a concern to protect them from vengeful acts by victorious forces. Similarly, most of the provisions on the treatment of the dead now codified in the Geneva Conventions relate to the military dead in international conflicts.[16]

The provisions in Geneva Convention IV relative to the protection of civilian persons are considerably more brief, as noted by Breau et al.[17] Article 16 provides only that 'each Party to the conflict shall facilitate the steps taken to search for the killed and wounded', and only '[a]s far as military considerations allow'. This obligation does apply to the whole of the population of the country in conflict, without any adverse distinction. More detailed provisions cover deaths of civilian internees, placing obligations on the detaining power regarding safekeeping and transmission of wills, medical certification 'showing the causes of death and the conditions under which it occurred', and maintenance and transmission of official records of death (Article 129); and honourable burial, maintenance and marking of

---

[13] Letter dated 13 October 1967, quoted in G Lewy, *America in Vietnam* (New York, Oxford University Press, 1978) n 66.

[14] See ICC, 'Elements of Crimes' (2011) www.icc-cpi.int/NR/rdonlyres/336923D8-A6AD-40EC-AD7B-45BF9DE73D56/0/ElementsOfCrimesEng.pdf, 29, 35, confirming that the war crime of 'committing outrages on personal dignity' under Art 8(2)(b)(xxi) and (c)(ii) of the ICC Statute also applies to dead persons, in both IACs and NIACs.

[15] *Barake v Minister of Defence of Israel and ors (Jenin (Mortal Remains)* case) HCJ 3114/02 (2002), paras 9, 15.

[16] These include detailed provisions relating to, inter alia, the search for the dead and prevention of their despoilment; the recording and communication of particulars of identity, date and place of death, and cause of death; preparation and forwarding of death certificates or duly authenticated lists of the dead; collection and forwarding of personal articles; careful (if possible, medical) examination of bodies; honourable interment, maintenance and marking of graves, organisation of a graves registration service, and possible return of human remains. See GC I, Arts 15–17; GC II, Arts 18–21; GC III, Arts 120–21.

[17] S Breau, M Aronsson and R Joyce, *Drone Attacks, International Law and the Recording of Civilian Casualties of Armed Conflict* (Oxford, Oxford Research Group, 2011) 16.

graves, and transmission of lists of graves with particulars of identity and location (Article 130). Furthermore, Article 131 provides:

> Every death or serious injury of an internee, caused or suspected to have been caused by a sentry, another internee or any other person, as well as any death the cause of which is unknown, shall be immediately followed by an official enquiry by the Detaining Power.

Such an enquiry should include the taking of evidence of any witnesses and the preparation of a report; where guilt is indicated, 'all necessary steps' should be taken to ensure the prosecution of those responsible.[18]

However, Protocol I contains extensive further provisions covering the recording and investigation of civilian deaths. Article 34 extends the personal scope of application of obligations on the maintenance and marking of gravesites beyond internees to all persons who have died 'for reasons related to occupation or in detention resulting from occupation or hostilities', a category that relates, according to the official commentary, to victims of armed conflicts, 'particularly of bombardments'.[19] But it is Article 33 on the search for missing persons that contains arguably the most important further obligations. Parties to the conflict are required to record detailed identification information about persons who have died 'during any period of detention' and

> 2(b) to the fullest extent possible, facilitate and, if need be, carry out the search for and the recording of information concerning such persons if they have died in other circumstances as a result of hostilities or occupation.

The commentary notes that, unlike a search after a battlefield clash, the search for the missing 'is not so much a question of combing a well-defined area, but of *carrying out a real investigation*'.[20] The commentary goes on to explain that if the first step of checking last known place of residence or detention centre registers—a minimum requirement—proves unsuccessful, 'it may be necessary to search for members of the family who could give information, to question neighbours and colleagues, in short, to carry out a true investigation'.[21] Sub-paragraph 2(b) applies again 'in particular to the registration of the missing and the dead after bombardments'.[22]

Paragraph 4 provides for agreements between parties for search teams to identify and recover the dead from battlefield areas. The official commentary notes that this supplements the relevant provisions in Geneva Convention I. However, given the wider personal scope of application of Protocol I,

---

[18] GC IV, Art 131.
[19] ICRC, 'Commentary on the Additional Protocols of 8 June 1977 to the Geneva Conventions of 12 August 1949' (1987) para 1300.
[20] ibid, para 1224 (emphasis added).
[21] ibid, paras 1233–34.
[22] ibid, para 1269.

it is clear that Article 33(4) also applies to civilian dead who may be found in 'battlefield areas', particularly as such areas have become less clearly defined in contemporary conflicts and often overlap, or are indistinguishable from, civilian areas.

The whole section of Protocol I on missing and dead persons is covered by a general principle, that implementation activities 'shall be prompted mainly by the right of families to know the fate of their relatives'.[23] Given that rights-holders in IHL are generally the high contracting parties and/or the parties to the conflict, this is a rare case of a reference to rights held by natural persons, and moreover civilians. There is, then, a certain tension between this right and the fact that the search and investigation obligations under Article 33 are triggered by a request from an adverse party. (The resulting information is then either transmitted to that party, or through the protecting power if one exists, and/or to the ICRC's Central Tracing Agency.[24]) However, it is argued that, in the light of the general principle, there is at the least an implied obligation on an adverse party to forward any requests it receives from families with missing relatives.[25] The *travaux préparatoires* also show that Article 33 was intended to cover additionally nationals of states not party to the conflict, as well as nationals of co-belligerents, the latter category becoming of particular relevance given the large multinational coalitions assembled to fight a number of contemporary conflicts.[26]

So far, we have only considered obligations arising in international armed conflicts. Protocol II relating to the protection of victims of NIACs contains only the one provision in Article 8 requiring all possible measures to be taken 'to search for the dead, prevent their being despoiled, and decently dispose of them'. The official commentary on Article 8, while noting that it would not have been realistic to lay down detailed rules in the Protocol, nonetheless emphasises 'how important it is for families to be informed of the fate of their missing relatives and, when appropriate, the location of their graves, particularly in an internal fratricidal conflict', and states that the responsible authorities should do so as far as possible, describing it as 'a fundamental humanitarian activity'.[27]

Although these last views were at the time arguably an expression *de lege ferenda*, the obligations have since been recognised as part of customary IHL. The ICRC study on customary international humanitarian law identifies a number of relevant rules, including those concerning the search and collection of the dead (Rule 112), disposal of the dead (Rule 115), the prohibition of enforced disappearances (Rule 98) and respect for family life

---

[23] AP I, Art 32.
[24] ibid, Art 33(3).
[25] ibid, Art 33(1).
[26] ICRC (n 19) 1257–58. There were no objections.
[27] ibid, 4657.

(Rule 105). Of particular importance here are those that concern accounting for the dead and the missing:

> Rule 116. With a view to the identification of the dead, each party to the conflict must record all available information prior to disposal and mark the location of the graves.

> Rule 117. Each party to the conflict must take all feasible measures to account for persons reported missing as a result of armed conflict and must provide their family members with any information it has on their fate.

According to the ICRC study, state practice establishes these rules as norms of customary international law applicable in both IACs and NIACs.[28] This is evidenced by consistent state practice, including military manuals which are applicable in non-international conflicts,[29] national legislation and case law.[30]

It is also evident in the practice of states not party to the Protocols. According to the 1997 Report on US Practice, 'it is the *opinio juris* of the United States that all measures should be taken to search for the dead',[31] and that 'the parties to *all* armed conflicts should take such action as may be within their power to provide information about missing persons'.[32] The United States also supports the principle in Protocol I that families have the right to know the fate of their relatives.[33] In fact, at the diplomatic conference that prepared the Protocols, the USA had stated that '[t]he statement of the right of families to know the fate of their relatives was of primary importance for the understanding of the Section'.[34]

Israel's 1998 Manual on the Laws of War and 2006 Manual on the Rules of Warfare similarly refer to Protocol I specifying the right of families to know the fate of their relatives.[35] In *Jenin*, a case involving the mortal remains of Palestinians killed in a battle in a refugee camp, Israel's High Court of Justice stated that the Israeli authorities 'are responsible for the location, identification, evacuation and burial of the bodies' and that the authorities furthermore accepted that this was their obligation under international law.[36]

---

[28] Henckaerts and Doswald-Beck (n 5) rr 116–17.

[29] The ICRC cites in this regard the military manuals of Benin, Canada, Croatia, Germany, India, Italy, Kenya, Madagascar, Senegal and Togo. See Henckaerts and Doswald-Beck (n 5) r 116, n 7.

[30] ibid, *Military Junta* case (Argentina); Colombia Council of State, Case No 10941.

[31] Report on US Practice (1997) ch 5.1.

[32] ibid, ch 5.2 (emphasis added).

[33] See US Center for Naval Warfare Studies, 'Annotated Supplement to the Commander's Handbook on the Law of Naval Operations' (Newport, Naval War College, 1997) para 11.4, n 19.

[34] CDDH Official Records, vol XII (1 June 1976) CDDH/II/SR.76, 232, paras 28–29.

[35] Israel Manual on the Laws of War (1998) 61; Israel Manual on the Rules of Warfare (2006) 39.

[36] *Jenin (Mortal Remains)* case (n 15) para 15.

There is also a long record of international practice regarding the require-ment to account for the missing and the dead. In 1974 the UN General Assembly passed a resolution calling on parties to conflict, 'regardless of their character or location, ... to take such action as may be within their power to help locate and mark the graves of the dead ... and to provide information about those who are missing in action'. The resolution explicitly refers to civilians as well as combatants, and includes persons belonging to other countries not parties to the conflict.[37] In country-specific resolutions, states and international organisations have also called for the missing to be accounted for in Bosnia and Herzegovina, Cyprus, East Timor, Guatemala, Kosovo and the former Yugoslavia, as well as in Western Sahara.[38] As the USA stated with respect to missing civilians in a UN Security Council debate on Bosnia and Herzegovina: 'We have a responsibility to investigate, to find out what we can.'[39]

C. 'All Feasible Measures': Means and Scope of the Duty

While the prohibition on mistreatment of the dead is absolute, the investiga-tory obligations outlined above are generally not obligations of result, but of means. The requirement under Rule 117 on accounting for the missing, for example, is to take 'all feasible measures' and investigations regarding conflict-related deaths under Article 33(2)(b) of Protocol 1 should be car-ried out 'to the fullest extent possible'. The official commentary identifies a number of factors that may influence the 'possibility of conducting such investigations', including the infrastructure and geography of the country, the willingness of its leaders, manpower available, as well as, of course, reduced or delayed access due to hostilities.[40]

However, while no party can be required to perform the impossible, the obligation is to employ *all* means at their disposal. With regard to Rule 116 on accounting for the dead, the measures envisaged according to state practice include autopsies and the recording of such, death certificates, records of disposal, individual burial and marking of graves.[41] While ter-ritorial control clearly may affect the capacity to undertake investigations, it is not determinative: the obligation in Article 33(2)(b) is to 'facilitate and, if need be, carry out' the investigation. The wording reflects the fact

---

[37] UNGA Res 3220 (XXIX) (6 November 1974).
[38] See Henckaerts and Doswald-Beck (n 5) r 117.
[39] UNSC Meeting No 3564 (10 August 1995) UN Doc S/PV.3564, 6.
[40] ICRC (n 19) 1233, 1237.
[41] Henckaerts and Doswald-Beck (n 5) r 116. 'Practice also suggests that exhumation combined with the application of forensic methods, including DNA testing, may be an appro-priate method of identifying the dead after burial.'

that in occupied territory, the job may well fall first to the local municipal authorities.[42] Equally, however, given the quality of visual imaging available in modern aerial warfare, the duty to facilitate would encompass the provision of such information for the purposes of identifying the dead and establishing cause of death in cases of bombardment when the party did not have territorial control on the ground.

In an asymmetric conflict, measures employed are not reduced to the lowest common denominator but depend on the means available to each party and may include preparations in advance of military operations.[43] The end of active hostilities is the latest point at which investigations can be commenced, but the obligation arises 'as soon as circumstances permit'.[44] The Article 33 commentary explains that this means that 'the situation should be assessed immediately, and then at regular intervals … the Parties must constantly bear in mind the interests of families and be aware of the terrible moral suffering inflicted on them by any delay'.[45] Although the conduct of investigations may be limited by means available, the obligation to transmit information available is an obligation of result.[46]

Finally, while the duty to account for the dead and missing is binding on all parties to an armed conflict, including armed opposition groups, it is not limited to them. Article 19 of Protocol I requires neutral and other states not party to the conflict to apply the relevant provisions 'to any dead of the Parties to that conflict whom they may find'. Although this does not of course bind states not party to the Protocol, enough has been said above regarding acceptance of duties towards the dead and the missing meeting a fundamental humanitarian need to suggest that the obligation to account for the dead is a duty that applies universally.

This section has described the content and scope of the general duty in IHL to account for the dead and the missing in armed conflicts. The duty is established by the Geneva Conventions, the Additional Protocols and by customary IHL, and it falls on all states and parties to conflict by virtue of humanitarian considerations, even if they are not responsible for the deaths in question. In the following sections we will look at the further obligations that entail where a possible violation of IHL has occurred, including, but not limited to, the suspected commission of war crimes.

---

[42] CDDH Official records CDDH/II/SR.35, para 46.

[43] *Physicians for Human Rights v Commander of IDF Forces in the Gaza Strip* (Judgment) HCJ 4764/04 (2004), para 27. 'Preparations for dealing with the dead should have been planned in advance. Clear procedures should be fixed regarding the different stages of the process.'

[44] AP I, Art 33; Henckaerts and Doswald-Beck (n 5) r 117, Interpretation.

[45] ICRC (n 19) 1237.

[46] Henckaerts and Doswald-Beck (n 5) r 117, Interpretation.

III. INVESTIGATION OF POSSIBLE VIOLATIONS OF IHL

The previous section identified a series of investigatory obligations on all parties under the international law protecting the victims of armed conflict, sometimes referred to, for historical reasons, as the 'law of Geneva'. In now turning to the investigation of possible violations of IHL, we consider in particular investigatory obligations falling on belligerents under 'Hague law', or the law regulating the conduct of hostilities.

A. The Obligation to Ensure Respect for IHL and to Suppress Violations

There has been renewed interest in recent years in the nature and extent of the obligation to investigate violations of IHL. This has been prompted partly by national and international public concern over civilian deaths in high-profile conflicts, including those in Israel/Gaza and Iraq;[47] and by the findings of national courts and international human rights courts and monitoring bodies,[48] in their turn leading to institutional and procedural reforms in national practice (including in Canada, Australia, the UK and the USA).[49]

On the key question of when an investigation is required under IHL, however, the small but growing scholarly literature exhibits views that diverge sharply, both from each other and from official reports.[50] Schmitt emphasises that 'investigations are required only if there is reasonable suspicion or a credible allegation of a war crime having been committed'.[51] At the other end of the spectrum, the UN Special Rapporteur on the promotion and protection of human rights and fundamental freedoms while countering terrorism has stated that:

> [H]aving regard to the duty of States to protect civilians in armed conflict ... in any case in which civilians have been, or appear to have been, killed, the State

---

[47] In addition to the Turkel Commission, see eg UNGA, 'Human Rights in Palestine and other Occupied Arab Territories; Report of the United Nations Fact-Finding Mission on the Gaza Conflict' (25 September 2009) UN Doc A/HRC/12/48 (Goldstone Report); UK Parliament, 'The Report of the Baha Mousa Inquiry' (8 September 2011).

[48] See further below.

[49] See A Cohen and Y Shany, 'Beyond the Grave Breaches Regime: The Duty to Investigate Alleged Violations of International Law Governing Armed Conflicts' in MN Schmitt and L Arimatsu (eds), *Yearbook of International Humanitarian Law 2011*, vol 14 (The Hague, TMC Asser Press, 2012) 39.

[50] See eg MN Schmitt, 'Investigating Violations of International Law in Armed Conflict' (2010) 2 *Harvard National Security Journal* 31–84; Cohen and Shany (n 49); A Margalit, 'The Duty to Investigate Civilian Casualties During Armed Conflict and its Implementation in Practice' in TD Gill et al (eds), *Yearbook of International Humanitarian Law 2012*, vol 15 (The Hague, TMC Asser Press, 2014).

[51] Schmitt (n 50) 83.

responsible is under an obligation to conduct a prompt, independent and impartial fact-finding inquiry and to provide a detailed public explanation.[52]

Sassòli and Olson limit that obligation to possible violations.[53] The Turkel Commission, meanwhile, draws a distinction between investigation and examination, positing 'a general duty to broadly *examine* all suspected violations of international humanitarian law' and 'an additional duty to *investigate* certain types of alleged violations known as "war crimes"'.[54]

Common Article 1 of the Geneva Conventions establishes the duty not just to respect the Conventions but also 'to ensure respect', a formulation, repeated in Protocol I, that emphasises the positive nature of the obligation.[55] In terms of preventing violations, the Conventions establish obligations for the penal repression of 'grave breaches' of the Conventions ('war crimes')[56] but also state: 'Each High Contracting Party shall take measures necessary for the suppression of all acts contrary to the provisions of the present Convention other than the grave breaches.'[57] The word 'suppression' here ('faire cesser' in the French text) is explained in the official 1958 Commentary as follows: '[T]here is no doubt that what is primarily meant is the repression of breaches other than the grave breaches listed and only in the second place administrative measures to ensure respect for the provisions of the Convention.'[58] Protocol 1 applies the same rubric to its own provisions, while also confirming that the duty to suppress violations applies to omissions as well as acts.[59]

Which investigatory obligations does the duty to suppress, or to repress ordinary breaches, entail? Article 87 of Protocol I requires military commanders to prevent, to suppress and 'to report to competent authorities' breaches of the Conventions and the Protocol, and 'to initiate disciplinary or penal actions against violators'.[60] The obligation to investigate can be assumed in both the making up of a report and in initiating punitive action (particularly bearing in mind the need to safeguard rights of the accused). The official commentary duly states that 'the starting point' for any action

---

[52] UNGA, 'Promotion and Protection of Human Rights and Fundamental Freedoms while Countering Terrorism' (18 September 2013) UN Doc A/68/389, para 78.

[53] M Sassòli and LM Olson, 'The Relationship between International Humanitarian Law and Human Rights Law Where It Matters: Admissible Killing and Internment of Fighters in Non-International Armed Conflicts' (2008) 90 *International Review of the Red Cross* 871, 615 n 77.

[54] Turkel Commission (n 3) para 22 (emphasis in original).

[55] And, arguably, its character *erga omnes*: see Henckaerts and Doswald-Beck (n 5) r 144.

[56] See s 4.

[57] GC IV, Art 147(3).

[58] J Pictet, *Commentary on the Geneva Conventions of 12 August 1949* (Geneva, ICRC, 1952–59) 594.

[59] AP I, Arts 85(1), 86(1).

[60] ibid, Art 87(1)–(3).

to suppress or punish a breach is 'to establish or ensure the establishment of the facts'.[61] Where necessary, it would involve remitting the case to the judicial authority 'with such factual evidence as it was possible to find'.[62] In this way, the commentary notes, 'a commander of a unit would act like an investigating magistrate'.[63] Schmitt concludes that the article 'contemplates a system of military self-policing that complements the broader duty of States to investigate and prosecute' and that 'extends throughout the chain of command'.[64]

Although Protocol II is silent on the question of suppressing violations, the obligation to suppress in the Geneva Conventions quoted above extends to 'all' acts in violation, thereby including violations of Common Article 3 applicable to NIACs. This is one of the factors cited by the Turkel Commission when it concluded that: '[T]here is no longer a difference between the law of international and non-international armed conflicts with regard to the existence of an obligation to examine and investigate imposed on the territorial State and the State of nationality of the suspect.'[65] An example of practice by both state and non-state actors in an internal conflict is the 1992 agreement by the parties to the non-international conflict in Bosnia and Herzegovina to undertake, when informed of an allegation of IHL violations, 'to open an enquiry promptly and pursue it conscientiously' and to punish those responsible.[66]

State practice more broadly supports the existence of a duty to report and perform some form of investigation in all cases of suspected violations. The US Department of Defense defines a 'reportable incident' as 'a possible, suspected or alleged violation of the law of war, for which there is credible information', and requires all such incidents to be 'reported promptly, investigated thoroughly, and, where appropriate, remedied by corrective action'.[67] If a unit commander receives information suggesting a reportable incident might have been committed by personnel under his command, he must conduct a preliminary inquiry to 'gather all reasonably available evidence bearing on guilt or innocence', and, once an allegation is confirmed,

---

[61] ICRC (n 19) 3560.

[62] ibid, 3562.

[63] ibid.

[64] Schmitt (n 50) 43.

[65] Turkel Commission (n 3) para 27. The Commission further noted that the duty flowed from 'the principle that conventions should be complied with (*pacta sunt servanda*)'; Vienna Convention on the Law of Treaties (adopted 23 May 1969, entered into force 27 January 1980) 1155 UNTS 331, 332–33 (VCLT) Art 26. See also Schmitt (n 50) 48 n71: 'Assuming a State accepts a purported norm as binding, it has no reason to object to an obligation to investigate its possible breach.'

[66] 'Agreement on the Application of IHL between the Parties to the Conflict in Bosnia and Herzegovina' (London, 27 August 1992) Art 5, quoted in Henckaerts and Doswald-Beck (n 5) 3947 r 158.

[67] DOD Directive 2311.01E.

he must initiate a formal investigation and notify the relevant military criminal investigative organisation.[68] The Code of Conduct for Canadian Forces Personnel requires any violation of the laws of armed conflict to be 'investigated rapidly in as impartial a manner as possible'.[69] Canadian legislation, as well that of Australia and the UK, explicitly requires investigation in cases of suspected service offences in addition to mandatory criminal investigations in cases of war crimes.[70]

Given the lack of clarity on this point in the literature, it bears emphasis that the duty to consider initiating a criminal investigation also applies in cases of 'ordinary' breaches of IHL that do not meet the gravity threshold of a war crime.[71] This is clear from the structure and the wording of the relevant provisions of the Geneva Conventions and Protocol I. States remain at all times responsible for the actions of their armed forces;[72] that responsibility includes the obligation to suppress violations other than grave breaches;[73] the obligation to suppress involves commanders initiating, where appropriate, 'disciplinary or penal action against violators'.[74] The official commentary to the Fourth Convention explains: 'The Contracting Parties who have taken measures to repress the various grave breaches of the Convention and have fixed an appropriate penalty in each case should at least insert in their legislation a general clause providing for the punishment of other breaches' and 'should institute judicial or disciplinary punishment'.[75]

In fact, if criminal penalties were unavailable for breaches of IHL other than war crimes, this would lead to perverse results. It needs to be appreciated that military law makes extensive use of penal sanctions, including for conduct (dereliction of duty, insubordination) that would not generally constitute an offence under ordinary criminal law. Given the necessary calibration of offences and punishment in criminal law, it would be clearly anomalous if a commander could be prosecuted, say, for falling

---

[68] Manual for Courts-Martial; Chairman of Joint Chiefs of Staff, Instr.5810.01D, 6(f)(4)(e)(2), quoted in M Drabik, 'A Duty to Investigate Incidents Involving Collateral Damage and the United States Military's Practice' (2013) 22 *Minnesota Journal of International Law* inline 15, 26–27.

[69] Office of Judge Advocate General Canada, para 3, quoted in Margalit (n 50) 165.

[70] See Cohen and Shany (n 49) 52–54.

[71] If some commentators appear to talk in terms of a dichotomy between war crimes and non-criminal violations of IHL, that may be because they are talking of criminalisation as a matter of *international* law; see Y Dinstein, *The Conduct of Hostilities under the Law of International Armed Conflict*, 2nd edn (New York, Cambridge University Press, 2010) para 657; Turkel Commission (n 3) 39. See section IV.

[72] AP I, Art 91. See also GC IV, Art 148, and Hague Convention No IV Respecting the Laws and Customs of War on Land and its annex: Regulations concerning the Laws and Customs of War on Land (adopted 18 October 1907, entered into force 26 January 1910) 36 Stat 2227 TS No 539 (Hague Convention IV) Art 3.

[73] GC IV, Art 147(3).

[74] AP I, Art 87(3).

[75] Pictet (n 58) 594.

asleep on operational duty but not for ordering forced religious conversions, or launching an attack with reckless disregard for incidental civilian casualties.[76]

The distinction is this: unlike war crimes, which are criminalised under *international* law, the choice of penalties applied in cases of other violations or ordinary breaches of IHL depends on *national* (ordinary and military) law.[77] The international law duty in such cases is to suppress violations and to do so effectively; that requires an investigation, with, where appropriate, the possibility of a criminal prosecution.[78] It is therefore incorrect to argue that there is no duty to investigate unless a war crime is suspected.

B. Assessing Precautions in Attack and the Principle of Proportionality

Where investigatory obligations under the duty to suppress *all* IHL violations arguably matter most with regard to the avoidance of civilian deaths is in cases of failure to take precautions in attack. For Schmitt, a 'paradigmatic example is the airstrike that causes unexpected civilian casualties despite being executed as planned'.[79]

Civilian deaths are not necessarily unlawful under IHL and indeed most IHL practitioners would regard some incidental loss of civilian life as unavoidable in conflicts of any intensity. Besides the prohibition on attacks targeted at civilians or civilian objects, however, indiscriminate attacks are also prohibited, including attacks that may be expected to cause civilian collateral damage which would be excessive in relation to the military advantage anticipated.[80] This principle of proportionality, codified in Protocol I, is now accepted as part of customary IHL applicable in both IACs and NIACs.[81] Its practical significance leads Dinstein to conclude

---

[76] Neither of these are war crimes according to the Geneva Conventions or the ICC Statute; see Pictet (n 58) 594; Rome Statute of the International Criminal Court (adopted 17 July 1998, entered into force 1 July 2002) UN Doc A/CONF 183/9 (ICC Statute) art 8 and discussion below.

[77] Commander Ian Park gives the hypothetical example of a UK soldier stealing a loaf of bread from a civilian during an armed conflict. This would not amount to a war crime but would nonetheless 'constitute an offence of theft, pursuant to the Armed Forces Act 2006 and be liable for prosecution as well as subject to administrative action, including dismissal from the armed forces'; I Park, 'The Obligation to Investigate Violations of IHL' *EJIL: Talk!* 30 September 2016, www.ejiltalk.org/joint-series-on-international-law-and-armed-conflict-the-obligation-to-investigate-violations-of-ihl/.

[78] Cohen and Shany (n 49) 46. See section IV for a discussion of how a failure to investigate may itself incur criminal liability.

[79] Schmitt (n 50) 72.

[80] AP I, Art 51(4).

[81] Henckaerts and Doswald-Beck (n 5) r 14; see also ICC Statute, Art 8(b)(iv); See *Prosecutor v Kupreškić et al*, ICTY-95-16 and *Prosecutor v Martić*, ICTY-95-11. See also AP II, Art 13: 'The civilian population and individual civilians shall enjoy general protection against the dangers arising from military operations.'

that: 'Proportionality is the true guarantee of robust civilian protection from the effects of attacks in wartime.'[82]

These measures of civilian protection are operationalised through the requirement to take precautions in attack. In addition to refraining from launching an attack expected to cause disproportionate civilian damage, this includes doing everything feasible to verify that the objective of an attack is indeed a military objective and taking all feasible precautions in the choice of means and methods of attack in order to avoid, or at least minimise, civilian death or injury or damage to civilian objects.[83]

Two cases from Iraq and Afghanistan illustrate what can go wrong. During the first Gulf war in 1991, the US Air Force destroyed the Amiriya air-raid shelter in Baghdad with two precision-guided missiles, in the mistaken belief that it was a military command and control bunker. Some 400 civilians were killed. Although the USA knew the facility had been used as a civil defence shelter during the Iran–Iraq war, it failed to give advance warning of the strike.[84]

In September 2009 in Kunduz in Afghanistan, up to 100 civilians were killed when a US fighter jet destroyed two fuel tankers that had been hijacked by Taliban insurgents. The strike was called in by a German Bundeswehr commander who feared that the tankers might be used as a bomb to attack a NATO base and had been told that those in the vicinity of the tankers (stuck in a river bed) were all insurgents. German prosecutors undertook a criminal investigation but no charges were brought against the commander on the basis that his actions were reasonable given the information available to him at the time. A military investigation, however, found that the intelligence had been misleading and that the perceived threat could have been dealt with by ground troops rather than an aerial attack.[85]

In neither of these cases was there a breach of the proportionality rule as such, but rather an arguable failure to take feasible precautionary measures, including obtaining adequate information to verify the target as a military objective, the provision of advance warning, and the choice of alternative means and methods of attack. On this basis, neither case would be categorised as a war crime (despite widespread public claims to that effect). The consequences in terms of loss of civilian life, however, could hardly have been more serious.

It should be noted that even if the facts on the ground appear to indicate the commission of a war crime, it may not be confirmed as such because the requisite *mens rea* cannot be established. At the diplomatic conference that

---

[82] Dinstein (n 71) para 320.
[83] AP I, Art 57.
[84] See Dinstein (n 71) para 315.
[85] See Margalit (n 50) 159–60.

drew up Protocol I, there were concerns that the proportionality rule was formulated too imprecisely to allow its violation to be categorised as a grave breach.[86] Where it is included in the listing of grave breaches in Article 85, therefore, the words 'may be expected to cause' are replaced by 'in the knowledge that such attack will cause', thereby only covering the case where a perpetrator knew with certainty that loss of civilian life, injury to civilians or damage to civilian objects would be disproportionate.[87] An attack, therefore, in which a commander accepted the possibility that civilian loss of life might be excessive in relation to the military advantage anticipated but still went ahead—ie behaved recklessly—would not qualify as a war crime.[88] However, under the rubric described above in section III.A, breaches of the duty to take precautions in attack are still violations of IHL and, this chapter contends, in serious cases should and could still attract criminal sanctions, particularly if they broke operational rules of engagement.

A number of states made reservations or declarations at the time of ratifying Protocol I to the effect that the key factor in taking feasible precautions is the information actually available to the commander at the time of the decision.[89] Does 'available' here mean that the commander should already be in possession of it, or that it should be held by his or her party? Or does 'available' also mean 'obtainable'? The official commentary, emphasising that identification of the objective should be carried out with great care, particularly when it is located at a great distance, adds that 'in case of doubt, even if there is only slight doubt, [the commander] must call for additional information and if need be give orders for further reconnaissance'.[90] In most situations of contemporary aerial warfare, with one side enjoying air supremacy, this may well be feasible, although it could be argued that in certain circumstances, when a threat was pressing or when a significant opportunity for military advantage presented itself, it would be unrealistic. However, where an object is normally dedicated to civilian purposes (eg a house or a school), the presumption in case of doubt should be that it is not being used for military purposes.[91]

Nonetheless, 'what ultimately counts', according to Dinstein, in gauging whether collateral damage is excessive 'is not the actual outcome of the attack but the initial expectation and anticipation'.[92] The indiscriminate nature of an attack 'is not a by-product of "body count" but derives

---

[86] ICRC (n 19) 3472.
[87] API, Art 85(3)(b). See also Art 85(3)(c). Compare Arts 51(5)(b) and 57(2)(a)(iii). See also ICC Statute, Art 8.2(b)(iv).
[88] ICRC (n 19) 3479.
[89] Dinstein (n 71) para 343.
[90] ICRC (n 19) 2195.
[91] AP I, Art 52(3). Although Dinstein, referencing the USA, notes that 'the doubt rule is not universally acknowledged in all situations': Dinstein (n 71) paras 303, 240.
[92] Dinstein (n 71) para 325.

from the "nonchalant state of mind" of the attacker'.[93] A detailed review of the factors involved in assessing proportionality is beyond the scope of this chapter, but it should be noted that a rigid distinction between information available ex ante and investigation ex post is not always realistic in the context of armed conflicts of any duration and intensity. Precautions in attack are governed by the general principle that 'constant care shall be taken to spare the civilian population'.[94] There is an obligation to cancel or suspend an attack if it becomes apparent that the objective is not a military one or that collateral damage will be disproportionate, and information needs to be up to date.[95] In the planning of a series of attacks as part of a campaign, information about civilian casualties in the earlier part of the campaign will surely be necessary to enable precautions to be taken in the planning of later attacks.

Dinstein reminds us that '[e]ven collateral damage to civilians and civilian objects is by no means determined by purely crunching numbers of casualties and destruction on both sides'.[96] While number crunching is clearly not sufficient, it is, however, necessary: when civilian casualties are incurred (either unexpectedly or expectedly) an investigation is required to find out what happened in order to enable an informed decision to be made about the risk to civilians in any subsequent attack(s). Commanders' decisions may be judged on the information available at the time, but they cannot be isolated from the feedback loop.

Writing about the earlier years of the Afghanistan war, for example, Dinstein writes that, despite US equipment being 'the most advanced', 'collateral damage to civilians has repeatedly occurred, with bombing mistakes reported almost as a matter of routine'.[97] The history of warfare, of course, is replete with mistakes and the 'fog of war' is such that a mistake can occur even if all feasible precautions have been taken. However, implicit in the notion of routine mistakes is the suspicion that lessons have not been learnt from past practice, that all feasible precautions have not been taken and therefore that a violation of IHL may have occurred, albeit one which may not meet the relevant standard of *mens rea* to entail individual criminal responsibility.

In fact, state and international practice indicates a development towards the investigation of all cases where an attack causes civilian deaths. At the end of 2008 the International Security Assistance Force in Afghanistan

---

[93] ibid, para 315.
[94] AP I, Art 57(1).
[95] AP I, Art 57(2)(b); LC Green, *The Contemporary Law of Armed Conflict*, 2nd edn (Manchester, Manchester University Press, 2000) 160.
[96] Dinstein (n 71) para 319(iii).
[97] ibid, para 332.

established a civilian casualty tracking cell to, inter alia, 'demonstrate proportionality, restraint and utmost discrimination in the use of firepower; [and] acknowledge civilian casualties immediately and transparently investigate allegations rapidly'.[98] This was mirrored by a similar tracking cell within US forces.[99] In general US practice, the definition of 'reportable incident' quoted above depends on a violation being suspected, but the threshold is set fairly low: credible information suggesting a possible violation. Statements by senior US officials further indicate that every case of civilian death is now subjected to 'detailed analysis'.[100] Canadian procedures in Afghanistan require every instance of death or injury caused by Canadian forces to be reported and subject to subsequent investigation, usually by the military national investigation service.[101] According to UK practice, a 'shooting incident review' in every case of civilian death has to be held by a commanding officer within 48 hours and involves collecting operational logs and relevant documents as well as reports from witnesses.[102] Australian military procedures require an incident to be notified in, inter alia, any case involving 'the death, serious injury or disappearance of non-Defence personnel ... (even where there may be no reasonable suspicion of an offence having been committed)'.[103]

Schmitt injects an important word of caution about interpreting such state practice as indicative of a customary rule when that practice may be 'mandated not by a sense of legal obligation emanating from IHL' but rather by domestic constitutional requirements, obligations under human rights treaties, or indeed be driven by policy considerations.[104] However, once it is accepted that the duty to investigate goes beyond cases of suspected war crimes to every case of a suspected IHL violation that has serious consequences, including the failure to take precautions in attack, the need to perform some kind of investigation in every case of civilian death becomes apparent. The duty is not just to refrain from causing *excessive* civilian loss of life or injury, but to take constant care to *spare* civilians and to *avoid* (ie reduce to zero) or at least *minimise* (reduce as close to zero as possible) civilian death and injury. That requires an examination or investigation in each case. What sort of investigation is required will be considered next.

---

[98] COMISAF Tactical Directive, HQ ISAF/COM/08. Contrast, however, NATO policy in Libya: 'In Strikes on Libya by NATO, an Unspoken Civilian Toll', *New York Times* 17 December 2011.

[99] UN Assistance Mission to Afghanistan, 'Annual Report on Protection of Civilians in Armed Conflict 2008' (2009).

[100] Margalit (n 50) 164. See also Drabik (n 68) 27–28.

[101] Margalit (n 50) 165.

[102] ibid, 164.

[103] Cohen and Shany (n 49) 53–54.

[104] Schmit, (n 50) 56, 77–78.

C. Investigatory Standards and the Contribution of Human Rights Courts: Applying IHL/IHRL as *Lex Specialis*

State practice under IHL may reflect the rule that all violations leading to the death of civilians need to be investigated, but it is human rights courts and monitoring bodies that have gone furthest in elaborating the standards for governing investigations. The ECtHR first recognised the right to an effective investigation in cases involving the use of lethal force by state agents in 1995 in *McCann and Others v the UK* by reading the protection of the right to life together with a state's general duty to secure rights under the ECHR to everyone within its jurisdiction.[105] Since then the Court has found that investigative obligations continue to apply in the context of armed conflict, including in south-east Turkey, in Chechnya in the Russian Federation, and in relation to UK forces operating in Iraq, although the conduct of an investigation will vary according to the circumstances.[106] In *Kaya v Turkey* the Court emphasised that:

> [N]either the prevalence of violent armed clashes nor the high incidence of fatalities can displace the obligation under Article 2 to ensure that an effective, independent investigation is conducted into deaths arising out of clashes involving the security forces, more so in cases such as the present where the circumstances are in many respects unclear.[107]

The fact that *any* death involving the state use of force will trigger the obligation to investigate under human rights law[108] has attracted comment for going much further than the corresponding obligation under IHL. It is submitted, however, following the reasoning outlined above, that the discrepancy only pertains to killings of combatants or fighters of the opposing party. Where the death is that of a non-combatant, or a person whose status is unclear, an investigation is required under both branches of law.

In *Isayeva (I)*, a case involving the indiscriminate bombing of escaping civilians by Russian planes outside Grozny, Chechnya, the Court stipulated four criteria to govern investigations: independence, effectiveness, promptness and 'a sufficient element of public scrutiny'.[109] The criteria were explained further in *Al Skeini*, a case involving the killing of Iraqi civilians

---

[105] European Convention for the Protection of Human Rights and Fundamental Freedoms (as amended by Protocols Nos 11 and 14, 4 November 1950) ETS 5 (ECHR) Arts 2 and 1, respectively. See *McCann and ors v UK* (n 7) para 161.

[106] See eg *Ergi v Turkey* (App no 40/1993/435/514) ECHR 28 July 1998; *Isayeva v Russia* (n 7); *Al-Skeini and ors v United Kingdom* (n 7).

[107] *Kaya v Turkey* (Judgment) (1999) 28 EHRR 1, para 91.

[108] eg *McCann and ors v UK* (n 7) para 161; *Ergi v Turkey* (n 106) para 82.

[109] *Isayeva v Russia* (n 7) para 836.

by UK forces, where the Court stated that the effectiveness standard produced an obligation of means:

> The authorities must take reasonable steps available to them to secure the evidence concerning the incident. ... Any deficiency in the investigation which undermines its ability to establish the cause of death or the person or persons responsible will risk falling foul of this standard.[110]

The agreement by the UN General Assembly in 2005 of the Basic Principles on the Right to a Remedy and Reparation marked a point of convergence between human rights law and IHL regarding standards for investigations, referring as the Principles do to both gross violations of human rights and serious violations of IHL. Investigations need to be carried out 'effectively, promptly, thoroughly and impartially', according to the Basic Principles.[111] By the time of the 2009 Goldstone report into the Gaza conflict, independence, effectiveness, promptness and impartiality were referred to as the 'universal principles' of investigation.[112] Although the principles were derived from the work of human rights bodies, Schmitt concludes that 'there is no inconsistency between the broad principles applicable in human rights and humanitarian law investigations'.[113]

However, while the understanding of the principles of effectiveness, promptness and impartiality is indeed similar under both branches of law, the treatment of independence and transparency (or 'public scrutiny') exhibits important differences. In *Al Skeini*, the Court found that because investigations could be initiated and terminated by the operational commanding officer, they were not sufficiently independent.[114] In fact, independence 'means not only a lack of hierarchical or institutional connection but also a practical independence'.[115] But investigations are conceived under IHL within the chain of command, at least in the early stages, with the commander acting as an 'investigating magistrate'. This is not just for reasons of convenience, or because the operational commander is present on the ground, but also for effectiveness. As the ICRC commentary on Protocol I remarks: 'At this level, everything depends on commanders, and without their conscientious supervision, general legal requirements are unlikely to be effective.'[116] The commander's role in investigating violations is equally important for the prompt incorporation of lessons learnt. State practice

---

[110] *Al-Skeini and ors v United Kingdom* (n 7) para 166.
[111] UNGA, 'Basic Principles and Guidelines on the Right to a Remedy and Reparation for Victims of Gross Violations of International Human Rights Law and Serious Violations of International Humanitarian Law' (16 December 2005) UN Doc A/RES/60/147, para 3(b).
[112] Goldstone Report (n 47) para 1611.
[113] Schmitt (n 50) 55.
[114] *Al-Skeini and ors v United Kingdom* (n 7) para 172.
[115] ibid, para 167.
[116] ICRC (n 19) 3550.

regarding investigations nonetheless exhibits a move towards greater institutional separation from the chain of command, often prompted by human rights jurisprudence.[117]

Where both IHL and international human rights law (IHRL) are applicable, the ICJ has held that an accommodation between the two sets of rules is achieved through application of the doctrine of *lex specialis derogat legi generali*.[118] In an armed conflict, for example, the general prohibition on arbitrary killing in IHRL gives way to, or needs to be interpreted in the light of, the more specialised rules of lawful targeting under IHL. There is a general assumption in the academic literature on IHL investigations that in situations of armed conflict IHL will always constitute the *lex specialis*.[119] However, this is not the only way of interpreting the *lex specialis* doctrine. The wholesale displacement of IHRL by IHL in such situations would in fact run counter to the repeated findings by international human rights courts and the ICJ that human rights continue to apply during armed conflict. Other scholars have argued that the branch of law which contains the more specialised rule on the matter in question should be treated as *lex specialis*.[120] Thus while IHL will govern the lawfulness of an attack in armed conflict, the standards to be applied to the investigation of violations will follow the more elaborated rules in IHRL.

Such an interpretation of the *lex specialis* doctrine is particularly pertinent with regard to the transparency of investigations. The claim is frequently made that operational considerations require the content of investigations to remain classified. But the basis for such claims is often unclear, particularly when similar attacks which did not result in civilian casualties are made the subject of PR campaigns to demonstrate publicly the accuracy or effectiveness of strike capability.

The UN Special Rapporteur on the promotion and protection of human rights while countering terrorism, writing about CIA involvement in lethal operations in Pakistan, has stated that the use of secret services in operations creates 'an almost insurmountable obstacle to transparency'.[121] It could be

---

[117] See Schmitt, 'Investigating Violations of International Law' (n 50) 78, citing the cases of *R v Généreux* (1992) 1 SCR 259; *Lane v Morrison* (2009) HCA 29; *Findlay v the UK* (1997) 24 EHRR 221.

[118] See *Legality of the Threat or Use of Nuclear Weapons* (Advisory Opinion) [1996] ICJ Rep 226, para 25; *Legal Consequences of the Construction of a Wall in the Occupied Palestinian Territory* (Advisory Opinion) [2004] ICJ Rep 136, para 106; *Armed Activities on the Territory of the Congo (Democratic Republic of the Congo v Uganda)* [2005] ICJ Rep 168, para 216.

[119] See eg Schmitt (n 50) 53–54; Margalit (n 50) 174.

[120] eg L Doswald-Beck, 'The Right to Life in Armed Conflict: Does International Humanitarian Law Provide All the Answers?' (2006) 864 *International Review of the Red Cross* 903.

[121] UNGA, 'Promotion and Protection of Human Rights' (n 52) paras 46, 48. In 2013 the USA announced that it would transfer control of certain lethal counter-terrorism operations from the CIA to the Department of Defense, partly to increase 'transparency and accountability'.

argued that as the content of the relevant rules on investigatory standards is much more developed in IHRL, it should constitute the *lex specialis*. The default therefore should be transparency unless military necessity presents a compelling operational reason why transparency is impossible.[122]

Such an approach receives further support from the right, explicitly recognised in IHL, of families to know the fate of their relatives.[123] Under the law of the ECHR, the 'degree of public scrutiny required may well vary from case to case'; '[i]n all cases, however, the next-of-kin of the victim must be involved in the procedure to the extent necessary to safeguard his or her legitimate interests'.[124] This includes relevant disclosure of evidence.[125]

Space does not permit a detailed review here of state practice regarding investigatory standards, but it is notable that the relative implementation of international standards will be affected by the institutional structure of national military investigation systems as well as national legislation. Commander Sylvaine Wong remarks that the heavy reliance on criminal investigations in the UK, while addressing the independence concern, decreases the transparency of the system because of the need for confidentiality. In the USA, the inability of agencies outside the military chain of command, including those representing the interests of civilian victims, to be involved contributes to the perception of lack of independence. There is a degree of transparency, however, due to the US statutory right to request investigative reports after the fact under freedom of information legislation.[126]

The argument for applying IHRL investigative standards as *lex specialis* during armed conflict is stronger in situations of occupation and/or where a party to conflict is engaged in law enforcement activities, as these will be situations where the party is exercising sovereign power. Citing the Basic Principles and other human rights standards, the Turkel Commission concludes that: '[W]here force causes any serious injury or death of an individual

---

[122] Such an exception would not extend, however, to the concept of 'state secrets' or general assertions of 'state secret privilege'; see the judgment of the ECtHR in a case concerning CIA rendition, *El-Masri v The Former Yugoslav Republic of Macedonia* (2012) 57 EHRR 25, paras 191–92. See also Joint Concurring Opinion of Judges Tulkens, Spielmann, Sicilianos and Keller on the right to the truth.

[123] AP I, Art 32; Henckaerts and Doswald-Beck (n 5) r 117.

[124] *Hugh Jordan v the UK* (App no 24746/94) ECHR 4 August 2001, para 109. See also the summary of procedural requirements for an investigation given in *R (Al Skeini and others) v Secretary of State for Defence* [2004] EWHC 2911, para 322.

[125] ibid. See also *Öğur v Turkey* (App No 21594/93) ECHR 20 May 1999, para 92.

[126] S Wong, 'Investigating Civilian Casualties in Armed Conflict: Comparing US Military Investigations with Alternatives Under International Humanitarian and Human Rights Law' (2015) 64 *Naval Law Review* 111–67. To increase transparency and 'pro-actively inform families and NGOs of the course of events', Commander Wong recommends that 'unclassified summaries of investigation reports should be made publically available in a timely manner as standard practice'.

in the context of law enforcement activities there is a duty to investigate.'[127] The Israeli High Court had already confirmed in 2011 a tightening of Israeli investigative policy in the West Bank, under which a military police investigation would be opened immediately in every case 'in which a civilian is killed, as a result of action of IDF forces', except in incidents of 'a real combat nature' in which case the decision to open a military police investigation would follow a preliminary operational inquiry.[128]

With regard to the distinction made by the Turkel Commission between the *investigation* required in cases of alleged war crimes and the *examination* of all other suspected violations, it suffices here to note that: (i) it is not just war crimes investigations that are governed by the standards described here but also command-type investigations, whether these are called examinations, investigations or inquiries (with the level of independence from the chain of command depending in practice on the seriousness of the suspected violation and whether criminal charges may be brought); and (ii) the initiation of a criminal investigation does not exhaust the responsibility of the party to ensure that the institutional circumstances of suspected violations are properly investigated with a view to their effective suppression. The additional obligations that apply in cases of suspected war crimes are briefly considered next.

IV. INVESTIGATIONS IN CASES OF SUSPECTED WAR CRIMES OR OTHER VIOLATIONS OF INTERNATIONAL CRIMINAL LAW

This section considers investigatory obligations in cases where a suspected violation of IHL may entail individual responsibility as a war crime or other crime under international law. As the obligation to investigate war crimes under IHL is universally accepted, it will only be treated briefly here, highlighting aspects of the obligation that are additional to those considered above applicable to all violations. It may well occur that in the course of investigating a possible IHL violation, evidence is uncovered which indicates the potential commission of a war crime, thereby triggering a criminal investigation.

War crimes are distinct from the ordinary criminal breaches or other violations described in the last section in the following respects:

— They constitute 'grave' breaches of the Geneva Conventions or Protocol I or certain 'serious' violations of the laws and customs of war as recognised under international law.[129]

---

[127] Turkel Commission (n 3) paras 53–54. The example given is 'forcefully clearing a residence of uninvolved civilians so that it may be used as a military position'.
[128] *B'Tselem et al v Judge Advocate General* HCJ 9594/03 (2011).
[129] ICC Statute, Art 8.

— They are criminalized under *international* law and subject to an international or transnational jurisdiction, either under the statute of an international criminal tribunal or under the *aut dedere aut judicare* principle (see below).

In contrast to the ordinary breaches discussed in the last section, where the duty to suppress entails an investigation with the possibility of either disciplinary *or* criminal sanctions, in cases of suspected war crimes the obligation to undertake a criminal investigation is mandatory.[130]

A. Investigations under the Obligation *aut Dedere aut Judicare* and the Provision of Mutual Legal Assistance

The system for repressing grave breaches established by the Geneva Conventions and Protocol I (and now recognized as customary IHL) furthermore requires states not just to investigate war crimes allegedly committed by their own nationals or armed forces, or on their territory, but also other war crimes over which they may have jurisdiction, with a view to having the suspects either extradited to face prosecution or prosecuting them themselves (*aut dedere aut judicare*).[131] This obligation also applies, mutatis mutandis, to other offences criminalised under international law which may be committed during armed conflict (as well as in peacetime), including torture, enforced disappearances and a growing number of terrorist offences including the taking of hostages.[132]

The obligation to prosecute (or in the terms of Geneva Convention IV, to 'search for' and bring 'before its own courts') is in fact an obligation to investigate with a view to prosecution; the initiation of a prosecution will depend on the evidence. In more recent treaties following the 'Hague' formula, the obligation is to 'submit the case to its competent authorities for the purpose of prosecution'.[133] The obligation 'arises as soon as the presence of the alleged offender in the territory of the State concerned is ascertained, regardless of any request for extradition'.[134]

---

[130] GC IV, Art 146; AP I, Art 85(1); Henckaerts and Doswald-Beck (n 5) r 158. According to Schmitt, this 'unquestionably reflects a customary norm'; see Schmitt (n 50) 44.

[131] Henckaerts and Doswald-Beck (n 5) r 158.

[132] United Nations Convention against Torture and Other Cruel, Inhuman or Degrading Treatment or Punishment (adopted 10 December 1984, entered into force 26 June 1987) 1465 UNTS 113 (UNCAT), Arts 6–8; United Nations Convention against the Taking of Hostages (adopted 17 December 1979, entered into force 3 June 1983) 1316 UNTS 205, Art 8; United Nations Convention on Enforced Disappearances (adopted 20 December 2006, entered into force 23 December 2010) 2716 UNTS 3 (UNCED) Arts 10–11.

[133] So called because the terminology was first used in the 1970 Hague Convention for the Suppression of Unlawful Seizure of Aircraft; compare the articles cited in the note above.

[134] International Law Commission (ILC), 'The Obligation to Extradite or Prosecute (aut dedere aut judicare)' (2014), para 40.

In the case concerning *Questions relating to the Obligation to Prosecute or Extradite*, the ICJ identified a number of elements in the obligation to investigate.[135] A preliminary inquiry must be made immediately,

> conducted by those authorities which have the task of drawing up a case file and collecting facts and evidence; this may consist of documents or witness statements relating to the events at issue and to the suspect's possible involvement in the matter concerned.[136]

In fulfilment of the obligation to conduct a preliminary inquiry, the cooperation should be sought of the authorities in the state where the alleged crime was committed or where complaints have been filed in relation to the case. Where an inquiry is being made on the basis of universal jurisdiction, the authorities concerned should abide by the same standards in terms of evidence as when they have jurisdiction by virtue of a link with the case in question.[137] While the choice of means for conducting the inquiry remains in the hands of states parties, steps must be taken in order to conduct an investigation as soon as the suspect is identified in the territory of the state; establishment of the facts becomes imperative, at the latest, when the first complaint is filed against the person.[138] 'As a general rule', summarises the International Law Commission, 'the obligation to investigate must be interpreted in light of the object and purpose of the applicable treaty, which is to make more effective the fight against impunity.'[139]

In addition, it should be noted that a number of international criminal law treaties have extensive provisions governing international cooperation and mutual legal assistance with regards to criminal investigations. Thus the ICC Statute requires states parties to cooperate fully with the Court in its investigation and prosecution of crimes, empowers the Court to request assistance from non-states parties, and provides a detailed list of forms of investigatory assistance.[140] The Convention on Enforced Disappearance requires states parties to afford one another 'the greatest measure' of mutual assistance in connection with criminal proceedings (including 'the supply of all evidence at their disposal') and 'in searching for, locating and releasing disappeared persons and, in the event of death, in exhuming and identifying them and returning their remains'.[141,142]

---

[135] *Questions relating to the Obligation to Prosecute or Extradite (Belgium v Senegal)* (Judgment) [2012] ICJ Rep, 422.

[136] ibid, 453, para 83.

[137] ibid, para 84.

[138] ibid, 454, para 86.

[139] ILC (n 134) para 20.

[140] ICC Statute, Arts 86, 87 and 93.

[141] UNCED, Arts 14–15.

[142] International assistance in criminal investigations, particularly in urgent cases, is often effected through the International Criminal Police Organisation (INTERPOL) which has created a dedicated unit to focus on war crimes, crimes against humanity, and genocide, and

B. Requirements for National Investigations under the ICC Statute

Under the complementarity principle, the ICC will only take on a case where states are unwilling or unable to carry out investigations or prosecutions. To determine the unwillingness test, the ICC Statute requires national-level investigations or prosecutions to meet the standards of independence, impartiality and promptness, but also imposes an additional general requirement that they be genuine. This means that they should not be undertaken for the purpose of shielding the person concerned from criminal responsibility or otherwise conducted in a manner inconsistent with an intent to bring the person concerned to justice.[143]

Most of the investigatory obligations detailed in this chapter are obligations of means and, even in a situation of state collapse, the parties to the conflict are required to use those means at their disposal, limited though they may be. However, it must at least be possible to obtain the necessary evidence and testimony, and to carry out proceedings.[144] The purpose of the inability test is to ensure that where a state's justice system fails completely in this regard, the ICC can act as a court of last resort.

C. Command Responsibility

Specific investigatory obligations are also created by virtue of the doctrine of command responsibility, under which commanders are criminally responsible for war crimes committed by their subordinates if they fail to prevent or punish them.[145] Under the ICC Statute, for example, military commanders are responsible if they knew or should have known forces under their command were committing war crimes and they failed to take preventive measures or 'submit the matter to the competent authorities for investigation

---

which provides specialist training in the investigation of such crimes with the aim of establishing standard practices, including in the collection and processing of evidence related to mass atrocities and extending capacity for the investigation and prosecution of sexual- and gender-based violence. Further initiatives to create standards of good practice in this field include UK Foreign and Commonwealth Office, 'International Protocol on the Documentation and Investigation of Sexual Violence in Conflict: Best Practice on the Documentation of Sexual Violence as a Crime or Violation of International Law' (London, 2017). See also Institute for International Criminal Investigations, 'Guidelines for Investigating Conflict-Related Sexual and Gender-Based Violence against Men and Boys' (The Hague, IICI, 2016).

[143] ICC Statute, Art 17.
[144] ibid, Art 17(3).
[145] This is described by the ICRC as a 'long-standing rule of customary international law'; Henckaerts and Doswald-Beck, *Customary International Humanitarian Law* (n 5) r 153. See also *Re Yamashita (No 61), 327 US 1 (1947)*.

and prosecution'.[146] In such circumstances, therefore, the failure to fulfil the obligation to investigate may expose a commander to potential prosecution for war crimes.[147]

This type of criminal responsibility should be distinguished from the general duties or responsibilities placed on commanders to suppress violations of IHL (of which it is one aspect), which were discussed in section III. A failure to investigate civilian deaths according to the obligations outlined in this chapter is itself a violation of IHL and could invite disciplinary sanctions or a criminal charge (eg for dereliction of duty). Under the international criminal law doctrine of command responsibility, however, the failure to investigate and take other measures to prevent and punish war crimes is not a separate offence but rather a mode of liability for the underlying war crimes committed by subordinates.[148] It thus imposes an additional, and potentially very severe, sanction on commanders to ensure that their duty to investigate in serious cases is properly undertaken.

In the first conviction under the basis of command responsibility before the ICC, in March 2016 Jean-Pierre Bemba was found guilty, as a person effectively acting as a military commander, of the crimes against humanity of murder and rape, and the war crimes of murder, rape and pillaging, committed by his Movement for the Liberation of the Congo (MLC) forces in the Central African Republic in 2002–03.[149] As one of the elements, Trial Chamber III assessed whether the accused failed to take all necessary and reasonable measures to prevent or repress the commission of the crimes or to submit the matter to competent authorities for investigation and prosecution. The Chamber drew on jurisprudence from the ICTY, directing that a trial chamber 'must look at what steps were taken to secure an adequate investigation capable of leading to the criminal prosecution of the perpetrators', described as a 'minimum standard' for measures that may fulfil the duty to punish.[150] Bemba had taken some measures, including the creation of two commissions of inquiry, but these were found by Trial Chamber III to be 'limited in mandate, execution and/or results' and in sum

---

[146] ICC Statute, Art 28(a).

[147] cf Turkel Commission (n 3) para 35: 'A breach of the obligation imposed on officers and superiors to investigate effectively violations committed by their subordinates may itself be a breach of international criminal law'.

[148] At least under the ICC Statute. See the similar provision in the Statute of the ICTY (adopted 25 May 1993, as last amended 17 May 2002) Art 7(3). For a discussion of the distinction between treating a failure of command responsibility as a separate offence or as a mode of liability based on omission, see R Darryl, 'How Command Responsibility Got so Complicated: A Culpability Contradiction, its Obfuscation, and a Simple Solution' (2012) 13 *Melbourne Journal of International Law* 1, 30–40.

[149] *Prosecutor v Jean-Pierre Bemba Gombo* (Judgment) ICC-01/05-01/08 (21 March 2016).

[150] ibid, para 207. The Chamber was citing *Popović et al* (Appeal Judgment) ICTY-05-88 (30 January 2015) para 1932.

a 'grossly inadequate response to the consistent information of widespread crimes committed by MLC soldiers'.[151] The inadequacy of the measures was aggravated by indicators that they were not genuine, the fact that only public allegations of crimes by MLC soldiers prompted any reaction, and that they were 'primarily motivated by Mr Bemba's desire to counter public allegations and rehabilitate the public image of the MLC'.[152] The chamber listed a number of measures that Bemba could have taken. In addition to ensuring that MLC troops were properly trained in the rules of IHL and adequately supervised, he could have, inter alia, 'initiated genuine and full investigations into the commission of crimes, and properly tried and punished any soldiers alleged of having committed crimes' and 'shared relevant information with the CAR authorities or others and supported them in any efforts to investigate criminal allegations'.[153]

V. CONCLUSION

This chapter has identified the parameters of the positive duty in international law to investigate civilian deaths in armed conflict, based on the obligation of parties to conflict to investigate *all* IHL violations, including a failure to take precautions in attack, underpinned by the universal humanitarian obligation to account for the missing and the dead. The duty is established by virtue of the relevant provisions of Geneva Convention IV, Additional Protocols I and II, and by customary IHL, and applies in both IACs and NIACs. More specifically, the components of the duty are as follows:

— The universal obligation on all states and on all parties to armed conflict to account for the dead and the missing, particularly after any engagement, including holding an official enquiry into deaths of civilian detainees and undertaking the identification and recording of information concerning other persons who have died as a result of hostilities or occupation, in furtherance of the right of families to know the fate of their relatives.

— The obligation on parties to conflict to investigate *all* suspected IHL violations, with a view to imposing disciplinary or criminal sanctions or operational reforms or other measures to suppress the violation, in furtherance of the requirement to take constant care to spare the civilian population and to avoid or at lease minimise civilian death or injury.

---

[151] ibid, paras 720, 727.
[152] Ibid, para 728.
[153] ibid, para 729.

— The additional obligation on all states or parties to conflict in cases of a suspected war crime or other crime under international law to undertake a mandatory criminal investigation and to prosecute the alleged perpetrator(s) or transfer them to another state willing and able to do so or to an international tribunal with jurisdiction.

These findings are significant in that they establish that the duty to investigate is far wider than just cases of suspected war crimes and extends to every case of civilian death as a result of armed conflict, within the bounds of feasibility.

Equally significantly, the duty is located within IHL itself and does not depend on the application of human rights law. Growing jurisprudence from international human rights courts concerning the right to an investigation in cases engaging the right to life in situations of armed conflict has partly driven attempts to assert the widest possible application of human rights law, including extra-territorially.[154] However, this chapter has sought to demonstrate that a strong duty to investigate exists independently in IHL and therefore clearly obtains even in situations where human rights obligations do not apply. Similarly, as IHL binds all parties to conflict, it unambiguously covers armed opposition groups whose obligations under IHRL remain unsettled.[155]

Human rights courts have nonetheless made an important contribution in further elaborating the standards by which investigations should be governed. The standards of effectiveness, promptness and impartiality are common to both branches of law, but the requirements regarding independence and transparency are significantly more exacting under IHRL. The stipulations regarding the involvement of next-of-kin in investigations can be seen as complementary to (or in certain cases providing specific content to) the general principle in IHL that families have a right to know the fate of their relatives.

Will the duty to investigate described here prove inoperable or even counterproductive in imposing a burden on parties to armed conflict which will impede their military effectiveness? State practice, including that of specially affected states and those not party to Protocol I, would seem to indicate that this is not the case. Indeed, recent trends indicate that, far from being an unmanageable burden, the practice of investigating every case involving the death of civilians is being driven by policy as well as legal grounds.

In contemporary wars often waged among the civilian population, including asymmetric conflicts, there is a need not just to take sufficient

---

[154] See eg *Bankovic and Others v Belgium and Others* (App No 52207/99) ECHR 12 December 2001; *Al-Skeini and ors v United Kingdom* (n 7).

[155] For an expansive view, see A Clapham, *Human Rights Obligations of Non-State Actors* (Oxford, Oxford University Press, 2006) 271–98.

precautions to avoid civilian casualties but also to demonstrate the measures taken. Transparency is key. The UK's *Manual of the Law of Armed Conflict* warns that the failure of belligerents 'to investigate and, where appropriate, punish the alleged unlawful acts of members of their armed forces can contribute to the loss of public and world support'.[156] In a case involving the failure to 'thoroughly and accurately report and investigate a combat engagement' in which twenty-four civilians were killed at Haditha in Iraq in 2005, the US investigating officer stated that the commander's actions 'belie a wilful and callous disregard for the basic [tenets] of counterinsurgency operations and the need for popular support and legitimacy'.[157]

But recognition of the duty to investigate in state practice can also be seen as a reflection of the need to maintain the integrity of IHL more broadly. As much of the system of implementation originally envisaged in the Geneva Conventions and Additional Protocols—based on the appointment of Protecting Powers and the investigatory role of the International Humanitarian Fact-Finding Commission—has fallen into disuse, it is natural that pressure should have increased to strengthen the existing system of self-implementation, supervised by a sufficient level of public scrutiny. To that system, the duty to investigate is fundamental.

---

[156] Ministry of Defence, 438, cited in Schmitt, 'Investigating Violations of International Law' (n 50) 46.

[157] D Jackson, 'Reporting and Investigation of Possible, Suspected or Alleged Violations of the Law of War' (2010) *Army Lawyer*, 96, 98. See also US Department of the Army HQ and Marine Corps Combat Development Command HQ, 'Counter-Insurgency Manual' (COIN Manual) (2006).

3

Protection by Process: Implementing the Principle of Proportionality in Contemporary Armed Conflicts

AMICHAI COHEN*

I. INTRODUCTION

IN 2012–13 US officials attempted to clarify the position of the Obama administration regarding 'targeted killings'. They came up with a 'presidential policy guidance', a series of rules and procedures governing the use of targeted killings operations. The *Playbook*, as it became known, was declassified in 2017. Among its various rules, it includes a specific ruling that a targeted killing operation was not to be undertaken unless there was near certainty that *no* civilian will be killed.[1]

Whether or not this is actually the way in which the United States executes targeted killings operations is debatable.[2] There are accounts of US attacks undertaken with the full knowledge that civilians will be killed.[3] The point is, however, that the formal position of the US administration seems to contradict all that we know about war. Certainly, there has long been a prohibition against *directing* attacks at civilian targets. However, it was always understood that excluded from this prohibition (the so-called 'principle of

* The author would like to thank Eyal Benvenisti and Stuart Cohen for their comments on an earlier version. Research for this work was supported by the Israel Science Foundation Grant No 1027/13.

[1] United States, 'Procedures for Approving Direct Action against Terrorist Targets Located Outside the United States and Areas of Active Hostilities', 22 May 2013, 15, available at: https://www.justice.gov/oip/foia-library/procedures_for_approving_direct_action_against_terrorist_targets/download. The existence of the document and its contents was first revealed by Charlie Savage: C Savage, *Power Wars: Inside Obama's Post-9/11 Presidency* (New York, Little Brown, 2015) 283–84.

[2] See eg J Serle and J Purkiss, 'Get the Data: Drone Wars' *Bureau of Investigative Journalism*, 1 January 2017, www.thebureauinvestigates.com/category/projects/drones/drones-graphs/.

[3] R Devereaux, 'Manhunting in the Hindu-Kush: Civilian Casualties and Strategic Failures in America's Longest War' *The Intercept*, 15 October 2015, theintercept.com/drone-papers/manhunting-in-the-hindu-kush/.

distinction') were those civilian casualties that can be classified as *collateral damage:* unintended consequences of attacks on legitimate targets. The principle of proportionality provided another layer of protection for civilians, but even this principle is generally understood to prohibit only those attacks in which the damage to civilians is *excessive* in relation to the military advantage. The idea that civilians enjoy complete, or nearly complete, protection during attacks on legitimate military targets seems to deviate from all traditional rules.[4]

And yet, the ruling laid down by the Obama administration is not a mistake. It is in line with statements of human rights organisation and scholars. There seems to be a growing unease with regards to any civilian casualty in war, irrespective of whether the attack that caused harm to a civilian was or was not directed against a legitimate military objective.

The purpose of this chapter is to offer an explanation for this seeming discrepancy in IHL. Some scholars believe that the growing intolerance for any civilian casualties reflects a profound change in the legal norms applicable to armed conflicts. They argue that the nature of modern conflicts requires a reinterpretation of the principle of proportionality, to better reflect the value of the right to life even at times of armed conflict.

Clearly, these scholars are correct in identifying that modern armed conflicts are very different from traditional wars in their goals and methods. I submit, however, that the real reason behind the change in the interpretation of the principle of proportionality is not the introduction of new weapons, or the emergence of different laws. Rather, the real change lies in the fact that current armed conflicts have become complex bureaucratised operations, based on procedures and legal advice. It is this latter change in the way armed forces conduct operations that resulted in new societal attitudes to civilian casualties penetrating the military sphere. In so doing it brought about significant shifts in the interpretation of 'proportionality'.

This chapter will proceed as follows. I will first briefly present the traditional understanding of the principle of proportionality in IHL. I will then explain why changes in the way states fight modern armed conflicts has caused scholars to change their view of the principle of proportionality. In the last part I will describe the way in which armed forces operationalise the principle of proportionality in modern asymmetrical armed conflicts.

---

[4] A Gillespie, *A History of the Laws of War*, vol 2: *The Customs and Laws of War with Regards to Civilians in Times of Conflict* (Oxford, Hart Publishing, 2011) 39–51.

II. TRADITIONAL PROPORTIONALITY IN IHL

Although the term 'proportionality' does not explicitly appear in any IHL treaty,[5] it boasts a long pedigree within the laws of war.[6] Indeed, the linkage between justified ends, means and effects instituted by the principle can be found in Articles 51(5)(b) and 57(2) of Additional Protocol I of 1977 ('Protocol I'),[7] as well as in some other specific IHL norms.[8] In the words of Judge Roslyn Higgins of the ICJ, the essence of the principle is that 'even a legitimate target may not be attacked if the collateral civilian casualties would be disproportionate to the specific military gain from the attack.'[9]

This principle is innovative. It makes the balance between military necessity and humanitarian interests horizontal rather than vertical: there are situations in which a future damage to civilians would actually prohibit a military operation. The principle of proportionality requires the attacking power to audit its proposed operation, comparing the foreseeable damage to the civilian population with the expected military advantage.[10] Damage to the civilian population becomes prohibited once it is seen to be excessive in relation to the military advantage.

---

[5] Note that this is not a mere oversight since there was a serious attempt, which failed, to include the term proportionality in the First Additional Protocol to the Geneva Conventions (1977). WJ Fenrick, 'The Rule of Proportionality and Protocol I in Conventional Warfare' (1982) 98 *Military Law Review* 91, 102–07.

[6] In fact, some scholars claim that the concept was already present in the Christian medieval corpus of laws of war, which posited that war could be deemed to be just, and hence legitimate, only if its gains exceeded the horrors that it wrought. JG Gardam, 'Proportionality and Force in International Law' (1993) 87 *American Journal of International Law* 391, 394–95.

[7] Protocol I Additional to the Geneva Conventions of 12 August 1949 and relating to the Protection of Victims of International Armed Conflicts (adopted 8 June 1977, entered into force 7 December 1978) 1125 UNTS 3 (AP I). One hundred and sixty-four states are party to this Protocol; Israel, the USA, India, Pakistan and some other states have not ratified it. On the status of ratification of the Protocol, see the ICRC website at www.icrc.org/ihl. nsf/WebSign?ReadForm&id=470&ps=P. However, the specific norm of proportionality in the protocol is considered customary international law, and hence obligatory upon all states. See JM Henckaerts and L Doswald-Beck, *Customary International Humanitarian Law*, vol I: *Rules* (Cambridge, Cambridge University Press, 2006) 46–47.

[8] See eg Declaration Renouncing the Use, in Time of War, of Explosive Projectiles Under 400 Grammes Weight (adopted 11 December 1868, entered into force 11 December 1868) which condemned the 'employment of arms which uselessly aggravate the sufferings of disabled men, or render their death inevitable'. Similarly, Art 35(2) AP I explicitly forbids the use of these arms. See Gardam (n 6) 406 ('This provision codifies the preexisting customary principle and is also based on proportionality'); see also M Bothe, HJ Partsch and WA Soft, *New Rules for Victims of Armed Conflict: Commentary on the Two 1977 Protocols Additional to the Geneva Conventions of 1949* (The Hague, Martinus Nijhoff, 1982) 195–97; C Pilloud et al (eds), *Commentary on the Additional Protocols of 8 June 1977 to the Geneva Conventions of 12 August 1949* (Geneva, ICRC, 1987) 401–02.

[9] *Legality of the Threat or Use of Nuclear Weapons* (Advisory Opinion) [1996] ICJ Rep 226, para 587.

[10] M Cohen-Eliya, 'The Formal and Substantive Meanings of Proportionality in the Supreme Court's Decision Regarding the Security Fence' (2005) 38 *Israel Law Review* 262, 288–89 (detailing the use of proportionality in the decisions of Israel's Supreme Court).

It is clear, however, that even this innovative protection of civilians was never intended to provide complete protection to all civilians. Moreover, states expressly rejected the idea that the prohibition on disproportional attacks would mean that the *actual results* of the attack would be evaluated against the anticipated military advantage. Rather, in a series of declarations attached to Protocol I they declared that the relevant consideration is the civilian damage that a reasonable military commander *could have anticipated* according to reasonably available evidence, before the attack took place.[11]

Moreover, the principle of proportionality was drafted in ambiguous terms, making its application in a specific context complicated.[12]

The first ambiguity results from the fact that the concept of proportionality suffers from a fault inherent in any attempt to balance rights of civilians and interests of armed forces—the concepts are incomparable.[13] What value should one assign to each of the competing variables?[14] In particular, how should one measure military advantage against human lives? How should one assess the worth of human lives on both sides of the conflict? Are the parties entitled to protect their own citizens or soldiers at the cost of endangering uninvolved enemy civilians, and if so, at what ratio?[15]

Second, in addition to these moral dilemmas, there are practical difficulties: since the proportionality test is applied ex ante, the military and humanitarian effects of the attack, as well as the harm it was designed to prevent, are merely speculative and ultimately depend on subjective risk assessments.

Lastly, the interpretations of the different variables of the formula of proportionality are unclear. The term 'attack' in the formula of Article 51(5)(b) is undefined. Does it refer to a specific operation or does it also include a large-scale military campaign? Likewise, the term 'military advantage' in the same article also lacks clarity.[16]

---

[11] For a summary of the various interpretative declarations in this matter, see J Gaudreau, 'The Reservations to the Protocols Additional to the Geneva Conventions for the Protection of War Victims' (2003) 849 *International Review of the Red Cross* 143, 156.

[12] For a more detailed analysis of debates concerning the application of the rule of proportionality, see eg J Gardam, *Necessity, Proportionality and the Use of Force by States* (Cambridge, Cambridge University Press, 2004) ch 4.

[13] A Kasher and A Yadlin, 'Military Ethics of Fighting Terror: An Israeli Perspective' (2005) 4 *Journal of Military Ethics* 3, 22.

[14] WJ Fenrick, 'Targeting and Proportionality during the NATO Bombing Campaign against Yugoslavia' (2001) 12 *European Journal of International Law* 489, 499.

[15] See E Benvenisti, 'Human Dignity in Combat: The Duty to Spare Enemy Civilians' (2006) 39 *Israel Law Review* 81, 92–93.

[16] The ICRC commentary interprets this to mean that the advantage should have a 'substantial and relatively close' causal relationship to the contemplated military action. See Pilloud et al (n 8) 684. But in many cases states adopt a more expansive interpretation, taking into account also strategic factors. Regarding the IDF's policy, see M Schmitt and J Merriam, 'The Tyranny of Context: Israeli Targeting Practices in Legal Perspectives' (2015) 37 *Pennsylvania Journal of International Law* 53, 75.

Hence, the formula of proportionality in Article 51(5)(b) of Protocol I remains quite ambiguous and difficult to implement. Because of this ambiguity, a clear answer to all the questions posed above as to the correct contents of the concept of proportionality cannot be offered.

Or in the words of the US Department of Defense Law of War Manual:

> The weighing or comparison between the expected incidental harm and the expected military advantage does not necessarily lend itself to empirical analyses.[17]

Indeed, the actual effect of the principle of proportionality in traditional wars was highly arguable. As long as both sides spared the lives of civilians, and did not use civilians as human shields, one could say that international law on the protection of civilians was being observed. However, as James Morrow has shown, during the twentieth century abuse of the rules protecting civilians was especially common, even more than were other violations of IHL. Soldiers attack civilians because in some cases they envisage that by doing so they will gain military or personal advantages, at very little cost. Moreover, the attacked party will respond by targeting civilians rather than the soldiers responsible for the original violation, which in any case is very difficult to monitor.[18]

In other words, proportionality was intended, and interpreted, as a requirement for reasonable and professional decision-making by commanders. Commanders were required to use professional standards and judgements regarding civilian casualties, exactly as they were required to do so with respect to tactical or logistical issues.[19] It constituted an attempt to embed humanitarian considerations into the military calculus. Commanders were required to ask themselves how to limit civilian casualties, and in what cases were civilian casualties excessive relative to the military objective. This, admittedly, is a very open-ended standard. It differs from commander to commander, from context to context, and from military culture to military culture. It is very hard to put in concrete terms, and actually, no such concrete terms are expected or required.[20]

---

[17] US Department of Defense Law of War Manual (June 2015) 245.

[18] JD Morrow, *Order within Anarchy: The Law of War as an International Institution* (Cambridge, Cambridge University Press, 2014).

[19] A Cohen, 'The Principle of Proportionality and Operation Cast Lead: Institutional Perspectives' (2009) 35 *Rutgers Law Record* 23.

[20] In a recent study, D Statman and RS Keinan presented to hundreds of experts a hypothetical scenario occurring in an IAC, and asked them to determine the number of permitted civilian collateral damages in the specific scenario they presented. Fifty per cent of the experts would not specify a number. Among the respondents that did do so, the results varied immensely. See Israel Democracy Institute, paper presented at the conference 'Proportionality in Armed Conflicts' (Jerusalem, 31 May 2016) (unpublished, presentation with data filed with the author). These results correspond with my claim that no precise 'number' exists in IACs.

This open-endedness is especially unsuited for criminal prosecution. The fact that there exists no clear standard means that judges will not usually be able to find a violation of this standard. Indeed, international tribunals and national courts adjudicating violations of IHL almost never find anyone guilty of violation of the principle of proportionality. Even when they have done, the violation was so extreme that it seems that it in fact constituted a case of violation of the principle of distinction, ie so many civilians were killed compared to the military advantage that it is hard to believe that civilians were not the actual target of the attack.

III. NEW WARS, NEW LAW

The flexible and indeterminate nature of the principle of proportionality in IHL was especially relevant in traditional wars, during which large armies conducted massive operations. In those conflicts, the best protection that law could provide was to demand that commanders take into account the suffering of civilian populations, in the fashion described above. However, contemporary armed conflicts are different. With very few exceptions, large battles are a matter of history. Current armed conflicts have different goals and are conducted according to different methods. This shift has also fundamentally affected our understanding of the need to protect civilians, and as a result, has generated changes in the interpretation of the principle of proportionality. This part of the chapter will begin by defining in which ways current armed conflicts differ from traditional wars, and then explain how this change in the nature of armed conflict affected the issue of proportionality.

A. The Changing Nature of War

Modern wars are very different from those being waged when IHL was originally formulated, and indeed from those that formed the context of the development of the IHL.[21] Even if some of the characteristics of current armed conflicts were apparent during wars of the past, the unique combinations present today necessitates a reconsideration of some of the basic tenets of IHL with regards to contemporary armed conflicts.

First, modern armed conflicts are hybrid. Very rarely do they comprise an ongoing set of large-scale military manoeuvres between comparable

---

[21] R Smith, *The Utility of Force: The Art of War in the Modern World* (New York, Alfred & Knops, 2007).

armies, during which both parties employ maximum force to achieve a definite battlefield success. Instead, modern conflicts consist of short bursts of intense conflicts punctuated by lengthy periods of ongoing small-scale operations.

Second, modern armed conflicts are asymmetrical.[22] The parties to the conflict are not equal. In most cases, one side consists of a state, with all its might and organised armed forces; the other side is a non-state actor, fighting a guerilla-style war. Modern conflicts are also asymmetrical in the legal sense: when a liberal democratic state confronts a non-state actor, it usually attempts to observe IHL. Conversely, the non-state actors tend to commit serious violations of IHL, and sometimes ignore it altogether.[23]

Even though current IHL expressly rejects the idea of reciprocity,[24] in its early stages of development, both sides were clearly expected to observe its provisions. Even after the obligation of one party to observe IHL was expressly declared independent of the actions of the other, on the ground reciprocity remained an important factor. As James Morrow has convincingly shown, once one party to the conflict violated IHL, the other parties were quick to respond with violations of their own.[25]

As has already been noted, in current armed conflicts between states and non-state actors there very rarely exists even a semblance of reciprocity. The expectation that non-state actors might observe IHL flies in the face of reality. It is the state, and only the state, that is the focus of efforts to implement and enforce IHL.[26]

Third, the nature of modern armed conflicts as hybrid and asymmetrical also means that it is very difficult to identify a point at which the war can be said to be 'won'. The sides do not fight great battles out of which one can emerge the victor, and the enemy hardly ever capitulates. The so-called 'war' consists of a series of very small-scale operations, intended to create pressure on the other side. Combatants rarely 'lose' the war in the military sense. Most of the conflicts in this category that have reached conclusion are those in which the parties have achieved some kind of political agreement.

Lastly, modern media, and especially social networks, have made wars extremely exposed. There are no secret wars, and the image of war becomes

---

[22] A Munkler, 'The Wars of the 21st Century' (2003) *International Review of the Red Cross* 849, 7–22.

[23] MN Schmitt, 'Asymmetrical Warfare and International Humanitarian Law' (2008) 62 *Air Force Law Review* 1.

[24] See eg AP I, Art 51(6).

[25] Morrow (n 18).

[26] I do not ignore the fact that nominally, at least, international organisations also criticize non-state actors for violations of IHL. However, this seems to me to be more lip-service than a real-life attempt to enforce IHL on non-state actors.

even more important than winning the battle or performing the operation. When an army completes its military mission but loses the war of images, the state is defeated.

All these changes in the nature of war cause states, and especially liberal democracies, to try to adapt the ways they fight in modern armed conflicts. Liberal democracies assume that in many cases it is costly and futile to put 'boots on the ground'.[27] These countries try to make use of recent advances in technology to change the ways in which they fight modern armed conflicts. One use of technology is surveillance: advanced states can now track the electronic and voice conversations of any civilian anywhere on earth and, by use of satellites, pinpoint the physical whereabouts of any suspect. Likewise, thanks to technology, states can and do now resort to cyberwars, designed to infiltrate an enemy's communications networks and render them inoperative.

Advancement in technology also changes the way in which states use force, which is the focus of this chapter. States that possess advanced technology prefer aerial surgical attacks—many times in the form of targeted killings, which are especially attractive since they allow their perpetrators to avoid putting their own soldiers at risk.

In the next part I shall briefly describe the policy of targeted killing operations, and the reasons that this policy changes the way in which we understand proportionality.

B. Targeted Killings

Nils Meltzer defines targeted killings as a military tactic that includes the following cumulative elements: (a) use of lethal force; (b) intent to kill; (c) specific individuals; (d) the targeted individuals are not in the custody of those targeting them; (e) the operation is attributable to states or other subjects of international law.[28]

Targeted killings operations became the prime method of warfare used by the Obama administration, and are reportedly frequently used by other countries as well.[29]

---

[27] See eg Remarks by the President of the US at the National Defense University (23 May 2013) www.whitehouse.gov/the-press-office/2013/05/23/remarks-president-national-defense-university (claiming that 'it is false to assert that putting boots on the ground is less likely to result in civilian deaths or less likely to create enemies in the Muslim world').

[28] N Melzer, *Targeted Killings in International Law* (Oxford, Oxford University Press, 2008) 4–5.

[29] For a general description of the use of the doctrine, see G Blum and P Heymann, 'Law and Policy of Targeted Killings' (2010) 1 *Harvard National Security Journal* 145. See also Savage (n 1). Israel has certainly used targeted killings. See S David, 'Targeted Killing: The Israeli Experience' in CA Ford and A Cohen (eds), *Rethinking the Law of Armed Conflict in Age of Terrorism* (Plymouth, Lexington Books, 2012) 71.

The policy of targeted killings, as developed in recent years by several states fighting non-state actors, epitomises much of what is new in modern armed conflicts. This policy is individualised, rather than collective. Moreover, since it is based on the fact that wars are asymmetrical, it incorporates an assumption that against non-state actors what is important is not winning a battle, but rather incapacitating their leaders. In targeted killing operations, armed forces use high-end technology: weapons that are extremely accurate; drones operated from afar; and very precise intelligence, without which such operations could not take place at all.

The legality of targeted killings is ambiguous. Some lawyers, especially in the early days of targeted killings, considered them illegal per se: a form of extra-judicial assassination.[30] It seems that most scholars today view the policy itself as legal, but there is much debate over the specific contexts in which it can be used, and under what conditions.[31]

Aside from the legality of targeted killings, their actual use has also raised questions regarding 'civilian collateral damage' in targeted killing operations. The accurate use of weapons and intelligence in these operations make the issue of the use of the principle of proportionality a very specific one: the attacking state knows in advance that civilians are to be found near the target. Often, thanks to the high level of intelligence, these civilians can be identified by name, gender and age, and it is possible to assess with some accuracy how many of them will be killed. Traditionally, the principle of proportionality called upon commanders to limit the damage to a *collective* civilian population, which was assessed against a *collective* military target. However, in targeted killing operations the entire equation becomes individualised—the target is specific, and the civilians are known. Under those circumstances, any attempt to adhere to the general and inaccurate interpretation of proportionality would appear inappropriate. Indeed, as I will show below, scholars and states have struggled with the application of the principle of proportionality in these new cases.

IV. REVISITING PROPORTIONALITY

A. The New Scholarship

During the course of the past decade or so, several scholars and practitioners have attempted to provide a more concrete understanding of what

---

[30] See eg Y Stein, 'By Any Name Illegal and Immoral' (2003) 17 *Ethics & International Affairs* 127.

[31] It has been especially criticised when in use not in a 'hot zone': see S Krebs, A Cohen and T Mimran, *'Don't Ask, Don't Tell': Secrecy, Security, and Oversight of Targeted Killing Operations* (Jerusalem, Israel Democracy Institute, 2015) and sources cited.

constitutes a violation of the principle of proportionality. Much of this renewed interest was fuelled by specific incidents or operations.[32] Some authors viewed the extended use of targeted killings and similar operations as an opportunity for a renewed discussion of the actual meaning of proportionality in modern warfare.

The next part of this chapter will deal with the new interpretations of the principle of proportionality (which I shall term the 'new scholarship') advanced in the context of targeted operations.

B. Human Rights and Individualist Claims

One branch of the 'new scholarship' of proportionality deals with issues regarding the correct interpretation of the term proportionality from a moral or human rights point of view.

The background for this discussion is an unresolved major doctrinal question, regarding the use of targeted killings operations outside actual battlefields. It is quite clear that when a battle erupts, and the state chooses to attack a specific individual, the applicable law is that of the 'international law of armed conflict' or IHL. Many scholars and practitioners agree that when used in this setting, IHL allows the targeting of individuals, and hence targeted killings are allowed.[33] However, few targeted killings take place on a conventional battlefield, where they are usually least effective. Rather, they are directed against targets not actually fighting or personally involved in an ongoing battle, but engaged in some other activity: sleeping, eating, praying or reading. Which is the applicable legal paradigm under those circumstances? The governments of the United States and of Israel have long held the view that since the *general* context is still that of armed conflict, IHL remains the applicable law. After all, the person targeted is part of an organised group participating in an armed conflict.

An alternative view is that the situation in these cases no longer corresponds to that of armed conflict. Rather it must be classified as a law enforcement operation in which (absent an actual battle) terrorists constitute criminals. In law enforcement operations IHL does not apply. Rather, the applicable governing law is that of human rights, as is the case in any other state action.[34]

---

[32] eg Operation Cast Lead.

[33] See eg D Kretzmer, 'Targeted Killing of Suspected Terrorists: Extra-Judicial Executions or Legitimate Means of Defense?' (2005) 16 *European Journal of International Law* 171.

[34] N Melzer, 'Interpretive Guidance on the Notion of Direct Participation in Hostilities under International Humanitarian Law' (2008) 90 *International Review of the Red Cross* 991. Further on this issue, see also chapters 4 and 5 in this volume.

For the purposes of this chapter, the difference between the armed conflict model and the law enforcement model affects the interpretation of
proportionality.[35] If the applicable law is that of IHL, then proportionality
in IHL allows the attacking power to operate even if it assumes that civilians
will be killed. However, the law enforcement model is governed by human
rights law, which lays down much stricter rules regarding proportionality.
Under human rights law, killing innocent civilians is only rarely allowed.
The right to life is a foundation of human rights law, which forbids the
intentional killing of a civilian, even only as collateral damage.

But even if the situation is categorised as an armed conflict, in which
IHL is applicable, the interpretation of proportionality might not remain
unchanged. Most scholars believe that even in armed conflicts, especially
of a hybrid nature, human rights law is applicable, as a complementary
system.[36] According to this view, the right to life has to play some role in
the understanding of proportionality. This is especially true in targeted killing operations, where the civilian is usually not an anonymous member of a
collective entity, but rather a specific person.

One major question which has signalled the shift in proportionality scholarship is the question of the certainty of civilian death. Just as the Obama
administration balked at the idea that civilian death would be a known and
accepted result of targeted killings, so did many scholars. This, however,
was exactly the original meaning of the principles of distinction and of proportionality when they were first articulated. There was no doubt in the eyes
of the framers of the conventions that states could legitimately kill civilians,
as long as the intention of the state was to attack a legitimate military target. The innovation in the principle of proportionality was that even when
a legitimate military target was the intended result, it was forbidden to kill
a quantity of civilians in excess of the military value of the target. No one
doubted that some civilians could be knowingly killed when an important
military target was attacked.

To modern scholars, human rights activists and (much) public opinion all
this seems to be incredibly wrong. In their view, the right to life, protected
by international human rights law, does not simply disappear in armed conflicts.[37] Attacking a target knowing that innocent civilians will be killed, not

---

[35] See M Newton and L May, *Proportionality in International Law* (Oxford, Oxford
University Press, 2014) 241.

[36] *Legal Consequences of the Construction of a Wall in the Occupied Palestinian Territory*
(Advisory Opinion) [2004] ICJ Rep 136.

[37] As M Milanovic claimed: 'If human rights accrue to human beings solely by virtue of
their humanity why should these rights evaporate merely because two states, or a state and a
non-state actor, have engaged in armed conflict? More limited these rights may be, but they
cannot be completely extinguished or displaced if their basic universality premise, that they
are immanent in the human dignity of every individual, is accepted. See M Milanovic, 'Norm

as a mistake, but as a foreseen result of the attack, constitutes a clear violation of the right to life.[38]

This disagreement over the interpretation of the principle of proportionality lies at the root of legal disagreements regarding several issues.

Take, for example, the issue of 'force protection': can an army choose a method of combat which would protect its soldiers, at the cost of civilian lives? This, in essence, was the discussion regarding the 'zero casualties' policy adopted by NATO in the Kosovo war. There, NATO forces flew and dropped bombs from high altitudes, above the range of Serbian anti-aircraft missiles. This, however, necessarily meant that targeting by those planes would become less accurate, and that more civilians would be killed. A committee formed by the Prosecutor of the ICTY famously ducked the issue, by indicating the difficulties of understanding the principle of proportionality.[39] However, it is not surprising that some modern scholars claim that adopting such a method of 'zero casualties' violates the proportionality principle. If the life of every human being, friend or foe, counts the same, as is mandated by the right to life, then there is no reason to prefer the lives of one's own soldiers to those of enemy civilians.[40]

A similar discussion takes place with regards to 'human shields'—civilians who are intentionally placed where they would be harmed if an attack were made on a legitimate military target. It is settled international law that IHL forbids forcing persons to become human shields (involuntary human shields).[41] But what is the correct application of the principle of

---

Conflicts, International Humanitarian Law, and Human Rights' in O Ban-Naftali (ed), *International Humanitarian Law and International Human Rights Law* (Oxford, Oxford University Press, 2011) 95, 101. It seems that Y Dinstein holds a different view, according to which the application of IHL in this matter means that there is no applicability to human rights except in the very general sense, and hence the right to life does not apply. See Y Dinstein, *Non-International Armed Conflicts in International Law* (Cambridge, Cambridge University Press, 2014) 224–30.

[38] B Orend, *The Morality of War*, 2nd edn (Peterborough, Ont, Broadview Press, 2013) 124.
[39] ICTY, 'Final Report to the Prosecutor by the Committee Established to Review the NATO Bombing Campaign Against the Federal Republic of Yugoslavia' (13 June 2000) 48: 'The main problem with the principle of proportionality is not whether or not it exists but what it means and how it is to be applied. It is relatively simple to state that there must be an acceptable relation between the legitimate destructive effect and undesirable collateral effects. ... Unfortunately, most applications of the principle of proportionality are not quite so clear-cut. It is much easier to formulate the principle of proportionality in general terms than it is to apply it to a particular set of circumstances because the comparison is often between unlike quantities and values. One cannot easily assess the value of innocent human lives as opposed to capturing a particular military objective.'
[40] In fact, the disagreement is even more extreme. Some, like M Walzer and A Margalit, think that the lives of soldiers should be considered less than the lives of civilians. See A Margalit and M Walzer, 'Israel: Civilians and Combatants' *New York Review of Books*, 14 May 2009, www.nybooks.com/articles/2009/05/14/israel-civilians-combatants/. Others believe that that protecting the lives of the state's soldiers should weigh more than the civilians of the enemy. See Kasher and Yadlin (n 13).
[41] Henckaerts and Doswald-Beck (n 7) 337, r 97.

proportionality when civilians voluntarily gather around a military target in order to deter an enemy attack? Are these still considered civilians for the purpose of application of the principle of proportionality?[42] Many scholars believe that an individual does not somehow diminish the value of his life by placing himself, even voluntarily, near a military target, attacks on which he thereby intends to prevent. The right to life cannot be ignored, simply because it becomes legally more complicated for the attacking army to attack a target.[43]

All the above discussions have only become relevant in the context of modern armed conflicts, of which targeted killings are an integral part. They have resulted in a reinterpretation of the principle of proportionality, which severely limits the powers of states to attack in cases where civilians deaths are inevitable.

C. The Attempt to Provide Precise Content to Proportionality

An alternative route developed in modern scholarship is the attempt to provide concise content to the principle of proportionality. Some scholars claim that proportionality is not a general directive to the military commander, but rather a specific formula which can be applied with equal effect in a wide spectrum of cases across various empirical contexts.

For instance, Professor Boaz Ganor translated the general framework of Article 51 to a specific equation, in which he identified all the possible advantages and potential damages that have to be taken into account, and illustrated how they might be compared.[44] The advantage of this work is that it offers, for the first time, a coherent and systematic attempt to provide militaries with a tool which would allow them to insert specific values into the proportionality principle. Apart from the obvious utility of this exercise, it also offers a solution to the issue of inequality in the application of the principle of proportionality. If specific values can be attached to the variables in the equation, then there is no reason to posit major differences between states, and between different commanders within a state.

On the other hand, there do seem to be some major problems with Ganor's work. To begin with, in order to operationalise his formula, Ganor must determine the correct answer to all the questions which we discussed in the previous section. But he does not provide us with any specific theory according to which such determinations will be made. A second difficulty

---

[42] Newton and May (n 35) 207.
[43] Melzer (n 34) 57.
[44] B Ganor, *Global Alert: The Rationality of Modern Islamist Terrorism and the Challenge to the Liberal Democratic World* (New York, Columbia University Press, 2015).

is that Ganor ignores the fact that according to Article 51 of Protocol I the prohibition on attack is only if the damage to civilians is 'excessive' compared to the military advantage attained. The term 'excessive' was intentionally inserted by the framers of that document in order to emphasise that the principle of proportionality allows the attacking party some flexibility, and indicates the impossibility of defining an exact equation.[45] There are also some specific problems with the variables that Ganor inserts into the formula. I will not detail these specific problems here. Suffice it to say that the existence of these disagreements serves to prove that the equation is not 'neutral' but reflects some pre-existing concept of proportionality.

These criticisms aside, the rationale behind Ganor's work seems to me to be grounded in the ways in which military organisations view the use of force in modern wars. As described earlier, modern wars seem to be conflicts in which force is used sparingly, and only in order to achieve a very specific goal. No attempts are made to conquer vast territories or to annihilate the enemy. Hence, military targets become much more specific, and the utility of every use of force needs to be evaluated specifically, in terms of cost–benefit analysis. The overuse of force and killing of civilians could become a serious liability on the state, and jeopardise the entire policy. Logically, this means that a very strict evaluation should be made also in terms of proportionality. Therefore, while I do not concur with Ganor that his formula represents a coherent and complete interpretation of the term in IHL, I fully accept the motivations behind it. In fact, I believe that it is exactly this motivation which is driving armed forces in liberal democracies to adopt what I term a 'bureaucratised' or 'procedural' understanding of the term, one that I shall explain in the next part of this chapter.

V. PROPORTIONALITY AS PROCEDURE

With respect to proportionality, as in many other areas of international law, military practice and scholarship have advanced in parallel tracks.[46] While scholars were asking the moral and quantitative questions described above, military lawyers were doing something completely different. Armed forces translated the principle of proportionality into a bureaucratic process,

---

[45] The ICC Statute was even clearer in this regard. The relevant article of the ICC Statute declares that the damage to civilians has to be 'clearly excessive' compared to the military advantage in order to criminalise a disproportionate attack. Rome Statute of the International Criminal Court (adopted 17 July 1998, entered into force 1 July 2002) UN Doc A/CONF 183/9 (ICC Statute) Art 8 (2)(b)(iv). (Note that the ICC Statute includes proportionality breaches as a crime only in IACs, and not in NIACs.)

[46] D Luban, 'Military Necessity and the Cultures of Military Law' (2013) 26 *Leiden Journal of International Law* 315.

which has become an essential part of the way in which the armed forces are operationalising the principle of proportionality.

A. The Legal Background

Formally, the issue turned on the importance of Article 57 to Protocol I, 'precautions in attack'.[47] This article requires the attacking force to evaluate not only the issue of proportionality, but also a much wider series of issues before embarking on an attack: it has to consider the possibility of advanced warning (Article 57(2)(c)); to use means and methods of warfare that will cause the minimal level of damage to civilians (Article 57(2)(b)); and military commanders have to select from among several military objectives those that are least harmful to civilians (Article 57(3)).

Traditionally, Article 57 was considered as a tool for use by commanders in order to implement different facets of the prohibitions contained in earlier articles in Protocol I. However, in current armed conflicts, and especially in planned operations such as targeted killings, Article 57 has become a much more important norm. Armed forces that resort to targeted killings have come to consider it to be a blueprint for planning and executing an attack. In this approach, the main duty of the armed forces, and of military lawyers, is to undertake a series of bureaucratic tests and processes, which take into account the existence of civilians.

B. Procedures

Contemporary armed conflicts have decidedly heightened public awareness of civilian casualties. Modern media bring the pictures of dead women and children to every home and in so doing foster public criticism not only of the specific operation in which civilians were harmed, but also of the overall military policy and strategy. This attention creates pressures on politicians and armed forces to avoid civilian casualties. It has also given rise to a

---

[47] Art 57 states the following:

1. In the conduct of military operations, constant care shall be taken to spare the civilian population, civilians and civilian objects.
2. With respect to attacks, the following precautions shall be taken:
   (a) those who plan or decide upon an attack shall:

   ...

   (ii) take all feasible precautions in the choice of means and methods of attack with a view to avoiding, and in any event to minimizing, incidental loss of civilian life, injury to civilians and damage to civilian objects;

phenomenon sometimes termed 'the strategic corporal', a non-commissioned officer whose actions in a remote part of the battlefield might create political and strategic problems for politicians and high command.[48]

Naturally, this problem would be minimised were it possible to train all soldiers to behave in ways that take into account all the strategic and political implications of their actions. Despite some attempts to attain that goal,[49] it has not always proved attainable. Soldiers tend to take their own safety into account, to follow their instincts, and some of them possess an ideological or cultural bias which is not necessarily identical to that of their military or political superiors. In short, soldiers are like every other agent—they act to promote their best interest, which does not necessarily dovetail with that of their principal.[50]

One way to control the way in which soldiers behave is to create specific procedures. Indeed all bureaucracies adopt procedures precisely in order to control the way every bureaucrat operates. Procedures ensure, to a certain extent, that the lower-level operative will enjoy only limited discretion. He will therefore have only a limited chance to deviate from the wishes and orders of the higher level in the organisation, in the military case—higher command, or the political echelon. However, military activity does not easily lend itself to control by procedure, especially during battles. The reasons are clear. Procedures are time consuming, and battles require alacrity. Winning battles is about innovation when confronted with uncertainties and the 'fog of war', whilst procedures are based on information and knowledge.

     (iii)   refrain from deciding to launch any attack which may be expected to cause incidental loss of civilian life, injury to civilians, damage to civilian objects, or a combination thereof, which would be excessive in relation to the concrete and direct military advantage anticipated;

  (b) an attack shall be cancelled or suspended if it becomes apparent that the objective is not a military one or is subject to special protection or that the attack may be expected to cause incidental loss of civilian life, injury to civilians, damage to civilian objects, or a combination thereof, which would be excessive in relation to the concrete and direct military advantage anticipated;

  (c) effective advance warning shall be given of attacks which may affect the civilian population, unless circumstances do not permit.

  3. When a choice is possible between several military objectives for obtaining a similar military advantage, the objective to be selected shall be that the attack on which may be expected to cause the least danger to civilian lives and to civilian objects.

[48] C Krulak, 'The Strategic Corporal: Leadership in the Three Block War' [1999] *The Marines Magazine*, www.au.af.mil/au/awc/awcgate/usmc/strategic_corporal.htm.

[49] See eg L Liddy, 'The Strategic Corporal: Some Requirements in Training and Education' (2013) 11 *Australian Army Journal* 2, 139, declaring that: '[T]he Australian Army must begin to foster a military culture that is aimed at preparing non-commissioned officers (NCOs) to become what has been described as "strategic corporals".'

[50] For a full analysis, see PD Feaver, *Armed Servants: Agency, Oversight and Civil–Military Relations* (Cambridge, Harvard University Press, 2005).

Winning a battle requires flexibility and attention to the specific context, whereas procedures are universal and dogmatic.[51]

Against that background, targeted killings assume special significance, principally because they so obviously deviate from the general pattern of tension between operations and procedure in battle. It is the very essence of targeted killings that they are preplanned, and hence allow adequate time for consideration of consequences. Such operations also require precise intelligence—specific knowledge regarding the whereabouts of the target, a requirement that further allows for the precise calibration of objectives at all levels of command. In short, targeted killings seem to be the perfect area in which modern armies could actually control the way in which operations take place by using procedures that can be implemented in these kinds of operations.

Given such considerations, it is not surprising that targeted killings have indeed become highly bureaucratised, especially concerning attention to civilian casualties. In a recent article, Gregory McNeal described the way in which the United States assesses collateral damage and the legality of targeted killings.[52] There is a strict evaluation of the possible damage to civilians, a requirement to gather information, and clear guidelines regarding who should be part of the decision-making process. There is also extensive use of scientific knowledge regarding the effects of different kinds of weapons, such as the radius of impact of different bombs or projectiles. All these considerations create a situation in which, before targeted killing operations are employed, a very detailed set of procedures need to be followed. This procedure has two basic goals: (i) to limit as much as possible the extent of civilian casualties; and (ii) to ensure that even if casualties are caused, their number will be known in advance, and that high-level military and political command can be made aware of the figure, and evaluate the consequences. Similarly, the Israeli assessment of targets and targeted killing operations is also heavily proceduralised.[53]

C. The Saleh Shehadeh Targeted Killing

This chapter is not the place to itemise in detail all the evidence relative to the development of the use of procedures in targeted killings. As an

---

[51] Indeed, this is the reason armed forces adopt alternative modes of control. Such, for example, is the adoption of IHL—which serves as a mode of control. See E Benvenisti and A Cohen, 'War is Governance: Explaining the Logic of the Laws of War from a Principal-Agent perspective' (2014) 112 *Michigan Law Review* 1363.

[52] GS McNeal, 'Targeted Killing and Accountability' (2014) 102 *Georgetown Law Journal* 681.

[53] Schmitt and Merriam (n 16) 75.

illustration of my claim that procedures have become the main focal point of the legal analysis of targeted killings I will focus on one case—the targeted killing of Saleh Shehadeh by the Israeli Defense Forces (IDF) in 2002. This case was extensively documented by a report of a special investigatory commission, headed by a retired Israeli supreme court justice, Tova Strasberg-Cohen.[54]

Saleh Shehadeh was head of the Operational Branch of Hamas in Gaza, had instigated a significant number of attacks on Israelis, and was responsible for the deaths of large numbers of Israeli military personnel and civilians. On 22 July 2002, an Israeli warplane dropped a one-tonne bomb on a house in Gaza City, and killed Shehadeh. The same bomb also simultaneously killed many other persons in the same house, amongst them Shehadeh's wife, another Hamas operative, Shehada's 15-year-old child, and thirteen more civilians, eight of whom were children. One hundred and fifty civilian bystanders were injured.[55]

Initially, the IDF refused to open an official investigation into the incident. However, in 2003 a petition to investigate was submitted to the Israeli Supreme Court (in its capacity as the 'High Court of Justice'—a court with authority to review all governmental activities in Israel). In late 2006, while the petition was under consideration, the court published its landmark judgment in the *Public Committee against Torture* case, in which it ruled that targeted killings are not prohibited by IHL, provided that they follow some specific conditions.[56] In 2008, after pressure from the court,[57] the government opted to form a commission to investigate the Shehadeh killing. The commission submitted its report in February 2011.

The commission's conclusions were that although some mistakes were made in the process leading up to the Shehadeh operation, there was no need for a criminal investigation. The commission detailed the process that took place, and indicated the mistakes that were made.

For the purposes of this chapter, what is important is the general framework that the commission specified for decision-making in future targeted killing operations.

---

[54] Report of the Special Investigatory Commission on the Targeted Killing of Saleh Shehadeh (27 February 2011), Salah Shehadeh-Special Investigatory Commission, www.mfa.gov.il/MFA/Government/Law/Legal%20Issues%20and%20Rulings/Salah_Shehadeh-Special_Investigatory_Commission_27-Feb-2011.htm.

[55] A Meyerstein, 'Case Study: The Israeli Strike Against Hamas Leader Salah Shehadeh' *Crimes of War*, 19 September 2002, www.crimesofwar.org/print/onnews/Shehadeh-print.html.

[56] *The Public Committee Against Torture in Israel v The Government of Israel* HCJ 769/02 (2006) (*Targeted Killings* case).

[57] *Hess v Military Advocate General* HCJ 8794/03 (unpublished 2008).

First, the commission interpreted the *Public Committee against Torture* judgment[58] to set out the following requirements for a targeted killing operation: (i) the operation should take place only after the attacking party gathers accurate and reliable information regarding the intended targets and whether they are civilians taking direct part in the hostilities; (ii) the attacking party should take every feasible measure to attempt to secure the results with non-lethal weapons. All feasible efforts should especially be made to use less lethal measures; (c) the principle of proportionality must be observed and the harm to uninvolved civilians must not be excessive; and (d) an investigatory committee should be established in order to investigate operations that result in exceptional outcomes.

In applying the normative framework to the specific case, the commission found that the Israeli security agencies responsible for the operation considered thirteen civilian deaths to constitute a disproportionate number of civilian deaths. The commission, however, concluded that no criminal responsibility existed, since the main failure in the operation was a mistaken intelligence assessment. Nevertheless, the commission considered the mistake to be avoidable. This was because the intelligence-gathering operation conducted by the Israeli Security Agency (ISA) principally focused on how to find Shehadeh and the correct operational time for him to be hit; insufficient attention was paid to gathering intelligence regarding the possibility of civilian casualties.

The commission's recommendations are telling: after a general remark that Israel is committed to the principle of proportionality, and a recommendation that all security forces be made continuously aware of this commitment, the committee never specified what this principle actually means. Rather, its recommendations are principally concerned with procedural requirements as to how the decision regarding targeted killings and proportionality assessment should be taken. Thus, the commission suggested that all decisions in matters of targeted killings should be recorded (recommendations 9 and 10); that final decisions should be taken by the political echelon, and be made only in writing (recommendation 13); that disagreements between the heads of the security services be brought before the political echelon, especially regarding harm to civilians (recommendations 14 and 15); that the Prime Minister and the Minister of Defense should make the decision only after consulting the Chief of Staff and the head of the ISA (recommendation 16); that lawyers should be more involved in decision-making regarding targeted killings, and that any disagreement that they may have with the recommendation of the professional echelon should be brought to the attention of the political echelon (recommendation 17).

---

[58] *Targeted Killings* case (n 56).

All these recommendations point to a specific conclusion—what can be said regarding targeted killing is the procedure that should be followed. This is the important part of the decision-making process, rather than the result. The inability thus displayed to determine the specific number of deaths to be considered disproportionate is not unique. It is a natural result of the problems associated with the proportionality formulae as described above. The commission's procedural recommendations are consistent with existing practice in a fundamental way: they reflect the tendency to frame proportionality as a set of procedural requirements. The decision-maker is not given a specific number by the lawyer. In fact, the lawyer has no specific number to give. All the lawyer can, and should, do is stipulate procedures that will ensure the decision-maker takes civilian casualties into account.

D. Effects of Procedures

As explained above, it is the need for control that explains why procedures for assessing proportionality are adopted. The question is, however, whether this approach to the principle of proportionality protects civilians. Is the adoption of procedures a good or relevant way to attain a balance between the necessities of war and the protection of human lives? I offer below, only briefly, three sets of justifications for the procedural approach to proportionality: reasonableness, responsibility and organisational culture.

i. Creating a Zone of Reasonableness

One important effect of the use of procedures is to create a 'zone of reasonableness'. As I claimed above, the principle of proportionality cannot be interpreted to provide a precise number of civilian casualties considered not to be excessive. What it can do, and does, is require that specific considerations are taken into account. It requires a commander to focus his/her attention, wherever possible, on the possibility that civilians are likely to be harmed. The commander is free to choose between various options, but all these options are presented within a general framework. The fact that the decision-maker takes civilian casualties into account is by itself a very important factor. An acknowledgement of the need for a professional assessment of the military advantage in relation to civilian casualties itself provides an assurance that the latter will be taken into account, and not ignored as legitimate collateral damage.

ii. Responsibility and Control

Procedural and bureaucratic mechanisms create a visible hierarchy. It is clear who needs to make the decisions, and where the responsibility for those decisions lies. This issue is at the heart of a general policy in current IHL to try to place responsibility for following IHL on the policy-makers, rather than on low-level soldiers. The move is evident in current international criminal law, which includes several sophisticated legal mechanisms intended to ensure that commanders would indeed face consequences for the actions of persons under their command.

Many of the procedures employed by armed forces in targeted killings are entirely in agreement with this general trend in IHL, since they concern the identity of the decision-maker. In both the United States and Israel, any chance that civilians would be killed requires moving the locus of decision-making up the chain of command, usually to the political level. This, too, improves the quality of assessment of the balance between military necessities and human lives. Moreover, the higher the level of decision-making, the higher the level of responsibility. Responsibility for taking the lives of civilians should lie at the top. Political leaders and senior military commanders are the only persons who can decide on military policy, and are those who should pay the price for decision failures. Hence, it makes sense that the decision would be made at their level.

iii. Organizational Culture

The requirement that decisions are reached in accordance with clear guidelines and procedures also ensures the involvement of a greater number of persons in the decision-making process. These participants, who are responsible for verifying that all procedures are followed, bureaucratise the use of military power. Since procedures consume time, this may mean that it will take longer to arrive at a decision. But it also ensures that the decision-making process involves more participants. The different participants in the process are likely to contribute their various points of view and interests. For example, some might be able to recall precedents from prior cases in the same country or abroad. Others could identify the effect of certain actions on media coverage, and integrate the position of the public into the decision-making.

Lawyers constitute a unique sector, one that is empowered by the emphasis on procedure. Because of their expertise in matters of procedures, the extensive use of procedures means that more lawyers will be involved in the process.[59] Lawyers, in turn, create even more pressure

---

[59] Regarding the role of lawyers in the US armed forces, see JL Goldsmith, *Power and Constraint: The Accountable Presidency after 9/11* (New York, Norton, 2012) ch 5. On the expanding role of lawyers in the IDF, see A Craig, *International Legitimacy and the Politics of Security: The Strategic Deployment of Lawyers in the Israeli Military* (Lanham, MD, Lexington Books, 2013). Schmitt and Merriam (n 16).

for adherence to bureaucratic processes. Clear bureaucratic processes allow lawyers to impose control over decision-making, create transparent decision-making, and aim for equality between different cases. They also create a 'paper trail' that can be evaluated and investigated if anything goes wrong.[60]

It is therefore unsurprising that in targeted killing operations, where procedures are so important, lawyers play an extremely important role. They are attached to the armed forces, and have a voice in major questions concerning uses of force.[61] Lawyers are involved in various stages of planning the attack; they indicate where difficulties arise; and propose alternative modes of action.[62]

VI. SUMMARY

Targeted killing operations are a modus operandi that reflects the way in which modern armed conflicts differ from traditional wars. One aspect of this difference is the way in which the principle of proportionality is interpreted in the context of targeted killing.

Scholarship has tended to focus on the moral problems of the application of the principle in the context of targeted killings, or on attempts to quantify the proportionality formula. In practice, however, the real change in the application of the principle of proportionality has been the prominence accorded to the procedures involved in the application of this principle in the context of targeted killings.

The consequence of the use of procedures is a more careful military, which takes into consideration the possibility of mistakes and failures. It is therefore not surprising that in the United States, as described in the introduction to this chapter, there is a tendency to limit civilian casualties, or even to declare that civilian causalities will avoided completely. This development does not reflect changes in law, or at least not a clear legal norm. Rather, it is indicative of the way in which US organisational culture now undertakes its cost–benefit analysis. The rise of bureaucratic process and lawyers has meant that the US armed forces are more hesitant about the way that they use their targeting capabilities. It is possible, of course, that US claims in

---

[60] The rise of lawyers in armed forces is connected to the rise in investigations, which are one of the main roles of the lawyers in armed forces. See eg Goldsmith (n 59).

[61] A Cohen, 'Legal Operational Advice in the Israeli Defense Forces: The International Law Department and the Changing Nature of International Humanitarian Law' (2011) 26 *Connecticut Journal of International Law* 367.

[62] Goldsmith (n 59), quoting military officers speaking of their units' lawyers as 'consigliere'.

this regard are not accurate. However, even these declarations mean that the United States attempts to create an image of a conflict with very few civilian casualties. Inevitably, this shift affects the positions taken by other countries. Other liberal democracies cannot ignore the US position on this matter. Hence, for some countries, the principle of proportionality significantly limits the scope of targeted killing operations.

4

Regulating Armed Drones and Other Emerging Weapons Technologies

STUART CASEY-MASLEN

I. INTRODUCTION

I N THE EARLY 1980s, Edward Teller declared during a press conference that 'the unmanned vehicle today is a technology akin to the importance of radars and computers in 1935'.[1] Writing three decades later, in 2015, Peter Singer observed that armed unmanned systems—remotely piloted vehicles known colloquially as drones—are a 'game-changer'.[2] This is due to their ability to be deployed to linger over and surveil, without direct risk to one's own personnel, for days, weeks and even months at a stretch, and then to kill at a minute's notice, which affords states a new and exceptionally valuable capability to use lethal force.

Some are availing themselves of this tactical asset at an accelerating rate. In Afghanistan, for example, 2015 was the first year that the United States launched more explosive ordnance from armed drones than it did from combat aircraft controlled by a pilot in the cockpit.[3] Drones have become effectively integrated into US combat operational doctrine to an extent that is arguably unparalleled.[4] By April 2016, another eighteen states were said

---

[1] Cited in S Shane, *Objective Troy* (New York, Tim Duggan Books, 2015) 70–71.

[2] P Singer, 'The Five Deadly Flaws of Talking About Emerging Military Technologies and the Need for New Approaches to Law, Ethics, and War' in PL Bergen and D Rothenberg (eds), *Drone Wars* (Cambridge, Cambridge University Press, 2015) 215, 216.

[3] J Smith, 'Exclusive: Afghan Drone War—Data Show Unmanned Flights Dominate Air Campaign' *Reuters*, 21 April 2016, uk.reuters.com/article/us-afghanistan-drones-exclusive-idUKKCN0XH2UZ.

[4] In *Hunter Killer*, a former drone pilot and later squadron commander describes the evolution of the Predator drone 'from an aviation backwater joke to the tip of the spear in the war against terrorism'. See TM McCurley and K Maurer, *Hunter Killer: Inside the Lethal World of Drone Warfare* (London, Allen & Unwin, 2016) xiii. A former US Special Forces commander in Afghanistan records seeing drone use 'progress from the early part of the decade when there was very limited reliance on drones at the tactical operational level to now when almost

to already possess armed drones.[5] Many others—and certain non-state actors[6]—are actively seeking to acquire the requisite technology.

Singer goes much further, though, by arguing that drones are a technology that acts to '*change* the rules of the game'.[7] Here we part company. For while it is true to say that elements of the existing international normative framework have been repudiated by the United States since 2001, and, since 2015, also by the United Kingdom, the rules have not changed; rather, it is the circumstances in which force is being used that have been transformed. Armed drones enable extrajudicial execution of suspected terrorists outside the realm of the conduct of hostilities from a distance of thousands of miles away at the push of a button, but this fact does not alter the law. Herein I argue that the customary international legal rule governing the intentional lethal use of force in law enforcement—that such force may only be lawful when strictly unavoidable to protect life—remains undiluted (though it is, admittedly, more than a little scarred). It is more accurate to say that new US doctrine governing use of lethal force 'outside the traditional battlefield' has not attained the status of hard law, but amounts only to 'legal-style guidance' in a new use-of-force paradigm.[8]

This chapter addresses these issues by focusing on the use of armed drones in counterterrorism outside the conduct of hostilities, especially, but not only, by the United States. Such use may, and often does, violate the rights to life and to humane treatment, along with the notion of human dignity that underpins these human rights. It begins by describing the development of armed drones and their use in operations within and outside armed conflict. Use in the conduct of hostilities gives rise to far fewer international legal concerns and is thus addressed succinctly; the protection of those who are targeted away from the battlefield is the focus of broader and deeper concern and thus the mainstay of this chapter's assessment of extant international law. My concluding remarks look at some of the other weapons technologies that are on the research and development (R&D) horizon and which may be expected to threaten the enjoyment of human rights in years to come.

---

every squad leader demands to have one': see M Waltz, 'Bring on the Magic' in Bergen and Rothenberg (n 2) 209.

[5] J Bamford, 'Terrorists Have Drones Now. Thanks, Obama' *Foreign Policy*, 28 April 2016, http://foreignpolicy.com/2016/04/28/terrorists-have-drones-now-thanks-obama-warfare-isis-syria-terrorism/.

[6] See eg Remote Control Project, 'Hostile Drones: The Hostile Use of Drones by Non-State Actors against British Targets' (2016) www.oxfordresearchgroup.org.uk/sites/default/files/Hostile%20use%20of%20drones%20report_open%20briefing_16.pdf, 11–13. The report's lead author is reported to have described drones as a 'game-changer in the wrong hands'. Bamford, 'Terrorists Have Drones Now' (n 5).

[7] Singer (n 2) 215 (added emphasis).

[8] S Issacharoff and RH Pildes, 'Drones and the Dilemma of Modern Warfare' in Bergen and Rothenberg (n 2) 401.

II. THE DEVELOPMENT OF ARMED DRONES

Indirectly, drone technology owes its existence to Nikola Tesla, who first demonstrated the remote control of vehicles at the end of the nineteenth century. In 1898, on a pond in Madison Square Garden, Tesla controlled a boat by means of a radio signal, the first such application of radio waves in history and arguably also 'the birthplace of modern robotics'.[9] As one human geography expert has put it: 'On that body of water floated enormous, and largely unrecognized, military potential.'[10]

Armed aerial drones have existed, at least in R&D programmes, since World War I. In 1918, following pioneering work by Elmer Sperry, the inventor of autopilot technology and the gyroscope, the US Army began experiments with the Kettering Bug, an unmanned biplane with gyroscopic guidance capable of carrying 180lb of explosives for some 40 miles before dive-bombing into a target.[11] In 1919, after the end of the war, Sperry successfully sunk a captured German battleship using a pilotless aircraft.[12] But through most of the twentieth century drones were unarmed. Surveillance and reconnaissance drones were first deployed on a significant scale by the US during the armed conflicts in Vietnam in the 1960s,[13] and then in Bosnia and Herzegovina[14] and over Kosovo[15] in the 1990s. The Lockheed D-21 Air Launched Drone reportedly flew at supersonic speeds as long ago as the second half of the 1960s.[16]

Israel is said to have realised the potential military applications of drones in the 1970s, during the Yom Kippur War with Egypt and Syria.[17] After losing many of their planes to surface-to-air missiles, Israel used Vietnam-era reconnaissance drones procured from the United States to locate anti-aircraft sites.

---

[9] IGR Shaw, 'The Rise of the Predator Empire: Tracing the History of US Drones' *Understanding Empire* (2014) understandingempire.wordpress.com/2-0-a-brief-history-of-u-s-drones/.

[10] ibid.

[11] Shane (n 1) 69.

[12] US Army UAS Center of Excellence, '"Eyes of the Army", US Army Unmanned Aircraft Systems Roadmap 2010–2035' (2010) ARMY.MIL No 4; see RP Barnidge, Jr, 'A Qualified Defense of American Drone Attacks in Northwest Pakistan under International Humanitarian Law' (2012) 30 *Boston University International Law Journal* 409, 413.

[13] D Cenciotti, 'The Dawn of the Robot Age: US Air Force Testing Air-Launched UCAVs Capable to Fire Maverick and Shrike Missiles in 1972' *The Aviationist*, 14 March 2012, theaviationist.com/2012/03/14/the-dawn-of-the-robot-age/.

[14] RQ-1 Predator drones have been operational in Bosnia and Herzegovina since 1995 in support of NATO, the United Nations, and US operations. See 'Predator RQ-1/MQ-1/MQ-9 Reaper UAV, United States of America', *Airforce-Technology.com* www.airforce-technology.com/projects/predator-uav/.

[15] D Abel, 'Downing the Drones' *Boston Globe*, 10 June 1999, davidabel5.blogspot.fr/2005/06/downing-drones.html.

[16] 'Lockheed D-21 Air Launched Drone' (revised 12 May 2010) www.wvi.com/~sr71webmaster/d21~1.htm.

[17] See JF Kreis, 'Unmanned Aircraft in Israeli Air Operations' (1990) 37 *Air Power History* 4, 46.

The aerial drones proved to be vital assets during combat and the Israelis began to develop their own unmanned aircraft.[18] Israel then used drones to effect in Lebanon, beginning in the 1980s. One authority claims that armed Israeli drones may even have attacked ground targets by dive-bombing into them[19] in a precursor to the Harpy, a weapons platform whose sensors autonomously identify and target radar sites.[20]

But the iconic combat drone was and remains the Predator,[21] produced by San Diego-based General Atomics.[22] Even prior to the 9/11 attacks, the United States was using drones to look for Osama bin Laden. On 25 April 2000, Richard Clarke, the White House counterterrorism adviser, proposed that the Central Intelligence Agency (CIA) fly Predator drones over Afghanistan. The drones are launched by line-of-sight pilots but then controlled in flight by personnel stationed in bases thousands of miles away in the United States. In September 2000, the resultant Project Afghan Eyes, run by the CIA's Counterterrorism Center, twice identified an individual they believed to be bin Laden. Analysts reportedly mused:

> What if the Predator toted a missile along with its camera? What if the instant they got confirmation of the tall guy's identity they could fire at the push of a button? What if, some morning between a boring early staff meeting and a desultory lunch, they could kill Bin Laden, spend the afternoon writing it up, and still get home for dinner with the kids?[23]

The armed version of the aircraft that was subsequently developed can fire two laser-guided air-to-ground Hellfire ('Helicopter-launched fire-and-forget') AGM-114 missiles against armour and personnel.[24] The standard explosive charge in a Hellfire missile is typically some 8 kg, with a reported kill radius of 15 metres and a wounding radius of 20 metres.[25] The first Predator strike in anger is said to have hit the camp of Mullah Omar, the

---

[18] D Tepper, V Mentasti and J Raab, 'Discover How Drones Are Made' *Time*, 23 October 2015, www.time.com/4001016/discover-how-drones-are-made/, citing D Rodman, 'Unmanned Aerial Vehicles in the Service of the Israel Air Force' *Rubin Center*, 7 September 2010, www.rubincenter.org/2010/09/rodman-2010-09-07/.

[19] RA Gabriel, *Operation Peace for Galilee: Israeli/Palestine Liberation Organization War in Lebanon* (New York, Hill & Wang, 1985) 99; see D Rodman, *Sword and Shield of Zion: The Israel Air Force in the Arab–Israeli Conflict, 1948–2012* (Brighton, Sussex Academic Press, 2014) 85–86.

[20] See eg 'Harpy Air Defense Suppression System' *Defense Update*, last updated 4 March 2006, www.defense-update.com/directory/harpy.htm.

[21] The first Predator prototype had its maiden flight in July 1994. R Whittle, *Predator: The Secret Origins of the Drone Revolution* (New York, Henry Holt, 2014) 85, 86.

[22] General Atomics, 'Aircraft Platforms' (2016) www.ga-asi.com/aircraft-platforms.

[23] Shane (n 1) 66–67.

[24] 'US Hellfire Missile Orders, FY 2011–2016' *Defense Industry Daily*, 16 February 2016, www.defenseindustrydaily.com/us-hellfire-missile-orders-fy-2011-2014-07019/.

[25] See eg G Chamayou, *La théorie du drone* (Paris, Editions de la Fabrique, 2013).

leader of the Taliban, on 7 October 2001, killing two of his bodyguards.[26] As *New York Times* journalist Scott Shane observed: 'A new era in warfare had begun, with unpredictable consequences. ... The Predator would be the first drone to become famous—and infamous—generating newspaper editorials, protest marches, secret legal opinions, and outlandish artworks.'[27]

The basic Predator has since been supplemented by the MQ-9 Predator B model, also propeller-driven, better known by its nickname, 'the Reaper'. The more powerful Reaper, which can carry four Hellfire missiles as well as laser-guided bombs with a higher explosive yield, such as the Paveway II and GBU-12, is currently the US Air Force's main armed drone. When used in the conduct of hostilities during an armed conflict, the drones must comply with the primary law of armed conflict rules, namely distinction and proportionality in attack. In theory, this should pose relatively scant challenge to the user, as the video feed allows sight of the target or at least the immediate area prior to, during and following the launch of missiles or the dropping of precision-guided munitions. Although mistakes are made with drones, and targets wrongly identified and wrongly hit, the technology allows for more accurate targeting and more limited unintentional battle damage than many, if not most, conventional ordnance delivery systems. As the quality of the images continues to improve, it is not credible to argue that, in general terms, the use of armed drones on the battlefield should be outlawed, let alone that they are illegal.

Far more controversial has been, and continues to be, the use of armed drones outside the conduct of hostilities. The Predator was the drone used for the first killing outside a 'conventional war zone'; this occurred in Yemen in 2002. The target was the head of al-Qaeda in Yemen, Qaed Salim Sinan al-Harithi, who was suspected of involvement in the suicide bombing attack against the USS *Cole* in Aden on 12 October 2000. In the drone strike one Hellfire missile missed its target but the second hit the car in which al-Harithi was travelling, killing him and the five other passengers.[28] The attack appeared akin to an assassination, an act whose commission had first been prohibited to the CIA by Presidential Executive Order 11905, signed by US President Gerald R Ford on 18 February 1976. The Order against 'political assassination' was enacted in response to the post-Watergate revelations that the CIA had staged multiple attempts on the life of Cuban President Fidel Castro.[29]

---

[26] AH Michel, 'How Rogue Techies Armed the Predator, Almost Stopped 9/11, and Accidentally Invented Remote War' *Wired*, 17 December 2015, www.wired.com/2015/12/how-rogue-techies-armed-the-predator-almost-stopped-911-and-accidentally-invented-remote-war/.

[27] Shane (n 1) 69.

[28] ibid, 77, 78.

[29] 'US Policy on Assassinations' *CNN*, 4 November 2002, www.edition.cnn.com/2002/LAW/11/04/us.assassination.policy/.

On 4 December 1981, President Ronald Reagan issued Executive Order 12333 on 'United States Intelligence Activities', section 2.11 of which— entitled 'Prohibition on Assassination'—provides:

> No person employed by or acting on behalf of the United States Government shall engage in, or conspire to engage in, assassination.

Section 2.12 of the order prohibits indirect participation in activities prohibited by the order, stating: 'No agency of the Intelligence Community shall participate in or request any person to undertake activities forbidden by this Order.'[30]

In August 2007, Barack Obama, then campaigning for the Democratic nomination for the presidency, criticised a decision by the Bush administration to cancel a planned raid to grab Ayman al-Zawahiri in Pakistan in 2005; the decision had been made on the basis that the operation was too risky. In a speech to the Woodrow Wilson Center in Washington DC, Obama said the failure to act was a 'terrible mistake'. He pledged: 'If we have actionable intelligence about high-value terrorist targets and President Musharraf will not act, we will.' His rival for the nomination, Hillary Clinton, would later note that he had 'basically threatened to bomb Pakistan, which I don't think was a particularly wise position to take'.[31]

At the time of the future President's speech in 2007, a dozen strikes had occurred in Pakistan and one in Yemen; President George W Bush would significantly increase the pace of drone attacks in the last six months of his second term, in part because the Pakistani authorities were believed to have been tipping off some of the targets.[32] According to Scott Shane, in combating terrorism Obama considered

> invading countries decidedly old school, something left over from the era of the telegraph. The drone, using some of the same technology that was now creating the smart phone boom, might be the new, more humane way to protect the country.[33]

President Obama's administration certainly availed itself of armed drones on a significant scale. It was reported by the Bureau of Investigative Journalism that, as at the end of January 2015, almost 2,500 people had been killed by covert US drone strikes since Obama's inauguration.[34] During 2015, the

---

[30] See EB Bazan, 'Assassination Ban and EO 12333: A Brief Summary', updated 4 January 2002, www.fas.org/irp/crs/RS21037.pdf.

[31] Shane (n 1) 126–28, and supporting citations at 342, 343.

[32] ibid, 130, 140.

[33] ibid, 131.

[34] J Serle, 'Monthly Updates on the Covert War: Almost 2,500 Now Killed by Covert US Drone Strikes since Obama Inauguration Six Years Ago: The Bureau's Report for January 2015' *Bureau of Investigative Journalism*, 2 February 2015, www.thebureauinvestigates. com/2015/02/02/almost-2500-killed-covert-us-drone-strikes-obama-inauguration/.

Bureau calculated that 13 drone strikes in Pakistan killed between 60 and 85 people,[35] while in Yemen, 10 strikes killed between 30 and 51,[36] and in Somalia, 11–12 strikes killed between 20 and 93.[37] Their estimated number of 'civilian' casualties for these covert drone strikes in 2015 was exceptionally low: a maximum of 5 in Pakistan, 0 in Yemen, and 4 in Somalia. In total for Pakistan from 2004 to February 2016, it reported that 423 strikes had killed between 2,497 and 3,999 people, of whom between 423 and 965 were believed to be civilians.[38] In contrast, in July 2016, the United States made the claim that no more than 116 civilians had been killed from 2009 through to the end of 2015 in 473 drone strikes[39] outside areas of 'active hostilities' such as Afghanistan, Iraq and Syria.[40]

One candidate for the USA's next-generation armed drone may be Northrop Grumman's X-47B, which in 2013 achieved the first aircraft carrier-based launch and recovery by an autonomous, unmanned aircraft, and in April 2015, conducted the first autonomous aerial refuelling of a drone.[41] The United States has also developed a series of 'stealth' drones. Lockheed Martin's RQ-170 Sentinel,[42] also known by its nickname 'Wraith', was used for reconnaissance during the deadly Navy SEAL raid on Osama bin Laden's compound in Pakistan in May 2011. Subsequently, after capturing a crashed RQ-170 on its border, Iran reverse-engineered the drone and equipped it with the capability to fire four precision-guided munitions in a version named the Thunderbolt.[43] The Sentinel has also been copied by China, which has released pictures of the copied drone along with other aircraft.[44] Proliferation is occurring both directly and indirectly.

---

[35] 'CIA and US Military Drone Strikes in Pakistan, 2004 to Present—Summary Tables and Casualty Rates', www.docs.google.com/spreadsheets/d/1NAfjFonM-Tn7fziqiv33HlGt09wg LZDSCP-BQaux51w/pubhtml#.

[36] 'US Strikes in Yemen, 2002 to Present—Summary Tables and Casualty Rates', www.docs. google.com/spreadsheets/d/1lb1hEYJ_omI8lSe33izwS2a2lbiygs0hTp2Al_Kz5KQ/pubhtml#.

[37] 'US Strikes in Somalia, 2007 to Present—Summary Tables and Casualty Rates', www. docs.google.com/spreadsheets/d/1-LT5TVBMy1Rj2WH30xQG9nqr8-RXFVvzJE_47NlpeSY/ pubhtml#.

[38] 'CIA and US Military Drone Strikes in Pakistan' (n 35).

[39] S Ackerman, 'Obama CLAIMS US DRONES STRIKES have Killed up to 116 Civilians' *Guardian*, 1 July 2016, www.theguardian.com/us-news/2016/jul/01/obama-drones-strikes-civilian-deaths.

[40] 'US: Up to 116 Civilians Killed in Drone, other Air Attacks' *Fox News*, 1 July 2016, www.foxnews.com/politics/2016/07/01/us-up-to-116-civilians-killed-in-drone-other-air-attacks.html.

[41] 'X-47B UCAS Makes Aviation History ... Again!' *Northrop Grumman*, 2015, www. northropgrumman.com/Capabilities/x47bucas/Pages/default.aspx.

[42] The RQ designation indicates that the Sentinel does not carry weapons; as of writing it was not known if an armed version exists or is planned.

[43] 'Iran Unveils Combat UAV Based on Captured US Spy Drone Design' *RT News*, updated 2 October 2016, www.rt.com/news/361311-iran-drone-replica-armed/.

[44] S Rogers, 'RQ-170 Sentinel Drone—The US Air Force's Stealth Drone' *Deployment Essentials*, 8 October 2014, www.deploymentessentials.com/rq-170-sentinel-drone/.

In September 2015, Pakistan became the fifth state known to have used an armed drone in combat, joining Israel, Nigeria,[45] the United Kingdom[46] and the United States.[47] The strike in the Shawal valley in North Waziristan formed part of Operation Zarb-e-Azb, a military assault launched by the army in June 2014 against militant sanctuaries in the province bordering Afghanistan.[48] At the end of the year, it was reported that Saudi Arabia and the United Arab Emirates had been using Chinese armed drones in their campaign against Yemen's Houthi rebels, while Iraq had reportedly used them in action against Islamic State forces in Ramadi.[49]

In May 2016, it was announced that the UK was planning to double its fleet of armed drones with the new upgraded generation of Predator aircraft, Certifiable Predator B. The new aircraft will be able to fly for nearly twice as long, equipped with more bombs and missiles, and able to fly in bad weather and survive ice, lightning and bird strikes.[50] The new General Atomics aircraft is expected to be named 'Protector' when used by the Royal Air Force from the end of the decade: defence chiefs have reportedly suggested the new name 'in an attempt to change public perceptions that drones are unaccountable killing machines'.[51]

III. THE INTERNATIONAL NORMATIVE FRAMEWORK

It is a mistake to characterise the debate as to the legality of drone strikes as one between the applicability of international human rights law (IHRL) and IHL. International law governing state use of force—and therefore the applicable international rules for drone strikes—is more accurately embodied as either law of law enforcement rules or, during the conduct of hostilities, law of armed conflict rules (known as Hague law). The decision as to which body of rules is to be applied is governed by the facts of each case,

---

[45] See eg 'Drone "Destroys Boko Haram Base" in Nigeria' *RT News*, 3 February 2016, www.rt.com/news/331186-boko-haram-drone-video/.

[46] UK missions began using armed drones in May 2008. 'Reaper MQ9A RPAS' *Royal Air Force*, www.raf.mod.uk/equipment/reaper.cfm.

[47] F Mangi and NO Pearson, 'Pakistan Kills Three with Burraq Armed Drone Experts Say is Based on China's CH-3' *Sydney Morning Herald*, 11 September 2015, www.smh.com.au/world/pakistan-kills-three-with-burraq-armed-drone-experts-say-is-based-on-chinas-ch3-20150911-gjkjq3.html.

[48] J Boone, 'Pakistani Army Claims it has Killed Three Militants Using its Burraq Drone' *Guardian*, 7 September 2015, www.theguardian.com/world/2015/sep/07/pakistan-army-burraq-drone-strike-kills-three-militants-shawal-reports.

[49] K Mizokami, 'For the First Time, Chinese UAVs Are Flying and Fighting in the Middle East' *Popular Mechanics*, 22 December 2015, www.popularmechanics.com/military/weapons/news/a18677/chinese-drones-are-flying-and-fighting-in-the-middle-east/.

[50] B Farmer, 'Ministry of Defence Unveils New Armed Drone that Can Spy on Targets for Twice as Long to Double RAF fleet' *Daily Telegraph*, 1 May 2016, www.telegraph.co.uk/news/2016/05/01/ministry-of-defence-unveils-new-armed-drone-that-can-spy-on-targ/.

[51] ibid.

not the desired choice of the party using force (though of course it is always possible, as a matter of policy, to use force more restrictively than international law demands).

A. Hague Law Rules Governing Drone Strikes in the Conduct of Hostilities

As noted above, compliance with Hague law rules on distinction and proportionality in attack, both of which are underpinned by the rule of precautions in attack, is not especially difficult in the case of drone strikes. This is against the backdrop of the two rules whose exposition in customary and conventional law is relatively uncontroversial, but which oftentimes are very challenging to apply, given a certain lack of clarity as to their substantive contours. Thus, for example, the basic rule of distinction is formulated as follows:

> In order to ensure respect for and protection of the civilian population and civilian objects, the Parties to the conflict shall at all times distinguish between the civilian population and combatants and between civilian objects and military objectives and accordingly shall direct their operations only against military objectives.[52]

The specific rule affording protection to civilians is as follows:

> The civilian population as such, as well as individual civilians, shall not be the object of attack.[53]

This begs the question, however, as to how accurate an attack must be to comply with the rule. Jurisprudence before the ICTY, which is internally inconsistent, appears to indicate that mortar attacks that miss a lawful military objective by more than 150 metres may be unlawful[54] but that artillery attacks that miss a target by 200 metres are not.[55] Mistakes are generally

---

[52] Protocol I Additional to the Geneva Conventions of 12 August 1949 and relating to the Protection of Victims of International Armed Conflicts (adopted 8 June 1977, entered into force 7 December 1978) 1125 UNTS 3 (AP I) Art 48. See similarly, in the case of NIAC, Protocol II Additional to the Geneva Conventions of 12 August 1949 and relating to the Protection of Victims of Non-International Armed Conflicts (adopted 8 June 1977, entered into force 7 December 1978) 1125 UNTS 609 (AP II) Art 13(2).

[53] AP I, Art 51(2). The ICRC affirms that the customary international legal rule, in so far as individuals is concerned, is as follows: 'The parties to the conflict must at all times distinguish between civilians and combatants. Attacks may only be directed against combatants. Attacks must not be directed against civilians.' ICRC, 'Customary International Humanitarian Law Study Rule 1: The Principle of Distinction between Civilians and Combatants', www.ihl-databases.icrc.org/customary-ihl/eng/docs/v1_cha_chapter1_rule1.

[54] See 'Scheduled Shelling Incident 3', in *Prosecutor v Galić* (Judgment) ICTY-98-29 (5 December 2003), paras 331ff.

[55] See *Prosecutor v Gotovina and Markač*(Appeals Judgement) ICTY-06-90-A (16 November 2012), paras 58ff.

not considered violations of Hague law rules unless they are the result of a high degree of negligence.

A similar lack of precision surrounds the rule of proportionality in attack, whose customary formulation is expressed by the ICRC as follows:

> Launching an attack which may be expected to cause incidental loss of civilian life, injury to civilians, damage to civilian objects, or a combination thereof, which would be excessive in relation to the concrete and direct military advantage anticipated, is prohibited.[56]

The meaning of the word 'excessive' is of course the nub of the challenge in applying the rule to any given situation. The US Department of Defense's assertion, in its 2015 Law of War Manual, that 'a very significant military advantage would be necessary to justify the collateral death or injury to thousands of civilians'[57] demonstrates how permissive the United States might consider this rule to be. This outlying view, insofar as it suggests that hundreds of expected civilian casualties would not require very significant military advantage, could not be considered to reflect the mainstay of state practice. Indeed, in its December 2016 iteration, the Manual materially amended the claim, replacing it with an assertion that 'an extraordinary military advantage would be necessary to justify an operation posing risks of collateral death or injury to thousands of civilians'.[58]

Advantages offered by armed drones when they are used in the conduct of hostilities are, as noted above, the video feed integrated into unmanned aircraft, and the relatively low explosive yield of the missiles often fired in drone strikes. These help compliance with 'feasible' precautionary measures required by Hague law[59] and thereby to minimise civilian harm.

But use of force in the conduct of hostilities is to be considered truly exceptional. A series of three prerequisites exist, each of which must be met before Hague law rules may be applied. These are the following:

— there must be an armed conflict in progress, whether international or non-international in character;[60]

---

[56] ICRC, 'Customary International Humanitarian Law Study Rule 14: Proportionality in Attack' www.ihl-databases.icrc.org/customary-ihl/eng/docs/v1_rul_rule14. See also Art 51(5) AP I.

[57] US Department of Defense, 'Law of War Manual' (2015) www.archive.defense.gov/pubs/law-of-war-manual-june-2015.pdf, para 5.12.4.

[58] US Department of Defense, 'Law of War Manual' (2015, updated December 2016) para 5.12.3.

[59] According to Rule 15: 'In the conduct of military operations, constant care must be taken to spare the civilian population, civilians and civilian objects. All feasible precautions must be taken to avoid, and in any event to minimize, incidental loss of civilian life, injury to civilians and damage to civilian objects.' ICRC, Customary International Humanitarian Law Study Rule 15: Precautions in Attack', www.ihl-databases.icrc.org/customary-ihl/eng/docs/v1_rul_rule15. See Art 57 AP I.

[60] A NIAC exists only when regular and intense armed violence is occurring between a state armed force and an organised armed group or between two organised armed groups. An IAC between two states requires only a very low threshold of armed violence.

— the action must be conducted by one party to the armed conflict against another, opposing party to the armed conflict; and
— the action must be conducted in an area of active hostilities, at least (and probably only) in the case where the relevant armed conflict is non-international in character.

The third of these criteria is controversial. One opposing argument holds that once a NIAC is in progress on the territory of any state, any act on that territory conducted by one party to the armed conflict against another, opposing party will be governed by Hague law. This flies in the face of both logic and, arguably, also jurisprudence. According to the ICTY:

> Although the Geneva Conventions are silent as to the geographical scope of international 'armed conflicts', the provisions suggest that at least some of the provisions of the Conventions apply to the entire territory of the Parties to the conflict, not just to the vicinity of actual hostilities. Certainly, some of the provisions are clearly bound up with the hostilities and the geographical scope of those provisions should be so limited. Others, particularly those relating to the protection of prisoners of war and civilians, are not so limited.

> The geographical and temporal frame of reference for internal armed conflicts is similarly broad. This conception is reflected in the fact that beneficiaries of common Article 3 of the Geneva Conventions are those taking no active part (or no longer taking active part) in the hostilities. This indicates that the rules contained in Article 3 also apply outside the narrow geographical context of the actual theatre of combat operations.[61]

This is, in the author's view, a correct statement of the application of the law of armed conflict, particularly in a NIAC. Geneva law, as set out, inter alia, in the 1949 Geneva Conventions, applies to relevant acts across the territory, while Hague law is limited 'to the vicinity of actual hostilities'. Violence outside this area falls outside Hague law unless and until it amounts to intense combat between opposing parties.

Thus, in any case, except one where a use of force occurs in the conduct of hostilities, as described above, law enforcement rules determine whether or not state acts are permissible under international law. While IHRL provides the overarching framework for the law of law enforcement, much of the detail of that body of international law, at least insofar as it regulates state use of force, is found in a combination of customary rules and two general principles of law: necessity and proportionality.[62] The two principles are cumulative: thus, violation of either principle will usually mean that the victim's human rights have been violated.

---

[61] *Prosecutor v Tadić* (Decision on the Defence Motion for Interlocutory Appeal on Jurisdiction) ICTY-94-1-A (2 October 1995).
[62] A third general principle of law enforcement has emerged in recent decades—the principle of precaution requires that states ensure that law enforcement operations are planned and conducted so as to minimise the risk of injury.

Many, though not all of the relevant rules were first articulated in two soft-law instruments[63] adopted under UN auspices: the 1979 Code of Conduct for Law Enforcement Officials[64] and the 1990 Basic Principles on the Use of Force and Firearms by Law Enforcement Officials.[65] The 1990 Basic Principles elaborate in greater detail on the norms on use of force set out in Article 3 of the 1979 Code of Conduct, which stipulates that law enforcement officials 'may use force only when strictly necessary and to the extent required for the performance of their duty'. Although the provisions of the two instruments were not incorporated within the confines of an international treaty, many of the key norms they espouse are widely regarded today as constituting generally binding international law. Both the ECtHR and the Inter-American Court of Human Rights have cited the 1990 Basic Principles as authoritative statements of international rules governing use of force in law enforcement.[66]

The Basic Principles and the Code of Conduct apply explicitly to the acts of any organs of the state when using force for the purpose of law enforcement. Thus, law of law enforcement rules govern not only the police, but also any other law enforcement agency, state security force, paramilitary force (such as a *gendarmerie*), or the military, whenever it is engaged in acts of law enforcement.[67] Law of law enforcement rules do not apply to the

---

[63] Soft-law instruments do not have the same normative value as a treaty since they are hortatory rather than legally binding.

[64] Code of Conduct for Law Enforcement Officials (1979) UN Doc A/RES/34/169. The Assembly decided to 'transmit it to Governments with the recommendation that favourable consideration be given to its use within the framework of national legislation or practice as a body of principles for observance by law enforcement officials'. See para 1.

[65] Basic Principles on the Use of Force and Firearms by Law Enforcement Officials (1990) (Basic Principles). The UN General Assembly in its Resolution 45/166, adopted without a vote on 18 December 1990, welcomed the Basic Principles and invited governments to respect them (para 4).

[66] See eg *Benzer et al v Turkey* (Judgment) (App no 23502/06) ECHR 12 November 2013, para 90; *Cruz Sánchez et al v Peru* (Judgment) Inter-American Court of Human Rights Series C No 292 (17 April 2015), para 264. The Court refers to the 1979 Code of Conduct in the same paragraph. In its draft general comment on the right to life (not yet finalised as of writing), the Human Rights Committee states as follows: 'In particular, all operations of law enforcement agents should comply with relevant international standards, including the Code of Conduct for Law Enforcement Officials ... and the Basic Principles on the Use of Force and Firearms by Law Enforcement Officials (1990), and law enforcement agents should undergo appropriate training designed to inculcate these standards so as to ensure, in all circumstances, the fullest respect for the right to life.' UN Human Rights Committee, 'Draft General Comment No 36' (7 September 2015) UN Doc CCPR/C/GC/R.36/Rev, para 19.

[67] 'In accordance with the commentary to Article 1 of the Code of Conduct for Law Enforcement Officials, the term "law enforcement officials" includes all officers of the law, whether appointed or elected, who exercise police powers, especially the powers of arrest or detention. In countries where police powers are exercised by military authorities, whether uniformed or not, or by State security forces, the definition of law enforcement officials shall be regarded as including officers of such services.' Basic Principles (n 64) n 1.

conduct of hostilities during a situation of armed conflict, but do apply to acts of law enforcement amid armed conflict.

B. Law Enforcement Rules Governing Drone Strikes

i. The Principles of Necessity and Proportionality

Any force used must be only the minimum necessary in the circumstances (the principle of necessity) and must be for a legitimate law enforcement purpose. Force must never, therefore, be meted out vindictively or as a form of punishment.

In addition, force used must be proportionate to the threat (the principle of proportionality). This principle as it applies to use of force for law enforcement is much misunderstood. Proportionality does not mean that force must be used in strict accord with any use-of-force continuum, or as a 'tit-for-tat' response to violence. Instead, it sets a ceiling as to what is lawful use of force, in accordance with the threat posed by an individual or group of individuals and the offence that has been or is about to be committed. It is particularly specific when lethal force is being countenanced.

ii. The Rule Governing Intentional Lethal Use of Force

A distinct and higher standard applies when law enforcement officials 'shoot to kill'. An example in law enforcement could be to stop a suicide bomber or a hostage-taker from killing others. According to the final sentence of 1990 Basic Principle 9: 'In any event, intentional lethal use of firearms may only be made when strictly unavoidable in order to protect life.' The UN Special Rapporteur on extrajudicial, summary or arbitrary executions has termed this the 'protect life' principle, whereby 'a life may be taken intentionally only to save another life'. This he describes as 'the guiding star of the protection of the right to life'.[68]

In this heightened standard, imminence is an integral part of the test of lawful use of force. If a suspect is not about to pull the trigger of a firearm aimed at a hostage's head, or to detonate a bomb, intentional lethal use of force cannot be said to be strictly unavoidable to protect life. The Special Rapporteur has further affirmed that:

A common sense understanding of the scope of application of Principle 9 suggests that all weapons that are designed and are likely to be lethal should be covered,

---

[68] Report of the Special Rapporteur on extrajudicial, summary or arbitrary executions, Christof Heyns (1 April 2014) UN Doc A/HRC/26/36, para 70.

including heavy weapons such as bombs and (drone) missiles, the use of which constitutes an intentional lethal use of force.[69]

Landmines should also be considered as such weapons according to jurisprudence before the ECtHR.[70]

iii. Case Studies of Drone Strikes

A case study of applying these standards is the US Central Intelligence Agency (CIA)'s use of armed drones in Pakistan, at least until the middle of 2014 when armed conflict broke out in North Waziristan between Pakistan and the Pakistan Taliban (Tehrik-i-Taliban Pakistan, TTP) as a result of Operation Zarb-e-Azb, launched on 9 June. Previously there were NIACs of only limited duration between 2004 and June 2014[71] (meeting the generally accepted definition of sustained and significant armed violence between the state and an organised armed group).[72] Notably these occurred during Operation Zalzala, which was initiated by the Pakistani armed forces at the beginning of 2008; Operation Black Thunderstorm, which began in the Swat valley on 26 April 2009; and Operation Rah-e-Nijat (Path to Salvation) launched against the TTP in South Waziristan on 19 June 2009. According to a retired Pakistan army brigadier:

> More than 1,000 extremists were killed in the Bajaur operation conducted in August–October 2008. The Taliban were controlling most part of Bajaur prior to the operation. Now they are confined to the Mamoond area only. ... The Taliban will resort to suicide bombing and other terrorist activities to pressurise the government, demoralise the public and divert army's efforts in other direction.[73]

---

[69] ibid, para 71. See also eg *Esmukhambetov et al v Russia* (Judgment) (App no 23445/03) ECHR 29 March 2011.

[70] In *Alkin v Turkey*, the ECtHR affirmed that injury resulting from landmines is a violation of Art 2 of the 1950 ECHR because the very nature of the weapon makes their use unlawful: '[T]he Court considers that the laying of such indiscriminate and inhumane weapons as anti-personnel landmines, which affect the lives of a disproportionate number of civilians and children, amounts to intentional use of lethal force.' *Alkin v Turkey* (Judgment) (App no 75588/01) ECHR 13 October 2009, para 30.

[71] Other commentators argue that armed conflict was ongoing during most, if not all, of the period since 2004. See eg ME O'Connell, 'Unlawful Killing with Combat Drones: A Case Study of Pakistan 2004–2009' in S Bronitt, M Gani and S Hufnagel, *Shooting to Kill: Socio-Legal Perspectives on the Use of Lethal Force* (Oxford, Hart Publishing, 2012); and LR Blank and BR Farley, 'Characterizing US Operations in Pakistan: Is the United States Engaged in an Armed Conflict?' (2011) 34 *Fordham International Law Journal* 2.

[72] The armed violence by the TTP is better characterised as terrorist in nature, absent the 'protracted, large-scale violence ... between governmental forces and organized insurgent groups' that the Tadić decision requires. *Prosecutor v Tadić* (n 60) para 71; and, in relation to terrorist violence, see *Prosecutor v Tadić* (Judgment) ICTY-94-1-T (7 May 1997) para 562: to 'distinguish an armed conflict from banditry, unorganized and short-lived insurrections, or terrorist activities, which are not subject to international humanitarian law'.

[73] A Munir, 'What Next?' *Pakistanpal's Blog*, 27 May 2009, pakistanpal.wordpress.com/tag/operation-zalzala/.

According to available information, the United States first used armed drones in Pakistan in 2004 in a CIA strike that killed up to eight people, including a local Taliban commander, Nek Muhammad Wazir, and two children, near Wana in South Waziristan. The Pakistani army initially claimed responsibility for a 'rocket attack'.[74] According to a 2013 report in the *New York Times*, the target was

> not a top operative of al-Qaeda, but a Pakistan ally of the Taliban who led a tribal rebellion and was marked by Pakistan as an enemy of the state. In a secret deal, the CIA had agreed to kill him in exchange for access to airspace it had long sought so it could use drones to hunt down its own enemies.[75]

Unless Mr Muhammad was directly participating in hostilities in an ongoing armed conflict at the time of the attack, which does not appear to be the case despite his role in renewed armed violence, this amounts to an extrajudicial execution that invokes the responsibility of both Pakistan and the United States.

According to Philip Alston, the former Special Rapporteur on extrajudicial, summary or arbitrary executions:

> Outside of armed conflict, killings by the CIA would constitute extrajudicial executions assuming that they do not comply with human rights law. If so, they must be investigated and prosecuted both by the US and the State in which the wrongful killing occurred.[76]

Professor Alston further asserted that:

> Outside the context of armed conflict, the use of drones for targeted killing is almost never likely to be legal. A targeted drone killing in a State's own territory, over which the State has control, would be very unlikely to meet human rights law limitations on the use of lethal force. …
>
> In addition, drone killing of anyone other than the target (family members or others in the vicinity, for example) would be an arbitrary deprivation of life under human rights law and could result in State responsibility and individual criminal liability.[77]

---

[74] M Mazzetti, 'A Secret Deal on Drones, Sealed in Blood' *New York Times*, 6 April 2013, www.nytimes.com/2013/04/07/world/asia/origins-of-cias-not-so-secret-drone-war-in-pakistan. html?pagewanted=all; see also 'Get the data: Drone Wars. The Bush Years: Pakistan strikes 2004–2009' *Bureau of Investigative Journalism*, 10 August 2011, www.thebureauinvestigates. com/2011/08/10/the-bush-years-2004-2009/.

[75] ibid. According to the report, the deal 'paved the way for the CIA to change its focus from capturing terrorists to killing them, and helped transform an agency that began as a cold war espionage service into a paramilitary organization'.

[76] Report of the Special Rapporteur on Extrajudicial, Summary or Arbitrary Executions, Philip Alston, Addendum: Study on Targeted Killings (28 May 2010) UN Doc A/HRC/14/24/ Add.6, para 70.

[77] ibid, paras 85, 86.

A second case that concerns intentional lethal use of force during law enforcement involved the UK's first drone strike outside the conduct of hostilities, but which took place during ongoing armed conflicts. This occurred in August 2015 when British-born Islamic State fighter Reyaad Khan was killed in a strike by an RAF-piloted drone in the Islamic State stronghold of Raqqah in Syria in an action justified on the grounds of national self-defence.[78] The UK Prime Minister at the time, David Cameron, told Parliament on 7 September 2015 that Mr Khan was involved in actively recruiting Islamic State sympathisers

> and seeking to orchestrate specific and barbaric attacks against the west, including directing a number of planned terrorist attacks right here in Britain, such as plots to attack high profile public commemorations, including those taking place this summer.

> We should be under no illusion; their intention was the murder of British citizens, so on this occasion we ourselves took action. Today, I can inform the House that in an act of self-defence and after meticulous planning, Reyaad Khan was killed in a precision airstrike carried out on 21 August by an RAF remotely piloted aircraft while he was travelling in a vehicle in the area of Raqqa in Syria. In addition to Reyaad Khan, who was the target of the strike, two ISIL associates were also killed, one of whom, Ruhul Amin, has been identified as a UK national. They were ISIL fighters, and I can confirm that there were no civilian casualties.

> We took this action because there was no alternative. In this area, there is no Government we can work with; we have no military on the ground to detain those preparing plots; and there was nothing to suggest that Reyaad Khan would ever leave Syria or desist from his desire to murder us at home, so we had no way of preventing his planned attacks on our country without taking direct action.[79]

It was unclear to some whether this was a law enforcement action or an act in the conduct of hostilities occurring in one of the armed conflicts ongoing in Syria at the time. In the same statement before Parliament, the Prime Minister said: 'I want to be clear that the strike was not part of coalition military action against ISIL in Syria; it was a targeted strike to deal with a clear, credible and specific terrorist threat to our country at home.' He also referred to the lack of personnel 'on the ground to detain those preparing plots', arguably a law enforcement requirement, not one required by the law of armed conflict. At the same time, Mr Cameron said:

> The strike was conducted according to specific military rules of engagement, which always comply with international law and the principles of proportionality

---

[78]   M Wilkinson, P Dominiczak and S Swinford, 'David Cameron: Britain Mounted Fatal Air Strike in Syria' *Daily Telegraph*, 7 September 2015, www.telegraph.co.uk/news/uknews/terrorism-in-the-uk/11848600/David-Cameron-Britain-mounted-fatal-air-strike-in-Syria-live.html.

[79]   'Oral Statement to Parliament—Syria: Refugees and Counter-Terrorism—Prime Minister's Statement' *Gov.uk*, 7 September 2015, www.gov.uk/government/speeches/syria-refugees-and-counter-terrorism-prime-ministers-statement.

and military necessity. The military assessed the target location and chose the optimum time to minimise the risk of civilian casualties. This was a very sensitive operation to prevent a very real threat to our country.[80]

Despite the seemingly contradictory position as set out by the Prime Minister, this should be considered a law enforcement action. As Harriet Moynihan has written: '[O]ne military strike in self-defence does not give rise to the intensity of action required to meet the threshold for a non-international armed conflict.'[81] This returns us to the standard of intentional lethal use of force. As Nehal Bhuta has argued:

> Self-evidently, killing Khan was not the only way of disrupting his planned attacks because British security services are also stated to have foiled more than one attack on the UK or its allies. So the concept of imminence here is not in the sense of 'interception' of an unfolding plot. Rather, the Prime Minister's language intimates that killing Khan was necessary because it was the only way to stop him trying again. As such, evaluating the 'imminence' of the threat posed by Khan would appear to be in the nature of a probabilistic risk assessment of his (high) propensity to plan and direct another terrorist attack in the UK; by virtue of his pattern of activity, his very continued life constituted an imminent risk. Also included in this extended concept of imminence is whether other opportunities to kill the target will present themselves, should he not be targeted now.[82]

Bhuta effectively demonstrates how the situation with Reyaad Khan fails to meet the requirements of applicable international law. It was not *strictly unavoidable in order to protect life*, as the law of law enforcement requires. The violation of the law of law enforcement rule constitutes an arbitrary deprivation of life—the notion of arbitrariness includes a failure to comply with international law—and therefore, a priori, a violation of the right to life.

IV. CONCLUDING REMARKS

As Edward Teller observed in 1981, 'unmanned vehicles become really useful when they are intelligent'.[83] Three decades later, however, in January 2015, Professor Stephen Hawking, Director of Research at the Department of Applied Mathematics and Theoretical Physics at the University of Cambridge, signed an open letter along with many artificial intelligence (AI)

---

[80] ibid.
[81] H Moynihan, 'UK Drone Strike on ISIS Raises Legal Questions' *Chatham House*, 15 September 2015, www.chathamhouse.org/expert/comment/uk-drone-strike-isis-raises-legal-questions?gclid=CJTLpbSu1skCFUK4GwodossJ0Q#sthash.ajKzJi6e.dpuf.
[82] N Bhuta, 'On Preventive Killing' *EJIL Blog*, 17 September 2015, www.ejiltalk.org/on-preventive-killing/.
[83] Cited in Shane (n 1) 71.

experts and others cautioning against researchers creating a technology that cannot be controlled.[84] In March 2016, Professor Nick Bostrom, founding Director of the Future of Humanity Institute at Oxford University, issued a similarly apocalyptic warning of the dangers posed by AI, suggesting that the products of this technology could wipe out the human race.[85]

Fully autonomous armed systems are on the brink of deployment. Each remotely piloted Predator requires a team of more than a hundred to operate it.[86] How much easier would it be for the military if the weapon system could do all the work, including targeting and deciding when to fire and on whom? An explicit exception allowing for a fully autonomous weapon system was already included in the 2008 Convention on Cluster Munitions in the form of a munition container dispensing explosive submunitions 'designed to detect and engage a single target object'.[87] Textron Systems claims that its CBU-105 sensor-fuzed cluster munition system disperses ten BLU-108 canisters each of which disperses four submunitions equipped with two-colour infrared sensors designed to identify a target such as an armoured vehicle that the munition then engages.[88] According to Human Rights Watch, the submunitions explode above the ground and project an explosively formed jet of metal and fragmentation downward.[89]

Fully autonomous systems currently deployed are mostly machine guns that use sensors to detect intruders. In 2011, it was reported that a South Korean company, DoDAAM Systems, had developed an automated, turret-based weapon platform capable of locking onto a human target 3 km away. The Super aEgis II, which supports a variety of weapons, from a standard machine-gun to a surface-to-air missile, uses thermal imaging software and camera systems to lock onto a human-sized target even in the dead of night. The system requires no human presence.[90] Subsequently, the Super aEgis II was reconfigured to require a human operator to enter a password into the computer system to unlock the turret's firing ability and manually 'permit'

---

[84] 'Research Priorities for Robust and Beneficial Artificial Intelligence' *An Open Letter*, futureoflife.org/ai-open-letter/.

[85] N Bostrom, 'Safety Issues in Advanced AI' (RSA Conference in San Francisco, 3 March 2016) www.rsaconference.com/events/us16/agenda/sessions/2724/safety-issues-in-advanced-ai; see also S Lee, 'Artificial Intelligence Is Coming, and it Could Wipe Us Out if We're Not Careful, Professor Warns' *Newsweek*, 4 March 2016.

[86] Shane (n 1) 72.

[87] Convention on Cluster Munitions (adopted 30 May 2008, entered into force 1 August 2010) 2688 UNTS 39, Art 2(2)(c).

[88] 'BLU-108 Submunition' *Textron Defense Systems* (2010) www.textronsystems.com/sites/default/files/pdfs/product-info/blu108_datasheet.pdf.

[89] Human Rights Watch, 'Yemen: Cluster Munitions Wounding Civilians', 14 February 2016, www.hrw.org/news/2016/02/14/yemen-cluster-munitions-wounding-civilians.

[90] T Cleary, 'South Korean "Super Gun" Packs Hi-tech Killing Power' *Reuters*, 14 February 2011, www.reuters.com/video/2011/02/14/south-korean-super-gun-packs-hi-tech-kil?videoId=187406842&videoChannel=2602; see also http://www.dodaam.com/eng/sub2/menu2.php.

it to shoot. A senior research engineer for DoDAAM explained that the original version 'had an auto-firing system. But all of our customers asked for safeguards to be implemented. Technologically it wasn't a problem for us. But they were concerned the gun might make a mistake.'[91]

The Phalanx Close-in Weapon System is a ship-based 20 mm gun system that autonomously detects, tracks and attacks targets. The Counter Rocket, Artillery and Mortar System is a land-based fixed weapon system that employs the same technology as the Phalanx to target and attack rockets, artillery and mortars.[92] The Harpy, referred to above, is an armed unmanned aircraft incorporating an explosive warhead. It autonomously detects electromagnetic emissions from radar equipment before dive-bombing it.[93] Over the longer term, miniaturisation, as with drone technology, will be an important facet of fully autonomous weapons systems. Thus, the US Army's 2010–35 roadmap for unmanned aerial vehicles foresees nano-drone swarms with autonomous capability to cooperate with each other.[94]

In April 2016, five states (Algeria, Chile, Costa Rica, Mexico and Nicaragua) called for a pre-emptive ban on lethal autonomous weapons systems during the third Convention on Certain Conventional Weapons (CCW) meeting on the issue. According to campaigners, this increased to fourteen the number of states seeking a total prohibition.[95]

Peter Singer advises that other weapons systems are in R&D, including 'bio-agents and genetic weaponry, also known as DNA bombs; space weaponry; and human performance modifications, chemical and hardware enhancements to the human body. ... These advances include taking a present game-changer—unmanned systems—a great leap forward.[96]

---

[91] S Parkin, 'Killer Robots: The Soldiers that Never Sleep' *BBC*, 16 July 2015, www.bbc.com/future/story/20150715-killer-robots-the-soldiers-that-never-sleep.

[92] ICRC, 'Autonomous Weapon Systems, Technical, Military, Legal and Humanitarian Aspects, Expert Meeting, Geneva, 26–28 March 2014' (November 2014) 65; see also www.msl.army.mil/Pages/CRAM/cram.html.

[93] See www.iai.co.il/2013/16143-16153-en/IAI.aspx.

[94] US Army UAS Center of Excellence, 'Eyes of the Army', US Army Unmanned Aircraft Systems Roadmap 2010–2035', 65.

[95] 'Ban Support Grows, Process Goes Slow' *Campaign to Stop Killer Robots*, 15 April 2016, www.stopkillerrobots.org/2016/04/thirdmtg/. The other nine states were: Bolivia, Cuba, Ecuador, Egypt, Ghana, Holy See, Pakistan, Palestine and Zimbabwe.

[96] Singer (n 2) 215–16.

5

The Globalisation of Non-International Armed Conflicts

PAVLE KILIBARDA AND GLORIA GAGGIOLI

I. INTRODUCTION

THE DECADES SINCE the adoption of the 1949 Geneva Conventions and their 1977 Additional Protocols have seen a general increase in the phenomenon of NIACs.[1] While the differences in the law applicable to both IACs and NIACs are arguably becoming ever more blurry in light of state practice and international jurisprudence,[2] the main instruments of IHL remain grounded in a fundamental separation between the two types.[3] Some substantial differences in the law applicable to IACs and NIACs also remain. These differences notably relate to the status of individuals under the respective legal frameworks. The notion of 'combatant privilege', understood as the 'the right to participate directly in hostilities,' is absent from NIACs, and consequently this body of law does not contain such status as that of prisoner of war (POW).[4] The question of NIACs is

---

[1] According to the Geneva Academy of International Humanitarian Law and Human Rights, out of at least 48 armed conflicts occurring in 2016, 36 were of a non-international character, taking place in the territory of 20 states. See A Bellal, 'The War Report: Armed Conflicts in 2016' (2017) *Geneva Academy of International Humanitarian Law and Human Rights* 15.

[2] The ICRC Customary IHL study identified a total of 161 rules of customary IHL, most of which are considered as applicable in both IACs and NIACs. For a full list, refer to JM Henckaerts and L Doswald-Beck, *Customary International Humanitarian Law*, vol 1: *Rules* (Cambridge, Cambridge University Press, 2006).

[3] In particular, while the 1949 Geneva Conventions (except for Common Article 3) and AP I are exclusively applicable to IACs, Additional Protocol II applies to NIACs.

[4] On the combatant's privilege, see Hague Convention No IV Respecting the Laws and Customs of War on Land and its annex: Regulations concerning the Laws and Customs of War on Land (adopted 18 October 1907, entered into force 26 January 1910) 36 Stat 2227 TS No 539 (Hague Convention IV) Art 1; Protocol I Additional to the Geneva Conventions of 12 August 1949 and relating to the Protection of Victims of International Armed Conflicts (adopted 8 June 1977, entered into force 7 December 1978) 1125 UNTS 3 (AP I) Art 43(2). In IHL provisions pertaining to NIACs, there are no equivalent provisions which recognise the combatant privilege. The majority view among scholars is therefore that such a privilege does not exist in NIACs. See eg ICRC, 'Protocol Additional to the Geneva Conventions of 12 August 1949, and

also still subject to a number of controversies both with respect to their typology and the geographical scope of application of IHL in such conflicts.

For the purposes of this chapter, the term 'globalisation' of NIACs involves two different phenomena. First, it refers to the increasing number of 'extraterritorial NIACs', such as the fighting of the International Security Assistance Force (ISAF) against the Taliban in Afghanistan in the years since the overthrow of the Taliban regime and establishment of the Afghan Interim Administration in December 2001, or the involvement of states such as France and the United States in the struggle against the so-called Islamic State (ISIS) in Syria and/or Iraq. All of these involve states fighting non-state armed groups outside their own territory, with or without the consent of the territorial state, and as such give rise to a NIAC.[5] In spite of the fact that the drafters of the Geneva Conventions had in all likelihood an essentially territorial scope of application in mind when adopting Common Article 3 (ie limited to 'civil wars' taking place in the territory of a High Contracting Party), the majority view among states and scholars today is that armed conflicts involving organised non-state armed groups are NIACs even if they take place outside the territory of the belligerent state. In an attempt to address the complexity arising from the multiplicity of NIACs, the ICRC has proposed a typology of seven categories of NIACs, among which five involve an extraterritorial element.[6]

The other aspect of globalisation present in contemporary NIACs involves legal theories attempting to justify the application of humanitarian law beyond the territory of belligerent parties, wherever a person qualified as a legitimate target under IHL is located, thus justifying, for instance, drone strikes against members of organised non-state armed groups in peaceful countries.[7] This second aspect of the 'globalisation' of NIACs concerns the geographical scope of application of IHL.

relating to the Protection of Victims of International Armed Conflicts (Protocol I), 8 June 1977: Commentary of 1987' (1987) para 4441; M Bothe, HJ Partsch and WA Soft, *New Rules for Victims of Armed Conflict: Commentary on the Two 1977 Protocols Additional to the Geneva Conventions of 1949* (The Hague, Martinus Nijhoff, 2013); N Melzer, *International Humanitarian Law: A Comprehensive Introduction* (Geneva, ICRC, 2016) 83.

[5] The question whether such conflict may at the same time give rise to an IAC if the state where the hostilities are taking place did not agree to the intervention is disputed. See eg ICRC, 'International Humanitarian Law and the Challenges of Contemporary Armed Conflicts: Report' (Geneva, 2015); D Carron, 'L'acte déclencheur d'un conflit armé international' (PhD thesis, University of Geneva, 2016).

[6] The ICRC distinguishes the following types of NIAC: 'traditional' internal NIACs; spillover NIACs; multinational NIACs; cross-border NIACs; and transnational NIACs. See ICRC, 'International Humanitarian Law and the Challenges of Contemporary Armed Conflicts: Report' (Geneva, 2011) 7–13.

[7] The first time a large unmanned combat aerial vehicle (UCAV) was allegedly used outside the scope of the battlefield was in 2002 when the CIA killed six purported al-Qaeda members in Yemen. At that time, it was quite clear that there were no hostilities between the government of Yemen and al-Qaeda and that the USA was not intervening in a pre-existing armed conflict

The evolution of warfare has led to the development of new theories that challenged the traditional understanding that IHL applied essentially on territories controlled by belligerent parties[8] and increasingly began to take into consideration the existence of a link, or nexus, between a specific act and an existing armed conflict situation in order to establish the applicability of the laws of armed conflict. Bearing in mind the persistently popular notion of IHL as *lex specialis* with respect to human rights law,[9] as well as the ongoing debate with respect to the extraterritorial application of the latter body of law, each of these theories has different implications for the protection of the civilian population.

IHL was initially conceived to protect victims of armed conflicts from unnecessary and/or inhumane conduct on the part of belligerent states in times of IACs. For example, as early as 1899 the Contracting Parties to the original Hague Regulations found that limiting 'the evils of war' was in 'the interests of humanity and the ever increasing requirements of civilization',[10] while the drafters of the revised Geneva Convention of 1906 found that they were led by 'the desire to lessen the inherent evils of warfare as far as is within their power'.[11] Such considerations, and striking a balance between the principles of military necessity and humanity, have therefore been the very *ratio legis* of IHL since its inception.

Thus, in 1949, when Common Article 3 was added to the Geneva Conventions, the objective was to introduce rules regulating hostilities between sovereign states and rebels on their own soil, an issue that had until then proven difficult to tackle for reasons of state sovereignty. Subsequent developments, particularly the state of affairs in the post-9/11 world, confirmed the understanding that NIACs were not necessarily confined to the territory of any one state. While this meant that states could not claim to have no obligations under international law when confronting organised armed groups abroad, it has also led to concerns that the fight against terror could generally be equated with an armed conflict situation. As a result, IHL has

---

on Yemeni soil. See eg D Kretzmer, 'Targeted Killing of Suspected Terrorists: Extrajudicial Executions or Legitimate Means of Defence' (2005) 16 *European Journal of International Law* 2, 171–72.

[8] See in this sense ICRC (n 5) 15.

[9] *Legality of the Threat or Use of Nuclear Weapons* (Advisory Opinion) [1996] ICJ Rep 226, para 25; *Legal Consequences of the Construction of a Wall in the Occupied Palestinian Territory* (Advisory Opinion) [2004] ICJ Rep 136, para 106.

[10] Hague Convention No II with Respect to the Laws and Customs of War on Land and its annex: Regulations concerning the Laws and Customs of War on Land (adopted 29 July 1899, entered into force 4 September 1900) 32 Stat 1803 TS No 403 (Hague Convention II) Preamble.

[11] Geneva Convention I for the Amelioration of the Condition of the Wounded and Sick in Armed Forces in the Field (adopted 12 August 1949, entered into force 21 October 1950) 75 UNTS 31 (GC I) Preamble.

been invoked to curtail the more generous protection granted in certain circumstances by international human rights law (IHRL).

In what follows, we shall attempt to analyse the phenomenon of globalisation of NIACs both with respect to their typology and the geographical scope of application of IHL. This will be done by examining the position of key stakeholders—states as well as non-state actors such as the ICRC—with respect to various landmark situations since the adoption of the 1949 Geneva Conventions. We shall examine how various ways of 'over-classification' of situations of armed violence as NIACs, particularly in the context of the fight against terrorism, may lead to a lesser scope of protection afforded to the civilian population. Bearing in mind existing conflict situations, we will revisit the question of typology of extraterritorial NIACs and that of the geographical scope of application of IHL, and offer our recommendations on how to meet persisting challenges to the protection of civilians with reference to other branches of international law such as IHRL.

II. THE EVOLUTION OF THE TYPOLOGY OF NON-INTERNATIONAL ARMED CONFLICT

A. Civil Wars as the Main or Only Type of NIAC in 1949 and 1977, Respectively

The atrocities committed during World War II gave the international community unprecedented impetus to take action and prevent such crimes from taking place in the future. Waging wars of aggression in the interest of territorial expansion, depriving the population of occupied territories of even the most basic rights and targeting millions of human beings for extermination on the grounds of their racial or national origin—all of these, and more, had been done on an unprecedented scale by the Nazi regime and its allies in Europe and elsewhere. It was clear that the previously untouchable doctrine of state sovereignty could no longer be used to justify the most heinous atrocities human beings had proven themselves capable of inflicting upon each other. Most disconcertingly, some of the more depraved acts of the Axis powers before and during the war had not, formally legally speaking, been prohibited by existing international law. Discussions about expanding the existing body of IHL began immediately after the war and culminated in the diplomatic conference that adopted the new Geneva Conventions of 1949.[12] In addition to improving and expanding international legislation, the conference also tackled questions that had not hitherto been regulated.

---

[12] For an assortment of documents relevant to the 1949 Diplomatic Conference, see Federal Political Department, 'Final Record of the Diplomatic Conference of Geneva of 1949' Vols I–III (Bern).

Beyond World War II, the early twentieth century had seen brutal civil wars, such as the ones surrounding the 1921 Upper Silesia plebiscite and, particularly, the Spanish Civil War; in both of these cases, the ICRC—which had long since been engaged with the victims of internal conflicts—managed to bring the belligerents to undertake to respect the principles of the Geneva Conventions then in force.[13] But only a general treaty obligation would suffice in the long term. Thus, the circumstances after World War II allowed the ICRC to spearhead the process that led to the adoption of Common Article 3 to the four Geneva Conventions. For the first time in modern history, the international community agreed upon a set of binding legal norms governing hostilities of a non-international character—hostilities that, at the time, would have been considered primarily a High Contracting Party's internal affair, constituting part of their *domaine réservé*. In the words of the ICRC's 1952 Commentary to Common Article 3:

> There is nothing astonishing, therefore, in the fact that the Red Cross has long been trying to aid the victims of internal conflicts, the horrors of which sometimes surpass the horrors of international wars by reason of the fratricidal hatred which they engender. ... In a civil war the lawful Government, or that which so styles itself, tends to regard its adversaries as common criminals.[14]

The *travaux préparatoires* to the 1949 diplomatic conference demonstrate the existence of considerable controversy with respect to the notion of extending the Conventions' scope of application to conflicts not of an international character, to such an extent that certain states were initially openly hostile to the suggestion. For example, the Greek government emphatically concluded that:

> [I]t can hardly be imagined that a legal State would, in the case of any armed conflict, be willing to have mutineers, rebels and even outlaws placed under the protection of a foreign Power, which would assume the duties of a Protecting Power, and agree that those who committed acts harmful to the integrity of the State should enjoy the special immunity privileges etc granted to those engaged in regular warfare.[15]

Certainly much of the aversion came from the initial suggestion of providing for the application of the whole of the Geneva Conventions to NIACs. In fact, Common Article 2 of the draft Conventions, which was to

---

[13] ICRC, 'Geneva Convention for the Amelioration of the Condition of the Wounded and Sick in Armed Forces in the Field of 12 August 1949: Commentary of 1952' (1952) 39.

[14] ibid.

[15] Propositions and Observations of the Governments for the Diplomatic Conference for the Establishment of International Conventions for the Protection of War Victims Convened at Geneva on April 21st, 1949 by the Swiss Federal Council: Memorandum by the Greek Government (Athens, April 1949) 2.

regulate their general scope of application and eventually became Common Articles 2 and 3, stated:

> In all cases of armed conflict which are not of an international character, especially cases of civil war, colonial conflicts, or wars of religion, which may occur in the territory of one or more of the High Contracting Parties the implementing of the principles of the present Convention shall be obligatory on each of the adversaries. The application of the Convention in these circumstances shall in nowise depend on the legal status of the parties to the conflict and shall have no effect on that status.[16]

The idea of fully applying the Conventions to NIACs was quickly abandoned, after a number of attempts had been made to limit the actual situations to which they might be applicable. Even certain delegations in favour of extending the application of IHL to all types of armed conflict did not consider it appropriate to extend in full the Geneva Conventions to NIACs.[17] The terminology, which at the time made specific reference to 'civil wars, colonial conflicts, or wars of religion' as examples of NIACs, was particularly controversial, and not because (as it might seem to a twenty-first-century lawyer) they were seen as too narrow, but rather because they were too broad.[18] In the end, the debate was resolved not by limiting the Conventions' scope of application, but rather the substantive law to be applied,[19] leading to the text of Common Article 3 as we know it today.[20] References to specific types of armed conflict ('civil wars, colonial conflict, or wars of religion') were dropped because, according to the ICRC, 'too much detail risked weakening the provision because it was impossible to

---

[16] See eg Working Document drawn up for the Diplomatic Conference for the Establishment of International Conventions for the Protection of War Victims Convened at Geneva on April 21st, 1949 by the Swiss Federal Council: Draft Convention for the Relief of Wounded, Sick and Shipwrecked Members of Armed Forces on Sea, Art 2(4).

[17] This position was summed up by the French representative, Mr Lamarle, who stated that he 'did not feel it was possible to extend automatically all the clauses of the Conventions to internal conflicts'. His concerns were echoed by the Soviet delegate, Mr Morosov. See 'Final Record of the Diplomatic Conference' (n 12) 47, 98.

[18] During the diplomatic conference, a special committee was convoked consisting of representatives of Australia, the USA, France, Greece, Italy, Monaco, Norway, the UK, Switzerland and the USSR; Burma and Uruguay were later also included in order to provide representation to Asian and Latin American states. The special committee was tasked with examining paragraph 4 of what was then draft Article 2 concerning the application of the Conventions in times of NIACs. Some delegations, notably Australia, called for substituting the term 'conflicts not of an international character' with 'civil war in any part of the home or colonial territory of a Contracting Party', but these suggestions were ultimately dismissed when the idea to fully extend the application of the Conventions was abandoned. For more detail on these discussions, see 'Final Record of the Diplomatic Conference' (n 12) 120–27.

[19] ICRC (n 13) 46–48.

[20] The final text of Common Article 3, which has occasionally been referred to as a 'mini-convention' in its own right, obliges belligerent parties in a NIAC to apply, 'as a minimum', certain standards of conduct with respect to persons *hors de combat* and prohibits acts such as the taking of hostages and summary executions.

foresee all future circumstances and because the armed conflict character of a situation was independent of its motives'.[21] On the whole, discussions at the diplomatic conference of 1949 indicate that the question of extraterritorial NIACs was not specifically considered at the time. Nevertheless, the final decision by the delegates not to commit to a definition of such conflicts which was too precise ultimately left room for interpreting Common Article 3 as being applicable to such conflicts.

Long before the ICTY developed the most widely accepted criteria for determining the existence of a NIAC in the oft-quoted *Tadić* case,[22] the ICRC had suggested its own list of what it considered to 'constitute convenient criteria' for the determination of the existence of such a conflict.[23] These criteria include

> that the Party in revolt against the *de jure* government possesses an organized military force, an authority responsible for its acts, acting within a determinate territory and having the means of respecting and ensuring respect for the Convention; that the legal government is obliged to have recourse to the regular military forces against insurgents organized as military and in possession of a part of the national territory; that the insurgents have been recognized as belligerents;

or that they

> have an organization purporting to have the characteristics of a State, that the insurgent civil authority exercises de facto authority over persons within a determinate territory, that the armed forces act under the direction of the organized civil authority and are prepared to observe the ordinary laws of war, and the insurgent civil authority agrees to be bound by the provisions of the Convention.[24]

All of these criteria seem to relate principally to a situation of widespread insurgency against a national government, presumably taking place in the territory of the High Contracting Party in question. In the words of Jelena Pejić, senior legal advisor at the ICRC:

> When the Geneva Conventions (ie common Article 3 thereto) were being drafted, the negotiators essentially had one, 'traditional', type of NIAC in mind: that between government armed forces and one or more organized armed groups within the territory of a single State.[25]

When the two Additional Protocols to the Geneva Conventions were adopted almost thirty years later, fears similar to the ones expressed in the

---

[21] ICRC, 'Geneva Convention for the Amelioration of the Condition of the Wounded and Sick in Armed Forces in the Field of 12 August 1949: Commentary of 2016' (2016) para 373.

[22] *Prosecutor v Tadić* (Decision on the Defence Motion for Interlocutory Appeal on Jurisdiction) ICTY-94-1-A (2 October 1995) para 70.

[23] ICRC (n 13) 49.

[24] ibid, 49–50.

[25] J Pejić, 'Extraterritorial Targeting by Means of Armed Drones: Some Legal Implications' (2015) 96 *International Review of the Red Cross* 893, 80.

process of the drafting of Common Article 3 persisted. While the draft-ers strove to expand the regime of Common Article 3, the scope of appli-cation of Additional Protocol II (regulating NIACs) was eventually made even more restrictive. As foreseen by Article 1(1), the Protocol applies to all NIACs that

> take place in the territory of a High Contracting Party between its armed forces and dissident armed forces or other organized armed groups which, under respon-sible command, exercise such control over a part of its territory as to enable them to carry out sustained and concerted military operations and to implement [the] Protocol.[26]

Apart from excluding armed conflicts fought between non-state armed groups without government involvement, the Protocol sets a high thresh-old with respect to organisation and intensity[27] and introduces the require-ment of control over the territory of the belligerent state by the dissident. Logically, all of these requirements were subordinate to the overarching and realistic necessity of having the non-state belligerent party able to imple-ment the Protocol in the first place, which should in equal measure be seen as an implicit requirement of Common Article 3 (although the obligations under the latter are admittedly more limited in scope and basically come down to fundamental guarantees, which should not be difficult even for less well-organised groups to implement). Of course, to the extent that Addi-tional Protocol II is nowadays still read in a geographically restrictive man-ner, it does not in any way alter the scope of Common Article 3.[28] This is important to highlight considering the evolution warranting the latter article's application.

---

[26] Protocol II Additional to the Geneva Conventions of 12 August 1949 and relating to the Protection of Victims of Non-International Armed Conflicts (adopted 8 June 1977, entered into force 7 December 1978) 1125 UNTS 609 (AP II), Art 1(1).

[27] According to the ICRC's 1987 Commentary: 'The three criteria that were finally adopted on the side of the insurgents—ie a responsible command, such control over part of the ter-ritory as to enable them to carry out sustained and concerted military operations, and the ability to implement the Protocol—restrict the applicability of the Protocol to conflicts of a certain degree of intensity. This means that not all cases of non-international armed conflict are covered, as is the case in common Article 3.' See ICRC (n 4) para 4453. The ICTY has taken a similar position: 'Additional Protocol II requires a higher standard than Common Article 3 for establishment of an armed conflict. It follows that the degree of organisation required to engage in "protracted violence" is lower than the degree of organisation required to carry out "sustained and concerted military operations".' See *Prosecutor v Boškoski and Tarčulovski* (Judgment) ICTY-04-82-T (10 July 2008) para 177.

[28] However, it should be pointed out that authors such as Kolb and Hyde consider that: 'The guarantees of Additional Protocol II apply today, as part of customary international law, under the same conditions as Common Article 3. Therefore, in order to properly reflect the current conditions of applicability, Additional Protocol II would have to be amended to align it to the conditions of application expressed in Common Article 3.' See R Kolb and R Hyde, *An Introduction to the International Law of Armed Conflicts* (Oxford, Hart Publishing, 2008) 79.

Finally, some of the greatest breakthroughs in interpreting the law of NIACs came not by means of treaty law, but rather the jurisprudence of international criminal tribunals, specifically the ICTY. In the above-mentioned *Tadić* case, the ICTY found that a NIAC exists whenever there is 'protracted armed violence between governmental authorities and organized armed groups or between such groups within a State'.[29] The Trial Chamber subsequently interpreted the Appeals Chamber's notion of 'protracted armed violence' as referring to the 'intensity of the conflict',[30] providing us with the contemporary formula of examining the thresholds of intensity and organisation in order to ascertain the existence of a NIAC.[31] Clearly, this proposed definition of NIACs based on two essential criteria—intensity and organization—does not take into account territory (in contradistinction with Additional Protocol II) and thus does not exclude the existence of extraterritorial NIACs.

To summarise the above, it is safe to say that, in 1949, the drafters of Common Article 3 contemplated primarily internal conflicts, although they did not exclude the possibility of extraterritorial NIACs. This is demonstrated by the decision to use the term 'non-international' rather than 'internal' armed conflicts in the final text of the Conventions. In 1977, the drafters of Additional Protocol II preferred to set a more restrictive scope of application for the new treaty, but nonetheless did not modify the criteria for the application of Common Article 3, as further indicated by the jurisprudence of the ICTY.

B. Post 9/11: Multiplication of NIACs in the Framework of the Fight against Terror and the Issue of Over-Classification

In today's post-9/11 world, the struggle against terrorism is increasingly described using the language of IHL, and a number of non-state armed groups engaged in armed conflict against various governments have indeed

---

[29] *Prosecutor v Tadić* (n 22) para 70.
[30] *Prosecutor v Tadić* (Judgment) ICTY-94-1-T (7 May 1997) para 562.
[31] In its various case law, the ICTY has enumerated a number of indicators that the intensity threshold for a NIAC has been met. In the *Boškoski and Tarčulovski* case, an ICTY Trial Chamber listed the following: the seriousness of attacks and whether there has been an increase in armed clashes, the spread of clashes over territory and over a period of time, any increase in the number of government forces and mobilisation and the distribution of weapons among both parties to the conflict, as well as whether the conflict has attracted the attention of the UN Security Council, and whether any resolutions on the matter have been passed. With respect to the threshold of organisation, the Tribunal has held that 'while the jurisprudence of the Tribunal requires an armed group to have "some degree of organisation", the warring parties do not necessarily need to be as organised as the armed forces of a State'. See *Prosecutor v Boškoski and Tarčulovski* (n 27) paras 177, 197.

been described as 'terrorist' by one or more credible stakeholders.[32] Even before 9/11, a number of states engaged in NIACs had tried to label dissident movements as 'terrorists', usually in order to diminish any real or potential political legitimacy such groups may have, and particularly to deny the existence of an armed conflict on their soil.[33] However, after 9/11, the menace of terrorism is ever more frequently invoked in order to claim the existence of an armed conflict and, therefore, broader authority for the executive than would be available under regular peacetime norms. Thus, the fight against al-Qaeda in Afghanistan, but also outside the 'hot battlefield', as well as the fight against Boko Haram in Nigeria or ISIS in Syria and Iraq, has been described as an armed conflict, to which IHL, rather than just IHRL, is applicable.[34]

Following the 9/11 attacks and the subsequent US-led invasion of Afghanistan, the Western coalition found itself pitted not only against the Taliban government, but al-Qaeda militants as well. Whatever the situation may have been in the beginning, there can be little doubt that the intensity of the fighting against al-Qaeda in Afghanistan remained sufficient to ascertain the existence of a NIAC after the fall of the Taliban government. The position of the Bush administration that the 'war on terror'—chiefly the engagement against al-Qaeda—was an armed conflict, but that the captured fighters were excluded from the protection of IHL, sparked debate in the international community as to what extent this body of law was appropriate to deal with these allegedly new armed conflict situations.[35]

---

[32] The UN Security Council has repeatedly described certain groups as 'terrorist' or 'violent extremist' organisations in its resolutions: see eg UNSC Res 2199 (12 February 2015) UN Doc S/RES/2199; UNSC Res 2253 (17 December 2015) UN Doc S/RES/2253; and UNSC Res 2255 (22 December 2015) Un Doc S/RES/2255.

[33] This was the approach of the governments of Russia and Turkey with respect to various cases brought before the ECtHR concerning the conflicts in Chechnya and against the PKK, respectively. See eg *Ergi v Turkey* (App no 40/1993/435/514) ECHR 28 July 1998; *Isayeva v Russia* (App no 57950/00) ECHR 24 February 2005; *Isayeva v Russia, Yusupova v Russia, Bazayeva v Russia* (Apps no 57947/00, 57948/00, 57949/00) ECHR 24 February 2005; *Khatsiyeva and Others v Russia* (App no 5108/02) ECHR 17 January 2008.

[34] It is the position of the US government that transnational groups such as al-Qaeda challenge traditional concepts of classification and the geographical scope of IHL and therefore a more flexible position towards the applicability of IHL must be taken. In addition, the official US position is that human rights law does not apply extraterritorially. For more information on the official US stance, see an interview with the US Army Legal Counsel to the Chairman of the Joint Chiefs of Staff in 'Interview with Brigadier General Richard C Gross' (2014) 96 *International Review of the Red Cross* 893, 20–24.

[35] For a discussion of the early US position on the 'war on terror' and its conformity with international law, see M Sassòli, 'La "guerre contre le terrorisme", le droit international humanitaire et le statut de prisonnier de guerre' (2001) 39 *Annuaire canadien de droit international* 211; and M Sassòli, 'The International Legal Framework for Fighting Terrorists According to the Bush and the Obama Administrations: Same or Different, Correct or Incorrect?' (2010) 104 *Proceedings of the Annual Meeting (American Society of International Law)* 277, 277–80.

Many of the initial discussions concerned the nature of the conflict between the United States and al-Qaeda: if there was an armed conflict, was it an IAC or a NIAC? The US government initially maintained that its conflict with al-Qaeda was international, as it was not an internal armed conflict, but that the modus operandi of the group's militants had rendered them illegible for POW status (mainly because of their engaging in terrorist acts and failure to distinguish themselves from the civilian population).[36] Additionally, the government had maintained that Common Article 3 did not apply because the conflict with al-Qaeda was 'international in scope'.[37] The debate was, to a large extent, settled by the US Supreme Court's verdict in the *Hamdan v Rumsfeld* case, which can be seen as the 'breaking point' regarding the extraterritorial application of Common Article 3.[38] The Supreme Court dismissed the USA's argument that al-Qaeda was not a 'High Contracting Party' and that the Geneva Conventions were inapplicable to the fight against them. It found that at least one provision of the Geneva Conventions was applicable 'even if the relevant conflict was not between signatories', and that was Common Article 3, which governed the conflict against al-Qaeda.[39] The Court also highlighted that the phrase 'not of an international character' refers to conflicts which are not between nations (and therefore, not necessarily limited to the territory of a single state party).[40] Although the *Hamdan* judgment was crucial and positive in altering US practice with respect to suspected al-Qaeda detainees,[41] it also granted further legitimacy to the idea that the fight against international terrorism is governed by IHL rather than (just) human rights law. It is not to be contested that the fighting against an organised armed group labelled as 'terrorist' may be sufficiently intense in order to reach the threshold of a NIAC. In the 2008 trial judgment in the *Boškoski and Tarčulovski* case, the ICTY—having taken into consideration the findings of the US Supreme Court in *Hamdan v Rumsfeld*—found that 'the view that terrorist acts may be constitutive of protracted violence is also consistent with the logic of international humanitarian law' and that 'it would be nonsensical that international humanitarian law would prohibit such acts if these were not considered to fall within the rubric of armed conflict'.[42] There can be little

---

[36] See the press conference of then-US Secretary of Defense Donald Rumsfeld of 8 February 2002, available in M Sassòli, AA Bouvier and A Quintin, *How Does Law Protect in War?*, 3rd edn (Geneva, ICRC, 2011) 2338–46.

[37] *Hamdan v Rumsfeld* 548 US 557 (2006) 67.

[38] ibid.

[39] ibid, 66.

[40] ibid, 67.

[41] See Office of the Secretary of Defense, 'Memorandum on the Application of Common Article 3 of the Geneva Conventions to the Treatment of Detainees in the Department of Defense' (7 July 2006) available at fas.org/sgp/othergov/dod/geneva070606.pdf.

[42] *Prosecutor v Boškoski and Tarčulovski* (n 27) para 187.

doubt that the struggle against well-organised groups such as ISIS in Syria and Iraq amounts to an armed conflict situation.[43]

Nevertheless, there are several ways in which the contemporary fight against terrorism has led to an 'overclassification' of NIACs. By 'overclassification' we refer to treating as governed by IHL situations more appropriately regulated by IHRL.

i. Treating Terrorism as Ipso Facto Giving Rise to a NIAC

The fact that terrorist acts are being perpetrated does not as such mean that there is an ongoing armed conflict and that IHL is applicable. Such acts should be considered in light of the requirements of intensity and organisation, and only if these conditions have been met will there be a NIAC. There is therefore an ongoing and serious risk that IHL and the conduct of hostilities paradigm will be erroneously applied to fighting against alleged terrorists under circumstances where the factual conditions for a NIAC have not been met and where the law enforcement paradigm is fully applicable. In brief, not all terrorist activities are the result of organised armed groups. For instance, if a 'lone wolf' is conducting a terrorist attack in London or Paris, this is not an 'act of war' but mainly a criminal act under domestic law that must be dealt with as part of the law enforcement powers and duties of states;[44] the issues of attribution and membership in an organised armed group, as well as the notion of 'affiliated/associated forces', will be discussed further below.

ii. The Notion of 'Transnational NIACs'

In spite of the *Hamdan* judgment, the US conflict with al-Qaeda continues to draw the attention of scholarship with respect to its classification. Sivakumaran sums up the situation very well:

> Dispute has also arisen as to whether there is one armed conflict—a global conflict without defined territorial limits—between the United States and Al-Qaeda;

---

[43] There have been many sources attesting the high organisation of ISIS. See eg B Hubbard and E Schmitt, 'Military Skill and Terrorist Technique Fuel Success of ISIS' *New York Times*, 27 August 2014. Also, several scholars have discussed if ISIS actually meets the criteria of statehood under international law: see Y Shany, A Cohen and T Mimran, 'ISIS: Is the Islamic State Really a State?' *The Israel Democratic Institute*, 14 September 2014, available at en.idi. org.il/articles/5219.

[44] On the growing trend of lone wolves, see R Pantucci, 'A Typology of Lone Wolves: Preliminary Analysis of Lone Islamist Terrorists' *The International London Center for the Study of Radicalisation and Political Violence*, March 2011, 39; R Spaaji, 'The Enigma of Lone Wolf Terrorism: An Assessment' (2010) 33 *Studies in Conflict and Terrorism* 9; and S Teich, 'Trends and Developments in Lone Wolf Terrorism in the Western World: An Analysis of Terrorist Attacks and Attempted Attacks by Islamic Extremists, International Institute for Counter-Terrorism' *IDC Herzliya*, October 2013, 23.

multiple armed conflicts between the United States and Al-Qaeda, for example in Afghanistan, in the Arabian Peninsula, and the like; an armed conflict between the United States and Al-Qaeda in one country but not another; or no armed conflicts aside from those in Afghanistan and Iraq, rather law-enforcement operations against Al-Qaeda. The issue is important as terrorist attacks in and of themselves do not amount to an armed conflict.[45]

The first part of this quotation highlights a second overclassification issue, ie the idea of a global or 'transnational NIAC' that is believed by some to currently exist between al-Qaeda and the United States.[46] This position means that, as a result of al-Qaeda's transnational nature and the existence of cells in many countries across the world, the engagement against al-Qaeda should be seen overall as governed by IHL regardless of where it takes place.[47] It may be difficult to discern whether this is, strictly speaking a classification issue (wherein the threshold of organisation of an armed group is understood to be met throughout multiple countries and regions), or a question of the geographical scope of application of IHL (where it is maintained that, while the criteria of organisation and intensity have been met in a single country, any operations undertaken against legitimate targets under IHL will be guided by the conduct of hostilities paradigm regardless of where they take place). This second possible interpretation will be dealt with further below.

There have been dissident voices with respect to the organisational threshold necessary for a NIAC to come into existence. Referring to the ICTY's *Limaj* case,[48] Peter Margulies argues that the ICTY ended up taking a more flexible approach to this criterion, meaning that what is required is actually only minimal organisation rather than a high degree of organisation:

In *Limaj* ... the ICTY found that the Kosovo Liberation Army (KLA) was organized even though evidence of discipline was 'scant' by the court's own admission. Witnesses differed widely on when the military police cited by the tribunal had been established. If the military police were a salient symbol of organizational discipline, this divergence in recollection seems odd. Moreover, as the ICTY

---

[45] S Sivakumaran, *The Law of Non-International Armed Conflicts* (Oxford, Oxford University Press, 2012) 233.

[46] ICRC (n 6) 10.

[47] The position is summarised by Brigadier General Richard C Gross as follows: 'Commentators will often say, "There is action being taken in Yemen, but we are not at war with Yemen." Well, of course we are not at war with Yemen, but the Yemeni authorities have given permission/consent for us to partner with them in actions taken there and so the conflict is not with Yemen or Yemen's enemies; the conflict is with Al-Qaeda. Of course, geography matters in some instances. But we cannot tie ourselves to one country and say that combat will only take place in that country, and not outside.' Richard Gross interview (n 34) 21.

[48] *Prosecutor v Fatmir Limaj, Haradin Bala and Isak Musliu* (Judgment) ICTY-03-66-T (30 November 2005).

acknowledged, there was no record of any imposition of discipline among KLA members.[49]

Margulies further argues that 'terrorist groups are more organized than their historical image suggests' and that 'today's terrorist groups, including Al Qaeda, also display far more organization than is commonly understood'.[50] Therefore, a 'network' of organisations such as al-Qaeda should be taken as constituting a single armed group no matter where individual groups constituting the network may be found.

Although there has been limited case law indicating a more flexible threshold of organisation for the purposes of a NIAC,[51] the level required has traditionally been seen as set higher than just minimal organisation. For example, when Additional Protocol II makes reference to 'organised armed groups', it sees them as being 'under responsible command' and as 'exercis[ing] such control over a part of its territory as to enable them to carry out sustained and concerted military operations and to implement this Protocol'.[52] While the threshold of organisation in Additional Protocol II may allegedly be different from that of Common Article 3,[53] it remains indicative of the level of organisation necessary for an armed group to be considered 'organised'.[54] It is submitted that the very raison d'être of the organisation criterion is to ensure that the armed group is capable of complying with IHL and that this is also inherent in the scope of Common Article 3. A key element to determine whether the level of organisation is met is thus, in our view, the existence of a certain *accountability structure* within the group.[55] To that end, in the *Limaj* case quoted by Margulies, the ICTY even took the existence of a 'military police' responsible for the discipline of the fighters as indicative that the threshold of organisation had been met.[56]

---

[49] P Margulies, 'Networks in Non-International Armed Conflicts: Crossing Borders and Defining "Organized Armed Group"' (2013) 89 *International Law Studies* 54, 63.

[50] ibid, 65–66.

[51] In the case of *Juan Carlos Abella v Argentina (La Tablada)*, the Inter-American Commission on Human Rights accepted that the siege of a military base by around 40 armed attackers amounted to a NIAC in spite of the brevity of the attack (which only lasted about 30 hours)—an issue that could be seen as relevant both with respect to the criteria of intensity and organisation. See *Juan Carlos Abella v Argentina* (1997) Inter-American Commission on Human Rights Case No 11.137, 271.

[52] AP II, Art 1.

[53] *Prosecutor v Boškoski and Tarčulovski* (n 27) para 177.

[54] According to Pejić: 'It is widely recognized that a non-state party to a NIAC means an armed group with a certain level of organization that would essentially enable it to implement international humanitarian law.' J Pejić, 'The Protective Scope of Common Article 3: More than Meets the Eye' (2011) 93 *International Review of the Red Cross* 881, 191–92.

[55] The organisational level should also be sufficient to enable the group to engage in a continuum of attacks rather than isolated strikes, which is a direct link with the threshold of intensity required for a NIAC.

[56] *Prosecutor v Limaj, Bala and Musliu* (n 48) para 113.

This case certainly seems to set a quite high (rather than low) standard of organisation; one that most terrorist groups simply do not achieve.

Therefore, it has generally been the stance of legal scholarship that the conflict between the United States and al-Qaeda is not 'transnational'.[57] The ICRC itself has explicitly rejected the actual existence (but not possible existence in the future) of such 'transnational armed conflicts' since '[a] single NIAC across space and time would, *inter alia*, require the existence of a "unitary" non-State party opposing one or more States';[58] something that has never been really demonstrated. In fact, some of the evidence offered by authors such as Margulies could just as readily (and perhaps more convincingly) be used to argue the existence of separate armed conflicts against different groups (members of the al-Qaeda 'network'), rather than a single, 'transnational' one.[59]

To be sure, there is nothing in IHL which would negate the existence of extraterritorial NIACs, including possibly 'transnational' NIACs. Indeed, there have been cases of a single armed group being based in the territory of more than one state: one need only think of ISIS in Syria and Iraq, where it forms a single entity across two countries.[60] However, the capacity of this entity as a single, unified command structure to exercise control over purported cells in countries as far as Libya, Afghanistan, France or Belgium is dubious, at best. The distinction is not based on law, but rather on facts: the conditions for a non-state armed group to exercise a sufficient level of control over its individual members in numerous and distant parts of the world are difficult to meet. Whereas there is no consensus on whether the fight against al-Qaeda or ISIS constitute actual transnational NIACs (whereby the global network is equated with the armed group), nothing indicates that this category of extraterritorial NIAC may not materialise in the future.

---

[57] 'Subsequent intelligence assessments, representing a significant portion of the United States' overall knowledge on terrorism networks, point to decentralized groups that spring up independently and operate with little, if any, connection to Al Qaeda. The burgeoning number of groups gather strategy, tactics, and inspiration from more than five thousand radical Islamic websites. The Central Intelligence Agency's Director offered in April 2006 that "new jihadist networks and cells, sometimes united by little more than their anti-Western agendas, are increasingly likely to emerge". Arguably, this cannot be a sufficient basis for classifying all these acts as part of a single, non-international armed conflict under existing international humanitarian law.' M Sassòli, 'Transnational Armed Groups and International Humanitarian Law' (2006) 6 *Harvard Program on Humanitarian Policy and Conflict Research* 1, 10–11. See also JD Ohlin, 'Targeting Co-Belligerents', in C Finkelstein, JD Ohlin and A Altman (eds), *Targeted Killings: Law and Morality in an Asymmetrical World* (Oxford, Oxford University Press, 2012) 60–89.

[58] Pejić (n 25) 83. See also the section on transnational NIACs in ICRC (n 6) 10–11.

[59] Marguiles considers al-Qaeda's affiliates in Pakistan, Afghanistan, Iraq, the Arabian Peninsula, North Africa, Somalia (al-Shabab), Yemen and elsewhere as forming a single organisation. See Margulies (n 49) 71–75.

[60] See CC Caris and S Reynolds, 'ISIS Governance in Syria' *Institute for the Study of War*, July 2014, available at www.understandingwar.org/sites/default/files/ISIS_Governance.pdf.

iii. The Notion of 'Associated Forces/Affiliates'

Another aspect of transnational NIACs is to consider, for instance, that al-Qaeda, as an armed group operating in one or more states, is supported by several 'associated forces' operating globally. In this sense, Richard Gross, a senior US army legal counsel, explains that the term 'associated forces' refers to

> a co-belligerent who has entered the fight alongside Al-Qaeda against the United States or its coalition partners. So, it is not just any group that shares Al-Qaeda's ideology and it is not just any group that may be fighting the US somewhere in the world. It has to be a co-belligerent; this component is critical.[61]

According to Margulies, the key criterion to consider regional groups as 'affiliates' (for the purpose of targeting) is whether al-Qaeda is exercising 'strategic influence' over such groups, ie that it is able to influence their choice of targets.[62] This could allegedly be inferred from as many factors as financing, training or exchange of information about operations.[63]

This aspect is not without its problems either. As highlighted by the Special Rapporteur on extrajudicial, summary or arbitrary executions, Philip Alston, in his 2010 Study on Targeted Killings:

> With respect to the existence of a non-state group as a 'party' [to an armed conflict], al-Qaeda and other alleged 'associated' groups are often only loosely linked, if at all. Sometimes they appear to be not even groups, but a few individuals who take 'inspiration' from al Qaeda. The idea that, instead, they are part of continuing hostilities that spread to new territories as new alliances form or are claimed may be superficially appealing but such 'associates' cannot constitute a 'party' as required by IHL—although they can be criminals, if their conduct violates US law, or the law of the State in which they are located.[64]

The notion of 'associated forces' or 'affiliates' remains entirely undefined and its implications can be grave. When does an armed group become an 'associate' or 'co-belligerent' of another armed group such as al-Qaeda and thus a party to the ongoing armed conflict with al-Qaeda? IHL does not provide a clear-cut answer to this question. Proposals such as the ones just presented comport the risk of including under the umbrella of 'affiliates' civilians who are not participating at all in hostilities (or only indirectly)

---

[61] Richard Gross interview (n 34) 22.
[62] Margulies (n 49) 75.
[63] ibid.
[64] UN Human Rights Council, 'Report of the Special Rapporteur on Extrajudicial, Summary or Arbitrary Executions, Addendum: Study on Targeted Killings' (28 May 2010) UN Doc A/HRC/14/24/Add.6, para 55.

such as persons who receive general training or who are financed/or who finance al-Qaeda.

One may argue that terrorist cells become co-belligerents—and a party to a pre-existing NIAC—as soon as they *support* an armed group such as al-Qaeda or ISIS based on an analogy with the so-called 'support-based approach'. The support-based approach was specifically developed to determine under which conditions IHL applies to multinational forces in a pre-existing NIAC; essentially what level of support to a party to the conflict is necessary for those forces to be considered as having become a party themselves.[65] It should be highlighted notably here that the multinational force must undertake 'actions related to the conduct of hostilities' for such a support to exist.[66] If the support-based approach were to be accepted in the context of non-state actors, this may lead to an expansion of existing NIACs as the threshold of intensity required for the existence of NIAC would not need to be met by the actions from and against small groups that are mere associates. So long as the latter support a belligerent party, they immediately become a party to a pre-existing NIAC. It is submitted, nevertheless, that—at the very least—for a group to be capable of becoming a 'co-belligerent' for the purposes of IHL, it must first meet the organisational criterion required by that body of law on its own.[67] Moreover, the baseline should be that 'co-belligerency' may be inferred only if the organised armed group undertakes actions that amount to direct participation in hostilities in support of another non-state organised armed group that is already involved in a pre-existing NIAC.[68]

---

[65] Under the support-based approach, these conditions are: there is a pre-existing NIAC ongoing in the territory where multinational forces intervene; actions related to the conduct of hostilities are undertaken by multinational forces in the context of that pre-existing conflict; the multinational forces' military operations are carried out in support of a party to that pre-existing conflict; and the action in question is undertaken pursuant to an official decision by the troop-contributing countries or international organisation in question to support a party involved in that pre-existing conflict. See T Ferraro, 'The Applicability of International Humanitarian Law to Multinational Forces' (2014) 95 *International Review of the Red Cross* 891/892, 584.

[66] ibid.

[67] Some of the proponents of the notion of 'associated forces' themselves seem to make reference to this requirement; for example, former US Department of Defence General Counsel Jeh Johnson: 'An "associated force," as we interpret the phrase, has two characteristics to it: (1) an organized, armed group that has entered the fight alongside al Qaeda, and (2) is a co-belligerent with al Qaeda in hostilities against the United States or its coalition partners. In other words, the group must not only be aligned with al Qaeda. It must have also entered the fight against the United States or its coalition partners. Thus, an "associated force" is not any terrorist group in the world that merely embraces the al Qaeda ideology.' JC Johnson, 'National Security Law, Lawyers, and Lawyering in the Obama Administration' (2012) 31 *Yale Law & Policy Review* 1, 146.

[68] See Ferraro (n 65) mutatis mutandis.

iv. Membership and Attribution to an Organised Armed Group

A last major issue in terms of overclassification that has arisen in the context of the fight against terror relates to excessively 'generous' interpretations in relation to *individual membership* in an armed group as well as *attribution* of initially private conduct to a non-state armed group.[69] It is not the place here to solve general (and unsettled) matters such as membership into and attribution to non-state armed groups.[70] A few comments will suffice here.

Membership in armed groups is difficult to determine as it has no basis in domestic law (in contradistinction with membership in armed forces) and it is not necessarily visible (through uniforms, fixed distinctive signs or identification cards).[71] The only real attempt at legally defining membership has been made by the ICRC in the context of its Guidance on Direct Participation in Hostilities. According to the ICRC, members of an armed group— for the purpose of targeting—are persons having a 'continuous combat function'. Members such as recruiters, trainers, financiers and propagandists would not be targetable under this position.[72] This position remains, however, very controversial. A number of states and experts consider notably that membership should be more broadly defined as encompassing anyone who belongs to the military wing of the group (including, for instance, the cook).[73] Irrespective of such debates, it is quite clear that mere claims by alleged terrorists that they belong to al-Qaeda or ISIS should not be sufficient to consider them as part of those groups.

In the same vein, the fact that groups such as ISIS acknowledge ex post facto apparently independent terrorist attacks should not be considered as

---

[69] It remains controversial whether an organised non-state armed group may assume responsibility for an act in the same way a state may in line with Art 11 of the ILC's Articles on the Responsibility of States for Internationally Wrongful Acts (ie by acknowledging or adopting conduct that is otherwise not attributable to it).

[70] The only real attempt to legally define membership in an armed group has been made by the ICRC in the context of its *Guidance on Direct Participation in Hostilities*. According to the ICRC, members of an armed group—for the purpose of targeting—are persons having a 'continuous combat function'. Members such as recruiters, trainers, financiers and propagandists would not be targetable under this position. See N Melzer, 'Interpretive Guidance on the Notion of Direct Participation in Hostilities under International Humanitarian Law' (2008) 90 *International Review of the Red Cross* 991, 27–36. See also chapter 1 in this volume.

[71] ibid, 32–33.

[72] ibid, 27–36.

[73] See MN Schmitt, 'Deconstructing Direct Participation in Hostilities: The Constitutive Elements' (2010) 49 *NYU Journal of International Law and Policy* 697. The Israeli government is also of the opinion that members of OAGs may be targeted solely by virtue of their membership unless they are *hors de combat* or entitled to special protection, as is the case with medical personnel. 'The 2014 Gaza Conflict: 7 July–26 August 2014: Factual and Legal Aspects' (May 2015) available at mfa.gov.il/ProtectiveEdge/Documents/2014GazaConflictFullReport.pdf, para 264. See also 'Chief Military Advocate General Mag Gen Dan Efrony's Comments on Contemporary Armed Conflict' *IDF Blog*, 17 February 2015, available at www.idfblog.com/chief-military-advocate-general-mag-gen-dan-efronys-comments-contemporary-armed-conflict/.

sufficient to establish membership or even attribution except in exceptional circumstances. It may be interesting to consider a limited analogy with the ICJ's 1980 judgment in the *USA v Iran* case.[74] In this case, the Court determined that the occupation of US diplomatic and consular premises in Tehran and the hostage-taking of US diplomatic and consular personnel performed by students (as private persons) became attributable to Iran after the state had acknowledged and encouraged their actions.[75] However, three issues need to be borne in mind in this analogy: first, Iran is a state, and attribution of unlawful conduct to a state is not controversial, which is not the case with non-state actors. The issue of attribution to organised non-state armed groups remains indeed a field almost completely unexplored in international law.[76] Second, the hostage-taking in that case represented a continuous act, which the state of Iran encouraged while it was still taking place. Had the acts already been finished by the time Iran acknowledged them, it is difficult to foresee if they would have equally been attributable to Iran.[77] Using this analogy with attribution of unlawful conduct to states with non-state actors, we could say that situations wherein ISIS (for instance) assumes responsibility for an attack by 'lone wolves' in Paris is not the same if that attack is finished by the time they do so (this is the case with most attacks), or if it is an ongoing act (eg a hostage crisis). Third, even if private acts may become attributable to a state, this does not mean that the private individuals become de facto organs of the state.[78] By analogy,

---

[74] *Case Concerning United States Diplomatic and Consular Staff in Tehran (United States of America v Iran)* [1980] ICJ Rep 3, para 25.

[75] ibid, para 74.

[76] This is understandable from a 'responsibility perspective' since there is no law/mechanism relating to the responsibility of organised non-state armed groups. To date, responsibility in this context is only based on individual criminal responsibility of members of the group. In any case, it is submitted that attribution issues remain important from an IHL perspective in order to assess, for instance, the intensity of violence (continuum of attacks performed by the armed group) and possibly to determine the legal regime applicable in relation to acts that have been performed for an armed group and in the context of an armed conflict (eg possibility for security detention).

[77] See ILC, 'Report of the International Law Commission on the Work of its 53rd Session' (23 April–1 June and 2 July–10 August 2001) UN Doc A/CN.4/SER.A/2001/Add.1 (ARS), 'Commentary to Art 11', 53: 'In that case it made no difference whether the effect of the "approval" of the conduct of the militants was merely prospective, or whether it made the Islamic Republic of Iran responsible for the whole process of seizure of the embassy and detention of its personnel ab initio. The Islamic Republic of Iran had already been held responsible in relation to the earlier period on a different legal basis, viz its failure to take sufficient action to prevent the seizure or to bring it into an immediate end. In other cases no such prior responsibility will exist. Where the acknowledgement and adoption is unequivocal and unqualified there is good reason to give it retroactive effect, which is what the tribunal did in the Lighthouses arbitration.'

[78] See *Application of the Convention on the Prevention and Punishment of the Crime of Genocide (Bosnia and Herzegovina v Serbia and Montenegro)* (Merits) [2007] ICJ Rep 43, paras 397ff.

even if a terrorist armed group acknowledges and adopts the acts of a lone wolf, this does not make him/her ipso facto member of the group, at least certainly not for the purposes of targeting. Although these arguments are still very much exploratory, one thing is certain: membership and attribution must be based on facts, not mere allegations for propaganda purposes.

In brief, the fight against international terrorism has, without doubt, contributed towards the present 'globalization' of NIACs, with many such conflicts being fought precisely against groups considered terrorist organisations.[79] It has constituted a fertile ground for 'overclassification' issues, with the consequence (intended or not) of lowering the protection of individuals suspected of terrorism and surrounding civilians by potentially applying an IHL framework to law enforcement situations.

III. A TYPOLOGY OF NIACs IN LIGHT OF CONTEMPORARY PRACTICE—IS TERRITORY REALLY IRRELEVANT?

The above analysis of different situations potentially governed by Common Article 3 to the Geneva Conventions demonstrates the necessity of producing a general typology of NIACs that would assist scholars and practitioners examining these situations. NIACs had previously usually been classified on the basis of the applicable law—primarily based on whether or not Additional Protocol II was applicable in addition to Common Article 3.[80] More recently, the ICRC has offered a general typology that may be seen as 'fact-based', rather than 'law-based', insofar as it relies on different sets of circumstances where Common Article 3 is said to apply.[81] The ICRC's seven-member typology concerns both internal and extraterritorial NIACs and is not based on any single criterion of differentiation, but rather lists all possible situations that have been referred to as NIACs whether the ICRC agrees with them or not. The US Department of Defense's 2015 Law of War Manual similarly differentiates between different situations amounting to a NIAC, with interesting results, although the purpose of the analysis is to compare circumstances that may give rise to a NIAC rather than to give an actual typology.[82]

---

[79] For an overview of ongoing NIACs in 2016 and their actors, see Bellal (n 1) 29–30.

[80] This is the approach adopted by a number of legal scholars, eg S Vité, 'Typology of Armed Conflicts in International Humanitarian Law: Legal Concepts and Actual Situations' (2009) 91 *International Review of the Red Cross* 873, 69–94; and Sassòli, Bouvier and Quintin (n 36) 123–24.

[81] The typology was published in ICRC (n 6) 9–11.

[82] The Law of War Manual specifically examines civil wars, internal armed conflicts, transnational or internationalised NIACs, guerrilla or unconventional warfare, rebellion or insurrection, terrorism and small wars or low-intensity conflicts. See US Department of Defence, 'Law of War Manual' (June 2015, updated May 2016) 1001–04.

There are different ways of sorting NIACs depending on the criteria chosen. One way is to differentiate between internal and extraterritorial, and this difference is certainly relevant. It is nevertheless useful to further break down various types of extraterritorial NIACs. This could be done based on whether the host state has given its consent to the foreign state's presence or not: one possible consequence of a lack of consent would be the parallel existence of an IAC between the two states if we accept the double classification approach as espoused in the ICRC's 2016 Commentaries to the Geneva Conventions.[83] Nevertheless, as this would have little bearing on the NIAC itself, we do not find that the issue of consent would play a very significant role in further distinguishing between different types of extraterritorial NIACs. Ultimately, the factor of geographical distance may be the most practical to describe and differentiate between different types of NIACs.

A. Internal NIACs

These are 'traditional' NIACs, confined to the borders of a single state, whether they are fought between that state and one or more local non-state armed groups, or between such groups without state involvement. As examples of the former, we may give the fighting between the forces of the Federal Republic of Yugoslavia and the KLA during the Kosovo conflict; the engagement of Russian forces against Chechen insurgents during both Chechen wars; and the conflict (or conflicts) between Turkey and the Kurdistan Workers' Party (PKK) in its various stages since at least the beginning of the first insurgency in 1984. The conflicts between left-wing and right-wing militias in Colombia and nationalists and Islamists in northern Mali are illustrative of NIACs fought between non-state armed groups. In addition to Common Article 3, some internal NIACs fought between states and dissident forces could also be governed by Additional Protocol II where the conditions for its application have been met.

B. Extraterritorial NIACs

These NIACs have in common that they take place beyond the borders of a single state. As shown previously, NIACs are not confined to internal conflicts: it is the fact that at least one of the belligerent parties is a non-state organised armed group that makes them a conflict 'not of an international

---

[83] ICRC (n 21) para 477. See, contra, Carron (n 5); and J Stewart, 'Towards a Single Definition of Armed Conflict in International Humanitarian Law: A Critique of Internationalized Armed Conflict' (2003) 85 *International Review of the Red Cross* 850.

character'. The following distinct situations may be considered extraterritorial NIACs:

1. *Cross-border or 'short-distance' NIACs.* These usually involve situations when an armed group fighting a state is primarily (or to a large extent) based and operates from the territory of a neighbouring state (the 'host state'). It is crucial that the armed group may not be considered as an agent of the host state, as the conflict would otherwise become international. Examples of such conflicts are rare. Insofar as Hezbollah was not an agent of the Lebanese government at the material time, the 2006 war between Hezbollah and Israel, which primarily took place on Lebanese territory, may be considered a cross-border NIAC.[84]

   Cross-border NIACs should be distinguished from so-called 'spillover' situations. 'Spillover' conflicts are situations wherein a NIAC has erupted and takes place in the territory of a single state, but hostilities extend to the territory of neighbouring countries—as often happens in armed conflict situations—in a quite limited manner.[85] Such a situation has been portrayed by the ICRC as a type of NIAC.[86] In our view, however, spillover is not a specific type of NIAC, but rather a phenomenon pertaining to the geographical scope of application of IHL. In fact, any type of NIAC may in practice 'spillover' into the territory of a neighbouring state. Therefore, it is not so much the existence of an armed conflict that is at stake here (classification issue) but rather the question whether IHL rules may apply beyond the territory of the belligerent state if the armed conflict spills over into the territory of the neighbouring state. Despite the fact that the spillover phenomenon requires further scrutiny, we will reserve this discussion for the next section on the geographical scope of application of IHL.

2. *Trans-border or 'long-distance' NIACs.* These armed conflicts involve one or more states fighting an armed group that is present neither on their own territory, nor on that of a neighbouring state.[87] Such conflicts may also involve international organisations, such as when multinational forces fight an armed group in a host country under a UN mandate.[88] The non-state armed group is based in the territory of one, or several,

---

[84] Here, the lack of consent by Lebanon to Israel's intervention implies the existence of a parallel IAC between Israel and Lebanon.

[85] See ICRC (n 6) 9–10; and Pejić (n 54) 194.

[86] ICRC (n 6) 9–10.

[87] It is to be noted that a hypothetical transborder NIAC limited to non-state armed groups can be imagined, although, to our knowledge, such conflicts have not occurred to date.

[88] In its typology, the ICRC has proposed two categories of 'multinational' NIACs to cover 'armed conflicts in which multinational armed forces are fighting alongside the armed forces of a "host" state—in its territory—against one or more organized armed groups'. It also distinguishes the category of multinational NIACs in which UN forces, or forces under the aegis of a regional organisation (such as the African Union) are sent to support a 'host' government

states that are distant from the belligerent state(s). The conflict between Western states and the Taliban and al-Qaeda in Afghanistan after the fall of the Taliban regime constituted a trans-border NIAC. This is also the case with the operations of the Russian Federation against rebel forces in Syria. However, in both of these situations, it may also be maintained that there existed a primary internal NIAC between the host state and local non-state organised armed groups, and that foreign powers merely became co-belligerents in those rather 'traditional' internal NIACs. This is also the case with air strikes launched by Western states against ISIS in Iraq, but not in Syria, as they may not be considered co-belligerents of the Syrian government (they do not have its consent to fight ISIS on its territory). Therefore, the situation in Syria may be considered prototypical of a 'trans-border' or 'long-distance' NIAC. It should be noted, however, that the fight opposing the coalition to ISIS in Syria has also sometimes been portrayed as a spillover from Iraq, since the United States and its allies initially supported the fight of the Iraqi government in Iraq against ISIS, which afterwards 'spilled over' to Syrian territory.[89]

3. *Transnational NIACs.* This highly controversial category, which has already been discussed in the previous section in relation to the fight against al-Qaeda and ISIS, bears superficial resemblance to trans-border NIACs, but is based on different legal considerations. Whereas trans-border NIACs rest on the idea that a non-state armed group may achieve a sufficient level of organisation to engage in a NIAC while based in the territory of a single state (or neighbouring states in a localised manner), a transnational NIAC relies on the idea that the armed group is a transnational one—ie a single identity with a worldwide scope. Consequently, it would not be necessary to prove, for instance, that al-Qaeda in Yemen or Pakistan are sufficiently organised as armed groups on their own (and no additional authority to use force against them at the national level may therefore be needed[90]), since they form part of the

---

involved in hostilities against one or more organised armed groups in its territory. Although it is useful to specify that these conflicts remain non-international ones despite the important international component, they do not differ substantially from other transborder or long-distance NIACs involving just one state. The difference merely pertains to the number of actors involved, and also their nature when the multinational forces act under the command and control of an international organisation. See ICRC (n 6) 10.

[89] This is notably how the Geneva Academy's Rule of Law in Armed Conflict (RULAC) Project treats this situation. See Geneva Academy, 'RULAC: Non-International Armed Conflicts in Syria' (28 July 2017) available at www.rulac.org/browse/conflicts/non-international-armed-conflicts-in-syria#collapse1accord.

[90] Just after the 9/11 attacks, the US Congress passed the Authorization for Use of Military Force, which authorised the US President 'to use all necessary and appropriate force against those nations, organizations, or persons he determines planned, authorized, committed, or aided the terrorist attacks that occurred on September 11, 2001, or harbored such

same al-Qaeda worldwide transnational armed group. In the same vein, a terrorist cell of five persons in Switzerland loosely connected to ISIS may be considered as part of this allegedly transnational armed group. This approach, which principally depends on a more flexible reading of the threshold of organisation, practically allows for ignoring territorial factors, thus possibly giving rise to a truly 'global' armed conflict against alleged transnational armed groups.[91] From an IHL perspective, nothing indicates that 'transnational armed groups'—ie groups that are transnationally organised—cannot exist. In other words, IHL requires that the armed group be sufficiently organised but does not 'localise' the assessment of this criterion. However, the criterion of organisation should not be interpreted too loosely as discussed above.[92] A thorough and careful empirical study of the structure and functioning of entities such as al-Qaeda and ISIS would be needed to definitively negate or confirm their transnational character, at least beyond regions (such as Afghanistan/Pakistan in relation to al-Qaeda or Iraq/Syria in relation to ISIS).

This typology has shown that extraterritorial NIACs are indeed numerous in our contemporary world. But, at the same time, it has also questioned the pervasive conception that the classification of a situation of violence as a NIAC is completely disconnected from territorial notions and relies only on the identity of the parties. By and large, contemporary extraterritorial NIACs are nothing more than a variation of traditional internal armed conflicts in which a third state, a coalition or an international organisation intervenes at the request or with the consent of the host state. Wars are still mainly fought on the territory of states and not merely between abstract entities in a vacuum. Concepts of borders and state sovereignty still have implications—as a matter of fact and law—for classification purposes.

---

organizations or persons'. US Congress, 'Authorization for Use of Military Force' Pub L No 107-40 (18 September 2001) Art 2(a). This has been understood as covering al-Qaeda, the Taliban and 'associated forces' within and outside Afghanistan. See 'Report on the Legal and Policy Frameworks Guiding the United States' Use of Military Force and Related National Security Operations' *The White House*, December 2016, available at www.justsecurity.org/wp-content/uploads/2016/12/framework.Report_Final.pdf.

[91] According to Brigadier General Gross, the possibility of a global war is nevertheless precluded by considerations of sovereignty: 'Carefully constrained by law and policy, we have to be able to go to the enemy, wherever the enemy may be. Now, that does not mean a global war. That does not mean we are everywhere. There are certainly principles of sovereignty. We have to respect the principles of international law, so you are not going to see a global war *per se*, but it is not just war confined to Afghanistan either.' See Richard Gross interview (n 34) 21.

[92] See above discussion on transnational NIACs in section II of this chapter.

IV. CONTEMPORARY PERSPECTIVES ON THE GEOGRAPHICAL SCOPE OF APPLICATION OF INTERNATIONAL HUMANITARIAN LAW

Closely related to the issue of the classification of armed conflicts is the question of the geographical scope of application of IHL in extraterritorial NIACs. Whereas the first aspect concerned the very existence, in the legal sense, of an armed conflict, the latter refers to the territory where IHL is applicable once an armed conflict is deemed to exist.

The IHL treaties themselves do not specify their geographical scope of application, although Common Article 1 requires High Contracting Parties 'to respect and to ensure respect for the present Convention in all circumstances'.[93] While the ICRC interprets this as covering 'not only the provisions applicable to international armed conflict, including occupation, as defined by common Article 2, but also those applicable to non-international armed conflict under common Article 3',[94] it nevertheless does not provide us with much information on the territory within which IHL is applicable. Again, the jurisprudence of international tribunals is relevant in this regard.

As we have seen above, in the *Tadić* case, the ICTY held that 'international humanitarian law continues to apply ... in the case of internal conflicts, [in] the whole territory under the control of a party, whether or not actual combat takes place there'.[95] Similarly, the ICTR found that: '[Common Article 3] must be applied in the whole territory of the State engaged in the conflict.'[96] However, the ICTY never determined that IHL may not be applicable beyond the borders of the state engaged in a NIAC, and the ICTR's own statute foresees its jurisdiction over 'persons responsible for serious violations of international humanitarian law committed in the territory of Rwanda and Rwandan citizens responsible for such violations committed in the territory of neighbouring States'.[97]

---

[93] See Art 1 common to GC I; Geneva Convention II for the Amelioration of the Condition of Wounded, Sick and Shipwrecked Members of Armed Forces at Sea (adopted 12 August 1949, entered into force 21 October 1950) 75 UNTS 85 (GC II); Geneva Convention III Relative to the Treatment of Prisoners of War (adopted 12 August 1949, entered into force 21 October 1950) 75 UNTS 135 (GC III); Geneva Convention IV Relative to the Protection of Civilian Persons in Time of War (adopted 12 August 1949, entered into force 21 October 1950) 75 UNTS 287 (GCIV). For a discussion of the obligations under Common Article 1, see K Dörmann and J Serralvo, 'Common Article 1 to the Geneva Conventions and the Obligation to Prevent International Humanitarian Law Violations' (2015) 96 *International Review of the Red Cross* 1.

[94] ICRC (n 21) para 125.

[95] *Prosecutor v Tadić* (n 22) para 70.

[96] *The Prosecutor v Jean-Paul Akayesu* (Judgment) ICTR-96-4-T (2 September 1998) para 635.

[97] Statute of the International Criminal Tribunal for Rwanda (accessed 8 November 1994, as last amended on 13 October 2006) Art 1.

Controversies persist with respect to the geographical scope of application of Common Article 3. These controversies relate to two different questions that we may portray as internal versus external: (i) Does IHL—and in particular conduct-of-hostilities rules—apply in the whole of the territories controlled by the belligerent parties? (internal aspect); (ii) May IHL—and in particular conduct-of-hostilities rules—apply beyond the territories controlled by the belligerent parties? (external aspect).

(i) Regarding the internal aspect of the geographical scope of application of IHL, the ICRC's 2016 Commentary acknowledges the issue by noting that:

> The question has arisen as to whether humanitarian law applies in the whole of the territory of the State concerned or only in areas where hostilities are occurring. In areas of a State where hostilities are few and far between or even non-existent it may seem questionable whether humanitarian law applies. There is concern that humanitarian law, and especially the rules on the conduct of hostilities, should not apply in regions where hostilities are not taking place, even in a State in which an armed conflict is occurring. In the more peaceful regions of such a State, the State's criminal law and law enforcement regimes, within the boundaries set by the applicable international and regional human rights law, may provide a sufficient legal framework.[98]

Concretely, this issue becomes of concern in light of the contemporary fight against terrorism. Consider, for instance, an alleged ISIS cell located in Paris. Since France is involved in an extraterritorial NIAC in Syria against ISIS, would the French government be allowed to engage this cell under a conduct-of-hostilities paradigm or is the more protective human rights law enforcement paradigm the only one applicable in such a situation (or else, the prevailing one)? When asked by a journalist if France was at war with ISIS, former French intelligence officer Alain Chouet replied: 'We are at war in the territories controlled by Daesh in the Middle East, but not in the Hexagon.'[99]

In order to subject this type of issue to further scrutiny, the ICRC called an expert meeting in 2012 on the question of the use of force in armed conflict situations—particularly the interplay between the law enforcement and conduct-of-hostilities paradigms. The meeting resulted in a detailed expert meeting report,[100] which notably includes questions relevant to the geographical scope of application of IHL in its internal aspect. This question is, of course, of particular relevance to this chapter, as the law enforcement

---

[98] ICRC (n 21) para 456.

[99] 'Terrorisme: La France est-elle vraiment en guerre contre Daech?' *LCI* (27 July 2016) www.lci.fr/international/terrorisme-la-france-est-elle-vraiment-en-guerre-contre-daech-1514033.html.

[100] G Gaggioli, 'The Use of Force in Armed Conflicts: Interplay Between the Conduct of Hostilities and Law Enforcement Paradigms' (ICRC, 2013).

paradigm, based on human rights law, is almost universally seen as more protective than the IHL-based conduct-of-hostilities paradigm.[101] The ICRC's report focuses on a number of case studies where the interplay between IHL and human rights is controversial, such as the 'isolated sleeping fighter example', wherein, in the context of an internal armed conflict, a government's forces locate 'a fighter belonging to [the dissident armed group] … sleeping at home with his family in a part of the territory controlled by the government'.[102] Under the circumstances, the fighter is arguably not an imminent threat, and the issue has been raised that, while a traditional interpretation of IHL would allow the fighter to be killed provided the principles of proportionality and precautionary measures have been respected, the law enforcement paradigm may appear more appropriate. For the purpose of this chapter, a crucial aspect of this thought experiment lies in the fact that the fighter is located outside of what has been referred to as the 'conflict zone', which 'is neither defined nor used in IHL treaties … [but is] frequently used, in practice, to describe an area where active hostilities are taking place'.[103] The ICRC takes note that, 'by a small margin', the majority of experts gathered at the meeting considered that IHL applies in the whole of the territory of the belligerent party and that the conduct-of-hostilities paradigm was, as a consequence, applicable to the use of force against a legitimate target under IHL in times of armed conflict and, as *lex specialis*, prevailed over IHRL.[104]

While it will certainly remain controversial for the time being, the opinion of the majority of experts as stated above may be seen as consistent with the ICTY's approach in *Tadić* (although in that case the Tribunal did not make a conclusive statement on the geographical scope of application of IHL or on the interplay between IHL and HRL—it merely found that IHL continued to apply beyond the immediate battlefield). From a protection aspect, there may be an alternative solution to the 'isolated sleeping fighter problem', such as the one raised in Chapter IX of the ICRC's *Interpretive Guidance on the Notion of Direct Participation in Hostilities under International Humanitarian Law*.[105] There, the ICRC finds that:

> [W]hile operating forces can hardly be required to take additional risks for themselves or the civilian population in order to capture an armed adversary alive, it would defy basic notions of humanity to kill an adversary or to refrain from giving him or her an opportunity to surrender where there manifestly is no necessity

---

[101] For a comparison of the two, see UNGA, 'Report of the Special Rapporteur on Extrajudicial, Summary or Arbitrary Executions, Philip Alston: Study on Targeted Killings' (2010) UN Doc A/HRC/14/24/Add.6, paras 28–92.

[102] Gaggioli (n 100) 13.

[103] ibid, 17.

[104] ibid, 19.

[105] Melzer (n 70) 77–82.

for the use of lethal force. In such situations, the principles of military necessity and of humanity play an important role in determining the kind and degree of permissible force against legitimate military targets.'[106]

This approach is based on an interpretation of the principles of military necessity and humanity, and has the advantage of remaining within the conduct-of-hostilities paradigm, while limiting its material scope. This approach has, however, been extremely controversial even among legal scholarship.[107] On the other hand, some states that do not consider themselves legally bound by considerations highlighted in Chapter IX of the ICRC Guidance have nevertheless adopted a kind of 'capture rather than kill approach' for policy reasons; for example, this has allegedly been US practice during the counterinsurgency in Afghanistan.[108]

(ii) The external aspect of the geographical scope of application of IHL is no less debated. The ICRC summarises this debate with the following question:

A person who would constitute a lawful target under IHL moves from a State in which there is an ongoing NIAC into the territory of a non-neighbouring non-belligerent State, and continues his or her activities in relation to the conflict from there. Can such a person be targeted under the rules of IHL by a third State in the territory of the non-belligerent State?[109]

Very broadly and in the interests of clarity, most views on the scope of IHL *ratione loci* may be seen as grounded either in the notion of control over territory (territory-based approach), or by establishing a link between the operation *in casu* and an existing armed conflict (nexus approach).

The territory-based approach limits the applicability of IHL to territory controlled by the belligerent parties stricto sensu; this territory may, or may not be restricted to the borders of a single state. It would preclude the possibility of applying the conduct-of-hostilities paradigm to persons who may otherwise constitute legitimate targets under IHL, but who are located in

---

[106] ibid, 82.

[107] While authors such as M Schmitt, W Boothby and K Watkin have criticised various aspects of the ICRC study, a particularly vehement attack against the ICRC's position in Chapter IX of the study was launched by Colonel W Hays Parks; see WH Parks, 'Part IX of the ICRC 'Direct Participation in Hostilities' Study: No Mandate, No Expertise, and Legally Incorrect' (2010) 42 *NYU Journal of International Law and Policy* 770. For Melzer's response to these various lines of criticism, see N Melzer, 'Keeping the Balance Between Military Necessity and Humanity: A Response to Four Critiques of the ICRC's Interpretive Guidance on the Notion of Direct Participation in Hostilities' (2010) 42 *NYU Journal of International Law and Policy* 831.

[108] See Gaggioli (n 100) 85–87 ('Appendix 5: Summary of the presentation by Richard Gross').

[109] The ICRC goes on to argue that there are two ways to answer the question, first by resorting to nexus, which may potentially lead to a 'global battlefield' scenario, and second, by finding that IHL is not applicable to such situations in the first place—which is preferable. See ICRC (n 5) 14–15.

the territory of non-belligerent states where the law enforcement paradigm would be much more appropriate under the circumstances.[110] This is the position of the ICRC, which does, however, allow for an exception whereby the scope *ratione loci* of IHL may expand to the territory of an adjacent non-belligerent State 'on an exceptional and *sui generis* basis'.[111] This is the 'spillover' situation.

According to the ICRC, the spillover theory

> is based on the understanding that the spill over of a NIAC into adjacent territory cannot have the effect of absolving the parties of their IHL obligations simply because an international border has been crossed. The ensuing legal vacuum would deprive of protection both civilians possibly affected by the fighting, as well as persons who fall into enemy hands.[112]

At first blush, this may seem contradictory with the territory-based approach. Sasha Radin points out, for instance, that:

> Considerable support exists for the position that borders do not matter when establishing Common Article 3 and the Tadić test's applicability to spill-over conflicts, and even to cross-border conflicts. The logic, however, seems to change when the discussion turns to 'global' conflicts. There appears to be a reluctance to accept that Common Article 3 and relevant customary international law may apply to 'global' conflicts without regard to State borders.[113]

Nevertheless, this inconsistency is not as significant as it might seem. In fact, the spillover theory still relies somehow on notions of territory and geographical proximity, rather than on nexus. The spillover theory also provides a pragmatic solution to situations where borders between neighbouring states are not clearly defined or identifiable.

Another potential criticism of 'spillover' is that there is actually very little legal ground for justifying this approach. In the words of Jelena Pejić: 'There is, admittedly, no readily accessible or detailed explanation for the legal reading that has been recognized by States and scholarly opinion with respect to spill-over NIACs.'[114] While the practical attractiveness of resorting to this interpretation is evident, we submit that additional research should be undertaken into the question of the legal basis for spillover.

For example, some states, notably the USA, have occasionally justified spillover by invoking the notion of 'hot pursuit', a term borrowed from the vocabulary of the law of the sea.[115] This concept basically involves the

---

[110] ibid, 15.
[111] ibid, fn 13.
[112] ICRC (n 6) 9–10.
[113] S Radin, 'Global Armed Conflict? The Threshold of Extraterritorial Non-International Armed Conflicts' (2013) 89 *International Law Studies* 696, 719–20.
[114] Pejić (n 25) 80–81.
[115] See 'Pakistan Fury over US "Hot Pursuit" Attack' *CNN*, 11 June 2008, edition.cnn.com/2008/WORLD/asiapcf/06/11/pakistan.troops.killed/.

extension of a state's criminal jurisdiction for acts committed on its sovereign territory and allows pursuit of the offending vessel beyond such territory, subject to limitations with respect to other states' sovereignty.[116] It is important to note that, in situations where the 'hot pursuit' analogy was made in armed conflict situations, it was always used as an argument to justify intrusion upon another state's territory rather than to claim the applicability of IHL—which is not in line with the way this concept exists in the law of the sea. The latter posits that the right of hot pursuit expires once the pursued vessel reaches another state's territorial waters.[117] Be that as it may, the hot pursuit analogy may—as a factual rather than legal analogy, and subject to a number of considerations—be an interesting and useful way of filling the 'spillover gap'. Bearing in mind that this notion is completely absent from IHL treaties, it may cover situations which, in practice, normally lead to spillover: for example, when the parties to a NIAC are fighting in the vicinity of a border of a neighbouring non-belligerent state, it is easy to imagine how they may stray into that state's territory. On the other hand, the hot-pursuit analogy would prevent the targeting of fighters who are located in that neighbouring state's territory, but are neither currently involved in the fighting, nor are located in the proximity of the border itself. This understanding of spillover would probably be more restrictive than the one adopted by the ICRC. With respect to norms on state sovereignty and the overarching principles of human rights law, we posit that this is an advantage of the hot-pursuit analogy, which merits further examination and elaboration elsewhere.

An alternative approach to the geographical scope of application is the nexus approach. The idea that a specific act may be linked to an existing armed conflict and therefore regulated by humanitarian law irrespective of where it takes place has also been accepted in practice by some states[118]

---

[116] Under the UN Convention on the Law of the Sea: 'Such pursuit must be commenced when the foreign ship or one of its boats is within the internal waters, the archipelagic waters, the territorial sea or the contiguous zone of the pursuing State, and may only be continued outside the territorial sea or the contiguous zone if the pursuit has not been interrupted.' UN Convention on the Law of the Sea (adopted 10 December 1982, entered into force 16 November 1994) 1833 UNTS 397 (UNCLOS), Art 111(1).

[117] For a broad discussion of the notion of hot pursuit, see NM Poulantzas, *The Right of Hot Pursuit in International Law*, 2nd edn (The Hague, Martinus Nijhoff, 2002).

[118] The US approach to transnational conflicts leans towards the nexus-based approach (although territory is not completely discarded either). For example, while the US DoJ memo relating to the targeted killing in Yemen makes an attempt to establish AQAP as an al-Qaeda faction or co-belligerent with a considerable presence in that country, this seems to be only a supplementary argument to justify the killing. See US Department of Justice, 'Memorandum for the Attorney General: Applicability of Federal Criminal Laws and the Constitution to Contemplated Lethal Operations against Shaykh Anwar al-Aulaqi' (16 July 2010) fas.org/irp/agency/doj/olc/aulaqi.pdf. See also Richard Gross interview (n 34) 21: 'Of course, geography matters in some instances. But we cannot tie ourselves to one country and say that combat will only take place in that country, and not outside. Now, the US also has a policy governing operations *outside* of what we call the "active zone of hostilities" or the "hot battlefield", in

and theorised by some prominent legal scholars. For instance, Lubell and Derejko give an example of an extraterritorial NIAC where they find the applicability of IHL established by reference to the nexus:

> Let us assume for the sake of argument that there is no question that state A and group X are engaged in an armed conflict that takes place in numerous parts of state A itself. Group X then sets up command and training camps just across the border in a remote area of state B, and which state B is not sponsoring but is unable to prevent. Group X leaders are based in this camp, their militants are based here and cross the border to carry out attacks before returning to camp, and rockets are even launched from the camp by group X against state A forces. Clearly a nexus exists, and operations by state A against this camp would be considered as part of the armed conflict and governed by IHL.[119]

The authors go on to argue that, were the camp *in casu* located further away from the border, the answer would nevertheless be the same, and that 'it is unclear why the precise number of miles should affect the applicability of IHL'.[120] They also find that there is no difference if the attack were to take place within state A's territory, but removed from the active battlefield, or in the territory of its neighbour, and that establishing a nexus is the best way of explaining this situation. Very importantly, they state that:

> [T]his approach does not allow for declaring open season on all past or present group X members around the globe. Neither the battlefield nor the hostilities relocate together with any individual who was on it or previously participating in it; if that were the case, it would be impossible to disengage from an armed conflict.[121]

Nevertheless, it seems that the authors would allow the targeting, under the conduct-of-hostilities paradigm, of persons who are a legitimate target under IHL regardless of their location; this is also how the ICRC understands the concept of nexus, finding that, 'under this approach, what is decisive is not where hostile acts occur but whether, because of their nexus to an armed conflict, they actually represent "acts of war"'.[122] As well as Noam Lubell,[123] Nils Melzer[124] and Michael Schmitt[125] have also advocated

---

other words Iraq and Afghanistan. So we have policy constraints for such types of operations as well, and I think those are important. They respect other countries' sovereignty and keep the conflict limited and focused on the enemy without being overly broad.'

[119] N Lubell and N Derejko, 'A Global Battlefield? Drones and the Geographical Scope of Armed Conflict' (2014) 11 *Journal of International Criminal Justice* 1, 81.

[120] ibid.

[121] ibid, 82.

[122] ICRC (n 5) 14.

[123] See also N Lubell's remarks at the ICRC's panel on the scope of IHL in 'Panel Discussion— Scope of the Law in Armed Conflict, ICRC' (19 February 2015) www.icrc.org/en/event/scope-of-law.

[124] N Melzer, 'Study on the Human Rights Implications of the Usage of Drones and Unmanned Robots in Warfare' (European Parliament, 2013) 21.

[125] MN Schmitt, 'Extraterritorial Lethal Targeting: Deconstructing the Logic of International Law' (2013) 52 *Columbia Journal of Transnational Law* 77, 97.

taking the nexus approach with respect to the geographical scope of application of IHL.[126]

While the nexus approach seems to represent a coherent approach to the question of application of IHL *ratione loci*, it suffers from at least two major setbacks. First, while it may be convenient to explain certain situations to which IHL applies by resorting to nexus (Lubell and Derejko invoke the situation of drone pilots, who are, according to them, legitimate targets under IHL irrespective of the fact that they are usually far removed from the active battlefield, or 'naval personnel who launch missiles from warships located hundreds of miles from their target destination' and who are similarly directly participating in hostilities, as best explained by this approach),[127] there may be simpler ways of explaining by using more well-established IHL concepts. For example, in the passage we quoted above, Lubell and Derejko are referring to what we would consider a cross-border NIAC in our typology. There, IHL would apply in the territory controlled by the belligerent parties; it should not be seen as applicable beyond it, except in very limited situations of spillover (perhaps in line with our tentative analogy with hot pursuit). This also leads us to the second point in contention, which is the very broad scope IHL would have if we were to resort to nexus. In our opinion, when fighters in a NIAC are located in territory where IHL is not applicable (eg in the territory of a non-neighbouring, non-belligerent state), then the conduct-of-hostilities paradigm is not the appropriate one. Finally, the argument used by authors such as Melzer that 'in the absence of express territorial limitations … humanitarian law applies wherever belligerent confrontations occur'[128] does not seem absolutely convincing for two reasons: first, the already-quoted ICTY jurisprudence in the *Tadić* case, while indeed not expressly limiting the application of IHL to any state's borders, nevertheless focuses on the notion of control over territory as the prerequisite of applying IHL.[129] Second, with respect to the notion that IHL holds no express territorial limitations on its application, it should be added for good measure that IHL provides no explicit basis for nexus either.

Based on the above considerations, we believe that a limited revival of the territorial criterion with respect to the geographical scope of application of

---

[126] The notion of nexus is completely absent from treaty law and is not limited to the geographical scope of application debate. It was first elaborated by the ICTY in the *Tadić* case in order to determine if a particular offence is a war crime or not, by linking it to an ongoing armed conflict. See *Prosecutor v Tadić* (Judgment) (n 30) para 573. It also plays a role in defining the notion of direct participation in hostilities (the 'belligerent nexus'). For more details on this, see N Melzer, *Targeted Killing in International Law* (Oxford, Oxford University Press, 2008); Melzer (n 70); Melzer (n 107); and Schmitt (n 73).

[127] Lubell and Derejko (n 119) 86.

[128] Melzer (n 124) 21.

[129] *Prosecutor v Tadić* (n 22) para 70.

IHL remains the most protective approach in the present context of globalisation of NIACs and with the development in technologies, such as drones and autonomous weapons, continuously expanding targeting options.[130] Bearing in mind the problem of 'overclassification' which is certainly present in the contemporary fight against terrorism, the problem would be further amplified by adopting an unlimited understanding of the geographical scope of application of IHL based on the undefined notion of nexus. IHL exists to provide protection in very extreme situations, and should not be invoked in order to diminish the standards of peacetime protection where the latter is the more fitting regime.

V. THE CHALLENGES OF THE GLOBALISATION OF NIACs FOR CIVILIAN PROTECTION

As demonstrated above, the globalisation of NIACs—understood both as the overall increase in the number of extraterritorial NIACs taking place around the world as well as the theoretical attempts at widening the application of IHL either by means of conflict classification or more flexible approaches to the question of its geographical scope—poses a considerable challenge from a protection aspect.

This challenge mainly lies in the trend of applying IHL too extensively and to the detriment of human rights protection. For example, consider a situation where an alleged cell of al-Qaeda (or ISIS) is present in a luxury hotel in Geneva, Switzerland, where it is clandestinely planning an attack against US personnel in Afghanistan (or Syria). If al-Qaeda or ISIS are perceived as transnational groups, engaged in transnational conflicts against Western powers, IHL would be deemed to apply in this scenario and allow (or at least not prohibit) the targeting of this cell in Switzerland, as not only is the cell constituted of individuals having a 'continuous combat function',[131] but, even if this concept were to be rejected, there is in any case little doubt that such preparatory measures aiming at carrying out a specific hostile act amount to direct participation in hostilities.[132] The United States would thus be entitled—under IHL—to target them under the conduct-of-hostilities paradigm provided that their expected military advantage from such an attack would outweigh potential civilian collateral damage and that all feasible precautions had been taken to that effect (the issue of Swiss sovereignty notwithstanding). This would also be the result of adopting the

---

[130] See G Gaggioli, 'Lethal Force and Drones: The Human Rights Question' in SJ Barela (ed), *The Legitimacy of Drones* (Burlington, VT, Ashgate Publishing, 2015) 91–115.
[131] Melzer (n 70) 27–36.
[132] ibid, 66.

nexus approach to the scope of IHL *ratione loci*. In a nutshell, the persons located in the Geneva hotel situated in Switzerland where there is no armed conflict could become the target of a legal drone strike. It is also often overlooked that the reverse would also be true, as per the principle of equality between belligerents. In other words, expansive interpretations in relation to IHL applicability could well serve the purposes of non-state organised armed groups (such as al-Qaeda or ISIS), which would under such an interpretation not violate IHL if they were to attack, for instance, US or French soldiers not only on their own territory but also when they are present in the territory of third states.

We disagree with the above approach. In our opinion, overextending the reach of IHL does not serve the interests of protection of the civilian population; the fact that IHL is not applicable to a particular situation does not imply a 'protection gap'. On the contrary, operations such as the one above would be covered by human rights law, which is both more protective and more appropriate under the circumstances. The applicability of human rights law does not cease in times of armed conflict[133] (although there remains, again, a minority of opinion challenging this notion).[134] Moreover, although a minority of influential states continue to deny the extraterritorial application of human rights treaties,[135] the extraterritorial application of human rights treaties—at least when there is control over territory (eg occupation) or authority over individuals (eg detention)—is now well established in legal practice[136]

---

[133] See *Legality of the Threat or Use of Nuclear Weapons* (n 9); *Legal Consequences of the Construction of a Wall* (n 9); and *Armed Activities on the Territory of the Congo (Democratic Republic of the Congo v Uganda)* [2005] ICJ Rep 168.

[134] *Legality of the Threat or Use of Nuclear Weapons* (n 9), para 24.

[135] For the US position, see eg Human Rights Committee, 'Statement of State Department Legal Adviser, Conrad Harper' (31 March 1995) UN Doc CCPR/C/SR 1405, para 20; US Department of State, 'Second and Third Periodic Report of the United States of America to the UN Committee on Human Rights Concerning the International Covenant on Civil and Political Rights' (2005) Annex 1; 'United States Responses to Selected Recommendations of the Human Rights Committee' (2007) 1–2. See also Human Rights Committee, 'Concluding Observations on the Fourth Periodic Report of the United States of America' (23 April 2014) UN Doc CCPR/C/USA/CO/4, para 4a. For legal writings on which the US government relies, see eg MJ Dennis, 'Application of Human Rights Treaties Extraterritorially in Times of Armed Conflict and Military Occupation' (2005) 99 *American Journal of International Law* 119. However, even within the US government, there have been dissenting opinions in this regard; see HH Koh, 'Memorandum Opinion on the Geographical Scope of the International Covenant on Civil and Political Rights' (19 October 2010). For the position of Israel, see eg Human Rights Committee, 'Sixty-Third Session. Summary Record of the 1675th meeting: Consideration of the Initial Report of Israel' (21 July 1998) UN Doc CCPR/C/SR.1675, paras 21, 27; Human Rights Committee, 'Addendum to the Second Periodic Report, Israel' (4 December 2001) UN Doc CCPR/C/ISR/2001/2, para 8.

[136] In its *Wall* Advisory Opinion, the ICJ confirmed that the International Covenant on Civil and Political Rights (ICCPR), the International Covenant on Economic, Social and Cultural Rights (ICESCR), and the Convention on the Rights of the Child (CRC) may apply extraterritorially. *Legal Consequences of the Construction of a Wall* (n 9) paras 107–13. This is also the opinion of the Human Rights Committee; see Human Rights Committee, 'General Comment

and scholarship.[137] The customary nature of rights, such as the right to life, has also been raised as an argument to maintain that these rights apply extraterritorially without jurisdictional limitation,[138] although this position has had its detractors.[139] While the interplay between IHL and IHRL—and especially the *lex specialis* maxim—remains subject to debate, the majority view revolves around complementarity and reciprocal influence, rather than mutual exclusion.[140] It has also been argued that even when there is a contradiction between applicable IHL and IHRL rules, the human rights law rule may under certain circumstances be considered as the *lex specialis*.[141]

Applying the law enforcement paradigm to the above-mentioned hypothetical terrorist cell in Geneva would mean that lethal force may only

No 31: The Nature of the General Legal Obligation Imposed on States Parties to the Covenant' (26 May 2004) UN Doc CCPR/C/21/Rev.1/Add. 1326, para 11. Similarly, the ECtHR has established the extraterritorial applicability of the ECHR: see eg *Issa and ors v Turkey* (2004) 41 EHRR 567; *Öcalan v Turkey* (App no 46221/99) ECHR 12 May 2005; and *Al-Skeini and ors, Bar Human Rights Committee (intervening) and ors (intervening) v United Kingdom* (2011) 53 EHRR 18. This has also been the approach of the Inter-American System: see *Ecuador v Colombia* (2010) Inter-American Commission on Human Rights Case No 112/10; *Disabled Peoples' International v USA* (1987) Inter-American Commission on Human Rights Case No 9213; *Salas v USA* (1993), Inter-American Commission on Human Rights Case No 10.573.

[137] See M Milanović, *Extraterritorial Application of Human Rights Treaties: Law, Principles and Policy* (Oxford, Oxford University Press, 2011); M Milanović, 'Extraterritorial Derogations from Human Rights Treaties in Armed Conflict', in N Bhuta (ed), *The Frontiers of Human Rights: Extraterritoriality and its Challenges* (Oxford, Oxford University Press, 2016) 55–88; G Gaggioli (n 130) 91–115; Melzer (n 124) 16–18; G Gaggioli, 'Remoteness and Human Rights Law' in JD Ohlin, *Research Handbook on Remote Warfare* (Cheltenham, Edward Elgar Publishing, forthcoming).

[138] ICRC (n 6) 22.

[139] It is unclear whether states such as the USA and Israel agree with this position. Their arguments against the extraterritorial application of human rights law are mostly (if not only) based on the jurisdictional clauses in human rights treaties. According to Professor Michael Schmitt, the USA has never rejected the extraterritorial application of the customary right to life. A counter-argument that could be raised is that, even if the right to life is indeed customary, it is still difficult to establish practice and *opinio juris* to the effect that it is not intrinsically accompanied by any jurisdictional limitation. This caveat is often raised by Professor Marco Sassòli, notably in his teachings and conferences. The fact that a number of non-binding human rights instruments such as the American Declaration on the Rights and Duties of Man or the Universal Declaration of Human Rights recognise the right to life without establishing jurisdictional limitation might nevertheless be seen as elements of relevant practice and *opinio juris*.

[140] See M Sassòli and LM Olson, 'The Relationship Between International Humanitarian and Human Rights Law Where it Matters: Admissible Killing and Internment of Fighters in Non-International Armed Conflicts' (2008) 90 *International Review of the Red Cross* 871; and M Milanović, 'Norm Conflicts, International Humanitarian Law and Human Rights Law' in O Ben-Naftali (ed), *Human Rights and International Humanitarian Law* (Oxford, Oxford University Press, 2010); see also G Gaggioli, *L'influence mutuelle entre les droits de l'homme et le droit international humanitaire à la lumière du droit à la vie* (Paris, Pedone, 2013).

[141] G Gaggioli and R Kolb, 'A Right to Life in Armed Conflicts? The Contribution of the European Court of Human Rights' (2007) 37 *Israel Yearbook on Human Rights* 118; Gaggioli (n 140) 42–60.

be used against it as a measure of last resort in the execution of a lawful arrest or the protection of any person from unlawful violence, and then only no more than absolutely necessary and strictly proportionate to such purposes.[142] In a nutshell, there would have to be an attempt to arrest the terrorists, rather than outright kill them. This does not only have a potential impact on the alleged terrorists' lives, but also on those of any civilians who may become the collateral damage of a potential lethal strike against them. While IHL allows, under certain circumstances, civilian collateral damage,[143] the status of incidental civilian losses when force is used lawfully under the law enforcement paradigm is less clear.[144] Nevertheless, IHRL remains the more protective branch of international law, as the standards of planning and control in law enforcement operations in order to prevent such losses are arguably higher.[145]

Another difference in the regimes of IHL and IHRL that would be relevant in such situations concerns detention. In times of IAC, IHL permits detention of POWs[146] and the internment of civilians for security reasons,[147] acting as legal basis for such deprivation of liberty and providing grounds and certain procedural safeguards such as regular review of the reasons for security internment.[148] With respect to NIACs, the situation is less clear, and it remains to be seen if IHL may be provided as a sufficient legal basis for security detention in such circumstances.[149] In any case, IHL does not say anything about the grounds for detention and procedure to be followed

---

[142] These requirements are shared by universal and regional human rights treaties, eg International Covenant on Civil and Political Rights (adopted 16 December 1966, entered into force 23 March 1976) 999 UNTS 171 (ICCPR), Art 6 and European Convention for the Protection of Human Rights and Fundamental Freedoms (as amended by Protocols Nos 11 and 14, 4 November 1950) ETS 5 (ECHR), Art 2, as elaborated under the relevant jurisprudence.

[143] See AP I, Art 51(5)(b). The principle of proportionality is considered by the ICRC to reflect a norm of customary law that is also applicable in times of NIAC; see Henckaerts and Doswald-Beck (n 2) 46–50.

[144] Human rights bodies have accepted very limited and unforeseen casualties among bystanders in rare cases. See *Andronicou and Constantinou v Cyprus* (App no 25052/94) ECHR 10 September 1997, para 194; ECHR, *Kerimova and Others v Russia* (App no 17170/04) ECHR 3 May 2011, para 246; and *Finogenov and Others v Russia* (App no 18299/03 and 27311/03) ECHR 20 December 2011.

[145] See *McCann and Others v UK* (App no 18984/91) ECHR 27 September 1995, paras 146–214.

[146] GC III, Art 21.

[147] GC IV, Arts 42, 68.

[148] ibid, Arts 43, 78.

[149] Both Common Article 3 and AP II take into consideration the position of persons deprived of liberty and extend them such guarantees as humane treatment, but they do not provide an explicit legal basis such as those that exist in IACs. This topic remains subject to intense debate amongst scholars and practitioners; for example, compare the ICRC's position on detention in armed conflict in ICRC, 'Internment in Armed Conflict: Basic Rules and Challenges' (November 2014), with the position taken by the UK Supreme Court in *Abd Ali Hameed Al-Waheed (Appellant) v Ministry of Defence (Respondent)* [2017] UKSC 2; *Serdar Mohammed (Respondent) v Ministry of Defence (Appellant)* [2017] UKSC 1.

with respect to persons deprived of liberty in the context of a NIAC.[150] On the other hand, IHRL proclaims the right to liberty and security of person and that no one shall be subjected to arbitrary arrest or detention,[151] and goes on to lay out procedural safeguards which are considered higher than those provided by IHL, such as the right to challenge before a judge the lawfulness of the detention (habeas corpus).[152] While universal treaties such as the International Covenant on Civil and Political Rights (ICCPR) may be seen as allowing security detention under certain limited circumstances,[153] this is not true of the ECHR, which provides an exhaustive list of grounds for lawful deprivation of liberty, and security detention is not listed among them.[154] Outside the context of an armed conflict, in order for such detention to be undertaken lawfully, a proper derogation to the right to liberty would previously have to be made.[155]

In a recent high-profile case, the ECtHR compared the regime of the IHL of IACs and that of the ECHR and determined that, while the Convention remained applicable to persons deprived of liberty in times of IAC, the Geneva Conventions may be taken as providing legal bases and grounds for detention even in the absence of a derogation from the Convention.[156] However, the Court has never yet taken such a position with respect to NIACs. Nevertheless, if we were to accept the interpretation that the IHL of NIACs provides legal basis and grounds for security detention, it is ipso facto less protective than the corpus of human rights. Without additional international case law to clarify this issue, we submit that decreased standards of detention (including an overall increase in arbitrary and unlawful deprivations of liberty) are one of the potential consequences of the ongoing globalisation of NIACs. The problem of overclassification could then lead to IHL being invoked in order to justify potentially indefinite internment for security reasons of alleged members of terrorist groups, as was allegedly the case of many persons detained in Guantánamo by the United States.[157]

---

[150] The ICRC, which interprets the IHL of NIACs as providing a legal basis for security detention, nevertheless accepts that 'additional authority' in domestic law, an international treaty or UN Security Council resolution or even army standard operating procedures (SOPs) would still be necessary with respect to the grounds and procedures of such detention. ICRC (n 149) 8. See the chapter in this volume by Françoise Hampson.

[151] ICCPR, Art 9(1); ECHR, Art 5(1); American Convention on Human Rights (accessed 22 November 1969, entered into force 18 July 1978) OAS TS No 36 (ACHR) Art 7(2)–(3); and African Charter on Human and Peoples' Rights (accessed 27 June 1981, entered into force 21 October 1986) CAB/LEG/67/3 rev 5, 21 ILM 58 (ACHPR) Art 6.

[152] ICCPR, Art 9 (4).

[153] Human Rights Committee, 'General Comment No 35: Article 9 (Liberty and Security of Person)' (16 December 2014) UN Doc CCPR/C/GC/35, para 15.

[154] ECHR, Art 5(1).

[155] ibid, Art 15.

[156] See *Hassan v United Kingdom* (App no 29750/09) ECHR 16 September 2014, paras 65–111.

[157] See Human Rights Committee (n 135) para 21.

Additionally, IHL does not provide equivalent monitoring mechanisms to the bodies established by various human rights treaties. Although human rights bodies have shown an increasing willingness to examine armed conflict situations under their respective mandates,[158] and to take into consideration IHL when doing so, they will always be limited to examining applications under the scope of the treaties they have been created to monitor.[159] Therefore, the more developed institutional structure of IHRL is submitted as an additional argument in favour of a more restrictive approach to the applicability of IHL to the fight against terrorism.

Finally, while the notion of state sovereignty is usually put aside when discussing *jus in bello* (and has therefore not been developed in the present chapter), we submit that an excessively fragmented approach to international law actually risks endangering individuals. *Jus ad bellum* considerations and state sovereignty remain an additional (or even a primary) protective layer that should not be overlooked. Jonathan Horowitz and Naz Modirzadeh[160] give an excellent example of how the notion of sovereignty can actually prove more protective than IHL itself. They posit a hypothetical situation in which the Syrian government is considering launching a strike against Syrian rebel commanders meeting US personnel on US soil. Provided that we accept that the rebels would remain targetable under IHL under such circumstances, such an attack may be lawful under IHL if the principles of distinction, proportionality and precautions were all respected. However, Horowitz and Modirzadeh argue that the Syrian government should nonetheless take into consideration that—even if *jus ad bellum* self-defence

---

[158] eg *Georgia v Russia (II)* (App No38263/08) ECHR 13 December 2011, para 72. However, the ECtHR has generally refused to apply IHL in situations which were arguably NIACs, but where the government did not invoke this body of law, see *Ergi v Turkey, Isayeva v Russia* and *Isayeva v Russia, Yusupova v Russia, Bazayeva v Russia* (n 33). See the chapter in this volume by Bill Bowring.

[159] The Inter-American Court explained this approach as follows: 'When a State is a Party to the American Convention and has accepted the contentious jurisdiction of the Court, the Court may examine the conduct of the State to determine whether it conforms to the provisions of the Convention, even when the issue may have been definitively resolved by the domestic legal system. The Court is also competent to determine whether any norm of domestic or international law applied by a State, in times of peace or armed conflict, is compatible or not with the American Convention. In this activity, the Court has no normative limitation: any legal norm may be submitted to this examination of compatibility. In order to carry out this examination, the Court interprets the norm in question and analyzes it in the light of the provisions of the Convention. The result of this operation will always be an opinion in which the Court will say whether or not that norm or that fact is compatible with the American Convention. The latter has only given the Court competence to determine whether the acts or the norms of the States are compatible with the Convention itself, and not with the 1949 Geneva Conventions.' *Las Palmeras v Colombia (Preliminary Objections)* Inter-American Court of Human Rights Series C No 67 (4 February 2000) paras 32–33.

[160] J Horowitz and N Modirzadeh, 'Guest Post: How International Law Could Work in Transnational Non-International Armed Conflicts: Part I of a Two-Part Series' *Opinio Juris*, 11 April 2013, opiniojuris.org/2013/04/11/guest-post-how-international-law-could-work-in-transnational-non-international-armed-conflicts-part-i-of-a-two-part-series/.

against non-state actors were an accepted notion—the rebels do not represent an 'immediate threat' for Syria.[161] At risk of legitimately being accused of unlawfully breaching US sovereignty, the authors argue that the Syrian government would be wise not to undertake the attack regardless of its lawfulness under IHL. Thus, with respect to the lives of the rebels and civilians who might be caught up in such an attack, it is the sovereignty of the United States that provides greater protection than IHL. This example reminds us of the necessity of taking into consideration more than a single branch of the law when determining the lawfulness of any particular conduct.

Based on all of the above, we consider that the overapplication of IHL may have a negative impact on the regime of protection provided by international law. We find little merit to arguments submitted in order to prove the existence of an ongoing 'transnational' NIAC. We similarly hold that the concept of nexus should not be used in order to expand the geographical scope of application of IHL. With respect to the notion of 'spillover', while it may indeed be necessary to use such notions to explain certain strictly defined situations that occur in practice, it should be used in a restrictive manner, as well as better conceptualised and circumscribed with additional legal arguments. Finally, the approach that seems to be most sound in a legal sense, as well as most protective overall, is to insist on the extraterritorial application of human rights law in light of existing case law by human rights bodies and to uphold the sovereignty of states as an indirect barrier to the overapplication of IHL.

---

[161] In the famous *Caroline* case, the right to self-defence was understood to mean 'a necessity of self-defence, instant, overwhelming, and leaving no choice of means, and no moment for deliberation'. This is still seen as a fundamental principle of international law. See MN Shaw, *International Law*, 6th edn (Cambridge, Cambridge University Press, 2008) 1131.

6

Administrative Detention in Non-International Armed Conflicts

FRANÇOISE J HAMPSON

I. INTRODUCTION

DETENTION HAS ALWAYS been a feature of armed conflicts.[1] This chapter addresses only internment or administrative detention, not detention with a view to criminal proceedings. What is being examined here is the internment regime itself. Who can be interned, on what grounds and subject to what form of review? It is in that area that difficulties have arisen in determining the norms applicable. The issue of the transfer of an internee from the detaining power to the territorial state or a coalition partner or to the home territory of the detaining power will not be discussed.[2]

In the recent past, internment appears to have given rise to a range of difficulties for states involved in armed conflicts. When considering those problems, it is necessary to distinguish between two quite different challenges. There is first the issue of implementation and enforcement, which is what is at issue when clear and agreed rules are violated. An example is forms of interrogation used on occasion by British interrogators in Iraq,[3] which were in breach of the undertaking given by Prime Minister Heath during the litigation concerning alleged torture in Northern Ireland.[4]

---

[1] On the history and evolution of rules applicable to armed conflict, including detention, see generally G Best, *Humanity in Warfare* (London, Methuen, 1983) and *War and Law since 1945* (Oxford, Clarendon Press, 1994).

[2] This has given rise to difficulties in recent extraterritorial NIACs in Afghanistan and Iraq. The challenges relate both to the legal rules applicable and to the uncertainty as to the actual treatment to which transferees are likely to be subjected. This can vary at different times, in different places and as between different detaining authorities.

[3] See W Gage, *The Baha Mousa Inquiry Report* (London, HMSO, 2011) www.gov.uk/government/uploads/system/uploads/attachment_data/file/279190/1452_i.pdf.

[4] ibid, para 1.39. See also *Ireland v UK* (App no 5310/71) ECHR 18 January 1978, para 101.

The second challenge involves alleged uncertainty as to the applicability and/or the existence or scope of an alleged rule. It is not possible to take appropriate corrective action unless a detailed diagnosis is undertaken of the causes of the aberrant result. It ought to be easier to address issues of implementation and enforcement, where there is agreement on the applicability, scope and interpretation of the norm in question.

The issue of *treatment* in detention, including during interrogation, will not be discussed in this chapter. Generally speaking, the rules regulating treatment in detention are accepted and clear, as is their applicability and their scope.[5] The issue there is implementation and enforcement, including the surprising alleged ignorance of those responsible for interrogation as to the norms applicable.[6] This text will also not consider detention with a view to criminal proceedings, whether conducted by the detaining state or another state.

Neither coalition operations, with or without a UN mandate, nor UN operations as such will be discussed. The latter raise particular issues concerning the degree to which the UN and UN forces are bound by treaties ratified by states.[7] Whilst the joint nature of such activities does give rise to certain challenges, many of the problems in the field of detention arise owing to the uncertainty as to norms applicable. It is not just that different states may have ratified different treaties. They may take a different view as to the existence and scope of their legal obligations, particularly in the field of customary law. If states individually disagree about that, it is inevitable that the disagreements will be highlighted in coalition operations. In other words, this text is looking at internment in operations such as those in Iraq and Afghanistan, particularly in the phase when states were present to assist the territorial state in dealing with an armed conflict against one or more organised armed groups.

In order to identify the legal issues, it is necessary to understand the situation on the ground that the rules are intended to address. Then the rules applicable in domestic emergencies and IACs will be considered briefly, in order to establish benchmarks of what is both feasible and necessary. The core of the text examines the rules in NIACs. After a discussion of what is

---

[5] The standards are similar under both the law of armed conflict (LOAC)—otherwise known as international humanitarian law (IHL)—and under human rights law (HRL). The standards themselves do not appear to be disputed, even if ensuring respect in practice is often challenging.

[6] Gage (n 3) with particular reference to the ignorance of the interrogators with regard to permitted techniques.

[7] A state participating in a UN-mandated operation is bound by its IHL obligations, if they are applicable. The controversial issue is rather whether the UN as such is bound by IHL or HRL; see UN Secretariat, 'Secretary-General's Bulletin: Observance by United Nations Forces of International Humanitarian Law' (6 August 1999) UN Doc ST/SGB/1999/13.

contained (or, more accurately, not contained) in the treaty law, the analysis will look first at NIACs within the territory of the state involved. To refer again to the examples given above, what were the rules regarding internment that applied to the governments of Iraq and Afghanistan, respectively? The analysis will then examine the rules applicable to internment in NIACs outside the territory of the detaining state. In other words, what rules applied to, for example, the UK and the USA in those situations? That is where the main problems seem to arise.

II. HOW AND WHY A PERSON MAY BE APPREHENDED AND INTERNED

A person may be apprehended because they were captured or surrendered after having fought. This includes capture whilst wounded or sick or following shipwreck. The reason for internment is to prevent those detained from rejoining their own forces. They are detained on account of being a member of the opposing armed forces,[8] in other words on account of their status. There is no punitive element to the internment. The object also determines for how long they may be detained; until the end of active hostilities.[9] There is another, more controversial, context in which internment may occur. The security forces may have intelligence suggesting that a given individual has been and continues to be involved in hostile activities. The information may not be of a type or quantity to permit detention with a view to criminal proceedings. The protection of sources and concern at revealing intelligence-gathering capabilities may also preclude such proceedings. The threat posed by the individual may be to the armed forces and/or to the civilian population, usually that of the territory in which the fighting is occurring but also possibly that of the intervening state. The person may be detained as a result of an operation in which capture was the object, or the person may be captured and it may emerge subsequently that he is of interest to the detaining authorities. It is likely, in such a situation, that the detaining authority wants *both* to take a threat off the streets *and* to pump the detainee for information about his associates and his exploits. The reason for the internment again suggests its duration. When the individual ceases to be a threat, he should be released. These reasons for needing to detain are both plausible and understandable. They enable the identification of the necessary grounds of detention: in the first case the status of the individual; and, in the second,

---

[8] See the discussion of POWs at section IV below.
[9] Geneva Convention III Relative to the Treatment of Prisoners of War (adopted 12 August 1949, entered into force 21 October 1950) 75 UNTS 135 (GC III) Art 118; for texts of the Geneva Conventions of 1949 and the Additional Protocols of 1977, see ICRC, 'Geneva Conventions and Commentaries', www.icrc.org/en/war-and-law/treaties-customary-law/geneva-conventions.

his behaviour or conduct. The armed forces also need to take account of the impact of the implementation of the detention policy in practice on the operation as a whole. An arbitrary application of the policy may cause people to call into question the detention regime itself.

The situation on the ground helps in the identification of appropriate grounds of detention. It also provides some indication as to the preconditions of release, which implies some form of review mechanism where the detention is based on the threat posed by the individual. It does not, superficially at least, afford much guidance as to treatment during detention or the due-process guarantees needed in the review process. In fact, that is an oversimplification. If a party to a conflict has the reputation of mistreating detainees, opponents are more likely to fight to death to prevent themselves from being detained. It is alleged that one reason so many Iraqis surrendered in the Gulf War of 1990–91 was that they believed they would be treated properly.[10] Mistreatment of detainees is also likely to affect the perceived legitimacy of the operation, both in the minds of the local population and of the population of the sending state. Inadequate due-process guarantees in the review process are likely to result in more flawed decision-making, however appropriate the detention policy itself. This, in turn, is likely to call into question the legitimacy of the detention regime.

Treatment includes both what is done or not done to the individual internee, whether as punishment or for some other reason, and also the general conditions of detention. The latter involves factors such as the provision of food, shelter, hygiene and meeting spiritual, medical and exercise needs. It also involves contact with the outside world, whether lawyers, doctors, friends or family. As already indicated, this text does not address the issue of treatment in detention.

The other principal issue that arises out of the fact of internment is the question of review of the need for detention. This includes the composition of the review mechanism, frequency of review, the test used to determine the need to continue internment, procedural rights in the review process and the legal status of the determination by the review mechanism. Does it bind those responsible for the detention? These issues will be discussed, since they concern the internment regime itself.

The totality of what happens to internees in detention is likely to have a significant impact on the perceived legitimacy of the detention regime as a whole, lawful or otherwise. Given the importance of winning 'the battle of hearts and minds' and retaining the support of public opinion in the state where the conflict is occurring and of the population of the intervening

---

[10] P Rowe (ed), *The Gulf War 1990–1991 in International and English Law* (London, Routledge, 2005) ch 9.

state, as well as of the international community as a whole, detention is of huge importance to security forces. If they fail to pay it sufficient attention or to allocate the resources necessary, states are likely to pay a heavy price. The negative effects of badly handled detention can arise both where people are arbitrarily detained, in other words on insufficient or inadequate grounds, or where they are ill treated.

It is important to consider what is likely to happen if internment is *not* an option, legally, politically or militarily. First, those who have been involved in killing and injuring civilians and members of the security forces will continue to engage in those activities. This raises the question of the scope of the positive obligation of the state to protect the lives of civilians and its security forces. Second, security forces faced with the frustration of dealing with the first consequence will find opportunities to kill members of the opposing forces, lawfully or otherwise. This may be as a result of individual or local initiatives or even ordered from higher up the chain of command, possibly through interpretation of the rules of engagement (ROE). There is also a risk that such people will be detained but outside any legal framework. This may even include not acknowledging the fact that they have been detained, known in human rights law as enforced disappearances. In other words, the alternative to internment is not as simple as liberty.

It is submitted that during armed conflict there is a need for an internment regime. It is important that it should not be arbitrary and that all aspects of the internment regime are required to meet appropriate legal standards. Some elements of the regime need to be absolute or almost absolute. That is to say, they should not vary in different contexts. That would include grounds of detention, the existence of a review mechanism, periodicity of review and the legally binding character of the decision. Some elements will need to show more flexibility, to cope with varying exigencies at different stages of detention, different stages of the conflict and between different conflict contexts. That said, there will be a minimum standard with regard to those elements. They include the information given to the internee as to the reasons for the internment and representation in the review process.

It is now possible to turn to the law to see to what extent it meets these needs. Two bodies of international law are relevant: human rights law (HRL) and the law of armed conflict (LOAC), also known as international humanitarian law (IHL). In this chapter, the latter body of rules will be referred to as IHL because detention is part of the law on the protection of victims which was the origin of IHL. (LOAC refers to both the rules on the conduct of hostilities and those on the protection of victims.) The questions to be asked of the applicable law include:

— Does it provide authority to intern?
— Does it provide appropriate grounds of internment?

— Does it provide for the existence of a review mechanism?
— Does it require that the composition of the review mechanism is such as to ensure its independence?
— Does it require the appropriate frequency of review?
— Does it provide for appropriate procedural rights in the review process, including representation, access to information as to grounds of internment and ability to call witnesses?
— Does it require that the determination of the review body be legally binding?

When looking at what the law provides, the starting point is treaty law. In interpreting treaty law, account may be taken of jurisprudence or case law. That is particularly important in the case of HRL. Human rights treaties only provide a skeleton. All the substantial flesh on the bones of HRL that now exists comes from case law. Where treaty law is silent, ambiguous or obscure, it will be necessary to consider customary international law.[11] It is important to remember that different players view the relationship between HRL and IHL from different standpoints. As far as the armed forces are concerned, the starting point is IHL. HRL is only relevant insofar as it modifies the IHL rule otherwise applicable. On the other hand, as far as a human rights monitoring or enforcement mechanism is concerned, the starting point is HRL, possibly modified by derogation.[12] The question then becomes whether, when and how should it take account of IHL.

Before examining internment in NIACs in some detail, it is useful to examine how the issue of internment is addressed in domestic emergencies that do not constitute armed conflicts and also in IACs. This should assist in identifying benchmarks that can be used to evaluate internment in NIACs. In the first situation, one is dealing only with HRL, possibly modified by derogation. In the second, both IHL and HRL may be relevant and therefore also the question of how human rights bodies handle the applicability and application of IHL.

---

[11] Customary international law is a source of equal legal standing to treaties. In practice, it is common to start with an examination of treaty law, because it is easy to determine whether there is a relevant rule, its contents and whether the state in question has ratified it. The existence of a customary norm and its formulation and scope may well be issues of dispute. The Statute of the ICJ defines customary law as 'evidence of a general practice accepted as law'; see Statute of the International Court of Justice (adopted 26 June 1945, entered into force 24 October 1945) 33 UNTS 993 (ICJ Statute) Art 38(1)(b).

[12] Derogation is a procedure set out in some human rights treaties, most notably the ICCPR, the ACHR and the ECHR, whereby in a situation of emergency threatening the life of the nation, the state may modify some but not all of its human rights obligations to the extent strictly necessary; see further below.

III. INTERNMENT IN DOMESTIC EMERGENCIES

The very first case before the ECtHR involved internment in a domestic emergency.[13] The challenges that an internment regime poses for HRL include the following:

— Is it necessary to derogate in order to be able to introduce such a regime or can it be done under 'normal' peacetime rules?
— How should the usual requirement of a procedure to determine the lawfulness of detention by a court be applied in a context in which the evidence justifying detention cannot be reviewed in open court?
— What are the requirements with regard to determining the continuing need for detention?

One difficulty in looking for precise answers to these questions is that human rights bodies have two principal functions. They may be required to address the general human rights situation in a state or the scope of an entire article.[14] In neither of those cases do they have the time or the space to answer precise questions. They offer general guidance. When determining an individual case, the bodies do have to deal with very particular facts but they only deal with the issues that have been raised and do not necessarily address related matters. It is striking how little guidance is afforded by HRL with regard to the precise requirements of internment. It is, however, possible to determine general directions of travel. If a state wishes to avoid finding itself at the receiving end of a judgment, it would be well advised to take account of how a human rights body is *likely* to rule, even if it has not yet done so.

Human rights treaties other than the ECHR simply prohibit arbitrary detention.[15] That leaves open whether internment is prima facie arbitrary, possibly requiring derogation to justify it or whether that is not necessary.

---

[13] *Lawless v Ireland* (App no 332/57) ECHR 1 July 1961. It is possible that nowadays the interpretation of Art 15 ECHR would require stricter conditions to be met to justify emergency measures.

[14] For example, the Human Rights Committee under the ICCPR receives periodic reports from states on implementation of its obligations and, following a dialogue with the state, produces Concluding Observations on the situation with regard to respect for the treaty in the state in question. Separately, and divorced from any consideration of a particular state, it produces General Comments, clarifying either the scope of an Article or discussing an issue.

[15] eg International Covenant on Civil and Political Rights (adopted 16 December 1966, entered into force 23 March 1976) 999 UNTS 171 (ICCPR) Art 9; American Convention on Human Rights (accessed 22 November 1969, entered into force 18 July 1978) OAS TS No 36 (ACHR) Art 7; African Charter on Human and Peoples' Rights (accessed 27 June 1981, entered into force 21 October 1986) CAB/LEG/67/3 rev 5, 21 ILM 58 (ACHPR) Art 6. See also the mandate of the Working Group on Arbitrary Detention, one of the UN Special Procedures.

In a General Comment on the relevant provision of the ICCPR, the Human Rights Committee stated that internment would

> normally amount to arbitrary detention as other effective measures addressing the threat, including the criminal justice system, would be available. If, under the most exceptional circumstances, a present, direct and imperative threat is invoked to justify the detention of persons considered to present such a threat, the burden of proof lies on States parties to show that the individual poses such a threat and that it cannot be addressed by alternative measures, and that burden increases with the length of the detention. States parties also need to show that detention does not last longer than absolutely necessary, that the overall length of possible detention is limited and that they fully respect the guarantees provided for by article 9 in all cases. Prompt and regular review by a court or other tribunal possessing the same attributes of independence and impartiality as the judiciary is a necessary guarantee for those conditions, as is access to independent legal advice, preferably selected by the detainee, and disclosure to the detainee of, at least, the essence of the evidence on which the decision is taken.[16]

It is striking that the Committee does not formally require derogation in order to justify internment, but the language used suggests that it will be difficult to justify such a policy outside a context in which derogation would be possible.

In a review of the concept of 'arbitrary detention', the Working Group on Arbitrary Detention[17] stated:

> Even though administrative detention per se is not tantamount to arbitrary detention, its application in practice is overly broad and its compliance with the minimum guarantees of due process is in the majority of cases inadequate.[18]

The situation under the ECHR was, and perhaps still is, different. Whilst other human rights treaties prohibit 'arbitrary detention', the ECHR lists exhaustively the only permitted grounds of detention. They do not include internment. In order to be able to intern, a state *must* derogate.[19] Provided that the situation is one in which the state can derogate and that it has done so, it may be able to introduce internment, on condition that it can establish the necessity for such a policy and that it is not implemented in a discriminatory fashion. Human rights law does not itself provide the authority for the policy. Domestic legislation is necessary to establish the authority to intern,

---

[16] UN Human Rights Committee, 'General Comment 35' (16 December 2014) UN Doc CPPR/C/GC/35, para 15, footnotes omitted.

[17] The Working Group on Arbitrary Detention (WGAD) is a UN Special Procedure, which means that all Member States of the UN can be subject to its scrutiny. This is in contrast to bodies established under treaties, such as the Human Rights Committee, which can only exercise their authority over states that have ratified the treaty in question.

[18] UN Human Rights Council, 'Report of the Working Group on Arbitrary Detention' (24 December 2012) UN Doc A/HRC/22/44, para 74.

[19] *Lawless v Ireland* (n 13); *Ireland v UK* (n 4); *Cyprus v Turkey* (1993) 15 EHRR 509.

which may then be recognised as legitimate under HRL. Domestic law will also have to address questions such as grounds of detention, review of the continuing need for detention, composition of the review mechanism and the end of internment. Both the law itself and its implementation need to be in conformity with human rights law.

The most important feature of HRL in situations of emergency is that the authority to intern comes from domestic, not international, law. That authority may, in appropriate circumstances, be recognised by HRL.

IV. INTERNMENT IN INTERNATIONAL ARMED CONFLICTS

An IAC is an armed conflict between two or more states. It arises whatever the degree of force used and however mismatched the parties may be militarily.[20] IHL began to be put into treaty form in the mid-nineteenth century. There was already a body of customary law regarding the detention of former fighters.[21] It was recognised that members of the armed forces of a state were not committing a crime merely because they participated in the conflict. They were, on all sides, merely responding to the call, lawful or otherwise, of their sovereign. In that sense, legally speaking, there was equality between the belligerents. There was no reason to punish a member of the opponent's armed forces but there was every reason to prevent his rejoining the fight. Once they had been removed from the battlefield, treating the detainees properly had no implications for the conduct of hostilities, beyond the general question of the diversion of resources to meet their needs.

The treaty regime has undergone constant modification and refinement, usually in the light of immediately prior experience in armed conflict. It should be remembered that, owing to the applicability of the 1929 Geneva Convention on Prisoners of War, generally speaking those captured by regular armed forces on the western front in World War II had a good survival rate, in contrast to those captured on the eastern front or in the Far East.[22]

The principal provisions on detention in IACs are now found in Geneva Conventions III and IV of 1949, with certain supplementary elements found in Additional Protocol I of 1977.[23] The Geneva Conventions have been universally ratified. Additional Protocol I has been widely but not universally ratified. Non-ratifiers include the USA, Israel and Turkey. They are bound by such of the provisions of Additional Protocol I as constitute customary law.[24]

---

[20] Common Article 2 of the four Geneva Conventions of 1949.
[21] Best (n 1).
[22] ibid.
[23] For texts and commentaries, see ICRC (n 9).
[24] JM Heckaerts and L Doswald-Beck, *Customary International Humanitarian Law* (Cambridge, Cambridge University Press, 2005); see also ICRC, 'Customary IHL Database', www.ihl-databases.icrc.org/customary-ihl/eng/docs/home.

This section will consider first the detention of those recognised as combatants, then that of those who have fought but who are not recognised as combatants, and finally that of civilians.

A. The Detention of Combatants

The term 'combatant' has a technical meaning; it does not simply mean a person who fights. Since 1977, a combatant is a person with the right, or legal authority, to fight.[25] That is to say that he cannot be prosecuted for the mere fact of fighting. Oversimplifying, that refers principally to the members of the state's armed forces and certain other categories characterised by their proximity to the armed forces. Before 1977 (and to this day for certain non-parties to Additional Protocol I) the term used to cover this status was 'privileged belligerent'.[26] There is an important balance between the benefits and the disadvantages of combatant status. The benefits include non-prosecution for the mere fact of fighting and detailed protection rules, whether wounded, sick, shipwrecked or a POW.[27] On the downside, a combatant may be targeted throughout the armed conflict, regardless of what he is doing and whether or not he constitutes a threat at the time, and may be detained until the end of active hostilities.

Authority to detain combatants is provided, arguably not by express provision but by necessary implication, under Geneva Convention III. Article 4 identifies those who, if captured, must be held as prisoners of war. Geneva Conventions I and II provide that captured combatants who are wounded or sick or shipwrecked have to receive the treatment their condition requires but they remain POWs.

In 1949, it was assumed that a person would want the status of a POW. For that reason, it was assumed that a person would only require access to a status determination mechanism if the detaining power was not going

---

[25] Protocol I Additional to the Geneva Conventions of 12 August 1949 and relating to the Protection of Victims of International Armed Conflicts (adopted 8 June 1977, entered into force 7 December 1978) 1125 UNTS 3 (AP I), Arts 43, 44.

[26] See generally C Garraway, 'Interoperability and the Atlantic Divide: A Bridge over Troubled Waters' (2006) 80 *Naval War College International Law Studies* 339–47. Some commentators do not use the terms with their technical meanings. In some languages there is only one word for both fighter and combatant. Legally speaking, fighter just describes someone who fights. It tells you nothing about his status. A combatant, on the other hand, is a person entitled to fight. It does not include civilians who take a direct part in hostilities, who would come within the normal meaning of fighter. The status of combatant only exists in IACs; see further below.

[27] Immunity from prosecution only applies to those who fight according to the rules. If a combatant commits a war crime (eg the intentional killing of civilians), he can be prosecuted. If convicted, he retains his POW status.

to give the person POW status. The mechanism was provided by Geneva Convention III Article 5. Status determination is undertaken on an individual, not a collective, basis.[28] The type of situation was intended to address was where the individual claimed to be a member of the state's armed forces but where for some reason the detaining authority thought the person was not such a member.[29]

Once a person has been determined to be a POW, he can be detained until the end of active hostilities.[30] That is the result of the basis for detention. The goal is to prevent the individual from rejoining his own forces during the existence of an armed conflict. It is not based on the threat the individual may pose. It also follows that review, once the determination has been made, would be pointless.

Additional Protocol I recognised that individuals detained as POWs might wish to deny that they had that status. The review mechanism under Article 45 can be used by either those claiming or those denying POW status.[31] One reason why a person might wish to object to the status is that detention may last to the end of active hostilities. Another reason, particularly where the alleged POW is detained in the territory of the other belligerent, is that he may in fact be an opponent of the regime against which that state is fighting.[32]

B. The Detention of Persons Who are Neither Entitled to Combatant Status nor Civilian

When Additional Protocol I was adopted in 1977, it was recognised that a person might not be a civilian but might not be entitled to POW status. Article 75 of Additional Protocol I, which is generally regarded as reflecting customary law, provides fundamental guarantees for those detained and not otherwise protected. An example would be a member of a militia group

---

[28] GH Aldrich, 'The Taliban, al Qaeda, and the Determination of Illegal Combatants' (ICRC, 2002) www.icrc.org/eng/assets/files/other/george_aldrich_3_final.pdf, responding to 'Memorandum Opinion of the Counsel to the President: Status of Taliban Forces under Article 4 of the Third Geneva Convention of 1949' (Office of Legal Counsel, 2002) fas.org/irp/agency/doj/olc/taliban.pdf. It should be noted that Aldrich was one of the principal US negotiators of the Additional Protocols to the Geneva Conventions.

[29] eg *Public Prosecutor v Oie Hee Koi (and Associated Appeals)* (Judgment) AC 829 [1968]. The case concerned the POW status of fighters detained during the Malayan insurgency.

[30] GC III, Art 118.

[31] AP I, Art 45(1).

[32] This was the case of some of the Iraqis detained as POWs by the UK in 1991; see FJ Hampson, 'The Geneva Conventions and the Detention of Civilians and Alleged Prisoners of War' (1991) *Public Law* 507–22.

fighting on the side of a party to the conflict but not incorporated into its own armed forces and where the group does not satisfy the requirements to obtain combatant status.[33] It does not appear to provide the authority to detain but recognises that such detention may occur. Paragraph 3 of Article 75 requires that such detainees 'be released with the minimum delay possible and in any event as soon as the circumstances justifying the arrest, detention or internment have ceased to exist'. No further clarification is provided with regard to grounds of detention or review. Paragraph 6 provides that internees shall benefit from the protections of the article until their release or repatriation, whenever that occurs. The principal protection concerns humane treatments but there are also due-process guarantees, in the event of criminal proceedings being brought against them. As people who do not have the status of combatants, they do not benefit from immunity from criminal proceedings from the mere fact of having fought.

C. The Internment of Civilians

The internment of civilians is addressed in Geneva Convention IV. It may arise in two different situations. First, there may be individuals from belligerent state B in the territory of state A at the outbreak of hostilities. Examples from World War II include German refugees in the UK and persons of Japanese origin in the USA. It should be remembered that, at that time, Geneva Convention IV was not in existence. More recently, the UK was the only member of the coalition established in 1990 to remove Iraqi forces from Kuwait who claimed the need to detain Iraqis in the UK.[34] Some of them were indisputably combatants. Others were held as combatants (ie POWs) but denied that they were members of the armed forces of Iraq. Yet others were indisputably civilians, usually students. The second situation envisaged the internment of civilians in situations of occupation. The obvious example is the internment of civilians in the Occupied Palestinian Territories. The same situation arose in the immediate aftermath of the war against Iraq in 2003, until the establishment of an Iraqi government.

---

[33] For a militia group to qualify as combatants, they are required: '1. To be commanded by a person responsible for his subordinates; 2. To have a fixed distinctive emblem recognizable at a distance; 3. To carry arms openly; and 4. To conduct their operations in accordance with the laws and customs of war': see Hague Convention No IV Respecting the Laws and Customs of War on Land and its Annex: Regulations respecting the Laws and Customs of War on Land (adopted 18 October 1907, entered into force 26 January 1910) 36 Stat 2227 TS No 539 (Hague Convention IV) Art 1. The same requirements are reflected in GC III, Art 4 with regard to the circumstances in which a militia group may qualify for POW status. Where the group does not satisfy these requirements, the individual fighter is not a civilian but is also not a combatant.

[34] Hampson (n 32).

The internment regimes are broadly similar.[35] The authority to detain is found in IHL itself. The grounds are 'imperative reasons of security'. There is provision for review at least twice a year. The review mechanism envisaged is not necessarily a court but can be an administrative board. Where the reasons for internment no longer exist, the person must be released. Internment is seen as an extreme measure and not something to be applied to whole groups. This detention regime is based on the threat posed by the individual and not on his status as a civilian belonging to an opposing belligerent. An individual does not lose civilian status just because he participated in the hostilities.

In IACs, the authority to intern is provided by international law. There is no need for domestic authority, unlike the situation in a domestic emergency. International law also provides for at least some of the incidents of the internment regime.

D. Whether Human Rights Bodies Recognise the IHL Internment Regimes in IACs

Both the Working Group on Arbitrary Detention (WGAD) and the ECtHR have recognised the existence of the internment regime under IHL in the case of *international* armed conflicts. The WGAD's Basic Principles and Guidelines on Remedies and Procedures on the Right of Anyone Deprived of His or Her Liberty by Arrest or Detention to Bring Proceedings before Court address situations of armed conflict.[36] In the case of IACs, they generally follow the regime outlined above.[37] The ECtHR had to address the issue in the case of *Hassan v United Kingdom*, which concerned detention during the period of occupation in Iraq following the 2003 war.[38] The Court stated that it would only interpret the ECHR in the light of IHL if the respondent state invoked IHL. It would not do so *proprio motu*.[39] The Court allowed

---

[35] Geneva Convention IV Relative to the Protection of Civilian Persons in Time of War (adopted 12 August 1949, entered into force 21 October 1950) 75 UNTS 287 (GC IV) Arts 41–43 (aliens in the territory of a party to the conflict) and Art 78 (internees in occupied territory).

[36] UNGA, 'Basic Principles and Guidelines on Remedies and Procedures on the Right of Anyone Deprived of His or Her Liberty by Arrest or Detention to Bring Proceedings before Court' (4 May 2015) UN Doc WGAD/CRP.1/2015. Certain of the principles and guidelines are controversial.

[37] See generally ibid, principle 16, paras 45–50 and guideline 17, paras 112–15. One exception is the assertion of a right to bring legal proceedings where he seeks repatriation or transfer if seriously injured or ill (para 48). The detaining power is not under an *obligation* to effect such repatriation or transfer under IHL.

[38] *Hassan v United Kingdom* (App no 29750/09) ECHR 16 September 2014.

[39] ibid, para 107. The American Commission and Court of Human Rights have used Common Article 3 of the Geneva Conventions *proprio motu* to clarify the scope of the relevant human rights provision, rather than to displace it. It is not clear what attitudes other human

the UK to rely on IHL even though it had not derogated.[40] The Court accepted that the authority to intern and the grounds of detention were to be found in IHL. The Court, which appeared to proceed on the basis that Hassan was detained under Geneva Convention IV, said that review could be conducted by an administrative board, which needed to be as independent as possible. It is not clear whether the Court required review by such a body in all cases or only those falling within Geneva Convention IV.[41]

V. INTERNMENT IN NON-INTERNATIONAL ARMED CONFLICTS[42]

A NIAC can be fought between the state and an organised armed group (OAG) or between OAGs. In order to be an armed conflict, it is necessary that the OAG be sufficiently organised and the fighting be of sufficient intensity.[43] In that event, the situation will be regulated by common Article 3 of the Geneva Conventions. If the state has ratified Additional Protocol II of 1977 and if the fighting involves the state against one or more OAGs and if the OAGs can mount sustained and concerted military operations, the situation may also be regulated by the Protocol.[44] In other words, whilst all

rights bodies will take to the following questions: (i) whether a state has to invoke IHL before allowing it to rely on that body of rules; and (ii) whether the state has to derogate in order to rely on IHL and whether the answer is different in the case of IACs and NIACs.

[40] In *Hassan v United Kingdom* (n 38) para 104, the ECtHR suggested that a state cannot invoke IHL without derogating in a NIAC. It is not clear whether the Court had in mind only NIACs in national territory or all NIACs. It should be noted that the case itself only concerned an IAC.

[41] ibid, para 106. It is submitted that either there should be no requirement of review in the case of POWs or else the status determination process should be treated as the review and should only be necessary at the outset.

[42] See generally L Hill-Cawthorne, *Detention in Non-International Armed Conflict* (Oxford, Oxford University Press, 2016). See also J Pejic, 'Procedural Principles and Safeguards for Internment/Administrative Detention in Armed Conflict and Other Situations of Violence' (2005) 87 *International Review of the Red Cross* 375–91; Y Shany, 'A Human Rights Perspective to Battlefield Detention: Time to Reconsider Indefinite Detention' (2017) 93 *International Law Studies* 102 and 'The Future of US Detention under International Law: Workshop Report' (2017) 93 *International Law Studies* 272.

[43] The clarification as to what constitutes a NIAC is the product of the case law of the ICTY and the International Criminal Tribunal for Rwanda (ICTR). It appears to have obtained general acceptance, as reflected in the definition in Rome Statute of the International Criminal Court (adopted 17 July 1998, entered into force 1 July 2002) UN Doc A/CONF/183/9 (ICC Statute) Art 8(2)(f).

[44] AP II applies to armed conflicts not covered by AP I and 'which take place in the territory of a High Contracting Party between *its* armed forces and dissident armed forces or other organized armed groups which, under responsible command, exercise such control over a part of its territory as to enable them to carry out sustained and concerted military operations and to implement this Protocol'; see Protocol II Additional to the Geneva Conventions of 12 August 1949 and relating to the protection of Victims of Non-International Armed Conflicts (adopted 8 June 1977, entered into force 7 December 1978) 1125 UNTS 609 (AP II) Art 1 (emphasis added).

NIACs are regulated by common Article 3, only some are, in addition, regulated by Additional Protocol II. Furthermore, by virtue of its wording, the Protocol only applies to the territorial state and an OAG; it does not appear to apply to states intervening to assist the territorial state.[45]

A. NIACs in National Territory

It is very common for states to deny the applicability of IHL to a NIAC in national territory. They tend to describe the situation as either below the threshold of common Article 3 or as one involving criminal/terrorist activity. Examples include 'the Troubles' in Northern Ireland and the situation in eastern Turkey in the early 1990s. This does not prevent such states from derogating under the ECHR, as was the case of the two states cited. That is to say that the states claim there is an emergency but deny that it is an armed conflict. This means that, in their opinion, the situation is regulated by HRL, with the benefit of derogation. A derogation can only be made where the emergency 'threatens the life of the nation', which implies a significant degree of disruption to normal life.[46] A derogation enables a state to modify (not eliminate) some, but not all, of their human rights obligations.[47] The notice of derogation has to specify which parts of which articles are being modified and what is replacing the usual provision. The most common derogation seeks to permit the state to detain people for longer than usual before bringing them before a judicial authority. As already indicated, a state may seek to introduce internment but this is far from being routine. For a period during 'the Troubles', the UK introduced internment. In the inter-state case *Ireland v United Kingdom*, the ECtHR ruled that the UK could justify the policy.[48]

Where a state denies the applicability of IHL, it would seem to be improper for them to seek to rely on IHL rules before a human rights body. The body does, however, need to make it clear that it is taking no position on the de jure applicability of IHL. It is simply accepting that the state is willing to be judged by what is usually a higher standard of protection. Since the derogation has to be consistent with the state's other obligations, any prohibitions

---

[45] ibid; the significance of the phrase 'its armed forces'.

[46] UN Human Rights Committee, 'General Comment No 29: Derogations during a State of Emergency' (31 August 2001) UN Doc CCPR/C/21/Rev.1/Add.11; see also *Lawless v Ireland* (n 13) and *Ireland v UK* (n 4).

[47] UN HRC (n 46). The provision on detention is potentially derogable in all human rights treaties with a derogation clause.

[48] There is an important policy question with regard to the use of internment in national territory. It may act as a recruiting drum for the organised armed group. Whether it does so in fact may depend on the manner in which the policy is executed and the detainees are treated, rather than on the existence of the internment regime itself.

contained in IHL, such as the prohibition of discrimination, can be incorporated into the derogation.[49]

Where a state denies the applicability of IHL, the situation will be the same as during a national emergency. That is to say that internment provided for by national law will be compatible with HRL on condition that the state can and does derogate and that the state can establish the necessity of internment. The national law will need to define the grounds on which a person can be interned, to establish some form of review mechanism that will need to be as independent as possible and to ensure that a detainee will be released when the grounds are no longer satisfied. Whilst it is likely that some form of due process before the review mechanism will need to be ensured, the precise content of those guarantees in such a situation is not, as yet, clear.

Where a state admits the applicability of IHL, whether or not it has derogated, it may still need formally to invoke IHL in order to be able to rely on it.[50] It is possible that the state will be required to derogate under HRL in order to be able to invoke IHL in a NIAC.[51] It may be more advantageous for a state to rely on domestic emergency measures, even where it admits the applicability of IHL. The next subsection will consider the implications of relying on IHL in a NIAC before a human rights body.

B. NIACs Outside National Territory

NIACs outside national territory are not new, even though the level of concern appears to be of recent date.[52] Such a situation can arise where a state fights an OAG in the territory of another state[53] or where a state

---

[49] Under ECHR, Art 15 (the derogation clause), Art 14, which deals with discrimination, is potentially derogable. A state wishing to derogate from the provision would have to establish the need to discriminate, which would be difficult. Any derogation has to be in conformity with a state's other obligations. Common Article 3 of the Geneva Conventions prohibits any form of discrimination.

[50] *Hassan v United Kingdom* (n 38).

[51] ibid.

[52] For example, when the USA was involved in an armed conflict against the Vietcong, assisting the government of Vietnam, it was involved in a NIAC. That was also true of the Soviet Union assisting the government of Afghanistan. It is possible for there to be simultaneously IACs and NIACs, eg in the conflict between Georgia and Russia, there was simultaneously an IAC between Georgia and Russia and a NIAC between Georgia and the South Ossetian militia, unless the latter was under the effective/overall control of Russia.

[53] eg Israel against Hezbollah in Lebanon 2006. The classification of the conflict between those two parties is without prejudice to the question of whether there also existed an IAC between Israel and Lebanon. The lawfulness of the resort to force by Israel in Lebanon is a completely separate legal question. That is part of the *jus ad bellum*. The rules on the conduct of hostilities, including the rules on classification of conflicts, form part of the *jus in bello*. See generally, E Wilmshurst (ed), *International Law and the Classification of Conflicts* (Oxford, Oxford University Press, 2012).

assists another state in dealing with a NIAC in the territory of the latter.[54] The national law of most states, at least with regard to detention, does not apply outside the borders of the state. In other words, the only law a state is able to rely on as providing authority to intern is international law. The question then becomes whether international law authorises internment in NIACs, in the way it does in IACs. There are two possible sources of such authority: IHL or Security Council resolutions.

There is no reference in common Article 3 of the Geneva Conventions to internment. It requires that those in detention be treated humanely but says nothing about who can be detained. That is hardly surprising. At the time of the negotiation of the Geneva Conventions, it was assumed that 'armed conflict not of an international character' referred to conflicts within the borders of a state with no external involvement. In such a situation, the negotiators could assume that domestic law would provide the detention regimes, including the possibility of internment. Where one or more states are assisting the territorial state in dealing with a NIAC, it is possible that the latter will have domestic law on internment on which the intervening states can rely.[55] Even in such a situation, that does not resolve all difficulties. First, do the interveners have to hand over anyone detained so that he is interned by the national authorities or can they intern him themselves? Second, at least in the case of parties to the ECHR, can they derogate with regard to a situation outside national borders? Do they need to derogate themselves or can they rely on a derogation by the territorial state? What if the territorial state has not derogated? Is it necessary for both the intervening and the territorial state to have derogated?

It is possible that the territorial state has no domestic law on internment. That was the case in Afghanistan. In so far as internment is an exceptional measure, the territorial state may not during a time of armed conflict be able or willing to pass the necessary legislation. Where there is no domestic authority to intern, states are dependent on international authority. As shown above, common Article 3 does not appear to provide it.

Additional Protocol II has the merit of at least referring to internment. Article 5 of Additional Protocol II refers 'to persons deprived of their liberty for reasons related to the armed conflict, whether they are interned or detained'. It does not, however, provide authority to intern. It simply sets out how those who may be interned are to be treated. Furthermore, as already explained, Additional Protocol II does not appear to apply to an intervening state.

---

[54] Most recently, Iraq after the installation of an Iraqi government and Afghanistan after the installation of President Hamid Karzai.

[55] Since the basis on which the operation is undertaken is the consent of the territorial state, it is likely that that state will have to give those states assisting it express authority to rely on the former's authority to intern.

It should be noted that there is no combatant status in a NIAC. There is therefore no parallel with Geneva Convention III. This has significant implications for review and the end of detention. It will be recalled that only in the case of POWs is there no need for review, once the determination as to status has been made, because the detention is status based and not threat based. Similarly, only in the case of status-based detention can the basis for its termination be the end of active hostilities.

If there is no equivalent to the authority provided by Geneva Conventions III and IV in IACs, one may ask whether the authority is provided by necessary implication? Additional Protocol II does, after all, refer to internment. That seems to be insufficient.[56] Furthermore, it would not address the need to establish the other elements in an internment regime, such as grounds for internment and the review mechanism.

Another possibility is establishing that the authority exists under customary international humanitarian law applicable in NIACs. In order to establish a customary norm, it is necessary to show that the practice is followed by a large majority of states and that it is followed as a matter of legal obligation, not policy.[57] That is a real challenge in NIACs. Where domestic law provides for internment, is that state practice for international law purposes or only evidence of practice with regard to domestic law? Another difficulty is that the formula for establishing customary law works well with regard to prohibitions or obligations but is problematic in the case of permissive rules. No one suggests that states are obliged to intern. The question is whether they have permission or authority to do so.

It seems clear that there is a customary prohibition of arbitrary detention for all parties in all types of NIAC.[58] It is not clear whether that derives from HRL or IHL. That still begs the question whether internment is a form of arbitrary detention.[59] Customary law is not ideally suited to something as detailed and technical as an internment regime, requiring as it does not just a definition of the grounds of detention but other elements as well.

We are faced with something of a paradox. There is no doubt that internment may be necessary. It is clearly permitted in certain circumstances in emergencies that do not constitute armed conflicts. It is also permitted in IACs.

---

[56] Pejic (n 42); he suggests that internment is authorised by necessary implication. This view was rejected by the High Court in *Serdar Mohammed v Ministry of Defence* [2014] EWHC 1369 (QB); see detailed discussion below. See also D Murray, 'Non-State Armed Groups, Detention Authority in Non-International Armed Conflict, and the Coherence of International Law: Searching for a Way Forward' (2017) 30 *Leiden Journal of International Law* 2; response of KJ Heller, 'IHL Does Not Authorise Detention in NIAC: A Response to Murray' *Opinio Juris*, 22 March 2017; response of D Murray, 'Examining Detention Authority in NIAC: A Response to Heller' *Opinio Juris*, 3 April 2017.

[57] See n 11.

[58] Henckaerts and Doswald-Beck (n 24) r 99.

[59] See nn 16, 17.

The apparent gap in NIACs is not the result of opposition to the idea. After all, the state can use its domestic law to create an internment regime in a purely internal NIAC and that will be recognised by HRL. It simply did not occur to states, in 1949 or 1977, that it might be necessary to provide international authority for detention outside national borders in a NIAC. National and international courts may feel that it is not their role to invent a detention regime in NIACs, however clear it may be as to what it should provide. States need to reach agreement on the contents of an internment regime applicable in NIACs outside national borders. At the current time, however, states have shown a remarkable reluctance to assume new obligations in the field of IHL, even where that would give them authority to act.[60]

The issue has been addressed squarely by the English courts in the case of *Serdar Mohammed v the Ministry of Defence*. In the High Court, Leggatt J ruled that authority to intern in Afghanistan was not provided by English domestic law. It was also not provided by either IHL treaties or customary IHL applicable in NIACs.[61] The Court of Appeal, on the basis of somewhat different reasoning, agreed.[62] The Supreme Court was divided but a majority agreed with the conclusions of Leggatt J on the lack of authority provided by IHL.[63] Some of them expressed the view that customary law was moving in the necessary direction.

The ECtHR has not yet had to deal with alleged customary IHL rules on internment in a NIAC. The *Al-Jedda* case was argued on the basis of Security Council resolutions.[64] The *Hassan* case concerned detention regulated by the IHL rules applicable in an IAC.[65] The Working Group on Arbitrary Detention has suggested that, in NIACs, internment can only be justified if authorised by the law of the territory where the detention occurs. This implies that it does not think that it is authorised by customary IHL.[66]

The only other possible source of an authority to intern is a Security Council resolution, adopted under Chapter VII of the UN Charter. There can

---

[60] At the last Conference of the International Red Cross, states were unwilling to take forward initiatives which they had previously supported in the field of procedural guarantees in detention and securing compliance and better implementation of IHL. There is a genuine and well-founded fear that any attempt to negotiate new rules would risk calling into question well-established rules.

[61] *Serdar Mohammed v Ministry of Defence* (n 56).

[62] *Serdar Mohammed & ors v Secretary of State for Defence* [2015] EWCA Civ 843.

[63] *Abd Ali Hameed Al-Waheed (Appellant) v Ministry of Defence (Respondent)* and *Mohammed & ors (Respondent) v Ministry of Defence (Appellant)* [2017] UKSC 2. It should be noted that, unusually, the Supreme Court sat as a nine-bench court.

[64] *Al-Jedda v the United Kingdom* (App no 27021/08) ECHR 7 July 2011. See J Pejic, 'The European Court of Human Rights' *Al-Jedda* Judgment: The Oversight of International Humanitarian Law' (2011) 93 *International Review of the Red Cross* 837–51. Pejic criticises the Court for not taking account of IHL but the government did not at any point invoke IHL to justify detention. It relied exclusively on Security Council resolutions.

[65] *Hassan v United Kingdom* (n 38).

[66] UNGA (n 36) para 116.

be little doubt that in principle the Security Council *could* authorise internment and provide all the details of an internment regime. The question is rather whether it has in fact done so. Where an operation as a whole receives a UN mandate, whether or not it is a UN operation as such, it is usual for the resolution to provide that those authorised may use 'all necessary means' to achieve the goals in question. The first issue is whether that formula is sufficient to provide authority for internment. If so, the second question becomes whether that is enough or whether it is also necessary for the resolution to provide at least a framework for the internment regime?

No Security Council resolution has, to date, specified the grounds on which a person can be interned, the frequency of review, the nature of the review body or the procedural guarantees in such proceedings. This issue was also addressed in the *Serdar Mohammed* litigation. In the High Court, where judgment was given after that of the ECtHR in *Al-Jedda* but before that in the case of *Hassan v United Kingdom*, it was held that a Security Council resolution could not provide authority to detain for more than 96 hours.[67] The Court of Appeal determined that the authority to detain was given to ISAF, rather than individual states.[68] The detention had, therefore, to conform to ISAF policy, which was that no one could be detained for more than 96 hours. The Supreme Court was divided on the significance of a Security Council resolution.[69] Most of the nine judges thought that the 'all necessary means' formula did authorise detention; Lords Reed and Kerr dissented. This required the majority to distinguish the case of *Al-Jedda v UK* before the ECtHR, involving detention in Iraq under different Security Council resolutions. They appeared to think that *Hassan*, which was based exclusively on IHL, had implications for the significance of Security Council resolutions. A minority of the judges thought that authority to detain was only given to the ISAF, as a result of which any detention had to conform to ISAF policy. Arguably a bare majority of the judges stated that authority was given to both ISAF and national contingents. Seven of the judges thought that the resolutions authorised detention on grounds resembling 'imperative reasons of security', which is the formula used in Geneva Convention IV. They did not address the question of the review mechanism or procedural guarantees.

An important question is the attitude a human rights body is likely to take to an argument based on a Security Council resolution. This has been addressed by the ECtHR in the case of *Al-Jedda v UK*.[70] The reasoning of the Court is a little opaque. It might appear that the Court would only allow

---

[67] See n 56.
[68] *Serdar Mohammed & ors v Secretary of State for Defence* (n 62).
[69] See n 63.
[70] *Al-Jedda v the United Kingdom* (n 64).

the state to rely on the resolution if it *required* internment.[71] A state wants to be permitted, not required, to intern. This is to oversimplify the issue. The ECtHR will only allow a Security Council resolution to displace the ECHR where the state is *required* to give effect to the resolution. Under Article 103 of the UN Charter, resolutions under Chapter VII of the UN Charter prevail over conflicting obligations. There can only be a conflicting obligation if the resolution *requires* a state to do something that would be prohibited under HRL or *prohibits* it from doing something required under HRL. Where the resolution *permits* a state to take certain action, there is no conflicting *obligation*. The resolution therefore cannot prevail over conflicting human rights law obligations.[72] It is difficult to see how this reasoning would lead to a different result if the case of *Serdar Mohammed* reached the ECtHR, unless the Court adopted a different line of argument. It is not clear how the Human Rights Committee would handle an argument based on a Security Council resolution.[73]

The implications of allowing all Chapter VII resolutions of the Security Council to prevail over all other obligations under international law would be very wide ranging. It would destabilise international law generally, not merely HRL. It would, in effect, prioritise might over right. A much better solution would be for states to take steps to generate clear evidence of customary law in the field of internment in NIACs outside national territory.

VI. THE WAY FORWARD[74]

States have sought to address the challenge posed by the lack of clarity of the rules on internment in extraterritorial NIACs. Denmark initiated

---

[71] ibid, para 101. 'Before it can consider whether Article 103 had any application in the present case, the Court must determine whether there was a conflict between the United Kingdom's obligations under United Nations Security Council Resolution 1546 and its obligations under Article 5 § 1 of the Convention. In other words, the key question is whether Resolution 1546 placed the United Kingdom under an obligation to hold the applicant in internment.'

[72] It is clear from *Hassan v United Kingdom* (n 38) para 99 that this is a correct reading of para 101 of *Al-Jedda*.

[73] In *Sayadi and Vinck v Belgium* (2008) Human Rights Committee CCPR/C/94/D/1472/2006, the Human Rights Committee had to address the impact of a Chapter VII Security Council resolution in the context of a counter-terrorism sanctions process. Rather than addressing the direct impact of the resolution on the relevant human rights norms, it analysed the situation in relation to the intermediary state. The Committee was of the view that the case did not concern the Security Council resolution itself but the compliance of national measures adopted by Belgium (in implementation of the Security Council resolution) with its human rights obligations. Whether or not one agrees with the reasoning in the case, it is submitted that it offers little guidance on whether the Human Rights Committee would consider that the 'all necessary means' formula is sufficient to authorise internment in a NIAC.

[74] See ICRC, 'Strengthening IHL Protecting Persons Deprived of their Liberty in Relation to Armed Conflict' (1 April 2017) www.icrc.org/en/document/detention-non-international-armed-conflict-icrcs-work-strengthening-legal-protection-0. The document sets out the steps

an intergovernmental discussion, called the Copenhagen Process, which resulted in very general guidelines.[75] They are too general to meet the need. On the assumption that there is a broad area of agreement as to the relevant elements of an internment regime and as to the content of those elements, mechanisms exist that could assist in the articulation of standards that could be found to represent customary law. It might be possible to obtain a non-binding UN General Assembly resolution in which states set out the contents of an internment regime in NIACs. At the regional level, the Steering Committee for Human Rights of the Council of Europe, a body composed of the representatives of states, could undertake a study. On the basis of its results, it could propose the adoption of a resolution by the Committee of Ministers, which would set out the contents of an internment regime in NIACs and confirm that they represented customary law. This would not bind the ECtHR but would afford it useful guidance. It would confirm that states are entitled, under customary IHL applicable in NIACs, to introduce an internment regime. Internment would be on the grounds of imperative reasons of security. The review mechanism would not need to be a court but would need to be as independent as possible. Those dealing with a case would need to be outside the chain of command of those responsible for the detention. Review of the need for internment would need to take place at least four times a year. Certain procedural guarantees would need to be identified but the precise contents of the guarantee would probably need to allow for considerable flexibility.[76] The current lack of precision in the rules is not fundamentally due to disagreement but to an accident of history.

---

taken since the Concluding Report; 'Strengthening International Humanitarian Law Protecting Persons Deprived of their Liberty' (Concluding Report of the 32nd International Conference of the Red Cross and Red Crescent, Geneva, October 2015) EN 32IC/15/19.1. States have rejected the idea of legally binding norms in this field and want the process to be in the hands of states as well as the ICRC.

[75] 'The Copenhagen Process Principles and Guidelines on the Handling of Detainees in International Military Operations', um.dk/en/~/media/UM/English-site/Documents/Politics-and-diplomacy/Copenhangen%20Process%20Principles%20and%20Guidelines.pdf; see also B Oswald and T Winkler, 'Copenhagen Process Principles and Guidelines on the Handling of Detainees in International Military Operations' (2012) 16 *ASIL Insights* 39; and J Hartmann, 'The Copenhagen Process: Principles and Guidelines' (2013) 16 *Yearbook of International Humanitarian Law* 3–32.

[76] Pejic (n 42).

7

The Crime of Rape in Military and Civilian Jurisdictions

LOIS MOORE AND CHRISTINE CHINKIN[1]

I. INTRODUCTION

INTERNATIONAL LAW SEEKS to protect civilians from rape and sexual violence in time of war through three complementary treaty regimes: through the rules and regulations that make up IHL (or the laws of war), effectively including a code of conduct for the military in the field during armed conflict and occupation; through international criminal law (ICL), which addresses individual criminal responsibility for the commission of the most serious such crimes; and through international human rights law (IHRL), which recognises gender-based violence against women[2] as violations of human rights.[3] These treaty regimes are supplemented by a customary international law prohibition of sexual violence[4] and by UN Security Council thematic resolutions on the protection of civilians in armed conflict, the protection of children in armed conflict and the Women, Peace and Security agenda. The substantive legal principles form the basis for prosecutions in international courts and, as incorporated into national legal systems,[5] in national courts.

International law of course regulates state behaviour; one of the challenges is the transposition from state obligation to criminal responsibility of

---

[1] The authors thank Dr Arimatsu for her helpful comments and suggestions.

[2] UN Committee on the Elimination of Discrimination against Women (UNCEDAW), General Recommendation No 19 'Violence against Women' (1992) UN Doc A/47/38.

[3] See especially Vienna Declaration and Programme of Action (25 June 1993) UN Doc A/CONF.157/23, para 38; Beijing Declaration and Platform of Action: Fourth World Conference on Women (4–15 September 1995) UN Doc A/CONF.177/20 and A/CONF.177/20/Add.1, paras 112–30.

[4] ICRC, 'Customary International Human Rights Law, Rule 93: Rape and Other Forms of Sexual Violence', www.icrc.org/customary-ihl/eng/docs/v1_rul_rule93.

[5] Either directly in so-called monist legal systems or through legislative action in dualist systems: J Crawford, *Brownlie's Principles of Public International Law*, 8th edn (Oxford, Oxford University Press, 2012) 48–50.

individual perpetrators, or those under whose authority they act. This is further complicated by the wide array of actors who commit sexual violence in conflict and are subject to different legal regimes. Perpetrators may include members of the regular armed forces, both those of the state where the act is committed and those of other states operating in the conflict-affected territory; civilians attached to state armed forces such as security contractors; UN peacekeepers;[6] members of irregular and rebel armed forces, who may or may not have an internal system of military discipline and respect for IHL; terrorist groups and even criminal gangs,[7] all of whom are unlikely to have any respect for IHL or IHRL in their operations; and civilians. With respect to the last, instances of rape and other forms of sexual violence committed by civilians (eg partners, family members) increase during conflict,[8] due perhaps to the general breakdown of law and order, to the tensions created by the violence, and to the impunity with which rape is being committed in the course of or as part of the conflict itself.

This chapter considers the implementation of IHL and ICL in national military and civilian criminal jurisdictions and addresses the question of how sexual violence should be prosecuted at the national level, which is essential if impunity for such crimes is to be addressed. It also examines the implications of states' IHRL obligations with respect to their approach to national implementation of IHL and ICL. In sum, it seeks to answer two key questions. First, should national military justice systems continue to have a role in prosecuting rape and sexual offences committed by military personnel and/or others in conflict, or should national civilian criminal justice systems take precedence? Second, should national criminal justice systems prosecute rape and sexual violence as war crimes and crimes against humanity, or as 'ordinary' domestic crimes? And how should rape and sexual violence be defined for these purposes?

The chapter concludes that national military justice systems are, generally speaking, inappropriate for prosecuting sexual violence in conflict; primary responsibility should rest with national civilian criminal authorities. There are real advantages in national prosecutions of sexual violence in conflict being made on the basis of war crimes and crimes against humanity, not least the increased stigma that may attach to a conviction for these crimes over that for sexual violence under ordinary national laws. However,

---

[6] UN peacekeepers are subject to specific regulation, which is outside the scope of this chapter.

[7] M Kaldor, *New and Old Wars: Organised Violence in a Global Era*, 3rd edn (Cambridge, Polity Press, 2012) 9–10.

[8] 'Conflicts exacerbate existing gender inequalities, placing women at a heightened risk of various forms of gender-based violence by both State and non-State actors.' UNCEDAW, General Recommendation No 30: 'Women in Conflict Prevention, Conflict and Post-Conflict Situations' (18 October 2013) UN Doc CEDAW/C/GC/30, para 34; Human Security Research Group, 'Human Security Report 2012' (Human Security Press, 2012) 33–37.

careful scrutiny is required to ensure that domestic legislation adequately incorporates the gender justice aspects of ICL as most recently reflected in the practice of the ICC.[9] International and regional human rights law also has an important role to play in clarifying and monitoring states' responsibility for addressing impunity for, and thus protection against, sexual violence in conflict. However, this complex network of legal regulation accords only limited protection against conflict-related sexual violence; despite the UN Security Council's exhortations, legislative, social and practical obstacles together with lack of political will all combine to deny adequate protection against such offences.

II. INTERNATIONAL CRIMINAL FRAMEWORK

A. International Conventions and Custom

Contemporary prohibitions of rape and sexual violence in armed conflict build upon a long history, from early warrior codes, military codes and manuals,[10] and, from the turn of the twentieth century, international agreements.[11] In tracing this history, Patricia Sellers has argued that the purpose of such early prohibitions was not to protect the civilian population per se but rather to serve during conflict 'as a means to guarantee continued economic productivity, and also to preserve a society as a unified political entity'.[12] The way in which war was waged was considered a matter for military discipline and reciprocity between the formal armed forces of states; protection of civilians, let alone prohibiting rape, was not the principal concern.

The 1949 Geneva Convention IV, the first international treaty exclusively devoted to the protection of civilians in time of international and non-international armed conflicts (IACs and NIACs respectively), expressly

---

[9] Office of the Prosecutor of the International Criminal Court, 'Policy Paper on Sexual and Gender-Based Crimes' (2014) www.icc-cpi.int/iccdocs/otp/OTP-Policy-Paper-on-Sexual-and-Gender-Based-Crimes--June-2014.pdf.

[10] Lieber Code: Instructions for the Government of Armies of the United States in the Field General Order No 100 (24 April 1863) Art 44. Interestingly, the penalty for rape was death.

[11] Hague Convention No IV Respecting the Laws and Customs of War on Land and its annex: Regulations Concerning the Laws and Customs of War on Land (adopted 18 October 1907, entered into force 26 January 1910) 36 Stat 2227 TS No 539 (Hague Convention IV) Arts 23, 25. Pursuant to Art 46, 'family honour and rights' must be respected in occupied territory. The 1899 Hague Convention II has the same provisions: Hague Convention No II with Respect to the Laws and Customs of War on Land and its Annex: Regulations Concerning the Laws and Customs of War on Land (adopted 29 July 1899, entered into force 4 September 1900) 32 Stat 1803 TS No 403 (Hague Convention II) Art 46.

[12] P Viseur Sellers, 'The Prosecution of Sexual Violence in Conflict: The Importance of Human Rights as Means of Interpretation' (UN Human Rights Commission, 2009) 6, www.ohchr.org/Documents/Issues/Women/WRGS/Paper_Prosecution_of_Sexual_Violence.pdf.

protects women against 'any attack on their honour'—rape, enforced prostitution and indecent assault.[13] This is not the language of prohibition,
although this is how the provision is now understood; nor did it spell out
where the responsibility for such protection lay. In NIACs 'outrages upon
personal dignity, in particular humiliating and degrading treatment' were
prohibited at any time and in any place.[14]

The establishment of the International Criminal Tribunal for the Former
Yugoslavia (ICTY) in 1993 and the International Criminal Tribunal for
Rwanda (ICTR) in 1994, followed by the various hybrid tribunals, fur-
thered international prohibitions of sexual violence and the framework for
their criminal prosecution. The jurisprudence developed by these tribunals,
the experience of actors focused on bringing gender issues to their consideration[15] and lobbying by women's organisations all contributed to international acceptance of the need for a permanent international criminal court
to prosecute the most serious violations of IHL. The ICC Statute, adopted in
1998,[16] provides the most forward-thinking (and feminist) approach to the
prosecution of sexual violence in conflict, and makes a number of significant
improvements to the legal protection of civilians from rape in conflict.[17] It
has a wider scope of application, covering both IACs and NIACs as well as
crimes against humanity committed outside of an armed conflict. It has a
modern definition of rape,[18] a significant expansion of the concept of other
types of sexual violence,[19] and important protections for victims and witnesses.[20] And it has enhanced the status of rape and sexual violence in the
pantheon of international crimes, by making them war crimes, violations
of the laws and customs of war, and crimes against humanity in their own
right. They are now understood as serious violations of bodily integrity and
sexual autonomy.[21]

---

[13] Geneva Convention IV Relative to the Protection of Civilian Persons in Time of War
(adopted 12 August 1949, entered into force 21 October 1950) 75 UNTS 287 (GC IV) Art 27.
[14] ibid, Art 3 (Common Article 3).
[15] S Brammertz and M Jarvis, *Prosecuting Conflict-Related Sexual Violence at the ICTY*
(Oxford, Oxford University Press, 2016).
[16] Rome Statute of the International Criminal Court (adopted 17 July 1998, entered into
force 1 July 2002) UN Doc A/CONF 183/9 (ICC Statute).
[17] Such protections apply to all victims of sexual violence; the UN Security Council recognises that sexual violence in armed conflict also affects men and boys: UNSC Res 2106
(24 June 2013) UN Doc S/RES/2106. UNCEDAW, General Recommendation No 30 (n 8)
para 20, states that: 'Under international humanitarian law, women affected by armed conflicts
are entitled to general protections that apply to both women and men.'
[18] ICC, Elements of Crimes (2002) UN Doc ICC-ASP/1/3, 108 (Elements of Crime)
Arts 7(1)(g)-1, 8(2)(b)(xxii)-1.
[19] 'Rape, sexual slavery, enforced prostitution, forced pregnancy, enforced sterilization' or
any other form of serious sexual violence are designated as crimes against humanity and war
crimes: ICC Statute, Arts 7(1)(g), 8(2)(e)(vi).
[20] ICC, Rules of Procedure and Evidence (2002) UN Doc ICC-ASP/1/3, 156 (Rules of Procedure) rr 70–72.
[21] '[T]he crime of rape ... constitutes a violation of women's right to personal security,
autonomy and bodily integrity.' *RPB v the Philippines* (2014) Committee on the Elimination

Alongside IHL and ICL, IHRL also prohibits sexual violence in the context of armed conflict. States' human rights obligations include the duty of due diligence, requiring: an effective criminal justice system to be established and implemented[22] for protection against sexual violence; the investigation, prosecution and punishment of perpetrators (both state actors and non-state actors) of human rights violations including sexual violence; an independent and impartial judicial system, including any military judicial system; and the necessary criminal legislation prohibiting sexual violence in conflict and in peace, including a definition of rape which avoids gender stereotypes. International and regional human rights law has also, for some time now, recognised the need to remove prosecution of crimes that constitute serious human rights violations from military justice systems.[23]

B. Enforcement of IHL and ICL

The overlapping systems of IHL and ICL, combined with enforcement mechanisms at both the international and national levels, result in a complex, multilayered enforcement regime for prohibitions on sexual violence in conflict.

Geneva Convention IV requires states to enact the necessary domestic legislation to enable them to prosecute grave breaches, actively search for offenders, and either prosecute them before their own courts, or extradite them to another state that will do so.[24] Perhaps not surprisingly, given its historic context, Geneva Convention IV does not expressly include rape as a grave breach;[25] nor does Additional Protocol I, nearly thirty years later.[26] In the case of other breaches, a state's obligation is limited to taking all necessary measures for their suppression.[27] There is no express obligation

of Discrimination against Women, CEDAW/C/57/D/34/2011, para 8.10; *Prosecutor v Kunarac et al* ICTY-96-23-T and IT-96-23/1-T (22 February 2001), para 457.

[22] UNCEDAW has stated that having a system in place to address the problem is insufficient: '[I]t must be supported by State actors, who adhere to the State party's due diligence obligations.' *Fatma Yildirim (deceased) v Austria* (2007) Committee on the Elimination of Discrimination against Women, CEDAW/C/39/D/6/2005, para 12.1.2; *Şahide Goecke v Austria* (2007) Committee on the Elimination of Discrimination against Women, CEDAW/C/39/D/5/2005, para 12.1.2.

[23] L Joinet, 'Issue of the Administration of Justice through Military Tribunals' (2002) UN Doc E/CN.4/Sub.2/2002/4.

[24] GC IV, Art 146.

[25] ibid, Art 147.

[26] Protocol I Additional to the Geneva Conventions of 12 August 1949 and relating to the Protection of Victims of International Armed Conflicts (adopted 8 June 1977, entered into force 7 December 1978) 1125 UNTS 3 (AP I) Art 85.

[27] GC IV, Art 146.

to have a legislative framework, and no concept of universal jurisdiction with respect to such non-grave breaches. Further, since rape and other types of sexual violence are not defined in Geneva Convention IV, each High Contracting Party was free to apply its own definitions and prosecution practice. This undoubtedly would have included many sexual stereotypes, such as the need for physical resistance by the victim, or proof of her chastity. Penile vaginal penetration was the principal actus reus of rape, discounting the other forms of physical invasion which have been practised in armed conflict settings. And the possibility of the rape of men and boys was not contemplated as a breach of IHL.[28]

States parties to the ICC Statute have reserved for themselves primary responsibility for prosecuting war crimes and crimes against humanity, under the principle of 'complementarity'. The ICC's jurisdiction is 'limited to the most serious crimes of concern to the international community as a whole'.[29] A case that has met the seriousness threshold (as determined by the ICC Prosecutor) is admissible before the ICC unless: it is being investigated or prosecuted by a state; that state is unwilling or unable genuinely to carry out the investigation or prosecution; or it is not of sufficient gravity to warrant further action by the ICC.[30] Any alleged rape as a war crime or crime against humanity that does not meet this seriousness threshold is exclusively within the jurisdiction of the relevant states parties. It will be for the state to determine whether any such case is prosecuted, and if so whether there is military or civilian jurisdiction; there is no requirement one way or the other in the ICC Statute.

The ICC alone (even in conjunction with other international criminal tribunals) is not able to end impunity for sexual violence in conflict. The Court's capacity to bring perpetrators to justice is limited due to resource constraints, its jurisdictional boundaries and its role as a court of last resort.[31] If impunity for rape and sexual violence in conflict is to be effectively addressed and thus protection of civilians enhanced, states must implement the responsibility they have reserved for themselves for investigation, prosecution and punishment of international crimes and give effect to their IHRL obligations.

---

[28] GC IV, Art 27 is gender-specific: 'Women shall be especially protected ... in particular against rape.' On rape and sexual violence against men, see S Sivakumaran, 'Sexual Violence against Men in Armed Conflict' (2007) 18 *European Journal of International Law* 2, 253.

[29] ICC Statute, Art 5(1).

[30] ibid, Art 17.

[31] R Grey, 'Sexual Violence against Child Soldiers' (2014) 16 *International Feminist Journal of Politics* 4, 601, 602–03.

C. Domestic Implementation of IHL and ICL

This concurrent applicability of ICL and IHL, together with both military and civilian justice systems at the national level, creates some complexity in determining how rape and sexual violence should be treated in national jurisdictions. The national implementation framework could include: domestic legislation, granting national courts jurisdiction to prosecute grave and other breaches of the Geneva Conventions, including those relating to rape and sexual violence, often dating from the 1950s; incorporation of ICC Statute provisions by granting national courts jurisdiction to prosecute rape and sexual violence as war crimes and crimes against humanity, usually enacted after 2000; and finally criminalisation of rape and sexual violence, in both civilian and military law, which would be relevant in peacetime as well as war. The last could date from any time, but there is some evidence that domestic criminal sexual violence laws are being updated post-2000.[32] National prosecutors may prefer to prosecute rape and sexual violence in conflict, not as international crimes, but under 'ordinary' domestic criminal law, making these laws equally relevant to prosecutions of these crimes committed during conflict.

In practice, in execution of their obligation to enforce the Geneva Conventions under national law, states have, by and large, included Geneva Convention IV provisions on rape in their military manuals and laws of armed conflict, often directly repeating their language.[33] Military manuals and laws of armed conflict generally apply to serving military personnel of state armed forces, whether conduct is committed in the home jurisdiction or during military operations abroad. States have also incorporated the Geneva Convention IV prohibition on rape into their domestic criminal law applicable to civilians (nationals or non-nationals), who could be tried in the ordinary civilian criminal courts.[34] Despite legislative efforts, there is little evidence that states have been active in prosecuting grave, or indeed any, breaches of the Geneva Conventions, either within their military justice

---

[32] F Ni Aolain, 'Gendered Harms and their Interface with International Criminal Law' (2014) 16 *International Feminist Journal of Politics* 4, 622.

[33] ICRC, 'Practice Relating to Rule 93: Rape and Other Forms of Sexual Violence' Part III, www.icrc.org/customary-ihl/eng/docs/v2_rul_rule93; ICRC, 'Customary Law Study, Practice Relating to Rule 156. Definition of War Crimes' Part III, Military Manuals, www.icrc.org/customary-ihl/eng/docs/v2_rul_rule156#_IIMiMa.

[34] ICRC, 'Practice Relating to Rule 93: Rape and Other Forms of Sexual Violence' Part IV, www.icrc.org/customary-ihl/eng/docs/v2_rul_rule93; ICRC, 'Customary Law Study, Practice Relating to Rule 156. Definition of War Crimes' Part IV, www.icrc.org/customary-ihl/eng/docs/v2_rul_rule156#_IIMiMa; ICRC, 'National Implementation of IHL', www.icrc.org/applic/ihl/ihl-nat.nsf/vwLawsByCountry.xsp.

systems or otherwise.[35] Indeed, the UK Ministry of Justice has confirmed that there have been no prosecutions under the Geneva Conventions Act 1957, the legislation that brought breaches of Geneva Convention IV into English law.[36]

There is no express requirement in the ICC Statute for states parties to incorporate into their domestic criminal legislation or military codes the ability to prosecute sexual violence as international crimes. However, the UN Security Council has urged Member States to 'include the full range of crimes of sexual violence in national penal legislation to enable prosecutions for rape and sexual violence in armed conflict'.[37] States also have a clear IHRL duty to put in place the necessary legislative provisions to enable them effectively to prevent and punish rape and sexual violence against women in conflict situations, and to implement such legislation.[38] Some of the legislative approaches taken by states in implementing the ICC Statute are discussed further below.

III. MILITARY v CIVILIAN CRIMINAL JURISDICTION

Neither IHL nor ICL specifies whether sexual violence in conflict by members of state armed forces or others should be prosecuted by national military or civilian courts.[39] Where the accused is a member of state armed forces,[40] states have the choice between exercising their jurisdiction over rape and sexual violence committed in conflict in military or civilian criminal courts. Military courts may also be authorised to prosecute any alleged

---

[35] NN Jurdi, *The International Criminal Court and National Courts: A Contentious Relationship* (Farnham, Ashgate Publishing, 2011) 1–2; JK Kleffner, *Complementarity in the Rome Statute and National Criminal Jurisdictions* (Oxford, Oxford University Press, 2008) 33–38.

[36] Ministry of Justice, 'Closing the Impunity Gap: UK Law on Genocide and Redress for Torture Victims' (2009) www.publications.parliament.uk/pa/jt200809/jtselect/jtrights/153/153we10.htm, para 3.

[37] UNSC Res 2106 (n 17) para 2. See also UN Human Rights Council Res 23/25, 'Accelerating Efforts to Eliminate All Forms of Violence against Women: Preventing and Responding to Rape and other Forms of Sexual Violence' (2013) UN Doc A/HRC/RES/23/25, para 7; African Commission on Human and Peoples' Rights, Resolution 283: Resolution on the Situation of Women and Children in Armed Conflict (2014) www.achpr.org/sessions/55th/resolutions/283/, para 1.

[38] UNCEDAW, General Recommendation No 30 (n 8) para 15.

[39] Only the Declaration on the Protection of All Persons from Enforced Disappearance and the Inter-American Convention on Forced Disappearance of Persons restrict the use of military justice for gross human rights violations. F Andreu-Guzman, *Military Jurisdiction and International Law: Military Courts and Gross Human Rights Violations* (Geneva, International Commission of Jurists, 2004) 12, 17.

[40] Geneva Convention III Relative to the Treatment of Prisoners of War (adopted 12 August 1949, entered into force 21 October 1950) 75 UNTS 135 (GC III) Art 4, determines who is a member of the state's armed forces for the purposes of defining prisoner of war status.

violation of international law, whether or not the accused is a member of the military.[41]

A. Role of Military Justice in Enforcement of IHL

At the end of World War II, international prosecutions for war crimes and crimes against humanity were undertaken in military tribunals—notably the Nuremburg Military Tribunal, the Tokyo Military Tribunal and trials in national jurisdictions.[42] However by the time of the ICTY and ICTR, reliance on military justice to ensure compliance with IHL was falling out of favour, so that neither of those tribunals, nor any of the hybrid tribunals which followed them, were constituted as military courts. Among the factors that have contributed to this change in attitude towards military justice systems as the preferred enforcement mechanism for IHL is the change in the nature of warfare during the latter half of the twentieth century, with a move away from international armed conflicts between states' armed forces to conflicts of national liberation and to what have been termed 'new wars'. Crimes against civilian populations—the paradigmatic nature of violence in new wars[43]—as crimes against humanity have been decoupled from IAC and NIAC and there has been an increasing recognition by the international community of the need for their prosecution to combat impunity.[44] Military tribunals were discredited because of their use by Latin American military dictatorships in the 1980s to shield government officials and military commanders from liability, whilst prosecuting civilians in a forum that lacked any concept of a fair trial and due process. Military courts generally appeared unwilling to prosecute soldiers for breaches of IHL, whether related to sexual violence or not. Military offenders were treated leniently, with enlisted soldiers, rather than officers, bearing the brunt of any prosecutions, despite most military justice systems recognising the concept of command responsibility. Failure by military justice systems to prosecute under command responsibility undermines the incentive on superior officers to

---

[41] The DRC is an example of military courts which had exclusive jurisdiction over war crimes and crimes against humanity committed by the state military and police as well as by combatants in non-state armed groups. Such jurisdiction has now been moved to civilian courts, by the adoption of legislation implementing the ICC Statute in January 2016.

[42] D Plesch, S Sa'Couto and C Lasco, 'The Relevance of the United Nations War Crimes Commission to the Prosecution of Sexual and Gender-Based Crimes Today' (2014) 25 *Criminal Law Forum* 349.

[43] C Chinkin and M Kaldor, 'Gender and New Wars' (2013) 67 *Journal of International Affairs* 1, 173; see also C Chinkin and M Kaldor, *International Law and New Wars* (Cambridge, Cambridge University Press, 2017) 11–13.

[44] SD Murphy, 'New Mechanisms for Punishing Atrocities in Non-International Armed Conflicts' (2015) 16 *Melbourne Journal of International Law* 298.

ensure compliance with IHL, thus detracting from its effectiveness in protecting civilians from sexual violence in conflict.

B. IHRL Obligations Regarding Military Courts

The Geneva Convention III judicial guarantees for POWs captured in the context of an IAC[45] are conferred on members of state armed forces and those accompanying them, and members of other militias or volunteer corps provided they meet certain criteria.[46] Contemporary non-state armed groups are unlikely to meet these criteria, and in any event are unlikely to be operating totally in an IAC. The requirement of Common Article 3 to provide trials by regularly constituted courts 'affording all the judicial guarantees which are recognized as indispensable by civilized peoples'[47] is applicable in NIAC. Common Article 3 establishes basic fair trial obligations on both military and civilian courts in a NIAC, whether operated by a state party or a non-state party to the conflict.

IHRL requires states to ensure that persons accused of criminal offences receive a fair and public hearing by a competent, independent and impartial tribunal established by law. This fundamental right is guaranteed in international and regional[48] treaties, most notably Article 14 of the ICCPR,[49] and applies equally to military and civilian court systems.[50] It provides protection for military defendants as much as for civilian defendants. But military courts do not always comply with IHRL standards,[51] in particular because they may lack independence and impartiality since they operate within the chain of command, and without adequate guarantees of independence. In 2006 the UN Commission for Human Rights endorsed Draft Principles

---

[45] GC III, Arts 99–108.

[46] ibid, Art 4.

[47] Common Article 3(1)(d); see also Protocol II Additional to the Geneva Conventions of 12 August 1949 and relating to the Protection of Victims of Non-International Armed Conflicts (adopted 8 June 1977, entered into force 7 December 1978) 1125 UNTS 609 (AP II) Art 6.

[48] European Convention for the Protection of Human Rights and Fundamental Freedoms (as amended by Protocols Nos 11 and 14, 4 November 1950) ETS 5 (ECHR) Art 6; Charter of Fundamental Rights of the European Union (adopted 2 October 2000, entered into force 26 October 2012) OJ C83/02, Arts 47, 48; American Declaration on the Rights and Duties of Man (entered into force April 1948) OAS Res XXX, Arts XVIII, XXVI; American Convention on Human Rights (adopted 22 November 1969, entered into force 18 July 1978) OAS TS No 36 (ACHR) Arts 8, 25; African Charter on Human and Peoples' Rights (adopted 27 June 1981, entered into force 21 October 1986) CAB/LEG/67/3 rev. 5, 21 I.L.M. 58 (ACHPR) Arts 7, 26.

[49] International Covenant on Civil and Political Rights (adopted 19 December 1966, entered into force 23 March 1976) 999 UNTS 171 (ICCPR).

[50] UN Human Rights Committee, General Comment No 32 'Article 14: Right to Equality before Courts and Tribunals and to a Fair Trial' (2007) UN Doc CCPR/C/GC/32 para 22.

[51] Andreu-Guzman (n 39) 10.

Governing the Administration of Justice through Military Tribunals (the Decaux Principles), which provide 'a minimum system of universally applicable rules'.[52] Both the Inter-American Court of Human Rights (IACtHR)[53] and the European Court of Human Rights (ECtHR)[54] have held that the failure of military courts to comply with the human rights standards of fair trials and due process constitutes a violation of their respective Conventions. The African Commission on Human and Peoples' Rights (ACHPR) has issued guidelines on the right to a fair trial in Africa, the provisions of which are fully applicable to military courts.[55] '[H]uman rights standards and principles relating to the administration of justice ... fully apply to military courts.'[56]

C. Jurisdiction of Military Courts

Two issues relevant to rape and sexual violence in conflict arise from the international and regional legal frameworks: personal jurisdiction and subject matter jurisdiction.

With respect to personal jurisdiction, a number of human rights instruments specify that military trials of civilians should be avoided.[57] For instance, the UN Human Rights Committee's view is that trials of civilians by military courts should be exceptional, limited to cases where such trials are necessary, justified by objective and serious reasons, and where the civilian courts are unable to undertake the particular trial.[58] This view is supported by the Special Rapporteur on the independence and impartiality of Judges and Lawyers[59] and by the Inter-American Commission and Court on Human Rights, the ECtHR, the Council of Europe and the ACHPR.[60]

[52] E Decaux, 'Issue of the Administration of Justice through Military Tribunals' (2006) UN Doc E/CN.4/2006/58 2 (Decaux Principles).

[53] *Palamara Iribarne v Chile* (Merits, Reparations and Costs) Inter-American Court of Human Rights Series C No 135 (22 November 2005) paras 256–57, 269(14)–(15); *Castillo Petruzzi et al v Peru* (Merits, Reparations and Costs) Inter-American Court of Human Rights Series C No 52 (30 May 1999) paras 221–222. See Andreu-Guzman (n 39) 113–21; Inter-American Commission on Human Rights (IACHR), 'Right to Truth in the Americas' (2014) OEA/Ser.L/V/II.152, paras 102–06.

[54] *Ergin v Turkey* (No 6) (2008) 47 EHRR 36, para 54 (also approving the Decaux Principles (n 52) para 24); *Martin v UK* (App 40426/98) ECHR 24 October 2006, paras 41, 51.

[55] ACHPR, 'Principles and Guidelines on the Right to a Fair Trial and Legal Assistance in Africa' (2003) DOC/OS(XXX)247, para L.

[56] G Knaul, 'Report of the Special Rapporteur on the Independence of Judges and Lawyers' (2013) UN Doc A/68/285, para 17.

[57] See eg D Orentlicher, 'Updated Set of Principles for the Protection and Promotion of Human Rights through Action to Combat Impunity' (2005) UN Doc E/CN.4/2005/102/Add.1, pr 29; ACHPR, 'Principles and Guidelines' (n 55) para L(c)); 'Report of the Working Group on Arbitrary Detention' (1999) UN Doc E/CN.4/2000/4, paras 67, 68.

[58] UN HRC, 'General Comment No 32' (n 50) para 22.

[59] Knaul (n 56) paras 100–05.

[60] IACHR, 'Right to Truth' (n 53) para 103; *Durand and Ugarte v Peru* (Merits) Inter-American Court of Human Rights Series C No 68 (16 August 2000) para 117; *Ergin v Turkey*

Several arguments are made that this blanket prohibition of military court jurisdiction over civilians may be inappropriate. For instance, non-military individuals attached to military forces operating outside of their home territory—dependants of military personnel and contractors—may be more appropriately tried in military courts in their home jurisdiction.[61] The more important debate in this context centres on the status of fighters, members of irregular non-state armed groups, significant perpetrators of rape and sexual violence.[62] In wars of national liberation in Africa and Asia, and in the military dictatorships in Latin America, some military justice systems prosecuted not only regular soldiers but also members of irregular forces who were taking part in combat activities, but were not state military personnel.[63]

In an IAC under IHL, the basic distinction is between combatants—members of regular state armed forces who operate within a system of military discipline and enjoy combatants' privilege[64]—and civilians—those taking no part in hostilities and who enjoy protections.[65] Irregular forces and groups, who are not combatants and do not enjoy combatants' immunity, but who are also not subject to civilian protections whilst engaging in hostilities, do not fit neatly into either of these categories, and it seems counterintuitive to regard them as civilians for the purposes of determining which courts should have jurisdiction over them. IHRL does not expressly indicate whether such persons should be treated as civilians or non-civilians for the purposes of determining whether they should be prosecuted for criminal offences in military courts, but the inference is that anyone other than serving members of a regular state armed force should be prosecuted outside of the military justice system.

In the United States, members of al-Qaeda and the Taliban were treated as unlawful enemy combatants and were made subject to the jurisdiction of

---

(n 54) paras 42–49; Council of Europe/European Court of Human Rights, 'Guide on Article 6 of the European Convention on Human Rights: Right to a Fair Trial (Criminal Limb)' (2014) www.echr.coe.int/Documents/Guide_Art_6_criminal_ENG.pdf, paras 83-86; ACHPR, 'Principles and Guidelines' (n 55) para L.

[61] DE Stigall, 'An Unnecessary Convenience: the Assertion of the Uniform Code of Military Justice ("UCMJ") over Civilians and the Implications of International Human Rights Law' (2009) 17 *Cardozo Journal of International and Comparative Law* 59; M Gibson, 'International Human Rights Law and the Administration of Justice through Military Tribunals: Preserving Utility while Precluding Impunity' (2008) 4 *Journal of International Law and International Relations* 1, 24; P Rowe, *The Impact of Human Rights Law on Armed Forces* (Cambridge, Cambridge University Press, 2005) 97–111.

[62] See eg the facts of *Prosecutor v Jean-Pierre Bemba Gombo* ICC-01/05-01/08 (21 March 2016). See generally E Crawford, *The Treatment of Combatants and Insurgents under the Law of Armed Conflict* (Oxford, Oxford University Press, 2010).

[63] Joinet (n 23) para 3.

[64] GC III, Art 4; AP I, Art 43.

[65] AP I, Art 51.

specialist military commissions, established to try certain alleged war criminals or terrorist suspects whose conduct was associated with armed conflict; civilian criminal courts were thought to be ill-equipped to deal with war crimes committed abroad.[66] The point is made that:

> Combatants who are accused of committing crimes during armed conflict are usually best and most fairly judged in military forums by their peers, fellow combatants who … have military acumen and practical experience regarding LOAC, battlefield conditions, operations, and customs. Given such specialized expertise, combatant peers can sensibly and more adequately evaluate and weigh armed conflict-related evidence of war crimes, defenses, aggravation, mitigation, and extenuation.[67]

Whatever the merits of this argument in the context of military operations, where decisions regarding choice of weaponry and tactics and judgments as to military necessity and proportionality of civilian harm are relevant, none of these considerations appertain to a prosecution for rape or sexual violence in conflict. It is therefore not an argument in favour of bringing such charges for these acts in military justice systems where the alleged perpetrators are not members of the regular state armed forces.

With respect to subject matter jurisdiction, Principle 8 of the Decaux Principles states that military justice systems should be limited to disciplining strictly military offences.[68] What this entails is debatable; the UN Special Rapporteur on the independence of judges and lawyers recommends that the subject matter jurisdiction of military tribunals 'be limited to criminal offences of a strictly military nature … such as desertion, insubordination or abandonment of post or command'.[69] Sexual violence in conflict does not fit into this category of strictly military offences.

There is a credible argument that all serious sexual violence allegations should be dealt with in civilian criminal jurisdictions, whether or not occurring in conflict. Rape is always a serious violation of a victim's human rights. Victims are entitled to know that their claims will be investigated by someone independent from the service to which their alleged attacker is attached.[70] There may also be entrenched gender biases in military tribunals, reflecting military cultures more broadly.[71] However, critics of this view argue that rape and sexual violence allegations are as much a matter of military discipline and morale as any other criminal offence, and should

---

[66] J Bialke, 'Al-Qaeda and Taliban Unlawful Combat Detainees, Unlawful Belligerency, and the International Laws of Armed Conflict' (2004) 55 *Air Force Law Review* 1, 70.

[67] ibid.

[68] 'Decaux Principles' (n 52) pr 8; Knaul (n 56) paras 98–99.

[69] Knaul (n 56) para 98.

[70] S Ogilvie and E Norton, 'Military Justice: Proposals for a Fair and Independent Military Justice System' (National Council for Civil Liberties, 2014) para 16.

[71] M Morris, 'By Force of Arms: Rape, War and Military Culture' (1995–96) 45 *Duke Law Journal* 651.

be maintained within the military justice system to ensure that the special circumstances of military discipline apply.[72] As two Canadian military commentators put it: 'To the extent that sexual assault offences have the potential to undermine morale and unit discipline, lessen mutual trust and respect, and ultimately impair military efficiency' removing them altogether from military discipline is problematic.[73]

In addition, Principle 9 of the Decaux Principles provides that:

> In all circumstances, the jurisdiction of military courts should be set aside in favour of the jurisdiction of the ordinary courts to conduct inquiries into serious human rights violations such as extrajudicial executions, enforced disappearances and torture, and to prosecute and try persons accused of such crimes.[74]

While this list does not expressly include rape, the Committee against Torture has established that rape in conflict is tantamount to torture,[75] as has the ICTY.[76] Rape and sexual violence in conflict should therefore be treated as serious violations of human rights for the purposes of determining military jurisdiction.

There is an argument that military courts are, in principle, capable of meeting IHRL standards regarding fair trials, and that, if they do so in a particular state, there is no reason why they should not be able to prosecute both military personnel and civilians for crimes that constitute serious human rights violations.[77] Given that the civilian status of members of non-state armed groups is contestable, there may be some practical justification for trying individual perpetrators captured in the field of operations in mobile military courts, given the desirability of prosecuting perpetrators in order to end impunity. Military courts accustomed to functioning in conflict zones may be able to deliver justice more swiftly, near the scene of the crime and with victims and witnesses readily available, thus enabling victims to see justice being speedily delivered.[78] Indeed, in conflict-affected and post-conflict states, the civilian criminal courts may be dysfunctional, not human rights compliant, or may simply not have the capacity or resources to deal

---

[72] Ogilvie and Norton (n 70) para 12; Knaul (n 56) para 70.

[73] J Pitzul and J Maguire, 'A Perspective on Canada's Code of Service Discipline' (2002) 52 *Air Force Law Review* 1, 15.

[74] See also Andreu-Guzman (n 39) 19–20; Colombia and Mexico have taken steps to remove serious human rights violations, including sexual violence, from military jurisdiction: Knaul (n 56) para 71.

[75] UN Committee Against Torture, General Comment No 2: 'Implementation of Article 2 by States Parties' (2008) UN Doc CAT/C/GC/2; *Sylvie Bakatu Bia v Sweden* (2011) Committee Against Torture, CAT/C/46/D/379/2009 and *Eveline Njamba and Kathy Balikosa v Sweden* (2010) Committee Against Torture, CAT/C/44/D/322/2007 (both rape by state officials in the DRC during armed conflict).

[76] *Prosecutor v Delalic et al* (Judgment) ICTY-96-21-T (16 November 1998) para 496.

[77] Rowe (n 61) 101.

[78] Gibson (n 61) 16–18.

with prosecutions of both the increased level of 'ordinary' domestic criminal offences committed during the conflict as well as serious human rights violations.

We believe that rape and sexual violence as war crimes and crimes against humanity should, generally, be prosecuted in civilian, not military, courts whether committed by members of a state's regular armed forces,[79] or by irregular armed forces, regardless of the status of the latter. However, it may be that exercise of personal and subject matter jurisdiction by military or civilian courts in any given state needs to be considered contextually in the light of the circumstances obtaining at the time, and the desirability of bringing perpetrators of such crimes to justice.

D. Reform of Military Justice Systems

There is a growing trend for reform of military justice systems in compliance with states' IHRL obligations, with some states reforming their legal systems to remove human rights violations entirely from the jurisdiction of military courts[80] and/or to remove civilians from such jurisdiction.[81] In addition, some states have amended their law so that all allegations of sexual assault, whether or not conflict-related, should or must be referred to the ordinary civilian criminal prosecutor, and not kept within the military justice structure.[82]

IV. WHAT CRIME SHOULD BE PROSECUTED?

A. International or Domestic Crimes?

The question as to what crimes should be prosecuted in national criminal courts encompasses two interrelated issues: whether states should prosecute sexual violence in conflict as war crimes and crimes against humanity, or under ordinary domestic criminal law concepts; and whether states should use the ICC Statute definitions of rape and sexual violence in their legislation adopting ICL and/or in their ordinary domestic criminal law.

Many, but by no means all, states parties to the ICC Statute have adopted, or are drafting, domestic laws to enable them to prosecute war crimes and

---

[79] Knaul (n 56) para 106.

[80] ibid, para 71; Andreu-Guzman (n 39) 161.

[81] Part II section II of Andreu-Guzman (n 39) 169–378, considers reform of various military justice systems; see also Joinet (n 23) para 23.

[82] See *Military Justice System: Adjudication of Sexual Offenses* (Washington, DC, Law Library of Congress, 2015) www.loc.gov/law/help/militaryjustice/index.php for steps being taken by certain countries to remove all sexual offences from the chain of command.

crimes against humanity in their national civilian criminal courts.[83] Since the ICC Statute does not expressly require implementing legislation, there is no guidance as to whether states parties must adopt its definitions of war crimes and crimes against humanity verbatim. Complementarity under the ICC Statute ignores gender justice in determining admissibility before the ICC. The 'unwilling or unable' criteria[84] look to the overall effectiveness of the national judicial system and do not consider whether that system will in fact result in gender justice for victims substantially equivalent to that which could (at least theoretically) be obtained at the ICC; nor does it clarify whether having national criminal law on sexual violence is sufficient to demonstrate that a state is willing and able to prosecute. States parties were unwilling to allow the ICC to enquire into their national laws and criminal practices.[85] Given that most cases of sexual violence in conflict will be prosecuted (if at all) at the national level, leaving the ICC with only the most serious cases, this is a potentially serious deficiency in the system of protection of civilians from rape in armed conflict provided by the ICC Statute.

But IHL, ICL and IHRL are complementary legal regimes. IHRL requires states to have domestic penal legislative provisions to prevent, punish and eradicate violence against women,[86] a requirement that overlaps with their responsibility to domesticate IHL and ICL relating to rape and sexual violence in armed conflict. Rape in war is now recognised as a violation of women's human rights under the Convention for the Elimination of All Forms of Discrimination against Women,[87] the Convention against Torture[88] and the ICCPR.[89] The ECtHR and the IACtHR have held that rape in conflict by a state's own personnel (military, police and security

---

[83] See ICC National Implementation Legislation Database, www.legal-tools.org/browse/national-implementing-legislation-database. A Carillo and A Nelson, 'Comparative Law Study and Analysis of National Legislation Relating to Crimes against Humanity and Extraterritorial Jurisdiction' (2014) 46 *George Washington International Law Review* 3, 481.

[84] ICC Statute, Art 17.

[85] L Chappell, *The Politics of Gender Justice at the ICC: Legacies and Legitimacy* (Oxford, Oxford University Press, 2015) 165–68.

[86] Inter-American Convention on the Prevention, Punishment and Eradication of Violence against Women (adopted 9 June 1994, entered into force 5 March 1995) 33 ILM 1534, Art 7(c); Convention on Preventing and Combating Violence against Women and Domestic Violence (adopted 11 May 2011, entered into force 1 August 2014) CETS No 210, Art 49; Protocol to the African Charter on Human and Peoples' Rights on the Rights of Women in Africa (Maputo Protocol) (adopted 11 July 2003, entered into force 25 November 2005) CAB/LEG/66.6, Art 11(3).

[87] *MEN v Denmark* (2011) Committee on the Elimination of Discrimination against Women /C/55/D/35/2011, para 8.8; UNCEDAW, General Recommendation No 30 (n 8).

[88] Committee Against Torture, General Comment No 2 (n 75); *Bakatu Bia v Sweden* (n 75); *Njamba and Balikosa v Sweden* (n 75).

[89] UN Human Rights Committee, General Comment No 28 'Article 3 (The Equality of Rights between Men and Women)' (2000) UN Doc CCPR/C/21/Rev.1/Add.10, para 8; *MI v Sweden* (2013) Human Rights Committee, CCPR/C/108/D/2149/2012 (rape is a violation of the ICCPR Art 7 prohibition on torture).

forces) violates their respective Conventions.[90] The ICC must take account of human rights law in its application and interpretation of the ICC Statute and other relevant legal instruments.[91] And states must comply with their human rights duty of due diligence in legislating against and prosecuting rape and sexual violence in conflict by non-state actors in national courts[92] under the principle of complementarity.

There are a number of reasons why prosecutions at the national level for sexual violence in conflict as war crimes or crimes against humanity are preferable to prosecutions under ordinary domestic criminal law on sexual offences, the reasons varying to some extent depending on whether the state in question is or is not a state party to the ICC Statute. First, prosecution for a grave breach, war crime or crime against humanity may incur more stigma than being prosecuted for ordinary domestic rape. Convictions on this basis should therefore carry more weight in dispelling the impression that impunity continues to apply to rape in war, which should increase the deterrence effect of prosecutions based on IHL and ICL. Second, the concept of command responsibility does not apply under ordinary domestic criminal law. The March 2016 conviction of Bemba by the ICC illustrates the importance of this basis for liability. Bemba was not convicted of direct participation in rape,[93] but solely on the basis of his command responsibility of non-state forces, an important holding for ending any assumption of impunity. Third, jurisdiction under national criminal law is primarily territorial (or in civil law countries based on the nationality of the offender) while prosecution for international crimes allows—indeed requires—extraterritorial jurisdiction. Territorial jurisdiction may not be the most appropriate for various reasons, including that, in the conflict-affected state, the government itself may be involved in the conduct. If war crimes and crimes against humanity are to be properly prosecuted, states other than those where the crimes occurred must be willing to prosecute in their national courts, using the concept of universal jurisdiction. However, despite this requirement for grave breaches of Geneva Convention IV, universal jurisdiction remains controversial.[94]

---

[90] *Aydin v Turkey* (App No 23178/94) ECtHR 25 September 1997; *Ana, Beatriz y Celia González Pérez v Mexico* (2001) Inter-American Commission on Human Rights Case No 11.565; *Miguel Castro-Castro Prison v Peru* (Judgment) Inter-American Court of Human Rights Series C No 181 (2 August 2008); *Raquel Marti de Mejia v Peru* (1996) Inter-American Commission on Human Rights Case No 10.90; *'Las Dos Erres' Massacre v Guatemala* (Judgment) Inter-American Court of Human Rights Series C No 251 (4 September 2012).

[91] ICC Statute, Art 21(3).

[92] UNCEDAW has recognised that states parties must regulate non-state actors in the prevention of gender-based violence in armed conflict under their due-diligence duty; UNCEDAW, General Recommendation No 30 (n 8) para 15; see also Committee Against Torture, General Comment No 2 (n 75) para 18.

[93] *Prosecutor v Jean-Pierre Bemba Gombo* (n 62) paras 693, 735 and 741–42.

[94] A Cassese, 'Is the Bell Tolling for Universality? A Plea for a Sensible Notion of Universal Jurisdiction' (2003) 1 *Journal of International Criminal Justice* 589.

Fourth, the IHL defences of military necessity and proportionality would not be available in ordinary domestic criminal prosecutions.[95] Whilst sexual violence against civilians can never be justified by military necessity or proportionality, these concepts may be relevant to other grave breaches, war crimes or crimes against humanity. Finally, any statutes of limitation in domestic criminal law should not be applicable to international crimes.

There may be other advantages to prosecuting as a war crime or crime against humanity if the state in question is a state party to the ICC Statute and has domestic legislation implementing it into national criminal law. First, provided that the definitions of rape and sexual violence in the ICC's Elements of Crimes have been properly incorporated into domestic implementing legislation (as to which see further below), prosecuting under the ICL concepts is likely to provide a more robust approach than may be the case under national criminal law. Second, once the national prosecutor has established that a coercive environment exists, individual victim non-consent to the rape should be irrelevant. This should not only make convictions more likely, with the deterrence effect that may bring, but should also increase the willingness of victims to come forward to testify. However, the additional (and unfamiliar) hurdle of demonstrating a sufficient nexus to armed conflict and a coercive environment may encourage national prosecutors to prosecute under normal domestic criminal law, even if ICL has been fully incorporated into national law. Third, if there is an appropriate investigation and appropriate charges are brought, then the case should be inadmissible before the ICC under the Article 17 criteria for admissibility. Finally, if there has been a proper trial, the *ne bis ad idem*[96] rule prevents the defendant being made subject to charges before the ICC in relation to the same conduct. It is not clear that a trial under domestic criminal law would displace the rule.[97]

If the state is not a party to the ICC Statute, or has not implemented it into domestic law, the position is somewhat different. Relying on the Geneva Convention IV approach to rape, undefined and treated as a violation of a woman's honour, may mean that national courts will apply outdated domestic concepts of rape and sexual violence. The national prosecutor must demonstrate that the conduct has a nexus to an IAC or NIAC[98] for it to be

---

[95] J Kelly, 'Re: Civilian Casualty Court Martial: Prosecuting Breaches of International Humanitarian Law using the Australian Military Justice System' (2013–14) 37 *Melbourne University Law Review* 342, 353.

[96] ICC Statute, Art 20.

[97] WA Schabas, *An Introduction to the International Criminal Court* (Cambridge, Cambridge University Press, 2014) 204.

[98] G Gaggioli, 'Sexual Violence in Armed Conflicts: A Violation of International Humanitarian Law and Human Rights Law' (2014) 96 *International Review of the Red Cross* 894, 513–17.

treated as a breach of Geneva Convention IV. This may appear to a busy prosecutor an unnecessary complication, and best avoided. A state that only applies the Geneva Conventions is unlikely to have a legal concept of crimes against humanity[99] committed in the context of or as part of a widespread or systematic attack directed against a civilian population with knowledge of the attack. This omission may limit the ability of national prosecutors to bring international criminal charges in relation, for instance, to crimes committed during an internal conflict that does not constitute a NIAC.[100]

If, over time, national prosecutors do prosecute perpetrators of rape and sexual violence in armed conflict in national courts under principles of IHL and ICL, this will enhance the work of the ICC and increase the deterrent effect of its prosecutions. Prosecutions brought in their own countries will also make justice more accessible to victims. However, this may not appeal to national prosecutors: one research study detected no successful efforts by state prosecutors to try conflict-period sexual violence in domestic courts; rather efforts to bring conflict-period sexual violence into national courts were initiated by civil society organisations.[101] It is therefore timely that the experience of prosecuting rape at the ICTY is being made available to national prosecutors to facilitate better outcomes in conflict-related sexual violence cases.[102]

B. Defining Conflict-Related Rape

How rape in conflict is incorporated in legislation enabling national courts to prosecute international crimes is critical in ensuring compliance with the ICC Statute and human rights jurisprudence on the elements of the crime.[103] Defining rape was the subject of substantial, and sometimes conflicting, jurisprudence at the ICTY and the ICTR, notably whether the non-consent of the victim had to be established as an element of the crime, as was the case in the national criminal laws surveyed by the two Tribunals.

---

[99] See eg, the USA, a non-state party to the ICC Statute, has no legislation enabling prosecution of crimes against humanity: D Scheffer, 'Closing the Impunity Gap in US Law' (2009) 8 *Northwest University Journal of International Human Rights* 30, 38; the Crimes Against Humanity Act of 2009 referenced in this article has not been enacted: See 'S 1346 (111th): Crimes Against Humanity Act of 2010', www.govtrack.us/congress/bills/111/s1346.

[100] See E Wilmshurst (ed), *International Law and the Classification of Conflicts* (Oxford, Oxford University Press, 2012) for a consideration of the classification of IAC and NIAC.

[101] UC Berkeley School of Law Human Rights Centre, 'The Long Road: Accountability for Sexual Violence in Conflict and Post-Conflict Settings—Kenya, Liberia, Sierra Leone, Uganda' (2015) 4.

[102] Brammertz and Jarvis (n 15) 384–86.

[103] See Amnesty International, 'Rape and Sexual Violence: Human Rights Law and Standards in the International Criminal Court' (2011) www.amnesty.org/en/documents/IOR53/001/2011/en/, 11.

Two approaches were manifested: coercion, where proof of a coercive environment precluded any need for enquiry into a victim's consent; or consent, where the consent had to be freely given and genuine.[104] The ICC Statute does not require non-consent to be proved as an element of the crime of rape. Instead, rape is committed where the invasion is committed:

> By force, or by threat of force or coercion, such as that caused by fear of violence, duress, detention, psychological oppression or abuse of power, against such person or another person, or by taking advantage of a coercive environment, or the invasion was committed against a person incapable of giving genuine consent.[105]

In *Bemba* the ICC considered for the first time the circumstances in which 'taking advantage of a coercive environment' would apply. It applied a broad interpretation, in particular that:

> [I]n addition to the military presence of hostile forces among the civilian population, there are other coercive environments of which a perpetrator may take advantage to commit rape ... [and] ... several factors may contribute to create a coercive environment.[106]

In cases that are serious enough to come before the ICC, a coercive environment will invariably be present and the perpetrators will almost certainly be taking advantage of it. Similarly, national courts prosecuting war crimes and crimes against humanity should adopt the coercion approach of the ICC Statute, regardless of any contrary provisions in ordinary domestic criminal law of that state. Domestic law concepts of consent should not be relied upon to establish the offence of rape as a war crime or a crime against humanity.[107]

The ICC's Rules of Procedure provide that evidence of, or questioning regarding, any alleged consent by a victim can only be raised by the defence if the ICC so determines following in camera proceedings as to the probity of the evidence.[108] Victims are also protected from intrusive questioning and against inappropriate inferences of consent from their conduct.[109] Nor is the ICC permitted to admit evidence of the prior or subsequent sexual conduct of a victim or witness.[110] These restrictions are required to protect victims from invasive and insulting questioning, to encourage more victims to come forward, and to address impunity, and therefore should be applied

---

[104] C MacKinnon, 'Defining Rape Internationally: A Comment on *Akayesu*', in C MacKinnon, *Are Women Human? And Other International Dialogues* (Cambridge, Harvard University Press, 2006) 237.

[105] Elements of Crime (n 18) Arts 7(1)(g)-1(2), 8(2)(b)(xxii)-1(2) and 8(2)(e)(vi)-1(2). A person may be incapable of genuine consent if affected by natural, induced or age-related incapacity.

[106] *Prosecutor v Jean-Pierre Bemba Gombo* (n 62) para 104.

[107] Brammertz and Jarvis (n 15) 136, 386.

[108] Rules of Procedure (n 20) r 72.

[109] ibid, rr 70 (a), (c) and (d).

[110] ibid, r 71.

at the national level. The focus of prosecutions for rape and sexual violence in conflict must be on the sexual autonomy of victims, not on the behaviour of victims.

The ability of a defendant to raise consent as a defence[111] should be sufficient protection for those situations where sexual contact between combatants and civilians has occurred with genuine consent. Other sexual offences committed in a conflict-affected state (ie ordinary civilian rape) are unlikely to be part of an organised plan, nor widespread or systematic, so are unlikely to be prosecuted as war crimes or crimes against humanity.

C. Deficiencies in National Implementation

That national implementing legislation may not incorporate adequately the important gender justice aspects of rape and sexual violence as international crimes is demonstrated by the following examples, illustrating a wide range of approaches:

— The Commonwealth Model Law on the ICC does not require that the Elements of Crime be taken into account in proceedings under domestic legislation providing national court jurisdiction over international crimes; the wording was recently changed from mandatory to permissive. It does not provide for adoption of the Rules of Procedure and instead allows defendants to raise any defence allowable under the relevant domestic criminal law.[112] That could enable a defendant to raise a defence of consent in circumstances where it would be impermissible in a trial before the ICC.
— The UK International Criminal Court Act 2001 defines war crimes and crimes against humanity by reference to Articles 8 and 7, respectively, of the ICC Statute and requires UK courts to take into account the ICC Elements of Crimes, but does not mention the Rules of Procedure.[113]
— The Australian implementing legislation does not define rape as a war crime or a crime against humanity by reference to the ICC Statute. It defines the actus reus of rape similarly to the ICC Statute, but includes the victim's non-consent as an element of the crime. The circumstances in which consent is not given include force or fear of force, incapacity and taking advantage of a coercive environment.[114]

---

[111] ibid, r 72.
[112] Model law to implement the Rome Statute of the International Criminal Court in 'International Criminal Court (ICC) Statute and Implementation of the Geneva Conventions' (2011) 37 *Commonwealth Law Bulletin* 4, 681, 689.
[113] UK International Criminal Court Act (2001), ss 50(1), (2).
[114] Australia Criminal Code Act (1995) Div 268.14.

— The list of sexual offences in the German Criminal Code Against International Law 2002 differs from that in the ICC Statute, and does not refer to the latter's definitions or Elements of Crime.[115]

— Canada's Crimes against Humanity and War Crimes Act 2000 criminalises sexual violence as war crimes and crimes against humanity under customary international law, and expressly includes Articles 7 and 8 of the ICC Statute as customary international law for these purposes.[116]

— The Belgian International Crimes Act 2003 makes rape and sexual violence war crimes and crimes against humanity using the same language as Articles 8 and 7, respectively, of the ICC Statute, but does not expressly refer to the Elements of Crimes or Rules of Procedure.[117]

— South Africa was one of the first African states to implement the ICC Statute into its domestic legislation. Its International Criminal Court Act 2002 mirrors the wording of Articles 7 and 8 of the ICC Statute.[118] It does not expressly incorporate the definitions in the Elements of Crimes, but does provide that South African courts shall consider and may take into account the provisions of the ICC Statute.[119] Since the express purpose of the Act is to ensure South African compliance with its international obligation of complementarity,[120] it is hoped that the national courts will take into account the ICC's gender justice approach to rape and sexual violence.

— The Philippine Act on Crimes Against International Humanitarian Law, Genocide, and Other Crimes Against Humanity reproduces the list of rape and sexual violence as war crimes and crimes against humanity as set out in Articles 8 and 7, respectively, of the ICC Statute.[121] There is no express reference to the ICC Statute or its definitions, but the Philippine courts are to be guided by principles of customary international law and by rulings of international courts and tribunals.[122] This is not specific, nor helpful given that some international jurisprudence may not be as up to date as the ICC Statute definitions, but it may give courts enough authority to enable them to apply the ICC Statute definitions.

---

[115] Germany Code of Crimes Against International Law of 26 June 2002 (2002), Arts 7(1) (6), 8(1)(4).

[116] Canada Crimes against Humanity and War Crimes Act (2000) c 24 ss 4(1), (3), (4) and ss 6(1), (3), (4).

[117] Belgium Act of 1999 Concerning the Punishment of Grave Breaches of International Humanitarian Law as amended International Crimes Act 2003, Art 1(2)(7).

[118] South Africa Implementation of the Rome Statute of the International Criminal Court Act (2002) (Act No 27, 2002) sch 1, pts 2, 3.

[119] ibid, Art 2.

[120] ibid, Art 3.

[121] Philippine Act on Crimes Against International Humanitarian Law, Genocide, and Other Crimes Against Humanity (Republic Act 9851, 2009) ss 4(b)(19), 6(g).

[122] ibid, ss 15(e), (f).

— The Uganda International Criminal Court Act 2010 cross-references Articles 7 and 8 of the ICC Statute without reproducing them.[123] It also expressly provides that Ugandan courts may have regard to the Elements of Crimes[124] and brings into Ugandan law the Rules of Procedure.[125] This is perhaps the most helpful approach of any of the states surveyed for this chapter.

Even in a monist state, where international treaty obligations automatically take effect in domestic law, the issue may not be straightforward. For example, although the DRC is such a state, the definition of rape and provisions regarding coercion and consent were not initially incorporated into military law. This resulted in some military judges prosecuting conflict-related sexual offences taking account of ICL and others not.[126] The DRC's legislation to implement war crimes and crimes against humanity fully into DRC law was only enacted in 2016,[127] so hopefully this situation will improve in time.

Since national prosecutors may prefer not to have to deal with proving a conflict context and charge conflict-related rape and sexual violence under ordinary domestic criminal law rather than as a war crime or crime against humanity, consistency between international and national definitions of these crimes is desirable. There is an emerging IHRL obligation to implement domestic rape legislation that is consistent with the coercion-based approach of ICL.[128] International, regional and national legislation regarding trafficking also tends to lend support for a severely limited 'lack of consent' element for sexual violence.[129]

Although it appears that more extensive concepts of sexual violence are being brought into domestic criminal legislation as states ratify the ICC Statute,[130] further work is needed to determine if these new provisions adequately take account of states' IHRL obligations, particularly if they are to be used in lieu of prosecutions for war crimes and crimes against humanity.

---

[123] Uganda International Criminal Court Act 2010 (Act No 11, 2010) ss 8, 9.

[124] ibid, s 19(4)(a).

[125] ibid, s 5(c).

[126] G Breton-Le Goff, 'Ending Sexual Violence in the Democratic Republic of the Congo' (2010) 34 *Fletcher Forum of World Affairs* 1, 13, 23; DP Zongwe, 'The New Sexual Violence Legislation in the Congo: Dressing Indelible Scars on Human Dignity' (2012) 55 *African Studies Review* 2, 37, 41–43, 47–48.

[127] See Parlamentarians for Global Actions, 'Democratic Republic of the Congo', www.pgaction.org/campaigns/icc/africa/drc.html and 'PGA Welcomes the Enactment of the Implementing Legislation of the Rome Statute of the ICC by the Democratic Republic of the Congo' (4 January 2016) www.pgaction.org/news/pga-welcomes-enactment-drc-implementing.html.

[128] See eg *Vertido v The Philippines* (2010) Committee on the Elimination of Discrimination against Women CEDAW/C/46/D/18/2008, para 8.9(b); *MC v Bulgaria* (App no 3972/98) ECtHR 4 December 2003, paras 102–07, 166; Council of Europe (n 86) Arts 36(1) and (2).

[129] Sellers (n 12) 36.

[130] Ni Aolain (n 32) 622–23.

There is a counterargument that prosecution under ordinary domestic criminal law should be sufficient, both to defeat the admissibility criteria of the ICC Statute and to provide adequate justice to victims. The point is made that a conviction under domestic criminal legislation, for instance for murder, would still attract very serious penalties.[131] But it may well be that there is a more widely shared concept of what constitutes murder than is the case with rape and sexual violence. Stereotypes persist leading to lack of prosecutions, reluctance of victims and witnesses to come forward to testify, and acquittals.[132] Nevertheless, a prosecution under domestic ordinary criminal law that does not meet ICC standards may still be subject to the double-jeopardy rule, precluding prosecution by the ICC, even if the defendant is acquitted at the national level.[133] It is therefore more important in the context of sexual violence in conflict for the international definitions to be applied than it is for other categories of war crimes and crimes against humanity.

V. CONCLUSION

International bodies, notably the Security Council and the international criminal tribunals, have played important roles in seeking an end to impunity for rape and other sexual violence in armed conflict. They have set and clarified normative standards for protecting civilians from these atrocities, and provided guidance and encouragement to states to condemn such crimes and to punish perpetrators.

However, international bodies alone are unable to address impunity for sexual violence in war, making it imperative that it is prosecuted at the national level as a war crime and a crime against humanity. Otherwise, achievements at the international level will not be realised in a way that will positively impact women's lives in armed conflict and in peace.

Most states have both military and civilian criminal justice systems. States have an obligation under IHRL to ensure that both systems provide competent, independent and impartial justice, recognising the concepts of due process and a fair trial. There may be an assumption that military courts are better suited to prosecuting conflict-related sexual violence because they have traditionally been responsible for enforcing IHL, and they recognise the concepts of command responsibility and extraterritorial jurisdiction.

---

[131] Schabas (n 97) 197–98.

[132] *Vertido v The Philippines* (n 128) paras 8.5–8.6; see generally RJ Cook and S Cusack, *Gender Stereotyping: Transnational Legal Perspectives* (Philadelphia, University of Pennsylvania Press, 2010).

[133] Jurdi (n 35) 62–64.

However, military courts within the military chain of command are now seen as inherently unlikely to meet the IHRL criteria of impartiality and independence, and therefore should not prosecute either civilians or military personnel for human rights violations, including sexual violence, except in exceptional circumstances. Although there may be circumstances where military justice may justifiably be applied, bearing in mind in particular the desirability of bringing perpetrators to justice promptly, investigation and prosecution of these crimes are generally best left to civilian criminal justice systems. It appears that there is a trend towards both improving the IHRL compliance of military justice systems, and removing prosecutions of sexual violence in conflict from military jurisdictions.

There are real advantages to sexual violence in conflict being prosecuted in national courts as war crimes and crimes against humanity, rather than under ordinary domestic criminal law, not least the increased stigma that may attach to convictions on those charges. However national legislation must be drafted carefully to encapsulate the gender justice protections in the ICC Statute, the Elements of Crimes, Rules of Procedure and policy statements. The small sample of national implementing legislation reveals a wide range of approaches, most of which would not import the full range of gender protections of the ICC.

If the establishment of the ICC is to contribute fully to protecting civilians from, and ending impunity for, rape and sexual violence in armed conflict, a consistent approach must be taken in implementing legislation on war crimes and crimes against humanity at the national level. International and regional human rights bodies have a critical role to play in this regard, monitoring states' adoption and enforcement of international standards. Although states were resistant to empowering the ICC to look into their domestic sexual offence legislation, international and regional human rights law has the potential to do just that.

This complex network of legal regulation, with its overlapping applicability of IHL, ICL and IHRL, with international and national prosecutions and with civilian and military jurisdictions, has, to date, provided only limited protection for civilians against rape and sexual violence in conflict. What is needed now, however, is not more international laws or bodies, but for states to comply with their international obligations and responsibilities. These responsibilities include: addressing the structural power inequalities that enable rape, both in and outside of armed conflict, to continue (prosecution of individual cases of sexual violence by the ICC or other international, hybrid or national tribunals will not change the complex set of gendered conditions in everyday life that perpetuates rape in war); adopting the necessary legislation to bring IHL and ICL into the jurisdiction of national civilian criminal courts; and taking effective steps to investigate and prosecute such crimes—simply adopting a legislative framework is not sufficient.[134] CEDAW has recommended that criminal accountability also be enhanced through 'strengthening the capacity of security, medical and judicial personnel to collect and preserve forensic evidence related to sexual violence in conflict and post-conflict contexts' and ensuring 'adequate protection measures for victims and witnesses, including non-disclosure of identity and the provision of shelters'.[135]

States must also be willing to bring prosecutions under the principle of universal jurisdiction in appropriate circumstances, rather than leaving the burden of ending impunity to conflict-affected and post-conflict states. As the G8 Group of Ministers stated after the 2013 Global Summit on Preventing Sexual Violence in Armed Conflict, those accused of rape in war should be brought to trial. 'There should be no safe haven for perpetrators of sexual violence in armed conflict.'[136]

---

[134] UNCEDAW, General Recommendation No 30 (n 8) paras 38 and 81.

[135] ibid, para 81(j), (k).

[136] Foreign & Commonwealth Office, 'Declaration on Preventing Sexual Violence in Conflict' (2013) www.gov.uk/government/publications/g8-declaration-on-preventing-sexual-violence-in-conflict, para 4.

Part II

Remedies

8

The Right to Reparation for Victims of Armed Conflict

CARLA FERSTMAN

I. INTRODUCTION

BOTH INTERNATIONAL AND internal armed conflicts continue to have an acute impact on civilians and entire communities. Millions of civilians have been subjected to extreme forms of violence during and while fleeing conflicts, including mass deaths, torture, rape, sexual slavery, mutilations, and other cruel and debilitating physical and psychological treatment, abductions, deportations and all sorts of destruction and looting to homes and communities. In addition to the impacts of these forms of targeted violence, the consequences of conflict for civilians include poverty, trauma, disease, family dislocation and displacement. Increasingly, women and children are targeted; they also face the brunt of the consequences of conflict. Added to this, the multiple destabilisations associated with conflict have a tendency to permeate post-conflict societies; weak law enforcement and infrastructure and lingering tensions continue to put civilians, particularly the most vulnerable ones, at risk of further violence long after the formal end of a conflict.

While these multiple and cross-cutting harms are increasingly being acknowledged, they are rarely addressed specifically. The fate of victims is often an afterthought in peace negotiations and justice processes and victims rarely receive reparations; reparations often having been subsumed by more negotiable or contingent notions of 'reconciliation', 'charity' or 'humanitarianism'.

'Reparation' is a concept with contested understandings depending on the discourse or discipline being used, which may include law, politics, international relations, religion, psychology, sociology, penology or any combination of them. It signifies the concepts of repair, 'making good', restoration, rehabilitation, vindication. In law, 'reparations' are understood as what is owed by a wrongdoer in response to a breach of an obligation.

Reparations feature in the law of armed conflict; however, the norms and procedures relating to the same are opaque, porous and largely insufficient. The legal lacunae relate to victims' limited standing to pursue claims, for what types of harms, against whom, in which forums and with which result, all of which are extenuated when claims are pursued extraterritorially. There are equally questions about the extent of states' and others' responsibility to afford reparations when wrongful conduct can be attributed to a number of actors.

The challenges facing victims seeking reparations are multiple and include a variety of practical access hurdles linked to poverty, marginalisation, discrimination and victims' typical lack of voice and political agency to compel those in positions of power to meet their rights and legitimate demands and needs. Who is understood to be deserving of reparations, particularly when a whole society may have suffered in different ways, can also introduce often sensitive and potentially divisive choices, which can turn the process of reparations into a political project. If not handled with care, reparations may engender further distrust and resentment within communities, or foster stigmatisation. There is also a tendency for decision-makers to simplify victims and victimhood; to ignore the various ways in which victims suffer and the gendered nature of that suffering. To acknowledge differences in victims' perspectives, wants and needs can be too complicated for the post-conflict political environment and somehow too stark: decision-makers may have a general sense of empathy for the notion of victims but they rarely want to get too close, even if this results in the voices of the most marginalised being obscured.

In this chapter, I explore some of the main challenges victims of armed conflict face in obtaining reparations, citing a variety of case examples. There have been some advances in victims' access to reparations largely as a result of the influences of human rights law on the law of armed conflict and a growing global movement to address the lacunae. However, progress has been piecemeal.

II. THE RIGHT TO REPARATION: AN OVERVIEW

The notion of a 'right' to reparation has progressively become accepted as a matter of law. It entails victims' right to access domestic remedies in response to a violation (the procedural component) and the right to receive adequate and effective forms of reparation, which aim at 'eliminating, as far as possible, the consequences of the illegal act and restoring the situation that would have existed if the act had not been committed',[1] and may entail

---

[1] *Case Concerning the Factory at Chorzów (Ger v Pol)* (1928) PCIJ Sr A No 17, para 47.

any combination of restitution, compensation, rehabilitation, satisfaction and guarantees of non-repetition (the substantive component).[2]

Victims' access to remedies is a hallmark of human rights protection—any person whose rights have been violated has the right to equal and effective access to justice before a court or like body before which a remedy can be sought.[3] It is active and participatory and acknowledges, and in fact fosters, the agency of the individual or group to decide if, when, how and in which forum to assert rights. The UN Basic Principles and Guidelines on the Right to a Remedy and Reparation for Victims of Gross Violations of International Human Rights Law and Serious Violations of International Humanitarian Law make clear that access must be fair and non-discriminatory, and procedures must be accessible and suitable to take account of victims' particular needs. In practice, discrimination and marginalisation can inhibit access to justice or associated reparations processes; often, key documents are not translated to local languages; information dissemination does not reach remote areas or reach those who cannot read; structures to ensure safety, privacy and dignity are not in place which can discourage many women and others who experience stigma from coming forward.[4] The Basic Principles and Guidelines underscore that measures should be taken to

> minimize the inconvenience to victims and their representatives, protect against unlawful interference with their privacy as appropriate and ensure their safety from intimidation and retaliation, as well as that of their families and witnesses, before, during and after judicial, administrative, or other proceedings that affect the interests of victims.[5]

In a post-conflict context, the regular justice institutions may not be functioning or will be under extreme strain. Even in the best of circumstances they would be ill equipped to deal with a flood of conflict victims with multiple harms. Practically, this has meant that in such circumstances specialist judicial or administrative structures are needed to give effect to victims' rights to lodge claims for reparations. The Basic Principles and Guidelines refer to such possibilities, indicating that '[i]n addition to individual access to justice, States should endeavour to develop procedures to allow groups of victims to present claims for reparation and to receive reparation, as appropriate'.[6] Remedies must be available to all persons within the

---

[2] Basic Principles and Guidelines on the Right to a Remedy and Reparation for Victims of Gross Violations of International Human Rights Law and Serious Violations of International Humanitarian Law (16 December 2005) UN Doc A/RES/60/147 (adopted without vote).

[3] MC Bassiouni, 'International Recognition of Victims' Rights' (2006) 6 *Human Rights Law Review* 203.

[4] C O'Rourke, F Ni Aolain and A Swaine, 'Transforming Reparations for Conflict-Related Sexual Violence: Principles and Practice' (2015) 28 *Harvard Human Rights Journal* 97, 137–39.

[5] Basic Principles and Guidelines (n 2) Art 12(b).

[6] ibid, Art 13.

state's jurisdiction, which has been understood to include non-citizens and instances when a state exercises effective control over an area outside its national territory.[7]

The standard of reparations first articulated by the Permanent Court of International Justice and which has thereafter framed the quantum and quality of inter-state claims is 'full', as needing to wipe out all the consequences of the illegal act and re-establish the status quo ante.[8] It is described in the International Law Commission's Articles on the Responsibility of States (ARS) which covers all internationally wrongful acts, in these same terms.[9]

However, in practice, reparation rarely meets the standard of 'full'. This is partly because of the impossibility of undoing or repairing the harm caused by most heinous acts, especially when perpetrated during conflict, such as killings, rapes, torture and forced displacement. But it is also because of the enormity of the victimisation and the limited resources available for reparations at the end of a conflict, and only varying degrees of political will. A question arises as to how this exceptionalism impacts on the overall clarity of the rule. It has been argued that the disconnect demonstrates the tenuousness or even absence of a right to reparation,[10] or the narrower point that it reveals the absence of a right to 'full' reparation.[11] Tomuschat, for example, has argued that:

> Whenever chaos and anarchy set in, the magnitude of the sums required for effective reparation makes it imperative not only on economic, but also on legal grounds, to call into question the seemingly invincible proposition that reparation must wipe out all of the negative consequences of an injurious act.[12]

However, it can and has been argued that the exigencies of particular situations do not lower the overall standards; the overarching rules remain

---

[7] *Ilaşcu v Moldova and Russia* (App no 48787/99) ECHR 8 July 2004; *Al-Saadoon v United Kingdom* (App no 61498/08) ECHR 2 March 2010.

[8] *Chorzów Factory Case* (n 1) para 29; *Legality of the Threat or Use of Nuclear Weapons* (Advisory Opinion) [1996] ICJ Rep 226, para 152.

[9] ILC, 'Report of the International Law Commission on the Work of its 53rd Session' (23 April–1 June and 2 July–10 August 2001) UN Doc A/CN.4/SER.A/2001/Add.1 (ARS), Arts 31, 34 and commentaries thereto. See Basic Principles and Guidelines (n 2) Art 18, which describes 'full and effective' reparation for gross human rights and serious IHL violations.

[10] C Tomuschat, 'Reparation for Victims of Grave Human Rights Violations' (2002) 10 *Tulane Journal of International and Comparative Law* 157, 177–80.

[11] *Jurisdictional Immunities of the State (Germany v Italy: Greece Intervening)* (Merits) [2012] ICJ Rep 143, para 94.

[12] C Tomuschat, 'Individual Reparation Claims in Instances of Grave Human Rights Violations: The Position under General International Law' in A Randelzhofer and C Tomuschat (eds), *State Responsibility and the Individual—Reparation in Instances of Grave Violations of Human Rights* (The Hague, Kluwer, 1999) 11.

even if, for practical reasons, the results are abridged.[13] It may be difficult for a wrongdoer to have all the necessary means for making the required reparation. However, that inadequacy cannot exempt a wrongdoer from the legal consequences resulting from its responsibility under international law. As Judge Yusuf recognises in his dissenting opinion in *Germany v Italy*: 'Such arrangements appear to have been resorted to for policy or practical reasons aimed at avoiding the prospect of innumerable private suits, or a delay in the conclusion of peace treaties and the resumption of normal relations between formerly belligerent States';[14] they do not imply an absence of individual rights.[15] The Basic Principles and Guidelines also take this approach, by recognising the importance for states to 'endeavour to develop procedures to allow groups of victims to present claims for reparation and to receive reparation', 'in addition to individual access to justice'.[16] The ILC has recognised the challenges posed by mass victimisation in the ARS. While an earlier version of the ARS exempted debtors from the need to afford full reparation when to do so would 'result in depriving the population of a State of its own means of subsistence',[17] the final text of the ARS omits this provision and instead introduces elements of equity and reasonableness. This is most evident with the reference to restitution, which is only required if it 'does not involve a burden out of all proportion to the benefit deriving from restitution instead of compensation'.[18] The commentaries make clear that the provision applies 'only where there is a grave disproportionality between the burden which restitution would impose ... and the benefit which would be gained, either by the injured State or by any victim of the breach'.[19] The text never strays from the principle of 'full' reparation. Flexibility is introduced in how it may be achieved;[20] however, there is no licence to restrict the quantum or quality of reparation that is owed should the amount prove difficult on the wrongdoer.

Reparation can come in a variety of forms—material, symbolic, individual and/or collective—which should be determined in light of what is most appropriate and effective to address the violations and resulting harms. Collective reparations may be appropriate to address situations in which collectives were specifically targeted (the destruction of religious or

---

[13] E Schwager and R Bank, 'Is There a Substantive Right to Compensation for Individual Victims of Armed Conflicts against a State under International Law?' (2006) 49 *German Year Book of International Law* 367, 393.

[14] *Jurisdictional Immunities of the State* (n 11) Judge Yusuf Dissenting Opinion, para 16.

[15] ibid, para 19. See also Basic Principles and Guidelines (n 2) Art 13.

[16] Basic Principles and Guidelines (n 2) Art 13.

[17] See Art 42(3) of a former version of the ARS (n 9) (not retained). International Law Commission (ILC), 'Report of the International Law Commission on the Work of its 48th session' (6 May–26 July 1996) UN Doc A/51/10, para 66.

[18] ARS (n 9) Art 35(b).

[19] ARS (n 9) Commentary to Art 35, para 11.

[20] ARS (n 9) Commentary to Art 36, para 4.

cultural property) or where the incidents that gave rise to the harm may have affected communities or large groups of persons in a similar if not identical way. Invariably, there will be a need for several forms of reparations to adequately address the harms. Experience shows that reparations processes should be highly consultative regardless of whether they are claimant led or more diffuse administrative programmes set up by governments or as part of settlement arrangements. Consultation with victim communities about their suffering, their particular wants and needs is particularly important when determining what reparations should look like, especially when it is impossible to re-establish the status quo ante, as will be the usual case with IHL violations. But victim engagement does not end there; it will be vital throughout the reparation process including during and following its implementation, if it is to empower and have meaning for the intended beneficiaries.

The reparation owed to victims may require differentiation in the awards in order to adequately account for the specificity of the harms caused to particular individuals or groups. This is important both from a compensatory perspective but also to publicly acknowledge the particular suffering of segments of society which is crucial for victims' empowerment and for peacebuilding and prevention. In addition to addressing immediate needs, reparations should also take account of any prior situations of marginalisation or discrimination or structural inequalities which caused or were a significant contributing factor to the violation. Reparation should have transformative potential.[21]

III. CLAIMING REPARATIONS FOR IHL VIOLATIONS

IHL treaties are silent on whether victims can claim reparations. Unlike human rights law, IHL treaties do not specifically oblige states to afford victims a procedural remedy, nor are there specialised international complaints mechanisms.[22] This may be due to the genesis of IHL as a set of rules applicable to states in their relations with each other;[23] particularly on the international plane, individuals were understood as the passive recipients of protections, not active participants. Traditionally, the right to receive

---

[21] One of the main purposes of the Nairobi Declaration on Women's and Girls' Right to a Remedy and Reparation (19–21 March 2007). See generally O'Rourke, Ni Aolain and Swaine (n 4).

[22] See J Kleffner and L Zegveld, 'Establishing an Individual Complaints Procedure for Violations of International Humanitarian Law' (2000) 3 *Year Book of International Humanitarian Law* 384, who argue that a specialised procedure should be established.

[23] R Dolzer, 'Settlement of War-Related Claims: Does International Law Recognize a Victim's Private Right of Action—Lessons after 1945' (2002) 20 *Berkeley Journal of International Law* 296, 336.

reparation was capable of being given effect in IHL through the laws on injury to aliens and diplomatic protection, however imperfect and discretionary the route. This passivity is out of step with human rights framings, which are focused much more on agency and empowerment. Also, the passivity tends to privilege the notion of reparation as a political project over and above any notion of rights and duty bearers because it increases the uncertainty around reparations (regarding both the decision of states to claim it, and when and what is afforded). The notion of injury to aliens is also ill suited to victims of internal armed conflict, and difficult to implement for victims who have fled their state of nationality or are otherwise unable to rely on that state to espouse their claims. The UN Claims Commission, for example, had to modify its inter-state procedures in order to allow certain international agencies to submit claims on behalf of stateless persons, who unlike other individuals could not rely on their governments to put forward claims on their behalf.[24]

Because of these deficiencies, there have been attempts to interpret or read in procedural rights to IHL.[25] The ICRC has posited 'a growing tendency to recognise the exercise of rights by individuals',[26] though it has avoided asserting this tendency as evidence of an established rule of customary international law or even an emerging one. Some commentators have sought to imply procedural rights from the fact that victims are the ultimate beneficiaries of reparation.[27] The obligation to afford the result of reparation arguably requires the entity with that obligation to ensure that there are effective procedures through which the ultimate beneficiaries

[24] See UNCC, Guidelines Relating to Paragraph 19 of the Criteria for Expedited Processing of Urgent Claims (23 October 1991) UN Doc S/AC.26/1991/5, paras 3–4, specifying that: 'A high number of individuals will most likely not be in a position to have their claims submitted by a Government. Among these individuals Palestinians represent the most numerous group. Furthermore, stateless persons and other individuals in the same position who still remain in Kuwait or who are situated on border lines are to be included in this category. The international community, represented by the UNCC, bears the overall responsibility for protecting the interests of the above-mentioned individuals.'

[25] See eg ILC, 'Reparation for Victims of Armed Conflict' (76th ILC Conference, 7–11 April, 2014) Res No 1/2014; Art 1 of the Resolution provides: 'Victims have a right to access an effective mechanism to claim reparation ("reparation mechanism").'

[26] ICRC, Customary International Law Database, r 150, www.icrc.org/customary-ihl/eng/docs/home, accessed 10 July 2016.

[27] L Zegveld, 'Remedies for Victims of Violations of International Humanitarian Law' (2003) 85 *International Review of the Red Cross* 497, 507; M Frulli, 'When Are States Liable Towards Individuals for Serious Violations of Humanitarian Law? The *Markovic* Case' (2003) 1 *Journal of International Criminal Justice* 406, 417. See also Y Sandoz, 'Unlawful Damage in Armed Conflicts and Redress under International Humanitarian Law' (1982) 22 *International Review of the Red Cross* 131, 137; F Kalshoven, 'State Responsibility for Warlike Acts of the Armed Forces: From Article 3 of Hague Convention IV of 1907 to Article 91 of Additional Protocol I of 1977 and Beyond' (1991) 40 *International and Comparative Law Quarterly* 827, 835–36.

may gain access to reparation.[28] Others have considered that the progressive evolution of human rights law has had an impact on the meaning of state responsibility and the recognition of procedural rights in the law on armed conflict.[29]

Invariably though, what is recognised is states' obligation to afford reparation and victims' right to *receive* it, not their independent right to *claim* it. IHL claims lodged by victims with domestic courts have usually failed on procedural grounds, because of the perceived incompatibility with peace settlements, sovereign immunity, act-of-state doctrine or the non-self-executing nature of the right to reparation under IHL. Making reference to implied rights has not helped to overcome such blockages.[30]

The nature of war and conflict will naturally produce extraterritorial elements. This may be because of the transnational nature of the conflict, the involvement of foreign states or multinational corporations in what might be construed as a non-international conflict, or because victims and/or perpetrators (including with their assets) may have fled to other jurisdictions. Those claims brought mainly by 'aliens' before the courts of the country said to be responsible for the violation have rarely been successful, a principle barrier being victims' lack of standing to pursue IHL claims and the non-self-executing nature of the right to reparation under IHL;[31] in the United States some such claims have failed on the basis of national security confidentiality.[32] When peace agreements have been negotiated by states, it is next to impossible for victims who feel aggrieved by the settlement process, or for some reason fall outside the bounds of that settlement, to seek compensation before the courts of their nationality (to complain about the settlement)[33] or the courts of the wrongdoing state (to argue that they were

---

[28] See Bassiouni (n 3) 217, who argues in relation to states' obligation to afford reparation, that, even though there is no explicit obligation to establish special procedures, those states whose existing legal frameworks are deficient must establish such procedures in order to ensure that they are capable of affording effective remedies, or else they would be implicitly violating their obligations.

[29] Letter dated 12 October 2000 from the President of the ICTY addressed to the Secretary-General (3 November 2000) UN Doc S/2000/1063, para 20. See also 'Report of the International Commission of Inquiry on Darfur' (25 January 2005) www.un.org/News/dh/sudan/com_inq_darfur.pdf, accessed July 2016, para 593; Schwager and Bank (n 13) 378, 391; R Hoffmann, 'Reparation for Victims of War and Non-state Actors?' (2007) 32 *South African Year Book of International Law* 291, 297. See also P Gaeta, 'Are Victims of Serious Violations of International Humanitarian Law Entitled to Compensation?' in O Ben-Naftali (ed), *International Humanitarian Law and International Human Rights Law* (Oxford, Oxford University Press, 2011) 310.

[30] Some of this jurisprudence is discussed in V Bílková, 'Victims of War and Their Right to Reparation for Violations of International Humanitarian Law' (2007) 4 *Miskolc Journal of International Law* 1. See also the following chapter in this volume.

[31] See eg *Varvarin Bridge* case (10 December 2003) No 1 O 361/02 affirmed by the German Federal Constitutional Court in a decision dated 13 August 2013, BVerfG, 2 BvR 2660/06.

[32] *El-Masri v Tenet*, 437 F Supp 2d 530 (2006) para 536; 479 F 3d 296 (2007).

[33] See eg the *Shimoda* case, a claim brought by Japanese Hiroshima and Nagasaki residents who argued that the Japanese government owed them compensation when it waived its right

not captured by the settlement)[34] because the rights have been understood to vest in their state of nationality. Claims brought by victims before the courts where they are based, against a foreign state, have mainly failed for reasons of immunity.[35] Exceptionally, such cases have been capable of proceeding where immunity is not at issue or where there has been specific domestic legislation allowing for a cause of action[36] though judges may nevertheless bar a claim on other grounds, such as *forum non conveniens* or the political questions or act-of-state doctrine. In some instances, the threat of pending or further suits has prompted political negotiations and settlements, benefiting large categories of victims.[37] Some claims have been able to proceed on the basis of human rights law because human rights law has been deemed to apply to the conflict context (usually for conflict of a non-international character or where the state being sued is adjudged to have had effective control over the particular events in the territory).[38] Furthermore, in civil law countries, a successful criminal law conviction opens up the possibility for civil parties to claim compensation from the convicted perpetrator.[39] These cases are important in that the victims can rely at least in part on

to seek compensation from the United States for the use of atomic bombs. The Tokyo District Court determined that: 'There is in general no way open to an individual who suffers injuries from an act of hostilities contrary to international law to claim damages on the level of international law.' *Shimoda* case (Judgment) Tokyo District Court (7 December 1963) (referred to in 'Customary International Law Database' (n 26) r 150).

[34] There are a few exceptions, including the Korean 'comfort women' case, where Japan was ordered to pay compensation because it had been aware of the violations but did not adopt legislation to compensate the plaintiffs. See *Ko Otsu Hei Incidents* case (Judgment) Yamaguchi Lower Court (27 April 1998) (referred to in 'Customary International Law Database' (n 26) r 150).

[35] *Jurisdictional Immunities of the State* (n 11). Note, however, that in the USA, claims have been able to proceed against foreign state officials who are not recognised as being immune from the jurisdiction of the courts for serious violations of human rights and humanitarian law. See *Samantar v Yousuf et al* 130 S Ct 2278 (2010).

[36] In the USA, several claims for damages against foreign defendants concerning IHL violations have proceeded on the basis of the Alien Tort Claims Act 28 USC, para 1350 such as *Kadic v Karadzic* 70 F 3d 232, 246 (1995); *Mushikiwabo v Barayagwiza* 1996 US Dist LEXIS 4409 (1996); *Altmann v the Republic of Austria*, 541 US 677 (2004); *Mehinovic v Vuckovic* 198 F Supp 2d 1322 (2002).

[37] This was the case with a number of the Holocaust-era restitution programmes set up in the 2000s. See *In re Holocaust Victim Assets Litigation* (2001) 2001 US App LEXIS 30154 which proceeded to settlement. See eg Federal Law on the Establishment of a Foundation 'Responsibility, Remembrance and Future' (amended on 4 August 2001) BGBl vol 2000-I, 1263; BGBl vol 2001-I, 2036.

[38] *Jaloud v the Netherlands* (App no 47708/08) ECHR 20 November 2014; *Al-Jedda v the United Kingdom* (App no 27021/08) ECHR 7 July 2011; *Al-Skeini and ors, Bar Human Rights Committee (intervening) and ors (intervening) v United Kingdom* (2011) 53 EHRR 18; *Al-Saadoon and Mufdhi v the United Kingdom* (App no 61498/08) ECHR 2 March 2010.

[39] See eg for a sampling of claims in the countries where the violations took place: Chad: Criminal Trial Judgment relating to 20 security agents and accompanying civil action for damages, N'Djaména (25 March 2015); Democratic Republic of the Congo: *Military Prosecutor v Massaba (Blaise Bongi)* RP No 018/2006, RMP No 242/PEN/06, ILDC 387 (24 March 2006); Peru: *Sentencia Alberto Fujimori* Exp No AV-19-2001 (7 April 2009). For extraterritorial

the prosecutor to prove the main facts of the case; however, the victims are dependent on there being a conviction to pursue the civil claims.

International claims procedures have been established in response to IHL violations, such as (in response to international armed conflicts) the Treaty of Versailles,[40] the UN Compensation Commission,[41] the Ethiopia–Eritrea Claims Commission,[42] and numerous Holocaust-era restitution programmes. Many property restitution commissions[43] have been instituted to resolve claims, and compensation schemes have been put in place by governments at the end of an internal armed conflict. For example, the Colombian Justice and Peace Law of 2005 provides extensive provisions for reparations by demobilised paramilitaries, and following a decision of the Colombian Constitutional Court, also by the state.[44] Reparation to Colombian conflict victims has also been a prominent feature of jurisprudence of the Inter-American Court of Human Rights.[45] Often these measures are partial, only applying to certain categories of conflict victims or to crimes which took place within an overly narrow timeframe. At times, measures have also been found to be exclusionary to women and other marginalised groups.

The degree of claimant engagement within these bodies has also varied. In some processes, injured individuals have no procedural involvement. In others, victims have been consulted usually in groups as to the harm suffered and their preferences for reparation, with or without needing to submit verifiable proof of individualised harm. In yet other instances, more rigorous processes have been established in which injured individuals may make a claim to an administrative procedure established precisely for that purpose or a court.

More simplified approaches tend to be taken when there is a large number of injured individuals who would be entitled to significant reparation that

claims, see The Netherlands: *The Netherlands v Mpambara* 22-002613-09 (2011); Norway: *The Public Prosecuting Authority v Mirsad Repak* 08-018985MED-OTIR/08 (2008); Senegal: *Case against Hissein Habré* (Decision on civil party claims) (29 July 2016).

[40] Treaty of Peace Between the Allied and Associated Powers and Germany (adopted 28 June 1919, entered into force 10 January 1920) 225 CTS 188 (Treaty of Versailles) Art 297(e).

[41] See UNCC, 'Arrangements for Ensuring Payments to the Compensation Fund' (2 August 1991) UN Doc S/AC.26/1991/1, para 14.

[42] Agreement between the Government of the State of Eritrea and the Government of the Federal Democratic Republic of Ethiopia (adopted 12 December 2000, entered into force 12 December 2000) 2138 UNTS 94, 40 ILM 260, Art 5.

[43] International Organization for Migration (IOM), 'Property Restitution and Compensation: Practices and Experiences of Claims Programmes' (2008) ref no 978-92-9068-450-3.

[44] Corte Constitucional, Sentencia C-370/06, Gaceta de la Corte Constitucional (18 May 2006) www.corteconstitucional.gov.co/relatoria/2006/c-370-06.htm, accessed 31 July 2016.

[45] See eg *Mapiripán Massacre v Colombia* (Merits, Reparations and Costs) Inter-American Court of Human Rights, Series C No 134 (15 September 2005) paras 355.7–355.17; *19 Merchants v Colombia* (Merits, Reparations and Costs) Inter-American Court of Human Rights Series C No 109 (5 July 2005) paras 283–84.

would be overwhelming for a court to adjudicate claim by claim, and/or when the nature of the violations is such that victims would not have the requisite proof to satisfy a court of their injuries using typical standards of proof.[46] These can be accompanied by processes that assign the secretariats of the claims commissions the task of gathering evidence to substantiate or corroborate the evidence supplied by applicants. For instance, the Legal Unit of the Commission for Real Property Claims of Refugees and Displaced Persons in Bosnia and Hercegovina amassed cadastral and property book records to verify the claims of applicants, in recognition of the difficulties that would be posed should they be required to collect this data from local municipalities directly.[47] Similarly, the lawyers and paralegals working at the secretariat of the first Claims Resolution Tribunal for Dormant Accounts in Zurich, Switzerland conducted legal and factual inquiries as well as historical research on the circumstances surrounding a case, and often sent requests for (additional) information to the bank or the claimant to inquire about information on the account and the account owner contained in the bank records or to inquire about and clarify specific aspects of a claim.[48]

The recent practice of international or internationally supported criminal courts that allows victims to apply for reparation upon a conviction of an individual perpetrator is an important procedural development, though both the procedures and the outcomes have proved to be highly restrictive thus far.[49] Given the subject matter jurisdiction of the ICC, reparations will only be afforded for crimes within the jurisdiction of the Court (genocide, war crimes, crimes against humanity and, potentially, aggression) and not for all violations that occur during conflict. Furthermore, access to reparations will be predicated upon the nature of the charges pursued by the

---

[46] See generally HM Holtzmann and E Kristjánsdóttir (eds), *International Mass Claims Processes: Legal and Practical Perspectives* (Oxford, Oxford University Press, 2007); M Bazyler and R Alford (eds), *Holocaust Restitution: Perspectives on the Litigation and its Legacy* (New York, New York University Press, 2006); P Hayner, *Unspeakable Truths: Transitional Justice and the Challenge of Truth Commissions*, 2nd edn (New York, Routledge 2010); E Kristjánsdóttir, 'International Mass Claims Processes and the ICC Trust Fund for Victims' in C Ferstman, et al (eds), *Reparations for Victims of Genocide, War Crimes and Crimes against Humanity: Systems in Place and Systems in the Making* (Leiden, Martinus Nijhoff, 2009) 170; M Henzelin, V Heiskanen and G Mettraux, 'Reparations to Victims before the International Criminal Court: Lessons From International Mass Claims Processes' (2006) 17 *Criminal Law Forum* 317.

[47] See C Ferstman and SP Rosenberg, 'Reparations in Dayton's Bosnia and Herzegovina' in Ferstman et al (n 46) 483.

[48] H Niebergall, 'Overcoming Evidentiary Weaknesses in Reparation Claims Programmes—The Mass Claims Context' in Ferstman et al (n 46) 145.

[49] Rome Statute of the International Criminal Court (adopted 17 July 1998, entered into force 1 July 2002) UN Doc A/CONF 183/9 (ICC Statute) Art 75; Internal Rules of the Extraordinary Chambers in the Courts of Cambodia (9 February 2009, amended 17 September 2010) www.eccc.gov.kh/en/document/legal/internal-rules, accessed July 2016, r 23.

Prosecutor. To date, this has posed a significant limitation on victims' access to Court-ordered reparations, as has the limited funds secured through fines and forfeitures, and raised through voluntary contributions to the ICC's Trust Fund.

IV. THE AWARD OF REPARATIONS

The substantive component of reparations—the obligation of states to afford reparations—is reflected in several international humanitarian law treaties, particularly Article 3 of the Hague Convention IV,[50] largely reproduced in Article 91 of Additional Protocol I.[51] It stems from the general obligation of states to afford reparation for internationally wrongful acts, as reflected in the ILC's Articles on the Responsibility of States for Internationally Wrongful Acts.[52] This approach has been followed by the ICJ in its *Wall* Advisory Opinion, where it held that Israel was obliged 'to make reparation for all damage caused by the construction of the wall ... to all the natural or legal persons concerned'[53] as a result of the various international obligations that Israel was said to have breached.[54] Thus, reparation is premised on the existence of a legal violation, and not simply on the existence of an injury. Consequently there is no obvious obligation under this framework to afford reparation to victims for 'legal' collateral damage during armed conflict.[55] This is despite the introduction of strict liability frameworks in other areas of the law.[56]

The ICRC has expressed the view that the state obligation to afford reparation for IHL violations constitutes a rule of customary international law, applicable in both IACs and NIACs.[57] The same view was expressed in

---

[50] Hague Convention No IV Respecting the Laws and Customs of War on Land and its annex: Regulations concerning the Laws and Customs of War on Land (adopted 18 October 1907, entered into force 26 January 1910) 36 Stat 2227 TS No 539 (Hague Convention IV) Art 3.

[51] Protocol I Additional to the Geneva Conventions of 12 August 1949 and relating to the Protection of Victims of International Armed Conflicts (adopted 8 June 1977, entered into force 7 December 1978) 1125 UNTS 3 (API).

[52] ARS (n 9) Arts 1, 12; *Case concerning the factory at Chorzow (Ger v Pol)* (Jurisdiction) PCIJ Sr A No 9, para 21. See also EC Gillard, 'Reparation for Violations of International Humanitarian Law' (2003) 85 *International Review of the Red Cross* 532.

[53] *Legal Consequences of the Construction of a Wall* (n 8) para 152.

[54] ibid, para 147.

[55] However, many troops have a practice of giving discretionary one-off payments without an admission of liability when civilians are killed or injured in the course of hostilities. For a review of such practices, see Center for Civilians in Conflict, 'Monetary Payments for Civilian Harm in International and National Practice' (Amsterdam International Law Clinic, 2013) https://civiliansinconflict.org/wp-content/uploads/2017/11/Valuation_Final_Oct_2013pdf.pdf.

[56] See eg ILC 'International Liability for Injurious Consequences Arising out of Acts not Prohibited by International Law' legal.un.org/ilc/guide/9.shtml, accessed July 2016.

[57] Customary International Law Database (n 26) r 150.

the final report of the International Commission of Inquiry on Darfur.[58] This is consistent with the approach taken by the ILC, which underscores that the reparations obligation automatically attaches to all internationally wrongful acts; it does not distinguish between IACs or NIACs.[59] However, the status of the rule is controversial, owing to the limited and variable practice, typically contingent on states' interests and settlement prerogatives. The rule has been particularly controversial for non-international conflicts, given that no compensatory obligation was included in Additional Protocol II.[60] Yet, a failure to recognise the reparations obligation in internal armed conflict may create discrepancies with other applicable law, given the significant if not complete overlap with non-derogable human rights obligations operating in such contexts.

With respect to IACs, compensation has typically been dealt with at the inter-state level in multilateral or bilateral peace treaties or settlement agreements through token lump-sum amounts which had little or no correlation with the precise scale of the damages and harm caused to individual victims, in spite of the general international law standard requiring *restitutio ad integrum*.[61] As Kalshoven has noted:

> [T]he agreements usually lay an obligation on the vanquished State to pay a more or less random amount, determined more by its perceived financial capabilities than by any serious attempt to assess the damage caused by the unlawful acts of either party's armed forces; and the victor State may or may not distribute (part of) the money to individual claimants.[62]

They emphasise *cy-pres* remedies, lump-sum payments to a large number of individuals calculated along the line of specific beneficiary groups, and symbolic and communitarian (as opposed to individual) forms of reparation determined by judicial, quasi-judicial or non-judicial mechanisms. 'Full' reparation is not afforded because it is unrealistic—the compensable amount would be too high, there would be too many victims to repair, or because it is politically undesirable in the context of the end of the conflict.[63] At times, treaties deliberately exclude or settle claims.[64]

---

[58] International Commission of Inquiry on Darfur, 'Report of the International Commission of Inquiry on Darfur' (25 January 2005) paras 76, 592, 593, www.un.org/News/dh/sudan/com_inq_darfur.pdf, accessed 24 July 2016. Note, however, that the compensation commission the Commission of Inquiry recommended was never established. For a contrary view on the law, see C Tomuschat, 'Darfur—Compensation for the Victims' (2005) 3 *Journal of International Criminal Justice* 579.

[59] ARS (n 9) Art 31.

[60] Protocol II Additional to the Geneva Conventions of 12 August 1949 and relating to the Protection of Victims of Non-International Armed Conflicts (adopted 8 June 1977, entered into force 7 December 1978) 1125 UNTS 609 (AP II).

[61] ARS (n 9).

[62] Kalshoven (n 27) 836.

[63] ICRC, 'Strengthening Legal Protection for Victims of Armed Conflicts' (28 November–1 December 2011) Doc No 31IC/11/5.1.1, 27.

[64] Considered in Dolzer (n 23).

Courts or formal adjudicative bodies that have considered reparation for violations occurring in the context of an IAC are limited. The ICJ has adjudicated IHL violations in a number of its cases; however, remedies have usually been left to the parties to decide after a finding of a violation. This occurred with the case *Armed Activities on the Territory of the Congo (Democratic Republic of the Congo v Uganda)*, which the ICJ decided on the merits in December 2005.[65] The Court found in the DRC's favour, holding that Uganda had violated the principles of non-use of force and non-intervention, as well as its obligations under international human rights law, IHL, and the other obligations incumbent upon it under international law. In particular, it held that Uganda's responsibility was engaged in respect of the wrongful acts of the Ugandan military as well as for any lack of vigilance in preventing violations of human rights and IHL by other actors present in the territory that Uganda occupied, including by rebel groups acting on their own account. In relation to a counter-claim brought by Uganda, the ICJ determined that the DRC had breached the 1961 Vienna Convention on Diplomatic Relations in a variety of ways, including when its military attacked the Ugandan embassy in Kinshasa and maltreated Ugandan diplomats and others on the embassy premises and the international airport. Both parties were obligated to afford reparation. The Court decided that, failing agreement between the parties, it would settle the question of reparation due to each of them, and reserved for that purpose the subsequent procedure in the case.

The DRC finally came back to the Court a decade later,[66] and the matter remains pending. In his declaration, Judge Cançado Trindade noted that this lapse of time 'already far exceeded a reasonable time, bearing in mind the situation of the victims, still waiting for justice' (para 3). He argued that the judgment should have been accompanied by the determination of a reasonable time limit for the provision of reparations for damages inflicted upon the victims. Unfortunately, however, there is currently no framework in place to ensure that those ultimate intended beneficiaries will benefit in any concrete way from reparations awarded in an inter-state process, regardless of how long that process will take. When reparations are awarded against several parties to a conflict, the reparations of each party tend to simply cancel each other out. Such was the case with the Eritrea–Ethiopia Claims Commission, which painstakingly reviewed the quantum and quality of numerous IHL violations of both parties, amongst other violations.[67] Because reparation

---

[65] *Armed Activities on the Territory of the Congo (Democratic Republic of the Congo v Uganda)* [2005] ICJ Rep 168.

[66] *Armed Activities on the Territory of the Congo (Democratic Republic of Congo v Uganda)* (Order) [2015] Gen List no 116.

[67] Writing about the Ethiopia and Eritrea Claims Commission, Murphy, Kidane and Snider note that the payments of approximately \$161.5 million awarded to Eritrea and approximately \$174 million awarded to Ethiopia were not implemented nor were they likely to be

is afforded to a state under the principle of injury to aliens, the reparation is owed formally to the state, not the individuals, even if the individuals are the ultimate intended beneficiaries.

Similarly, those international criminal courts and tribunals that allow reparation claims have not privileged the concept of 'full' reparation; quite the opposite, judgments to date have emphasised that, given the sui generis statutory or rules frameworks, and taking into account the numbers of potential beneficiaries and often impecunious convicted perpetrators, a 'collective' or symbolic approach should be taken.[68] At the time of writing, bureaucratic wrangling at the ICC about reparations has meant that four years after the Court's first decision on reparations in the *Lubanga case*, not a single victim has benefited from Court-ordered reparations.[69]

With respect to conflicts of a non-international character, reparations are sometimes included in the mandate of transitional justice processes, such as compensation or land restitution commissions or specialised government programmes which undertake vetting, establish new institutions, contribute to truth-telling and memorialization, or provide victims with access to rehabilitation and health services, pensions or other benefits. In these cases, the adequacy of the adopted measures tends to depend on the degree of victim engagement, the transparency of decision-making and the inclusiveness of the process (fairness and non-discrimination). Some processes have been inaccessible to victims outside of the country or to non-citizens; at times processes have required victims to undertake onerous procedural steps to comply or have taken a narrow view of victimisation that has led to the exclusion of entire categories of victims from the programme. Occasionally, victims have sought to address the weaknesses or inadequacies of such reparations programmes through the courts or through sustained advocacy. Sometimes this has led to improvements or additions.

In civil law countries where individual perpetrators have been prosecuted and reparations have been awarded as part of civil damages adhesion processes, the reparation payments often remain unimplemented. This is because individual perpetrators are often impecunious, or in instances

---

implemented. They set out some of the rather limited steps undertaken by the Commission to encourage the parties to implement the awards, though these were not heeded, and recommend a number of ways in which courts, commissions or similar bodies could strengthen the prospects for reparations to be paid, and for the reparations to reach their ultimate intended beneficiaries. See SD Murphy, W Kidane, TR Snider, *Litigating War: Mass Civil Injury and the Eritrea–Ethiopia Claims Commission* (Oxford, Oxford University Press, 2014) 407–10.

[68] *Prosecutor v Thomas Lubanga Dyilo* (Appeal on Reparations) ICC-01/04-01/06-3129 (3 March 2015); *Co-Prosecutors v Kaing Guek Eav alias Duch* (Appeal Judgment) 001/18-07-2007-ECCC/SC (2 February 2012) 281–20, 630–717.

[69] *Prosecutor v Thomas Lubanga Dyilo* (Request Concerning the Feasibility of Applying Symbolic Collective Reparations) ICC-01/04-01/06-3219 (15 July 2016).

when an award is made jointly and severally against the individual perpe-trator and the state, the procedures to enforce claims against the state have been unwieldy and inaccessible.[70] In Chad, a local criminal court convicted twenty former members of the security service in March 2015 and ordered that 7,000 victims be compensated (a total amount of 75 billion CFA). The Chadian government was ordered to contribute half the funds but at the time of writing, no progress had been made with the release of funds or establishment of a commission to oversee payment.

V. FORMS OF REPARATION

The Articles on the Responsibility of States identify cessation, assurances and guarantees of non-repetition, and reparation, which may take the form of restitution, compensation or satisfaction.[71] This is consistent though somewhat more narrowly framed than the Basic Principles and Guidelines, which refer to restitution, compensation, rehabilitation, satisfaction and guarantees of non-repetition.

A. Restitution

Restitution is understood in most IHL treaties as the main obligation, failing which compensation or other forms of reparation should be afforded.[72] It is a particularly relevant and important component of reparation for conflict violations. The restoration of citizenship, the return of land and property or assets, the release of prisoners—all forms of restitution—are key means by which those that have been displaced or otherwise affected by conflict can begin to resume their lives. Restitution in some of these areas has the

---

[70] See eg *SA v the Democratic Republic of the Congo*, claim filed with the African Commis-sion on Human and Peoples' Rights (21 November 2014) www.redress.org/downloads/engcom-munication-sa-v-drc20-nov-2014.pdf, accessed 25 July 2016. See also REDRESS et al, 'Right to Reparation for Survivors: Recommendations for Reparation for Survivors of the 1994 Gen-ocide against Tutsi' (October 2012) www.redress.org/downloads/publications/121031right_ to_rep.pdf, accessed 25 July 2016.

[71] ARS (n 9) Arts 30(a),(b), 31.

[72] See eg Geneva Convention I for the Amelioration of the Condition of the Wounded and Sick in Armed Forces in the Field (adopted 12 August 1949, entered into force 21 October 1950) 75 UNTS 31 (GC I) Arts 34, 35; Geneva Convention IV Relative to the Protection of Civilian Persons in Time of War (adopted 12 August 1949, entered into force 21 October 1950) 75 UNTS 287 (GC IV) Art 55; Protocol for the Protection of Cultural Property in the Event of Armed Conflict (adopted 14 May 1954, entered into force 7 August 1956) 249 UNTS 358, Art 3; UNHCR, Guiding Principles on Internal Displacement (Geneva, 1998) UN Doc E/CN.4/1998/53/Add.2, principle 29(2); Convention for the Protection and Assistance of Inter-nally Displaced Persons in Africa (adopted 22 October 2009, entered into force 6 December 2012) Art 12.

potential to be transformative: for instance, land, property and succession laws that restrict female inheritance have sometimes been changed in post-conflict contexts.[73]

IHL treaties include the need to ensure that transferred detainees receive appropriate treatment, failing which, the transferring authority has the obligation to 'take effective measures to correct the situation or shall request the return of the prisoners of war'.[74] They also make specific reference to the requirement to return requisitioned property at the end of a war, failing which, compensation is required.[75] Similar restitution obligations are mentioned in the Convention for the Protection of Cultural Property and its first protocol.[76] With respect to refugees and displaced persons, the obligation to facilitate return and assist them to recover property is also a primary objective, failing which, compensation or other forms of reparation may sometimes be acceptable alternatives.[77]

There are numerous examples of post-conflict restitution. Sometimes restitution has been incorporated into peace settlements, such as to address mass displacement, as occurred in Bosnia and Herzegovina.[78] In other cases, restitution has been pursued by states at the end of an international conflict, particularly when the property or assets are state owned, such as the return of stolen cultural property or to delimit the boundary of states' territories.[79]

---

[73] See eg Centre on Housing Rights and Evictions, 'Promoting and Protecting the Inheritance Rights of Women: A Survey of Law and Practice in Sub-Saharan Africa' (2004).

[74] Geneva Convention III Relative to the Treatment of Prisoners of War (adopted 12 August 1949, entered into force 21 October 1950) 75 UNTS 135 (GC III) Art 12.

[75] eg GCI, Arts 34, 35; GCIV, Art 55. For a judicial determination on the obligation to restitute cultural sites, see *The Islamic Community in Bosnia and Herzegovina v The Republika Srpska* (Decision on Admissibility and Merits) CH/96/29 (11 June 1999) and *The Islamic Community of Bosnia and Herzegovina ('Prnjavor Graveyard')* CH/99/2177 (February 2000). These decisions and the challenges to their implementation are discussed in Ferstman and Rosenberg (n 47) 495–98.

[76] Convention for the Protection of Cultural Property in the Event of Armed Conflict (adopted 14 May 1954, entered into force 7 August 1956) 249 UNTS 240, Art 18(b); Protocol for the Protection of Cultural Property (n 72) Art 3. The obligation to return cultural property is set out in several UN Security Council resolutions, such as UNSC Res 686 (2 March 1991) UN Doc S/RES/686, para 2(d); Res 1483 (22 May 2003) UN Doc S/RES/1483, para 7; Res 2199 (12 February 2015) UN Doc S/RES/2199, para 17. In contrast, the Second Protocol to the Hague Convention of 1954 for the Protection of Cultural Property in the Event of Armed Conflict (adopted 26 March 1999, entered into force 4 March 2004) 38 ILM 769 reinforces the obligation to prevent the destruction of cultural property and adopts a framework for individual criminal responsibility.

[77] Guiding Principles on Internal Displacement (n 72) principle 29(2); Convention for the Protection and Assistance of Internally Displaced Persons (n 72) Art 12.

[78] See Annex 7 of the General Framework Agreement for Peace in Bosnia and Herzegovina (the Dayton Peace Agreement) 21 November 1995 which affirmed the right of refugees and displaced persons to have their property restored to them (or to be compensated where restitution is not possible) and included the general responsibility to create 'conditions suitable for return' such as the repeal of discriminatory laws and prevention of incitement of ethnic hostility.

[79] Agreement between the Government of the State of Eritrea and the Government of the Federal Democratic Republic of Ethiopia (Algiers Agreement) 12 December 2000 (2001) 40 ILM 260.

Restitution of privately owned property, such as art, homes, bank accounts, or the restoration of private rights, such as citizenship, has at times been initiated by claimant litigation. These cases can, however, be plagued by lack of documentatory evidence of ownership lost in the conflict and its aftermath and the vagaries of the passage of time. Property and assets cases are further complicated by determinations as to whether any sale from the original owner was a product of duress, and whether any subsequent sales to bona fide parties give rise to legal interests on their part that must be taken into account. Looted art cases, for instance, will often turn on which country's law is being applied, given significant differences in how limitation periods are calculated and applied, and the rules concerning the rights of bona fide purchasers. This has led to several attempts at standardisation across jurisdictions.[80] It also suggests a need for special procedures to be employed, to avoid the excessive formalism of courts which are not always best placed to take account of the limitations of victims' evidence.

Occasionally restitution claims have resulted not only in the settlement of an individual's claim but in agreements for much wider restitution programmes covering large classes of beneficiaries. Restitution may also result from advocacy as part of wider processes of transition within a country. Where done well, restitution can also complement wider development goals, particularly in the area of land and property where security of tenure can be strengthened through such processes.

Victims have sometimes used the courts to complain about the adequacy and fairness of restitution programmes, which have occasionally been found to discriminate against certain potential beneficiary groups.[81] Such complaints have not always been successful, however. The ECtHR has dismissed claims relating to the inadequacy of state administrative compensation schemes (which had the effect of extinguishing private claims relating to Nazi slave labour), on the basis that the state should have a wide margin of appreciation to strike an appropriate balance in the general interest.[82]

The ECtHR has considered a number of cases in which individuals have been dispossessed of property and other assets as a result of conflict.[83]

---

[80] See eg Unidroit Convention on Stolen or Illegally Exported Cultural Objects (Rome, 24 June 1995); Washington Conference Principles on Nazi-Confiscated Art (Washington, DC, 3 December 1998); Holocaust Expropriated Art Recovery Act of 2016 (114th Congress 2015–16) introduced 7 April 2016.

[81] *Ivica Kevesevic v the Federation of Bosnia and Herzegovina* CH/97/46 (10 September 1998); *García Lucero et al v Chile* (Preliminary Objection, Merits and Reparations) (28 August 2013).

[82] *Poznanski and others v Germany* (Decision on Admissibility) (App no 25101/05) ECHR 3 July 2007.

[83] Principal among these is *Loizidou and Cyprus (intervening) v Turkey* (1997) 23 EHRR 513.

Chiragov v Armenia concerned an application brought by Azerbaijani Kurds who were forced to flee from their homes to Baku in the context of the Nagorno-Karabakh conflict. They have since been unable to return to their homes and properties because of Armenian occupation. The Grand Chamber, in finding for the Applicants, noted that:

> [I]t would appear particularly important to establish a property claims mechanism, which should be easily accessible and provide procedures operating with flexible evidentiary standards, allowing the applicants and others in their situation to have their property rights restored and to obtain compensation for the loss of their enjoyment.[84]

Restitution programmes to redress both Holocaust-era injustices and subsequent nationalisation programmes put in place under communist rule have had less success, given that the Court's restrictive interpretation of its temporal jurisdiction has barred the majority of claims regarding the unlawful expropriations, considering only the fairness of the later restitution procedures.[85]

B. Compensation

Compensation is understood to cover any financially assessable damage, both material and moral, and loss of profit,[86] as well as the costs for legal or expert assistance, medicine, and psychological and social services.[87] Under international humanitarian law, protections afforded to individuals (and concomitant rights to reparation when the protections are breached) are determined according to their nationality (citizen, enemy citizen, neutral party's citizen) and status (civilian or combatant). Article 3 of Hague Convention IV as well as Article 91 of Additional Protocol I refer to compensation 'if the case demands', which is understood to require compensation if and when restitution is impossible.[88]

Compensation

> should be provided for any economically assessable damage, as appropriate and proportional to the gravity of the violation and the circumstances of each case ..., such as: (a) physical or mental harm; (b) lost opportunities, including employment, education and social benefits; (c) material damages and loss of earnings, including

---

[84] *Chiragov and Others v Armenia* (App no 13216/05) ECHR 16 June 2015, para 199.
[85] See eg *Malhous v the Czech Republic* (App no 33071/96) ECHR 13 December 2000.
[86] ARS (n 9) Art 36.
[87] Basic Principles and Guidelines (n 2) Art 20.
[88] API, Art 91; ICRC, '1949 Conventions and Additional Protocols, and their Commentaries—Commentary to Art 91', www.icrc.org/applic/ihl/ihl.nsf/vwTreaties1949.xsp, accessed 24 July 2016.

loss of earning potential; (d) moral damage; (e) costs required for legal or expert assistance, medicine and medical services, psychological and social services.[89]

As was held by the Inter-American Court of Human Rights in the *Velásquez Rodríguez* case, 'it is appropriate to fix the payment of "fair compensation" in sufficiently broad terms in order to compensate, to the extent possible, for the loss suffered'.[90]

Judicial reparations processes tend to privilege compensation over other forms of reparation, although, as indicated earlier in this chapter, compensation has rarely been 'full'.

C. Rehabilitation

Rehabilitation includes measures for physical and psychological treatment[91] as well as legal and social services,[92] and access to social benefits.[93] Certain specialist thematic IHL conventions emphasise the importance of targeted victim assistance and rehabilitation, such as the Convention on Cluster Munitions.[94] The Optional Protocol to the Convention on the Rights of the Child on the involvement of children in armed conflict[95] specifies that:

> States Parties shall take all feasible measures to ensure that persons within their jurisdiction recruited or used in hostilities … are demobilized or otherwise released from service. States Parties shall, when necessary, accord to such persons all appropriate assistance for their physical and psychological recovery and their social reintegration.[96]

It also indicates that: 'States Parties shall cooperate … in the rehabilitation and social reintegration of persons who are victims of acts contrary thereto, including through technical cooperation and financial assistance.'[97]

Rehabilitation has been awarded or confirmed by the Inter-American Court of Human Rights in a number of cases relating to conflict victims.

---

[89] Basic Principles and Guidelines (n 2) Art 20.
[90] *Case of Velásquez Rodríguez v Honduras* (Interpretation of the Compensatory Damages) Inter-American Court of Human Rights Series C no 9 (17 August 1990) para 27.
[91] *Plan de Sánchez Massacre v Guatemala* (Reparations) Inter-American Court of Human Rights Series C no 116 (19 November 2004) paras 106–08.
[92] Basic Principles and Guidelines (n 2) Art 21.
[93] UN Human Rights Committee, 'Concluding Observations on the Second Periodic Report of Bosnia and Herzegovina, adopted by the Committee at its 106th session (15 October– 2 November 2012)' (13 November 2012) UN Doc CCPR/C/BIH/CO/2, para 8.
[94] See Convention on Cluster Munitions (adopted 30 May 2008, entered into force 1 August 2010) 2688 UNTS 39, Art 3.
[95] Optional Protocol to the Convention on the Rights of the Child on the Involvement of Children in Armed Conflict (adopted 25 May 2000, entered into force 12 February 2002) 2173 UNTS 222.
[96] ibid, Art 6.
[97] ibid, Art 7.

For instance, in the *Barrios Altos* case against Peru, which resulted in an agreement on reparations between the parties, Peru agreed to cover the health expenses of the beneficiaries, granting them free care at the respective health centre, in respect of diagnostic procedures, medicine, hospitalisation, surgery, childbirth, traumatological rehabilitation, and mental health.[98] In other cases, the Court has taken a broader approach to rehabilitation, incorporating not only health rehabilitation, but also housing and educational programmes.[99] The ICC's Trust Fund for Victims has emphasised rehabilitation as part of its assistance work with victims of crimes coming within the jurisdiction of the Court. It has reported on both psychological and emotional support and physical rehabilitation work, including referrals for medical care, orthopaedic or plastic surgery, fitting of prostheses, treatment of wounds or infections, fistula treatment and other types of care.[100]

D. Satisfaction and Guarantees of Non-Repetition

Mass victimisation is the norm for both IACs and NIACs. As indicated, 'full' reparations, the clear standard for inter-state claims set out in the articles on state responsibility, have not been capable of implementation in practice. This is made worse in contexts when particular victims' situations of vulnerability or marginalisation preclude them from benefiting fully from any reparations offered, or results in an unjust distribution of reparations.

The challenges posed by mass victimisation are also evident when it comes to determining what forms of reparation are most suitable. It is not obvious how to adapt individual remedies to the context of mass victimisation when it is often claimed that collective reparations, particularly in the area of satisfaction and guarantees of non-repetition, might be better suited to balance individual and collective interests. Collective reparations can be problematic when the beneficiaries do not see themselves as a collective, either because they are dispersed or because of the nature of the violation. Even when the violation was perpetrated against a community or group, designing reparations (whether judicial or administrative) can also present challenges, as there is risk of compounding stereotypes, confounding reparations with development or appearing tokenistic.

---

[98] *Barrios Altos v Peru* (Reparations and Costs) Inter-American Court of Human Rights Series C No 87 (30 November 2001) para 42. See also *Cantoral Benavides v Peru* (Reparations and Costs) Inter-American Court of Human Rights Series C No 88 (3 December 2001) para 51(b); *Molina Theissen v Guatemala* (Reparations and Costs) Inter-American Court of Human Rights Series C No 108 (3 July 2004) paras 58(2), 71.

[99] See eg *Moiwana v Suriname* (Preliminary Objections, Merits, Reparations and Costs) Inter-American Court of Human Rights Series C No 124 (15 June 2005) paras 213–15; *Yakye Axa v Paraguay* (Merits, Reparations and Costs) Inter-American Court of Human Rights Series C No 125 (15 June 2005) paras 205–06, 221.

[100] ICC Trust Fund for Victims, 'Programme Progress Report' (2015) 17–18.

Satisfaction, understood as an exceptional remedy in the articles on the responsibility of states, has been frequently ordered in human rights jurisprudence to address injuries which involve breaches of trust, which acknowledgement and commemoration may help to remedy. Satisfaction has been awarded by courts and recommended by treaty bodies considering an array of violations occurring in the context of conflict. For instance, it was the remedy, and controversially the sole remedy (in the form of a declaration of responsibility), awarded by the ICJ against Serbia for its failure to prevent genocide in the *Bosnia Genocide* case.[101]

Criminal investigations have also been ordered as a form of satisfaction;[102] amnesties and related procedural bars on investigations and prosecutions have been disallowed for many crimes occurring during (and outside of) conflict, including genocide, war crimes, crimes against humanity, torture and enforced disappearances.[103] Cessation, as a form of satisfaction, has been emphasised as a remedy for continuing violations such as disappearances, wherein full disclosure of the truth, public acts of recognition and the need to locate and identify remains are understood as central to satisfaction.[104] What constitutes meaningful and appropriate satisfaction in response to an IHL violation requires decision-makers to consult with the widest possible constellation of victims.

Guarantees of non-repetition have included creating specific obligations to prevent new violations,[105] strengthening the administration of justice, improving monitoring mechanisms and other procedural safeguards, changing policies or legislation, vetting public officials, and setting up new institutions and commissions of inquiry.[106] These measures are most meaningful

---

[101] *Application of the Convention on the Prevention and Punishment of the Crime of Genocide (Bosnia and Herzegovina v Serbia and Montenegro)* (Merits) [2007] ICJ Rep 43, para 463.

[102] Bassiouni (n 3) 263–64.

[103] *Bautista de Arellana v Colombia* (1995) Human Rights Committee, CCPR/C/55/D/563/1993, paras 8.2, 10.

[104] *Neira-Alegría v Peru* (Reparations and Costs) Inter-American Court of Human Rights Series C No 29 (19 September 1996) para 69; *Plan de Sanchez Massacre v Guatemala* (Reparations) Inter-American Court of Human Rights Series C No 116 (19 November 2004) paras 93–103; UN Human Rights Committee, 'Concluding Observations on the Second Periodic Report of Bosnia and Herzegovina, Adopted by the Committee at its 106th session (15 October–2 November 2012)' (13 November 2012) UN Doc CCPR/C/BIH/CO/2, para 9; *Ferida Selimović et al v the Republika Srpska* (Decision on Admissibility and the Merits) CH/01/8365 (7 March 2003).

[105] See the Second Protocol to the Hague Convention (n 76). A number of UN Security Council resolutions have emphasised the impermissibility of the trade of cultural objects removed from conflict zones, such as UNSC Res 661 (6 August 1990) UN Doc S/RES/661 on the situation between Iraq and Kuwait; Res 1483 (22 May 2003) UN Doc S/RES/1483 concerning Iraq; Res 2199 (12 February 2015) UN Doc S/RES/2199 concerning Iraq and Syria.

[106] *Institute for Human Rights and Development in Africa (on behalf of Esmaila Connateh & 13 others) v Angola* Comm no 292/04 (7–22 May 2008) para 87.

when they respond specifically to marginalisation or structural inequalities operating in society and actively seek to break discriminatory patterns.

Guarantees of non-repetition are also linked with general measures of deterrence and prevention of future violations. For instance, UN Security Council Resolution 2199 of 12 February 2015 recognised the link between financial sanctions, bans on the trade in arms, oil, and Iraqi and Syrian looted cultural property, and the disruption of armed groups and the prevention of terrorism.

VI. CONCLUSIONS

The right to reparation for victims of armed conflict exists as a matter of law, but what the law says is required is disconnected from what happens in practice. Part of the difficulty is the limited standing for victims to pursue claims to assert their interests, which results in a piecemeal approach largely contingent on states' prerogatives. But there is also a discord between the rigidity of the law and practice. There is an absence of rules regarding 'second-best' remedies and reparation, particularly how to assess when a state or other wrongdoer is justified even on a temporary basis in affording anything other than 'full' reparation, and what standards should be employed to assess such 'second-best' measures. There are a range of approaches that have been taken by administrative bodies as to how best to address such challenges with a view to realising adequate and effective forms of reparation that correspond to the greatest possible extent to the harm. Language such as 'appropriate', 'effective', 'capable of responding to the harm', etc, suggests that 'second-best' measures must seek to approximate, to the greatest possible extent, 'full' reparation. However, there is nonetheless a tendency for states to start from the standpoint of 'anything goes', with victims struggling to fight for greater rights, which remains an uphill battle.

9

Arguing International Humanitarian Law Standards in National Courts—A Spectrum of Expectations

SHARON WEILL

D OMESTIC JUDGES ARE bound by the rule-of-law principles; they are supposed to be independent, impartial, accessible, and to provide an effective and equal enforcement of the law. In sum, they are entrusted to apply the law, while making a solid distinction between politics and law (or at the very least have to be perceived as doing so). This task is particularly challenging when national courts are adjudicating cases that involve international law issues in politically sensitive cases, such as in situations of armed conflicts.

Critics have shown that international law is interrelated with international politics, both in its formation, definition and in its enforcement.[1] Therefore, when courts apply international law, this will inevitably involve political interest, as the law itself is indeterminate and inherently political. This chapter illustrates the contradictory and often incoherent position in which national courts place themselves when applying international law, despite being formally expected to comply with the rule-of-law principle. Here, two distinct aspects come into play—the national legal framework that empowers national courts to apply international law (the structural aspect) and the court's de facto application of international law (the functional aspect). While national systems may comply with the structural requirements, such as the structural independence of judges or the incorporation

---

[1] M Koskenniemi, *From Apology to Utopia—The Structure of International Legal Argument* (New York, Cambridge University Press, 2005) 591. On the political nature of the international legal enforcement mechanism, see eg R Nollez-Goldbach and J Saada (eds), *Justice Penal International face aux Crimes de Masse: Approches Critiques* (Paris, Editions Pédone, 2014).

of international law in domestic legislation,[2] it may well be that the de facto function of the court will not correspond to these principles. The analysis made in this chapter focuses on the functional role of courts in their application of international law, and identifies five functional roles: (i) the apologist role of courts, in which they serve as a legitimating agency of the state's illegal actions; (ii) the avoiding role of courts, in which they, for policy considerations, avoid exercising jurisdiction over a case; (iii) the deferral role of courts, in which they apply the law in part and in part defer back to the other branches of the government; (iv) the limiting role of courts, in which they apply the law as required by the rule of law; and (v) the utopian role of courts, in which they introduce moral judgments for the protection of the individual, beyond the requirements of international law.[3] Each of these functions is illustrated through a critical legal analysis of national case law from different jurisdictions, in which both the legal argument and the political context are examined. Through such an analysis, special attention is given to interpretation of the legal norm, to the process of fact-finding and to the political context in which a particular decision was rendered.

As this chapter shows, national judges have developed nuanced approaches to deal with situations in which although being expected to act as neutral legal actors, they have included political judgments—yet without appearing to have let the political past their courtroom's iron gate.

I. THE APOLOGIST ROLE

One of the functions of national courts within a democratic system is the granting of legitimacy to the government and its policies. Studies from the fields of sociology of law and political science suggest that states rely on courts as a legitimising agent.[4] It is argued that courts have been accorded

---

[2] National courts will not be able to apply international law beyond the competence accorded to them by their national constitutional framework. Therefore, the applicability of international law norms within domestic systems and the competence of courts to enforce them must be guaranteed at the national level. In view of the fact that international norms are not always sufficiently detailed to be enforced by a court, even in states where courts may directly apply IHL, treaty law and customary law, states should enact adapting legislation. In order to make these laws enforceable, access to the courts must likewise be guaranteed by legislation. For further details on the structural requirements, see S Weill, 'Building Respect for IHL through National Courts' (2014) 96 *International Review of the Red Cross* 895/896, 862–64.

[3] S Weill, *The Role of National Courts in Applying International Humanitarian Law* (Oxford, Oxford University Press, 2014).

[4] R Cotterrell, *The Sociology of Law* (London, Butterworths, 1984) 234, 245; M Shapiro, *Courts: A Comparative and Political Analysis* (Chicago, University of Chicago Press, 1981) 17–28, 297; DD Caron, 'Towards a Political Theory of International Courts and Tribunals' (2007) 24 *Berkeley Journal of International Law* 401, 407.

competence to exercise judicial review over the political branches, and the level of independence required for the judiciary to have authority in the eyes of the public, precisely in order to provide this legitimating effect.[5] Shamir has shown that courts, in order to legitimise state policies, must first secure their own legitimacy as being independent.[6] They do so through the rare landmark cases in which they rule against the interest of the state. These exceptional decisions are usually not significant for their own merits as their actual impact is often negligible, but rather for the reinforcement of the legitimacy of courts, and the attribution of the necessary semblance of independence. After establishing their own legitimacy as an institution not seen as linked to any political interests, they can be then used to legitimate all the other cases in which similar policies are often approved. This section examines that legitimating role of the Israeli High Court of Justice (HCJ) with regard to the separation wall.

A. The Role of the Israeli HCJ in Legitimating the Separation Wall

In 2002 Israel started to build a wall between itself and the Occupied Palestinian Territories (OPT). In order to include Israeli settlements built beyond the 'Green Line' (separating Israel proper from the OPT), the wall was built within Palestinian land in many parts. Following the request of the UN General Assembly, on 9 July 2004 the ICJ gave an Advisory Opinion on the legality of the wall constructed in the OPT. The ICJ found that Israel had no authority to build the wall beyond the 'Green Line', ie beyond Israel's internationally recognised territorial sovereignty. It further found that the chosen route of the wall aimed at protecting illegal settlements, and that it amounted to de facto annexation of Palestinian land.[7] A few months later the Israeli HCJ rendered its own decision on the legality of the wall in the *Mara'abe* case (2005). *Mara'abe* concerned the legality of a part of the wall that was built in order to protect the settlement of Alfei Menashe, which has a population of approximately 5,700 Israelis.

---

[5] Cotterrell (n 4) 234, 245.

[6] R Shamir, 'Landmark Cases and the Reproduction of Legitimacy: The Case of Israel's High Court of Justice' (1990) 24 *Law & Society Review* 3, 781, 782–83. See also M Shapiro (n 4) 124. According to Benvenisti, courts within a state's democratic system are required to balance these two conflicting vectors: the institutional necessity of any government to rely on the court as a legitimising agent, and the need for the courts' to be seen as independent. See E Benvenisti, 'United We Stand: National Courts Reviewing Counterterrorism Measures' in A Bianchi and A Keller (eds), *Counterterrorism: Democracy's Challenge* (Oxford, Hart Publishing, 2008) 275.

[7] *Legal Consequences of the Construction of a Wall in the Occupied Palestinian Territory* (Advisory Opinion) [2004] ICJ Rep 136, paras 120–22.

Unlike the ICJ, the Israeli HCJ ruled that whether the settlements were established in violation of international law was an irrelevant question;[8] and that the military commander had the authority to build a security fence, as it was undertaken for security reasons: '[I]t is not a political consideration which lies behind the fence route at the Alfei Menashe enclave, rather the need to protect the well-being and security of the Israelis.'[9] As a result of the construction of the wall in this area, the well-being and security of Israeli settlers was guaranteed through the near-total encirclement of the Palestinian city of Qalqiliya (with 40,000 Palestinian inhabitants) by an 8-meter wall and a 50-metre-wide barbed-wire fence. In addition, five small Palestinian villages became trapped within 'the Israeli side' of the wall. These villages, whose populations found themselves unable to maintain their regular life as integrally linked with Qalqiliya and the West Bank, were the petitioners in this case.

After the HCJ established the general authority of the state to build the wall, the Court was prepared to strike out a specific segment of the planned route of the wall if the authority was not exercised in a proportionate manner. This assessment was conducted through the 'proportionality test' borrowed from Israeli administrative law.[10] The proportionality test enabled the Court to provide remedies to Palestinian individuals in extreme cases without having to challenge the entire policy.

In *Mara'abe* the Court found that the route chosen amounted to a disproportionate decision due to its effect on the Palestinian population.[11] However, a closer look at the proportionality test—or more specifically, at which facts entered into the justices' consideration and which facts were excluded—is required.

---

[8] *Mara'abe et al v Israel Prime Minister et al* HCJ 7957/04 (2005), para 19: 'The military commander is authorized to construct a separation fence in the area for the purpose of defending the lives and safety of the Israeli settlers in the area. It is not relevant whatsoever to this conclusion to examine whether this settlement activity conforms to international law or defies it, as determined in the Advisory Opinion of the International Court of Justice at the Hague. For this reason, we shall express no position regarding that question.'

[9] ibid, paras 101, 99.

[10] For a definition of the proportionality test consisting of three elements, see ibid, para 30.

[11] ibid, paras 112–14: 'Is it possible to ensure the security of Israelis through a different fence route, whose impingement upon the rights of the local residents would be a lesser one? ... [W]e have by no means been convinced that the second subtest of proportionality has been satisfied by the fence route creating the Alfei Menashe enclave. It seems to us that the required effort has not been made.'

Figure 1: Route of the Separation Wall (detail)

As surprising as it may appear from a simple look at the map shown in Figure 1, the Court's finding against the state, which strengthened its reputation as an independent judicial institution after the ICJ's advisory opinion, dealt only with an almost insignificant part of the route of the wall. The proportionality test was conducted between the settlement of Alfei Menashe (5,700 Israeli inhabitants) and the five small Palestinian villages (1,200 inhabitants) that had become trapped within the 'Israeli side' of the wall. The consequences for the 40,000 inhabitants of the city of Qalqilya in the northern part were simply not included in the HCJ's proportionality test. This factual issue remained somehow obscured by the Court's narrow selection of what it considered to be the affected populations. A more reasonable description of the facts would dictate a different balance, namely: can and should the needs of a small number of settlers be guaranteed by the encirclement of more than 40,000 persons in the Palestinian city of Qalqilya? However, this fact was simply not put into Judge Barak's balancing test.

The Court's remedy was to move the wall's route with regard to a specific segment in order to relocate Palestinians from five, already abandoned, small villages, to the 'Palestinian side' of the wall. Consequently, this decision had a negligible impact on the ground, and the Qalqilya wall became indirectly legitimised by the Court. Even more astonishing is the fact that the situation in Qalqilya was not entirely absent from the Court's ruling.

Its plight is described in detail, yet not in the sections 'relevant' to the case. The story of Qalqiliya appears as a non-binding opinion of the Court, or an obiter, under a section of the ruling entitled 'The Advisory Opinion of the ICJ at the Hague and the *Beit Sourik* Case'. In this section of the ruling, the HCJ cited parts of the UN reports written by Professors Dugard and Ziegler, which describe well the situation in Qalqiliya.[12] These reports were among the documents that constructed the factual basis for the ICJ's Opinion. Justice Barak's aim in citing these reports was to show how the two courts had two different fact-finding processes. The Court provided an extensive analysis of the different opinions of both courts (the ICJ and the Israeli HCJ) and attempted to explain their disparity by noting that 'the difference between the factual bases upon which the courts relied is of decisive significance'.[13] This observation could not have been formulated any better. Thus, Qalqiliya is not portrayed in this ruling as a relevant fact of the actual petition, but in the obiter section of the judgment, to illustrate the point that the facts that lay before the ICJ were not examined through a security lens.

The methodology chosen by the Israeli HCJ to review only specific segments of the wall was not a neutral choice. A general petition on the legality of the wall was pending before the Court. Yet, the Court decided to examine as a matter of policy only the legality of small segments of the wall.[14] In this way, as each segment of the wall reviewed by the HCJ is stripped from its broader factual context, the political intention of the de facto annexation became easier to ignore. At the same time, in exceptional cases, the Court could declare small segments of the wall to be illegal. In reality, these rulings had almost no impact on the ground. It allowed, however, the Israeli Court not only to legitimise the illegal policy as a whole, but also to reinforce its own reputation as an independent and effective judicial institution, which imposes limits on the state. Not surprisingly, the *Mara'abe* case, which was the first Israeli wall case rendered after the ICJ Advisory Opinion, and which gained the attention of the international legal community, was among the rare cases in which the route of the wall was found to be disproportionate.

---

[12] ibid, para 40: 'The city of Qalqiliya is encircled by the barrier with entrance and exit possible from one gate only. Thus the town is isolated from almost all its agricultural land. The villages surrounding it are separated from their markets and services.' See also para 45: '[A]lmost completely imprisoned by the winding route of the wall, including 40,000 residents of Qalqiliya.'

[13] ibid, para 68. Here Judge Barak explained that: 'It was not mentioned that Qalqiliya lies two kilometers from the Israeli city of Kfar Saba; that Qalqiliya served as a passage point to Israel for suicide bomber terrorists, primarily in the years 2002–2003, for the purpose of committing terrorist attacks inside of Israel; the Trans-Israel highway (highway 6) [built beyond the Green Line] whose users must be protected, passes right by the city.'

[14] S Arieli and M Sfard, *The Wall of Folly* (Tel Aviv, Yediot Sfarim, 2008) 157–60 (in Hebrew).

Finally, the fact that such an extreme situation as the Qalqiliya enclave could be indirectly legitimised while ruling on the disproportionality of a negligible part of the wall is also related to the legal procedure. The petitioners in this case were from the five small villages trapped on the 'Israeli side'. Therefore, the Court could ignore the Qalqiliya enclave in the north in the name of 'the relevant facts'. This case also reveals how some human rights lawyers came to doubt whether petitioning the HCJ did a greater service to the interest of the state than to their clients, even when they won their cases.[15]

B. The Apologist Role and the Rule of Law

The apologist role of courts is in opposition to the founding principles of the rule of law that relate to the function of the judiciary. It defies the fundamental requirement that the judiciary be independent and impartial. A court that serves as legitimating agency for the state's illegal action does not maintain its neutral position, and it becomes no more than an arm of the executive. In addition, the right to access a court cannot be realised effectively. Koskenniemi observes a structural bias within the international legal order.[16] This observation also seems to be valid for national courts that apply IHL. The inherent impartiality of national judges is related to the combination of a number of factors that influence judges' willingness to serve their state's national interest while applying IHL. First, the subjective default orientation of the judge herself tends to defend and favour her own national interest. This is especially true in times of armed conflict. Courts are state institutions—they consist of judges who are citizens of the state, and who therefore share the same sociological and psychological mindset.[17] Second, when two sides fall into a conflict that they cannot resolve between themselves, it is natural for them to resort to a third party to resolve the conflict. This is the prototype triadic structure of courts (ie two disputing parties and a third-party decision-maker). The condition for this structure

---

[15] M Sfard, 'The Price of Internal Legal Opposition to Human Rights Abuses' (2009) 1 *Journal of Human Rights Practice* 1, 37–50; see also John Reynolds, *Legitimising the Illegitimate?: The Israeli Court of Justice and the Occupied Palestinian Territory* (Al-Haq, Ramallah, 2010) n 106 and accompanying text.

[16] M Koskenniemi, *From Apology to Utopia: The Structure of International Legal Argument* (New York, Cambridge University Press, 2006) 607: 'Out of any number of equally "possible" choices, some choices—typically conservative or status quo oriented choices—are methodologically privileged in the relevant institutions.'). See also D Kennedy, *A Critique of Adjudication* (Cambridge, Harvard University Press, 1997) 59–60.

[17] B Leiter, 'American Legal Realism' in DM Patterson (ed), *A Companion to Philosophy of Law and Legal Theory*, 2nd edn (Oxford, Blackwell, 2010) 249. See also JJ Toharia, 'Judges' in JD Wright (ed), *International Encyclopedia of the Social & Behavioral Sciences*, 2nd edn (Amsterdam, Elsevier, 2015) 879–84.

to be legitimate is for the conflict-solver to be perceived as independent and impartial vis-à-vis the two parties to the conflict. As the judge is a state agent, in cases where the state is a party to the proceedings (and to the armed conflict), the triadic structure is necessarily weakened, as one of the parties may perceive the third party as an ally of its adversary. Presumptions, the burden of proof and other general rules may serve as legal tools to mask this structural bias through factual determination. In this respect, when the state is a party to IHL proceedings, and evidentiary or normative presumptions are made in its favour, the bias in favour of the state is only reinforced. In many legal systems, despite the complexity of establishing the facts in IHL cases (in which the state usually possesses exclusive information, already giving it an advantage over its adversary), additional presumptions are granted in favour of the state, further weakening the triadic structure. The authorities' version of the facts is given special weight. The general presumptions of honesty, good faith and integrity afforded to agency officials assume that the authority's factual claims are true.[18] Moreover, it becomes extremely difficult to prove that the authority's decision was arbitrary. The factual presumption, taken together with the more general presumption that the judiciary does not have more expertise than the authorities on certain matters, prevents courts from intervening effectively in a decision that was taken according to a professional authority's assessment. This means that where state authorities claim they were guided by reasonable considerations, their rationale will generally be upheld by courts. Finally, the complex political relations between the states involved in an IHL case often lead to a selective enforcement of the law that depends on the nationality of the victim and the identity of the responsible state or individual.

II. THE AVOIDING ROLE OF COURTS

Given that political objectives may be in certain situations irresistible (such as during ongoing hostilities, in which the total independence of courts is not always feasible) national judges have developed avoidance doctrines.[19] These doctrines permit judges to refrain from exercising competence despite

---

[18] See, for example, the ruling of the DC Circuit Court of Appeals when dealing with habeas corpus claims filed by detainees in Guantanamo. In *Latif v Obama* 666 F.3d 746 (2011), it instructed that lower courts should presume the accuracy of evidence presented by the government. In that case, although intelligence and interrogations reports had previously been found by the district court to be unreliable evidence, they were entitled to a presumption of regularity. The decision provided a significant reduction of burden of proof in favour of the government that radically reduced the chances of a successful habeas claim before US civilian courts.

[19] E Benvenisti, 'Judicial Misgivings Regarding the Application of International Norms: An Analysis of Attitudes of National Courts' (1993) 4 *European Journal of International Law* 2, 183.

jurisdiction being established, shielding states from judicial scrutiny before national courts.[20] By avoiding a case through the use of doctrines such as the act-of-state doctrine, the principle of non-justiciability, or the political question doctrine, the legal question remains outside the realm of justice and is left to the political arena. Recourse to avoidance doctrines may be justified in light of the difficulty in assessing evidence in foreign affairs cases and in applying legal standards to policy questions, as well as the question of expertise of judges in these matters and the institutional fear of judges that a decision will be ignored by the executive.[21] However, avoidance doctrines usually serve political goals, which are not always made public. When a case is declared by the court as non-justiciable, it may appear that the judiciary is not only deferring to the political branch, but is also implicitly condoning the action.[22] As is demonstrated in this section, avoidance doctrines have no definite borders. This is notwithstanding the judicial enumeration of 'neutral' factors for their application. While in one jurisdiction an issue may not be justiciable, in another the same issue would be. Thus, it clearly appears that a policy choice (and not a legal one) motivates the decision of a court invoking the avoidance doctrine.

A. Targeted Killing: To Avoid or Not to Avoid? It Depends on Whom You Ask[23]

On 30 August 2010, the American Civil Liberties Union and the Center for Constitutional Rights filed a suit in the US District Court of Columbia in the name of Nasser Al-Aulaqi against President Obama and others, challenging their decision to authorise the targeted killing of Al-Aulaqi's son, a US citizen, in Yemen. They claimed that the US policy of targeted killing violates the Constitution and international law, and requested the court to declare that according to US constitutional law and international law, the US government is prohibited from carrying out the targeted killing of its citizens where no armed conflict exists.[24] The US District Court of Columbia

---

[20] L Henkin, 'Is There a "Political Question" Doctrine?' (1976) 85 *Yale Law Journal* 5, 599.

[21] TM Franck, *Political Questions/Judicial Answers: Does the Rule of Law Apply to Foreign Affairs?* (Princeton, Princeton University Press, 1992) 45–60.

[22] Deeper examinations of cases in which these doctrines are not applied—through their rejection or by defining their exceptions—support this assumption. Study has shown that a court is more likely to render a decision on the merits in cases involving foreign relations or military affairs when the case results in a finding in favour of the state. See J Yates and A Whitford, 'Presidential Power and the US Supreme Court' (1998) 51 *Political Research Quarterly* 2, 539–50.

[23] For a complete analysis, see S Weill, 'Reducing the Security Gap through National Courts: Targeted Killings as a Case Study' (2016) 21 *Journal of Conflict and Security Law* 1, 49–67.

[24] *Al-Aulaqi v Obama* (Complaint for Declaratory and Injunctive Relief) (2010) ccrjustice.org/files/Al-Aulaqi%20v.%20Obama%20Complaint.pdf.

ruled that the case was dealing with political questions and was therefore not justiciable. The court took the position that the questions posed required both 'expertise beyond the capacity of the judiciary' and the need for 'unquestioning adherence to a political decision by the Executive' as well as an assessment of 'strategic choices directing the nation's foreign affairs [that] are constitutionally committed to the political branches'.[25] Thus, the US court ruled that the question of the legality of a targeted killing of a US citizen, who challenged a violation of his constitutional rights, was outside the realm of judicial law enforcement.

Even the court appeared to be uneasy with the result: '[I]t does not appear that any court has ever—on political question doctrine grounds—refused to hear a US citizen's claim that his personal constitutional rights have been violated as a result of US government action taken abroad.'[26] While the court was ready to acknowledge that it is a 'drastic measure' for the US to employ lethal force against one of its own citizens abroad, even if that citizen was an active part of a terrorist group, the court only expressed its discontent in a commentary within its own judgment, and not as a basis for the decision that it took: 'To be sure, this Court recognizes the somewhat unsettling nature of its conclusion—that there are circumstances in which the Executive's unilateral decision to kill a US citizen overseas is "constitutionally committed to the political branches" and judicially unreviewable.'[27]

The Israeli HCJ was asked to rule on the justiciability of targeted killings and responded differently than its US counterpart. The legality of the Israeli policy of targeted killing in the OPT was challenged before the HCJ in 2002. The petitioners submitted that by the end of 2005 close to 300 members of alleged terrorist organisations had been killed in targeted killings as well as approximately 150 civilians, who were close to the scenes of the killings.[28] The petitioners' claim was that the targeted killing policy was illegal as it violated international humanitarian and human rights law. In his ruling on the case, Judge Barak discussed at length the role of non-justiciability doctrines in the Israeli legal system.[29] The HCJ found that although its judgment was likely to have political or military implications, the Court determined that the question of whether or not to employ a 'State policy of preventive strikes which cause the death of terrorists and at times of nearby innocent

---

[25] *Al-Aulaqi v Obama* 727 F Supp 2d 1 (2010) 76–77. See also 80: 'Because decision-making in the realm of military and foreign affairs is textually committed to the political branches, and because courts are functionally ill-equipped to make the types of complex policy judgments that would be required to adjudicate the merits of plaintiff's claims, the Court finds that the political question doctrine bars judicial resolution of this case.'

[26] ibid, 74.

[27] ibid, 78.

[28] *The Public Committee Against Torture in Israel v The Government of Israel* HCJ 769/02 (2006), para 1.

[29] ibid, paras 48–49.

civilians' is a question of legal character.[30] Therefore, it rejected the non-justiciability claim based on that being a political question.

Interestingly, the reasoning in both the Israeli and the US decisions could have each led to the opposite result in those specific cases. In the US case the claim involved the allegation of a violation of the constitutional rights of a US citizen.[31] In Israel, the case challenged a policy of a general nature and not an individual case, which was previously ruled to be non-justiciable.[32] However, their decisions reflect different attitudes, arguably a result not of a legal consideration but of their different institutional policy on such matters.

B. Avoidance—Negative and Positive Aspects

From the perspective of the rule of law, the avoiding role of courts is highly problematic as it violates several of its basic principles, most notably the right of access to a court and the requirement of a legal system to enforce the law in an equal and effective manner. While courts have established criteria for the application of an avoidance doctrine, it has not always been possible to predict when courts would render a judgment on the merits of a case, as extralegal considerations are often involved. This entails that the law is often applied in a selective mode, in breach of the equality principle, which most often corresponds to the state position. Having said that, the positive aspect of avoidance doctrines is that when avoiding a case, courts at least do not produce a distorted jurisprudence that may be cited by other courts or jurisdictions in order to legitimise states' illegal acts by serving as apologists for states.

III. THE DEFERRAL ROLE OF COURTS

In recent years, there has been a growing trend of exercising judicial review over matters that had been traditionally avoided, such as courts' review of state acts during conflicts, even beyond their territorial jurisdiction. In order to deal with the inherent political complexity of international law,

---

[30] ibid, paras 51, 52: 'The question is whether or not to employ a policy of preventative strikes which cause the deaths of terrorists and at times of nearby innocent civilians. The question is—as indicated by the analysis of our judgment—legal ... the question is of the norms of proportionality applicable to the issue. The answers to all of those questions are of a dominant legal character.'

[31] See, for example, recent Canadian and Australian cases, eg *Hicks v Ruddock et al* (2007) FCA 299; *Habib v Commonwealth of Australia* (2010) FCAFC 12. In these cases the claims were based on violations of the Constitution, and therefore the courts ruled that avoidance doctrines cannot be applied.

[32] *Bargil v The State of Israel* HCJ 4481/91 (1993) 210.

courts have developed a nuanced and gradual way to address their own role of appropriately applying international law to executive acts through the use of the deferral technique and an open dialogue with the legislative and executive branches.[33] As the cases discussed in this section illustrate, courts are increasingly willing to exercise their competence over questions of international law, especially cases dealing with protection of human rights of the individual. However, they are still reluctant in such cases to overturn a decision by the executive on the merits and tend to show significant deference to the executive.

A. The UK *Abbasi* Case as a Case Study

The deferral role of courts is clearly apparent in a number of Guantánamo cases in different jurisdictions.[34] For example, the UK *Abbasi* case, decided in 2002, was among the first 'war on terror' cases dealt with by a court of a US-allied state. Abbasi, a British national, was captured by US forces in Afghanistan during the armed conflict there. In January 2002, Abbasi was brought to Guantánamo Bay. At the time of his appeal he had been held captive for eight months without access to a court or any other form of tribunal, or even being allowed access to a lawyer. Abbasi sought judicial review over the UK's decision not to afford him diplomatic protection, and asked the Court of Appeal to compel the UK Foreign Office to make representations on his behalf to the United States. Abbasi claimed that his fundamental right not to be arbitrarily detained had been infringed and that the state was obliged under English public law to take positive steps to redress this violation.

The first non-justiciability claim raised by the UK government was that the relief sought by the claimant was founded on the assertion that the US government was acting unlawfully. The UK government argued that, as English courts should not examine the legitimacy of actions taken by a foreign sovereign state, in this case the legality of the detention of prisoners at Guantánamo, the claim was not justiciable as 'for the court to rule on that assertion would be contrary to comity and to the principle of State immunity'.[35] This argument was firmly rejected by the Court as the case concerned a 'clear breach of international law, particularly in the context of human rights'.[36] The second non-justiciability claim raised by

---

[33] Benvenisti (n 6) 257.

[34] ibid. For other US and Canadian cases, see Weill (n 3) 121–34.

[35] *R (Abbasi) v Secretary of State for Foreign and Commonwealth Affairs* [2002] EWCA Civ 1598, [2003] UKHRR 76 CA, paras 28–57.

[36] ibid, para 57: 'Albeit that caution must be exercised by this court when faced with an allegation that a foreign state is in breach of its international obligations, this court does not need the statutory context in order to be free to express a view in relation to what it conceives to be a clear breach of international law, particularly in the context of human rights.'

the UK government was that the conduct of the UK Foreign Secretary, and his decision not to provide diplomatic assistance to Mr Abbasi, involved a question that could not be reviewed by a court, as his decision was based on foreign policy considerations entirely confined to the political branch.[37] This claim was also rejected by the Court on the grounds that the law of judicial review has developed and included 'the invasion of areas previously immune from review, such as the exercise of the prerogative',[38] affirming that the issue of justiciability depended not on a general principle, but on subject matter and suitability in a given case.[39] On the merits of the claim, however, the Court was unwilling to take a decision, deferring entirely to the executive's judgment: '[W]hether to make any representations in a particular case, and if so in what form, is left entirely to the discretion of the Secretary of State.' With regard to the right to habeas corpus, the Court declared that it could offer no direct remedy as 'the United States Government is not before the court, and no order of this court would be binding upon it', and furthermore, the respondent in this case, the UK, 'has no direct responsibility for the detention'.[40] While the remedy was entirely deferred to the state by granting the executive a very broad margin of discretion, at the same time the Court openly questioned the legality of the detention in Guantánamo in what was, at that time, an unprecedented situation:

> In apparent contravention of fundamental principles recognised by both jurisdictions and by international law, Mr Abbasi is at present arbitrarily detained in a 'legal black hole'. ... What appears to us to be objectionable is that Mr Abbasi should be subject to indefinite detention in territory over which the United States has exclusive control with no opportunity to challenge the legitimacy of his detention before any court or tribunal.[41]

Moreover, the English court addressed the US courts, in a remarkable attempt to engage in dialogue with and guide the American judges, who were expected to rule on the right of habeas corpus of British citizens detained in Guantánamo:

> On the face of it we find surprising the proposition that the writ of the United States courts does not run in respect of individuals held by the government. ... It is important to record that the position may change when the appellate courts in the United States consider the matter.[42]

---

[37] ibid, paras 68–106. This claim corresponds to the US political question doctrine; see Weill (n 3) 154–59.

[38] *Abbasi v Secretary of State* (n 36) para 80.

[39] ibid, para 106: 'It is not an answer to a claim for judicial review to say that the source of the power of the Foreign Office is the prerogative. It is the subject matter that is determinative.'

[40] ibid, para 67.

[41] ibid, paras 64, 66.

[42] ibid, paras 15, 66. See also para 18: 'There have been widespread expressions of concern, both within and outside the United States, in respect of the stand taken by the United States government in cases such as *Hamdi*.'

Even if the litigation in the *Abassi* case did not succeed on the merits, the English Court of Appeal went far beyond a cautious line in declaring that Abbasi was arbitrarily detained and in labelling Guantánamo Bay a 'legal black hole'.[43] Second, the decision not to avoid judicial review in this case allowed the English court to engage in an audacious judicial dialogue with US courts on the policy of detention in Guantánamo Bay during the early days of the 'war on terror'. It is, however, difficult to estimate the weight of this call and its influence on US jurisdiction.[44] While *Abbasi* was mentioned in several *amici curiae* briefs submitted to the US Supreme Court, in its ruling on the legality of the detention in Guantánamo and the right to habeas corpus in 2004, this Court did not make any reference to *Abbasi*. It is quite possible that, in the eyes of the American judiciary, the English court went beyond the limits of the usual comity between states' respective judicial institutions. At the same time, the influence of the *Abbasi* decision over the destiny of the British detainees in Guantánamo cannot be overestimated, at least with regard to the UK context.[45] By January 2005, following diplomatic pressure, Abbasi and the three other British citizens still detained at Guantánamo were transferred to UK custody. It can reasonably be assumed that the *Abbasi* judgment was among the factors that influenced that decision.[46]

B. From Deferral Towards a More Assertive Role?

The deferral technique allows an important transition from the avoidance role toward the exercise of judicial review in politically sensitive cases. If today, courts' rulings on the merits may end with a similar result (ie in pursuance of state policy), the importance of deferring to the executive should not be underestimated. Once the gates of judicial review are open, courts start a process in which they establish their legitimacy and independency, and their climbing further up the ladder of judicial review is thus only a matter of time.[47] However, the risk with the use of the deferral technique is

---

[43] ibid, para 64.

[44] When the decision in the *Abbasi* case was rendered in 2002, the question of the legality of the detention of the deteinees in Guantanamo was still pending before the US Court of Appeals for the District of Columbia Circuit. A year later, on 11 March 2003, the US Court of Appeals did not follow the English court's stance, and dismissed the claimants' action. The US Supreme Court overruled the lower court's decision in *Rasul v Bush* in 2004. See *Al Odah v United States* 321 F.3d 1134 (2003) and *Rasul v Bush* 321 F.3d 1134 (2004).

[45] RG Murray, 'The Ripple Effect: Guantanamo Bay in the United Kingdom's Courts' (2010) 1 *Pace International Law Review Online Companion* 9, 42. See also P Sands, 'The "Political" and the "Legal": Comments of Professor Tushnet's Paper' (2007) 3 *International Journal of Law in Context* 319, 322.

[46] Murray (n 45) 25.

[47] Benvenisti (n 6).

that if the state misuses the discretion allocated by the judiciary, instead of fulfilling their role as limiting abuses of the law, courts may instead facilitate a state's illegal policy, leading them to perform an apologist role.

IV. THE LIMITING/NORMATIVE ROLE OF COURTS

Under the limiting/normative role of national courts, which probably fulfils best the requirements of the rule of law, the principle of the independence of the courts takes a dominant role. In other words, courts exercise their role as independent institutions that apply international law and, if required, impose limits on the executive and offer protection against governmental abuse of power in accordance with the principle of separation of powers.

A. Imposing Limits on the Criminal Trials Currently Held in Guantánamo Bay

An interesting example of such a role is the limiting role performed by US civilian courts when reviewing on appeal the cases prosecuted at the military commissions at Guantánamo Bay.[48] Since the creation of the commissions in November 2001, eight cases have been completed in the following order.[49] In 2007, after more than five years at Guantánamo, the Australian David Hicks was the first detainee to appear before the military commissions under the Military Commissions Act of 2006. He was convicted in a plea bargain for providing material support for terrorism and sentenced to seven years imprisonment, but most of the sentence was suspended and he was transferred to an Australian prison from which he released in December 2007. Salim Hamdan, Osama bin Laden's driver, was the second individual to be tried beginning in the summer of 2008.

---

[48] The Military Commission Act of 2009 enlarged the possibility of appeal before US regular courts. As clarified by JK Elsea, once internal appeals are exhausted, 'the accused may appeal the final decision to the United States Court of Appeals for the District of Columbia Circuit, with respect to the findings and sentence ... DC Cir appellate decisions may be reviewed by the Supreme Court under writ of certiorari. ... Other review by a civilian court, including review on petition of habeas corpus, is no longer expressly prohibited.' See JK Elsea, 'The Military Commissions Act of 2009 (MCA 2009): Overview and Legal Issues' (2014) *Congressional Research Service*, www.fas.org/sgp/crs/natsec/R41163.pdf.

[49] Three other cases, including the 9/11 case that involves five defendants, have been ongoing. Declassified court documents are available at www.mc.mil. Ironically, although the military commissions' website bears the title phrase 'fairness—transparency—justice', at time of writing, the commissions' website was inaccessible outside of the United States. For a good media coverage of these cases by Carol Rosenberg, see 'Guantánamo: By the Numbers' *Miami Herald*, 25 October 2016, www.miamiherald.com/news/nation-world/world/americas/guantanamo/article2163210.html.

Like Hicks, Hamdan was convicted for providing material support for terrorism and sentenced to five years. However, in November 2008, he was transferred to Yemeni custody and released from prison in January 2009. Third, bin Laden's Yemeni 'media secretary', Ali Hamza al-Bahlul was convicted in November 2008 and sentenced to life imprisonment. He remains segregated alone as a convict in Guantánamo Bay's Camp 6 Convict's Corridor, while his case is slowly appealed in the DC federal courts. In 2010 Ibrahim al-Qosi, a Sudanese, agreed to a plea bargain for providing material support for terrorism and conspiracy to commit terrorism. He was released to Sudan two years later. In an earlier habeas corpus claim submitted in a federal court in 2004, al-Qosi was the first prisoner to complain of torture before the US federal judiciary, but, as part of his plea agreement, he withdrew his habeas petition including the torture claims. Omar Khadr, a Canadian citizen and only a teenager when arrested, was convicted in 2010 through a plea bargain for murder in violation of the laws of war; attempted murder in violation of the laws of war; conspiracy; providing material support for terrorism; and spying.[50] Khadr was repatriated to Canada in 2012 and released on bail from Canadian prison in 2015. Noor Uthman Mohammed pleaded guilty in 2011 to providing material support to terrorism, including a provision in the agreement to be transferred to Sudan if he testified for the government at federal and military trials until his release. All but thirty-four months of a fourteen-year sentence was suspended, and Uthman Mohammed was released and transferred to Sudan in December 2013. Majid Khan, a Pakistani citizen, was convicted in February 2012 through a plea bargain in which it was agreed to postpone his sentencing until he testified against other so-called 'high-value' defendants. According to the Senate Select Committee on Intelligence Report on the CIA Rendition, Detention, and Interrogation Program—commonly known as the 'Torture Report'—Majid Khan's 'lunch tray', consisting of hummus, pasta with sauce, and nuts and raisins, was 'pureed' and rectally infused on at least one occasion during his CIA captivity.[51] Ahmed Al Darbi, a Saudi national, pleaded guilty to several charges in February 2014 as an accomplice in the 2002 terrorist attack against the French oil tanker, MV *Limburg*, which was carried out while Darbi was *already* imprisoned at Guantánamo. He agreed to testify before the military commission in exchange for return to a Saudi Arabian prison in 2018. The agreement explicitly requested that:

> Once my guilty plea is accepted by the Military Commission, I will not initiate any legal claims against the United States Government, any United States Government

---

[50] The plea bargain is available at media.miamiherald.com/smedia/2010/10/26/10/stip. source.prod_affiliate.56.pdf.

[51] The Senate Select Committee on Intelligence, 'Committee Study of the Central Intelligence Agency's Detention and Interrogation Program' (December 2014) fn 584. See also fn 497.

Agency or official, or any civilian or civilian agency regarding my capture, detention, or confinement conditions prior to my plea. I further agree to withdraw or dismiss without prejudice any pending litigation regarding my capture, detention, confinement conditions, or alien unlawful enemy combatant or alien unlawful enemy belligerent status.[52]

Revealingly, four of these eight convictions were overturned on appeal by the DC Circuit.[53] According to US federal jurisprudence, military courts have competence to try non-nationals for violations of the international law of war.[54] While a number of convicts were charged for material support for terrorism, the US Court of Appeals for the District of Columbia Circuit ruled in 2012 in *Hamdan v United States* ('*Hamdan* II') that material support for terrorism was not proscribed as a war crime by international law. Thus, the military commissions lack the competence to try this offence.[55] The significance of the *Hamdan* II ruling is that if conduct only violates domestic US law but not also international law, then it can only be prosecuted in a civilian court, not a military tribunal. As a consequence, the charges and convictions for providing material support for terrorism against Noor Uthman Muhammed and David Hicks were also vacated—although the defendants themselves had all already been set free.[56] A similar case was decided by the same DC Court of Appeals in the *al-Bahlul* case in June 2015 in the context of the charge of 'conspiracy'—another cornerstone offence used in most of the ongoing and past Guantánamo Bay prosecutions. Judge Tatel from the

---

[52] *United States v Al Darbi* (Offer for pretrial agreement) ISN 00768 (2013) para 11. However, even without the plea bargain any procedure of this kind is prevented by US legislation. In a recent decision the US district court ruled that civil courts lack subject matter jurisdiction to hear any such case involving a torture complaint; see *Jawad v Former Secretary of Defence* No 15-5250 (2016). In this case, former prisoner Jawad filed a complaint in a district court seeking damage from the USA arising out of his alleged mistreatment while in detention. The district court dismissed the complaint as it found that Art 7(a) of the 2006 MCA barred the court from hearing any (non-habeas) claims arising out of Jawad's detention. The ruling was confirmed by the DC Circuit Court of Appeals. See 28 USC, para 2241(e)(2), which was introduced by s 7(a) of the 2006 MCA: '[N]o court, justice, or judge shall have jurisdiction to hear or consider any [non-habeas] action against the United States or its agents relating to any aspect of the detention, transfer, treatment, trial, or conditions of confinement of an alien who is or was detained by the United States and has been determined by the United States to have been properly detained as an enemy combatant or is awaiting such determination.' Unlike the habeas corpus stripping provision—which was found to be invalidated by the US Supreme Court in *Boumediene*—this provision remains valid in the view of the courts.

[53] See the convictions against S Hamdan, D Hicks, NU Muhammed and AH al-Balul, all discussed below. Al-Balul is the only one who is still imprisoned.

[54] See US Supreme Court jurisprudence; in *Ex Parte Quirin*, the Supreme Court determined the competence of the military commission and ruled that enemy belligerents may be tried for violations of the 'law of war'; *Ex Parte Quirin* 317 US 1 (1942).

[55] *Hamdan v United States* 696 F.3d 1238 (2012).

[56] See decisions of the US Court of Military Commissions Review of 9 January 2015 and 18 February 2015, which vacated the convictions of Hicks and Noor Uthman Muhammad, available at www.mc.mil.

Court of Appeals had explicitly expressed her position on her role as guardian of the rule of law:

> Despite the government's protestations this court's holding will not 'inappropriately restrict' the nation's ability to ensure that those who conspire to commit terrorism are appropriately punished. After all, the government can always fall back on the apparatus it has used to try federal crimes for more than two centuries: the federal courts.[57]

This decision had the potential to invalidate most of the cases, and to jeopardise the competence of the commissions to continue ongoing prosecutions. Therefore, the government petitioned the court for a rehearing *en banc*. On 25 September 2015 the DC Circuit Court of Appeals vacated its previous judgment and granted the government's petition. Thus, the *al-Balul* case is pending before the entire bench of the same Court: nine judges will decide whether 'conspiracy' will attract a similar fate as providing material support to terrorism.

B. Conditions Promoting the Normative Role of Courts

Courts may encounter difficulty in their attempts to impose the law on a state's acts during conflicts, because of the court's institutional limits within the state in which it operates and its need to maintain institutional authority and reputation. Several criteria may reinforce the authority of courts and legitimate their active role. The duration of the conflict, the timing of the review and the length of time that has elapsed since the armed conflict took place are important factors for courts in determining their willingness to exercise their authority. An active and independent civil society and media, which could influence public opinion and increase the demand for judicial scrutiny during the period after the conflict, are equally important factors. The initial stages of armed conflicts are typically characterised by a strong sense of patriotism and unity of the state in support of the executive. As courts are state institutions, and judges are citizens of their states, they form an integral part of the state system. However, this sense is not necessarily as strong when the review is carried out months or years after the facts (which frequently happens when a case is heard in a second or third instance). The time interval, and public opinion that has meanwhile crystallised due to media, NGO and academic reports concerning IHL violations, may have an impact on the willingness of courts to exercise their authority. Once the conflict becomes protracted, it becomes easier for a court to exercise its authority and to rule against the state—a situation that is barely imaginable during the initial stages of a full-scale military operation.

---

[57] *Al-Bahlul v the US* CMCR-09-001 (2015) 9–10.

There is another temporal aspect that is particular to serious violations of IHL. War crimes are not subject to statutory limitations. Therefore, war crimes trials can be held long after the crimes occurred. When the courts of the responsible state in a post-conflict setting deal with war crimes cases, courts may have an easier time in ruling against one of their own citizens. This is especially the case if there exists a consensual historical narrative that has identified individuals responsible for committing war crimes, and if enough time has passed to ensure that the people directly involved in the violations no longer belong to the circle of decision-makers.

Another aspect to be taken into account is the fact that national courts are part of a global legal order, a development that domestic courts are increasingly becoming aware of when adjudicating IHL cases. Thus, if international tribunals or leading national courts have already reviewed the same issue, it may be legally and politically easier for other courts to take a more active or assertive role.

V. THE UTOPIAN ROLE OF COURTS

Utopian decisions are decisions rendered when national courts interpret a rule beyond its purpose and the intention of the drafters, in the name of ethical values. These decisions, usually made against the state or government position, typically trigger a significant political or legal response.

The case of Judge Baltasar Garzón in Spain is an example of the court playing an activist role, which has resulted in far-reaching consequences. Following a petition filed by family members and associations representing victims of the Franco regime before the Spanish court on 14 December 2006, Judge Garzón opened a criminal investigation into allegations of crimes against humanity committed during the Spanish civil war and the period of Franco's rule. On 16 October 2008, he delivered a decision that recognised the Court's jurisdiction over the case, ruling that the Spanish Amnesty Law of 15 October 1977, which afforded amnesty for Franco-era crimes, did not apply to crimes against humanity.[58]

This decision did not pass unnoticed. Jurisdiction was denied on appeal,[59] and Judge Garzón was indicted under Spain's prevarication law, which

---

[58] Audiencia Nacional, *Juzgado Central de Instrucción No 5*, Diligencias Previas Proc Abreviado 399/2006 V (Judgment of 16 October 2008). Jurisdiction was assumed, inter alia, over crimes committed by Franco and his high command during the war and the post-war period in respect of 'crimes against the state', which under Arts 23.2, 23.4 and 65.1 of the Ley Organica Judicial corresponds to the jurisdiction of the Audiencia Nacional, carried out in the context of and connected to crimes against humanity.

[59] Audiencia Nacional, Sala de lo Penal, *Juzgado Central de Instruccion No 5*, Pleno, Diligencias Previas Proc Abreviado 399/2006 V, Auto (2 December 2008).

allows judges to be prosecuted for unjust judgments.[60] Garzón was in addition suspended from his judicial functions.[61]

While Garzón's interpretation arguably went beyond the purpose of the Spanish Amnesty Law, it was consistent with principles of international criminal law. Indeed, Spanish courts have consistently affirmed, in cases based on universal jurisdiction, that amnesties granted by third states that aim to prevent accountability for international crimes are not binding on Spanish courts.[62] Ironically, the Garzón case suggests that Franco's crimes can only be prosecuted in third states, based on universal jurisdiction.

VI. CONCLUSION

The relations between international law and politics are being constantly shaped. The nuanced way domestic courts reflect these relations of power, as illustrated in this chapter, is merely an expression of the broader ongoing struggle between different political visions, translated into legal norms and behaviours.

International law stands at a crossroads. It could provide a common legal basis for representing values such as equality and human security, applied within the rule of law framework. Alternatively it could serve as a tool to enable the exercise of a state's arbitrary power or economic interest and to allow abuses against persons under the cloak of legality. The ability of the law to serve as a tool of protection depends on the strength of our political demands to define its content and the nature of its enforcement.

---

[60] The complaint was filed by 'Manos Limpias', a right-wing political organisation on 26 January 2009 before the Criminal Chamber of the Supreme Court of Spain. Judge Garzón was indicted in April 2010 for the crime of *prevaricación*, alleging the abuse of his judicial authority by opening the inquiry into the Franco-era crimes. The crime of *prevaricación* is defined in Art 446 of the Spanish Criminal Code: 'The judge or magistrate who, knowingly, dictates an unjust sentence or resolution.' On 24 March 2011 Judge Garzón brought a case to the ECtHR challenging the lawfulness of his criminal prosecution, alleging a violation of Arts 6, 7, 8 10 and 18 of the ECHR, available at: www.interights.org/userfiles/Garzon_ECHR_Application_final_full.pdf.

[61] Unanimous Decision of the Spanish General Council of the Judiciary. See D Makosky, 'Spain Judicial Panel Suspends Judge Garzon over Franco Probe' *Jurist*, 14 May 2010, jurist.org/paperchase/2010/05/spain-judicial-panel-suspends-judge-garzon-over-franco-probe.php.

[62] See decision of the Central Investigative Court No 5 of the Audiencia Nacional of 1 September 2000 (indictment of Miguel Angel Cavallo); decision of 20 September 1998 of the Central Investigative Court No 6 (Pinochet case).

10

The Death of Lex Specialis? *Regional Human Rights Mechanisms and the Protection of Civilians in Armed Conflict*

BILL BOWRING[1]

I. INTRODUCTION

IN THIS CONTRIBUTION I engage with one of the thorniest and most controversial topics to bedevil international law concerning the protection of civilians in armed conflict. First, I outline the various approaches to the problem from 1996 onwards, and my own—radical perhaps—response in 2009. Next, I turn to the fruitful jurisprudence of the Inter-American Commission and Court of Human Rights. Third, I engage with the refusal, perhaps wisely, of the ECtHR to engage with the spectre of *lex specialis* as a means of resolving the apparent tension between international human rights law (IHRL) and IHL or the law of armed conflict. This culminated in the 2014 Grand Chamber judgment in *Hassan v UK*. Lastly, I turn to a recent intervention by the African Commission on Human and Peoples' Rights.

II. WHAT ARE THE ISSUES?

The issue of the application of IHRL and IHL was posed in 1996 in paragraph 25 of the ICJ's Advisory Opinion on the Legality of the Threat or Use of Nuclear Weapons.[2]

---

[1] I wish to acknowledge the tremendous research assistance given to me by Birkbeck PhD candidate Leticia Da Costa Paes, especially as to the Inter-American system; and by my own PhD student, Ali RaissTousi.
[2] *Legality of the Threat or Use of Nuclear Weapons* (Advisory Opinion) [1996] ICJ Rep 226.

The Court observed that 'the protection of the International Covenant of Civil and Political Rights does not cease in times of war', with the exception, of course, of those rights that, under Article 4, may be derogated from '[i]n time of public emergency which threatens the life of the nation'. This means that '[i]n principle, the right not arbitrarily to be deprived of one's life applies also in hostilities'.

The Court observed, however, that 'the test of what is an arbitrary deprivation of life … falls to be determined by the applicable *lex specialis*, namely, the law applicable in armed conflict'. It concluded therefore that:

> [W]hether a particular loss of life, through the use of a certain weapon in warfare, is to be considered an arbitrary deprivation of life contrary to Article 6 of the Covenant, can only be decided by reference to the law applicable in armed conflict and not deduced from the terms of the Covenant itself.

In 2004 Vera Gowlland-Debbas explained that:

> The Court accepts the continuing applicability of the Covenant in time of armed conflict, from which it may be inferred that it acknowledges the complementarity of human rights and humanitarian law. Its reference to the *lex specialis* cannot therefore mean the displacement of human rights by humanitarian law, at least to the extent of the nonderogable rights, in time of armed conflict. It should be pointed out that the maxim *lex specialis derogat generali* was traditionally applied only as a discretionary aid in interpreting conflicting but potentially applicable treaty rules. It is not relevant in determining the incremental or complementary nature of treaty rules.[3]

In 2007 Nancie Prud'homme sought to 'demonstrate the inadequacy of the theory of *lex specialis* and the hazard of opting for such a model to articulate the parallel application of international humanitarian law and international human rights law'.[4] She wanted to lay the foundations for alternatives. However, in 2008, Françoise Hampson, referring to three judgments of the ICJ,[5] stated that three interrelated propositions had emerged.[6] First, human rights law remains applicable even during armed conflict. Second, it is applicable in situations of conflict, subject only to derogation. Third, when both IHL and human rights law are applicable, IHL is the *lex specialis*. But the

---

[3] V Gowlland-Debbas and F Kalshoven, 'The Relevance of Paragraph 25 of the ICJ's Advisory Opinion on Nuclear Weapons' (2004) 98 *Proceedings of the Annual Meeting (American Society of International Law)* 358.

[4] N Prud'homme, 'Lex Specialis: Oversimplifying a More Complex and Multifaceted Relationship?' (2007) 40 *Israel Law Review* 2.

[5] *Legality of the Threat or Use of Nuclear Weapons* (n 2), para 25; *Legal Consequences of the Construction of a Wall in the Occupied Palestinian Territory* (Advisory Opinion) [2004] ICJ Rep 136, para 106; *Armed Activities on the Territory of the Congo* (Democratic Republic of the Congo v Uganda) [2005] ICJ Rep 168, paras 216–20.

[6] F Hampson, 'The Relationship between International Humanitarian Law and Human Rights Law from the Perspective of a Human Rights Treaty Body' (2008) 90 *International Review of the Red Cross* 871, 550.

relation between IHL and IHRL had not been resolved. She suggested that the Inter-American Court of Human Rights had shown the way, at least as regards the manner in which IHL can be taken into account.[7] However, her reference was to the Inter-American Commission, which had only dealt with such situations under the Inter-American Declaration of Human Rights, under which it did not deliver binding legal judgments.[8]

I took a more radical position in 2009,[9] when I suggested that: 'Chalk is being compared with, or even substituted by, cheese. Or still worse, the two are being mixed together: chalky cheese is horribly indigestible, while cheesy chalk is no good at all for writing on black-boards.'[10] I argued that at the most superficial level, IHL and IHRL have much in common.[11] Both are bodies of law ratified by states and binding on states. In both cases there are large multilateral treaties, ratified by most states. But there the similarity ends. There are significant differences between the law of armed conflict and human rights law.

The first relates to history. IHL is far older than IHRL. It is to be found at the beginning of recorded history, on the earliest recorded interactions between polities.[12] IHRL, on the other hand, did not exist in any form before the eighteenth century, when it first emerged in the declaration and bills of the French and American revolutions.[13] Even then, it formed part of domestic, constitutional law rather than international law, and only found its place in international law after World War I.

The second concerns the character of the normative structures themselves. IHL is, I asserted, intrinsically conservative, taking armed conflict as a given, as indeed it always has been in human society. Prior to the Red Cross codification, IHL was known as 'the laws and customs of war'. There is, on the other hand, no such prehistory for IHRL, which is in principle and has in my opinion always been revolutionary, scandalous in its inception,

---

[7] ibid, 572.

[8] ibid, 565; her footnote referred to the US operations in Grenada which were at issue in *Disabled Peoples' International v the United States* (1987) Inter-American Commission on Human Rights Case No 9213; *Coard et al v the United States* (1999) Inter-American Commission on Human Rights Case No 10.951; and the invasion of Panama in *Salas v the United States* (1993) Inter-American Commission on Human Rights Case No 10.573. The United States disputed the jurisdiction of the Inter-American Commission.

[9] B Bowring, 'Fragmentation, Lex Specialis and the Tensions in the Jurisprudence of the European Court of Human Rights' (2009) 14 *Journal of Conflict and Security Law* 485. The next section of this contribution draws from that article.

[10] ibid, 485.

[11] ibid, 489–90.

[12] See eg J Ober, 'Classical Greek Times' in M Howard, GJ Andreopoulos and MR Shulman (eds), *The Laws of War: Constraints on Warfare in the Western World* (Yale University Press, New Haven, 1994).

[13] In this I concur with A MacIntyre, *After Virtue: A Study in Moral Theory*, 2nd edn (Notre Dame, University of Notre Dame Press, 1990).

inspired by collective action and struggle, and threatening to the existing state order.[14]

The third follows from the second, and relates to the nature of the redress provided. Breaches of IHL had, until the creation of the ICC, called for action by one state against another, as in the *DRC v Uganda* case,[15] or, as with the Geneva Conventions, punishment of 'grave breaches' carried out by individuals. The individuals concerned must be investigated and prosecuted by states, or more recently by bodies created by states, through the agency of the Security Council or treaty bodies. In either case, the actor seeking redress was the state or its surrogate. The victim has had (until the victim provisions in the ICC Statute) no standing as such.

Despite having been established by private actors, the ICRC is a mediator between states, or, as in Additional Protocol II, non-state actors with the capacity to control territory. I emphasise that while by virtue of the Geneva Conventions states bind themselves to 'respect and ensure respect' for the conventions, the mechanism of enforcement is primarily that of national and international criminal law.

IHRL is the diametric opposite. It is the province of individual complaint, before the World War II to national courts, and following WWII to treaty bodies and mechanisms in which states, and not individuals, are brought to account. However, it must be emphasised that the initial claimants of the first-generation rights were the revolutionary movements against absolutism in the eighteenth century; those of the second generations were typically trade unions and other social movements, whose struggles attained legal recognition with the creation of the International Labour Organization in 1919. And those of the third generation were, as is well known, peoples, notably colonised peoples, fighting for their independence. The first and most important of the rights of the third generation is the right of peoples to self-determination, finally recognised in common Article 1 of the 1966 International Covenants on human rights.[16]

From this point IHL has been profoundly marked by developments in IHRL. The anticolonial struggles were largely aimed at securing independence within defined, overseas, territories—ie the so-called 'salt-water self-determination', in respect of territories separated from the colonial metropolis by seas and oceans, the territories to which the UN 'colonial'

---

[14] See B Bowring, *The Degradation of the International Legal Order? The Rehabilitation of Law and the Possibility of Politics* (Oxford, Routledge, 2008) 111–18; and B Bowring, 'Misunderstanding MacIntyre on Human Rights' in K Knight and P Blackledge (eds), *Revolutionary Aristotelianism: Ethics, Resistance and Utopia* (Stuttgart, Lucius & Lucius, 2008).

[15] *Armed Activities on the Territory of the Congo* (n 5) paras 216–17.

[16] See the key collection, which awakened my own interest in international law: J Crawford (ed), *The Rights of Peoples* (Oxford, Clarendon Press, 1988); and Bowring, *Degradation* (n 14) 69–98.9–38.

declaration of 1960 was directed.[17] The non-state protagonists were the 'national liberation movements'.[18] That was the period, up to the collapse of the USSR, when the use of force by self-determination movements— national liberation movements—was not, as is so often the case today, characterised as 'terrorism'.[19]

Until 1977, when two Additional Protocols were promulgated, there was no successful attempt to update the rules of conduct of hostilities from those contained in the Geneva Conventions of 1949 so as to take account of use of force in the cause of self-determination, as Hampson and Salama had pointed out.[20] They suggested that 'this may have been partly attributable to the reluctance, after both the first and second world wars, to regulate a phenomenon which the League of Nations and later the United Nations were intended to eliminate or control'.[21] However, this is to downplay the significance of the Protocols. It is of course the case that, as they note, Additional Protocol I dealt with IACs, updating provisions on the wounded and the sick and formulating rules on the conduct of hostilities, while Additional Protocol II dealt, for the first time, with high-intensity NIACs.

In this, they followed Doswald-Beck and Vité, in whose view the most important contribution of Additional Protocol I 'is the careful delimitation of what can be done during hostilities in order to spare civilians as much as possible'.[22] However, of a number of scholars recently publishing on the tension (or clash) between IHRL and IHL, only William Abresch recognised that the Additional Protocols aimed to extend the reach of the existing treaties governing international conflicts to internal conflicts: '[T]hus, Protocol I deemed struggles for national liberation to be international conflicts.'[23] In other words, if an armed conflict is a struggle for national liberation against 'alien occupation' or 'colonial domination' it is considered an 'international armed conflict' falling within Additional Protocol I.[24]

---

[17] UNGA Res 1514(XV) (14 December 1960).

[18] See the excellent analysis of the legal issues in J Faundez, 'International Law and Wars of National Liberation: Use of Force and Intervention' (1989) 1 *African Journal of International and Comparative Law* 85; and HA Wilson, *International Law and the Use of Force by National Liberation Movements* (Oxford, Oxford University Press, 1990).

[19] See GJ Andreopoulos, 'The Age of National Liberation Movements' in Howard, Andreopoulos and Shulman (n 12); and B Bowring, 'Positivism versus Self-Determination: The Contradictions of Soviet International Law' in S Marks (ed), *International Law on the Left: Re-examining Marxist Legacies* (Cambridge, Cambridge University Press, 2008).

[20] For a useful brief summary of the history of IHL, see F Hampson and I Salama, 'Working Paper on the Relationship between Human Rights Law and Humanitarian Law' (21 June 2005) UN Doc E/CN.4/Sub.2/2005/14, 25–26.

[21] ibid, 26

[22] L Doswald-Beck and S Vité, 'International Humanitarian Law and Human Rights Law' (1993) 293 *International Review of the Red Cross* 94, 99.

[23] W Abresch, 'A Human Rights Law of Internal Armed Conflict: The European Court of Human Rights in Chechnya' (2005) 16 *European Journal of International Law* 741, 742.

[24] AP I, Art 1(4). See also Abresch (n 23) 753.

This, I suggested, was the key to understanding the significance of both Additional Protocols. They were the response of the ICRC, and then the overwhelming majority of states that had ratified the Protocols, to the new world of 'internationalised' internal conflicts, in the context of armed struggle for self-determination by national liberation movements. In this way the international legal recognition of the right of peoples to self-determination impacted directly on IHL.

Writing in 2012,[25] Jean d'Aspremont and Elodie Tranchez noted that most lawyers and judges have 'presupposed that norms of IHL and human rights law (HRL) belong to the same legal order and the same legal regime and are, at the surface, in conflict with one another'. On the contrary, these authors argue that 'the relations between IHL and HRL ought to be construed in terms of competition rather than conflict'. Their starting point is that 'these two branches of international law have long lived side by side ignoring one another'.[26] They further point out that 'direct and strict conflicts between IHL and HRL norms hardly exist. Indeed, as was explained above, there can be no conflict of norms short of direct and strict incompatibilities.'[27] Their central argument was that:

> [T]he scopes of HRL and IHL are now competing *ratione loci*, *ratione personae* and *ratione temporis*. *Ratione loci* since from now HRL is not held to bind States only in their territory but also in territories which come under their effective control; *ratione temporis* since HRL is no longer confined to times of peace but also extends to times of war; and *ratione personae* as a result of the application of HRL to intrastate conflict situations.[28]

Most recently, Françoise Hampson and Daragh Murray returned to the issue in an *EJIL Talk* blog,[29] concluding that:

> [I]t is essential that human rights bodies address situations of armed conflict in a manner that is fully cognisant of the reality of armed conflict. The law of armed conflict was established specifically for the purposes of regulating armed conflict. International human rights law was not. While it is perfectly possible to apply international human rights law during situations of armed conflict—and while it is appropriate and even beneficial that this occurs—doing so requires adapting

---

[25] J D'Aspremont and E Tranchez, 'The Quest for a Non-Conflictual Coexistence of International Human Rights Law and Humanitarian Law: Which Role for the Lex Specialis Principle?' in R Kolb and G Gaggioli (eds), *Research Handbook on Human Rights and Humanitarian Law* (Cheltenham, Elgar, 2013) 223–50.

[26] ibid, 224.

[27] ibid, 232.

[28] ibid, 233.

[29] FJ Hampson and D Murray, 'ESIL-International Human Rights Law Symposium: "Operationalising" the Relationship Between the Law of Armed Conflict and International Human Rights Law' *EJIL Talk!*, 11 February 2016, www.ejiltalk.org/esil-international-human-rights-law-symposium-operationalising-the-relationship-between-the-law-of-armed-conflict-and-international-human-rights-law/.

international human rights law in order to acknowledge the distinct context of conflict, and the distinct requirements of the law of armed conflict. Accordingly, human rights bodies must ensure that they obtain sufficient expertise in relation to the law of armed conflict, and States must ensure that they argue their cases coherently and effectively. Importantly, States should also ensure that they intervene as third parties in relevant cases, so as to assist human rights bodies in appropriately operationalising the relationship between the two bodies of rules.

They were referring in particular to the case of *Hassan v UK*,[30] to which I will return. These topics continue to excite the interest of many scholars of international law.[31]

III. THE ISSUES IN THE INTER-AMERICAN SYSTEM

The Inter-American Commission of Human Rights was the first international body to adjudicate cases in which it directly applied IHL, and found states in breach of these norms. On 30 October 1997 the Inter-American Commission in the *La Tablada* case, Argentina, examined for the first time whether it was competent to apply IHL directly.[32] The case concerned an attack launched by 42 armed persons on military barracks of the national armed forces in 1989 at La Tablada, Argentina. The attack precipitated a battle lasting approximately 30 hours, resulting in the deaths of 29 of the attackers and several state agents. The Commission understood that it was 'competent to apply directly rules of international humanitarian law or to inform its interpretations of relevant provisions of the American Convention by reference to these rules'.[33] The Commission argued that: 'It is understandable that the provisions of conventional and customary humanitarian law generally afford victims of armed conflicts greater or more specific protections than do the more generally phrased guarantees in the American Convention and other human rights instruments.'[34] It understood that its competence to apply humanitarian law rules was supported by the text of the American Convention, by its own case law, as well as by the jurisprudence of the Inter-American Court of Human Rights: '[T]he American Convention itself authorizes the Commission to address questions of humanitarian law in cases involving alleged violations of Article 25.'

---

[30] *Hassan v United Kingdom* (App no 29750/09) ECHR 16 September 2014.
[31] See the newly published, at the time of writing, J Ohlin (ed), *Theoretical Boundaries of Armed Conflict and Human Rights* (Cambridge, Cambridge University Press, 2016), in particular M Milanovic, 'The Lost Origins of Lex Specialis: Rethinking the Relationship between Human Rights and International Humanitarian Law', 78–117.
[32] *Juan Carlos Abella v Argentina* (1997) Inter-American Commission on Human Rights Case No 11.137.
[33] ibid, para 157.
[34] ibid, para 159.

However, the *Las Palmeras v Colombia* case, decided by the Inter-American Court in 2001,[35] articulated a jurisdiction limitation in the area of IHL. The Commission brought Las Palmeras to the Court after completing an investigation in Colombia into the deaths of at least six victims who had been killed extrajudicially by members of the National Police Forces, aides by the Colombian armed forces. This was the first case in which the Court addressed the application of IHL.

The Commission stated in the preliminary objections, as a declaration of principle, that:

> [T]he instant case should be decided in the light of the norms embodied in both the American Convention and in customary international humanitarian law applicable to internal armed conflicts and enshrined in Article 3, common to all the 1949 Geneva Conventions.

The Commission reiterated its belief that both the Court and the Commission were competent to apply this legislation.[36]

But the Court understood that the American Convention had only given the Court competence to determine whether the acts or the norms of the states parties are compatible with the American Convention itself, and not with the 1949 Geneva Conventions. Therefore, the Court decided to support the third preliminary objection filed by the state (lack of competence of the Court).

Although *Las Palmeras* was not a specific case about *armed conflict*, the Court reinforced its opinion in relation to IHL in later cases addressing internal conflict.

In the *Serrano Cruz Sisters v El Salvador* case before the Court in 2005, the Commission in the preliminary objections (2004) had not requested the Court to apply IHL, but to apply the American Convention in order to establish the international responsibility of El Salvador for the forced disappearance of the Serrano Cruz sisters.[37]

The Court referred to the 'complementarity between international human rights law and international humanitarian law and the applicability of the former in times of peace and during armed conflict', and also repeated that the it is 'empowered to interpret the norms of the American Convention in light of other international treaties'.[38] The Court also remembered that it had protected members of communities by adopting provisional measures

---

[35] *Las Palmeras v Colombia* (Judgment) Inter-American Court of Human Rights Series C No 67 (4 February 2000) para 29.
[36] ibid.
[37] *Serrano-Cruz Sisters v El Salvador* (Judgment) Inter-American Court of Human Rights Series C No 118 (23 November 2004) para 109.
[38] ibid, para 111.

'in light of the provisions of the American Convention and international humanitarian law', given that they were in a situation of extreme gravity and urgency in the context of an armed conflict.[39] The Court mentioned a wide range of IHL instruments as to the protection of victims of international armed conflicts. Also, the Court observed that:

> [T]he State cannot question the full applicability of the human rights embodied in the American Convention, based on the existence of a non-international armed conflict. The Court considers that it is necessary to reiterate that the existence of a non-international armed conflict does not exempt the State from fulfilling its obligations to respect and guarantee the rights embodied in the American Convention to all persons subject to its jurisdiction, or to suspend their application.[40]

In the *Bamáca Velazquez* case,[41] the Court confirmed its rejection of the direct application of IHL, but recognised once again the role of IHL as an interpretative reference for cases of armed conflict. The Commission had once again insisted that Guatemala was in breach of both the American Convention and Common Article 3 of the Geneva Conventions, as a result of the Guatemala military's torture and murder of a guerrilla fighter during the conflict there.[42] But the Court found violations only of the American Convention, confirming its lack of competence to find state violations of a treaty that was not explicitly contemplated in the Convention. However, the Court observed that:

> Although the Court lacks competence to declare that a State is internationally responsible for the violation of international treaties that do not grant it such competence, it can observe that certain acts or omissions that violate human rights, pursuant to the treaties that they do have competence to apply, also violate other international instruments for the protection of the individual, such as the 1949 Geneva Conventions and, in particular, common Article 3.[43]

---

[39] cf 'Order of the Inter-American Court of Human Rights—*Matter of the Pueblo Indigena de Kankuamo*' (5 July 2004) para 11; 'Order of the Inter-American Court of Human Rights—*Matter of the Communities of Jiguamiandó and Curbaradó*' (6 March 2003) para 11; and 'Order of the Inter-American Court of Human Rights—*Matter of the Peace Community of San José de Apartadó*' (18 June 2002) para 11.

[40] *Serrano-Cruz Sisters v El Salvador* (n 37) para 118.

[41] *Bámaca-Velásquez v Guatemala* (Judgment) Inter-American Court of Human Rights Series C No 70 (25 November 2000).

[42] The Commission stated that the purpose of the application was for the Court to decide whether the state had violated the following rights of Efraín Bámaca Velásquez: Art 3 (Right to Juridical Personality), Art 4 (Right to Life), Art 5 (Right to Humane Treatment), Art 7 (Right to Personal Liberty), Art 8 (Right to a Fair Trial), Art 13 (Freedom of Thought and Expression), Art 25 (Right to Judicial Protection) and Art 1 (Obligation to Respect Rights), all of the American Convention, and also Arts 1, 2 and 6 of the Inter-American Convention to Prevent and Punish Torture and Common Art 3 of the Geneva Conventions (*Bámaca-Velásquez v Guatemala* (n 41) para 2).

[43] *Bámaca-Velásquez v Guatemala* (n 41) para 208.

The Court 'has already indicated in the *Las Palmeras Case* (2000), that the relevant provisions of the Geneva Conventions may be taken into consideration as elements for the interpretation of the American Convention'.[44] Hence, the organs of the Inter-American System can employ IHL as an interpretive tool.

The Court's jurisprudence has reaffirmed on many occasions the importance of contextualising human rights law within the broader scope of public international law, arguing that IHL can be extremely useful to achieve better interpretation of the human rights law in a context in which IHL applies. In the *Mapiripán Massacre v Colombia* case the Court held:

> While it is clear that this Court cannot attribute international responsibility under International Humanitarian Law, as such, said provisions are useful to interpret the Convention, in the process of establishing the responsibility of the State and other aspects of the violations alleged in the instant case. These provisions were in force for Colombia at the time of the facts, as international treaty agreements to which the State is a party, and as domestic law, and the Constitutional Court of Colombia has declared them to be *jus cogens* provisions, which are part of the Colombian 'constitutional block' and are mandatory for the States and for all armed State and non-State actors involved in an armed conflict.[45]

In the 2012 case of *The Santo Domingo Massacre v Colombia*,[46] the Court reaffirmed its capacity to use IHL as *lex specialis* when adjudicating an alleged breach of human rights under the American Convention that had occurred in a context of armed conflict. This interpretation of the jurisdictional limits within the American Convention resulted in an end to the Commission's capacity to find direct violations of IHL by states.

Despite this, the use of IHL as an interpretive tool within the Inter-American system has remained useful and necessary.

In *Santo Domingo* the Court conducted its analysis in part on the basis of the rules of IHL governing the conduct of hostilities. The Court addressed the rules of proportionality and of distinction, but its analysis focused on the obligation to take *precautionary measures*. The Court highlighted a range of factors about the cluster munition that was used, including the wide impact area of its six submunitions. It called the cluster munition an imprecise weapon ('una arma imprecisa') and considered that the use of any air-dropped explosive weapon ('armamento explosivo') to be dangerous, and therefore requiring to be strictly controlled to ensure that damage would only be caused to the selected target. The Court found that the

---

[44] ibid, para 209.
[45] *Mapiripán Massacre v Colombia* (Merits, Reparations and Costs) Inter-American Court of Human Rights Series C No 134 (15 September 2005) para 115.
[46] See 'Santo Domingo Massacre v Colombia (IACtHR)' *Weapons Law Encyclopedia*, 1 December 2013, www.weaponslaw.org/cases/iacthr-santo-domingo-massacre.

instructions given for the weapon's employment were imprecise, especially with respect to the minimum distance of the strike location to the village, and noted that military manuals in use in December 1998 indicated that this type of weapon should not be used in or near a populated area. In view of the weapon's lethality and its limited accuracy ('capacidad letal y la precisión limitada') the Court concluded that the use of the cluster munition in or near the village of Santo Domingo violated the attacker's precautionary obligations under IHL, and consequently, amounted to a violation, by Colombia, of the rights to life and to physical, mental and moral integrity under the American Convention.[47]

After these cases before the Court in which the use of IHL as *lex specialis* was established, in the limited sense of a tool for helping interpret human rights under the Convention, the Commission had to deal with many cases involving armed conflict and the application of IHL. It seems that the Court's decision has changed the Commission's position. The Commission started following the Court, using IHL as an interpretative tool, but declining to find direct violations of IHL legal instruments, as in *Rio Frio Massacre v Colombia*[48] and *Ana, Beatriz and Celia González Pérez v Mexico*.[49]

The evolution of the Court's jurisprudence can be seen in the 2014 case of *Rodriguez Vera et al (The disappeared from the Palace of Justice) v Colombia*.[50] This case concerned one of the most notorious events in recent Colombian history. In 1985, the Palace of Justice, Colombia's Supreme Court, was stormed and seized by members of the M-19 guerilla group. State security forces used disproportionate and excessive force in their fight to retake the Palace of Justice. As a result, many hostages in the building were killed by the use of automatic weapons, grenades, bombs and the fires that ensued. Further, once the Palace of Justice had been retaken, special forces detained many innocent survivors, and transferred them to military locations, where they were tortured, beaten and ultimately executed. The Court found that the state had violated the American Convention, the Inter-American Convention to Prevent and Punish Torture and the Inter-American Convention on Forced Disappearance of Persons.

The Court held in terms that are worth setting out in full:

> In the instant case, neither the Commission nor the representatives have asked the Court to declare the State responsible for possible violations of norms of international humanitarian law. In accordance with Article 29(b) of the American

---

[47] ibid.

[48] *Río Frío Massacre v Colombia* (2000) Inter-American Commission on Human Rights Case No 11.654, para 758.

[49] *Ana, Beatriz and Celia González Pérez v Mexico* (2000) Inter-American Commission on Human Rights Case No 11.565, para 1097.

[50] *Rodriguez Vera et al (The disappeared from the Palace of Justice) v Colombia* (Judgment) Inter-American Court of Human Rights Series C No 287 (14 November 2014).

Convention and the general rules for the interpretation of treaties contained in the 1969 Vienna Convention on the Law of Treaties, the American Convention can be interpreted in relation to other international instruments. Starting with the case of *Las Palmeras v Colombia*, the Court has indicated that the relevant provisions of the Geneva Conventions may be taken into account as elements for interpreting the American Convention. Therefore, when examining the compatibility with the Convention of a State's actions or norms, the Court may interpret the obligations and the rights contained in this instrument in light of other treaties. In this case, by using international humanitarian law as a norm of interpretation that complements the Convention, the Court is not ranking the different laws, because the applicability and relevance of international humanitarian law in situations of armed conflict is not in doubt. It merely means that the Court may observe the rules of international humanitarian law as a specific law in the matter, in order to apply the norms of the Convention more precisely when defining the scope of the State's obligations. Hence, if necessary, the Court may refer to provisions of international humanitarian law when interpreting the obligations contained in the American Convention in relation to the facts of this case. Consequently, the Court rejects this preliminary objection.[51]

As will be seen, the Inter-American Court has worked its way to a position very similar to that of the Strasbourg Court.

IV. THE STRASBOURG COURT: TURNING A BLIND EYE TO THE ISSUES?

Immediately prior to the public hearing at the ECtHR of the first six Chechen cases against Russia,[52] the applicants' lawyers, including the present author, argued between themselves whether it would assist their clients, the victims of gross violations of the right to life and other ECHR rights, to refer to or to rely upon the jurisprudence of the ICTY. They decided—rightly—not to.

Arnold and Quenivet are the coeditors of a book suggesting that there is a 'new merger' between IHL and IHRL.[53] As the introduction puts it: 'At the heart of the enquiry is whether the two bodies of law, IHL and IHRL have finally merged into a single set of laws.'[54] The editors cite Cerna's remark that IHL 'evolved as a result of humanity's concerns for the victims of war,

---

[51] ibid, para 39.
[52] These were: the bombing of the civilian refugee column in October 1999 (*Isayeva, Yusupova and Bazayeva v Russia* (App no 57947/00, 57948/00 and 57949/00) ECHR 24 February 2005); the massacre in the Staropromyslovskiy district of Grozny (*Khashiyev and Akayeva v Russia* (App no 57942/00 and 57945/00) ECHR 24 February 2005); and the indiscriminate bombing of the village of Katyr-Yurt in February 2000 (*Isayeva v Russia* (App no 57950/00) ECHR 24 February 2005).
[53] R Arnold and N Quenivet (eds), *International Humanitarian Law and Human Rights Law: Towards a New Merger in International Law* (Leiden, Martinus Nijhoff, 2008).
[54] ibid, 1.

whereas human rights law evolved as a result of humanity's concern for the victims of a new kind of internal war—the victims of Nazi death camps'.[55]

It will be plain from my remarks above that, *pace* Cerna, this is as far from what actually happened as could be the case. I repeat that laws and customs of war have accompanied the use of armed force since the beginning of history, while human rights are much more recent, but pre-existed the Holocaust.

In her own chapter in the collection, commenting on the Chechen cases, Quenivet asserted that the Strasbourg Court

> never assessed whether military operations conducted by state authorities were carried out in order to gain a military advantage. This is certainly linked to the fact that the very notion of military advantage is one encapsulated in IHL, and is therefore beyond the legal remit in which the [Court] assesses violations of the ECHR.[56]

She concluded: 'Without explicitly recognising that it is appraising the compliance of states with the core principles of IHL in non-international armed conflicts, the [Court] is in fact referring to the main principles of the lex specialis.' And further: 'What is remarkable is that the Court applies the detailed provisions applicable in times of international armed conflict to situations of non-international armed conflict.'[57] I hope I have shown that the Court would very likely have reached a quite different result if it had been confronted with applying IHL to individual commanders. In my view, the ECtHR was able to make the findings of fact it did precisely because it was applying different standards within a very different conceptual framework.

William Abresch, on the other hand, believed that the ECtHR had applied the doctrines it had developed on the use of force in law enforcement operations (eg by the police), to high-intensity conflicts involving large numbers of insurgents, artillery and aerial bombardment.[58] He correctly observed that for lawyers trained and practising within IHL, the law of IAC would be the ideal proper law for internal armed conflict. He called this an 'internationalizing trajectory'.[59] However, he contended that the ECtHR has broken

---

[55] CM Cerna, 'Human Rights in Armed Conflict: Implementation of International Humanitarian Law Norms by Regional Intergovernmental Human Rights Bodies' in F Kalshoven and Y Sandoz (eds), *Implementation of International Humanitarian Law* (The Hague, Kluwer, 1989) 31, 34.

[56] N Quenivet, 'The Right to Life in International Humanitarian Law and Human Rights Law' in Arnold and (n 53) 341.

[57] ibid, 353.

[58] Abresch (n 23) 742.

[59] ibid, 742.

from such a trajectory, in order to derive its own rules from the 'right to life' enshrined in Article 2 of the ECHR. His prognosis was that:

> [G]iven the resistance that states have shown to applying humanitarian law to internal armed conflicts, the ECtHR's adaptation of human rights law to this end may prove to be the most promising base for the international community to supervise and respond to violent interactions between the state and its citizens.[60]

He therefore continued to believe that IHL was the proper law to be applied to situations such as the Chechen (or the Kurdish) conflicts.

Abresch's approach was in reality therefore not so far from that of Hampson, who clearly considers that the Strasbourg Court should take IHL into account to the extent of applying it, and believed that despite the fact that the Court has never referred to the applicability of IHL, 'there is an awareness of the type of analysis that would be conducted under IHL'.[61] In this she follows the 'classical' model of Doswald-Beck and Vité, who considered that: '[T]he obvious advantages of human rights bodies using [IHL] is that [IHL] will become increasingly known to decision-makers and the public, who, it is hoped, will exert increasing pressure to obtain respect for it.'[62]

Similarly, Aisling Reidy, who was one of the lawyers in the Turkish Kurdish cases, together with Hampson and the present author,[63] considered that in the cases against Turkey, the Strasbourg Court was 'borrowing language from [IHL] when analysing the scope of human rights obligations. Such willingness to use humanitarian law concepts is encouraging.'[64] She too saw this development as 'certainly welcome in so far as it contributes to a stronger framework for the protection of rights'.[65] I disagree. I cannot see how the use of the alien framework of IHL in such a case would be 'encouraging'.

I can illustrate these points by further reference to the Chechen cases at the ECtHR.[66] These were cases brought by individual Chechen 'victims' against the Russian Federation. There could have been an inter-state case, and perhaps should have been; but this would still have been a complaint of violation of individual rights. The Chechen applicants in many ways spoke for the whole of their people. Their objective in the proceedings was not to obtain monetary compensation. What they wanted was the vindication,

---

[60] ibid, 743.

[61] Hampson and Salama (n 20) 18.

[62] Doswald-Beck and Vité (n 22) 108.

[63] See B Bowring, 'The Kurds of Turkey: Protecting the Rights of a Minority' in K Schulze, M Stokes and C Campbell (eds), *Nationalism, Minorities and Diasporas: Identities and Rights in the Middle East* (London, IB Tauris, 1996).

[64] A Reidy, 'The Approach of the European Commission and Court of Human Rights to International Humanitarian Law' (1998) 324 *International Review of the Red Cross* 513, 521.

[65] ibid, 521.

[66] References for the first six cases are given above, n 52.

at the highest level, of the truth of their account of what had happened to them and to the mass of Chechens. At this level Russia's right to sovereign action was at stake.

One by-product—entirely contingent as it happens—of the judgments in their favour was the naming of perpetrators in the case of *Isayeva v Russia*, which concerned the indiscriminate bombing of the village of Katyr-Yurt in February 2000 ordered by two senior Russian officers, General Shamanov and General Nedobytko. Findings of fact that amount to the commission of war crimes placed their investigation with a view to prosecution firmly on the agenda. In their submissions to the Council of Europe's Committee of Ministers on compliance with the judgments in October 2005,[67] the applicants argued that:

> [T]hese two officers were found to have been responsible for a military operation which involved the 'massive use of indiscriminate weapons' and which led, inter alia, to the loss of civilian lives and which has been found to have violated Article 2 of the European Convention on Human Rights. The applicants submit that in the light of the Court's findings …, criminal proceedings should be opened in respect of both of them.

It goes almost without saying that Russia never opened such proceedings.

Finally, I turn to Alexander Orakhelashvili.[68] He noted 'interdependence' of IHRL and IHL as explained by the ICJ in the *Wall* opinion, and 'parallelism' as displayed in *DRC v Uganda*. He cited the *Kunarac* case for the proposition that IHRL and IHL are 'mutually complementary'[69] and that 'their use for ascertaining each other's content and scope is both appropriate and inevitable'.[70] He commented in detail on the first six Chechen cases,[71] and concluded that:

> [T]he European Court's approach allows it to secure the legal outcome required under both human rights law and humanitarian law, even though it does not directly apply the provisions of the latter body of law, as norms falling outside its competence.[72]

This, I respectfully submit, is simply wrong. I have sought to show above that the defendant(s), the burden and standard of proof, and the evidential issues would have been quite different had IHL been the proper

---

[67] See 'Implementation of ECtHR Judgments in Chechen Cases' [2008] *EHRAC Bulletin* 6, www.ehrac.org.uk/wp-content/uploads/2014/10/Issue-10-ENG-ONLINE.pdf#page=6.

[68] A Orakhelashvili, 'The Interaction between Human Rights and Humanitarian Law: Fragmentation, Conflict, Parallelism, or Convergence?' (2008) 19 *European Journal of International Law* 1.

[69] *Prosecutor v Kunarac, Kovac and Vucovic* (Judgment) ICTY-96-23-T and ICTY-96-23/1-T (22 February 2001) para 467.

[70] Orakhelashvili (n 68) 164.

[71] ibid, 170–74.

[72] ibid, 174.

body of law for these cases. Orakhelashvili's conclusion, with which I also disagree, is that: '[T]he Court's approach should be based, as it mostly is, on the implicit application of the standards of humanitarian law, albeit cloaked in the Convention-specific categories of legitimacy, necessity and proportionality.'[73] I return to the metaphor of chalk and cheese: these categories have an entirely different origin and content from those of IHL.

A. *Hassan v UK*

The first case in which the ECtHR expressly considered the relation between IHRL and IHL was the Grand Chamber judgment in *Hassan v United Kingdom*.[74] Under the heading 'Relevant International Law' the Court listed 'Relevant Provisions of the Third and Fourth Geneva Conventions' (paragraph 33); The Vienna Convention on the Law of Treaties, 1969, Article 31 'General Rule of Interpretation' (paragraph 34); the 'Case-Law of the International Court of Justice Concerning the Inter-relationship between International Humanitarian law and International Human Rights Law' (paragraphs 35–37), notably the Advisory Opinion on *The Legality of the Threat or Use of Nuclear Weapons* (8 July 1996), paragraph 31; the Advisory Opinion on *The Legal Consequences of the Construction of a Wall in the Occupied Palestinian Territory* (9 July 2004) paragraph 106; the judgment in *Armed Activities on the Territory of the Congo (Democratic Republic of Congo (DRC) v Uganda*, (19 December 2005), paragraphs 215–16; The Report of the Study Group of the International Law Commission on Fragmentation of International Law (paragraph 38) and the Analytical Study of the Study Group on the same topic, dated 13 April 2006 (A/CN.4/L.682), paragraph 104; The House of Lords' judgment in *Al-Jedda* (paragraph 39); 'Derogations Relating to Detention under Article 15 of the European Convention on Human Rights and Article 4 of the International Covenant on Civil and Political Rights' (paragraphs 40–42).

The Applicant submitted, as summarised by the Court:

> 83. The Court had often applied the Convention in situations of armed conflict and recognised that in principle it was not displaced (the applicant referred to the following cases: *Ahmet Özkan and Others v Turkey*;[75] *Varnava and Others v Turkey* [GC];[76] *Al-Jedda*, § 105; *Al-Skeini*, §§ 164–167). This was, moreover, supported by the advisory opinion of the International Court of Justice in

---

[73] ibid, 182.

[74] *Hassan v the United Kingdom* (n 30).

[75] *Ahmet Özkan and Others v Turkey* (App no 21689/93) ECHR 6 April 2004, paras 85, 319.

[76] *Varnava and Others v Turkey* (App no 1, 16065/90, 16066/90, 16068/90, 16069/90, 16070/90, 16071/90, 16072/90 and 16073/90) EHCR 18 September 2009, para 191.

The Legal Consequences of the Construction of a Wall in the Occupied Palestinian Territory, § 106. In the applicant's submission, the International Court of Justice was recognising in this passage that there might be some rights that fall within the scope of international humanitarian law but to which no human rights convention extended. In the applicant's view, the position was that at most, the provisions of international humanitarian law might influence the interpretation of the provisions of the Convention. For example, they might be relevant in determining what acts were strictly required by the exigencies of the situation for the purposes of a derogation from Article 2. In the context of Article 5, this might, in an appropriate case, inform the Court's interpretation of 'competent legal authority' and 'offence' in Article 5 § 1(c). However, it was not right that Article 5 was displaced in circumstances in which the Geneva Conventions were engaged. The Convention was a treaty aimed at protecting fundamental rights. Its provisions should not be distorted, still less ignored altogether, to make life easier for States which failed to use the mechanism within the Convention that expressly dictated how they were to reconcile its provisions with the exigencies of war.

84. The applicant further contended that, in any event, the Government had not identified anything that United Kingdom forces were required to do by the Geneva Conventions that would have obliged them to act contrary to Article 5. The Iraq war was a non-international armed conflict following the collapse of Saddam Hussein's forces and the occupation by coalition forces. There was considerably less treaty law applicable to non-international armed conflicts than to international armed conflicts. International humanitarian law stipulated minimum requirements on States in situations of armed conflict but did not provide powers. In reality, the Government's submission that the Convention should be "displaced" was an attempt to re argue the question of Article 1 jurisdiction which was decided in *Al Skeini*. If the Government's position were correct, it would have the effect of wholly depriving victims of a contravention of any effective remedy, since the Third and Fourth Geneva Conventions were not justiciable at the instance of an individual. Such a narrowing of the rights of individuals in respect of their treatment by foreign armed forces would be unprincipled and wrong.

85. Finally, even if the Court were to decide that Article 5 should be interpreted in the light of the Third and Fourth Geneva Conventions, Tarek Hassan was arrested and detained as a means of inducing the applicant to surrender. The detention was arbitrary, it did not fall within any of the lawful categories under Article 5 § 1 and it was not even permissible under international humanitarian law.

The Government submitted:

86. ... that the drafters of the Convention did not intend that an alleged victim of extra-territorial action in the active phase of an international armed conflict, such as a prisoner of war protected by the Third Geneva Convention, who might nonetheless wish to allege a breach of Article 5, would benefit from the protections of the Convention. There was nothing to suggest any such intent within the Convention or its *travaux préparatoires*, or indeed in the wording or *travaux préparatoires* of the 1949 Geneva Conventions, which would have been at the forefront of the minds of those drafting the Convention as establishing the relevant

applicable legal regime. Furthermore, such intent would be inconsistent with the practical realities of conduct of active hostilities in an international armed conflict, and also with such Convention jurisprudence as there was bearing on the issue.

The Human Rights Centre at the University of Essex made extensive submissions which were summarised by the Court in paragraphs 91–95.

The Court recognised (paragraph 99) that:

> This is the first case in which a respondent State has requested the Court to disapply its obligations under Article 5 or in some other way to interpret them in the light of powers of detention available to it under international humanitarian law.

The Court continued (paragraph 100) that:

> The starting point for the Court's examination must be its constant practice of interpreting the Convention in the light of the rules set out in the Vienna Convention on the Law of Treaties of 23 May 1969 (see *Golder v the United Kingdom*, judgment of 21 February 1975, Series A no 18, § 29, and many subsequent cases).

The Court observed (paragraph 101) that:

> The practice of the High Contracting Parties is not to derogate from their obligations under Article 5 in order to detain persons on the basis of the Third and Fourth Geneva Conventions during international armed conflicts. ... Moreover, it would appear that the practice of not lodging derogations under Article 15 of the Convention in respect of detention under the Third and Fourth Geneva Conventions during international armed conflicts is mirrored by State practice in relation to the International Covenant for the Protection of Civil and Political Rights.

Having reviewed the ICJ case law, the Court held:

> 103. In the light of the above considerations, the Court accepts the Government's argument that the lack of a formal derogation under Article 15 does not prevent the Court from taking account of the context and the provisions of international humanitarian law when interpreting and applying Article 5 in this case.

> 104. Nonetheless, and consistently with the case-law of the International Court of Justice, the Court considers that, even in situations of international armed conflict, the safeguards under the Convention continue to apply, albeit interpreted against the background of the provisions of international humanitarian law.

> ...

> 107. Finally, although, for the reasons explained above, the Court does not consider it necessary for a formal derogation to be lodged, the provisions of Article 5 will be interpreted and applied in the light of the relevant provisions of international humanitarian law only where this is specifically pleaded by the respondent State.

The Court's conclusion was (paragraph 110): '[I]t would appear that Tarek Hassan's capture and detention was consistent with the powers available to the United Kingdom under the Third and Fourth Geneva Conventions, and was not arbitrary.'

This long-awaited clarification has aroused considerable discussion.[77]

As always, the *EJIL Talk* blog provided excellent rapid reaction. For Lawrence Hill-Cawthorne,[78] the Court had

> effectively read into Article 5(1) ECHR an extra permissible ground for detention where consistent with the Third and Fourth Geneva Conventions, and it read down the requirement of habeas corpus in Article 5(4) to allow for the administrative forms of review under the Fourth Geneva Convention.

As to positive points in the Court's judgment, he pointed out that: '[T]he Court rejected the UK's principal argument that IHL as the *lex specialis* precluded jurisdiction arising under Article 1 ECHR (para 77). To have followed this would effectively have been to displace the entire Convention where IHL applies.' Second, the Court had refused to follow the UK

> on the notion of *lex specialis*. Instead, its reasoning rests on two tools of treaty interpretation under Article 31(3) of the Vienna Convention on the Law of Treaties (VCLT), namely subsequent practice (Article 31(3)(b)) and other relevant rules of international law applicable in the relations between the parties (Article 31(3)(c)) (paras 100–102).

Furthermore, 'the Court does not simply submit Article 5 ECHR to the more permissive treaty standards in the Third and Fourth Geneva Conventions. Rather, its approach to this relationship is more symbiotic.'

His first criticism of the Court was that

> whilst its reliance on Articles 31(3)(b) and (c) VCLT over the *lex specialis* maxim did, as noted, encourage greater clarity, it is not clear that either subsequent practice or Article 31(3)(c) quite so readily points to the conclusion at which the Court arrived.

He identified the Court's reliance on state practice of non-derogation. He also raised a 'more general question about the propriety of using subsequent practice in a manner that effectively modifies treaty obligations'.

Marko Milanovic followed with 'some thoughts on the practical impact of Hassan, its bottom line and possible future influence'.[79] As to the bottom line, he emphasised that:

> [W]henever the military forces of a European state capture any individual, no matter where that individual is located … the Convention will apply by virtue

---

[77] Se, eg R English, 'Law of Armed Conflict Means that Anti-Detention Provision in ECHR May Be Disapplied re Iraqi Detainee' *UK Human Rights Blog*, 16 September 2014, ukhumanrightsblog.com/2014/09/16/law-of-armed-conflict-means-that-anti-detention-provision-in-echr-may-be-disapplied-re-iraqi-detainee/.

[78] L Hill-Cawthorne, 'The Grand Chamber Judgment in Hassan v UK' *EJIL Talk!*, 16 September 2014, www.ejiltalk.org/the-grand-chamber-judgment-in-hassan-v-uk/.

[79] M Milanovic, 'A Few Thoughts on Hassan v United Kingdom' *EJIL Talk!*, 22 October 2014, www.ejiltalk.org/a-few-thoughts-on-hassan-v-united-kingdom/.

of the personal conception of Article 1 jurisdiction as authority and control over individuals. ... In short, European soldiers carry the ECHR with them whenever they engage in capture operations.

Moreover, 'the most striking features of the judgment are its refusal to apply (or even mention) the *lex specialis* principle, and the fact that it is confined to situations of international armed conflict only'. Of course, 'the Court's re-interpretation of Article 5 is tantamount to its amendment'. Judgment in the case of *Jaloud v Netherlands* followed swiftly on 20 November 2014, but did not shake the approach taken in *Hassan*.[80]

Shaheed Fatima QC published a two-part commentary, under the heading 'Reflections on *Hassan v UK*: A Mixed Bag on the Right to Liberty'.[81] She was also critical of the Grand Chamber, in particular its starting point that state practice regarding both the ECHR and ICCPR is not to enter derogations regarding detentions made pursuant to the Geneva Conventions III and IV:

> This premise does not support the GC's conclusion because the state practice simply begs the questions: what are the reasons explaining the state practice and what (if anything) do those reasons say about whether IHL may be used when assessing the human rights' lawfulness of detentions? The GC should have considered these questions. In particular, the GC should have considered whether the state practice is explicable (partly at least) by reference to jurisdictional issues and therefore whether it has any continuing relevance to the relationship between IHL/IHRL.

Finally, Diane Webber, in *ASIL Insights*, wrote in 2015 under the heading: 'Hassan v United Kingdom: A New Approach to Security Detention in Armed Conflict?'[82] She concluded by suggesting that:

> [A] subtle difference can be discerned between the approach of the ECHR and [UN Human Rights Committee] HRC. The ECHR requires armed conflict security detention to comply with Section 5 European Convention, whereas the HRC assumes in principle that armed conflict security detention complies with Section 9 ICCPR. So parties to the European Convention are required to be satisfied that armed conflict detention is not arbitrary, whereas parties to the ICCPR are not required to take that extra step. States that are parties to both Conventions might

---

[80] *Jaloud v The Netherlands* (App no 47708/08) ECHR 20 November 2014. See A Sari, 'Jaloud v Netherlands: New Directions in Extra-Territorial Military Operations' *EJIL Talk!*, 24 November 2014, www.ejiltalk.org/jaloud-v-netherlands-new-directions-in-extra-territorial-military-operations/.

[81] F Shaheed, 'Reflections on Hassan v UK: A Mixed Bag on the Right to Liberty (Part 1)' *Just Security*, 10 October 2014, www.justsecurity.org/16170/reflections-hassan-uk-mixed-bag-liberty-2/; see also F Shaheed, 'Reflections on Hassan v UK: A Mixed Bag on the Right to Liberty (Part 2)' *Just Security*, 14 October 2014, www.justsecurity.org/15942/reflections-hassan-uk-mixed-bag-liberty/.

[82] D Webber, 'Hassan v United Kingdom: A New Approach to Security Detention in Armed Conflict?' (2015) 19 *American Society of International Law* 7.

be advised to ensure that security detentions in armed conflict comply with the more stringent requirements enumerated by the ECHR.

What is clear is that the spectre of *lex specialis* has been definitely laid to rest by the Grand Chamber in *Hassan*.

V. THE AFRICAN SYSTEM GETS INVOLVED

In November 2015, the African Commission on Human and Peoples' Rights (the Commission) adopted General Comment (GC) no 3 on the right to life.[83] The GC deals with a variety of issues surrounding the right to life, inter alia, the death penalty, use of force in law enforcement and armed conflict, investigations and accountability, and extraterritoriality. The GC also considers the relationship between the African Charter on Human and Peoples' Rights and IHL.

The GC states:

> 32. In armed conflict, what constitutes an 'arbitrary' deprivation of life during the conduct of hostilities is to be determined by reference to international humanitarian law. This law does not prohibit the use of force in hostilities against lawful targets (for example combatants or civilians directly participating in hostilities) if necessary from a military perspective, provided that, in all circumstances, the rules of distinction, proportionality and precaution in attack are observed. Any violation of international humanitarian law resulting in death, including war crimes, will be an arbitrary deprivation of life

On 7 June 2016 Vito Todeschini commented on *EJIL Talk*.[84] He pointed out that this paragraph was

> interesting in respect of three elements: the concept of 'arbitrariness' with regard to acts of deprivation of life in armed conflict; the interpretive principle employed to connect the ACHPR and IHL; and the legal consequences arising from IHL violations when human rights law also applies.

Furthermore, like the Strasbourg Court, the Commission 'refrained from invoking *lex specialis* to read the interplay between IHL and human rights law', and confirmed that 'systemic integration, not *lex specialis*, is the appropriate interpretive principle to operationalise the relationship between norms of IHL and human rights law'.

---

[83] African Commission on Human and Peoples' Rights, 'General Comment No 3 on the African Charter on Human and Peoples' Rights: The Right to Life (Article 4)' (2015).

[84] V Todeschini, 'The Relationship between International Humanitarian Law and Human Rights Law in the African Commission's General Comment on the Right to Life' *EJIL Talk!*, 7 June 2016, www.ejiltalk.org/the-relationship-between-international-humanitarian-law-and-human-rights-law-in-the-african-commissions-general-comment-on-the-right-to-life/.

Most importantly, the Commission had affirmed that:

> [A]n attack causing death in violation of IHL rules amounts to an arbitrary deprivation of life. ... For the first time, a human rights treaty body made it explicit that, when human rights law norms are placed in the background to favour the application of IHL norms, a breach of the latter entails a violation of the former.

This has momentous consequences for the availability of remedies:

> The acknowledgment that a breach of the IHL targeting rules resulting in death amounts to an arbitrary deprivation of life opens the way to individuals for obtaining redress for IHL violations via the right to a remedy under human rights law.

I very much agree with Todeschini's conclusion: 'Overall, the African Commission's GC may constitute a significant contribution to strengthen the enforcement of victims' right to reparation for both IHL and human rights violations in armed conflict.'

VI. CONCLUSION

The invitation to prepare this contribution has come at an auspicious time, when some much-needed clarity has emerged as to the relationship between IHRL and IHL. While I do not retract my remarks as to chalk and cheese, and the very different origins of the two branches of law, all three regional human rights systems have now taken giant steps to augmenting the protection of civilians caught up in armed conflict.

11

Extraterritorial Obligations under Human Rights Law

CEDRIC RYNGAERT[1]

U NDER IHL, CIVILIAN victims of out-of-area military operations largely lack remedies against the states (and international organisations) whose acts caused harm. This explains why aggrieved individuals have set their eyes on the promises held by human rights law. Human rights framing notably has procedural advantages as human rights norms can often be invoked against the state before domestic courts, and in some regions, even before supranational courts, eg the ECtHR in the Council of Europe area. The substantive question then arises whether such human rights norms are applicable to out-of-area operations. More technically, this is the question whether such norms have *extraterritorial application* (EA), or conversely, whether a state has *extraterritorial human rights obligations*, ie obligations to secure the human rights of individuals located beyond its borders.

Doctrinally speaking, the geographical scope of human rights treaties such as the ECHR and the ICCPR, and thus the reach of primary human rights obligations, crucially depends on the interpretation of the notion of 'jurisdiction'. Indeed, Article 1 ECHR provides that '[t]he High Contracting Parties shall secure to everyone *within their jurisdiction* the rights and freedoms defined in Section I of this Convention', whereas Article 2(1) ICCPR provides that 'each State Party … undertakes to respect and ensure to all individuals within its territory and *subject to its jurisdiction*' (emphasis added). A variety of interpretations have been given to the notion of jurisdiction. Looking at state and institutional practice, one can discern a majority view, which construes 'jurisdiction' in light of territorial and/or personal 'control', and a minority view, treating 'jurisdiction' as coextensive with state territory. As will be discussed in sections I and II, the ECtHR adheres to the former view, whereas the US position on the reach of the

[1] The author appreciates the financial support from the European Research Council (Proposal 336230—UNIJURIS) and the Dutch Organization for Scientific Research (No 016.135.322).

ICCPR is emblematic of the latter. The main goal of this contribution is, however, not to give an overview of the different existing constructions of the notion of human rights jurisdiction. A brief overview is necessary to set the stage, but then I go on to critique more fundamentally the territorial and control-based understanding of human rights jurisdiction. Highlighting the incongruities of the recent *Mothers of Srebrenica* decision before a Dutch court (2014), which attributed a host of acts to the extraterritorially acting state, but only established jurisdiction in respect of one, I suggest, drawing on earlier work done by Tzevelekos and Jackson,[2] to approximate the concept of human rights jurisdiction with the international law of state responsibility (section III). For this body of law, territorial location is not relevant; what counts is that a state actor committed or failed to prevent a wrongful act. In practical terms, this comes close to a plea for a cause-and-effect form of jurisdiction, which has so far been resisted by the ECtHR, at least in its official discourse.[3]

I admit that such an expansive approach to jurisdiction, while conceptually sound, risks being overbroad, which may in turn alienate states, both the extraterritorially acting states and the territorial ones. In this respect, I engage with, and reject, the argument that EA is a device of imperialism and intervention by stealth; EA aims to ensure civilian protection and accountability for military activities gone wrong (section IV). I also engage with the argument that there is a certain risk that human rights talk could legitimise situations of occupation, but argue that this risk has been overblown by some writers (section V). In spite of all the doom scenarios being conjured up, critics of EA would generally do well to realise that expansive EA only applies *in principle*: the principled application of human rights abroad does not say anything about possible norm conflicts, contextual interpretations and permissible derogations, which could sometimes drastically restrict EA in practice. In section VI, I argue that in situations of armed conflict, the content of human rights in extraterritorial operations should be interpreted in light of the relevant context, including the coapplication of IHL. Such contextual interpretation, as already applied by the ECtHR for that matter,[4]

---

[2] VP Tzevelekos, 'Reconstructing the Effective Control Criterion in Extraterritorial Human Rights Breaches: Direct Attribution of Wrongfulness, Due Diligence, and Concurrent Responsibility' (2014) 36 *Michigan Journal of International Law* 129; see also M Jackson, 'Freeing Soering: The ECHR, State Complicity in Torture, and Jurisdiction' (2016) 27 *European Journal of International Law* 3. In favour of a cause-and-effects text, arguably underlying the state agent control model, see A Orakhelashvili, 'Human Rights Protection During Extra-Territorial Military Operations: Perspectives at International and English Law' in N White and C Henderson (eds), *Research Handbook on Conflict and Security Law* (Cheltenham, Edward Elgar, 2012) 608; see also N Bhuta, 'The Frontiers of Extraterritoriality—Human Rights as Global Law' in N Bhuta (ed), *The Frontier of Human Rights* (Oxford, Oxford University Press, 2016) 11.

[3] *Banković and ors v Belgium and ors* (2007) 44 EHRR SE5, para 75.

[4] *Hassan v United Kingdom* (App no 29750/09) ECHR 16 September 2014.

may go quite some way to soothe concerns over a possible inflexible application of human rights in difficult circumstances. As I submit in section VII, this contextualisation can be brought on even firmer legal footing by states formally derogating from human rights treaties.

Accordingly, doctrinal tools are sufficiently available to states and courts to limit the fall-out of an expansive interpretation of the EA of human rights treaties. Built-in constraints to interpretation and derogation, as well as the applicability of IHL in armed conflict, should normally ensure that the rights and interests of civilians are properly taken into account.

I. THE EUROPEAN POSITION: THE APPROACH OF THE EUROPEAN COURT OF HUMAN RIGHTS

While a number of other international supervisory organs have addressed the EA of human rights treaties and have favoured it,[5] the notion and its scope have mainly been developed by the ECtHR. It is not the aim of this contribution to list and discuss the relatively extensive EA case law of the ECtHR; a large number of scholarly publications have already done so.[6] To grasp the arguments made later in the contribution, it suffices here to mention a number of EA milestones in the case law. Given the theme of this volume—the protection of civilians in armed conflict—the emphasis lies on EA in respect of military operations abroad and situations of occupation.

It is recalled that whether, and to what extent, the ECHR is given EA depends on the interpretation given to the notion of jurisdiction in Article 1 ECHR. In a judgment in 1995, *Loizidou v Turkey*, the Court fatefully linked 'jurisdiction' with the notion of 'effective control' by holding that the Article 1 obligation to secure the ECHR rights and freedoms within a Contracting Party's jurisdiction 'derives from the fact of such control whether it be exercised directly, through its armed forces, or through a subordinate local administration'.[7] In all subsequent jurisdiction cases, this effective control standard became the metric by which to measure the EA of the ECHR. As *Loizidou* pertained to a situation of occupation, the effective control standard initially took on a particularly territorial flavour: as evidenced by the famous *Bankovic* decision, individuals finding themselves in areas

---

[5] *Lopez Burgos v Uruguay* (1981) Human Rights Committee, IHRL 2796; *Coard et al v United States* (1999) Inter-American Commission on Human Rights Case No 10.951, para 37; *Legal Consequences of the Construction of a Wall in the Occupied Palestinian Territory* (Advisory Opinion) [2004] ICJ Rep 136, paras 108–11.

[6] See eg M Gondek, 'Extraterritorial Application of the European Convention on Human Rights: Territorial Focus in the Age of Globalization?' (2005) 52 *Netherlands International Law Review* 3; M Milanovic, *Extraterritorial Application of Human Rights Treaties* (Oxford, Oxford University Press, 2011); K Da Costa, *The Extraterritorial Application of Selected Human Rights Treaties* (Leiden/Boston, Martinus Nijhoff Publishers, 2012).

[7] *Loizidou and Cyprus (intervening) v Turkey* (1997) 23 EHRR 513, paras 62, 64.

over which the contracting party does not exercise full territorial control, eg in areas that were bombed by the latter from the air, did not fall within the state's human rights jurisdiction.[8] The strict territorial control standard subsequently gave way to a more relaxed 'state agent control' model in *Issa v Turkey*, pursuant to which

> a State may also be held accountable for violation of the Convention rights and freedoms of persons who are in the territory of another State but who are found to be under the former State's authority and control through its agents' operating ... in the latter State.[9]

In *Al Skeini v United Kingdom*, the latest restatement of the principles governing EA, however, the Court fell short of fully endorsing an autonomous personal model of jurisdiction, instead opting for a curious blend of the territorial and personal model.[10] In this case, the Court held that assuming abroad 'the exercise of some of the public powers normally to be exercised by a sovereign government', in particular the 'exceptional circumstances' of 'assuming authority and responsibility for the maintenance of security', established a jurisdictional link between the state and the individuals killed in the course of the state's extraterritorial security operations, for the purposes of Article 1 of the Convention.[11] This blend of models speaks to the Court's unwillingness to fully disavow the territorial model of *Bankovic*. As a result, it remains an open question as to whether killings in areas *not under the territorial control* of the state, eg targeted killings through drone strikes, can be addressed by the *Al Skeini* jurisdictional model.[12] The UK High Court endorsed the state agent control model for acts of *extraterritorial* physical violence of this kind in the case of *Al-Saadoon*,[13] but the decision was quashed on appeal.[14]

---

[8] *Banković v Belgium* (n 3).

[9] *Issa and ors v Turkey* (2004) 41 EHRR 567, para 71.

[10] *Al-Skeini and ors, Bar Human Rights Committee (intervening) and ors (intervening) v United Kingdom* (2011) 53 EHRR 18.

[11] ibid, para 149.

[12] Some authors, however, have argued that drone programmes in foreign airspace may amount to the exercise of public powers under the *Al-Skeini* model. See eg PV Kessing, 'The Extraterritorial Use of Armed Drones and International Human Rights Law: Different Views on Legality in the US and Europe?' in EA Andersen and EM Lassen (eds), *Europe and the Americas: Transatlantic Approaches to Human Rights* (The Hague, Brill, 2015) 377; R Frau, 'Unmanned Military Systems and Extraterritorial Application of Human Rights Law' (2013) 1 *Groningen Journal of International Law* 1, 10.

[13] *Al-Saadoon v Secretary of State for Defence* [2015] EXHC 715, para 106: 'Whenever and wherever a [state party] purports to exercise legal authority or uses physical force, it must do so in a way that does not violate [ECHR] rights.'

[14] *Al-Saadoon v Secretary of State for Defence* [2016] EWCA Civ 811. See for my comments, C Ryngaert, 'Al-Saadoon v United Kingdom: Another Shot at Human Rights Accountability for the Extraterritorial Use of Lethal Force', *UCall Blog*, 2016, blog.ucall.nl/index.php/2016/09/al-saadoon-v-united-kingdom-another-shot-at-human-rights-accountability-for-the-extraterritorial-use-of-lethal-force/.

Questions also remain as to the *scope* of a state's extraterritorial human rights obligations. In *Al Skeini*, the ECtHR held in this respect that the state is only under an obligation to secure the Convention rights 'that are relevant to the situation' of the individual, and thus that rights (or more accurately: state extraterritorial obligations) can be 'divided and tailored'.[15] As the Court gave no more specific guidance, states may obviously face uncertainty as to their exact extraterritorial human rights obligations. Nevertheless, the rule of thumb that (negative) obligations to respect human rights abroad apply in a relatively unfettered manner, whereas the scope of positive obligations depends on the context, may ease some concerns.[16]

II. THE US POSITION

In Europe, as a result of the ECtHR's case law, the EA of human rights may no longer be seriously contested as a matter of principle. The main debate has shifted to delimiting the *scope* of this application, in particular what 'control' means, and what human rights obligations—and to what extent— apply extraterritorially. The United States, in contrast, has so far steadfastly *rejected* the EA of human rights treaties, in particular the ICCPR. It has done so apparently out of fear that its policy of extraterritorial targeted killings (eg via drone strikes) and surveillance (snooping on foreigners by the National Security Agency), and more generally its foreign military and law-enforcement ventures would be subject to international scrutiny.

The US position *against* the EA of the ICCPR is of relatively recent vintage: it was only enunciated in 1995, in an oral response by the then-Legal Adviser during the presentation of the USA' (first) Initial Report to the Human Rights Committee (HRC).[17] This interpretation has been sustained ever since. Again in its Fourth Periodic Report to the HRC (2012) the United States holds on to its restrictive view,[18] even if it acknowledges contrary views expressed by the HRC itself (General Comment No 31), the ICJ and other states parties.[19] Leaked memoranda, published by the *New York*

---

[15] *Al-Skeini v United Kingdom* (n 10) para 137.

[16] Note that one and the same ECHR provision could contain a negative *and* a positive obligation. For instance, the right to life under Art 2 ECHR has a substantive dimension, meaning that a state should *respect* the right to life by only using lethal force in extreme circumstances, as well as a procedural one, meaning that a state should *investigate* incidents concerning the use of lethal force. The ECtHR case of *Jaloud*, the first post-*Al-Skeini* ECtHR decision on EA, precisely revolved around the latter dimension. See *Jaloud v The Netherlands* (App no 47708/08) ECHR 20 November 2014. The case is discussed below.

[17] UN Human Rights Committee, 'Statement of State Department Legal Adviser, Conrad Harper' (24 April 1995) UN Doc CCPRIC/SR 1405.

[18] UN Human Rights Committee, 'Consideration of Reports Submitted by States Parties under Article 40 of the Covenant' (22 May 2012) UN Doc CCPR/C/USA/4.

[19] ibid, para 505.

Times in 2014,[20] have demonstrated, however, that the official US view is internally fiercely contested: the 2010 memorandum, drafted by then-Legal Adviser Harold Koh himself advocated *abandoning* the 'strict territoriality'-based position of the USA.[21] In a later memorandum of 2013, Koh made a similar argument with respect to the Convention against Torture (CAT).[22] In 2014, this argument did, at least to a certain extent, carry the day in the third, fourth, and fifth US reports to the Committee against Torture, in which the United States acknowledged that 'the Convention ... applies to "certain areas beyond" its sovereign territory', and more specifically to 'all places that the State party controls as a governmental authority'.[23] It is likely that this change of position was informed by reputation losses caused by interrogation practices in such places as Guantánamo and Bagram. It is not fully clear, however, whether this shift implies that the United States recognises the EA of the CAT in all situations of torture committed by US agents abroad. Observers have in any event voiced some concern that a restrictive reading of 'controlling as a governmental authority' may yet place secret prisons controlled de facto, but not de jure by the United States outside the jurisdictional scope of the CAT.[24] However that may be, the US acknowledgement that the CAT, as a human rights treaty, could at least in some circumstances apply extraterritorially may pave the way for the EA of other human rights treaties such as the ICCPR. Indeed, in the face of contrary positions taken by US allies and international institutions, and persistent reputation losses, the United States may one day well decide to abandon its opposition against the principled EA of the ICCPR. Instead, it may then want to concentrate its argumentation on drawing the contours of such application, on the relationship between human rights law and international humanitarian law in times of armed conflict (the latter arguably constituting *lex specialis*),[25] and possibly on (limited) derogation from human rights treaties (see sections VI and VII).

---

[20] C Savage, 'Secret US Memo Made Legal Case to Kill a Citizen', *New York Times*, 8 October 2011, www.nytimes.com/2011/10/09/world/middleeast/secret-us-memo-made-legal-case-to-kill-a-citizen.html?_r=0.

[21] US Department of State, 'Memorandum Opinion on the Geographic Scope of the International Covenant on Civil and Political Rights' (19 October 2010).

[22] US Department of State, 'Memorandum Opinion on the Geographic Scope of the Convention Against Torture and Its Application in Situations of Armed Conflict' (21 January 2013).

[23] Committee Against Torture, 'Concluding Observations on the Third to Fifth Periodic Reports of the United States of America' (20 November 2014) UN Doc CAT/C/USA/CO/3–5, para 10.

[24] For an overview of reactions, see A Szpak, 'A Change of the US Position Regarding the Extraterritorial Prohibition of Torture—Is it a Breakthrough?' (2015) 17 *International Community Law Review* 496, 508–09.

[25] See in this respect also B Van Schaack, 'The United States' Position on the Extraterritorial Application of Human Rights Obligations: Now Is the Time for Change' (2014) 90 *Naval War College International Law Studies* 20.

It is of note that the USA is not the only state which opposes as a matter of principle the EA of human rights law, and the ICCPR in particular. Israel—confronted with the issue of applying the ICCPR in the Occupied Palestinian Territories (OPT)—also does so, at least since 2010,[26] even if at an earlier stage it implicitly seemed to accept the Convention's EA by making the (second-order) *lex specialis* argument.[27] That being said, the Israeli High Court of Justice, which has often demonstrated an independent streak, *did* accept the EA of the ICCPR, by notably finding Article 9(1) ICCPR on the right to liberty and security of the person applicable to arrests carried out by Israel in the OPT.[28] Also the US Supreme Court, for that matter, has recognised, in *Boumediene v Bush*, that aliens detained at Guantánamo Bay, ie outside the US, have 'extraterritorial' habeas corpus rights—although these rights were held to apply under US constitutional law rather than international human rights law (IHRL).[29]

III. EXPANDING JURISDICTION: BEYOND THE CONTROL STANDARD

One of the bizarre results of the current, even so-called 'progressive' interpretation of the jurisdictional clause in human rights treaties as mandated by the ECtHR is that persons adversely affected by an internationally wrongful act that is undeniably attributable to a state do not necessarily fall within the human rights jurisdiction of that state. Thus, a person may be unlawfully killed by an aerial bombardment, or by gunfire from a military patrol, and yet not fall within the jurisdiction of the responsible state, per *Al Skeini*, on the ground that the latter does not exercise effective control or public powers over the relevant territory or situation. On its face, this situation appears to be unacceptable. To remedy it, a more expansive concept of jurisdiction inspired by, and even based on, the rules of state responsibility may be called for.

[26] UN Human Rights Committee, 'Replies of the Government of Israel to the List of Issues To Be Taken up in Connection with the Consideration of the Third Periodic Report of Israel' (12 July 2010) UN Doc CCPR/CI/SR/Q/3/Add.1, 3: 'The Convention, which is a territorially bound Convention, does not apply, nor was it intended to apply, to areas outside its territory.'

[27] UN Human Rights Committee, 'Comments by the Government of Israel on the Concluding Observations of the Human Rights Committee' (24 January 2007) UN Doc CCPR/C0/78//SR/Add.1. For a longer discussion of the Israeli position, see US Department of State, 'Memorandum Opinion on the Geographic Scope of the International Covenant on Civil and Political Rights' (19 October 2010) 45–48; O Ben-Naftali and Y Shany, 'Living in Denial: The Application of Human Rights in the Occupied Territories' (2004) 37 *Israel Law Review* 17, 100–01.

[28] For a discussion of the relevant case-law, see A Gross, 'The Righting of the Law of Occupation' in Bhuta (n 2) 26–27.

[29] *Boumediene v Bush* 553 US 723 (2008). All the same, the US received plaudits for this decision from the UN Human Rights Committee. See UN Human Rights Committee, 'Concluding Observations on the Fourth Periodic Report of the United States of America' (23 April 2014) UN Doc CCPR/C/USA/CO/4, p 3.

In particular the *Mothers of Srebrenica* judgment of the District Court of The Hague[30] shows how courts may consider attribution and jurisdiction as analytically distinct hurdles that need to be successively taken before (often rather limited) state responsibility can be established vis-à-vis the victims of human rights violations, in this case liability of the Dutch state for failing to protect Bosnian Muslim men from violations of their right to life perpetrated by a Bosnian Serb militia. In its reasoning, the Court first attributed to the Netherlands *seven* actions carried out by the Dutch troop contingent (Dutchbat) in the Srebrenica area.[31]

This discrepancy is explained by the workings of the concept of human rights jurisdiction, as clarified in *Al Skeini*. According to the Court, the Netherlands only had 'effective control as understood in the *Al Skeini* judgment over the compound', as '[t]he compound was a fenced-off area in which Dutchbat had the say and over which the UN after the fall of Srebrenica exercised almost no actual say any more'.[32] In contrast, in the Court's view, the Netherlands had no such control over the much larger safe area, which as designated by UN Security Council Resolutions 819 and 836 (1993) was to be protected using 'all necessary means, including the use of force'. Dutchbat's deployment purportedly 'did not concern the exercise of *"public powers"* by *the State* in the form of *"executive or judicial functions"* in the *safe area* that would normally be implemented by the Government of Bosnia-Herzegovina'.[33] Nor, according to the Court, was there anything 'to show that through Dutchbat the State had *"physical power and control"* ... over the populace in the *safe area*' nor over 'the refugees who after the fall of Srebrenica remained in [a] *mini safe area*'.[34]

Thus, this case shows how detrimental to the interests of the civilian population the *Al Skeini* jurisdictional standard could be: whereas a host of acts were attributed to the Netherlands (and could arguably be wrongful too), only a handful of persons who had found refuge on the compound of Dutchbat were considered to fall within the jurisdiction of the Netherlands. Only to those persons would the Netherlands owe any (human rights) obligations. No obligations were owed to the 7,000 other Bosnian Muslims from

[30] *Mothers of Srebrenica v State of the Netherlands* ECLI:NL:RBDHA:2014 (2014). The case is currently under appeal. I have discussed the judgment at some length in C Ryngaert, 'Srebrenica Continued. Dutch District Court Holds the Netherlands Liable for Cooperating with Bosnian Serbs' (2014) 61 *Netherlands International Law Review* 3.
[31] *Mothers of Srebrenica* (n 30) para 4.144: '(i) Abandoning the *blocking positions*; (ii) Not reporting war crimes; (iii) Not providing the refugees with adequate medical care; (iv) Handing in weapons and other equipment to the Bosnian Serbs; (v) Maintaining the decision not to allow refugees into the compound during the transitional period; (vi) Separating the men from the other refugees during the evacuation; (vii) Cooperating in evacuating refugees who had sought refuge in the compound.'
[32] ibid, para 4.160.
[33] ibid, para 4.156 (emphasis in original).
[34] ibid, para 4.159 (emphasis in original).

the safe area killed in mass executions. The discrepancy between the results of the attribution test and the jurisdiction test is conveniently reasoned away by the District Court by reference to a diverging *control standard* applicable to attribution and jurisdiction, respectively.[35] However, one is left to wonder whether it makes sense to employ substantively different control standards, and ultimately whether the control standard for jurisdictional purposes is appropriate in the first place. As far as the latter point is concerned, it is recalled that the jurisdictional clauses of the human rights treaties, such as Article 1 ECHR, do *not* feature the notion of control. 'Jurisdictional control' is a jurisprudential creation,[36] as a result of which individuals adversely affected by—potentially wrongful—acts duly attributed to the state under the well-accepted control standard in the law of the state responsibility may nevertheless not fall under the 'jurisdictional human rights' control of that very state. As courts have created the latter control mode, they may possibly de-create it too, and bring human rights jurisdiction more in line with the law of state responsibility. After all, it is an anomaly that for one and the same act affecting internationally protected individual rights, a state can incur responsibility under general international law, but not under human rights law. In practice, in any event, this evolution has been under way for some time, as courts, interpreting the reach of Article 1 ECHR, at least with respect to the direct use of force by states, have edged closer to a free-standing state agent control model of jurisdiction.[37] This model resembles the state responsibility-based attribution model insofar as the *location* of the act is irrelevant; what simply matters is that the purportedly wrongful act is committed by a state actor, and thus attributed to the state, *wherever it may have occurred*.[38] The next jurisprudential step is to be more explicit about the interlinkage between the jurisdictional control model and the concept of attribution in the law of state responsibility.

---

[35] ibid, para 4.158: 'It is important to draw a distinction between the *effective control* criterion in the context of attributing actions to the State and in the context of the jurisdiction of the State which criterion is applied in both cases according to the circumstances of the case. In this way a state can have *effective control* over an area without exercising *effective control* over the specific actions of individuals in that area and vice versa.'

[36] *Loizidou v Turkey* (n 7).

[37] This holds true even if courts may formally reject the cause-and-effect model equating attribution and jurisdiction. See eg in *Al-Saadoon* (n 13) paras 104–05, where the UK High Court argued that it is only when 'the act involves the use of coercive physical force over an individual ... that the affected individual is brought within the state's jurisdiction wherever in the world the exercise of such power takes place', as deciding otherwise would collapse the distinction between jurisdiction and breach (para 108). At the same time, however, it held that the instantaneous extraterritorial use of physical force—a state proximately causing harm to an individual—triggered the human rights jurisdiction of the UK (para 102). See also *Al-Skeini v United Kingdom* (n 10) para 648, where the ECtHR found that the extraterritorial use of force by a state's agents against an individual can bring that individual under the state's jurisdiction, if the state agent physically commands control over the individual in question.

[38] Tzevelekos (n 2) 152.

Connecting jurisdiction with the general law of state responsibility may not only result in the EA of classic negative human rights obligations (prohibition of lethal force, torture), but also allow for a novel conceptualisation of the EA of a state's *positive* obligations, of the kind held by the Netherlands in the aforementioned *Mothers of Srebrenica* case. Vassilis Tzevelekos has observed in this respect that: 'The state should, simply enough, be pragmatically connected to a situation requiring it to put its means at the services of whoever is in need of them.'[39] This 'connection' is not necessarily related to control, but rather to a due-diligence-based capacity to effectively influence a state of affairs that risks giving rise to human rights violations. This nexus argument resembles the one made by the claimants in *Mothers of Srebrenica* (but ultimately rejected by the Court), namely that 'first and foremost' 'Dutchbat's actions fall under the jurisdiction of the State since the deployment of military personnel to protect civilians is part of the core tasks of any state', and that 'Dutchbat was the only military power of any significance in the *safe area* that had to protect the civilians against the Bosnian Serbs and Dutchbat's presence was of crucial importance for the existence of the *safe area*'.[40]

A state-responsibility, due-diligence-based rather than control-based approach to human rights jurisdiction could, in case wrongfulness is established, also lead to a finding of responsibility in another scenario, namely in respect of *extraterritorial state complicity*. Such complicity occurs when one state aids and assists another state to commit a wrongful act, on the latter's territory, eg when the UK assists a foreign state using enhanced interrogation techniques. This conduct could undeniably engage the complicit state's responsibility under Article 16 of the ILC Articles on the Responsibility of States for Internationally Wrongful Acts. However, as Miles Jackson has pointed out, in such a scenario the victim of the wrongful act does not fall within the human rights jurisdiction of the complicit state, as the latter does not exercise authority and control over the victim per the *Al Skeini* standard. As a result, the victim cannot formulate a human rights claim against the complicit state, even if it is crystal clear that a human rights violation (torture) has been committed.[41] Extrapolating the ECtHR's *Soering* principle—which considers the act of extraditing or expelling an individual to a third state where he could foreseeably be exposed to an ECHR violation to fall within the ECHR jurisdiction of the extraditing state,[42]

---

[39] ibid, 174.
[40] *Mothers of Srebrenica* (n 30) para 4.155. On a subsidiary basis, they relied on an extensive version of the control standard when submitting that 'the jurisdiction of the State alongside that of the UN exists because Dutchbat was in fact the only military power in the *safe area* and as such exercised *"effective control"* over the *safe area*' (para 4.157).
[41] Jackson (n 2) 4.
[42] *Soering v United Kingdom* (1989) 11 EHRR 439, para 86.

Jackson argues that also acts of aiding and assisting a third state where it is foreseeable that a human rights violation will occur fall within the complicit state's jurisdiction.[43] This approach is commendable, as it narrows the existing accountability gap resulting from the absence of remedies under the general law of state responsibility and (oftentimes also) under the law of the territorial state where the violation occurred.

These progressive approaches to jurisdiction—both relating to negative and positive obligations—remain to be tested in higher courts, and the ECtHR in particular. However, as in more recent cases the ECtHR has de facto departed from *Bankovic*, one could imagine that the Court may also one day shed the strictures of *Al Skeini*. Nevertheless, I expect that, if the Court proves willing to go down this path, it will somehow have to merge the concepts of attribution and due diligence with the control standard; the latter is so much ingrained in its case law on EA that the Court is unlikely just to give it up.

IV. EXTRATERRITORIAL APPLICATION OF HUMAN RIGHTS AS INTERVENTION?

As the EA of human rights expands, fears may be stoked that EA is just another legal ploy to justify (Western) intervention in the affairs of other states. When Western states apply—and are even obliged to apply—their own version of human rights abroad, are they not supplanting the regulatory and enforcement choices made by the territorial state? This concern arguably underlies the ECtHR's choice in *Bankovic* to interpret the notion of jurisdiction on the basis of *general international law*: as the Court held, 'from the standpoint of public international law', jurisdiction, defined as state competence, is 'primary territorial' and 'as a general rule, defined and limited by the sovereign territorial rights of the other relevant States'.[44] This public international law approach to the concept of jurisdiction in human rights treaties may subsequently have been discredited,[45] largely on the ground that 'state jurisdiction' in general international law has a prohibitive/permissive dimension, whereas in human rights law it has an obligatory one.[46] Nevertheless, the ECtHR's *Bankovic* reference to the

---

[43] Jackson (n 2) 6–12.

[44] *Bankovic v Belgium* (n 3) para 59. In *Ilaşcu and ors and Romania (intervening) v Moldova and Russian Federation* (2005) 40 EHRR 1030, para 312, the Court also toed this line, presuming jurisdiction 'to be exercised normally throughout the State's territory'.

[45] M Milanovic, *Extraterritorial Application of Human Rights Treaties* (Oxford, Oxford University Press, 2011), 19–34.

[46] Compare S Ratner, *The Thin Justice of International Law* (Oxford, Oxford University Press, 2015) 268, (arguing that EA of human rights and jurisdiction are 'distinct doctrinal boxes and labels'). It is noted that jurisdiction in general international law uses a limited number of permissive principles justifying a state's jurisdictional assertion; any assertions beyond

'sovereign territorial rights of the other relevant States' speaks to a concern that EA may well violate the principle of non-interference on which the edifice of modern international law has been built.

This concern is largely overblown, however. Especially in respect of extraterritorial state obligations to respect, one would be hard pressed to find another sovereign's territorial rights trampled upon by extensions of the geographical reach of human rights treaties. To the contrary, far from being offended by the EA of human rights treaties, territorial states may tend to *support* human rights claims filed against extraterritorially active states, and argue that their extraterritorial interventions—which may have been unlawful to begin with—come with certain (human rights) obligations. Surely in *Bankovic* the former Yugoslavia did not take issue with the human rights claims being brought by its own nationals against NATO Member States. EA of human rights could thus hardly be seen as a tool of neo-imperialism, enabling Western states to impose their own version of human rights on non-Western states.[47] Instead, it could be said to *partly compensate* for ill-advised Western interventionism.[48] It is no surprise that a territorial state has never protested instances of EA of human rights law. Accordingly, under the public international law of jurisdiction, which is concerned with horizontally delimiting states' competence and for which foreign protest is thus the ultimate test of legality, such application would be lawful.

V. EXTRATERRITORIAL APPLICATION OF HUMAN RIGHTS LEGITIMISING OCCUPATION?

As argued in section IV, EA should not be viewed as interventionism. It remains the case nevertheless that the diagonal human rights relationship between the state and individuals based abroad may, under certain circumstances, raise sovereignty concerns. This applies notably to positive obligations that may require increased regulatory penetration, and in particular in situations of military occupation or quasi-occupation.

---

these principles are considered as presumptively unlawful and as interferences in the internal affairs of other states. In contrast, jurisdiction under human rights treaties pertains to the geographical scope of primary human rights obligations; it identifies the group of persons to whom a state owes obligations.

[47] See also Milanovic (n 45) 94 (arguing that the issue is not whether EA is contrary to the cultural mores of the territorial state, but rather whether obligations can reasonably be complied with).

[48] *Al-Skeini v United Kingdom* (n 10) para 37 (writing that it 'ill behooves a state that imposed its military imperialism over another sovereign State ... to resent the charge of having exported human rights imperialism to the vanquished enemy'). See also Tzevelekos (n 2) 150 (characterizing a denial of access to justice for victims of extraterritorial human rights violations as 'neo-colonialism').

On the initiative of Eleanor Roosevelt, going by the *travaux prépara-toires* of the ICCPR, the drafters had already been aware of the conflicts with the territorial sovereign to which an overbroad construction of the notion of jurisdiction could give rise, notably in the relationship between the state and individuals in occupied territories in the aftermath of World War II. The drafters ultimately settled that states would not be obliged to enact legislation regarding persons under short-term military occupation. Such persons were deemed to be subject to the concurrent jurisdiction of the territorial state, and 'conflicting authority' with local sovereignty could result if the extraterritorially acting state were to have obligations too.[49] Despite the *travaux* of the ICCPR with respect to situations of (extraterritorial) occupation, it is now widely accepted that human rights *do* apply to occupied territories. As much has been held indeed by both the ICJ[50] and the ECtHR.[51] This evolution is arguably grounded in a purposive interpretation of the relevant human rights conventions, and may be tracking a more encompassing humanisation tendency in international law, which puts the individual and—in armed conflict—civilians centre stage.[52] From the standpoint of protecting civilians, this may seem to be unobjectionable and, in fact, deserving full support, especially where occupation has become almost permanent, as in the case of Palestine.

Nevertheless, concern has been voiced that a rights-based relationship between occupying states and the occupied population confers a degree of legitimacy on the hostile occupation; notably, invoking human rights may allow the occupier to justify its 'transformative' occupation, and bring about 'human rights-mandated' institutional changes to the legal framework of the occupied territory,[53] in violation of relevant rules of (international humanitarian) occupation law which precisely prohibit such changes in the interest

---

[49] UN Human Rights Commission, Summary Record of the Hundred and Ninety-Third Meeting (1950) UN Doc E/CAN/SR.193; UN Human Rights Commission, Summary Record of the Hundred and Ninety-Fourth Meeting, (1950) UN Doc E/CAN/SR.194. See at length, US Department of State, 'Memorandum Opinion on the Geographic Scope of the International Covenant on Civil and Political Rights' (19 October 2010) 15–25.

[50] *Legal Consequences of the Construction of a Wall in Occupied Palestinian Territory* (n 5) para 106; *Armed Activities on the Territory of the Congo (Democratic Republic of the Congo v Uganda)* [2005] ICJ Rep 168, para 211.

[51] *Loizidou v Turkey* (n 7); *Cyprus v Turkey* (2002) 35 EHRR 731; *Demopoulos v Turkey* (2010) 50 EHRR SE14.

[52] See T Meron, 'The Humanization of Humanitarian Law' (2000) 94 *American Journal of International Law* 2; RG Teitel, 'Humanity's Law: Rule of Law for the New Global Politics' (2001) 35 *Cornell International Law Journal* 2.

[53] NK Modirzadeh, 'The Dark Sides of Convergence: A Pro-Civilian Critique of the Extraterritorial Application of Human Rights Law in Armed Conflict' (2010) 86 *US Naval War College International Law Studies* 349, 375: 'I do not want that State to be in a position to argue that it has to engage in certain institutional changes in order to be able to comply with its human rights obligations back home. I do not want a State that has no relationship to civil society in my country, has no long-term understanding of my population, its history, its religious values, etc, to have a hand in shaping its human rights framework simply by virtue of its choice to invade.'

of the occupied people.[54] This right to self-determination-informed 'slippery slope' argument against the EA of human rights law is somewhat overblown, however. With respect to long-term occupations pervasively affecting the daily life of the occupied population, it cannot be denied that the occupier is the most natural human rights obligor around. Admittedly, given the inherent hostility between occupier and occupied, the substantive content of the human rights to be respected and ensured risks lacking democratic legitimacy; after all, this content normally gradually comes into being through sustained vertical interactions between a (more or less representative) government and the governed. However, the democratic legitimacy argument should not be used to dismiss the application of human rights out of hand. Human rights norms are in large part consubstantial norms, meaning that they exist under both domestic and international law.[55] Thus, insofar as the extraterritorially acting state, including the occupying state, does not export its own national or regional interpretations of human rights law but adheres to internationally recognised human rights interpretations, the danger of intervention could be considerably lessened. This danger could even be averted altogether when the occupier, as a caretaker, only vicariously enforces the human rights obligations to which the occupied state had previously subscribed, at least as far as positive obligations—generally considered as more intrusive—are concerned. In case doubts as to the good intentions of the occupier-cum-human rights obligor cannot be dispelled, the safest option would be to fall back on the IHL of occupation as *lex specialis* in armed conflict. Arguably, occupation law does not feign a relationship of trust between occupier and occupied that could potentially be abused, as human rights law would; instead, acknowledging a hostile situation, it provides for suitable protection for the occupied population.

The protection offered by occupation law may for that matter, somewhat counterintuitively perhaps, at times confer a higher degree of protection on civilians than human rights law. As Aeyal Gross has argued, especially in horizontal relationships where the rights of one person or group are balanced against those of another, the application of human rights law may well go to the detriment of the rights of the population living under occupation, especially in property rights cases where the balance of rights may swing in favour of the legitimate interests of the occupier's (transferred) citizens.[56] IHL, in

---

[54] Geneva Convention IV Relative to the Protection of Civilian Persons in Time of War (adopted 12 August 1949, entered into force 21 October 1950) 75 UNTS 287 (GC IV) Art 64.

[55] A Tzanakopoulos, 'Judicial Dialogue as a Means of Interpretation' in HP Aust and G Nolte, *The Interpretation of International Law by Domestic Courts: Uniformity, Diversity, Convergence* (Oxford, Oxford University Press, 2016) 82.

[56] Gross (n 28) 43, 47 (criticising the ECtHR's judgment in *Demopoulos v Turkey*, in which the Court held in para 116 that 'it would risk being arbitrary and injudicious for it to attempt to impose an obligation to effect restitution [to individuals belonging to the occupied country] in all cases').

contrast, may be more protective of the rights of the occupied population in such cases, as Article 49(6) of Geneva Convention IV prohibits the settlement of citizens of the occupying country in the occupied country. A deceptively simple way out of this conundrum of whether to apply human rights law or IHL is, in line with the theme of this volume, to apply the norm that is most protective of the rights of civilians. This rule of thumb, however, perhaps just begs the question: not only may it not be obvious which norm is the most protective, as the property rights example demonstrates, but also the issue of *which* civilians deserve protection may inform what law (human rights or IHL) to choose.[57]

VI. FLEXIBLE EXTRATERRITORIAL APPLICATION OF HUMAN RIGHTS: FROM *LEX SPECIALIS* TO CONTEXTUALISED INTERPRETATION

Accepting that international human rights obligations enjoy wide EA does not necessarily mean that states are required to respect and ensure abroad the entire panoply of rights. Human rights may apply extraterritorially in an expansive fashion *in principle*, whereas in practice this application may be hemmed in by various restraining devices. The latter may soothe concerns over the overbroad EA of human rights.

As could already be gleaned from the discussion on occupation law, states could argue that IHRL, as the law of the peace, does not and should not fully apply in situations of armed conflict, to which the—partly rival—regime of IHL applies. IHL norms could then apply as *lex specialis*. Furthermore, it is arguable that the scope of human rights obligations is, and should be, a function of the degree of control exercised by the state, or the state's capacity to influence the enjoyment of human rights abroad. In this respect, as the ECtHR also held in *Al Skeini*, human rights can be 'divided and tailored'.[58] Finally, states could, in some circumstances, including armed conflict, derogate from many of their human rights treaty obligations, in spite of the latter's principled EA.

It would lead me too far to delve in detail into the overall relationship between human rights and IHL; this relationship is discussed in other contributions to this volume.[59] Nevertheless, it bears emphasis that the human rights/IHL interface is analytically not entirely distinct from the question

---

[57] Along the same lines Y Ronen, in her work on transitions from illegal territorial regimes, has demonstrated that *Prinzipienreiterei*, evidenced by the automatic application of the international duty of non-recognition of illegal regimes and their acts, may sometimes harm the legitimate expectations and human rights of individuals living under such regimes. Y Ronen, *Transition from Illegal Regimes under International Law* (Cambridge, Cambridge University Press, 2011).

[58] *Al-Skeini v United Kingdom* (n 10) paras 136–37.

[59] Inter alia, see the Introduction and the chapter by Bowring.

of the EA of human rights treaties: the more such treaties are given EA, the more the question of the contours of the application of human rights in armed conflict will come to the fore. As is known, for a rather long time now, the principled co-application of human rights and IHL in armed conflicts has been recognised by the ICJ. In its 1996 Advisory Opinion on the *Legality of the Threat or Use of Nuclear Weapons*, the ICJ acknowledged the applicability of the ICCPR in times of war, bar derogation under Article 4 ICCPR.[60] Relying on this *dictum*, in its *Wall* opinion and its *Armed Activities* judgment, the ICJ went on to characterize IHL as *lex specialis* vis-à-vis human rights law in armed conflict.[61] The Court remained silent, however, on the precise circumstances under which IHL would operate as *lex specialis*. Currently, two concrete issues stand out of human rights law and IHL being at daggers drawn: (i) whether the use of extraterritorial lethal force, eg in drone strikes, is always permissible in situations of armed conflict;[62] and (ii) what standards of detention apply in armed conflict.[63] On the first question, IHL would reply that lethal force, if used against combatants or those who directly participate in hostilities is lawful, whereas human rights law would argue that, in light of the human right to life, lethal force could only exceptionally be used.[64] On the second question, IHL would reply that persons posing a security threat could be detained without judicial review,[65] whereas under human rights law, they would be entitled to the right to liberty, meaning that they could challenge their detention before a regularly constituted court.[66]

The technique of derogation from human rights treaties, discussed in the next section, is probably the most elegant and legally sound one to ensure that human rights do not unduly jeopardise the state's legitimate security interests in extraterritorial military operations. Absent derogation, a compromise solution of co-applying IHL and human rights law has to be found. This could be done, in a somewhat similar manner to derogation, by relying on built-in exceptions regarding the scope of particular human rights. For instance, Article 6(1) ICCPR provides that '[n]o one shall be *arbitrarily* deprived of his life' (emphasis added), a formulation which creates room for considering killings that are lawful under IHL to also pass muster under

---

[60] *Legality of the Threat or Use of Nuclear Weapons* (Advisory Opinion) [1996] ICJ Rep 226, para 25.

[61] *Legal Consequences of the Construction of a Wall in Occupied Palestinian Territory* (n 5) para 106; *Armed Activities on the Territory of the Congo* (n 50) para 216.

[62] See the chapter by Casey-Maslen.

[63] See the chapter by Hampson.

[64] Convention for the Protection of Human Rights and Fundamental Freedoms (European Convention on Human Rights, as amended) (ECHR), Art 2.

[65] See eg GC IV, Art 42.

[66] ECHR, Art 5.

human rights law (such killings not being 'arbitrary').[67] Alternatively, when no exception is explicitly made in the treaty, an interpretation of the relevant human rights provision that is alive to the operational challenges on the battlefield and the applicability of IHL may be called for. The ECtHR's judgment in *Hassan v United Kingdom* evidences such a compromise; in that case, the Court held that: '[T]he grounds of permitted deprivation of liberty [under Article 5 ECHR] should be accommodated, as far as possible, with the taking of prisoners of war and the detention of civilians who pose a risk to security under [the Geneva Conventions].'[68] Interpreting the procedural safeguards of human rights law 'in a manner which takes into account the context and the applicable rules of [IHL]'[69] eventually brought the Court to recognise an ex parte administrative review by a panel of military lawyers as a sufficient safeguard in a situation of armed conflict. Similar flexibility was also envisaged in *Al Saadoon*, in which the UK High Court, after acknowledging the application of the ECHR to the extraterritorial use of force, favoured an interpretation of Article 2 ECHR, enshrining the right to life, that would make the use of lethal force lawful under IHL; as to the procedural dimension of Article 2 ECHR (the state duty to investigate killings), the Court called on the courts to 'recognise their lack of institutional competence' and to afford armed forces wide latitude in dealing with such cases.[70]

As Bhuta has noted, this accommodation exercise in the context of the EA of human rights law yields 'a law of extraterritorial human rights', ie 'one in which human rights norms become flexible abstract principles' adapted to transnational armed conflicts and other formerly exceptional situations.[71] However, flexibility does not necessarily amount to applying the *lex specialis* rule, in which case the human rights norm would be disapplied.[72] Rather, it points to a *contextual interpretation* of international human rights norms, which preserves the core of the human rights norm while acknowledging the difficulties of uncritically applying it to the difficult circumstances reigning

---

[67] See *Legality of the Threat or Use of Nuclear Weapons* (n 60) para 25: '[W]hether a particular loss of life, through the use of a certain weapon in warfare, is to be considered an arbitrary deprivation of life contrary to Article 6 of the [ICCPR], can only be decided by reference to the law applicable in armed conflict and not deduced from the terms of the Covenant itself.'

[68] *Hassan v United Kingdom* (n 4) para 106.

[69] ibid, para 107.

[70] *Al-Saadoon* (n 13) paras 108–11.

[71] Bhuta (n 2) 17.

[72] See also JJ Paust, 'Human Rights on the Battlefield' (2016) 47 *George Washington International Law Review* 3 (stating that '[t]here is no *lex specialis* law of war override of human rights law during war', and that instead 'some law of war requirements provide contextually relevant meaning', and even that 'compliance with the laws of war on a foreign battlefield should assure compliance with global human rights law').

on the battlefield.[73] This method of reconciling human rights and IHL is appropriate, since a decontextualised application of the ECHR may undermine states' continuous support for the Convention, including its case law on the EA of human rights.

A failure to heed states' concerns may create the risk that states call into question the principled EA of the ECHR, with the attendant, and entirely undesirable, result that no human rights at all apply beyond the state's borders.[74] Alternatively, even if states accept the ECtHR's case law, the Court's interpretation of the substantive scope ECHR protections may well remain unimplemented, ie an equally undesirable result. As I have argued elsewhere with Friederycke Haijer, in *Jaloud v the Netherlands*[75]—the latest ECtHR judgment on the EA of the ECHR—the Court may have somewhat overreached by paying insufficient attention to the challenges that a state faces in investigating the extraterritorial use of lethal force (even if its position on jurisdiction is largely defensible).[76] While the Court was aware of 'the particularly difficult conditions prevailing in Iraq at the relevant time' (where the Dutch were present, between 2003 and 2005, as participants in the Stabilization Force in Iraq, under British command), it did hold that the Netherlands had failed to discharge its procedural obligations under Article 2 ECHR with respect to the killing of an Iraqi civilian from a checkpoint, citing insufficient cooperation with Dutch judicial authorities, witness collusion, an unsatisfactory autopsy, and disappeared evidence.[77] The Court failed to explain, however, how it weighed the local conditions in Iraq, which were undeniably relevant for the grounds of non-cooperation.[78] In our opinion, this failure to set out clear requirements for (and limitations to) the duty to investigate extraterritorial killings may adversely affect

---

[73] To a certain extent, inspiration could be found in the ECtHR's margin-of-appreciation doctrine, which developed however only in a *domestic*, as opposed to an extraterritorial context. See eg *Belgian Linguistic Case (No 2)* (1968) 1 EHRR 252: '[T]he Court cannot disregard those legal and factual features which characterize the life of the society in the State which ... has to answer for the measure in dispute'; see also *Handyside v United Kingdom* (1976) 1 EHRR 737: 'By reason of their direct and continuous contact with the vital forces of their countries, State authorities are in principle in a better position than the international judge to give an opinion on the exact content of these requirements [relating to the freedom of speech] as well as on the 'necessity' and of a 'restriction' or 'penalty' to meet them.'

[74] Compare more generally Ratner (n 46) 88–89 (arguing that when suggesting more just legal norms, we must take into account prospects for compliance by global actors, although conceding that 'ideas for morally better rules should not be abandoned simply because they will not command *immediate* acceptance *by all*' (emphasis in original).

[75] *Jaloud v the Netherlands* (n 16).

[76] F Haijer and C Ryngaert, 'Reflections on *Jaloud v the Netherlands*' (2016) 19 *Journal of International Peacekeeping* 1–2.

[77] *Jaloud v the Netherlands* (n 16) paras 226–27.

[78] Haijer and Ryngaert (n 76) 182. Compare also *Jaloud v the Netherlands* (n 16) joint concurring opinion of judges Casadevall, Berro-Lefevre, Šikuta, Hirvelä, López Guerra, Sajó and Silvis.

prosecutorial reforms and more thorough investigations in future cases of civilian casualties.[79] This being said, states, aware of their extraterritorial human rights obligations, have, regardless of judicial instructions, designed policies to investigate civilian casualties in armed conflict.[80]

VII. DEROGATION

Even if, in principle, human rights treaties can be applied extraterritorially, states may consider derogating from the treaties with a view to escaping from extraterritorial obligations. So far, states have not yet derogated from human rights treaties to this effect, possibly because, at least in the recent past, they considered the treaties not to apply extraterritorially in the first place. However, as Milanovic has pointed out, derogations may 'be necessary and desirable, as part of the price worth paying for the extensive and effective application of treaties outside states' boundaries'.[81] Not all observers, however, agree that derogation would be permissible in the context of extraterritorial military ventures. Some British judges in particular, hearing cases concerning the UK's military operations abroad, have voiced scepticism in this regard. In *Al Jedda*, Lord Bingham of the House of Lords wrote that: 'It is hard to think that [the conditions for derogation] could ever be met when a state had chosen to conduct an overseas peacekeeping operation.'[82] This view was echoed by Lord Philips and Lord Hope in two later Supreme Court cases.[83] In *Serdar Mohammed*, however, Justice Leggatt wrote that the phrase 'war or other public emergency threatening the life of the nation' in Article 15 ECHR, the Convention's derogation clause, should be interpreted as 'including, in the context of an international peacekeeping operation, a war or other emergency threatening the life of the nation on whose territory the relevant acts take place'.[84] This view is also

---

[79] Haijer and Ryngaert (n 76), 189.

[80] On the US system at length, see S Wong, 'Investigating Civilian Casualties in Armed Conflict: Comparing US Military Investigations with Alternatives under International Humanitarian and Human Rights Law' (2015) 64 *Naval Law Review* 111. See for the Netherlands, 'Brief d.d. 20 november 2006 van het College van procureurs-generaal gericht aan de hoofdofficier van justitie te Arnhem, inhoudende de Handelwijze bij geweldsaanwending militairen, Staatscourant' (29 November 2006) nr 233. See also the chapter by Lattimer.

[81] M Milanovic, 'Extraterritorial Derogations from Human Rights Treaties in Armed Conflict' in Bhuta (n 2) 58.

[82] *R (Al-Jedda) v Secretary of State for Defence* [2007] UKHL 58, [2008] 1 AC 332, para 38, Lord Bingham.

[83] *R (Smith) v Secretary of State for Defence* [2010] UKSC 29, para 57 (Lord Philips referring to 'circumstances falling short of those permitting derogation under Article 15 ECHR'); *R (Smith) v Minister of Defense* [2013] UKSC 41, paras 59–60 (Lord Hope arguing that no derogation for overseas operations is possible).

[84] *Serdar Mohammed v Ministry of Defence* [2014] EWHC 1369 (QB) paras 155–56.

held by Milanovic, who on the basis of a careful analysis of the drafting history of the ECHR and the ICCPR, came to the conclusion that the conventions' derogation clauses could well apply to extraterritorial military operations.[85] The more courts edge closer to an expansive cause-and-effect model of jurisdiction, the more states may perceive the necessity to actually activate these clauses. It is observed, however, that derogation is not a blank cheque for disapplying human rights or creating a lawless environment; any measures are subject to rather strict legal scrutiny. Article 15(1) ECHR only allows contracting parties to derogate 'to the extent strictly required by the exigencies of the situation, provided that such measures are not inconsistent with its other obligations under international law'. Article 4(1) ICCPR adds that these measures 'do not involve discrimination solely on the ground of race, colour, sex, language, religion or social origin'.

The reference to 'other obligations under international law' in the derogation clauses, for that matter, creates a window, or even a legal basis, for importing IHL into the conventional human rights regimes,[86] enabling the application of IHL as *lex specialis* vis-à-vis human rights law in extraterritorial military operations. On closer inspection, however, the oblique reference to IHL in the derogation clauses of the ICCPR and the ECHR demonstrates that use of the *lex specialis* rule is not entirely apt in the context of derogations. In the strict sense, *lex specialis* arguably only serves a purpose when there is a *norm conflict*, eg when an IHL norm directly clashes with a human rights norm, with the one then prevailing over the other. In the case of derogation, however, human rights norms are *disapplied* on the basis of the human rights treaty itself, and only the relevant IHL norms remain applicable.[87] In any event, in order to safeguard the rights and interests of civilians caught up in armed conflict and extraterritorial military operations, it is advisable that states activate derogation clauses rather sparingly and, in light of our argument in the previous section, preserve the core tenets of the relevant human rights norm when derogating.

VIII. CONCLUDING OBSERVATIONS

In this contribution, I have demonstrated that human rights treaties—especially the ECHR—have been given extraterritorial application in an exceedingly liberal fashion, notably with a view to protecting civilians caught up in armed conflict. Hold-outs such as the United States may soon

---

[85] Milanovic (n 81).

[86] DS Goddard, 'Applying the European Convention on Human Rights to the Use of Physical Force: *Al-Saadoon*' (2015) 91 *International Law Studies Series. US Naval War College* 402, 423.

[87] Compare Milanovic (n 81) 84: 'My own view is that *lex specialis* exists only in its weak variant, as an aid to interpretation.'

abandon their opposition to the principled application of human rights treaties. However, the doctrine of EA, incrementally developed by the case law, is not fully consistent. Moreover, it is too strongly wed to the control standard, the introduction of which was not at the time properly explained. Instead, this contribution has advocated the approximation of the doctrine of EA with the law of state responsibility. This technique would enable civilian victims to fall within a state's human rights jurisdiction, as soon as they have suffered injury as a consequence of an internationally wrongful act attributable to that state, including its failure to act. The resulting expansive EA should not raise alarm bells, however. There are multiple valid mitigating legal devices that can take into account the challenges for the state in fully applying human rights norms extraterritorially, such as contextual interpretation, *lex specialis* (IHL) and derogation. Awareness of these possibilities may persuade states to support expansive iterations of the EA of human rights treaties.

12

What Duties Do Peacekeepers Owe Civilians? Lessons from the Nuhanović Case

LIESBETH ZEGVELD[1]

I. JULY 1995

THE ICJ QUALIFIED the massacre of many thousands of Muslim men from the safe area of Srebrenica in July 1995 as genocide.[2] At the time a Dutch battalion (Dutchbat) was stationed there in the context of the United Nations Protection Force (UNPROFOR).[3] The mandate given to Dutchbat was to protect the local population in the safe area of Srebrenica. On 11 July 1995, Srebrenica was taken by force of arms by the Bosnian-Serb army under the command of General Mladić. After the fall of the safe area a stream of refugees fled to the Dutchbat compound near Srebrenica, seeking protection against the Bosnian-Serb forces. While the majority of the refugees had to stay outside the compound, Dutchbat admitted some 5,000 refugees into the compound.[4] Amongst these refugees admitted into the compound were around 239 men of military age, ie between the ages of 16 and 60.

Immediately after the fall of Srebrenica, the deputy commander of UNPROFOR, General Gobillard, instructed the commander of Dutchbat, Lieutenant Colonel Karremans, to '[t]ake all reasonable measures to protect

---

[1] The author represented Nuhanović in all instances before the Dutch courts between 2004 and 2013 and is Professor of War Reparations at the University of Amsterdam.

[2] *Application of the Convention on the Prevention and Punishment of the Crime of Genocide (Bosnia and Herzegovina v Serbia and Montenegro)* (Merits) [2007] ICJ Rep 43.

[3] In Resolution 819 of 16 April 1993 the Security Council designated Srebrenica as a 'safe area' and demanded that the Bosnian-Serb army withdraw from surrounding areas. In Resolution 836 of 4 June 1993 the Security Council called upon the Member States to contribute armed troops and logistic support to UNPROFOR. The Netherlands placed a battalion of the Airborne Brigade at the disposal of UNPROFOR.

[4] A far larger number of refugees (around 27,000) had to stay outside the compound in the open air.

refugees and civilians in your care'.[5] Furthermore, the UN instructed Dutchbat that 'after having provided support, it is prohibited to send persons away if that would expose them to physical danger'.[6]

Amongst the refugees who were admitted into the compound were the brother and parents of Hasan Nuhanović. Nuhanović was employed as an interpreter by the United Nations. He worked for the Military Observers for the United Nations (UNMOs). Hasan Nuhanović had a UN pass and was on the list of local personnel who would be evacuated with Dutchbat if need be. When it became evident that the enclave of Srebrenica would fall into the hands of the Bosnian Serbs, Nuhanović accommodated his younger brother Muhamed, father Ibro, and mother Nasiha to the compound, where they stayed in the temporary UNMO office. Nuhanović hoped that as he would be evacuated with Dutchbat, the battalion would take his family members along.

On 12 July 1995 the Bosnian-Serb army started transporting the thousands of refugees who were staying outside the compound in the open air. The able-bodied men were separated from the rest and deported. Women and children were evacuated to Kladanj, a safe territory in the Muslim Croatian Federation. Once all the refugees outside the compound had been removed, in the course of 13 July, the Dutch soldiers started to expel the refugees from inside the compound. Once outside, they were taken away by the Bosnian Serbs, the men separated from the women and children.

Contrary to Nuhanović's hope and expectations, Dutchbat was not prepared to keep his family inside the compound. In an effort to prevent especially his brother from being sent away, Nuhanović tried to convince Dutchbat that his brother should be added to the list of local personnel allowed to evacuate with Dutchbat. Dutchbat refused because Muhamed did not have a UN pass. Other desperate attempts by Nuhanović to keep his family inside the compound also failed.

Nuhanović's brother and parents were the very last to be sent away from the compound, into Bosnian-Serb hands. Nothing has ever been heard of them since.[7]

Dutchbat, the UNMOs and the others remaining behind on the compound, including Hasan Nuhanović, were evacuated ten days later, on 21 July 1995.

In the years that followed, Hasan Nuhanović desperately sought for signs his brother and parents might still be alive. When he came to realise that such signs could no longer be expected, he started another search: for justice. Nuhanović sought to bring suit in the court of the state that contributed

---

[5] *Hasan Nuhanović v The Netherlands* (Appeal Judgment) LJN: BR5388 (2011) para 2.16.
[6] ibid.
[7] Nuhanović learned in 2007 and 2010 that the mortal remains of his father and brother, respectively, had been recovered from a mass grave.

troops to UNPROFOR in Srebrenica in July 1995: the Netherlands. As this country was totally foreign to him, this was not an easy task, both financially and practically. However, with the help of Pax, a Dutch NGO, Nuhanović managed to gain access to the Dutch courts. The procedures lasted from 2004 until 2013. I represented Hasan Nuhanović in all instances in the Dutch court.

II. NUHANOVIĆ'S CLAIM IN THE DUTCH COURT

In 2004 Nuhanović took the case of his younger brother and father to the Dutch court.[8] He argued that the state of the Netherlands (hereinafter: the state, or the Netherlands) had committed a wrongful act against him and that it was liable to pay compensation. The wrongful act consisted of sending away Nuhanović's brother and father from the UN compound. Dutchbat did so after the Nuhanović family had fled to the compound to seek protection against the enemy, the Bosnian-Serb army. Nuhanović argued that Dutchbat was fully aware of the danger his family members were facing when they were given into the hands of the Bosnian Serbs.

The Netherlands' defence was essentially that the actions of Dutchbat should be attributed exclusively to the United Nations and not to the state contributing troops to a UN peacekeeping mission. This claim was grounded in the fact that the Dutch peacekeepers were international personnel acting under Security Council authorisation and placed under the operational command and control of the United Nations.

Nuhanović acknowledged that Dutchbat acted under a UN flag. However, he pointed out that at the time not only was a UN flag flying on the roofs of the halls inside the compound, but also a Dutch flag. More specifically, Nuhanović argued that during the crisis of the fall of Srebrenica, the Netherlands (also) exercised control over Dutchbat's conduct. In his view, this should lead to responsibility.

Nuhanović's claim was not an easy one and legally almost unprecedented.[9] Prior to this claim, the accepted view was that control over peacekeepers is

---

[8] He initially also included the death of his mother in the case. But in the appeal case and in the case before the Supreme Court he limited his claim to the death of his younger brother and father.

[9] In a similar case the Belgian court found that the conduct of the troops in Rwanda, stationed there to prevent the killing of the Tutsis in the 1994 Rwandan genocide, could be attributed to Belgium in a situation where Belgium had withdrawn from the peacekeeping mission; see *Mukeshimana-Ngulinzira and others v Belgium and others* (Judgement) RG No 04/4807/A, 07/15547/A, ILDC 1604 (2010). After the rulings in the *Nuhanović* case, the district court in The Hague issued a similar ruling in favour of male Srebrenica victims who were expelled from the UN compound; see *Mothers of Srebrenica v State of the Netherlands* ECLI:NL:RBDHA:2014 (2014). This judgment has been appealed by both parties.

transferred to the UN, leading to a legal connection only with the UN and not with the troop-contributing state. The legal state of affairs was based on the idea of overall control of the UN over peacekeeping missions, whereas Nuhanović demanded that the court look into the specific situation that had arisen after the fall of the Srebrenica enclave, which had led to the deportation of the Muslim men and the evacuation of Dutchbat. His claim was that during this transitional period, it was not the UN, or at least not only the UN, that exercised control, but also the government of the Netherlands.

In first instance, the district court of The Hague allowed the Netherlands' defence, ruling that Dutchbat's conduct was exclusively attributable to the UN and not (also) to the Netherlands.[10] This ruling was overturned by the court of appeal of The Hague.[11] The Netherlands appealed to the Supreme Court, which dismissed the appeal, resulting in a final judgment that the Netherlands bore responsibility for the death of Nuhanović's brother and father, Muhamed and Ibro Nuhanović.[12]

The proceedings centred around two questions: (i) Could Dutchbat's conduct be attributed to the Netherlands? And (ii) Was Dutchbat's conduct wrongful? In this chapter I address both issues.

III. STATE VERSUS UN RESPONSIBILITY

The key question in this case was whether responsibility can be shared between a state contributing troops to a UN peacekeeping mission and the UN itself. Could both the Netherlands and the UN be responsible for Dutchbat's conduct on 13 July 1995 when it sent away Nuhanović's brother and father? Or can responsibility in peacekeeping missions as a matter of principle only be attributed exclusively to either one?

In first instance the district court took the view of exclusive attribution: Dutchbat's behaviour could only be attributed to one actor. The district court subsequently found that operational command and control over the Dutch military had been transferred to the UN, a fact that was not disputed.[13] Once command and control over Dutch troops had been transferred to the United Nations, responsibility for Dutchbat's conduct could no longer be attributed to the Netherlands. The court applied the ILC Articles on State Responsibility, arguing that when a state places its troops under the

---

[10] *Hasan Nuhanović v The Netherlands* (Judgment) LJN: BF0181/265615 (2008).

[11] *Hasan Nuhanović v The Netherlands* (Appeals) (n 5).

[12] *Hasan Nuhanović v The Netherlands* (Judgment) ECLI:NL:HR:2013:BZ9225 (2013).

[13] The Dutch government had not been able to produce the written legal agreement with the UN governing its contribution of personnel and equipment to UNPROFOR, but the Dutch courts in all instances accepted the claim of the Netherlands that such an (written or unwritten) agreement existed.

command of another state, the conduct of those troops is then considered the conduct of the latter state.[14] The court engaged this rule of state responsibility by means of analogy to the attribution of actions of armed forces made available to the UN.[15]

In the district court's view this rule of exclusive attribution could not be set aside by gross negligence or serious failure of supervision over forces.[16] The only exception to exclusive attribution, the district court ruled, would be if the government of the Netherlands or its army command structure had cut across the UN command structure, undermining the factual basis in July 1995 for attribution to the United Nations. Only in that case would there be scope for attribution to the Netherlands.[17] Accordingly, the court analysed whether orders had been given to Dutchbat by the Dutch authorities to disregard or disobey UN orders. Also, the court considered whether Dutchbat, with the agreement of the authorities in the Netherlands, had backed out of the UN command structure. The court could not, however, find a factual basis for such attribution to the Netherlands. The court concluded that Dutchbat's 'acts and omissions should be attributed strictly, as a matter of principle, to the United Nations'.[18] It determined that although Dutchbat might have acted wrongfully, this was of no avail to Nuhanović 'because the acts and omissions of Dutchbat during the evacuation should be considered as those of the United Nations'[19] and of the United Nations only.

At appeal the court took a different approach, which was affirmed by the Supreme Court. Rather than taking the transfer of operational command and control as a relevant criterion, the appeal court started from effective control as the key concept for attributing responsibility.[20] The appeal court relied on the ILC Draft Articles on the Responsibility of International Organisations (DARIO).[21] In particular, it applied Article 7 DARIO, which stipulates:

> The conduct of an organ of a State or an organ or agent of an international organisation that is placed at the disposal of another international organisation

---

[14] International Law Commission (ILC), Articles on Responsibility of States for Internationally Wrongful Acts (2001) UN Doc A/56/10, 2001, Art 6.

[15] *Hasan Nuhanović v The Netherlands* (Judgment) (n 10) para 4.8.

[16] ibid, para 4.13.

[17] ibid, para 4.14.1.

[18] ibid, paras 4.11, 4.13.

[19] ibid.

[20] The position taken by the Court of Appeal was quite similar to the standpoint defended by Tom Dannenbaum in an article on division of liability during peacekeeping operations. As counsel of Nuhanović, the author submitted this article to the court. T Dannenbaum, 'Translating the Standard of Effective Control into a System of Effective Accountability: How Liability Should be Apportioned for Violations of Human Rights by Member State Troop Contingents Serving as United Nations Peacekeepers' (2010) 51 *Harvard International Law Journal* 1, 113.

[21] ILC, Draft Articles on the Responsibility of International Organisations, with commentaries (3 June and 4 July–12 August 2011) UN Doc A/66/10 (DARIO).

shall be considered under international law an act of the latter organisation if the organisation exercises effective control over that conduct.[22]

It rejected the state's argument that Dutchbat's conduct should in principle always be attributed to the UN because Dutchbat had been placed under command and control of the UN and UNPROFOR had been created under Chapter VII of the UN Charter. The state underpinned its argument with Article 6 DARIO, provision stipulates that the conduct of organs of an international organisation shall be attributed to that organisation.[23] However, the state's reasoning was wrong in that troop contingents are not organs of the UN but organs of their states.[24] The Supreme Court rejected the state's view, pointing out that while in peacekeeping situations states transfer command and control over their troops to the UN, they maintain certain powers. Members of the national contingent remain, for example, in the service of the sending state, which keeps control over the personnel affairs of its military. Sending states also retain disciplinary and criminal authority over their military.[25] Moreover, and particularly relevant to this case, the troop-sending state at all times preserves the power to withdraw its troops and stop its participation in the mission.[26] Therefore, the UN does not possess full operational command and control. Hence, while the UN has always maintained that during the exercise of their mandate, peacekeepers

---

[22] *Hasan Nuhanović v The Netherlands* (Appeals) (n 5) para 5.8. The Appeal Court referred to Art 6 of a previous draft of the DARIO, which is currently Art 7.

[23] See Art 6 DARIO: '1. The conduct of an organ or agent of an international organisation in the performance of functions of that organ or agent shall be considered an act of that organisation under international law, whatever position the organ or agent holds in respect of the organisation. 2. The rules of the organisation apply in the determination of the functions of its organs and agents.'

[24] Nevertheless the UN itself also maintains that peacekeeping troops are to be considered subsidiary organs of the UN. See ILC, 'Responsibility of International Organisations: Comments and Observations Received from International Organisations' (17 February 2011) UN Doc A/CN.4/637/Add.1, 10, para 3.

[25] Accordingly, in 2010, Nuhanović filed a criminal complaint against the Dutch commander and deputy commander of Dutchbat with the Dutch prosecution office. The Dutch prosecutors in 2013 refused to open a criminal investigation. The complaint is available online at www.prakkendoliveira.nl/en/news/surviving-relatives-of-srebrenica-victims-file-criminal-complaint-re-crimes-committed-in-july-1995/, accessed 24 June 2016. The decision of the prosecution office is available at www.om.nl/vaste-onderdelen/zoeken/@31682/persbericht/, accessed 24 June 2016. Nuhanović has subsequently submitted a request for review at the Military Chamber of Appeal in Arnhem, which rejected his request. Nuhanović then filed a complaint before the ECtHR. The ECtHR is still to decide on the admissibility of the complaint.
Another matter that falls exclusively under state jurisdiction is the selection of competent persons for the troop contingent. The Dutchbat commander was often complained of as being wholly incompetent to be in charge of the battalion in difficult circumstances. See eg S Zboray, 'Karremans' falen was oorzaak van de val van Srebrenica' *Trouw*, Amsterdam, 12 April 2002, www.trouw.nl/tr/nl/5009/Archief/article/detail/2799684/2002/04/12/Karremans-falen-was-oorzaak-van-de-val-van-Srebrenica.dhtml, accessed 23 June 2016.

[26] See Commentary on Art 7 DARIO. *Hasan Nuhanović v The Netherlands* (Appeals) (n 5) para 5.10.

'are under the sole authority of the organisation and not that of their respective States',[27] this claim does not reflect reality.

Importantly, the Dutch court of appeal and the Supreme Court did not rule out the possibility that more than one actor has effective control as this is, according to the courts, a generally accepted principle of law.[28] This means that conduct can be attributed to more than one person or entity. Indeed, Article 48 DARIO explicitly provides for dual attribution.[29] The same conduct can therefore be attributed to both an international organisation and a state. The Dutch courts' finding was novel.[30] In *Behrami* and *Saramati*, the ECtHR denied admissibility of these cases, ruling that the acts or omissions in question were attributable to the United Nations and therefore no longer to the troop-contributing states, thereby excluding the possibility of dual attribution.[31] In *Al-Jedda*, handed down two days after the Nuhanović case, the ECtHR seemed to have taken a different approach, however, ruling that possible attribution of the impugned acts to the UN would not exclude attribution to the United Kingdom.[32]

---

[27] U Palwankar, 'Applicability of International Humanitarian Law to United Nations Peace-Keeping Forces' (1993) 294 *International Review of the Red Cross* 227.

[28] *Hasan Nuhanović v The Netherlands* (Appeals) n 5, para 5.9.

[29] See Art 48 DARIO: 'Where an international organisation and one or more States or other international organisations are responsible for the same internationally wrongful act, the responsibility of each State or organisation may be invoked in relation to that act.'

[30] The notion of dual attribution has been accepted by some legal scholars. A Sari, 'Jurisdiction and International Responsibility in Peace Support Operations: The Behrami and Saramati Cases' (2008) 8 *Human Rights Law Review* 165, 167; N Tsagourias, 'The Responsibility of International Organisations for Military Missions' in M Odello and R Piotrowisz (eds), *International Military Missions and International Law* (Leiden, Martinus Nijhoff Publishers, 2011) 6, 7.

[31] *Behrami and Behrami v France* (App no 71412/01) and *Saramati v France, Germany and Norway* (App no 78166/01) ECHR 2 May 2007, para 64. In these cases the ECtHR observed that the applicants in Behrami and Behrami complained about the impugned inaction of KFOR troops and that Saramati complained about his detention by, and on the orders of, KFOR. The ECtHR considered that the question raised by the cases was whether the ECtHR was competent to examine under the ECHR those states' contribution to the relevant civil and security presence exercising control of Kosovo. The ECtHR considered that issuing detention orders fell within the security mandate of KFOR and that the supervision of de-mining fell within the mandate of UNMIK. It went on to ascertain whether the impugned action of KFOR (detention of Mr Saramati) and inaction (the alleged failure to de-mine in the Behrami case) could be attributed to the UN. In that respect, the ECtHR first established that Chapter VII of the UN Charter could provide a framework for the delegation of the UNSC's security powers to KFOR and of its civil administration powers to UNMIK. Since KFOR was exercising lawfully delegated Chapter VII powers of the UNSC and since UNMIK was a subsidiary organ of the UN created under Chapter VII, the impugned action and inaction was, in principle, 'attributable' to the UN which had a legal personality separate from that of its Member States and was not a contracting party to the Convention.

[32] *Al-Jedda v the United Kingdom* (App no 27021/08) ECHR 7 July 2011, para 81. The case concerned the detention of Al-Jedda by British troops in Iraq over a long period of time, allegedly violating his rights under Art 5 ECHR. However, it should be noted that the ECtHR based its ruling on both effective control and 'ultimate control and authority' of the UK, the latter criterion raising questions whether the alleged human rights violations could indeed be attributed to more than one actor.

The considerations of the Dutch courts in the case of Nuhanović meant that the responsibility of the Netherlands and the UN could in fact coexist. The removal of Nuhanović's family from the UN compound could therefore in principle be attributed to both the Netherlands and the UN. Whether indeed Dutchbat actions should be attributed to the Netherlands depended on whether Dutch authorities in The Hague exercised effective control over these actions, a question I will address now.

IV. EFFECTIVE CONTROL OF THE NETHERLANDS

The attribution of Dutchbat's conduct to the state of the Netherlands thus depended on the factual control that the Dutch authorities exercised over Dutchbat's actions back in 1995.[33] In court an array of factors determined whether such authority had been exercised: orders that had been given by The Hague, decisions that had been made in the capital, telephone calls from the Dutch minister of defence to the Dutchbat commander in Srebrenica. A close analysis of the available facts showed that the Dutch government had not backed away from exercising considerable control over its military after the fall of the enclave.

After the fall of Srebrenica, the peacekeeping mission had failed. Serious worries arose about the safety of the refugees as well as of Dutchbat personnel. Dutch Defence Minister Voorhoeve was the first, on the afternoon of 11 July, to decide that Dutchbat would be withdrawn. In the evening of the same day, two senior Dutch military took a plane to Zagreb to talk with the UN Force Commander.[34] They agreed that both Dutchbat and the refugees would be evacuated. Furthermore, it was decided that the UNHCR would have primary responsibility for the evacuation of the refugees.[35] It was this meeting that led the appeal court to conclude that the Dutch government had taken part in the decision-making at the highest level:

> The Court can only conclude that the decision for the evacuation of Dutchbat and the refugees resulting from the consultations between Janvier [UN Force Commander], Van den Breemen [Dutch Chief of the Dutch Defence Staff] and Van Baal [Deputy Commander of the Royal Netherlands Army] was actually taken

---

[33] See also the Commentary to Art 7 DARIO, under 4: 'The criterion for attribution of conduct either to the contributing State or organisation or to the receiving organisation is based according to article 7 on the factual control that is exercised over the specific conduct taken by the organ or agent placed at the receiving organisation's disposal.'

[34] Force Commander of UNPF, which was the new name from 1 April 1995 of what had originally been known as UNPROFOR.

[35] *Hasan Nuhanović v The Netherlands* (Appeals) (n 5) paras 5.11–5.16; *Hasan Nuhanović v The Netherlands* (Supreme Court) (n 12) paras 3.2, 3.12.2.

by mutual agreement between Janvier on behalf of the UN on the one hand and by Van den Breemen and Van Baal on behalf of the Dutch government on the other. In the opinion of the Court it is not plausible that two of the highest ranking Dutch military officers had only travelled to Zagreb to be informed about what General Janvier, after being told about their wishes, would decide regarding the evacuation. The Court interprets the background of the consultations of that evening in such a manner that, considering the concerns that existed in The Hague for the safety of both Dutchbat and the refugees, in practice they could only take a decision on the evacuation that not only The Hague but also (the Force Commander of) the UN would approve of. The fact that Gobillard [deputy commander of UNPROFOR] and Nicolai [Dutch Chief of Staff of the Headquarters of UNPROFOR in Sarajevo] also took the decision to evacuate does not detract from the above conclusion, because what has been decided at the highest level must be decisive. Apparently both the UN and the Dutch Government considered this decision to be of such importance that they left it up to the Force Commander Janvier and two of the highest Dutch military officers. The Dutch Government participated in that decision-making at the highest level.[36]

The Dutch government also gave direct orders to the commander of Dutchbat in Srebrenica regarding the evacuation of the refugees. In the early morning of 12 July 1995, Defence Minister Voorhoeve spoke on the telephone to Karremans. During this telephone conversation Voorhoeve told Karremans to 'save whatever can be saved'.[37]

Other instructions, such as that Dutchbat was not allowed to cooperate in implementing separate treatment of the Muslim men, were issued by the Dutch government to Dutchbat through Dutch General Nicolai in Sarajevo. While prior to 11 July Nicolai had only served as chief of staff of the headquarters of UNPROFOR in Sarajevo, after the fall of the enclave Nicolai took on a double role, acting both as a UN and a Dutch officer. During preliminary witness hearings in the Dutch court procedure, Nicolai was clear about the fact that after the fall of Srebrenica he also received orders from The Hague:

> It was a turning point; Dutchbat's mission had ended and we were going to focus on getting the battalion back to the Netherlands. In itself this is also a national affair, but apart from that there were additional UN interests and that is why I also acted as the authorized representative for UNPROFOR. In that sense, I kind of had a double role. In this case things went a little further. Normally I did not receive any orders from the Netherlands, but only from the UN. At this moment the Netherlands also participated in the decision-making.[38]

---

[36] *Hasan Nuhanović v The Netherlands* (Appeals) (n 5) para 5.12.
[37] *Hasan Nuhanović v The Netherlands* (Supreme Court) (n 12) para 3.2.
[38] *Hasan Nuhanović v The Netherlands* (Appeals) (n 5) para 5.13.

Nicolai stated that the Dutch ministry of defence phoned him as the Dutch government feared for the Muslim men in Srebrenica:

> The Hague phoned me, because The Hague was concerned about the fate of the men and that is why we had to make sure in any case that they would not be treated as an individual group.[39]

As the Dutch chief of staff of the UNPROFOR headquarters in Sarajevo, Nicolai referred to himself as 'the authorized negotiator for the Netherlands'. Dutch Defence Minister Voorhoeve explained that after the fall of Srebrenica Nicolai no longer acted only for the UN and that it was only 'logical' that 'Dutch concerns' were communicated to him.[40] This was a consequence of the fact that the mission had ended and Dutchbat found itself in a transitional period. But it was also a consequence of the dysfunction of the UN, not only in this last transitional phase but throughout the peacekeeping mission. The Dutch Defence Minister was quite outspoken about the malfunctioning of the UN:

> My observation that the command structure did not function was based on a long period, a whole year, of noticing that certain parts of the command structure in particular did not function. Pointing at the highest national military officer is common use, also in peacekeeping operations that are proceeding well.[41]

According to the court of appeal, the Dutch government had given orders and not just transmitted its wishes or expressed its concerns. In the words of General Nicolai: '[I]f the Dutch Government says something like that, as a military officer you just carry it out.'

Based on these facts, the court of appeal concluded that the Netherlands had exercised effective control over Dutchbat actions. Given this control, the court found that the Dutch government could also have *prevented* Dutchbat from removing the Nuhanović family from the compound. There was no evidence that The Hague had instructed Dutchbat to remove the refugees. The decision to remove all the refugees from the compound seemed to have been made on the spot by the Dutchbat commanders; they had not been ordered to do so by the Dutch government. However, this did not prevent the court from arguing that The Hague should have used its power to stop Dutchbat acting as it did. It found that the degree of power of the Dutch authorities over Dutchbat allowed this conclusion. The court came to this finding without having established that the government was aware of the removal of the Muslims from the compound. Apparently the court found that the government should have informed itself of the local situation. In the words of the court:

> [I]t is beyond doubt that the Dutch Government was closely involved in the evacuation and the preparations thereof, and that it would have had the power to

39 ibid.
40 ibid.
41 ibid, para 5.15.

prevent the alleged conduct if it had been aware of this conduct at the time. The facts do not leave room for any other conclusion than that, in case the Dutch Government would have given the instruction to Dutchbat not to allow [Muhamed] Nuhanović (as well as his father Ibro Nuhanović) to leave the compound or to take him along respectively, such an instruction would have been executed.[42]

Clearly the court considered Dutch control over Dutchbat to be fully effective. The liability the court attached to the Netherlands goes beyond attribution of liability for giving orders. It also entailed liability for the failure to give orders to do or not to do something.

In sum, once Srebrenica had fallen, and Dutchbat was going to be evacuated, the battalion was (also) under command of the Dutch government. Dutch authority over Dutchbat had not only a theoretical nature, but was also exercised in practice: Dutchbat implemented instructions from the government in The Hague. The Netherlands thus had effective control over the conduct of which Dutchbat is accused by Nuhanović. This conduct therefore was attributable to the Netherlands.

The question whether the UN also had control over Dutchbat was left open. In any case, if the UN had control, it did not have exclusive control. This conclusion underlies the courts' rulings in the Nuhanović case and is in line with the finding that conduct can be attributed to more than one actor.

The next question was whether Dutchbat's conduct had been wrongful.

V. WRONGFULNESS OF DUTCHBAT'S CONDUCT

Did the removal of the Nuhanović family contravene the law? Nuhanović based his claim primarily on the domestic law of Bosnia-Herzegovina, being the law of the state where the wrongful acts had been committed and hence the law that was applicable according to Dutch private international law. He also invoked Articles 2 and 3 ECHR, ie the right to life and the prohibition of inhuman treatment, respectively.

Nuhanović argued that his brother and father were within the 'jurisdiction' of the Netherlands as referred to in Article 1 ECHR when they were expelled from the UN compound, triggering the applicability of the ECHR. Such a conclusion did not require an extension of the concept of 'jurisdiction' beyond what logically followed from the Convention. The Supreme Court assumed Dutch jurisdiction on the basis of Dutchbat's authority over the UN compound. While jurisdiction is 'primarily' territorial, extraterritorial jurisdiction has developed as an essential component of the protection offered by the Convention. In its casebook judgment *Loizidou v Turkey* the ECtHR stipulated that extraterritorial jurisdiction can flow from *effective*

---

[42] ibid, para 5.18.

control of an area.[43] Such control can also be limited to a smaller portion of the territory.[44] In the Nuhanović case, the Supreme Court pointed out that Dutch jurisdiction over the UN compound existed both legally and in practice. Its legal authority derived from the agreement on the status of UNPROFOR in Bosnia and Herzegovina concluded between the UN and Bosnia and Herzegovina. Pursuant to this agreement the Netherlands was competent, through Dutchbat, to exercise jurisdiction within the meaning of Article 1 ECHR inside the compound. In addition, the court observed, after the fall of the enclave on 11 July 1995 and, in particular, at the moment of Dutchbat's disputed conduct, the Netherlands also exercised de facto jurisdiction inside the compound. The compound was manned by Dutchbat and by Dutchbat only. Dutchbat decided who was allowed inside the compound and who could or must leave. Moreover, the Bosnian-Serb army respected Dutchbat's authority over the compound. After the fall of Srebrenica Dutchbat had withdrawn to the compound until its departure on 21 July 1995. Therefore, because of Dutchbat legal and factual control inside the UN base, the Netherlands exercised jurisdiction within the meaning of Article 1 ECHR.

Of course, the Supreme Court could only have come to this conclusion once it had established that the Netherlands exercised effective control over Dutchbat, leading to attribution of Dutchbat's conduct to the Netherlands. Could Dutchbat's conduct not have been attributed to the Netherlands due to a lack of effective control over its troops, control of Dutchbat could in turn never have led to jurisdiction of the Netherlands over the compound. So it was the situation of effective control over agents that led to the assumption of control over the territory inside the UN compound.

This raises the question of whether it was necessary for the Supreme Court to establish territorial jurisdiction inside the compound or whether its finding that the Netherlands had effective control over Dutchbat sufficed to establish jurisdiction within the meaning of Article 1 ECHR.

I believe that the finding of effective control over the Dutchbat military would indeed have sufficed to establish Dutch jurisdiction in terms of Article 1 ECHR. It is true that the question of attribution is to be distinguished from that of jurisdiction. The former deals with the question of ascribing to a subject of international law the acts or omissions of individuals or bodies under its effective authority or acting on its behalf. The notion of jurisdiction essentially 'refers to the territorial principle, State agent authority and control, effective control over an area and the Convention legal space'.[45] Hence, the legal concepts should not be mixed.

---

[43] *Loizidou and Cyprus (intervening) v Turkey* (1997) 23 EHRR 513, para 52.
[44] *Issa and ors v Turkey* (2004) 41 EHRR 567, para 74.
[45] Concurring opinion of Judge Spielman, joined by Judge Raimondi in the case of *Jaloud v the Netherlands*, criticising the ECHR's references in the case of *Jaloud v the Netherlands* to the law on attribution as unnecessary: '[T]he unnecessary references to the case-law of

However, the concept of effective control over state agents is applied both in the case of attribution of conduct creating liability as well as in the case of jurisdiction triggering the applicability of the ECHR. The ECHR has been found to apply in various cases involving jurisdiction based on *state agent authority*, departing from the notion of territory or space as the (only) basis for jurisdiction.[46] In *Issa and others v Turkey*, the ECtHR found that:

> Moreover, a State may also be held accountable for violation of the Convention rights and freedoms of persons who are in the territory of another State but who are found to be under the former State's authority and control *through its agents* operating—whether lawfully or unlawfully—in the latter State.[47]

In *Al-Skeini v the United Kingdom*[48] and, more recently, in *Jaloud v The Netherlands*[49] the ECtHR has also acknowledged that jurisdiction is exercised by a state when it assumes, through the consent, invitation or acquiescence of the government of a territory, all or some of the public powers normally exercised by that government. When a state acts in the exercise of these functions, jurisdiction is incurred.

It seems to me that effective control over its troops with a view to attribution of the acts of these troops to the state and effective control over troops with a view to creating jurisdiction within the meaning of Article 1 ECHR do in fact overlap. Both require the same analysis of facts and circumstances to establish the degree of control exercised by a state over its troops. The finding of the Dutch court that the territory of the UN compound fell within the jurisdiction of the Netherlands was thus unnecessary to trigger jurisdiction under the convention. The court's previous findings that the Dutch government exercised effective control over Dutchbat (and so its human rights

---

the International Court of Justice (see paragraphs 95–97) and to the International Law Commission's Articles on State Responsibility in the part of the judgment setting out the relevant international law, is ambiguous, subsidiary and incomprehensible. Ambiguous, because the majority's reasoning takes care to point out that the test for establishing the existence of "jurisdiction" under Article 1 of the Convention has never been equated with the test for establishing a State's responsibility for an internationally wrongful act under general international law. … There was therefore no need to examine the non-issue of "attribution", which is completely separate from the question of "jurisdiction". More fundamentally, the Court should in any event be careful not to conflate the notions of jurisdiction under Article 1 with the concept of State responsibility under general international law. Efforts to seek to elucidate the former by reference to the latter are conceptually unsound and likely to cause further confusion in an already difficult area of law.' *Jaloud v The Netherlands* (App no 47708/08) ECHR 20 November 2014.

[46] See eg *X v Germany* (App no 7705/76) ECHR 5 July 1977, para 168; *Hess v United Kingdom* (App no 6231/73) ECHR 28 May 1975, paras 73–74; *Cyprus v Turkey* (2002) 35 EHRR 731, paras 75, 76; and *Banković and ors v Belgium and ors* (2007) 44 EHRR SE5, para 73.

[47] *Issa and ors v Turkey* (n 44) para 71 (emphasis added).

[48] *Al-Skeini and ors, Bar Human Rights Committee (intervening) and ors (intervening) v United Kingdom* (2011) 53 EHRR 18.

[49] *Jaloud v the Netherlands* (n 45) paras 139–54.

abuses could be attributed to the Netherlands) would have sufficed. These factual findings provided a sufficient basis for the view that the Netherlands, through Dutchbat, was actually able to ensure compliance with the human rights enshrined in Articles 2 and 3 ECHR in relation to Muhamed and Ibro Nuhanović.

Subsequently, arriving at the human rights violations allegedly committed by Dutchbat, the appeal court granted Hasan Nuhanović's primary claim that the battalion should not have sent his brother Muhamed and his father Ibro away from the compound. The court reiterated that Nuhanović's father and brother had sought refuge at the compound to seek protection from the Bosnian-Serb enemy. It pointed out that Dutchbat knew of the crimes that had already been committed against the Muslim men by the Bosnian Serbs before as well as after the fall of the safe area of Srebrenica.[50]

The state had argued that Nuhanović's brother had left on his own free will, a defence that was, given the available facts, brushed aside by the court. This defence had more factual basis with regard to Nuhanović's father, however. At the very last moment before Ibro and Muhamed Nuhanović were ordered by Dutchbat to leave the base, the Dutchbat deputy commander told Nuhanović's father that he could stay, because he had represented the refugees in the meetings between the Dutchbat commander and the Bosnian-Serb commander, General Mladić. Asking what this would mean for his youngest son, the Dutchbat deputy commander told Nuhanović's father that his son could not stay and that it was 'up to him' (ie Nuhanović's father) what he chose to do. Confronted with an impossible choice, Ibro Nuhanović decided to join his youngest son and both left the UN compound. The court of appeal considered that the Netherlands had not acted wrongfully towards Ibro as he had permission to stay at the compound. However, the court found that

> his death may be considered to be the result of the wrongful acts with respect to Muhamed and therefore may be attributed to the State. After all, the Court deems it understandable and predictable that, under the given circumstances, Ibro would choose to go along with his minor son.[51]

The court concluded that according to domestic Bosnian law and the ECHR it is not allowed to surrender civilians to the armed forces if there is a real and predictable risk that the latter will kill or submit these civilians to inhuman treatment. By doing so, Dutchbat had also acted contrary to the instruction given by UN General Gobillard 'to take all reasonable measures to protect refugees and civilians in your care'.[52] The court believed that Muhamed and Ibro would still be alive if the state had not acted wrongfully towards them.

---

[50] *Hasan Nuhanović v The Netherlands* (Appeals) (n 5) para 6.7.
[51] ibid, para 6.20.
[52] ibid, para 6.8.

In addition to the finding that Dutchbat should have kept Nuhanović's brother and father inside the compound, the question also arose whether Dutchbat should have evacuated them to a safe area. While Nuhanović's primary claim was that his family should have been allowed to stay on the compound, alternatively he argued that his father and brother should have been taken along with the battalion.

The Netherlands had argued that only persons who possessed a UN pass were allowed to be evacuated together with Dutchbat. Muhamed did not work for the UN and hence did not have such a pass. According to the state, the Bosnian Serbs knew exactly who was working for Dutchbat. Dutchbat justifiably feared, according to the state, that the Bosnian Serbs would closely inspect the departing convoy. Therefore, taking along persons without a UN pass would imply enormous risks for the other participants in the convoy.

The court disagreed. It found that it had not been established that the possession of a UN pass was a requirement that had been demanded by the Bosnian Serbs.[53] Moreover, the court observed that it would have been possible to make a UN pass for Muhamed at the compound.[54] The court accepted that taking Muhamed along would have implied a certain risk. But it believed that

> considering the great interests of Muhamed that were at stake, the possible risks that were related to taking Muhamed along with or without a UN pass in reasonableness should not have resulted in the decision not to take him along.[55]

The court concluded that the Netherlands acted wrongfully towards Hasan Nuhanović by forcing his brother and father to leave the compound and that it was liable to pay the damages that Nuhanović has suffered and will suffer as a result of their death.

VI. CONCLUDING OBSERVATIONS

There are currently more than 100,000 soldiers wearing blue helmets. Their responsibility for the protection of civilians is enormous. And yet the liability for misbehaviour by these UN soldiers is often left undetermined. The legal action brought by Hasan Nuhanović over the death of his brother and father has changed this. The liability framework applied by the Dutch courts, which is based on effective control, enhances the access of victims to reparation.

---

[53] ibid, para 6.16.
[54] ibid, para 6.17.
[55] ibid, para 6.18.

In the Nuhanović case, the Netherlands repeatedly issued an often-heard warning: a negative ruling will have an adverse effect on the implementation of peace operations by the United Nations, in particular on the willingness of Member States to provide troops for such operations.[56] This is a strange argument. The possibility of liability should enhance the performance of peacekeepers and prevent recurrence of events such as occurred in the context of Dutchbat's conduct at Srebrenica. If there is a risk of another Srebrenica, states should indeed think twice if and how they can contribute to peacekeeping to the best of their ability. If this leads to fewer peacekeepers, that may be an acceptable consequence.

In theory national contingents are under UN authority, but it is common knowledge that states never relinquish full control to the UN.[57] Not only do national contingents regularly communicate with their domestic governments, but the case of Nuhanović makes clear that their contacts may go much further than consultation.

It has been said that the right question for establishing state liability is: who is giving the orders?[58] However, orders to commit human rights abuses are generally not given by states. Hence, this question may not always answer the question of who exercised effective control.[59] After the Nuhanović case the question can be more specific: who should have given the orders? The control of the Dutch government over Dutchbat, both legally and in practice, was so real that the Dutch court of appeal held that the Dutch government could have prevented the decision of Dutchbat to send away the Nuhanović family. Nollkaemper has commented that this 'may be opening the door rather wide. ... [f]or it would seem that a troop-contributing state always has the possibility to send orders or instructions to its nationals who serve in a UN-operation'.[60] However, if making effective use of this ability leads to prevention of human rights abuses, this indeed seems to be a fair scheme of liability.

---

[56] The Supreme Court rejected the state's argument, considering that '[t]his should not, after all, prevent the possibility of judicial assessment in retrospect of the conduct of the relevant troop contingent.' *Hasan Nuhanović v The Netherlands* (Supreme Court) (n 12) para 3.18.3.

[57] R Murphy, 'UN Military Operations and International Humanitarian Law: What Rules Apply to Peacekeepers?' (2003) 14 *Criminal Law Forum—An International Journal* 2, 174; R Murphy, 'The Legal Framework of United Nations Peacekeeping Forces and the Issue of Command and Control' (1999) 4 *Journal of Armed Conflict Law* 41–73. See also Dannenbaum, 'Translating the Standard of Effective Control' (n 20) 148.

[58] M Milanovic and T Papic, 'As Bad as it Gets: The European Court of Human Rights' Behrami and Saramati Decision and General International Law' (2009) 58 *International and Comparative Law Quarterly* 282.

[59] According to Dannenbaum, this explains why the ILC discusses in its commentary to Draft Article 7 not orders but 'command and control' more generally; see Dannenbaum (n 20) 156, 157, fn 193.

[60] A Nollkaemper, 'Dual Attribution: Liability of the Netherlands for Conduct of Dutchbat in Srebrenica' (2011) 9 *Journal of International Criminal Justice* 1143, 1148.

It should be stressed, however, that the Dutch courts did not issue this rule—who could have prevented the wrongful conduct—as a general theoretical norm. It firmly based it on the exceptional facts and circumstances of the Nuhanović case. Dutchbat and the Dutch government operated in a transitional period. The mission to protect Srebrenica had failed. It was 'out of the question' that Dutchbat or UNPROFOR would resume the mission.[61] States take back control in dire situations when their own military are at risk. And perhaps even rightly so. If the UN cannot take responsibility for their safety, states should take their responsibility if they have the power to do so. Evacuation of national troops in case of emergency is without doubt a national matter.

These special circumstances may limit the relevance of this judgment for victims of future peacekeeping operations. In this regard, it should also be borne in mind that the Nuhanović case is an extremely tragic and difficult one. Dutchbat in a most flagrant way disregarded UN instructions to protect the refugees as much as possible. The fact that Dutchbat had done nothing whatsoever to save Nuhanović's brother is likely to have influenced the court's interpretation of the applicable legal norms.

The facts therefore are likely to have played an extremely important role in this case. As lawyers we are inclined to focus on the law. However, the facts often determine the outcome of a case to a much greater degree.[62] Nuhanović was fortunate to have access to the facts necessary to underpin his case. However, it is often very difficult for victims to establish facts that have occurred during a peacekeeping mission. The UN, states and individual peacekeepers usually do have the facts. However peacekeepers return to their home country, taking the reports about their mission with them. The evidence is then held in at least two countries or held by the UN (giving the victims left behind the run-around). The victims do not have access to the reports of the military operations. If they consider obtaining the facts via a production-of-exhibits procedure at a national court, they are faced with the limited jurisdiction of the national courts. Individuals or organisations in other countries cannot be forced to collaborate and submit documents on the orders of a court.[63] It is also not unusual for peacekeepers

---

[61] *Hasan Nuhanović v The Netherlands* (Appeals) (n 5) para 5.11; *Hasan Nuhanović v The Netherlands* (Supreme Court) (n 12) para 3.12.2.

[62] The 'Basic Principles and Guidelines on the Right to a Remedy and Reparation' stress 'the victim's right to … access to relevant information concerning violations'. UNGA Res 60/147 (16 December 2005) UN Doc A/RES/60/147, principle 11. Principle 24 stipulates: '[V]ictims and their representatives should be entitled to seek and obtain information on the causes leading to their victimization and on the causes and conditions pertaining to … the serious violations of international humanitarian law and to learn the truth in regard to these violations.'

[63] L Zegveld, 'Restoration of Rights for Victims of Violations of International Humanitarian Law' (2008) Inaugural Lecture Leiden University, media.leidenuniv.nl/legacy/restoration-of-rights.pdf, accessed 23 June 2016.

to intentionally destroy information. Dutchbat destroyed documents before their departure from the Srebrenica enclave in 1995.[64]

The Netherlands has carried out various investigations into the acts and omissions of Dutchbat. These investigations—occasioned by rumours about misconduct—were good as they provided Nuhanović and other victims with access to information. It is strange, however, that although the victims were the subject of the investigations, they were seldom involved in them. In 2002, the Parliamentary Committee of Inquiry investigated the fall of Srebrenica. One of the objectives of this committee was to investigate how, in 1995, the pros and cons were weighed between Dutchbat's safety and that of the population in Srebrenica. For that purpose, the Committee only heard from the Dutch military and politicians.[65] The Committee apparently did not think it necessary to hear the other side of the story, the side of the local population.[66] The reason for not involving the victims was perhaps a practical one. The victims were far away and the military and politicians lived nearby. Or perhaps there was a wish to keep emotions out. Whatever the reason, it was remarkable because the victims could have provided first-hand information.

A final question that is still very much left undiscussed is the question of UN liability. One would expect that the fear of state liability, a fear that has materialised with the Nuhanović case, would motivate states to rethink UN liability. As noted, the responsibility of troop-sending states and the UN can coexist. Although the UN is likely to have less control than individual states, to the extent UN control can be established it leads to (co)responsibility of the organisation.

However, absolute immunity of the UN often makes UN liability an illusion. In the very early stages of his court case in the Netherlands, in November 2002, Nuhanović wrote a letter to the UN, holding it responsible for the death of his family. In its reply, the UN dismissed all liability. In the same letter, the organisation reserved all its immunities in respect to the claim of the victims, including its immunity from all forms of legal process, as provided for in Article 105 of the UN Charter and the Convention on the Privileges and Immunities of the United Nations. This immunity was confirmed in a recent judgment in a different case initiated by a large group of victims of Srebrenica. On 13 April 2012 the Dutch Supreme Court

---

[64] The Netherlands Institute for War Documentation (NIOD), *Srebrenica, een 'veilig' gebied: reconstructie, achtergronden, gevolgen en analyses van de val van een Safe Area* (Amsterdam, Boom, 2002) part I, 15.

[65] See Parliamentary Committee of Inquiry on Srebrenica, 'Mission without Peace' (27 January 2003) Parliamentary Papers II 2002/03 28506, p 11.

[66] ibid: 'If necessary for the purpose of the investigation, other military and surviving relatives can also be heard.' This has not, however, happened.

confirmed the immunity of the UN in Dutch courts. The fact that the case concerned genocide could not alter this, according to the court.[67]

There is thus a lack of independent legal control of UN peacekeeping operations at the UN level. It seems that the states and the UN are aware of the problem. The Nuhanović ruling should have increased their awareness. But an effective remedy has not been provided. The standing claims commission the UN has agreed to establish has never in reality been established.[68]

To guarantee the rule of law and prevent counterproductive effects on peacekeeping operations, this matter should be taken up by states and the United Nations in a responsible manner. All states should have an objective interest in the settlement of damage they have caused in peacekeeping missions and provide proper recourse to a remedy.

---

[67] *Stichting Mothers of Srebrenica v The Netherlands* (Judgment) ECLI:NL:PHR:2012: BW1999 (2012). For the ECtHR decision regarding the same case, see *Stichting Mothers of Srebrenica and Others v the Netherlands* (App no 65542/12) ECHR 11 June 2013.

[68] Art 48 of the Status of Forces Agreement between the UN and Bosnia-Herzegovina provides for the establishment of such a commission: '[A]ny dispute or claim of a private law character to which UNPROFOR or any member thereof is a party and over which the courts of Bosnia and Herzegovina do not have jurisdiction because of any provision of the present Agreement shall be settled by a standing claims commission to be established for that purpose. One member of the commission shall be appointed by the Secretary-General of the United Nations, one member by the Government and a chairman jointly by the Secretary-General and the Government.' See 'Agreement between the United Nations and the Government of Bosnia and Herzegovina on the Status of the United Nations Protection Force in Bosnia and Herzegovina. Signed at Sarajevo on 15 May 1993' [1993] *United Nations Juridical Yearbook* 47. See also M Kamminga, 'Pleidooi voor een claims commission voor Srebrenica' (2010) 85 *Nederlands Juristenblad* 1111, 1416. The UN did establish so-called 'claims review boards' in Bosnia-Herzegovina. However these claims review boards have only limited jurisdiction. They examine straightforward claims, such as damage caused by UN personnel in car accidents. Such claims must be submitted within six months of the damage occurring.

13

Civilian Protection and the Arms Trade Treaty

BLINNE NÍ GHRÁLAIGH*

I. INTRODUCTION

T
HE ARMS TRADE Treaty (ATT)[1] entered into force on Christmas Eve 2014 to rapturous acclaim. It is the first comprehensive global treaty to regulate the estimated US$70 billion international trade in conventional arms, previously less regulated than the international trade in armchairs.[2] It was widely lauded as an 'epoch-making'[3] 'victory for the world's people',[4] which was to 'build a better and safer world for all'.[5]

It is the first international treaty to recognise explicitly the 'security, social, economic and humanitarian consequences' of the international trade in conventional weapons,[6] and to identify 'reduc[ing] human suffering' as one of its primary purposes, alongside contributing to 'international and regional peace, security and stability', and promoting 'cooperation, transparency and responsible action' by states in the international trade in conventional weapons.[7] In order to achieve those purposes, the ATT places human rights

---

* I would like to thank Professor Andrew Clapham for his comments on an earlier draft.
[1] Arms Trade Treaty (adopted 2 April 2013, entered into force 24 December 2014) UNGA Res 67/234B (ATT).
[2] Ban Ki-Moon, as reported in: 'Absence of Global Standards for Arms Trade "Defies Explanation", but after Long Journey, Final Destination in Sight, Secretary-General Tells Conference', UN Press Release, 18 March 2013, www.un.org/press/en/2013/dc3420.doc.htm.
[3] 'First Committee Speakers Greet Arms Trade Treaty as "Epoch-Making" Achievement Capable of Restraining Proliferation If Backed by Strict Export Controls', UN Press Release, 29 October 2013, www.un.org/press/en/2013/gadis3489.doc.htm.
[4] United Nations Secretary-General (UNSG) Ban Ki-Moon statement on the adoption of the ATT, as reported in: 'Arms Trade Treaty Will Generate "Much-Needed Momentum" for Other Global Disarmament, Non-Proliferation Efforts, Secretary-General Says' UN Press Release, 2 April 2013, www.un.org/ News/Press/docs/2013/sgsm14919.doc.htm.
[5] 'Secretary-General's Remarks at a Reception Marking the Opening of the Arms Trade Treaty for Signature' UN Press Release, 3 June 2013, www.un.org/sg/en/content/sg/statement/2013-06-03/secretary-generals-remarks-reception-marking-opening-arms-trade.
[6] ATT (n 1) Preamble.
[7] ibid, Art 1.

316 Blinne Ní Ghrálaigh

and humanitarian law considerations at the very heart of the international conventional arms trade that it regulates, requiring states parties to consider each and every potential weapons export through their lens.

The ATT is not, however, a human rights or humanitarian law treaty. It is, as its name suggests, an arms trade treaty, supported and promoted by many of the world's leading arms-exporting states. It expressly recognises that 'civilians, particularly women and children, account for the vast majority of those adversely affected by armed conflict and armed violence',[8] fuelled by the international arms trade. However, it nevertheless equally explicitly recognises—and legitimises—the 'political, security, economic and commercial interests of States' in the international trade in those very weapons.[9] Therein lies an inherent tension in the ATT, reflected in its drawn-out and frequently contentious negotiation process, and enshrined in its final text. It is a tension which its critics claim was ultimately resolved by giving 'priority ... to profit over human suffering',[10] under a false veneer of human rights and humanitarian law concern. On such a view, the ATT represents not a victory for the world's people, but 'a historic and momentous failure',[11] which weakens—rather than strengthens—the human rights and humanitarian law obligations and protections that it purports to champion, precisely by linking them to a legitimised trade in arms, so inherently inimical to them.

This chapter suggests that the reality of the ATT is somewhere between the lofty claims of its proponents and the damning judgement of its detractors. It recognises that the ATT's provisions are imperfect, borne as they are out of significant—and perhaps supererogatory—compromises in its negotiating process, impacting on its scope and prohibitions. It acknowledges with concern the reluctance—and indeed refusal—by many states to reaffirm their commitment to fundamental principles of international law in the context of the regulation of the arms trade, reflecting a more general, troubling trend of the early twenty-first century. However, it argues that, notwithstanding those limitations, the ATT's provisions and the obligations placed on states thereunder *are* nevertheless robust and far-reaching, and

---

[8] ibid, Preamble.

[9] ibid. For critiques regarding the legitimising role of the ATT, see eg A Stavrianakis, 'Legitimising Liberal Militarism: Politics, Law and War in the Arms Trade Treaty' (2016) 37 *Third World Quarterly* 840; and DB Kopel, P Gallant and JE Eisen, 'The Arms Trade Treaty: Zimbabwe, the Democratic Republic of the Congo, and the Prospects for Arms Embargoes on Human Rights Violators' (2010) 114 *Penn State Law Review* 101.

[10] Statement by Bolivia quoted in 'Overwhelming Majority of States in General Assembly Say "Yes" to Arms Trade Treaty to Stave off Irresponsible Transfers that Perpetuate Conflict, Human Suffering' UN Press Release, 2 April 2013, www.un.org/press/en/2013/ga11354.doc. htm.

[11] K Jackson, 'The Arms Trade Treaty: A Historic and Momentous Failure' *Ceasefire*, 29 April 2013, www.ceasefiremagazine.co.uk/failure-arms-trade-treaty.

that this young treaty could yet, *if rigorously enforced*, become 'a powerful new tool in our efforts to prevent grave human rights abuses or violations of international humanitarian law'.[12]

In making that argument, this chapter is divided into five sections, including this introduction and a conclusion. Section II provides a brief overview of ATT and its contentious, consensus-based negotiating process. Sections III and IV provide an analysis of ATT Articles 6 and 7, which lie at the heart of the treaty's civilian protection regime, setting out the bases on which states must refuse weapons exports.

II. AN OVERVIEW OF THE ATT AND ITS NEGOTIATING HISTORY

The ATT is still a very young treaty, having entered into force on 24 December 2014. It represents the culmination of a nearly two-decade-long global campaign, led by civil society, including Nobel Peace Laureates, NGOs, grassroots campaigners, communities, survivors, researchers, academics and legal practitioners alike,[13] for an international treaty to regulate the international trade in conventional weapons. The treaty was adopted by the UN General Assembly (UNGA), with an overwhelming majority of 154–3 states voting in favour.[14] It entered into force a year and a half later, having secured the ratification of fifty states[15]—one of the shortest timelines ever for a multilateral UN treaty,[16] evidencing the strong support it received amongst states. It currently counts ninety-two states parties, including five

---

[12] UNSG Ban Ki-Moon (n 4).

[13] For a comprehensive history of the civil society campaigns behind the adoption of the ATT, see eg S Parker, 'Breaking New Ground? The Arms Trade Treaty' in *Small Arms Survey 2014: Women and Guns* (Cambridge, Cambridge University Press 2014) 76, 78–79; Amnesty International 'The Long Journey Towards an Arms Trade Treaty' (27 March 2013) www.amnestyusa.org/news/news-item/the-long-journey-towards-an-arms-trade-treaty; M Bolton et al, 'The Arms Trade Treaty from a Global Civil Society Perspective: Introducing Global Policy's Special Section' (2014) 5 *Global Policy* 433; E Kytömäki, 'Promoting Discussion on an Arms Trade Treaty, EU-UNIDIR Project: Final Report' (2011) UNIDIR 51 www.unidir.org/files/medias/pdfs/final-report-eng-0-145.pdf; and D Garcia, *Disarmament Diplomacy and Human Security: Regimes, Norms and Moral Progress in International Relations* (New York, Routledge, 2011) 50–53.

[14] Iran, North Korea and Syria represented the three no votes, with twenty-three states (including China, India, Russia and the Gulf states) abstaining: see UN Bibliographic Information System, 'The Arms Trade Treaty Voting Record' (2 April 2013) UN Doc A/RES/67/234B unbisnet.un.org:8080/ipac20/ipac.jsp?profile=voting&index=.VM&term=ares67234b.

[15] The ATT opened for signature on 3 June 2013, two months after its adoption by way of UNGA vote. In accordance with Art 22.1 ATT, it entered into force ninety days after the deposition with the UN of the fiftieth instrument of ratification.

[16] ATT Monitor, 'ATT Monitor Report 2016' (2016) armstreatymonitor.org/en/the-2016-report/, p 10.

of the top eight arms-exporting States (France, Germany, Italy, Spain and the UK),[17] and a further thirty-eight state signatories (including the USA),[18] signalling the limited impact those exporting states expected it to have on their own arms trading.

The ATT's final text was negotiated, at the insistence of the United States,[19] on the basis of consensus,[20] a consensus that ultimately failed at the final hurdle, leading to the aforementioned UNGA vote. While the rule of consensus often has the benefit of fostering strong, lasting collective support amongst negotiating parties, it necessarily requires considerable compromise and risks resulting a 'lowest common denominator' agreement, to which nobody objects.[21] There is no doubt that, but for the rule of consensus, the ATT's negotiations would have resulted in a more broad-ranging treaty, with strengthened prohibitions of arms trades.[22] This was made clear on ratification by numerous states, which underscored that the ATT represents 'the floor and not the ceiling' in the regulation of conventional weapons.[23]

The object of the ATT is to establish common standards for regulating and improving—but not curtailing or restricting—the *licit* international arms trade, and to prevent and eradicate the *illicit* international trade in conventional arms and prevent their diversion,[24] including to human rights abusers. It applies to seven broad categories of conventional weapons, namely: battle tanks, armoured combat vehicles, large-calibre artillery systems, combat aircraft, attack helicopters, warships, and missiles and

---

[17] Stockholm International Peace Research Institute (SIPRI), 'SIPRI Yearbook 2017: Armaments, Disarmament and International Security Summary' (2015) www.sipri.org/sites/default/files/2017-09/YB17-summary-eng.pdf, pp 14–15.

[18] UN Office for Disarmament Affairs (UNODA), 'The Arms Trade Treaty', www.un.org/disarmament/convarms/att/. The United States is the largest supplier of arms worldwide.

[19] See 'Key US Redline in the Negotiations', US Department of State, www.state.gov/t/isn/armstradetreaty/. The USA signed the ATT on 25 September 2013 but has not ratified it to date.

[20] As provided for in the UNGA, 'Provisional Rules of Procedure of the Conference' (7 March 2012) A/Conf.217/L.1 rules 33 and 34 www.un.org/ga/search/view_doc.asp?symbol=A/CONF.217/L.1&Lang=E.

[21] R Wolfrum and J Pichon, 'Consensus' in *Max Planck Encyclopedia of Public International Law* (October 2010) para 20. The full text provides an overview of the consensus principle, its benefits and disbenefits.

[22] G Nystuen and K Egeland, 'The Potential of the Arms Trade Treaty to Reduce Violations of International Humanitarian Law and Human Rights Law' in C Bailliet and K Larsen (eds), *Promoting Peace Through International Law* (Oxford, Oxford University Press, 2015) 214.

[23] See eg the statements made on behalf of Japan and other states, as recorded in 'Overwhelming Majority of States' (n 23); see also Egyptian statement to the UN at the General Debate of the First Committee of the UNGA (16 October 2014) unoda-web.s3-accelerate.amazonaws.com/wp-content/uploads/assets/special/meetings/firstcommittee/69/pdfs/GD_16_Oct_Egypt.pdf, para 10.

[24] ATT (n 1) Art 1.

missile launchers,[25] together with small arms and light weapons (SALW), such as machine guns.[26] It also applies—albeit to a more limited extent[27]—to weapon parts and components 'in a form that provides the capability to assemble' the above seven categories of weapons,[28] and—importantly—to ammunition/munitions capable of being 'fired, launched or delivered' by them.[29] The inclusion of ammunitions/munitions within the ATT's scope, one of the most contentious issues in the entire ATT negotiations process,[30] marked a victory for those seeking an arms trade treaty capable of fulfilling its goal of 'reduc[ing] human suffering', including by protecting civilians from rampant gun violence. However, it was only a partial victory: ammunition/munitions that are launched manually or not launched at all, such as hand grenades and manually positioned landmines, still fall entirely outside the ATT's scope, despite their proliferation and the untold amount of human suffering they cause. So too does surveillance equipment, including surveillance drones, guidance systems and technology, deliberately removed from the draft ATT text during the negotiation process,[31] raising real fears that the ATT is not 'future proofed'.[32] That represents a significant weakness in the ATT, only mitigated to a limited extent by the ATT's exhortation that states apply its requirements 'to the broadest range of conventional arms',[33] current and future.

The ATT governs not just the trade but the 'transfer' of the above items, involving their 'export, import, transit, trans-shipment and brokering'.[34] However, it does not include the international movement of weapons without a change of ownership, such as a transfer by a state to its own military bases overseas. It is also unclear if it relates to non-commercial transactions, such as gifts, which are neither explicitly referenced in the ATT text (largely due to opposition from China)[35] nor expressly excluded.

---

[25] The ATT's first seven categories correspond to the seven major conventional weapons categories listed in the United Nations Register of Conventional Arms (UNROCA) (1991) www.un.org/disarmament/convarms/register/.

[26] ATT (n 1) Art 2(1). For an account on the fraught negotiations leading to the inclusion of SALW within the ATT's scope, see L Lustgarten, 'The Arms Trade Treaty: Achievements, Failings, Future' (2015) 64 *International and Comparative Law Quarterly* 569, 571–72.

[27] Ammunition/munitions are not subject to the ATT's record-keeping and reporting requirements, as per one of the US's 'redline' positions: see US Department of State (n 19).

[28] ATT (n 1) Art 4.

[29] ibid, Art 3.

[30] S Casey-Maslen et al, *The Arms Trade Treaty: A Commentary* (Oxford, Oxford University Press, 2016) para 3.02.

[31] For a discussion on this, see Lustgarten (n 26) 582–83.

[32] See eg S O'Connor 'Up in Arms: A Humanitarian Analysis of the Arms Trade Treaty and its New Zealand Application' (2013) 11 *New Zealand Yearbook of International Law* 73, 85.

[33] ATT (n 1) Art 5(3).

[34] ibid, Art 2(2).

[35] See eg 'China and the Arms Trade Treaty—Prospects and Challenges' *Saferworld*, May 2014, www.saferworld.org.uk/downloads/pubdocs/china-and-the-att.pdf.

This too represents a possible serious loophole in its application, born of the consensus process.

The key obligations binding on ATT Member States are set out in Articles 6 and 7.[36] Frequently referred to as the 'heart' of the ATT, they require states parties to refuse authorisation for arms transfers in certain defined circumstances, including if they would be used in attacks against civilians or civilian populations. The ATT's other important obligations relate, inter alia, to documentation and reporting, intended to increase the transparency and scrutiny of the international arms trade.[37] States are required to give effect to their ATT obligations in a 'consistent, objective and non-discriminatory manner':[38] weapons transfer decisions are to be made in good faith, without political influence or bias. States must also establish national control systems, including national control lists.[39] These are intended to ensure that states assess weapons authorisation requests consistently, objectively and dispassionately, in accordance with their obligations arising under international law, including under ATT Articles 6 and 7, and domestic laws and regulations.

Crucially, states parties are also mandated to take 'appropriate measures to enforce national laws and regulations that implement the provisions of this Treaty', to ensure the effective enforcement of the ATT.[40] In the absence of an ATT-specific dispute-resolution or enforcement procedure, this provision is key to the effectiveness of the ATT in practice and to its capacity to fulfil its goal of protecting civilians in conflict. That is because it serves to subject states' compliance with their ATT obligations to the scrutiny of domestic mechanisms, including—in many if not all ATT jurisdictions—to the scrutiny of national courts. The extent to which courts prove themselves willing to take up the baton to ensure that states are held to their ATT obligations will be the litmus test of whether the treaty does indeed become the 'powerful new tool' for the prevention of 'grave human rights abuses or violations of international humanitarian law' that it was promised to be.[41]

The ICJ itself could also come to play an important role in this regard. That is because, despite the negotiating parties' failure to establish

---

[36] ATT (n 1) Arts 6, 7. Those articles operate alongside Arts 8–11, which set out more limited obligations on states parties, relating to the import, transit and trans-shipment, brokering and diversion of weapons.

[37] ibid, Arts 12, 13; as above, they do not apply to ammunition/munitions. For a comprehensive overview of the reports submitted by ATT state parties to date, see R Stohl and P Holtom, 'Reviewing Initial Reports on ATT Implementation: Analysis and Lessons Learned' ATT-Baseline Assessment Project (2016) www.stimson.org/sites/default/files/file-attachments/The-ATT-Initial-Reports-Reviewing-ATT-Implementation-Lessons-Learned.pdf.

[38] ATT (n 1) Art 5(1).

[39] ibid, Art 5(2).

[40] ibid, Art 14.

[41] UNSG Ban Ki-Moon (n 4).

a mandatory supranational dispute settlement mechanism for the ATT, over 50 ATT states parties, including three of the world's leading arms exporters (Germany, Spain and the UK),[42] have separately accepted the mandatory jurisdiction of the ICJ under Article 36(2) of its statute.[43] That means that the ICJ has prima facie jurisdiction over any dispute arising regarding the interpretation or application of the ATT as between any of those states. This affords the Court an important potential future role in ensuring states' compliance with their obligations and in ensuring that the pursuit of profit does not serve to trump the ATT's human rights and humanitarian objectives.

III. CIVILIAN PROTECTION AND THE PROHIBITION OF WEAPONS TRANSFERS UNDER ATT ARTICLE 6

Article 6 of the ATT—together with its Article 7—constitutes the core of the ATT's civilian protection capability. It is the first of two mandatory assessments a state party must undertake before authorising *any* transfer of arms or related items within the scope of the ATT. It identifies three circumstances in which states are *absolutely prohibited* from making a transfer: first, if such transfer would breach a binding UN Security Council resolution; secondly, if it would violate the state's obligations under other international treaties; and thirdly, if it would be used to violate certain fundamental provisions of international law. The list is short, states having, deeply troublingly, refused to agree to add other express prohibitions, including on transfers that would violate customary international law and international human rights law (IHRL). Nevertheless, the scope of the three agreed prohibitions is capable of broad interpretation, and is therefore capable of mitigating that refusal at least to some extent, as the following analysis demonstrates.

A. Prohibition on Transfers in Breach of Binding UN Security Council Decisions

Article 6(1) prohibits any arms transfer that would contravene a binding decision of the UN.[44] It refers specifically to mandatory UN arms embargoes, of which there are currently thirteen in force,[45] often more respected

---

[42] SIPRI (n 17).

[43] Statute of the International Court of Justice (adopted 26 June 1945, entered into force 24 October 1945) 33 UNTS 993 (ICJ Statute) Art 36(2).

[44] Charter of the United Nations (signed 26 June 1945, entered into force 24 October 1945) 557 UNTS 143 (UN Charter) Art 39. See also Arts 40–51, to which Chapter VII relates.

[45] For a full list, see SIPRI, 'Arms Embargoes Database', www.sipri.org/databases/embargoes.

in their breach than their observance.[46] Given that states parties are already bound, pursuant to the UN Charter itself, to accept and carry out binding decisions of the UN Security Council,[47] Article 6(1) does not in itself create any *new* substantive obligations, but it does subject those to the ATT's reporting obligations, and render them susceptible to domestic challenge.[48]

B. Prohibition on Transfers in Violation of International Agreements

Article 6(2) is also largely concerned with a state's pre-existing obligations. In prohibiting a state from making any transfer that would violate other agreements to which it is a party, Article 6(2) ensures that the ATT holds the baseline position: states cannot purport to rely on the ATT to avoid more onerous obligations binding on them pursuant to other treaties.

Article 6(2) refers 'in particular' to international agreements 'relating to the transfer of, or illicit trafficking in, conventional arms'. This plainly relates to other weapons-related treaties to which the transferring state is party.[49] However, it also encompasses *any* other international agreement capable of being violated by a transfer of weapons or ammunition, such as: the UN Charter itself, by which *all* current ATT states parties are bound, prohibiting any transfer that would be used in an act of aggression or an unlawful use of force;[50] IHL agreements, such as Additional Protocol II to the four Geneva Conventions, prohibiting, in NIACs, attacks on medical

---

[46] A wide-scale study of arms embargoes conducted by Control Arms in 2006 found that 'every one of the 13 United Nations arms embargoes imposed in the last decade has been systematically violated'. See Amnesty International, 'UN Arms Embargoes: An Overview of the Last Ten Years' (16 March 2006) www.amnesty.eu/static/documents/2006/06_03_16_UN_arms_embargoes.pdf citing B Wood, 'Strengthening Compliance with UN Arms Embargoes—Key Challenges for Monitoring and Verification' in *UNODA Occasional Paper Series No 10: Verifying Non-Proliferation & Disarmament Treaties Today* (2006). See also S Parker, 'Implications of States' Views on an Arms Trade Treaty' (UN Institute for Disarmament Research, 2008) 49.

[47] UN Charter, Arts 2(5), 25, 48.

[48] ATT (n 1) Art 14.

[49] See eg treaties relating to anti-personnel mines (Convention on the Prohibition of the Use, Stockpiling, Production and Transfer of Anti-Personnel Mines and on their Destruction (adopted 18 September 1997, entered into force 1 March 1999) 2056 UNTS 211 (Ottawa Convention)); firearms (Protocol against the Illicit Manufacturing of and Trafficking in Firearms, their Parts and Components and Ammunition (adopted 31 May 2001, entered into force 3 July 2005) 2326 UNTS 208); and cluster munitions (Convention on Cluster Munitions (accessed 3 December 2008, entered into force 1 August 2010) 2688 UNTS 39).

[50] UN Charter. See in relation to transfers to non-state parties, *Military and Paramilitary Activities in and against Nicaragua (Nicaragua v United States of America)* [1984] ICJ Rep 392, para 242. For a further discussion, see Casey-Maslen et al (n 30) paras 6.56–6.67. Protocol II Additional to the Geneva Conventions of 12 August 1949, and relating to the Protection of Victims of Non-International Armed Conflicts (adopted 8 June 1977, entered into force 7 December 1978) 1125 UNTS 609 (AP II) Arts 11, 14 and 16, respectively.

units and places of worship, and the destruction of objects indispensable to the survival of the civilian population, for any of its 168 states parties;[51] and—importantly—international and regional human rights agreements to which the transferring state is a party (a point made clear in a political declaration delivered by Mexico on behalf of no fewer than ninety-eight ATT States),[52] including the ICCPR, the ECHR[53] and the Refugee Convention of 1951.[54] The scope and application of Article 6(2), and the strict prohibitions on exports that it imposes are therefore both broad and significant.

C. Prohibition on Transfers in Violation of Specific Provisions of International Humanitarian and International Criminal Law

Article 6(3) also prohibits a state party from making a transfer where it 'has knowledge at the time of authorisation' that the arms or related items 'would be used' to commit genocide, crimes against humanity, grave breaches of the four Geneva Conventions, attacks against civilians and civilian objects, or war crimes as defined in international agreements to which it is a party.[55] These concepts are all well understood and well defined in international customary and treaty law.[56] '[O]ther war crimes as defined by international agreements to which the State is a party', in particular, would include not only all war crimes under Article 8 of the 1998 Rome Statute of the ICC

---

[51] AP II, Arts 11, 14 and 16, respectively.

[52] 'Adoption of the ATT by the UN General Assembly, Political Declaration Delivered by Mexico on behalf of 98 States' (New York, 2 April 2013) mision.sre.gob.mx/onu/images/disc_att_2abril13.pdf.

[53] This broad interpretation of Art 6(2) is underscored by UNODA in its 'Arms Trade Treaty Implementation Toolkit Module 5: Prohibitions on Transfers', unoda-web.s3-accelerate.amazonaws.com/wp-content/uploads/2015/08/2015-08-21-Toolkit-Module-5.pdf, 4.

[54] Convention Relating to the Status of Refugees (adopted 28 July 1951, entered into force 22 April 1954) 189 UNTS 137 (Refugee Convention).

[55] ATT (n 1) Art 6(3).

[56] See Convention on the Prevention and Punishment of the Crime of Genocide (adopted 9 December 1948, entered into force 12 January 1951) 78 UNTS 277 (Genocide Convention); crimes against humanity as codified in the Rome Statute of the International Criminal Court (adopted 17 July 1998, entered into force 1 July 2002) UN Doc A/CONF 183/9 (ICC Statute) Art 7; and the grave breaches regime of the four Geneva Conventions: Geneva Convention I for the Amelioration of the Condition of the Wounded and Sick in Armed Forces in the Field (adopted 12 August 1949, entered into force 21 October 1950) 75 UNTS 31 (GC I) Art 50; Geneva Convention II for the Amelioration of the Condition of Wounded, Sick and Shipwrecked Members of Armed Forces at Sea (adopted 12 August 1949, entered into force 21 October 1950) 75 UNTS 85 (GC II) Art 51; Geneva Convention III Relative to the Treatment of Prisoners of War (adopted 12 August 1949, entered into force 21 October 1950) 75 UNTS 135 (GC III) Art 130; Geneva Convention IV Relative to the Protection of Civilian Persons in Time of War (adopted 12 August 1949, entered into force 21 October 1950) 75 UNTS 287 (GC IV) Art 147.

(for any of its 124 states parties),[57] but also serious violations of the norms contained in Common Article 3 of the four Geneva Conventions (which enjoy universal ratification),[58] and the grave breaches regime of Additional Protocol I (for any of its 174 states parties),[59] relating respectively to the protection of victims of NIACs and IACs.

The prohibition on transfers of weaponry, ammunition or related items that would be used in 'attacks against civilian objects or civilians protected as such' reflects one of the most fundamental principles of customary international law.[60] It concerns not only *deliberate* attacks on civilians and civilian objects (eg schools, hospitals, and religious and historical buildings) but also *indiscriminate* attacks that fail to distinguish between military objectives and civilian objects, or in which weapons that are incapable of so discriminating are deployed. It also relates to attacks that are *disproportionate* as against the anticipated military advantage in terms of the expected incidental injury to civilians or damage to civilian objects, and/or in relation to which insufficient or inadequate precautions have been taken.[61] It is therefore an extremely important inclusion in Article 6's list of absolute prohibitions on weapons transfers, which goes a considerable way towards mitigating the regrettable and reprehensible failure by the negotiating parties to agree on an express prohibition of transfers that would violate customary international law.

The test that Article 6(3) sets down for a State Party to refuse a transfer is where the state has 'knowledge', 'at the time of the authorisation', that the

[57] ICC, 'States Parties to the Rome Statute—Chronological List' asp.icc-cpi.int/en_menus/asp/states%20parties/Pages/states%20parties%20_%20chronological%20list.aspx.

[58] A specific reference to Common Article 3 in an earlier version of the Treaty did not make it into the final text of the ATT, despite significant efforts on behalf of a number of negotiating states, including Switzerland and the ICRC. However, states parties to the four Geneva Conventions are necessarily bound by its provisions, despite its omission. Switzerland made a declaration on the adoption of the ATT, asserting that: 'It is our understanding that the words ... encompass, among others, serious violations of Common Article 3 to the 1940 Geneva Conventions—instruments that enjoy universality.' Switzerland's declaration was endorsed by other states, including Ireland. See in this regard 'Overwhelming Majority of States' (n 10).

[59] ICRC, 'Treaties, States Parties and Commentaries', ihl-databases.icrc.org/ihl/INTRO/470, prot 1.

[60] It reflects AP II, Art 13(2) and Protocol I Additional to the Geneva Conventions of 12 August 1949 and relating to the Protection of Victims of International Armed Conflicts (adopted 8 June 1977, entered into force 7 December 1978) 1125 UNTS 3 (AP I) Art 51(2), which provide that: 'The civilian population as such, as well as individual civilians, shall not be the object of attack.'

[61] See in this regard the jurisprudence of the ICTY, in particular *Prosecutor v Galić* (Appeal Judgment) ICTY-98-29-A (30 November 2006), paras 132–33, 57; *Prosecutor v Blaškić* (Appeals Judgment) ICTY-95-14-A (29 July 2004), para 159; *Prosecutor v Kordić and Čerkez* (Appeals Judgment) ICTY-95-14/2-A (7 December 2004), paras 47, 57, 105; *Prosecutor v Gotovina and Markač* (Judgement) ICTY-06-90-T (15 April 2011), para 1841 (analysis not overturned on appeal). For a further discussion see Casey-Maslen et al (n 30) paras 6.160–165.

arms, ammunition/munitions or items 'would be used' in the commission of any of the above breaches. The provision proved to be one of the most controversial in the drafting history of the ATT, and its meaning, including the meaning of each of the terms or clauses in italics, takes some unpacking. The meaning of 'knowledge' can be gleaned from the drafting history of Article 6(3). An earlier draft of the provision had prohibited transfers made 'for the purposes of facilitating' breaches of IHL, war crimes or crimes against humanity.[62] That earlier draft echoed both the ICC Statute's standard for secondary liability for an international crime (applicable where a person 'for the purpose of facilitating the commission of ... a crime, aids, abets or otherwise assists in its commission')[63] and the test for secondary responsibility under the International Law Commission's 'Draft Articles on Responsibility of States for Internationally Wrongful Acts' (which comments that a State is internationally responsible for an unlawful act by another if its aid or assistance was given 'with a view to facilitating the commission of that act').[64] The revision to the text of Article 6 can properly be seen as a deliberate rejection of a purposive standard that would have at best undermined the Article's effectiveness, and at worst emptied it of practical effect. As underscored by the ICRC:

> A State ... that intends to facilitate crimes against humanity, genocide, or war crimes is unlikely to admit that a transfer of arms is 'for the purpose' of facilitating these acts, and would therefore never apply the prohibition.[65]

A more pertinent analogy of the ATT's 'knowledge' standard is to be found in the jurisprudence of the ICJ, in cases involving an alleged breach by one state of its obligation to prevent breaches of international law by another. In the *Case Concerning the Application of the Convention on the Prevention and Punishment of the Crime of Genocide (Bosnia v Serbia)*, for example, the ICJ held, in relation to a state's obligation to prevent genocide, that 'knowledge' includes constructive knowledge of matters of which the state 'should normally have been aware'.[66] It found that:

> [A] State may be found to have violated its obligation to prevent even though it had no certainty, at the time when it should have acted, but failed to do so,

---

[62] RULAC, 'The Draft of the Arms Trade Treaty' (2012) UN Doc A/CONF.217/CRP.1, www. geneva-academy.ch/RULAC/pdf/Comprehensive-Draft-Arms-Trade-Treaty-of-26-July-2012. pdf.

[63] ICC Statute, Art 25(3).

[64] ILC, 'Draft Articles on Responsibility of States for Internationally Wrongful Acts, with Commentaries' (2001) vol II part 2, 66, para 5.

[65] Casey-Maslen et al (n 30) para 6.13. See also Mexico's declaration, referred to in the same text para 6.13.

[66] *Application of the Convention on the Prevention and Punishment of the Crime of Genocide (Bosnia and Herzegovina v Serbia and Montenegro)* (Merits) [2007] ICJ Rep 43. See also *Corfu Channel Case (United Kingdom v Albania)* (Merits) [1949] ICJ Rep 4, para 433.

that genocide was about to be committed or was underway; for it to incur responsibility on this basis it is enough that the State was aware, or should normally have been aware, of the serious danger that acts of genocide would be committed.[67]

As regards the meaning of the expression 'would be used', the forward-looking exercise to be undertaken by a state is similar to that required of it under other international agreements, notably those dealing with the possible 'transfer' of individuals to another state in breach of their fundamental rights.[68] The requisite test is whether there are 'substantial grounds for believing' that the person would face a 'real risk' of human rights violations upon deportation.[69] The UN Committee against Torture has underscored that the risk of serious violation must 'go beyond mere theory or suspicion', but that it 'does not have to meet the test of being highly probable'.[70] If there is such a risk, the deportation or 'transfer' is strictly prohibited.

It goes without saying that, in assessing the future risk, the transferring state must have regard to all the evidence available, including any past allegations or evidence of violations by the receiving state.[71] A state cannot escape its responsibilities by failing to conduct adequate due diligence: it will be deemed to have constructive knowledge of the information that it chose to ignore or disregard. That being said, what matters is the state's actual or constructive knowledge 'at the time of the authorisation'—not at the time of the transfer itself. This represents an unfortunate and avoidable weakness in the ATT and an apparent prioritising of 'done deals' over IHL and IHRL protections, in circumstances where months and sometimes years can lapse between authorisation of a transfer and its actual shipment, during which time the circumstances in the receiving state could change significantly.

---

[67] *Bosnia and Herzegovina v Serbia and Montenegro* (n 66) para 432.

[68] See eg Refugee Convention, Art 33(1); United Nations Convention against Torture and Other Cruel, Inhuman or Degrading Treatment or Punishment (adopted 10 December 1984, entered into force 26 June 1987) 1465 UNTS 113 (UNCAT) Art 3; International Covenant on Civil and Political Rights (adopted 16 December 1966, entered into force 23 March 1976) 999 UNTS 171 (ICCPR) Art 7.

[69] As per the determinations of UNCAT and the ECtHR, see eg Committee Against Torture, *CT and KM v Sweden* (17 November 2006) UN Doc CAT/C/37/D/279/2005, para 7.3; *Soering v United Kingdom* (1989) 11 EHRR 439, para 91 (requiring 'substantial grounds ... for believing the existence of a real risk of treatment contrary to Article 3'). The Human Rights Committee and the Inter-American Commission similarly rely on a 'real risk' standard; see eg *ARJ v Australia* (1997) Human Rights Committee, CCPR/C/60/D/692/1996, para 6.9; and *Report on the Situation of Human Rights of Asylum Seekers Within the Canadian Refugee Determination System* (2000) Inter-American Commission on Human Rights Case No OEA/Ser.L/V/II.106, Doc. 40 Rev, para 154.

[70] *SMR and MMR v Sweden* (1999) Committee Against Torture, CAT/C/22/D/103/1998, para 9.4.

[71] UNODA (n 53) 4.

D. The Capacity of Article 6 to Ensure the Protection of Civilians in Conflict

As the above analysis demonstrates, Article 6 is hardly ground-breaking in its content, building as it does on substantial obligations already binding on states—including non-ATT states parties—under customary international law and international treaties. Its novelty and import lies in expressly marrying those fundamental legal obligations regarding the protection of civilians and the reduction of violence to a system of international arms control.

Understood in that context, the refusal by negotiating states to agree to a strict prohibition on transfers in violation of IHRL marked a particularly low point in the ATT's negotiation and is a troubling reflection on states' current lack of commitment to their binding IHRL obligations. It has led to a significant weakness in the ATT text, which is difficult to reconcile with the treaty's stated principles of 'respecting and ensuring respect for human rights'.[72] More troubling still was states' failure to agree on express prohibitions relating to breaches of customary international law, including peremptory norms: this indicates an apparent lack of commitment by those states to its fundamental international legal strictures and an unwillingness to be bound by them in the arms export context. It also gives rise to a real danger that states parties and non-state parties alike may seek to rely on Article 6's 'lowest common denominator' express prohibitions to seek to escape obligations binding on them under customary law and IHRL.

That danger is capable of being mitigated to a significant extent—at least with regard to ATT states parties—as the above analysis demonstrates, through a broad interpretation of Article 6(2) and (3). Article 6's three prohibitions, although limited in number, are capable of broad interpretation and application, drawing within the scope of the ATT a whole gamut of obligations under IHL and IHRL, including certain customary law strictures. Article 6 places all those commitments centre stage of any arms transfer decision, and subjects them to its reporting and regulatory framework, and to the scrutiny of domestic mechanisms. Further and importantly, as the above analysis has demonstrated, Article 6 sets a standard for prohibiting transfers that is more stringent than that applicable pursuant to the secondary rules of state responsibility under customary international law. As regards the potential use of the weapons against civilians and civilian objects, in particular, the ATT *absolutely prohibits* states from making a transfer if they are aware, or should normally be aware, at the time of authorisation, of a real risk that the transferred items would be used not

---

[72] ATT (n 1) 'Principles'.

only in deliberate or indiscriminate attacks on civilians, but also in attacks launched without precaution, or in attacks that would be disproportionate in terms of their incidental impact on civilians or civilian objects. If that analysis is undertaken by states 'fairly, in a consistent, objective and non-discriminatory manner',[73] as mandated by the ATT, 'bearing in mind the principles referred to in this Treaty',[74] including the objective of 'reducing human suffering', it is clearly capable of having a significant impact on the supply of weapons worldwide and on the resultant protection of civilians in conflict.

IV. CIVILIAN PROTECTION UNDER ATT ARTICLE 7: EXPORT RISK ASSESSMENT

If a proposed arms export is not strictly prohibited under Article 6, an exporting state party must then proceed to conduct a mandatory risk assessment of the export under Article 7. This requires the state to evaluate the risk of a number of negative and positive impacts of a weapons export. These include: its contribution to peace and security,[75] whether it could be used to commit or facilitate a serious violation of IHL or IHRL,[76] and whether it could be used to commit offences under international agreements relating to terrorism or transnational organised crime.[77] A state must also 'take into account' the risk of the proposed export being used to commit or facilitate serious acts of gender-based violence or serious acts of violence against women and children.[78] Like Article 6, Article 7 is a provision clearly concerned with the protection of civilians in conflict, and its capacity to impact thereon is more far-reaching. Its three-step process is considered below.

A. The Article 7 Assessment Process

The 'objective and non-discriminatory' assessment that an exporting state is required to carry out under Article 7 is much broader still than the determination required of it under Article 6.

First, the 'serious violations of international humanitarian law' with which Article 7 is concerned are considerably broader than the grave breaches

---

[73] ibid, Art 5.
[74] ibid.
[75] ibid, Art 7(1)(a).
[76] ibid, Arts 7(1)(b)(i)–(ii).
[77] ibid, Arts 7(1)(b)(iii)–(iv). Consideration of these provisions is outside the scope of this chapter.
[78] ibid, Art 7(4).

regime of the four Geneva Conventions, breaches of their Common Article 3, and attacks against civilians and civilian objects (including indiscriminate and disproportionate attacks, and attacks launched in breach of the precautionary principle) which are—expressly or impliedly—prohibited under Article 6.[79] They also include all other serious violations of the laws and customs of war, including the use of prohibited weapons, the use of human shields and starvation as a method of warfare.[80] They necessarily include, for all ATT states parties, violations of the norms contained in Additional Protocol I to Geneva Convention IV and in Article 8 of the Rome Statute (now broadly accepted to reflect customary international law),[81] together with violations of the norms contained in other war crimes under customary international law,[82] capable of being committed in IACs or NIACs.

Secondly, Article 7 refers explicitly to 'serious violations of international human rights law'. Although not precisely defined in the ATT or in international legal usage,[83] the term can be understood as referring to a wide range of human rights violations that are particularly serious due to their nature, the manner in which they are committed, or their impact on civilians.[84] That would plainly include breaches of peremptory norms (*jus cogens*), including the prohibitions on torture and slavery.[85] It would also include other rights capable of being violated by the use of conventional weapons, such as the rights to food, health and housing and to freedom of assembly and religion.[86]

---

[79] JM Henckaerts and L Doswald-Beck, *Customary International Humanitarian Law*, vol I: *Rules* (Cambridge, Cambridge University Press, 2006) rs 1, 7. For a developed discussion on this, see P Sands, A Clapham and B Ní Ghrálaigh, 'The Lawfulness of the Authorisation by the United Kingdom of Weapons and Related Items for Export to Saudi Arabia in the Context of Saudi Arabia's Military Intervention in Yemen', Legal Opinion prepared on instructions from Amnesty International UK, Oxfam and Saferworld (11 December 2015) paras 5.42–5.43.

[80] Henckaerts and Doswald-Beck (n 79) 599–603.

[81] See eg K Dörmann, 'War Crimes under the Rome Statute of the International Criminal Court, with a Special Focus on the Negotiations on the Elements of Crimes' (2003) 7 *Max Planck Yearbook of United Nations Law* 341; M Scharf, 'Accelerate Formation of Customary International Law' (2014) 20 *ILSA Journal of International & Comparative Law* 305; F Pocar, 'To What Extent Is Protocol I Customary International Law?' in AE Wall (ed) *Legal and Ethical Lessons of NATO's Kosovo Campaign*, vol 78 (International Law Studies, 2002).

[82] See ICRC, 'What Are "Serious Violations of International Humanitarian Law"? Explanatory Note', www.icrc.org/eng/assets/files/2012/att-what-are-serious-violations-of-ihl-icrc.pdf.

[83] NB: the UN Security Council appears to use the terms 'grave' and 'serious' interchangeably in relation to violations of international human rights.

[84] Geneva Academy of International Humanitarian Law and Human Rights, 'What Amounts to "A Serious Violation of International Human Rights Law"? An analysis of Practice and Expert Opinion for the Purpose of the 2013 Arms Trade Treaty', Academy Briefing No 6 (August 2014) www.sipri.org/sites/default/files/research/disarmament/dualuse/pdf-archive-att/pdfs/20140800_ga_what-amounts-to-a-serious-violation-of-international-human-rights-law.pdf.

[85] M C Bassiouni, 'International Crimes: Jus Cogens and Obligatio Erga Omnes' (1996) 59 *Law and Contemporary Problems* 63, 68.

[86] See Sands, Clapham and Ní Ghrálaigh (n 79) para 5.43.

Thirdly, Article 7 is not restricted to the *commission* of international law violations, but relates also to their *facilitation*. Exporting states must therefore assess both the potential direct and indirect involvement of an export in serious violations of international law, eg whether a weapon could be used to facilitate sexual violence or to round up people for summary execution by other means.[87]

Fourthly, Article 7 requires an exporting state to 'take into account' the 'risk' of the weapons 'being used to commit or facilitate serious acts of gender-based violence or serious acts of violence against women and children'.[88] The inclusion of the provision represents an important step in formally recognising the impact of the international arms trade on sexual violence in particular.[89] However, despite efforts from over 100 negotiating states,[90] it was not included in the formal Article 7 assessment process—another regrettable consequence of the negotiating rule of consensus. That means that a state is not mandated to refuse an export unless the 'serious acts of violence' in question also constitute a threat to peace and security, or a serious violation of IHL or IHRL, such as, for example, the use of rape as a weapon of war or the forcible recruitment of child soldiers.

Fifthly and finally, the 'peace and security' concerns to which a state must have regard are broad. Examples of negative impacts would include the potential use of the weapons to breach the *jus ad bellum*, to escalate regional tensions, or to enable a state to oppress its citizens or a minority thereof. The risk of diversion of weapons to other states or armed groups would also plainly be relevant to considerations of peace and security—as well as to the risk of serious violations of IHL and IHRL.

As the above analysis demonstrates, the scope of the Article 7 assessment process is considerably broader than the determination required of states under Article 6. Where Article 7 is *more* restricted than Article 6 is in relation to its application: it applies exclusively to *exports* and not to other forms of transfer. That means that the *only* limitations on the import transit or trans-shipment of weapons, ammunition or on their brokering are the prohibitions contained in Article 6.

The nature of the Article 7 risk-assessment process, like the analysis under Article 6, is forward looking, focused on the 'potential' future use and impact

---

[87] Casey-Maslen et al (n 30) para 7.35.

[88] ATT (n 1) Art 7(4).

[89] For a more in-depth discussion, see C Green et al, 'Gender Based Violence and the Arms Trade Treaty: Reflections from a Campaigning and Legal Perspective' (2013) 21 *Gender and Development* 551, 553; Amnesty International, 'Applying the Arms Trade Treaty to Ensure the Protection of Human Rights' (2015) www.amnesty.org/download/Documents/ACT3000032015ENGLISH.PDF, 13–14.

[90] R Acheson, M Butler and S Tuvestad, 'Preventing Armed Gender-Based Violence: A Binding Requirement in the New Draft ATT text' (2013) 6(9) *Arms Trade Treaty Monitor* 9, reachingcriticalwill.org/images/documents/Disarmament-fora/att/monitor/ATTMonitor6.9.pdf.

of the weapons. Questions that a state should reasonably be expected to consider in undertaking the assessment would include: Would the proposed export provoke or prolong any armed conflict or aggravate existing tensions? Has the importer previously committed or facilitated serious violations of international law? Has the importing state integrated international law into its national laws, military doctrine and manuals? Has it prosecuted and punished members of its own armed forces responsible for violations?[91] In answering those questions, a state must 'tak[e] into account relevant factors'.[92] The sources to which it should have regard are the same as those relevant to its Article 6 determination, including intelligence received from other states, reports from UN and regional human rights monitoring bodies and tribunals, and NGO and credible press reports.[93] A state may also properly consider information and assurances provided by the receiving state—and indeed, pursuant to Article 8, an importing state is *required* to provide all 'appropriate and relevant information' requested by an exporting state, to assist it in making its Article 7 determination.[94]

As with regard to Article 6, the Article 7 assessment of risk takes place prior to *authorisation* not prior to transfer.[95] The considerable concern regarding this limitation raised during the negotiating process was not translated into textual revision: in its final version, Article 7 merely 'encourage[s]' but does not oblige states to 'reassess' any authorisation if they become aware pre-transfer of new information that would have been relevant to their Article 7 assessment. This is another significant textual weakness in the ATT.

B. Mitigation Measures under Article 7

When assessing the possible risks of an export, the exporting state must consider whether there are 'available mitigating measures' that might assist in reducing such risks. Examples would include confidence-building measures, and jointly developed and agreed programmes between the exporting and importing states, such as the provision of training to the importing state's armed forces. However, the measures must, necessarily, be capable

---

[91] UNODA (n 53) 3–4. See also ICRC, 'Arms Transfer Decisions: Applying International Humanitarian Law and International Human Rights Law Criteria—A Practical Guide' (May 2007) www.icrc.org/eng/resources/documents/publication/p0916.htm, 5–15; Amnesty International (n 89).

[92] ATT (n 1) Art 7.

[93] UNODA (n 53) 6.

[94] ATT (n 1) Art 8.

[95] R Acheson, 'News in Brief' (2013) 6(7) *Arms Trade Treaty Monitor 5*, reachingcriticalwill. org/images/documents/Disarmament-fora/att/monitor/ATTMonitor6.7.pdf; R Acheson, 'News in Brief' (2013) 6(8) *Arms Trade Treaty Monitor 7*, reachingcriticalwill.org/images/documents/Disarmament-fora/att/monitor/ATTMonitor6.8.pdf.

of mitigating the risk in relation to the particular export in question, at the time of its export.[96]

C. The Article 7 Determination

Having conducted an 'objective and non-discriminatory' assessment,[97] and having had regard to mitigating measures, the exporting state must then reach a determination on whether to grant the export. Here again, the ATT's text is not straightforward, and its meaning requires some unpacking.

The first factor an exporting state must assess is the potential that the export 'would undermine peace and security', notwithstanding any possible mitigating measures. If the state determines that the impact of a proposed export on 'peace and security' would be negative, the export *must* be refused. In this way, this part of the assessment process acts in a manner akin to the absolute prohibitions of Article 6. Conversely, if the state considers that the export *would* contribute to peace and security (eg if the weapons would be used to deter or defend against unlawful aggression or to assist a state in controlling its borders against infiltration by foreign fighters), it must still refuse the export if it determines that there is nevertheless an 'overriding risk' of the export being used to commit or facilitate a serious violation of IHL and IHRL. It is only if the state, having regard to mitigating measures, determines that the risk that the export could be used to commit or facilitate a serious violation of IHL or IHRL is not 'overriding', that it may authorise it.[98]

The term 'overriding risk' contained in Article 7(3) was perhaps the most contentious clause of the entire ATT. It is a concept without pedigree in international law, inserted into the ATT at the insistence of the United States, on the meaning and application of which the negotiating parties were unable to agree. The *Oxford English Dictionary* for its part defines 'overriding' as 'more important than any other considerations', a definition that underscores the term's relativity and lack of inherent measurability.[99]

In fact, the vast majority of states had been in favour of a clear, measurable test that would preclude an export being authorised if there were a 'substantial risk' of it undermining peace and security or of it being used to commit or facilitate a serious violation of IHL or IHRL.[100] Negotiations on

---

[96] See Casey-Maslen et al (n 30), paras 7.88–89; Sands, Clapham and Ní Ghrálaigh (n 79) paras 5.44–5.45.

[97] ATT (n 1) Arts 5, 7.

[98] Casey-Maslen et al (n 30) paras 7.90–7.95; see also Sands, Clapham and Ní Ghrálaigh (n 79) para 5.34.

[99] *Oxford English Dictionary*, 'Overriding', en.oxforddictionaries.com/definition/overriding.

[100] See eg N Goldring, 'Groundhog Day?' (2013) 6(8) *Arms Trade Treaty Monitor* 4;

K Prizeman, 'News in Brief' (2013) 6(2) *Arms Trade Treaty Monitor* 6, reachingcriticalwill.org/images/documents/Disarmament-fora/att/monitor/ATTMonitor6.2.pdf. See also eg UN

the clause were protracted and contentious; the USA, in particular, dug in its heels, precluding the possibility of consensus.[101] The rationale for the insistence by the USA on an 'overriding risk' standard appears to have been an attempt to ensure for itself the possibility of authorising an export, notwithstanding the substantial risk of it being used in serious violation of IHL or IHRL, if it deemed that some other undefined benefit to 'peace and security' would flow from it.[102] Such an 'end justifies the means' rationale is anathema to the theory and practice of IHL and IHRL,[103] is incompatible with the non-derogable nature of peremptory norms, and would undermine the long-established civilian protections contained therein. It is also manifestly incompatible with states' obligations under Common Article 1 to the four Geneva Conventions, 'to respect and ensure respect for the Conventions in all circumstances',[104] itself enshrined as one of the fundamental principles of the ATT.[105] Such an interpretation would—needless to state—weaken rather than strengthen civilian protection under international law.

This interpretation found little support amongst other states, leading some to make formal declarations on ratification, indicating that they would interpret 'overriding' as meaning 'more likely to materialise than not'[106] or 'substantial'.[107] The test that EU Member States are bound in any event to apply under the EU's parallel arms export regime is that of a 'clear risk'.[108] These declarations are capable of constituting state practice and could therefore serve to crystallise the meaning of Article 7 over time.[109] In the meantime, taking into account state practice and the object and

---

Conference on the Arms Trade Treaty, 'Compilation of Views on the Elements of an Arms Trade Treaty: Background Document Prepared by the Secretariat' (10 May 2012) UN Doc A/CONF.217/2 108 www.un.org/ga/search/view_doc.asp?symbol=A/CONF.217/2 which records the support of various states, including the UK, for a 'substantial risk' test.

[101] 'The President Scrubs Up Pretty Well' *Arms Trade Treaty Legal Blog*, 20 March 2013, armstradetreaty.blogspot.co.uk/2013/03/the-president-scrubs-up-pretty-well.html; R Acheson, 'A Meaningful ATT is Our "Overriding" Priority' (2013) 6(4) *Arms Trade Treaty Monitor* 1, reachingcriticalwill.org/images/documents/Disarmament-fora/att/monitor/ATTMonitor6.4.pdf.

[102] Casey-Maslen et al (n 30) para 7.32.

[103] A Clapham, 'The Arms Trade Treaty: A Call for an Awakening' (2013) 2 *European Society of International Law Reflections* 5.

[104] GC I, GC II, GC III and GC IV, Art 1.

[105] ATT (n 1) 'Principles'.

[106] 'Declaration of Liechtenstein upon ratification of the ATT' (16 December 2014) treaties. un.org/doc/Publication/MTDSG/Volume%20II/Chapter%20XXVI/XXVI-8.en.pdf, 4.

[107] ATT Monitor, 'ATT Monitor Report 2015' (2015) 42.

[108] Council of the European Union, 'Council Common Position 2008/944/CFSP of 8 December 2008 Defining Common Rules Governing Control of Exports of Military Technology and Equipment' (8 December 2008) eur-lex.europa.eu/legal-content/EN/TXT/PDF/?uri=CELEX:32008E0944&from=EN, Art 2.

[109] See Vienna Convention on the Law of Treaties (adopted 23 May 1969, entered into force 27 January 1980) 1155 UNTS 331, 332–33 (VCLT) Art 31(3)(b), which provides that, in interpreting a treaty '[t]here shall be taken into account, together with the context ... (b) any subsequent practice in the application of the treaty which establishes the agreement of the parties regarding its interpretation'.

purpose of the ATT, Article 7 is most plausibly to be interpreted as only permitting a state to authorise an export if it determines that the potential risk of a serious violation of IHL or IHRL would not be so grave as to override any positive contribution the export might make to peace and security.[110] Such an interpretation is not only consistent with states' obligations under international law, but also with the purpose of the ATT of 'reducing human suffering' and 'contributing to peace, security and stability'.[111]

D. The Capacity of Article 7 to Ensure the Protection of Civilians in Conflict

Like Article 6, Article 7 is clearly an imperfect tool for the protection of civilians in conflict. Its very structure, appearing to assert a false dichotomy between considerations of 'peace and security' and 'human rights and humanitarian law', fails to recognise explicitly that serious violations of IHL and IHRL are themselves capable of undermining peace and security.[112] It is rightly criticised for appearing to provide legal cover to states to continue weapons exports notwithstanding a significant risk that they would be used to commit or facilitate serious violations of IHL or IHRL, either: on the grounds that the risk only materialised *after* the state conducted its authorisation process, but before it actually made the transfer; or—crucially—on the basis of political interests, couched as 'peace and security' considerations. It is regrettable that some states, including states that have to date failed to ratify the ATT, were able, in the negotiations, to water down what could have been a stronger protection for victims of violence and conflict.

However, the suggestion by some critics that the final wording of Article 7, including, in particular, its 'overriding risk' test is 'enough to render the treaty worse than useless' is a criticism too far.[113] That is because it ignores the fact that states typically seek to present themselves as IHL and IHRL *champions*, rather than their violators.[114] States will often go to considerable lengths to legitimise and justify their conduct as *complying* with fundamental principles of IHL and IHRL, rather than admit to their breach. In relation to the ATT, it is unlikely therefore that a state would admit,

---

[110] Sands, Clapham and Ní Ghrálaigh (n 79) para 5.49. See also Amnesty International (n 89) pp 19–20.

[111] ATT (n 1) Art 1.

[112] This is at odds with the ATT's Preamble, which acknowledges that 'peace and security and human rights are interlinked and mutually reinforcing'.

[113] R Acheson, 'The ATT Is Needed for Saving Lives, Not Profits' (2012) 5(17) *Arms Trade Treaty Monitor* 1, http://reachingcriticalwill.org/disarmament-fora/att/negotiating-conference/att-monitor/6436-26-july-2012-vol-5-no-17.

[114] For an in-depth discussion of this, see H Koh, 'Why Do Nations Obey International Law?' (1997) 106 *Yale Law Journal* 2599. See also eg J Alvarez, 'Torturing the Law' (2006) 37 *Case Western Reserve Journal of International Law* 175.

openly, to exporting weapons notwithstanding its assessment of a significant risk of them being used to commit a serious violation of IHL or IHRL: indeed any such admission could constitute an internationally wrongful act in and of itself, and could give rise to international criminal responsibility on the part of the decision-maker. A state is much more likely simply to deny that such a risk arises, including by refuting any factual evidence, or by equivocating about or seeking to undermine the very nature of civilian protections under international law. The difficulties resulting from such denial, while deeply problematic, are not inherent to the ATT itself, or dependent on the precise formulation of its Article 7 test.

Importantly, the ATT provides a response and a solution to any such denial. It does so in mandating that states undertake the Article 7 risk assessment process in 'an objective and non-discriminatory manner'.[115] Pursuant to the treaty's provisions, states are obligated to undertake the Article 7 assessment reasonably and in good faith, on the basis of objective, detailed criteria, applied in a consistent, uniform manner to *all* proposed exports without discrimination.[116] Not only that, but their ultimate assessment under Article 7—just like their determination under Article 6—is subject to the scrutiny and oversight of domestic mechanisms, which include—in many if not all ATT Member States—the scrutiny of domestic courts.[117]

This means the role of civil society—of campaigners, activists and lawyers—which was at the ATT's genesis and which was responsible for securing its entry into force, remains critical in these early years for the treaty: it is only by ensuring that transfer decisions are subject to strict scrutiny and review that the ATT's far-reaching provisions will avoid becoming the irrelevant dead letter the treaty's critics accuse it of being. Indeed, it is the very extent to which civil society is able to challenge states' determinations under Articles 6 and 7, and the extent to which domestic mechanisms, and in particular domestic courts, prove themselves willing and able to scrutinise those determinations, and to hold governments to their obligations under the ATT that will prove in time to be the true litmus test for the efficacy of the treaty and its ability to become the 'victory for the world's people' it was hailed as being.

V. CONCLUSION

Three years on from the entry into force of the ATT, there is little evidence of the 'better and safer world for all', that this 'epoch-changing' treaty was portended to bring about. The Middle East alone—from Saudi Arabia to Syria, Israel to Iraq, Egypt to Libya—is awash with weapons procured from ATT

---

[115] ATT (n 1) Art 7.
[116] ibid.
[117] ATT (n 1) Art 5(2).

states parties, which are being used to commit the most serious violations of IHL and IHRL and to cause untold human suffering. Respect for the fundamental rules of international law by states appears to be waning rather than waxing throughout the world.

Domestic mechanisms have not to date proven effectual in holding states to their ATT obligations: in early 2017, in the first case brought since the entry into force of the ATT against an ATT state party for breach of its arms export obligations,[118] the High Court of England and Wales reviewed the decision by the UK Secretary of State for International Trade to continue to authorise and transfer arms exports to Saudi Arabia,[119] for use in its military campaign in Yemen.[120] The NGO Campaign Against the Arms Trade (CAAT) challenged the UK government's continued export of weapons to Saudi Arabia, in circumstances where authoritative allegations abound of serious violations of IHL and IHRL by the Saudi-led military coalition.[121] Airstrikes by the coalition are reportedly the 'single largest cause of casualties' in the conflict, responsible for over two-thirds of civilian deaths,[122] and for over two-thirds of the damage to civilian objects, which—together with a Coalition-imposed blockade on aid and other essential goods—have devastated the already impoverished country and led it to the brink of

---

[118] The proceedings were brought for breach of the UK's 'Consolidated EU and National Arms Export Licencing Criteria', dated 25 March 2014, which implement in domestic law the UK's obligations arising under the ATT, the EU Council Common Position 2008/944/CFSP of 8 December 2008, defining common rules governing the control of exports of military technology and equipment, binding on all EU Member States, and the Organisation for Security and Cooperation in Europe (OSCE) Principles Governing Conventional Arms Transfers (25 November 1993) DOC.FSC/3/96.

[119] *R (on the application of Campaign Against the Arms Trade) v Secretary of State for International Trade & Intervenors*, [2017] EWHC 1754 (Admin), judgment 10 July 2017 ('the CAAT case'). The author was instructed as counsel in the case on behalf of the second intervenors (Oxfam).

[120] Arms sales from the UK, an erstwhile so-called 'champion state' of the ATT, have increased by 500 per cent since Saudi began its military campaign in the impoverished state: see L Dearden, 'UK Sales of Bombs and Missiles to Saudi Arabia Increase by Almost 500% since Start of Yemen War' *The Independent*, 8 November 2017, www.independent.co.uk/news/uk/home-news/uk-british-weapons-arms-sales-saudi-arabia-yemen-war-increase-500-civilians-war-crimes-export-a8042871.html.

[121] For a summary, see Sands, Clapham and Ní Ghrálaigh (n 79). See also the three reports by the UN Security Council's Panel of Experts on Yemen, available at: https://www.un.org/sc/suborg/en/sanctions/2140/panel-of-experts/reports; OHCHR, 'Zeid Urges Accountability for Violations in YEMEN' (25 August 2016) www.ohchr.org/EN/NewsEvents/Pages/DisplayNews.aspx?NewsID=20411&LangID=E6; UNOCHA, 'UN Humanitarian Chief Calls for Urgent Protection of Civilians and Scaling Up of Support to Yemen' (4 October 2016) www.reliefweb.int/sites/reliefweb.int/files/resources/Press%20release%20USG%20Yemen%204.10.16.pdf; written evidence to Committees on Arms Export Controls by Save the Children, ADS, Mwatana Organization for Human Rights (July 2016).

[122] See eg R Colville, 'Press Briefing Notes on Yemen, Central African Republic and Escalating Tensions in East Jerusalem and West Bank' 29 September 2015, www.ohchr.org/EN/NewsEvents/Pages/DisplayNews.aspx?NewsID=16518&LangID=Ep 13; and Action on Armed Violence, 'Unacceptable Harm: Monitoring Explosive Violence in 2015' (26 April 2016) aoav.org.uk/wp-content/uploads/2016/05/AOAV-Explosive-Monitor-2015.pdf.

widespread famine.[123] The High Court acknowledged 'a substantial body of evidence suggesting that the Coalition has committed serious breaches of International Law in the course of its engagement in the Yemen conflict'.[124] However, having considered all the evidence, including 'closed material', ie secret information not made available to the claimants or the public,[125] the Court nonetheless opined that, in the assessment of risk, 'past and present conduct is one indicator' but is not determinative 'as to future behaviour and attitude towards International Humanitarian Law'.[126] In a deeply disappointing judgment, notable for its degree of deference to the executive and for its failure to engage with the substance and detail of international law, the Court held that the UK's governmental decision-making process, informed by knowledge of and close contact with Saudi Arabia, was sufficiently robust, and that the decision to continue supplying weapons to Saudi Arabia was not 'irrational', and therefore not unlawful.[127] On that basis, the Court dismissed the claim for judicial review.[128] An application for permission to appeal has been made by CAAT to the Court of Appeal. Civil society is anxiously awaiting the decision.

Is the 'lowest common denominator' political compromise embodied in the ATT to blame for the seemingly ever-increasing supply of arms, including from ATT state parties, to states with poor IHRL and IHL records? Would a more strongly worded treaty have compelled a different decision in the High Court? That is far from clear: the more robust wording and obligations contained in EU regulations, which were considered by the Court in the CAAT case, have similarly failed to date to stem the flow of weapons from EU Member States: individual export refusals by EU Member States still constitute rare 'exceptions in an overall export friendly environment'.[129]

---

[123] See eg UNOCHA, 'Yemen: "One Step Away from Famine"' (31 October 2016) www.unocha.org/top-stories/all-stories/yemen-%E2%80%9Cone-step-away-famine% E2%80%9D; UNOCHA, 'The Humanitarian Situation in Yemen in Facts and Figures' (13 September 2017) https://www.unocha.org/sites/unocha/files/dms/FF_updated_13092017.pdf; and UN News Centre, 'Famine May Be Unfolding 'Right Now' in Yemen, Warns UN Relief Wing' (17 November 2017) www.un.org/apps/news/story.asp?NewsID=58116#.WhxX4MacbUo.

[124] CAAT case, para 86.

[125] 'Closed Material Procedures', first introduced, pursuant to the Special Immigration Appeals Commission Act 1997, for certain immigration appeal hearings, were made more broadly available in civil proceedings pursuant to the Justice and Security Act 2013. They are controversial secret court procedures, which allow the government to rely on so-called 'sensitive' material in legal proceedings, without having to disclose it to the other side, on the grounds of asserted national security.

[126] CAAT case, para 181(iii).

[127] ibid, paras 198 and 210.

[128] ibid, paras 213–14.

[129] ST Hansen and N Marsh, 'Normative Power and Organized Hypocrisy: European Union Member States' Arms Export to Libya' (2015) 24 *European Security* 264, 279–80. Notably, other EU Member States, including France, Germany, Italy, the Netherlands and Spain, all ATT states parties, have also completed sales to Saudi Arabia since it began its military campaign in Yemen. See ATT Monitor (n 16) 5.

The simple and regrettable reality is that no treaty text, in and of itself, can compel states to cease waging or fuelling war. If that were so, the signing in 1928 of the General Treaty for Renunciation of War as an Instrument of National Policy, otherwise known as the Kellogg–Briand pact,[130] would have ended conflict almost a century ago. The signing of an international arms trade treaty was similarly never, realistically, going to bring the international arms trade to a juddering halt. Neither was its entry into force going to suddenly ensure respect by states for their IHL and IHRL obligations, or robust and intensive scrutiny of governmental export decisions by every domestic court.

What this chapter has shown is that the ATT framework, imperfect as it is, contains within it the necessary elements and mechanisms to ensure its efficacy as a tool to 'reduce human suffering' caused by conflict. Its far-reaching obligations binding on states parties are capable of ensuring a renewed international commitment to civilian protections arising under IHL and IHRL, as mainstreamed into each and every arms transfer decision they make. However, domestic enforcement mechanisms, including domestic courts, are critical to ensuring that states parties are held to that commitment. The ICJ may also in time have a role to play.

The ATT is still a very young treaty, and it would be premature to dismiss it out of hand as a failure. Importantly, it is 'only, and ultimately only, a framework'.[131] Its ultimate success will depend on the extent to which the obligations at the heart of the ATT, requiring states to assess every arms transfer through the lens of IHL and IHRL, serve to reaffirm and reinforce rather than undermine and eviscerate respect for those bodies of law and the inviolability of the protections they afford civilians in conflict. Said otherwise, it is only if states ensure—or are compelled by civil society and by the courts to ensure—that the ATT's threefold purposes of 'reduc[ing] human suffering', contributing to 'international and regional peace, security and stability', and promoting 'cooperation, transparency and responsible action' by states in the international trade in conventional weapons, prevail over profit in their application of the ATT, that the treaty will be effective. For the countless civilians around the world who find themselves under the ever-increasing hail of ATT state party-supplied weapons, the stakes could not be higher.

---

[130] General Treaty for Renunciation of War as an Instrument of National Policy (Kellogg–Briand Pact) (adopted 27 August 1928, entered into force 24 July 1929) 2137 UNTC 94.

[131] Australia's Foreign Minister Julie Bishop quoted in J Garrett, 'International Humanitarian System is Increasingly Stretched: Julie Bishop' *ABC News*, 14 November 2013, www.gunpolicy.org/firearms/citation/news/311.

Part III

Developments

14

A Path Towards Greater Respect for International Humanitarian Law[*]

VALENTIN ZELLWEGER AND FRANÇOIS VOEFFRAY[1]

> Caminante, son tus huellas
> el camino, y nada más;
> caminante, no hay camino,
> se hace camino al andar.
> *Antonio Machado*
> *Proverbios y cantares XXIX, Campos de Castilla* (1912)

I. INTRODUCTION

CONTEMPORARY ARMED CONFLICTS—such as in Syria, Iraq, Afghanistan, Libya, South Sudan or central Africa—illustrate how complex armed conflicts have become today and the resulting challenges for the implementation of international humanitarian law (IHL). The existence of internal armed conflict is obviously not a new phenomenon, but most of the ongoing armed conflicts nowadays are particularly complex. They involve several non-state armed groups and, at the same time, some degree of internationalisation, due to the involvement of one or more third countries. The war in Syria is emblematic of this new complexity, with several hundred

[*] This chapter was written in the summer 2016. An appendix at the end of this chapter reflects the latest developments since then.

[1] Valentin Zellweger is the former Legal Adviser of the Swiss Federal Department of Foreign Affairs and the current Permanent Representative of Switzerland to the United Nations and other international organisations in Geneva. François Voeffray is a former Ambassador-at-Large for International Humanitarian Law at the Swiss Federal Department of Foreign Affairs and is since 2016 the Deputy Ambassador of Switzerland in the United Kingdom. The authors would like to express their sincere gratitude and heartfelt thanks to Rochus Peyer, Legal Officer, Directorate of International Law, Swiss Federal Department of Foreign Affairs, for his valuable input and revision of this text.

armed groups and factions, unclear command structures and changing ties of allegiance. The fighting often takes place in densely populated areas, with disastrous consequences for civilians. This proliferation of actors, combined with a lack of clarity about who is in charge, is one of the most daunting challenges in the implementation of IHL. The list of current challenges also includes the denial of humanitarian access and assistance to people in need, the use of new means and methods of warfare, the mix between terrorism, counterterrorism and classical warfare, as well as what has been broadly termed 'hybrid warfare', a medley of semi-clandestine operations, information warfare and computer hacking. The latter two developments pose a whole new set of problems, not least because they fundamentally blur the boundaries between war and peace.[2]

In spite of all the new and recurring challenges, the rules of IHL—which are enshrined by treaty and customary international law—remain fully relevant. Although the nature of warfare is constantly evolving, it is largely acknowledged by states that IHL remains, by and large, an adequate legal framework for regulating the conduct of parties to an armed conflict and for providing protection to the victims of armed conflicts—ie all those who do not (or no longer) take part in the hostilities. The fact that a few normative gaps need to be addressed does not detract from the overall accuracy of this statement.[3] In order to reduce human suffering during armed conflict, one does not primarily need new rules, or different rules, but greater respect for those that already exist. In other words, the main problem nowadays is not of a normative nature. The most pressing challenge is the widespread flouting of the existing laws of war.

The latest reports of the United Nations Secretary-General on the protection of civilians seem to indicate that the situation is worsening in a number of areas.[4] Indiscriminate attacks on civilians are widespread in many contemporary conflicts. Schools and medical personnel and facilities are regularly and increasingly targeted. Access restrictions for humanitarian workers impede the delivery of assistance.[5] A growing number of parties to armed conflicts seem to openly disregard long-established rules of IHL in the conduct of hostilities or with regard to the protection of persons no longer taking part in hostilities. The wars of old were certainly no less cruel

---

[2] See ICRC, *International Humanitarian Law and the Challenges of Contemporary Armed Conflicts* (Geneva, ICRC, 2015).

[3] See ICRC, 'Protection of Victims in Armed Conflict' (Report) (2011).

[4] See Report of the Secretary-General, 'Annual Report on the Protection of Civilians in Armed Conflict'(2016) UN Doc S/2016/447.

[5] It is disconcerting to see that even the delivery of impartial healthcare in armed conflict, which is at the heart of the first 1864 Geneva Convention, is affected by this lack of respect. See ICRC, 'Healthcare in Danger: Making the Case' (2011) www.icrc.org/eng/publication/4072-health-care-danger-making-case.

than today's conflicts. For centuries, the laws and customs of war remained in an embryonic stage. And they were breached repeatedly. But nowadays war can no longer be considered as a period of lawlessness, where no rules apply. States have defined a detailed set of rules under international law to prohibit or at least limit the excesses of armed violence. What has also changed is global awareness, helped by today's world of instant information. Nowadays, modern technology enables us to find out what is going on across the world far more quickly and comprehensively than ever before. We cannot turn a blind eye to these violations, nor can we ignore our shared responsibility to respond to the violations being committed.

According to a recent survey by the International Institute for Strategic Studies, the number of armed conflicts has decreased over the past years, but the number of casualties has significantly increased.[6] These worrying tendencies stress the need to strengthen efforts to disseminate IHL and to persuade parties to armed conflicts to comply with the rules by which they are bound. Conflicting parties must be reminded time and again that even wars have rules, and that these rules apply to everyone.

Beyond the direct human consequences, lack of compliance with IHL may also affect its solidity and credibility. A few drops of water do not leave marks on a rock, but a constant flow will end up eroding it. Similarly, isolated violations do not have a serious impact on IHL, but repeated and serious breaches may eventually erode it and/or affect its credibility among conflicting parties.

Since IHL applies during the adverse circumstances of war, it is a matter of course that it is at greater risk of being violated than other bodies of international law. However, military necessity cannot be used by the conflicting parties as an argument or excuse for not complying with their obligations under IHL treaty and customary law. Designed for the specific circumstances of war, IHL adequately takes into account military necessity and establishes for each situation specific and judicious balances between this and humanitarian principles.

This chapter focuses on the need to generate greater respect for IHL. It discusses the deficiencies in the existing mechanisms provided for in the IHL treaties and the lack of a forum specifically dedicated to IHL. It also describes the ongoing diplomatic process facilitated by the ICRC and Switzerland and explains how bridging the current institutional gap could constitute a path towards greater respect for this crucial body of law.

---

[6] According to this 2015 IISS survey, 63 armed conflicts in 2008 led to 56,000 fatalities, whereas 180,000 people—more than three times as many—died in 2015 in a total of 42 conflicts. The numbers reflect the use of extreme violence in Syria and Iraq as well as the increase of casualties in Afghanistan.

II. DEFICIENCIES IN THE EXISTING IHL IMPLEMENTATION
MECHANISMS

A. Brief Overview of the Implementation Mechanisms Established under the IHL Treaties

The drafters of the Geneva Conventions of 1949 and their Additional Protocols of 1977 were fully aware of the difficulties in ensuring adherence to this body of law. Common Article 1 of the Geneva Conventions reflects the recognition that the implementation of IHL requires particular attention. In this provision, the states parties have undertaken to 'respect and ensure respect' for the Conventions in all circumstances. Common Article 1 goes beyond restating the general principle of international law of *pacta sunt servanda*. It stresses the special nature of the Geneva Conventions, which protect collective interests, and thereby underlines that states need to take specific measures to ensure that the Conventions are respected in all circumstances—not only by the organs under their authority, but also by other states parties to the Conventions and non-state entities.[7]

The drafters of the Geneva Conventions further translated this general provision into specific mechanisms that are aimed at facilitating proper implementation of the Conventions and their Additional Protocols. The first set of mechanisms pertains to measures that need to be taken in peacetime—ie before or after an armed conflict—notably with a view to implementing and disseminating the rules, and to prosecuting possible violations or making them stop.[8] For the Geneva Conventions and their Additional Protocols to serve their purpose, states must take a number of preparatory measures even before a war breaks out. As Jean Pictet put it in his commentary: '[O]ne of the worst enemies of the Geneva Conventions is ignorance.'[9] Domestic legislation and procedures must already be in place in order to enforce observance in situations of armed conflict before a war occurs.

---

[7] See ICRC, 'Commentary of the First Geneva Convention' (2016) https://ihl-databases.icrc.org/applic/ihl/ihl.nsf/Comment.xsp?action=openDocument&documentId=72239588AFA662 00C1257F7D00367DBD; N Levrat, 'Les consequences de l'engagement pris par les Hautes Parties Contractantes de "faire respecter" les Conventions humanitaires' in F Kalshoven and Y Sandoz (eds), *Mise en oeuvre du droit international humanitaire* (Dordrecht, Martinus Nijhoff, 1989); L Boisson de Chazournes and L Condorelli, 'Common Article 1 of the Geneva Conventions Revisited: Protecting Collective Interests' (2000) 837 *Review of the International Red Cross* 67; R Geiss, 'The Obligation to Respect and to Ensure Respect for the Convention' in A Clapham, P Gaeta and M Sassòli (eds), *The 1949 Geneva Conventions: A Commentary* (Geneva/Oxford, Oxford University Press, 2015). Regarding the responsibility of third states not involved in a given armed conflict, see in particular K Dörmann and J Serralvo, 'Common Article 1 to the Geneva Convention and the Obligation to Prevent International Humanitarian Law Violations' (2015) 895/896 *International Review of the Red Cross* 1.

[8] On domestic implementation, see generally A Ziegler and S Wehrenberg, 'Domestic Implementation' in Clapham, Gaeta and Sassòli (n 7).

[9] J Pictet, *Commentary on the First Geneva Convention* (Geneva, ICRC, 1952) 348.

Specific measures must be taken to ensure that the rules are well known and understood, not only within armed forces, but also by the relevant authorities and the general public. Before a war breaks out, states must also take the necessary measures to ensure that potential violations will be prosecuted and stopped. With the exception of the subject of criminal repression, these mechanisms have received relatively little attention in academic writing, which may have contributed to the widespread perception that IHL is entirely devoid of compliance mechanisms.

These preparatory and preventive measures are complemented by procedures that apply in wartime. Contrary to the obligations discussed above, their application is not simply a matter of domestic implementation. It is with these mechanisms that this chapter is mainly concerned. Their working modalities will be briefly reviewed so as to understand why they hardly play a significant role today in improving respect for IHL.

The first mechanism provided for in the Geneva Conventions and Additional Protocol I is the institution of protecting power on the basis of which a third state (the protecting power) may be entrusted by one of the concerned states (the power of origin) to safeguard its interests or those of its nationals vis-à-vis the other state which is involved in the armed conflict (the receiving state).[10] The institution of protecting power has a long tradition in the area of diplomatic relations where it has existed since the sixteenth century. It was transposed to armed conflicts as early as the Franco-Prussian War of 1870–71. This institution was actively and regularly used until World War II, but since its codification in the 1949 Geneva Conventions, states have had recourse to it in only five armed conflicts, the last occasion being the Falkland/Malvinas war of 1982 in which Switzerland safeguarded the interests of the United Kingdom and Brazil those of Argentina. As a result of the decline of this institution, the ICRC nowadays often plays the role of a de facto substitute for a protecting power. The reasons for such decline are manifold and to a large extent similar to those that affect the use of the other mechanisms provided for in the Geneva Conventions and their Additional Protocols. The first and main reason is probably the fact that the institution of protecting powers was originally designed for and applied in international armed conflicts, whereas most of today's armed conflicts are of an internal nature. In the context of non-international conflict, it

---

[10] See Arts 8/8/8/9 and 10/10/10/11 common to the 1949 Geneva Conventions; see also Art 5 AP I. On the institution of protecting powers in IHL, see ICRC, 'Commentary of the First Geneva Convention' (n 7) as well as G Abi-Saab, 'The Implementation of Humanitarian Law' in A Cassese (ed), *The New Humanitarian Law of Armed Conflict* vol I (Napoli, Editoriale scientifica, 1979); R Kolb, 'Protecting Powers' in Clapham, Gaeta and Sassòli (n 7); M Sassòli, 'Mise en oeuvre du droit international humanitaire et du droit international des droits de l'hommes: une comparaison' (1987) *Annuaire suisse de droit international* 59; R Wolfrum and D Fleck, 'Enforcement of International Humanitarian Law' in D Fleck (ed), *The Handbook of International Humanitarian Law*, 2nd edn (Oxford, Oxford University Press, 2008).

is obviously much more difficult to obtain the agreement of the conflicting parties, especially of the government side. These reasons will be further examined below. An additional and specific reason for the decline of this institution is the fact that the tasks of the Protecting Power may be demanding and politically sensitive. A state may hesitate to accept such a burdensome and costly mandate, especially with regard to protracted conflicts.

In the first decades of the development of modern IHL, much hope was also placed in the conciliation and enquiry procedures, with specific provisions for this being integrated in the four 1949 Geneva Conventions.[11] The purpose of such procedures is to elucidate the questions under dispute, to ascertain contested facts and to make settlement proposals to the conflicting parties. But here again, the modalities as well as the scope of these procedures must be agreed upon by the interested parties. As a result of these factors—having to grant explicit consent and the reluctance of states to accept independent investigative institutions—the conciliation and enquiry procedures established under the Geneva Conventions have almost never been used. Not a single enquiry has been carried out on the basis of the relevant provisions of the Conventions. This has led to a situation in which the UN system is frequently used to impose such investigative bodies. There has been over the last decades a proliferation of fact-finding missions *and* commissions of inquiry created outside the scope of the IHL treaties. The UN Security Council, the Human Rights Council and other international bodies have established a number of ad hoc fact-finding missions and commissions of inquiry to investigate alleged violations of international human rights and humanitarian law in conflict and post-conflict contexts.[12] Two observations can be made in this regard. First, it should be noted that the enquiry procedure was already provided for in Article 29 of the Geneva Convention

---

[11] See Arts 11/11/11/12 (conciliation procedure) and 52/53/132/149 (enquiry procedure) common to the 1949 Geneva Conventions. On the conciliation and enquiry procedures, see generally the 2016 updated ICRC Commentary on the First Geneva Convention. See also M Bothe, 'Fact-Finding as a Means of Ensuring Respect for International Humanitarian Law' in W Heintschel von Heinegg and V Epping (eds), *International Humanitarian Law Facing New Challenges* (Berlin, Springer, 2007); T Boutruche, 'Good Offices, Conciliation and Enquiry' in Clapham, Gaeta and Sassòli (n 7); L Condorelli, 'The International Humanitarian Fact-Finding Commission: An Obsolete Tool or a Useful Measure to Implement International Humanitarian Law' (2001) 83 *International Review of the Red Cross* 842; M Sassòli, A Bouvier and A Quintin (eds), *How Does Law Protect in War?*, 3rd edn (Geneva, ICRC, 2011) vol I, 386; vol II, 1713; S Vité, *Les procédures d'établissement des faits dans la mise en oeuvre du droit international humanitaire* (Brussels, Bruylant, 1999).

[12] eg, the UNSC created international commissions of inquiry on Darfur in 2004 and on the Central African Republic in 2013. For its part, the UN Human Rights Council has mandated a number of fact-finding missions, commissions of inquiry, special rapporteurs and independent experts. Currently, these mandates cover the situations in Syria, the Central African Republic, Mali, Somali, the Sudan, the Occupied Palestinian Territories and Libya. Fact-finding missions were also created by regional international institutions. For instance, the EU mandated fact-finding missions on the conflict in Georgia in 2008 and 2011, and the African Commission on Human and People's Rights sent a fact-finding mission to Darfur in 2004.

of 1929 for the Amelioration of the Condition of the Wounded and Sick in Armies in the Field. In other words, fact-finding was identified early on as a useful instrument for the implementation of IHL and codified in the IHL treaties at an early stage, but it has almost never been used under these treaties. By contrast, the appearance of fact-finding in the field of human rights is much more recent, where it is now frequently used by international human rights bodies such as the UN Human Rights Council. Second, while the purposes of such ad hoc commissions of inquiry are numerous and depend on the specificities of the mandate assigned to them, the focus has in many cases shifted from establishing whether violations have occurred to holding perpetrators accountable for these violations and initiating criminal prosecutions. As a consequence, states may have lost sight of the initial purpose of the conciliation and enquiry procedures established under the IHL treaties, namely their confidence-building component. This may have reinforced the reluctance of states involved in armed conflicts to use them.

In light of the shortcomings of the enquiry procedure under the 1949 Geneva Conventions, another attempt to facilitate the triggering and use of fact-finding was made at the Diplomatic Conference of 1974–77 that led to the adoption of Additional Protocol I to the Geneva Conventions of 1949. Article 90 of Additional Protocol I provides for the institution of the International Humanitarian Fact-Finding Commission, which is composed of fifteen independent members and is competent to (i) enquire into any facts alleged to be a grave breach or other serious violation of the 1949 Geneva Conventions and Additional Protocol I; and (ii) to facilitate, through its good offices, the 'restoration of an attitude of respect' for the Geneva Conventions and Additional Protocol I. The triggering of this mechanism is facilitated by the fact that states parties to Additional Protocol I can unilaterally declare in advance that they accept the competence of the Commission based on Article 90 with regard to any future armed conflict involving another state that has made a similar declaration. If both states involved in an armed conflict have recognised its competence in advance, the Commission may be triggered at the simple request of one of the parties to the conflict concerned. In all other cases, an enquiry may be instituted only if all concerned parties to the armed conflict give their consent. Although seventy-six states have accepted the competence of the Commission to date,[13] its services have not yet been called upon. One of the reasons is that most contemporary conflicts are of a non-international nature. The Commission may offer its services to the parties to a NIAC, and it has done so repeatedly, but its intervention cannot be triggered unilaterally on the basis of the recognition declarations mentioned above, since they are only made among states parties to Additional Protocol I.

---

[13] The list of states accepting the competence of the International Humanitarian Fact-Finding Commission based on Art 90 AP I is available at www.ihffc.org.

B. Why Have These Mechanisms Rarely if Ever Been Used in the Past Decades?

The reasons most frequently put forward to explain why the mechanisms under the IHL treaties are not used are the lack of political will and the reluctance of states involved in an armed conflict to implicate a third party. However, one must ask whether these mechanisms were not flawed from the very beginning. It is a matter of fact that the way in which they were configured and the lack of an appropriate institutional anchorage have severely impacted their use.

As discussed earlier, the three main compliance mechanisms established under the IHL treaties require the consent of all parties involved. They are based on the premise that states involved in an armed conflict have the will and capacity to propose instituting the mechanism in question to the other party or, in the case of the enquiry procedure, to both agreeing on its modalities. This approach is based on an expectation that is not likely to be fulfilled in the current geopolitical context, especially with regard to non-international and mixed international armed conflicts. It is a fact that no branch of international law dealing with the protection of persons that has been developed subsequently to the Geneva Conventions relies exclusively on mechanisms that are configured in this way.

Furthermore, the mechanisms established under IHL lack an attachment or anchorage in a broader institutional compliance structure. The Geneva Conventions and Additional Protocols do not provide for states to meet on a regular basis to discuss issues of common concern in the implementation or interpretation of their provisions and/or to perform other functions aimed at increasing respect for IHL. The absence of such an anchorage means that the three compliance mechanisms lack the institutional support that is necessary to make them known and be utilised, to facilitate the performance of their tasks, and to assist in any follow-up that may be appropriate. Triggering the mechanisms relies solely on the political will of the parties concerned, and it is also for these states to shoulder the financial costs. This has proven to be a very difficult obstacle to overcome.

In addition to these inadequacies, it should also be underlined that these mechanisms were originally designed and developed for international armed conflicts. Their design and scope of applicability are limited in a way that does not reflect the reality of contemporary armed conflicts. As is well known, the large majority of armed conflicts today are of a non-international nature. It is also in these conflicts that the necessity to increase respect for IHL is currently felt the strongest, and where humanitarian needs are the most evident.

The above diagnosis bears on the question of whether and how these mechanisms could be revitalised. This is a tricky topic. From a technical legal perspective, adapting the procedures established by the relevant provisions so that they correspond better to today's needs would require amending the

Geneva Conventions of 1949 and Additional Protocol I. The way in which the mechanisms were designed poses some limits to their reinvigoration. Although legally it is not unthinkable to transpose these mechanisms to situations of NIACs, it is obvious that the conciliation and enquiry procedures and the institution of the protecting power were set out in the IHL treaties with IACs in mind. States are generally reluctant to recognise non-state parties to an armed conflict as equal partners, which is a precondition for triggering these two mechanisms as they were originally designed and provided for in the 1949 Geneva Conventions.

Regarding the situation of the International Humanitarian Fact-Finding Commission, the assessment is slightly more optimistic. The Commission has the distinct advantage that it is a standing body composed of independent experts. It operates on the basis of a confidentiality procedure where there is no naming and shaming, which should be seen favourably by the conflicting parties. Furthermore, its way of operation is predetermined and does not therefore require the involved parties to find an agreement on that matter. It is a mechanism that is aimed at building confidence and restoring an attitude of respect for the law rather than one that antagonises the belligerent parties or is aimed at instigating criminal investigations. That explains why the procedure and findings of the Commission remain confidential.[14] While its competence is compulsory when both states involved have recognised the Commission in accordance with Article 90 of Additional Protocol I, the services of the Commission may also be sought on an ad hoc basis. In other words, nothing in Article 90 of Additional Protocol I would prevent a state from requesting the services of the Commission in a NIAC.

III. BRIDGING THE INSTITUTIONAL GAP

A. The Need for a Dedicated Forum for IHL

As mentioned above, the Geneva Conventions of 1949 and their Additional Protocols of 1977 and 2005 lack a conference of states parties or a similar institutional forum in which the parties to these instruments can regularly and systematically discuss and address the challenges they face in the implementation of IHL. The most important multilateral treaties are equipped with a much more elaborate system which generally includes a conference of states parties or another kind of institutional forum where states parties regularly meet to discuss the implementation of the treaty provisions. This is also in stark contrast to other instruments of international law aimed at the protection of persons. The Geneva Conventions are in this regard a striking exception among modern multilateral treaties.

---

[14] While the Commission works as a rule on the basis of confidentiality, states involved are free to opt out of this by agreement and to accept the publication of the Commission's findings.

Contrary to the Geneva Conventions of 1949, Additional Protocol I provides in Article 7 for the depositary to convene a Meeting of the High Contracting Parties to this instrument.[15] According to this provision:

> [The] depositary of this Protocol shall convene a meeting of the High Contracting Parties, at the request of one or more of the said Parties and upon the approval of the majority of the said Parties, to consider general problems concerning the application of the Conventions and of the Protocol.

The 26th International Conference of the Red Cross and Red Crescent provided a complementary basis for 'the Depositary to organise periodical meetings of the States Parties to the 1949 Geneva Conventions to consider general problems regarding the application of international humanitarian law.' This basis is broader than Article 7 of Additional Protocol I in three regards: first, it mentions the application of IHL in general, and not only of Additional Protocol I and the Geneva Conventions; second, it opens up these meetings to all states parties to the Geneva Conventions of 1949; and third, it does not require a formal request by one or more parties to the treaties, giving the depositary the authority to act *proprio motu*. However, it does not do away with other limitations and does not amend the process for convening such a meeting, which is burdensome. Not only must a majority of the states parties consent to the convening of the meeting, but a majority of them must also approve the topics to be addressed. As a consequence, since Additional Protocol I came into force, Switzerland has never received a request fulfilling the requirements of this provision. Acting as depositary of the four Geneva Conventions and their Additional Protocols, as well as on the basis of Resolution 1 of the 26th International Conference, Switzerland convened *proprio motu* a First Periodical Meeting on general problems relating to the application of IHL. The meeting took place in Geneva in January 1998 and dealt with two topics agreed in advance: the security of humanitarian workers, and armed conflicts linked to the disintegration of state structures. The outcome was a non-binding report reflecting the chairman's personal view.[16] This experience showed, however, that the procedure to convene such a meeting was complex and that the burden rested entirely on the depositary. As a matter of fact, it does not ensure the desirable involvement and ownership by the state parties to the Geneva Convention regarding the convening of the meeting, the selection of the topics, the participation in the discussions and the possible outcome. Due to these limitations, the depositary has not convened another

---

[15] On this provision, see generally G Abi-Saab, 'The Implementation of Humanitarian Law' in Cassese (n 10); Y Dinstein, 'Article 7 of Additional Protocol I' (2005) 24 *Australian Yearbook of International Law* 65; ICRC Expert Seminars, *Improving Compliance with International Humanitarian Law* (Geneva, ICRC, 2003); PY Fux and M Zambelli, 'Mise en oeuvre de la Quatrième Convention de Genève dans les territoires palestiniens occupés: historique d'un processus multilatéral (1997–2001)' (2002) *Revue internationale de la Croix-Rouge* 661.

[16] See (1998) 323 *International Review of the Red Cross* 366.

additional meeting. In other words, given its limitations, Article 7 of Additional Protocol I—combined or not with the 1995 resolution—does not provide an adequate basis for discussing, in a regular and systematic manner, current IHL implementation challenges. Therefore, it cannot serve to fill the current institutional gap and ensure that IHL receives the attention it deserves on the multilateral agenda.

The comparison with the human rights system is particularly salient. Both at the international and regional levels, a myriad of complementary mechanisms have been put in place to facilitate the implementation of human rights (although in the framework of the human rights system, too, one cannot fail to observe the discrepancy between states' obligations and the reality on the ground). At the universal level, the UN Human Rights Council has proven to be a particular active and lively forum. It addresses an ever-increasing number of thematic issues and geographic situations. Furthermore, the universal human rights treaties adopted under the auspices of the UN have established proper compliance mechanisms, notably in the form of committees of independent experts. There are in addition extensive regional regimes to protect human rights, including regional organisations and supranational human rights courts.

The IHL institutional vacuum described above has led to a situation where other international institutions—namely the UN Human Rights Council and the UN Security Council—are increasingly focusing on IHL issues. In itself, this is a positive development. But these institutions have their own mandates and logically focus on them. They address IHL issues from the perspective of their specific mandates—promoting human rights, and maintaining peace and security, respectively—and do not always adequately address the specificities of IHL or sufficiently involve the relevant stakeholders, namely experts working at national ministries of defence and justice.

B. The Diplomatic Process Facilitated by the ICRC and Switzerland

Based on these considerations—the current insignificant role played by the existing mechanisms in facilitating respect for IHL and, in particular, the institutional vacuum in implementing the law—the ICRC and Switzerland proposed a diplomatic process aimed at identifying options to improve respect for IHL in the wake of the international conference organised in 2009 to commemorate the sixtieth anniversary of the 1949 Geneva Conventions.[17]

---

[17] ICRC, '60 ans des Conventions de Genève et les décennies à venir' (Geneva, 9–10 November 2009) www.eda.admin.ch/dam/eda/fr/documents/publications/Voelkerrecht/Konferenzpapier-60-Jahre-Genfer-Konventionen_fr.pdf.

The starting point was a study[18] carried out by the ICRC in view of the 31st International Conference of the Red Cross and Red Crescent, which took place in late 2011. The ICRC examined the humanitarian problems arising from contemporary armed conflicts and whether IHL, as it existed at the time, provided an adequate response to these problems. It noted that:

> international humanitarian law continues to provide an appropriate framework for regulating the conduct of parties engaged in armed conflicts. ... In most cases, what is required to improve the situation of victims of armed conflicts is stricter compliance with the existing legal framework, rather than the adoption of new rules.[19]

Of the four areas of IHL that were examined in the report, states agreed in Resolution 1 of the 31st International Conference of the Red Cross and Red Crescent to 'pursue further research, consultation and discussion'[20] on two of them, namely the protection of persons deprived of their liberty in relation to armed conflict; and the issue of strengthening respect for IHL. In relation to the second issue, the 31st International Conference mandated the ICRC and Switzerland to facilitate the relevant work among states.

Following the 31st International Conference, the ICRC and Switzerland jointly led a large consultation process open to all states parties to the Geneva Conventions of 1949. States' views on a variety of topics were sought in the course of the consultations. Initially, the states examined the inadequacies of the existing mechanisms and options for their revitalisation. In that regard, the view was largely shared that, while the mechanisms remain at the disposal of states who wish to resort to them in accordance with the relevant provisions of the 1949 Geneva Conventions and Additional Protocol I, these mechanisms cannot substitute what was felt to be lacking the most in the current system: an institutional space for dialogue and cooperation among states to address the common challenges more systematically and to collectively develop ways to overcome them. In further consultations, the various opinions gradually converged on the possible contours of a new compliance system for IHL centred on a regular Meeting of States.[21] The process led to the submission of a concluding report[22] to the 32nd International Conference of the Red Cross and Red Crescent as well as a draft resolution.

---

[18] ICRC, Draft Resolution and Report on 'Strengthening Legal Protection for Victims of Armed Conflicts' (2011).

[19] ICRC (Resolution 1 of the 31st International Conference), 'Strengthening Legal Protection for Victims of Armed Conflicts' (2011) para 4.

[20] ibid, para 6.

[21] For an overview of the discussions, consult the documents available at www.eda.admin. ch/eda/en/home/aussenpolitik/voelkerrecht/humanitaeres_voelkerrecht/ikrk-initiative.html.

[22] ICRC, 'Concluding Report: Strengthening Compliance with International Humanitarian Law' (2015) available at www.rcrcconference.org/wp-content/uploads/sites/3/2015/04/32IC-Concluding-report-on-Strengthening-Compliance-with-IHL_EN.pdf.

In a nutshell, the proposal made by the ICRC and Switzerland, which was based on a very extensive consultation process, recommended the establishment of a regular Meeting of States. The draft resolution also laid out—without making a final decision on these aspects—the basic modalities and features of the future Meeting of States, including the general purpose of the Meeting of States, its functions, the participation of observers and the institutional structure. As regards the functions of this new forum, the draft resolution suggested holding thematic discussions on IHL issues[23] and setting up a national reporting procedure on the implementation of IHL.[24] These functions were designed so as to operate in a non-politicised and non-contextual manner, ie without reference to any specific situations. Under the reporting function, states would periodically submit a report on implementing IHL at the national level. Given the non-contextual nature of the forum, reports would not be scrutinised individually but become part of a single follow-up document to be discussed among all states in the forum. The reports would also help to identify possible thematic issues that might be addressed in more depth in thematic discussions held by the Meeting of States. Other possible functions, including, for example, fact-finding, were also examined by the states in the consultation process but did not generate sufficient support to be included in the draft resolution.

The draft resolution recommended the establishment of such a Meeting of States within one year and proposed that Switzerland be invited to convene the forum after a further preparatory process within an open-ended working group of states. It also underlined that participating in the future Meeting of States would be voluntary and of a non-legally binding nature, so as to take into account the clear reluctance of states to enter into a treaty-making exercise and with the aim of facilitating and encouraging broad participation in the new mechanism. Trying to create a legally binding mechanism would have significantly reduced the number of states willing to participate and therefore the usefulness and efficiency of such a forum. Furthermore, a codification process would have necessitated years of negotiations without any prospect of gathering the significant number of ratifications needed to implement a meaningful compliance mechanism.

While there were a significant number of countries that supported this draft resolution, a group of states introduced a parallel resolution just three days before the opening of the International Conference.[25] This text made no mention of the proposed Meeting of States and suggested instead that the International Conference should only endorse the enhancement of existing

---

[23] ibid, 21–23.
[24] ibid, 17–21.
[25] This group of states, led by Russia, included India, Syria, Cuba, Venezuela, Nicaragua, North Korea, Tajikistan and Belarus.

IHL mechanisms such as the voluntary, bilateral and confidential dialogue between states and the ICRC, and recommended exploring alternative ways, namely by making better use of regional forums on IHL as well as the Red Cross and Red Crescent Conference to be held in 2019. A third group of countries, mainly from the Arab Group and the Organisation of Islamic Cooperation, generally supported the idea of a Meeting of States as such, but alleged that the process was moving too fast and were reluctant to commit to some elements that had been set out in the official draft resolution, in particular the reporting function. They also insisted that the resolution be adopted by consensus.

After three days and nights of negotiations, the 32nd International Conference adopted a resolution that departs in several points from what had been proposed in the official draft resolution. But it does mark a turning point, since all states agreed by consensus to engage in an intergovernmental process which will serve to

> find agreement on features and functions of a potential forum of States and to find ways to enhance the implementation of IHL using the potential of the International Conference [of the Red Cross and Red Crescent] and IHL regional forums.[26]

This new process will be state-driven and of an 'intergovernmental nature', which means a shift from the consultations of the last four years to conducting negotiations among states. Although it was the common understanding upon the formal adoption of the resolution that Switzerland and the ICRC will continue to jointly facilitate this new process, this shift to a negotiation process will presumably entail more state ownership of the work to come. Furthermore, while the official draft focused on the Forum of States and recommended its establishment within one year, the resolution adopted by consensus also includes the search for ways to enhance the IHL implementation 'potential' of the International Conference and of regional fora and recommends submitting the outcome of this process to the next International Conference to be held in four years. It should be noted that this exploration will take place alongside discussions on a future forum of states, reflecting the fact that the different approaches are not opposed, but in fact complementary.

The resolution adopted by consensus is obviously much shorter and less detailed than the original draft. From the perspectives of the ICRC and Switzerland, as co-facilitators of this process, it is, nevertheless, probably the best that could have been obtained under the given circumstances, in an unfavourable international climate which clearly played a part in how events unfolded. The fact that all states expressed their readiness to initiate an intergovernmental process for strengthening respect for IHL is a significant step.

---

[26] ICRC (Resolution 2 of the 32nd International Conference), 'Strengthening Compliance with International Humanitarian Law' (2015).

States are now committed to negotiating the functions to be exercised by such a forum dealing with IHL as well as its operating features. They have also decided to explore, in a complementary manner, how to make better use of the Red Cross and Red Crescent Conference and the regional forums. This new process will not start from scratch but will benefit from the work that has been accomplished during the last four years of the consultation process.

IV. CONCLUSION

The need to enhance respect for IHL is clear and undisputed. The idea of establishing a forum of states on IHL that has emerged within the process facilitated by Switzerland and the ICRC would fill a long-standing gap in the IHL system of implementation. International humanitarian law would benefit in various ways from such institutional development. The forum would provide an opportunity for those involved at the national level in the implementation of IHL—notably from the ministries of defence and justice, alongside diplomatic experts—to regularly discuss and assess the state of implementation of IHL. It would serve as a venue to exchange experiences and lessons learned and thus identify best practices with a view to enhancing the respective capacities of states to live up to their obligations under IHL. Such a forum would also increase the visibility of IHL on the international agenda. Its focus would not, however, be on cases widely covered by the media—in which the rules were not respected—but rather highlight the challenges that parties to armed conflicts face in implementing IHL and bring to light the measures that may be taken to overcome these difficulties. In so doing, it would build trust and confidence among states to engage with each other on this topic, which remains highly politically sensitive for many. This would also help them to identify weaknesses in their national toolkits and generate greater cooperation among states so as to limit possible gaps in their respective capacities to uphold IHL norms.

This process shows a concrete and constructive path towards improving respect for IHL. At the same time, such a forum is not a panacea and should be seen as complementary to other ongoing efforts and initiatives, since it will obviously not be sufficient to meet all the needs and requirements in the implementation of IHL.

Navigating through the process decided upon by the 32nd International Conference may prove to be difficult. It will require patience from those States that wanted to proceed more rapidly, and constructive engagement by those that were reluctant to do so. Only time will tell if the decision taken at the Conference regarding this forum will mark the beginning of 'a chronicle of a death foretold' or one step back in order to leap forward—and ensure greater respect for international humanitarian law, in the common interest to uphold a minimum of humanity in times of armed conflict.

APPENDIX

As chapter 14 reflects the events until summer 2016, it might be useful to briefly describe developments that have taken place in the meantime in the framework of the initiative on IHL jointly conducted by Switzerland and the ICRC.

Following the resolution adopted by the 32nd International Conference of the Red Cross and Red Crescent in 2015, States initiated the Intergovernmental Process on Strengthening Respect for International Humanitarian Law in order to fulfil its mandate. The task given by the International Conference was twofold: on the one hand States were invited to envisage a potential forum of States and on the other hand to assess how they might use the potential of the International Conference of the Red Cross and Red Crescent and of the IHL regional forums to strengthen respect for IHL. Throughout 2016 and 2017, States met on a regular basis and engaged in fruitful discussions.

States agreed first on the modalities of the process and how to be organized in order to foster the adoption of an outcome to be presented to the 33rd International Conference of the Red Cross and Red Crescent in 2019. They subsequently discussed both parts of the above mentioned mandate. In doing so, States renewed their commitment to continue their efforts to find ways of enhancing implementation of IHL. The exchanges also allowed for the presentation and discussion of more than 20 proposals made by States in order to promote a focused dialogue among States on IHL.

The regular and constant active participation of States in this process demonstrates the importance of the initiative and States' awareness of the need to develop common solutions to ensure greater respect for IHL. The growing gravity of the situations that affect civilians in today's conflicts necessitates a joint effort by all States. Switzerland remains determined to promote a successful outcome of the process that will allow States to have new means at their disposal to fulfill their commitments and overcome this acute challenge.

Geneva, March 2018

Jean-Pierre Reymond
Ambassador-at-Large for International Humanitarian Law

15

The Responsibility to Protect and Non-State Armed Groups

JENNIFER M WELSH

T HE MAJORITY OF chapters in this volume address the question of how legal mechanisms, situated within the 'zone between' international human rights and humanitarian law, can better protect civilians against both old and new threats to their security. The discussion here, by contrast, considers the potential of an expressly *political* instrument: the principle of the 'responsibility to protect' (R2P) populations from genocide, war crimes, crimes against humanity, and ethnic cleansing. As I will show, R2P was designed by its advocates to serve as a means of enhancing compliance with existing bodies of law that aim to protect civilian populations, but also, more broadly, of fostering greater political will and institutional capacity to prevent and respond to atrocity crimes.[1] After setting out the rationale and function of R2P, I suggest how its initially state-centric focus might be expanded to address the challenge of non-state armed groups (NSAGs) as threats to civilians. I begin with an analysis of how we might conceive of both the legal and political responsibilities of these actors, before setting out potential strategies for combating or mitigating the protection challenges such actors create. The next section examines the difficult questions of whether and how states can call upon military assistance from the international community to assist them in addressing the threat posed by NSAGs. The chapter concludes with an analysis of the responsibilities that can be assigned to states for the actions of NSAGs over which they have a degree of control, particularly when those actions include grave violations of human rights or IHL.

---

[1] I use the term 'atrocity crimes' exclusively to refer to the four acts specified in para 138 of the 2005 World Summit Outcome. Genocide, war crimes and crimes against humanity are defined in international criminal law; ethnic cleansing, while not established as a distinct crime, includes acts that will regularly amount to one of the crimes, in particular genocide and crimes against humanity.

I. THE POLITICAL ROLE OF THE 'RESPONSIBILITY TO PROTECT'

At the 2005 World Summit marking the sixtieth anniversary of the United Nations, more than 170 heads of state and government unanimously accepted three interlinked responsibilities, which together constitute the principle of the R2P. The first, set out in paragraph 138 of the Summit Outcome Document, is the primary responsibility of states to protect their own populations from genocide, war crimes, crimes against humanity and ethnic cleansing, which includes a responsibility to prevent the occurrence of these acts (including their incitement). Secondly, in paragraph 139, states pledged to assist one another in fulfilling their protection responsibilities. And finally, as members of the international community, they declared their readiness to take collective action, in a timely and decisive manner, if any state were 'manifestly failing' to protect its population from atrocity crimes.[2] These three provisions are now commonly summarised in academic and diplomatic discourse as the three 'pillars' of R2P.[3]

The primary purposes of R2P were twofold: to address the failures of collective action to respond to atrocity crimes, as represented by the genocides in Rwanda and Srebrenica in the 1990s; and to build a stronger culture of prevention that could forestall the negative dynamics leading to such crimes. These specific goals were underpinned by a broader argument about the changing nature of sovereignty. According to the International Commission on Intervention and State Sovereignty, whose report gave rise to the terminology 'responsibility to protect', state sovereignty was no longer understood as undisputed control over territory, but rather had become a conditional right dependent upon a state's adherence to minimum standards of human rights protection. In other words, sovereignty implied responsibility.[4] Nevertheless, the role of the international community was conceived as supportive and remedial, and not as replacement for the primary responsibility of sovereign states to protect their own populations. Indeed, the development of the principle of R2P was based on the conviction that 'state sovereignty is enhanced through more effective protection of populations from atrocity crimes'.[5] Sovereignty and R2P were to be allies rather than adversaries.

---

[2] '2005 World Summit Outcome' (16 September 2005) UN Doc A/Res/60/1.

[3] UNGA, 'Report of the Secretary-General on Implementing the Responsibility to Protect' (23 July 2009) UN Doc A/63/677.

[4] International Commission on Intervention and State Sovereignty (ICISS), 'The Responsibility to Protect: Report of the International Commission on Intervention and State Sovereignty' (2001).

[5] UNGA, 'Report of the Secretary-General on a Vital and Enduring Commitment: Implementing the Responsibility to Protect' (13 July 2015) UN Doc A/69/981.

In pursuing the dual purpose set out above, the advocates of R2P (which included individual 'norm entrepreneurs', NGOs and particular Member States of the UN) were concerned more with changing cultures of indifference than they were with creating new legal obligations. As the then Secretary-General Kofi Annan stressed, the legal framework in international human rights, humanitarian and refugee law was already sufficient; the challenge was to close the gap between the law's promise and the actual suffering of civilians.[6] Annan's understanding of R2P as a political commitment resonated with a variety of states, which, for very different reasons, opposed the crystallisation of the principle into a new law of responsibilities to prevent and respond to atrocity crimes. This included several developing countries, who worried about permitting too much intervention and a gradual erosion of sovereignty under the rubric of R2P, as well as the United States, which has consistently been uneasy about creating new legal obligations that might reduce its sovereign right to decide upon the use of force. As a result, the most than can be said of R2P from a legal point of view is that it stands as an authoritative interpretation of existing legal regimes[7]—including the UN Charter provisions relating to the power of the Security Council to authorise coercive means when it deems the existence of a threat to international peace and security.

Given R2P's political nature, its functions fall into three main types. First, the principle has helped to forge a political consensus that the imminent threat or commission of atrocity crimes are matters of international concern, thereby creating a 'duty of conduct'[8] on the part of the international community. UN Member States have pledged to identify when atrocity crimes are being committed or are imminent and to deliberate on how different actors (national, regional and international) can and should respond—an achievement that was by no means a given when states began to discuss R2P at the beginning of the twenty-first century.

This more general consensus has also translated into agreement amongst UN Member States on *how* to prevent and respond to atrocity crimes. The progress is largely due to the particular formulation of R2P in the Summit

---

[6] B Jones, 'Implementing "In Larger Freedom"' in P Heinbecker and P Goff (eds), *Irrelevant or Indispensable? The United Nations in the 21st Century* (Waterloo, Wilfred Laurier University Press, 2005).

[7] This conclusion rests on the view that General Assembly resolutions (like the one that affirmed the content of the 2005 Summit Outcome Document) are themselves not sources of international law, though they can be taken as authoritative interpretations of existing legal regimes. See E Strauss, 'A Bird in the Hand is Worth Two in the Bush: On the Assumed Legal Nature of the Responsibility to Protect' (2009) 1(3) *Global Responsibility to Protect* 291–323; JM Welsh and M Banda, 'International Law and the Responsibility to Protect: Clarifying on Expanding States' Responsibilities?' (2010) 2(3) *Global Responsibility to Protect* 213–31.

[8] JM Welsh, 'Norm Contestation and the Responsibility to Protect' (2013) 5 *Global Responsibility to Protect* 365–96.

Outcome Document, which limits the principle to the most serious international crimes; firmly establishes that the primary R2P falls upon national authorities, and that this responsibility entails prevention; encourages a broad perspective on the types of instruments the international community can use to prevent and respond to atrocity crimes; and ensures that the resort to any coercive means of prevention or response are rooted firmly within the existing collective security provisions of the UN Charter (ie requiring Security Council authorisation). As a result, while there is continued contestation about particular aspects of R2P—as there is over much older normative advancements, such as human rights—the points of contention among Member States have diminished substantially over the past decade.

Second, the clear articulation of the means available to address atrocity crimes and the actors responsible for protection enabled the UN Secretary-General to develop and elaborate a robust framework for implementation based on the three mutually reinforcing pillars. This framework has helped to inspire a rapidly growing body of academic and policy literature that improves our understanding of how to anticipate and mitigate the risks associated with atrocity crimes.[9] In turn, this analysis has helped to inform new tools for analysing situations of concern as well as the creation of new or enhanced early warning mechanisms—both inside and outside of the United Nations.

R2P's final contribution is in catalysing the creation of new institutional capacity to prevent and respond to atrocity crimes. According to a growing number of scholars who study the impact of norms, these kinds of policy mechanisms are crucial for moving from rhetorical commitment to 'real-world' implementation, as they help to routinise compliance.[10] For example, more than 50 Member States of the UN and the European Union have now joined the Global Network of R2P Focal Points, by appointing a senior official responsible for promoting implementation of the R2P at the national level and fostering international cooperation on atrocity crime prevention and response. At the international level, there has been enhanced coordination and engagement among a variety of actors and institutions in cases where atrocity crimes have been committed, or were imminent, such as Kyrgyzstan, Cote d'Ivoire, Guinea, Kenya and—most recently—Burundi. These conscious efforts to forestall the commission of atrocity crimes, even if not fully effective in all cases, illustrate how the remedial responsibility of the international community is being activated and implemented.

---

[9] S Straus, *Making and Unmaking Nations* (Ithaca, Cornell University Press, 2015); S Rosenberg, T Galis and A Zucker (eds), *Reconstructing Atrocity Prevention* (Cambridge, Cambridge University Press, 2015); S Sharma and JM Welsh (eds), *The Responsibility to Prevent: Overcoming the Challenges of Atrocity Prevention* (Oxford, Oxford University Press, 2015).

[10] A Betts and P Orchard, *Implementation and World Politics: How International Norms Change Practice* (Oxford, Oxford University Press, 2014).

II. R2P AND NON-STATE ARMED GROUPS

The development of R2P at the turn of the last century grew out of a concern for the phenomenon of state-led atrocity crimes. Yet there has been a growing awareness that while the majority of instances of such crimes have been perpetrated by governments, or the factions they support, the protection crises confronting the international community over the past decade have been exacerbated by NSAGs that target civilians as an explicit part of their conflict strategy, as well as by the emergence of violent extremists—such as ISIS, Boko Haram and Al-Shabaab—who openly violate IHL and glorify their crimes. An Arria Formula meeting of the UN Security Council in December 2015, organized by non-permanent members Spain and Chile, acknowledged that the initial conception and formulation of R2P had been too 'state-centric', and thus had failed to appreciate other perpetrators of atrocity crimes and the urgent priority to deny such actors the space, time and resources to commit such acts.[11]

A. Segmenting the Category of 'Non-State Armed Group'[12]

In addressing the question of how the principle of R2P might accommodate the particular challenges posed by NSAGs, the first step is to unpack this category and acknowledge the wide array of actors it encompasses. The differences among them affect not only how they behave but also how strategies to counteract their threats to civilians might be designed. Alex Bellamy has gone the furthest thus far in examining how the originally state-centric nature of R2P could expand to include NSAGs. In so doing, he differentiates these actors along five axes—objectives, organisational type, ideology, strategies and tactics, and degree of territorial control—and from this analysis concludes that only a subset is relevant from the perspective of preventing and responding to atrocity crimes.[13]

The first axis, objectives, can range from pushing for government reform (eg the FARC in Colombia), to secession (eg the LTTE in Sri Lanka), to regime overthrow (eg the Houthis in Yemen), to the creation of a new

---

[11] E Luck, 'Briefing to the United Nations Security Council: Arria Formula Meeting on the Responsibility to Protect and Non-State Actors' (New York, 15 December 2015).

[12] For the purposes of this chapter, I follow the organisation Geneva Call in defining an NSAG as 'any organized group with a basic structure of command operating outside state control that uses force to achieve its political or allegedly political objectives'. See A Sjöberg, *Armed Non-State Actors and Landmines*, vol III: *Towards a Holistic Approach to Armed Non-State Actors?* (Geneva, PSIO, 2007).

[13] AJ Bellamy, 'Non-State Armed Groups and the Responsibility to Protect', Discussion Paper for the seminar 'Fulfilling the Responsibility to Protect: The Threat of Non-State Armed Groups and Their Increased Role in Perpetrating Atrocity Crimes', Brussels, 22 March 2016.

territorial and political order (eg the case of ISIS). The more concrete the overall political objective, Bellamy argues, the more likely the group is to engage with negotiators if such engagement contributes to achieving that overriding goal. Conversely, the lack of a clear political objective can frustrate political engagement and often intensifies the nature of the violence used. The second axis along which NSAGs vary is organisational type. Some have state-like features, with clear chains of command and a leadership that exercises effective control over all the group's elements. Indeed, many anti-colonial and secessionist movements have organised themselves in this hierarchical fashion in order to demonstrate their approximation to sovereign states.[14] However, most NSAGs are divided into competing factions with ambiguous lines of command and weak control by the 'centre'.[15] In fact, as Bellamy and others have noted, some NSAGs consciously embrace fragmentation and rely on loosely allied self-managing units in order to strengthen their resilience and protect themselves from decisive attacks on their 'core' organisation.[16]

The presence and strength of ideology is the third differentiating factor, as ideologies both inform agendas and justify the specific ways in which NSAGs operate. As Bellamy rightly observes, some ideologies do *not* justify or support atrocity crimes and might even serve to restrain the behaviour of members of NSAGs. By contrast, for violent extremists, such as those that have operated in Syria, Iraq and Afghanistan, ideologies construct threats and attribute guilt, and serve to justify the targeting and extermination of members of particular groups. 'Atrocity-justifying ideologies' thus provide a powerful resource for those in positions of power—who decide that mass violence is necessary—as well as for those 'direct or indirect killers' who carry out the policy of atrocity.[17] Turning to Bellamy's fourth axis, the strategies and tactics of NSAGs, there is also considerable variation, ranging from groups that consciously attempt to adhere to principles of IHL, such as those that have signed 'Deeds of Commitment' brokered by Geneva Call,[18] to extremists, such as ISIS, that intentionally flout international

---

[14] N Caspersen, 'Democracy, Nationalism and (Lack of) Sovereignty' (2011) 17 *Nations and Nationalism* 337–56.

[15] KG Cunningham, *Inside the Politics of Self-Determination* (Oxford, Oxford University Press, 2014); LJM Seymour, KM Bakke and KG Cunningham, 'E Pluribus Unum, Ex Uno Plures: Competition, Violence, and Fragmentation in Ethnopolitical Movements' (2016) 53 *Journal of Peace Research* 3–18.

[16] Bellamy (n 13); I Briscoe, 'Non-Conventional Armed Violence and Non State Actors: Challenges for Mediation and Humanitarian Action' (Norwegian Peacebuilding Resource Centre, 2013).

[17] JL Maynard, 'Combating Atrocity-Justifying Ideologies' in S Sharma and JM Welsh (eds), *The Responsibility to Prevent* (Oxford, Oxford University Press, 2015).

[18] See the discussion of Deeds of Commitment at www.genevacall.org/how-we-work/armed-non-state-actors/.

legal obligations—either for the ideological reasons suggested above or to frighten opponents or populations under their control. For the latter, engagement is unlikely to mitigate threats to civilians, and usually gives way to efforts to degrade the capacity and/or territorial control of NSAGs. But diplomatic and other forms of engagement with groups at the moderate end of the spectrum can produce positive effects for civilian populations—even if temporary.

The final axis along which NSAGs are distributed is the nature of the relationship to territory and the civilian population. For those groups engaged in self-determination struggles, the claim to a particular national or ethnic territory—and international recognition for that claim—is paramount. Other NSAGs draw their support from a particular sector of the community and try to deepen that support by providing social services and other governance functions to enhance their legitimacy.[19] By contrast, some groups, such as the Lord's Resistance Army, do not attempt to hold territory or provide services to civilians, making them less susceptible to traditional forms of pressure from the outside. ISIS, or so-called Islamic State, is even harder to categorise, as it is both diffuse and territorially rooted (with its strategy of capturing key cities, supply routes and infrastructure). Moreover, while other NSAGs have sought to carve out territory from within an existing sovereign state, through secessionist claims, ISIS's goals have been more expansionist: radically altering the map of the Middle East by attempting to eradicate two existing states (Syria and Iraq) and creating one unified caliphate. And as it advanced on cities and villages, it waged a campaign of violence against certain populations whose identity and religious beliefs are viewed as incompatible with ISIS's particular interpretation of Islam. Some argue that it is the transnational nature of ISIS's operations, with nodes connected to several countries, which weakens the organisation's reliance on and connection to local communities—leading them to use greater violence to maintain control.[20]

The conclusion to be drawn from this brief survey is that 'non-state armed group' is a broad umbrella, which includes entities with varying propensities and capacities to commit the crimes specified by the R2P. The different types of NSAG in turn call for different strategies of response from the international community, and only those that systematically violate (or threaten to violate) IHL and and international human rights law (IHRL) are of specific concern for the implementation of R2P.

---

[19] C Metelits, *Inside Insurgency: Violence, Civilians, and Revolutionary Group Behaviour* (New York, New York University Press, 2009); ZC Mampilly, *Rebel Rulers: Insurgent Governance and Civilian Life During War* (Ithaca, Cornell University Press 2011).

[20] Bellamy (n 13).

B. Establishing the Responsibilities of NSAGs

The preceding analysis of the ways in which NSAGs vary in their goals and operations also hints at the different degrees of threat they pose to civilian populations and the challenges in holding them accountable for the commission of the most serious international crimes. But although it may be easier to conceive of and implement the notion of *state* responsibility for protection, the principle of R2P should logically extend to consideration of the responsibilities of non-state actors as well. Failing to do so, as Bellamy maintains, 'would be to condemn civilian populations living in areas controlled by NSAGs to second class protection'.[21]

The first point to recall is that NSAGs do not operate in a vacuum: these groups are bound by a considerable range of relevant obligations under existing IHL and *individual members* of such groups can be subject to international criminal law in instances where they commit international crimes.[22] Common Article 3 of the Geneva Conventions, for example, binds all parties to a NIAC to refrain from using violence against individuals taking no active part in hostilities. Additional Protocol II also requires NSAGs to respect and protect civilian populations. While the original Protocol applies only to situations in which such groups control territory, many of its provisions are now recognised to form part of customary law and are thus also applicable where NSAGs are not in full control.[23]

In addition, while IHRL is relatively limited with respect to NSAGs (given that it is focused on obligations of the state towards individuals within its jurisdiction), developments in international criminal law—particularly the broadening of the scope of crimes against humanity and war crimes to include acts committed in NIACs—have created possibilities for establishing individual criminal responsibility for members of NSAGs.[24] Hence, in the context of Syria, the Independent International Commission of Inquiry's 2016 Report underscored the need for *all* groups to be held accountable to violations of IHL that amounted to war crimes[25]—for example, those specified in Article 8(2)(c) and (e) of the ICC Statute. All of these advances have worked towards addressing an imbalance in the impunity enjoyed by non-state and state actors. It is now the gravity of the crime, rather than

---

[21] ibid, 4.

[22] A Clapham, 'Rights and Responsibilities of Non-State Actors: Legal Landscape & Issues Surrounding Engagement' (2010) http://dx.doi.org/10.2139/ssrn.1569636.

[23] JM Henckaerts, and L Doswald-Beck, *Customary International Humanitarian Law*, vols I and II (Cambridge, Cambridge University Press, 2005).

[24] W Schabas, 'Punishment of Non-State Actors in Non-International Armed Conflicts' (2002) 26 *Fordham International Law Journal* 907.

[25] UN Human Rights Council, 'Report of the Independent International Commission of Inquiry on the Syrian Arab Republic' (11 February 2016) UN Doc A/HRC/31/68.

the requirement of statehood, that has become significant for criminal accountability.[26] Finally, it is crucial to underline that international criminal law establishes the responsibility of individual members of NSAGs for international crimes not committed in the context of armed conflict (and thus outside the ambit of IHL), including genocide and crimes against humanity.

Establishing responsibility becomes more complex, however, in situations where international criminal law cannot be applied or where the protection of populations requires more than general compliance with Common Article 3. In these situations, fulfilment of the R2P depends upon the consent and compliance of armed groups themselves[27]—a reality that has fostered the attempts by Geneva Call to encourage NSAGs to sign public pledges ('Deeds of Commitment') to follow the principles of IHL. An even more difficult and controversial question is whether NSAGs that have significant control over populations can be said to have responsibilities that extend beyond compliance with IHL and the prohibition of atrocity crimes.

Given R2P's status as a *political* principle, this latter question is not a matter of new legal rights or responsibilities. Rather, the principal considerations for the international community are how to extend protection to vulnerable populations and who—in practical terms—exerts effective control over those populations.[28] While states generally retain the primary responsibility to protect populations from atrocity crimes, non-state actors that exert effective control can also be said to have political responsibilities, flowing from the principle of R2P. As Bellamy suggests, these would entail the prevention of atrocity crimes or their incitement—including prevention

---

[26] In situations of violence that do not amount to an armed conflict, the attribution of responsibility to NSAGs is more controversial. Here, the question is whether and to what extent IHRL creates obligations for such groups. The Independent Commission of Inquiry on Syria, in its earlier 2012 report, determined that the Free Syrian Army (FSA) at that time did not exercise any effective control over territory, thus making IHL inapplicable and leaving IHRL as the only normative framework to assess its conduct. The Commission affirmed that 'at a minimum, human rights obligations constituting peremptory international law (*jus cogens*) bind States, individuals and non-State collective entities, including armed groups'. Thus, acts violating *jus cogens* (such as torture or forced disappearance) could not be justified. See UN Human Rights Council, 'Report of the Independent International Commission of Inquiry on the Syrian Arab Republic' (22 February 2012) UN Doc A/HRC/19/69. The current position of the Office of the High Commissioner for Human Rights, as well as a number of human rights treaty bodies, is that 'non-State actors that exercise government-like functions and control over a territory are obliged to respect human rights norms when their conduct affects the human rights of the individuals under their control' (Geneva Academy of International Humanitarian Law and Human Rights, 2016). I am grateful to E Gillard for directing me to this source and more general debate. See also CF Moran, 'Beyond the State: The Future of International Criminal Justice', International Crimes Database Brief No 7 (September 2014).

[27] M Sassoli, 'Taking Armed Groups Seriously: Ways to Improve their Compliance with International Humanitarian Law' (2010) 1 *International Humanitarian Legal Studies* 5.

[28] Given that R2P explicitly refers to the protection of *populations*, it is control over populations, and not the more demanding standard of control over territory, that is most relevant for application of the principle.

of such acts by third parties operating within the space that they control—and the provision of humanitarian access.[29]

Sceptics of this approach might argue that by attributing political responsibilities to NSAGs, the international community would effectively legitimise them and endow them with state-like attributes. But this step is not necessarily implied. Geneva Call's engagement with NSAGs expressly eschews legitimisation in favour of delivering more robust protection to populations. The organisation's goal is to set expectations for behaviour with respect to a population over which an NSAG exerts control, rather than to judge on the rightness or wrongness of that control. So too with the political principle of R2P. The protection responsibilities it establishes for NSAGs derive from practical 'facts on the ground', Bellamy writes, and are distinct from the primary responsibility to protect populations under the R2P framework 'which is held exclusively by states'.[30]

III. COUNTERING THE THREATS POSED BY NSAGs

R2P's framework for protecting populations from atrocity crimes is multi-dimensional, including prevention as well as response and non-coercive as well as coercive tools. Indeed, the implementation framework for Pillars I and II outlines the ways in which states can become more resilient to the dynamics that can lead to atrocity crimes—through reform of societal and state institutions—and how the international community can assist states in fulfilling their protection responsibility—particularly through technical advice and capacity building.[31] Preventing and countering the atrocity crimes committed by NSAGs requires the same kind of comprehensive approach, which stretches from deeper forms of so-called structural prevention to mechanisms for immediate crisis response. The task is made particularly challenging by the fact the problem posed by NSAG perpetrators of atrocity crimes 'reaches all the way from complex transnational networks down to deeply ingrained practices within local communities and sub-groups within them'.[32]

One solution to this challenge is to create greater complementarity between the approaches designed to prevent atrocity crimes and violent extremism. As noted in the 2015 Report of the Secretary-General on the

---

[29] Bellamy (n 13) 6.

[30] ibid, 6.

[31] UNGA, 'Report of the Secretary-General on Responsibility to Protect: State Responsibility and Prevention' (9 July 2013) UN Doc A/67/929; UNGA, 'Report of the Secretary-General on Fulfilling our Collective Responsibility: International Assistance and the Responsibility to Protect' (11 July 2014) UN Doc A/68/947.

[32] Bellamy (n 13) 12.

Responsibility to Protect, the environments that are conducive to the rise of violent extremism often mirror those where there is the greatest risk of atrocity crimes:

> Both phenomena are more likely in societies where the rule of law and good governance are weak; where economic and political inequalities between identity-based groups are pronounced; where human rights are systematically violated and individuals face institutionalized forms of discrimination and marginalization; and where there is a pervasive culture of impunity.[33]

A comprehensive strategy for tackling the risks posed by these environments would thus prioritise four key elements, ranging from the 'up stream' to the 'down stream': creating inclusive governance and communities and consciously building 'inhibitors' to atrocity crimes;[34] countering narratives of grievance or hatred that are used both to justify violence and to recruit and motivate violent extremists and perpetrators of atrocity crimes; addressing the lack of accountability for inciting or committing atrocity crimes; and tackling the transnational flows of ideas, arms and people that enable the perpetration of crimes and systematic violations of human rights. The UN's Plan of Action to Prevent Violent Extremism emphasises that any such strategy must extend beyond purely military responses to addressing deeper structural challenges, informed by a better assessment of the local contexts in which extremism flourishes.[35] It also follows that any comprehensive approach to preventing violent extremism and atrocity crimes requires coordinated action at different levels; national policy alone is insufficient.

Nonetheless, under the R2P framework, states have the primary responsibility to protect their populations from atrocity crimes, irrespective of the perpetrator. International law also makes clear that a state is obliged to exercise due diligence and do all it can to protect all persons under its jurisdiction against the threats that non-state actors, including de facto authorities and armed groups, pose to the enjoyment of human rights.[36] Given these political and legal responsibilities, states could take a number of concrete steps to strengthen their capacity to prevent atrocity crimes by NSAGs, whether at home or abroad. These include adopting national legislation (in accordance

---

[33] UNGA, 'Report of the Secretary-General on Mobilizing Collective Action: The Next Decade of the Responsibility to Protect' (22 July 2016) Un Doc A/70/999.

[34] The UN Secretary-General has identified the key inhibitors as including: professional and accountable security sectors; impartial institutions for overseeing political transitions; independent judicial and human rights institutions; national capacity to assess risk and mobilise early action; local capacity to resolve conflicts; media capacity to counteract prejudice and hate speech; and the capacity for effective and legitimate transitional justice. UNGA, 'Report of the Secretary-General on Fulfilling our Collective Responsibility' (n 31).

[35] UNGA, 'Report of the Secretary-General on a Plan of Action to Prevent Violent Extremism' (24 December 2015) UN Doc A/70/674.

[36] International Law Commission (ILC), 'Draft Articles on State Responsibility for Wrongful Acts', vol II (Yearbook of International Law, 2001) Arts 8, 9, 10.

with Security Council Resolution 2178) to prevent nationals from travelling abroad to commit international crimes; developing programmes to counter radicalisation and extremist ideologies; prohibiting NSAGs from profiting from the trade in raw materials, antiquities, hostages or foreign donations (as required by Security Council Resolution 2199); and fully supporting the protection of individuals and communities in other jurisdictions, whether through compliance with refugee and asylum law, the provision of humanitarian assistance, or the implementation of collective security measures authorised by the UN Security Council.

A. Support to States in Managing the Threat from NSAGs

In his implementation plan for R2P released in 2009, the then UN Secretary-General Ban Ki-Moon recognised that, in certain circumstances, collective international military assistance can be a critical means to support states in addressing the challenge posed by NSAGs.[37] This acknowledgement demonstrates that the use of military assets and armed forces to implement the R2P can, and often does, proceed with the consent of the host state.

Two examples illustrate how such assistance can enhance the protection of populations. The preventive deployment of UN peacekeeping forces to the Former Yugoslav Republic of Macedonia, from 1992 to 1999, helped to prevent conflict spillover from other parts of the Balkans, provided humanitarian assistance, and engaged in targeted actions to forestall inter-ethnic violence. The Regional Assistance Mission to the Solomon Islands (RAMSI), established in 2003 at the request of the government of the Solomon Islands (with the full participation of the Pacific Islands Forum), provided comprehensive military, civilian and police support to reduce ethnic conflict and initiate the rebuilding process. RAMSI assisted national authorities to protect their population by disarming military and criminal groups, establishing the rule of law, and holding perpetrators accountable through the criminal justice system.

Regional organisations have also supplied additional military capacity and expertise to help national authorities stabilise crises and protect vulnerable populations. The African Union Mission in Somalia, the African Union-led International Support Mission to Mali, and the European Union Training Missions to Somalia and Mali have each provided critical additional capacity to national security and law enforcement forces. Regional assistance also reinforced Nigerian efforts to combat the terrorist organisation Boko Haram and strengthened the response of several states in the region to the threat posed by the Lord's Resistance Army.

---

[37] UNGA, 'Report of the Secretary-General' (n 3) para 40.

Despite these concrete examples, the practice of providing military assistance in contexts where non-state actors commit or threaten to commit atrocity crimes is not without its challenges. The first set of issues is legal in nature.

In instances where the Security Council or regional organisations authorise stabilisation and assistance missions (as in the case of Macedonia and the Solomon Islands) the legality of military action by third-party actors is relatively straightforward. States have also claimed and recognised the legality of third-party military action in the territory of a sovereign state where that state explicitly requests international assistance. In the case of military action in Iraq in 2014 against ISIS, for example, Western powers argued that the general prohibition on the use of force in international law did not apply, given the request and consent of the reconstituted Iraqi government.[38] In a letter to the President of the UN Security Council on September 2014, the Iraqi Minister of Foreign Affairs had formally sought additional international support and assistance in his country's fight against ISIS. The stated aim of such military action was to 'end the constant threat to Iraq, protect Iraq's citizens and, ultimately arm Iraqi forces and enable them to regain control of Iraq's borders'.[39]

But while external support for the Iraqi government can be considered legal in this case, not all instances of 'intervention by invitation' or 'military assistance on request' have been free of controversy.[40] In the 1980s, prominent legal scholars[41]—as well as the British government—took the view that in cases of civil war (as opposed to situations of internal unrest), customary law had developed such that there was a duty *not* to intervene militarily without multilateral authorisation, unless there had been prior foreign intervention against the government. More recently, international lawyers have argued that while consent for intervention by third parties has a foundational character in international law,[42] and thus can preclude the wrongfulness of acts otherwise considered illegal (ie the use of force),

---

[38] UK Government, 'Summary of the Government Legal Position on Military Action in Iraq Against ISIL' (25 September 2014) www.gov.uk/government/publications/military-action-in-iraq-against-isil-government-legal-position/summary-of-the-government-legal-position-on-military-action-in-iraq-against-isil.

[39] UNSC, 'Letter dated 20 September 2014 from the Permanent Representative of Iraq to the United Nations addressed to the President of the Security Council' (22 September 2014) UN Doc S/2014/691.

[40] D Akande, 'Classification of Armed Conflicts: Relevant Legal Concepts' in E Wilmhurst (ed), *International Law and the Classification of Conflicts* (Oxford, Oxford University Press, 2012) 33–79.

[41] L Doswald-Beck, 'The Legal Validity of Military Intervention by Invitation of the Government' (1985) 56 *British Yearbook of International Law* 1.

[42] C Gray, *International Law and the Use of Force*, 3rd edn (Oxford, Oxford University Press 2008) 81.

it should be interpreted restrictively such that it gives only limited forms of legitimation.[43] In the specific context of analysing US justifications for its programme of drone strikes in Pakistan, Yemen and Somalia, legal commentators have emphasised that the scope of consent must be 'bounded': its legitimating force operates only to the extent that an act remains within the limits of a host state government's consent. They have also argued that the 'exculpatory potential' of consent does not extend to the *type* of force that is used. Consent therefore cannot preclude the wrongfulness of military actions that contravene IHL or peremptory norms of international law.[44]

The legality of third-party military action by invitation becomes particularly controversial in two instances. The first are circumstances in which a government's entitlement to request international assistance is contested due to a loss of territorial control and/or popular support. The second is where a government's consent is either coerced or assumed (rather than expressly stated). According to the Draft Articles on State Responsibility, consent must be 'valid' for it to facilitate an otherwise unlawful act: it should emanate from a legitimate government that speaks for the state, and be both freely given and clearly established.[45] In the context of US drone strikes, some have claimed that with respect to so-called weak states—ie states that are deemed unable to effectively act against NSAGs on their territory—consent for outside assistance can be implied. But as Byrne contends, this interpretation neglects the principle of agency that is at the very heart of consent, and shifts the grounds for determining validity to the capacity of a state to address threats emanating from within their sovereign jurisdiction.[46]

Military action by third-party states against NSAGs is also legally contested when it takes place on an adjacent territory that does not give its consent, but is alleged to be providing a staging ground for attacks on the country requesting international assistance. The ongoing air strikes by the US-led coalition on ISIS forces in Syria is the most prominent example. Critics of the claim that these strikes represent a form of collective self-defence in response to attacks by NSAGs in Iraq argue that this rationale could be invoked only if ISIS is deemed to be a direct agent of Damascus and is under its operational control.[47] Otherwise, as is implied by the ICRC's revised

---

[43] The broad outlines of the law concerning 'intervention by invitation' can be found in International Law Commission (ILC), Articles on Responsibility of States for Internationally Wrongful Acts (2001) UN Doc A/56/10, 2001 (ARS) Art 20.

[44] M Byrne, 'Consent and the Use of Force: An Examination of "Intervention by Invitation" as a Basis for US Drone Strikes in Pakistan, Somalia and Yemen' 3(1) *Journal on the Use of Force and International Law* 3–4, 25–26.

[45] ILC, 'Draft Articles on State Responsibility' (n 36) Art 20(6).

[46] Byrne (n 44) 8.

[47] This was the standard for collective self-defence set by the ICJ in the case of *Nicaragua v the United States of America. Military and Paramilitary Activities in and against Nicaragua (Nicaragua v United States of America)* [1984] ICJ Rep 392.

commentary to Common Article 2 of the Geneva Conventions,[48] the use of armed force against a NSAG on the territory of another state, without that state's consent, effectively creates an *international* armed conflict.

The second set of issues raised by international assistance to combat NSAGs is political, and relates to the dilemmas that third parties face in either offering such assistance themselves, or condoning it when it is offered by others. One such dilemma arises in situations in which the government that is requesting outside military assistance to combat NSAG perpetrators of atrocity crimes is *itself* engaged in military or police activities that could constitute grave violations of human rights. In this case, international assistance efforts to protect populations from one set of actors can become complicit in the criminal actions of another. Third-party states confronted this dilemma of complicity in Nigeria, when the government allegedly engaged in extrajudicial executions and attacks on unarmed civilians in the north-east of the country in the course of its response to the threat of Boko Haram.[49] Critics of Russia and Iran's support for the Assad government throughout Syria's long and bloody conflict have also raised the spectre of complicity with war crimes. A second dilemma stems from the mixed motives that frequently characterise third-party actors providing assistance to governments. Uganda's support to the government of South Sudan during 2014, and the creation of a joint military agreement in October of that year, provoked criticism from regional and international actors who not only suspected larger geopolitical aims on the part of the Ugandans but also believed that it would escalate fighting between government forces and rebels rather than protect the South Sudanese population from further atrocity crimes. Thus, while the R2P framework can furnish a normative basis and political rationale for international assistance to states struggling with NSAGs, there are circumstances in which third parties will have to pull back from providing or applauding that support.

These political dilemmas do not rule out the potential that international actors can effectively assist states—including through various forms of military support—in addressing the threats posed by NSAG perpetrators of atrocity crimes. However, they do illustrate how the R2P framework can, in practice, all too easily blend into the powerful agenda of counter-terrorism. Proponents of R2P must remain acutely conscious of this possibility, and work to ensure that security imperatives are not permitted to

---

[48] ICRC, 'The Geneva Conventions of 1949 and Additional Protocols and their Commentaries' (2016) ihl-databases.icrc.org/applic/ihl/ihl.nsf/Comment.xsp?action=openDocument&documentId=BE2D518CF5DE54EAC1257F7D0036B518, Art 2.

[49] 'Nigeria: War Crimes and Crimes Against Humanity as Violence Escalates in North-East' *Amnesty International*, 31 March 2014, www.amnesty.org/en/news/nigeria-war-crimes-and-crimes-against-humanity-violence-escalates-north-east-2014-03-31.

consistently trump or compromise fundamental humanitarian and human rights commitments.

IV. STATE RESPONSIBILITY FOR THE ACTS OF NSAGs

The articulation of the 'responsibility to protect' in the 2005 Summit Outcome Document was designed to remind states of their primary role in protecting populations from atrocity crimes, and both to activate and deepen the international community's supportive role. But as Ban Ki-moon lamented in his last report to the General Assembly on R2P, there remains a significant gap between rhetorical commitment and action on the ground. In identifying the barriers to implementation of R2P, the Secretary General pointed to cases in which—rather than preventing atrocity crimes—states have positively enabled their perpetration through forms of external support to NSAGs who serve as 'proxies' for the objectives of external powers. In some situations, third-party states have supplied the weapons that are used to commit war crimes, genocide or crimes against humanity, in contravention of their obligations under the Arms Trade Treaty, while in other cases they 'have turned a blind eye to their trade and transportation'.[50] Ban was particularly concerned in the final year of his tenure with the conflict in Yemen, where outside powers had used force in support of both state and non-state actors responsible for widespread and systematic violations of human rights and IHL.

Given the fact that, in a large number of today's civil wars, external actors support one or more of the parties, the political responsibilities associated with R2P are of particular relevance. These include the negative responsibility to deny perpetrators the means to commit atrocity crimes—or not to knowingly provide arms or illicit financing that would facilitate these actors. But they also extend to the positive responsibility to ensure respect for IHL and—arguably—to the broader responsibility to contribute to the resolution of deadly conflict.

International law has a different but complementary approach to regulating the conduct of states in proxy wars, and to preventing states from becoming complicit in the crimes of other actors. It serves these functions through two main kinds of legal judgments: first, determining when the involvement of an outside state is of a sufficient level to 'internationalise' a conflict; and second, determining when the acts of an NSAG can be attributable to a foreign state (under the law of state responsibility). In the *Tadić* case, the ICTY took the view that the ICJ's standard from the earlier

---

[50] UNGA, 'Report of the Secretary General' (n 33) para 30.

Nicaragua case—'effective control'—was too stringent. Instead, the Appeals Chamber suggested that a foreign state would be responsible for the acts of an NSAG if it exercised 'overall control' over that actor. This test would be satisfied

> when the State (or, in the context of an armed conflict, the Party to the conflict) has a role in organizing, coordinating or planning the military actions of a military group, in addition to financing, training and equipping or providing operational support to the group. Acts performed by the group or members thereof may be regarded as acts of de facto State organs regardless of any specific instruction by the controlling State concerning the commission of each of those acts.[51]

After applying this test, the Appeals Chamber held that because the Bosnian Serbs were under the 'overall control' of the Federal Republic of Yugoslavia, the conflict between that group and the Muslim-led Bosnian government was an IAC (with all of the legal responsibilities that flowed from that determination).

Nevertheless, there are issues related to the ICTY's interpretation of earlier jurisprudence and its own standard of 'overall control', with important implications for how we might consider the legal responsibilities of states for the actions of NSAGs.[52] These can be seen from the more recent case before the ICJ, the *Bosnian Genocide* case, in which the Court clarified its position. As the reasoning from this case shows, the ICJ in the *Nicaragua* case had not one, but *two* tests for determining when acts of an NSAG can be attributable to those of a foreign state. The first is a test by which *all the acts* of a group can be attributed to a state. The standard is one of strict control, or complete dependence: where an NSAG is completely dependent upon a foreign state, then that group can be deemed a de facto organ of that state (under Article 4 of the Articles on State Responsibility)—and therefore the actions of that group can be attributable to the foreign state. However, where a group is not completely dependent, and thus not a de facto organ of the foreign state, the *specific acts* of that group could still be attributable to the supporting state. In this case there is a second test, to determine whether such acts were committed under the instruction of a foreign state or its 'effective control'.[53]

This reasoning does set a higher bar, when compared with the standard of the ICTY, for establishing the responsibility of states for the actions of NSAGs. But the strictness seems warranted. As Akande puts it: 'A State

---

[51] *Prosecutor v Tadić* (Judgment) ICTY-94-1-T (7 May 1997) para 139.
[52] Akande (n 40) 58–60; M Milanovic, 'State Responsibility for Genocide' (2006) 17 *European Journal of International Law* 553.
[53] *Application of the Convention on the Prevention and Punishment of the Crime of Genocide (Bosnia and Herzegovina v Serbia and Montenegro)* (Merits) [2007] ICJ Rep 43, paras 385–402.

should only be held to be legally responsible for acts which are really its own.'[54] However, this jurisprudence does not necessarily weaken either the political injunction or the legal responsibility for states to take steps to prevent and respond to international crimes and to avoid complicity in these wrongful acts. While there is no explicit rule that prohibits support to NSAGs per se, there is an obligation under the terms of the Genocide Convention that would be relevant if there is apprehension that such a group is likely to commit acts that could constitute genocide. As the ICJ argued in the *Bosnian Genocide* case, a foreign state can be held responsible in certain cases for its own failure to act—namely to prevent the acts of a proxy group where specific rules of international law impose an obligation on it to do so. Under this logic, the ICJ held Serbia responsible for its *failure to prevent* the Srebrenica genocide rather than holding it responsible for *committing* genocide.[55] Within the broader political framework of the R2P, a focus on the actual behaviour of states and their complicity in the commission of crimes—eg through their failure to control the behaviour of proxies or their creation of a situation that permits atrocity crimes to occur—is likely to be a more powerful strategy for implementing RtoP in relation to NSAGs.

The issue of the legal obligations of states in relation to NSAGs becomes more contentious when we move from the crime of genocide to the other acts specified by the 'responsibility to protect'—namely war crimes and crimes against humanity.

It could be argued, for example, that the obligation to ensure respect for the Geneva Conventions (Common Article 1) creates a duty to prevent violations by NSAGs that a state is actively supporting. The counter-argument presented by some states is that this obligation to ensure respect applies narrowly, encompassing only the need to ensure respect by the forces of one's own side and not by the forces of other actors.[56] But clearly the political discourse around states' support for NSAGs that violate IHL suggests that this restrictive approach to interpreting the duty to 'ensure respect' is less tenable. The question of whether there is an obligation not to support proxies committing crimes against humanity is more complex, given that we still lack treaty text for these crimes. Furthermore, the legal basis for crimes against humanity is rooted in human rights law, thereby raising the general issue of the conditions under which states have extraterritorial human rights

---

[54] Akande (n 40) 60.

[55] *Bosnia and Herzegovina v Serbia and Montenegro* (n 53).

[56] An additional counter-argument is that the Geneva Conventions apply to IACs and thus the obligation to ensure respect is likely to have limited relevance in relation to the behaviour of NSAGs. However, it is important to recall that Common Article 3 of the Geneva Conventions applies to NIACs; thus, the Common Article 1 obligation to ensure respect for the Geneva Conventions can also entail an obligation to ensure respect for Common Article 3. I am grateful to D Akande for raising this point, as well as for directing me to the wider set of possibilities for holding states responsible for atrocity crimes committed by NSAGs.

obligations. Nonetheless, in situations where a state has control over an NSAG and that group controls territory, it has been accepted that the state has human rights obligations with respect to the people in that territory.[57] There may thus be scope to extend this reasoning to situations where there are allegations of complicity in the commission of crimes against humanity. More broadly, legal scholars such as Miles Jackson contend that given the seriousness of the obligations that international law places on non-state actors with respect to the commission of international crimes, and the prospect that international law will likely develop to recognise additional possibilities of unlawful wrongdoing by non-state actors, it logically follows that the ways in which states might participate in wrongful acts—not simply through the provision of assistance but also through influence—must be 'adequately sanctioned' via the application of notions of complicity.[58]

V. CONCLUSION

The criminal acts specified by the 'responsibility to protect' are a deep affront to the very idea of common humanity. The commission of atrocity crimes can also exacerbate wider protection needs, turning existing crises into more severe humanitarian emergencies and threatening international peace and security through their impact on neighbouring countries or their production of refugee flows and internal displacement. The effects are wide ranging and cast a long shadow. In addition to the tangible costs that are incurred through interruptions to economic growth, recovery efforts, or reversals in development, the perpetration of systematic violence based on victims' identity eats away at the fabric of societies, with consequences that pass through the generations.

Although R2P was designed primarily to confront the spectre of state-led atrocity crimes, its political role and function can and should extend to addressing the threat posed by NSAG perpetrators. The legal responsibilities of these groups to comply with humanitarian and human rights principles, while different from those of states, remain real and substantial. But their broader *political* responsibilities—and those of the states that support them—must also be asserted, so that the normative framework provided by R2P does not sideline those populations whose security is imperilled by non-state actors with both the motive and the means to commit the most serious international crimes.

---

[57] An example given by Akande is the situation of Turkey's control of Northern Cyprus through an entity that is not recognised as a state and is thus regarded as equivalent to an NSAG.

[58] M Jackson, *Complicity in International Law* (Oxford, Oxford University Press, 2015) 210–14.

16

Protecting Civilians by Criminalising the Most Serious Forms of the Illegal Use of Force: Activating the International Criminal Court's Jurisdiction over the Crime of Aggression

CARRIE McDOUGALL[1]

I. INTRODUCTION

THE CRIME OF aggression was born out of the overwhelming devastation inflicted by World War II, including its human toll of some 60 million dead, in addition to those left alive but irrevocably scarred. The crime against peace, the predecessor of the crime of aggression, was the centrepiece of the Nuremberg and Tokyo trials, famously described by Robert H Jackson, the US prosecutor appearing before the International Military Tribunal, as 'the supreme international crime', which 'contains within itself the accumulated evil of the whole'.

The question of whether there is a 'supreme' international crime and, if so, whether that crime is the crime of aggression, is ripe for debate. But Jackson's central thesis—that the wars of aggression prosecuted by Nazi Germany both engendered and enabled the slaughter that took place—is difficult to dispute.

---

[1] Dr Carrie McDougall is Legal Adviser at Australia's Permanent Mission to the United Nations in New York. This chapter was written in her personal capacity and should not be taken to reflect the views of the Australian government.

This chapter was drafted in early 2017, and finalised in Autumn 2017. In December 2017, the ICC Assembly of States Parties adopted a resolution that activated the ICC's jurisdiction over the crime of aggression from 17 July 2018 (see ICC-ASP/16/Res.5 'Activation of the Jurisdiction of the Court over the Crime of Aggression', https://asp.icc-cpi.int/iccdocs/asp_docs/Resolutions/ASP16/ICC-ASP-16-Res5-ENG.pdf).

The crime of aggression—the criminalisation of the most serious forms of the illegal use of inter-state armed force—is anchored in the *jus ad bellum*. A sharp distinction has always been drawn between the *jus ad bellum* and the *jus in bello*: one of the fundamental tenets of public international law is that IHL applies equally to the parties to a conflict—regardless of whether one of those parties was responsible for an unlawful use of force. It should also be acknowledged that while IHL provided the historical foundation for what is now referred to as the protection of civilians, deeper understandings of protection threats, needs and responses have developed, such that the protection of civilians is now widely understood to include all activities aimed at ensuring full respect for the rights of civilians in accordance with the law, including international human rights, criminal and refugee law, in addition to IHL. The key point in the current context is that the relationship between the crime of aggression and the protection of civilians is not a legal one, but rather one of cause and effect. Not all unlawful uses of inter-state armed force result in armed conflict, or otherwise cause widespread civilian deaths and injuries. And it is certainly not the case that all civilian deaths and injuries are triggered by an unlawful use of inter-state armed force. Nonetheless, it is undeniably true that unlawful uses of inter-state armed force all too often trigger the type of violence that leads to countless civilians—of both the victim and the aggressor state—being killed, injured, or otherwise wrenched from their ordinary lives and thrown into a dark fight for survival. It is for this reason that while the damage caused to sovereignty and territorial integrity by violations of the *jus in bellum* is significant, the harm that flows to innocent civilians has, from the outset, been a driving force behind the criminalisation of the most serious forms of the unlawful use of force.

2017 is likely to see the activation of the ICC's jurisdiction over the crime of aggression. And yet, despite the potential deterrent effect on the unlawful use of inter-state armed force, a number of states, led by the Permanent Five Members of the United Nations Security Council (P5), remain opposed to this endeavour. The reasons behind their opposition and the prospects that other states parties to the Rome Statute[2] of the ICC will be able to overcome their reservations is the subject of this chapter. The importance of these arguments goes beyond the immediate circumstances of 2017 to address the merits of the effective exercise of the ICC's jurisdiction over aggression in the years to come.

* * *

---

[2] Rome Statute of the International Criminal Court (adopted 17 July 1998, entered into force 1 July 2002) UN Doc A/CONF 183/9 (ICC Statute).

At the First Review Conference of the ICC Statute, held in Kampala, Uganda in 2010, states parties decided to criminalise the most serious forms of the illegal inter-state use of armed force.[3] Article 8*bis*(1) of the ICC Statute defines the crime of aggression as the

> planning, preparation, initiation or execution, by a person in a position effectively to exercise control over or to direct the political or military action of a State, of an act of aggression which, by its character, gravity and scale, constitutes a manifest violation of the Charter of the United Nations.

Paragraph 8*bis*(2) provides a list of qualifying acts of aggression that are capable of constituting the state act element of the crime.

Conditions for the exercise of the Court's jurisdiction over the crime are set out in Articles 15*bis* and 15*ter*. Under Article 15*ter*, the Court may exercise jurisdiction over a crime of aggression occurring within a situation referred to the Court by the UN Security Council under Article 13(b). Article 15*bis*, which governs state referrals and *proprio motu* investigations, is markedly more complicated. It provides that the Prosecutor may proceed with an investigation in respect of a crime of aggression where the Security Council has made a determination of an act of aggression committed by the state concerned (paragraphs 6 and 7). If the Council fails to make such a determination within six months of the UN Secretary-General being notified of the situation before the Court, provided that the Pre-Trial Division authorises the commencement of the investigation and the Security Council has not deferred ICC action under Article 16, the Prosecutor may proceed (paragraph 8).

Critically, at the time of the amendments' adoption, the ability of the ICC to exercise jurisdiction over the crime of aggression was made subject to two, cumulative, conditions. First, the Court may exercise jurisdiction only in respect of crimes of aggression committed one year after the ratification or acceptance of the amendments by thirty states parties. And second, the exercise of jurisdiction is subject to a decision of states parties to be taken after 1 January 2017.

The target of thirty ratifications was reached in June 2016: at the time of writing, thirty-four states parties have ratified the amendments, with many more ratifications in train.[4] The calendar has now also passed

---

[3] See ICC, 'The Crime of Aggression' (11 June 2010) Res RC/Res.6, which annexed the amendments to the ICC Statute, as well as elements of the crime and interpretive 'understandings' relating to both the definition of the crime and the conditions for the exercise of the Court's jurisdiction.

[4] At the time of writing, the amendments have been ratified by: Andorra, Argentina, Austria, Belgium, Botswana, Chile, Costa Rica, Croatia, Cyprus, Czech Republic, El Salvador, Estonia, Finland, Georgia, Germany, Iceland, Latvia, Liechtenstein, Lithuania, Luxembourg, Malta, the Netherlands, Poland, Portugal, Samoa, San Marino, Slovakia, Slovenia, Spain, the State of Palestine, Switzerland, the former Yugoslav Republic of Macedonia, Trinidad and Tobago and Uruguay.

1 January 2017, and it is clear that the majority of states parties are in favour of the Assembly of States Parties (ASP) deciding to activate the Court's jurisdiction over the crime of aggression at the next regular ASP meeting in December 2017.[5]

And yet there is a small but powerful group of states, led by the P5, that has outstanding concerns in relation to the prospect of the ICC exercising jurisdiction over the crime of aggression. The P5's position is not new. In the lead up to, and during, the Review Conference, all the P5 states expressed reservations in relation to the crime. The United States made it clear that it had outstanding concerns in relation to its definition. All members of the P5 also objected to the alleged inconsistency of the various models of the jurisdictional provisions that were on the table with their preferred interpretation of the UN Charter, which they argued gives the Security Council an exclusive right to identify an act of aggression. In the most strident example, France, following the adoption of the amendments, stated that it could not 'associate itself with the draft text' on the basis that Article 15*bis*(8) 'contravenes the Charter of the United Nations under the terms of which the Security Council alone shall determine the existence of an act of aggression'.[6]

In Kampala in 2010 these statements seemed somewhat hollow. Whatever concerns were held by the P5, they had not been sufficient for them to stand in the way of consensus—something that could readily have been achieved had they so desired. And yet, seven years on, it seems that, if anything, positions have hardened.

II. KEY CONCERNS RELATING TO THE DEFINITION OF THE CRIME OF AGGRESSION

The United States remains vocal in criticising what it describes as the 'uncertain' definition of the crime of aggression, in respect of which it asserts

---

[5] This is reflected in Operative Paragraph 121 of the annual Assembly of States Parties (ASP) 'omnibus resolution' (formally titled 'Strengthening the International Criminal Court and the Assembly of States Parties', 26 November 2016) ICC-ASP/15/Res.5, which 'welcomes the fact that more than 30 States Parties have deposited their instruments of ratification of the amendments on the crime of aggression, enabling the Assembly to take a decision to activate the Court's jurisdiction over the crime of aggression in 2017'. Op para 122 'calls upon all States Parties to consider ratifying or accepting these amendments and resolves to activate the Court's jurisdiction over the crime of aggression *as early as possible*, subject to a decision to be taken after 1 January 2017 by the same majority of States Parties as is required for the adoption of an amendment to the Rome Statute' (emphasis added). As the majority of states parties consider activation to be a straightforward matter, they were of the view that it was unnecessary to convene a Review Conference to make the decision. It was also considered unnecessary to convene a special session of the ASP given that the first precondition will not be fully satisfied until June 2017 (one year after the thirtieth ratification), just six months ahead of the regular ASP meeting.

[6] Statement by France, *Official Records*, ICC Doc RC/11 (2010), Annex VIII: 'Statements by States Parties in Explanation of Position after the Adoption of Resolution RC/Res.6 on the Crime of Aggression', 122.

there is 'little clarity or consensus'.[7] The definition found in Article 8*bis* is based on a definition of 'aggression' adopted by the UN General Assembly in 1974.[8] According to the United States, the ICC Statute strips this definition of key nuances (notably the exceptions and caveats built into the GA definition, which was only ever intended to serve as guidance in the making of the Security Council's political judgements).[9] The USA also argues that by expanding the definition of the state act element of the crime beyond 'wars of aggression' (which was at the heart of Nuremberg and Tokyo definitions of crimes against peace) the ICC Statute definition has strayed beyond customary international law.[10]

According to the United States, the risk of these cumulative failings is that the ICC will be cast 'into treacherous political waters that would threaten to undermine both the Court's credibility and that of the greater international criminal justice project'.[11] A variation on this argument has been put forward by China, which has argued that in light of its 'limited membership', small number of completed cases and strong criticism from some African countries, 'the Court does not have the standing to make an authoritative determination on such a sensitive question' as the legality of a use of force.[12]

A linked concern is the impact that ICC decisions on the crime of aggression could have on the *jus ad bellum*. As former State Department Legal Adviser Harold Koh and Special Coordinator of the Office of Global Criminal Justice Todd Buchwald (who together led the US delegation in Kampala) put it:

> [T]he adoption of the definition in a treaty as significant as the Rome Statute might well affect the way that states and others in the international community view customary international law, as is often said to have happened with respect to definitions of 'war crimes' and 'crimes against humanity' in the Rome Statute.'[13]

I have some sympathy for the criticisms of the definition that the USA has advanced. I have put forward detailed critiques of the definition myself.[14]

---

[7] S Sewall, 'Remarks' (9 April 2015) www.state.gov/j/remarks/240579.htm.

[8] UNGA, 'Resolution on the Definition of Aggression' (14 December 1974) UN Doc A/RES/3314.

[9] Sewall (n 7). See also HH Koh and TF Buchwald, 'The Crime of Aggression: The United States Perspective' (2015) 109 *American Journal of International Law* 257, 269.

[10] Koh and Buchwald (n 9) 270.

[11] ibid, 263.

[12] Z Lulu, 'China' in C Kress and S Barriga (eds), *The Crime of Aggression: A Commentary*, vol 2 (Cambridge, Cambridge University Press, 2017) 1131, 1136. This chapter was written in Lulu's personal capacity and an opening footnote states that it does not represent the views of China or the Chinese Ministry of Foreign Affairs. However, the views outlined echo positions put forward by China in public statements at the UN.

[13] Koh and Buchwald (n 9) 271.

[14] C McDougall, *Crime of Aggression under the Rome Statute of the International Criminal Court* (Cambridge, Cambridge University Press, 2013) 62–166.

Indeed, the less than ideal definition could well result in the ICC having to make difficult decisions regarding the content of the *jus ad bellum*—which, I would argue, is not how international criminal law should work. While I consider that the ICC has established itself as a responsible part of the international peace and security architecture and thus do not share China's reservations about the standing of the Court, I do consider that the lack of guidance provided by the definition has increased the likelihood that (legitimately or not) the mere making of decisions about the use of force (correct or not) will provide states with ammunition to criticise the Court.

This is not a reason, however, to stand in the way of the activation of the ICC's jurisdiction over the crime of aggression. In the first place, it would be implausible to suggest that the ICC Statute is otherwise a perfect instrument, with all other crimes defined in watertight provisions. A degree of interpretation is inevitable.

It is also naïve to suggest that decisions made by the ICC in relation to war crimes, crimes against humanity and genocide are devoid of politics. Establishing the requisite intent for genocide, the 'widespread or systematic attack' elements of crimes against humanity, or the 'plan and policy', 'large scale commission' or 'international armed conflict' elements of war crimes may cause the Court to examine various governmental actions and policies. There is no basis to suggest that such determinations are any less political than decisions relating to the use of inter-state armed force.[15]

More importantly, I do not consider the lack of certainty surrounding the definition to be fatal—indeed, the benefits of criminalisation—in particular the potential deterrent effect on unlawful uses of force—far outweigh the risks of the ICC adjudicating issues relating to the use of force.

In this context I agree with the USA that the crime of aggression is likely to have an impact on the *jus ad bellum*. Article 10 of the ICC Statute makes it clear that the aggression amendments can neither limit nor prejudice 'in any way existing or developing rules of international law' for purposes other than the ICC Statute. Article 25 further stipulates that nothing in the ICC Statute 'shall affect the responsibility of States under international law'.[16] As such, as a matter of law, ICC jurisprudence will not have any direct effect on the content of the *jus ad bellum*. I do, however, consider it likely that states will express views on cases before the Court and on any

---

[15] For similar views, see A Reisinger Coracini and P Wrange, 'The Specificity of the Crime of Aggression' in Kress and Barriga (n 12) 307, 331–33.

[16] These provisions are underlined in Understanding 4, adopted alongside the aggression amendments, which provides that: 'It is understood that the amendments that address the definition of the act of aggression and the crime of aggression do so for the purpose of this Statute only. The amendments shall, in accordance with Article 10 of the Rome Statute, not be interpreted as limiting or prejudicing in any way existing or developing rules of international law for purposes other than this Statute.'

future decisions it may hand down, which could provide a rich source of state practice and *opinio juris*, thereby shaping customary international law, as well as interpretations of Article 2(4) of the UN Charter.

However, while I appreciate that the status quo serves some interests, as an international lawyer I think that any process that allows for dynamic interpretations of the prohibition of the use of force and helps clarify the law, potentially eliminating uncertainties that states can hide behind, is likely to lead to fewer violations of the prohibition—which objectively can only been seen as a good thing.

Of course, states parties should do what they can to make sure that ICC decisions on the crime of aggression are as credible as possible. States parties should take this into account in making decisions about the election of judges.

* * *

A separate, specific, concern is that the definition risks criminalising humanitarian interventions, thus impeding action designed to prevent the commission of ICC Statute crimes. In the words of former US Under Secretary for Civilian Security, Democracy and Human Rights, Sarah Sewall: 'We fear that one of the effects of activating the ICC's aggression jurisdiction will be to create new potential obstacles to military action when it is urgently needed to save innocent lives.'[17]

In my view, this concern is overstated: the better interpretation (one shared by a majority of commentators involved in the negotiations) is that unauthorised humanitarian interventions fall outside the definition of the crime of aggression.

This is not to assert that a humanitarian intervention exception to the prohibition on the use of force has crystallised under customary international law. On the contrary, like a majority of states and use-of-force experts, I am of the view that such uses of force violate Article 2(4) of the UN Charter. In my opinion, however, *genuine* humanitarian interventions are likely to be viewed by many in the international community as legitimate, despite the fact that they are unlawful. As such, while humanitarian interventions fall foul of the *jus ad bellum*, a majority do not consider that such uses of force should attract criminal sanction.

More to the point, the exclusion of humanitarian interventions was a key consideration in the crafting of the manifest violation threshold: indeed, it was frequently cited as the prime example of why a threshold was needed to exclude certain acts from the definition's scope.[18] As a member of the

---

[17] Sewall (n 7).
[18] Notes of the June 2006, June 2007, December 2007 and June 2008 Special Working Group on the Crime of Aggression, on file with author.

Australian Delegation to successive meetings of the Special Working Group on the Crime of Aggression (SWGCA), I can also personally attest to going to some lengths to ensure that certain meeting reports recorded the fact that the intention behind the threshold was to exclude acts of insufficient seriousness, as well as acts of contested legality.[19]

A very significant number of states affirmed that humanitarian interventions were excluded from the definition of the crime when the USA tabled a draft understanding at the Review Conference that would have made this explicit.[20] My reading is that the proposed understanding was rejected, not because a majority of states parties took a different view; rather, the majority considered the understanding to be unnecessary in light of the fact that the issue had been settled during the SWGCA's negotiations (as well as the fact that there was no desire to reopen negotiations at the late stage at which

---

[19] See Report of the Special Working Group on the Crime of Aggression (June 2008) ICC-ASP/6/20/Add.1: Report of the Special Working Group on the Crime of Aggression (June 2009) ICC-ASP/8/INF.2. This view is shared by others involved in the negotiations: S Barriga, 'Negotiating the Amendments on the Crime of Aggression' in S Barriga and C Kress (eds), *The Travaux Préparatoires of the Crime of Aggression* (Cambridge, Cambridge University Press, 2012) 29; C Kress, 'Time for Decision: Some Thoughts on the Immediate Future of the Crime of Aggression: A Reply to Andreas Paulus' (2009) 20(4) *European Journal of International Law* 1138; J Potter, 'The Threshold in the Proposed Definition of the Crime of Aggression' (2008) 6 *New Zealand Yearbook of International Law* 155, 165. See also Understanding 6, which provides that: 'It is understood that aggression is the most serious and dangerous form of the illegal use of force; and that a determination of whether an act of aggression has been committed requires consideration of all the circumstances of each particular case, including the gravity of the acts concerned and their consequences, in accordance with the Charter of the United Nations.' Understanding 7 provides: 'It is understood that in establishing whether an act of aggression constitutes a manifest violation of the Charter of the United Nations, the three components of character, gravity and scale must be sufficient to justify a 'manifest' determination. No one component can be significant enough to satisfy the manifest standard by itself.' The conclusions outlined here are reflected in a recent commentary by one of South Africa's legal advisers, who writes that the threshold provides important protection against the use of force pursuant to Art 4(h) of the Constitutive Act of the African Union (which refers to the right of the Union to intervene in Member States pursuant to a decision of the Assembly in respect of grave circumstances, namely: war crimes, genocide and crimes against humanity) being considered aggression: A Stemmet, 'South Africa' in Kress and Barriga (n 12) 1271, 1275. Similar conclusions are reached by M Gillett, 'The Anatomy of an International Crime: Aggression at the International Criminal Court' (2013) 13 *International Criminal Law Review* 829, 853; J Root, 'First Do No Harm: Interpreting the Crime of Aggression to Exclude Humanitarian Intervention' (2013–14) 2(4) *University of Baltimore Journal of International Law* 63; J Trahan, 'Defining the "Grey Area" where Humanitarian Intervention May Not Be Fully Legal, but Is Not the Crime of Aggression' (2015) 2(1) *Journal on the Use of Force and International Law* 42.

[20] The US proposal read: 'It is understood that, for the purposes of the Statute, an act cannot be considered to be a manifest violation of the United Nations Charter unless it would be objectively evident to any State conducting itself in the matter in accordance with normal practice and in good faith, and thus an act undertaken in connection with an effort to prevent the commission of any of the crimes contained in Articles 6, 7 or 8 of the Statute would not constitute an act of aggression.'

the USA—which had absented itself from the SWGCA's discussions—tabled its proposal).[21]

One might argue that there is nothing to prevent a politically motivated prosecutor from nonetheless seeking to investigate and prosecute humanitarian interventions. However, at the very least I think it is fair to say that it would be an unwise prosecutor who sought to use the resources of the Office of the Prosecutor to pursue an investigation into a genuine humanitarian intervention given the difficulty of proving that the definition of the crime was satisfied beyond reasonable doubt, not least because of the high degree of attention this issue has already received and the number of states parties on the record as expressing the view that there was an intention to exclude humanitarian interventions from the definition of the crime.

Thus, while any number of geopolitical considerations are likely to continue to make states hesitant to use force that has not been authorised by the Security Council to prevent or halt mass atrocity crimes, I do not share the view that this is a reason not to activate the ICC's jurisdiction over the crime or to promote wider ratification of the aggression amendments.

III. KEY CONCERNS RELATING TO THE JURISDICTIONAL PROVISIONS

The first and foremost concern of all of the P5 is that the jurisdictional provisions governing the Court's exercise of jurisdiction over the crime of aggression do not respect the Council's exclusive prerogative to determine the existence of acts of aggression under Article 39 of the UN Charter.

The P5's argument has primarily rested on assertions about the proper meaning of Articles 24 (conferring on the Council the 'primary responsibility for the maintenance of international peace and security'), 39 (stating that '[t]he Security Council shall determine the existence of any ... act of aggression') and 103 (providing that in the event of a conflict between the obligations of States under the Charter and their obligations under any other international agreement, 'their obligations under the present Charter shall prevail').

France has said that consistency with the Charter is 'an essential condition to be met for the credibility and universality of the Court', suggesting that

---

[21] Claus Kress, a member of the German Delegation, who facilitated the final negotiation of the Understandings adopted alongside the amendments to the Statute, shares this assessment: see C Kress and L von Holtzendorff, 'The Kampala Compromise on the Crime of Aggression' (2010) 8 *Journal of International Criminal Justice* 1179, 1205. It is important to note that some states parties were also not prepared to support express language that could be interpreted to suggest that humanitarian interventions are lawful.

any other approach 'would imperil the conditions for its success'.[22] According to Russia, this is not a matter of 'excessive formalism' or an attempt to safeguard the P5's special powers, '[r]ather, it is a position in defence of the integrity of the UN Charter and the international legal order created by it'.[23]

Russia is equally concerned about the effect of conflicting decisions of the ICC and the Council, which it says runs the risk of 'undermining the stability of international relations and the credibility of international criminal justice'.[24] According to China, this would have a polarising effect on the international community as it tries to address a threat to international peace and security and thus risks destabilising the international legal order.[25]

The idea that the Security Council has the exclusive competence to identify acts of aggression is something that the overwhelming majority of states have rejected, and I would argue is unsustainable as a matter of law. As I have detailed elsewhere,[26] the mandatory language in Article 39 in relation to the identification of acts of aggression relates to the requirement that the Council identify acts of aggression (or threats to, or breaches of, the peace) as a precondition to making recommendations or taking enforcement action under Chapter VII of the UN Charter. The Council's powers under Article 39 in relation to the maintenance or restoration of international peace and security are not relevant to any judicial processes, not least the determination of individual criminal responsibility. The notion that the Council enjoys an exclusive right to identify acts of aggression is equally illusory: the ICJ has stressed that the Council's responsibilities under Article 24 are *only* primary, not exclusive. Indeed, both the General Assembly and the ICJ can determine the existence of an act of aggression. As such, it is difficult to see the P5's position as anything other than a blatant attempt to protect the P5's vested interest in an expansive reading of the Council's powers.

The problem of a conflict between the Council and the ICC is also exaggerated. UN Member States are acutely aware that Council decisions are often made on the basis of political expediency, and that at other times the Council is paralysed by the use, or threat of use, of the veto. I do not think that any state would be surprised if the ICC reached a conclusion that a crime of aggression had been committed in a situation where the Council had failed to act. The different decision-making processes of the Council and the Court are well understood. As such, it is difficult to accept that the

---

[22] E Belliard, 'France' in Kress and Barriga (n 12) 1143, 1147–48. The opinions expressed in this chapter are stated to be personal, but echo views expressed publicly by France at the UN. See also, for the UK's position, C Whomersley, 'United Kingdom' in Kress and Barriga (n 12) 1285, 1287. This appears to be a statement of official UK views.

[23] G Kuzmin and I Panin, 'Russia' in Kress and Barriga (n 12) 1264, 1267. This appears to be a statement of official Russian views.

[24] ibid, 1267.

[25] Lulu (n 12) 1137.

[26] See McDougall (n 14) 205–34.

Council's role in the maintenance of international peace and security would be undermined—or at least not undermined to any greater degree than it has already been on the basis of existing critiques—by an ICC determination that an act of aggression had been committed in respect of a situation where the Council had been silent.

This conclusion is strengthened by the fact that the Security Council and the ICJ can exercise concurrent jurisdiction, which necessarily implies a possibility of different conclusions being reached by those two bodies in relation to a use of force.[27] Indeed, the possibility of conflicting decisions between the Council and the ICC already exists: consider, for example, the need for the ICC to determine whether there was an IAC in the context of its deliberations on war crimes. As such, there is no basis for claims that the exercise of the ICC's jurisdiction over aggression has the potential to throw the international security system into disarray.

* * *

The compromise reached in order to evade the Security Council's exclusive control over prosecutions for the crime of aggression was a regime that, in the case of state referrals and *proprio motu* investigations, completely excludes the nationals of non-states parties from the ICC's jurisdiction (Article 15*bis*(5))[28] and allows states parties to opt out of the Court's jurisdiction over the crime (Article 15*bis*(4)).

The proper interpretation of the 'opt-out provision' is the primary focus of a number of states parties that have outstanding reservations in relation to the crime. It thus deserves to be examined in some detail.

Article 15*bis*(4) provides that:

> The Court may, in accordance with Article 12, exercise jurisdiction over a crime of aggression, arising from an act of aggression committed by a State Party, unless that State Party has previously declared that it does not accept such jurisdiction by lodging a declaration with the Registrar. The withdrawal of such a declaration may be effected at any time and shall be considered by the State Party within three years.

The key question requiring resolution is whether ratification of the aggression amendments by the state that is the victim of an act of aggression is sufficient to enable the Court to exercise jurisdiction over the national of a non-ratifying aggressor state (provided the aggressor state has not opted out

---

[27] R St J MacDonald, 'Changing Relations Between the International Court of Justice and the Security Council of the United Nations' (1993) 31(3) *Canadian Yearbook of International Law* 17.

[28] Art 15*bis*(5) ICC Statute reads: 'In respect of a State that is not a party to this Statute, the Court shall not exercise its jurisdiction over the crime of aggression when committed by that State's nationals or on its territory.' As such, individuals are excluded from the Court's jurisdiction regardless of whether their state of nationality was the purported victim or aggressor state.

before committing an act of aggression). Put another way, can states parties avoid the ICC's jurisdiction over aggression by not ratifying the amendments, or do they actively need to opt out?

The case being made by the USA,[29] the UK,[30] France,[31] China[32] and others is that Article 15*bis* was adopted under Article 121(5) of the ICC Statute and must be read as subject to it. Article 121(5) provides that the amendments that it governs

> shall enter into force for those States Parties which have accepted the amendment one year after the deposit of their instruments of ratification or acceptance. In respect of a State Party which has not accepted the amendment, the Court shall not exercise its jurisdiction regarding a crime covered by the amendment when committed by that State Party's nationals or on its territory.

According to these states, Article 121(5) must be read as limiting the Court's jurisdictional reach over perpetrators of crimes covered by an amendment when committed by a national or on the territory of a state party that has not accepted the amendment—regardless of whether the amendments have been accepted by another state whose nationals or territory are involved—thereby derogating from the ICC Statute's jurisdictional regime as set out in Article 12(2).[33] In other words, it is asserted that both the aggressor and the victim state must have ratified the amendments (and the aggressor state must not have opted out) in order for the Court to have jurisdiction.

This interpretation, however, disregards both the negotiating history of the jurisdictional provisions and key elements of the text of both the amendments and Resolution RC/Res.6 under which they were adopted.

In the SWGCA, there were two key debates about jurisdiction and entry into force that are relevant here. First, there was a debate over which amendment provision of the ICC Statute (Article 121(4) or (5))[34] should govern the aggression amendments, arising from the fact that the amendment provisions were finalised in Rome in 1998 in parallel with the crime of

---

[29] Koh and Buchwald (n 9) 279.
[30] Whomersley (n 22) 1288.
[31] Belliard (n 22) 1147.
[32] Lulu 1138–39.
[33] In relevant part, Art 12(2) provides that the Court will have jurisdiction where at least one of the states on whose territory the conduct in question occurred, or the state of nationality of the alleged perpetrator, has ratified the amendments.
[34] Art 121(4) ICC Statute provides that: 'Except as provided in paragraph 5, an amendment shall enter into force for all States Parties one year after instruments of ratification or acceptance have been deposited with the Secretary-General of the United Nations by seven-eighths of them.' Art 121(5), quoted above, applies to 'any amendment to articles 5, 6, 7 and 8'. The problem was that while Art 121(5) appears to have been intended to apply to amendments to the definitions of ICC Statute crimes, with the exception of the deletion of the aggression placeholder in Art 5(2), the aggression amendments (Arts 8*bis*, 15*bis*, 15*ter* and consequential changes made to Arts 9(1) and 20(3) and the addition of para 3*bis* to Art 25) do not concern the Articles to which Art 121(5) is stated to apply.

aggression placeholder being negotiated and, on their face, neither clearly applies.

Second, there was a debate over the proper interpretation of the second sentence of Article 121(5) and whether it in fact has the effect outlined above (known as the 'negative interpretation'), or whether it was intended to provide that the fact a crime was committed by a national of a state party that has not accepted the amendments, or on the territory of such a state party, does not confer jurisdiction on the Court—but at the same time does not preclude the ordinary exercise of the ICC's jurisdiction in accordance with Article 12 (known as the 'positive interpretation').[35]

There was essentially a difference of views between one group of states that was firmly of the view that the alleged aggressor state must have consented before the ICC could exercise jurisdiction, and an opposing camp that hoped to secure protection from crimes of aggression through the operation of the ICC Statute's ordinary jurisdictional regime.

These debates were unresolved at the opening of the Review Conference in Kampala. The breakthrough proposal, which contained the key elements of the compromise that was ultimately adopted (ie the availability of the opt-out for states parties plus the complete exclusion of non-states parties, in the case of state referrals and *proprio motu* investigations), was jointly made by the authors of competing proposals and proponents of the two opposing camps: Canada (in favour of aggressor state consent) and Argentina, Brazil and Switzerland (in favour of the application of the Article 12 jurisdictional regime). In its original formulation the 'CABS' proposal articulated the matter clearly:

> The Court may exercise its jurisdiction over the crime of aggression committed by a State Party's nationals or on its territory in accordance with article 12, unless that State Party has filed a declaration of its non-acceptance of the jurisdiction of the Court under paragraph 4 of this article.

In essence, Article 15*bis*(4) provides a soft consent-based regime, where the consent of existing ICC Statute states parties is assumed—unless they opt out.[36] As the President of the Assembly of States Parties at the time

---

[35] Importantly, states parties agreed that although the conduct of a perpetrator responsible for the crime of aggression typically occurs on the territory of the aggressor state, the crime can equally be said to have been committed on the territory of the victim state, where the consequences of that conduct are felt. As such, the reference in Art 12(2) to 'the State on the territory of which the conduct in question occurred' is understood to apply to the territory of both the aggressor and victim states. See Report of the Special Working Group on the Crime of Aggression (November 2008) ICC-ASP/7/SWGCA/1, paras 28–29 and Report of the Special Working Group on the Crime of Aggression (February 2009) ICC-ASP/7/SWGCA/2, paras 38–39.

[36] That this was the effect of the CABS proposal is confirmed in a commentary by the Brazilian contributors to the joint proposal: see M Biato and M Bohlke, 'Brazil' in Kress and Barriga (n 12) 1117, 1128.

(Liechtenstein's Permanent Representative to the UN, Christian Wenaweser) and his legal adviser (Stefan Barriga), who were intimately involved in the negotiation of the jurisdictional provisions, have written, this was not a compromise that was at the mid-point of the two opposing camps, rather: 'It was much closer to the position of the consent-oriented delegations, since it excluded non-States Parties entirely and since opting out was—at least legally—extremely easy to do.'[37]

As Wenaweser and Barriga explain, what had to be done at the Review Conference after this breakthrough proposal was tabled was to reconcile the emerging consensus for an opt-out system with the second sentence of Article 121(5). Their approach was 'to stress the unique position of the crime of aggression in the Rome Statute':[38]

> [W]e came to the conclusion that the legal key for an opt-out approach was to read article 121(5) in the context of other provisions of the Rome Statute, including articles 5 and 12. We therefore emphasized that States Parties to the Rome Statute had already opted into the Court's jurisdiction over the crime of aggression, precisely by ratifying the Statute in its original version. The first paragraph of article 12 of the Rome Statute states that any party to the Rome Statute 'accepts the jurisdiction of the Court with respect to crimes referred to in article 5', which explicitly includes the crime of aggression.[39]

This sui generis approach, which essentially provides that the second sentence of Article 121(5) does not apply to the aggression amendments, was amply recorded in Kampala. Subsequent versions of the jurisdictional provisions circulated among delegations added a reference to the Court exercising jurisdiction in accordance with Article 12(1). To give this phrase any meaning, it has to be understood as importing the ordinary jurisdictional regime of the ICC Statute. Competing 'understandings' on the positive and negative interpretation were also deleted—on the basis that the question had become moot. The draft resolution under which the amendments were to be adopted incorporated new references to Articles 5(2) and 12(1) and stressed in operative paragraph 1 (OP1) that a state party can lodge an opt-out declaration prior to ratification or acceptance of the amendments. OP1 also states that the amendments are adopted in accordance with Article 5(2) (as distinct from Article 121(3), which is the provision on adoption that directly relates to Article 121(5)). In addition, OP1 states that the amendments 'shall enter into force' in accordance with Article 121(5). The second

---

[37] C Wenaweser and S Barriga, 'Forks in the Road: Personal Reflections on Negotiating the Kampala Amendments on the Crime of Aggression' in S Linton, G Simpson and WA Schabas (eds), *For the Sake of Present and Future Generations: Essays on International Law, Crime and Justice in Honour of Roger S Clark* (Lieden, Brill Nijhoff, 2015) 283, 290–91.

[38] ibid, 292.

[39] ibid, 291. See also Biato and Bohlke (n 36) 1128.

sentence of Article 121(5) does not relate to entry into force; rather it determines the conditions for the exercise of jurisdiction. And of course there is nothing in Article 15*bis*(4) that limits its scope to state party aggressors that have ratified the amendments—rather it applies to all states parties.

For completeness, it should also be noted that Article 15*bis*(5), which exempts non-states parties from the Court's jurisdiction over the crime of aggression, mirrors the language of Article 121(5)'s second sentence. The very fact that Article 121(5) language has been employed with regard to non-states parties but not in relation to states parties not accepting the amendments points to the fact that a distinction must be made between the operation of the two paragraphs. Article 15*bis*(5) provides that the Court 'shall not exercise jurisdiction' over non-states parties and provides no exceptions thereto. In contrast, under Article 15*bis*(4), the Court 'may … exercise jurisdiction over' a state party 'unless' that party has lodged an opt-out declaration. The variances between these two paragraphs highlight the differences between Article 15*bis*(4) and Article 121(5)'s second sentence.

As emphasised by Wenaweser and Barriga, the interpretation being advocated for by the USA, the UK, France and others represents something above and beyond what the proponents of the negative interpretation of Article 121(5) pressed for in the lead up to Kampala, and is not consistent with a good-faith interpretation of the amendments. Lodging an opt-out declaration without ratifying the aggression amendments also only makes sense if the Court can exercise jurisdiction over a state party that has not ratified the amendments on the basis of a jurisdictional link under Article 12(2) created by another state's acceptance of the amendments. In their own words:

> Of course an opt-out clause only makes sense if the default position is 'in'! Otherwise, the system would first require States Parties to opt in, and then allow them to opt out—an entirely absurd approach in this context, and one that no delegation ever advocated for during and prior to Kampala.[40]

That some creativity was employed in devising the jurisdictional provisions is not in dispute. But it is equally beyond doubt that the amendment provisions were not a neat fit for the crime of aggression and that no solution (short of amending the amendment provisions, which was not something

---

[40] Wenaweser and Barriga (n 37) 292. See also S Barriga and N Blokker, 'Conditions for the Exercise of Jurisdiction Based on State Referrals and *Proprio Motu* Investigations' in Kress and Barriga (n 12) 657, 669–70. It has been argued that a state party that ratifies the amendments and then opts out receives the benefit of protection against acts of aggression, in that a crime of aggression committed against an opting-out state party by a national of a ratifying state party that has not opted out would fall within the Court's jurisdiction. However, as this would be an abrogation of the negative interpretation of Art 121(5)'s second sentence, the argument provides little proof of the applicability of the second sentence or the negative interpretation thereof. There is also no rational explanation for why states parties opposed to the negative interpretation would not only have agreed to its application but also to additional provisions that provide even greater benefits to non-accepting aggressor states parties.

that states parties were willing to consider) could have escaped the charge of invention. While Japan in particular has argued to the contrary,[41] I am firmly of the view that states parties had the power to adopt an interpretation of the amendment provisions that was fit for purpose.[42]

That the Court may exercise jurisdiction over the crime of aggression in situations where the victim state has ratified the amendments and the aggressor state has not ratified them but also not opted out represents the prevailing view—particularly among those most intimately involved in the crime-of-aggression negotiations.[43] It is further supported by the first opt-out declaration to have been lodged (by Kenya, which has not ratified the amendments).[44]

---

[41] Statements of Japan in *Official Records*, ICC Doc RC/11 (2010), Annex VII: Statements by States Parties in Explanation of Position before the Adoption of Resolution RC/Res.6 on the Crime of Aggression (at 121) and Annex VIII: Statements by States Parties in Explanation of Position after the Adoption of resolution RC/Res.6 on the Crime of Aggression (at 122). While written in his personal capacity, see also I Komatsu, 'Japan' in Kress and Barriga (n 12) 1217, 1231.

[42] The same conclusion is reached by S Barriga and N Blokker, 'Entry into Force and Conditions for the Exercise of Jurisdiction: Cross-Cutting Issues' in Kress and Barriga (n 12) 621, 632. It is emphasised in this context that Understanding 2 states that, in the case of Security Council referral, the Court may exercise jurisdiction over a crime of aggression 'irrespective of whether the State concerned has accepted the Court's jurisdiction in this regard'. That the Court should be able to exercise jurisdiction over non-ratifying states parties in the case of Security Council referral was never subject to any real dispute—despite the fact that this contradicts the wording of the second sentence of Art 121(5), which does not make an exception for Council referrals. Equally, Art 121(5) is silent as regards to non-states parties—but proponents of the negative interpretation were not comfortable with non-states parties being treated any differently to non-ratifying states parties, and thus insisted that they have like treatment under the provision. This demonstrates that even the strongest proponents of the negative interpretation were unwilling to apply it without modification. See further DM Ferencz, 'Current US Policy on the Crime of Aggression: History in the Unmaking' (2016) 48 *Case Western Reserve Journal of International Law* 189, 208.

[43] YS Kim, 'Republic of Korea (South Korea)' in Kress and Barriga (n 12) 1234, 1237–38; D Momtaz and EB Hamaneh, 'Iran' in Kress and Barriga (n 12) 1174, 1185; AR Coracini, 'The International Criminal Court's Exercise of Jurisdiction Over the Crime of Aggression—at Last … in Reach … Over Some' (2010) 2(2) *Goettingen Journal of International Law* 768–69; Kress and von Holtzendorff, (n 21) 1179; R Clark, 'Amendments to the Rome Statute of the International Criminal Court Considered at the first Review Conference on the Court, Kampala, 31 May–11 June 2010' (2010) 2 *Goettingen Journal of International Law* 2; W Schabas, 'The Kampala Review Conference: A Brief Assessment' (17 June 2010) huamrightsdoctorate. blogspot.com/2010/06/kampala-review-conference-brief-assessment; Ferencz (n 42) 208. For my own more detailed analysis, see McDougall (n 14) 234–62. It should be noted that at least Koh and Buchwald have misrepresented this common position in their written commentaries. They have described the argument as stating that 'the Court would—upon ratification by thirty states and the making of the necessary decision after January 1, 2017—exercise jurisdiction over any case of aggression involving a Rome Statute party *even if none of the alleged "aggressor states" and none of the alleged "victim states" had ratified the amendments*, on the theory that the Rome Statute party had already accepted the Court's jurisdiction by becoming party to the Rome Statute' (Koh and Buchwald (n 9) 285). As outlined above, this is not what I, or others involved in the negotiations who share this view, are in fact arguing.

[44] See Note Verbale, 'Declaration of Non Acceptance of Jurisdiction of the International Criminal Court Pertaining to the Crime of Aggression Pursuant to Paragraph 4 of Article 15bis of the Rome Statute Government of Kenya' (30 November 2015) MFA. INT. 8/14A VOL. X (86).

Contrary to what the USA has alleged, the interpretation outlined above does not violate the *pacta tertiis* rule: the aggression amendments do not create either obligations or rights for non-ratifying states parties without their consent—just as Article 12 of the ICC Statute does not create rights or obligations for non-states parties. Rather it creates a mechanism to enforce the existing right to prosecute individuals on the basis of the territorial or nationality bases of criminal jurisdiction.[45]

The real issue of course is that states parties that have outstanding reservations regarding the Court's exercise of jurisdiction over the crime of aggression would like to avoid the political cost of having to lodge opt-out declarations. But this was precisely the point behind the jurisdictional regime that was constructed. The Court's jurisdiction can be avoided—but not without undermining the ability of the state concerned to claim that its uses of force are lawful, and not without weakening the legitimacy of such states' wish to police the use of force.

That said, this debate does strike me as something of a storm in a teacup. As Liechtenstein has pointed out to states parties that wish to maintain an alternative interpretation of Article 15*bis*(4), in order to escape the Court's jurisdiction all they need do is lodge an opt-out declaration providing that, in their view, as a matter of law, they do not accept that the Court can exercise jurisdiction over alleged crimes of aggression committed by their nationals unless and until they ratify the amendments.[46] Proffering such a legal interpretation in the form of an opt-out declaration would have exactly the same effect as saying that one merely did not wish to be subjected to the Court's scrutiny—although it could be sold to constituents as upholding the rule of law, rather than trying to hide from it.

IV. KEY CONCERNS RELATING TO THE SUPPOSED IMPACT ON INTERNATIONAL PEACE AND SECURITY

Separate to concerns about the shape of the amendments adopted in 2010, a number of concerns have been raised by sceptics in relation to the supposed impact that the amendments will have on international peace and security.

It has been argued that activating the crime of aggression will overburden the Court and distract it from its 'core mandate', which, according to the

---

[45] The USA made a similar argument in relation to Art 12(2) of the ICC Statute when it was adopted, which has been widely rejected. See AR Coracini, '"Amended Most Serious Crimes": A New Category of Crimes within the Jurisdiction but Out of the Reach of the International Criminal Court?' (2008) 21 *Leiden Journal of International Law* 699, 703; MP Scharf, 'The ICC's Jurisdiction over Nationals of Non-Party States: A Critique of the US Position' (2001) 64 *Law and Contemporary Problems* 67, 98; D Akande, 'The Jurisdiction of the International Criminal Court over Nationals of Non-Parties: Legal Basis and Limits' (2003) 1 *Journal of International Criminal Justice* 618, 620.

[46] 'Seminar for States Parties to the Rome Statute of the ICC on the Activation of the Court's Jurisdiction over the Crime of Aggression' (17–18 June 2016) on file with author.

United States, is deterring and punishing war crimes, crimes against humanity and genocide. While stressing the USA's support for the Court, Sewall has argued that the ICC is still working to 'establish and sustain a record of effectiveness in the basic functions by which its success will be measured, such as apprehending defendants, protecting its witnesses, and prosecuting cases already underway'. In that context she asks: 'How will a Court that is already struggling to fulfil its core mandate respond to the additional burden of the kind of decisions it would make under the Kampala amendments?'[47]

This is another exaggeration. The notion that the Court is going to become inundated with aggression prosecutions is based neither on the past precedent of its practice, nor on the frequency of the commission of acts of aggression that could plausibly be said to meet the manifest-violation threshold beyond a reasonable doubt. Indeed, if anything, it seems more likely that investigations and prosecutions for the crime of aggression will be few and far between. And of course, it is the responsibility of states parties to ensure that the Court has all of the resources that it needs to execute its mandate.

The USA has asserted that the activation of the aggression amendments also risks making conflicts more difficult to resolve. Noting that peace agreements commonly avoid assigning blame for the initiation of a conflict, it has suggested that while there is now a broad consensus that amnesties should not be extended to other ICC Statute crimes, it is not clear that there is a similar consensus view that crimes of aggression should not go unpunished.[48]

This is an assertion that it is difficult to accept. State leaders already face investigation and prosecution for genocide, crimes against humanity and war crimes, which are perpetrated in the context of many unlawful uses of inter-state armed force. There is, moreover, no plausible reason to draw a distinction between aggression and other ICC Statute crimes when it comes to the benefits of transitional justice: punishing leaders for crimes of aggression may usefully signal a break with the past, blunting the desire for revenge in the target state and creating the conditions for a return to peace. And the objective, of course, is that as a result of the criminalisation of acts of aggression there will be fewer IACs in the first place.

Perhaps most tellingly, the USA has argued that leaders' fears about prosecution for the crime of aggression will have a chilling effect, such that the crime will discourage states from using lawful and appropriate force.[49] Of course, states that are committed to acting in accordance with their

---

[47] Sewall (n 7). See also Koh and Buchwald (n 9) 262; HH Koh and TF Buchwald, 'United States' in Kress and Barriga (n 12) 1290, 1295.

[48] Sewall (n 7). See also Koh and Buchwald (n 9) 263.

[49] Koh and Buchwald (n 9) 272.

international legal obligations in relation to the use of force have no reason to fear the activation of the ICC's jurisdiction over the crime of aggression, or to back away from their military alliances. In this regard, it is important to note that a number of NATO members have ratified, or are in the process of ratifying, the aggression amendments, suggesting that the USA's arguments are not gaining traction with its allies. Of course, any ambiguity about the legality of the use of force could always be avoided by a Security Council authorisation. In this way, the activation of the ICC's jurisdiction over the crime of aggression, so long resisted by the P5, may ironically become a strong argument for why the Council should step up and meet its responsibilities in relation to the maintenance and restoration of international peace and security.

Most importantly, however, given the inevitable death and destruction occasioned by any inter-state use of armed force, the fact that leaders may pause for thought before committing their militaries to international operations is not a bad thing.

V. CONCLUSION

The above-outlined critiques are not the only ones that have been directed toward the aggression amendments, but they are the ones that have been voiced by states with outstanding concerns in relation to the activation of the ICC's jurisdiction over the crime. It should also be emphasised that these concerns do not exclusively belong to the P5 (just that it is their views that dominate the public record).

At the time of writing, states parties are considering these issues in a facilitation on the activation of the ICC's jurisdiction over the crime of aggression established by the ASP.[50] The ASP agreed to establish the facilitation in order to give states parties a forum to air outstanding concerns, and in the hope that an activation decision can be made by consensus.

It remains to be seen whether states parties will resist what seems likely to be an inordinate amount of pressure from P5 members to reshape the aggression amendments or to thwart their effective implementation. My hope is that a majority of states parties will honour the commitment made in Kampala in 2010 to activate the Court's jurisdiction over the amendments as soon as possible, and ratify the amendments. In doing so, states parties will demonstrate their support for the ICC, help strengthen the rule

---

[50] See 'Strengthening the International Criminal Court' (n 5) Annex I to ICC-ASP/15/Res.5, para 18(b). The facilitation is mandated to 'make every effort to reach consensus' and to 'submit a written report directly to the Assembly ahead of its sixteenth session'. It is open to states parties only.

of law, underline their commitment to meeting their obligations in relation to the use of force, and—most importantly—help to deter the most serious forms of the illegal use of force. For the importance of the crime of aggression will not be measured by the number of sentences handed down by the Court.[51] Rather, it will be reflected in the caution taken by parliaments responsible for the authorisation of the use of force and in the decisions of leaders for whom the prospect of criminal punishment will be a factor in foreign policy decision-making. While this may be a concrete consideration for the leaders of states parties only, the court of public opinion will be able to point to the definition of the crime, which will create pressure to abide by international law's obligations even without the spectre of trial and punishment. In this way, the crime of aggression has the potential to prevent the deaths of countless victims. For this reason it deserves our support.

---

[51] S Wasum-Rainer, 'Germany' in Kress and Barriga (n 12) 1149, 1152.

17

Elements and Innovations in a New Global Treaty on Crimes Against Humanity

LEILA NADYA SADAT

I. THE EMERGENCE OF CRIMES AGAINST HUMANITY AT NUREMBERG

I N THE 1930s and 1940s, the world was shaken to its core. Germany, led by Adolf Hitler, launched a war of aggression, beginning with the invasion of Poland in September 1939. The conflict led to an estimated 50 million deaths and a campaign of atrocities so barbaric in its conception and savage in its implementation that statesmen and international lawyers struggled to find language that could fully describe the scope—and the illegality—of the horror it generated. Racial and religious discrimination became legalised; slave labour was used to support the war effort; ghettos effectively incarcerated, facilitating the destruction of entire populations; trains conveyed men, women and children in abject and inhumane conditions to work in extermination camps; human beings became the subjects of ghastly medical experiments—all as the war itself was carried out with atrocious ferocity.[1] Faced with the devastation that the war had wrought, a controversial decision was taken to conduct a trial of the Nazi leaders (and, subsequently, the Japanese)[2] after the war had been won on the grounds that the actions of the accused were 'so calculated, so malignant, and so

---

[1] See 'Trial of Major War Criminals before the International Military Tribunal', vol I (Nuremberg, 14 November–1 October 1946) 226–53.

[2] *Punishment for War Crimes. The Inter-Allied Declaration Signed at St James's Palace, London, on 13 January 1942, and Relative Documents. Issued by the Inter-Allied Information Committee, London* (HMSO, 1942). For a history of the debates concerning whether or not to conduct a trial, see WR Harris, *Tyranny on Trial* (Dallas, Southern Methodist University Press, 1999).

devastating, that civilization cannot tolerate their being ignored, because it cannot survive their being repeated'.[3]

Thus it was that 'crimes against humanity' entered the international lexicon.[4] This new crime was defined in the Charters of the International Military Tribunals at Nuremberg[5] and Tokyo,[6] which were tasked with the conduct of the trials, as murder, extermination, deportation, enslavement, persecutions and 'other inhumane acts' committed against a civilian population.[7]

This sparse definition provided more questions than answers about the nature of crimes against humanity and its legal elements, as did the judgments of the International Military Tribunals, which were relatively laconic on the subject. Moreover, although the trials may have been necessary preconditions to the re-establishment of peace and the reckonings of wrongs, they were not sufficient to fully heal the world from events that 'sprang from the darkest zone of man'.[8] Indeed, no purely legal definition could fully capture the suffering of their victims or the horror of those bearing witness to their terror. Their widespread nature, their systematicity, their extraordinary cruelty and their debasement of what it means to be human—all these elements were included in one terrible crime, charged at Nuremberg and Tokyo, and subsequently adopted by the UN General Assembly[9] and the International Law Commission.[10] In theory, this transformed 'crimes against humanity' from rhetorical flourish to a category of offences condemned by international law for which individuals could be tried and punished. In fact, however, because no global treaty on crimes against humanity was ever proposed or negotiated, their effective prosecution remained tenuous and uncertain.

---

[3] 'Trial of Major War Criminals before the International Military Tribunal' (n 1) vol II, 98–99.

[4] The crime has a long historic pedigree, however. LN Sadat, 'Crimes Against Humanity in the Modern Age' (2013) 107 *American Journal of International Law* 334, 337 n 16 and sources cited. See also S Szurek, 'Historique: La Formation du droit international pénal' in H Ascensio, E Decaux and A Pellet (eds), *Droit International Pénal*, 2nd edn (Paris, Editions A Pedone, 2012) 21, 21–23.

[5] Agreement for the Prosecution and Punishment of Major War Criminals of the European Axis, and Establishing the Charter of the International Military Tribunal (IMT) (8 August 1945) 82 UNTS 279 (IMT Charter).

[6] Charter of the International Military Tribunal for the Far East (entered into force 19 January 1946, as amended 26 April 1946) TIAS No 1589 (IMFTE Charter).

[7] IMT Charter (n 5) Art 6(c) and IMFTE Charter (n 6) Art 5(c).

[8] E Wiesel, *Night* (London, Macmillan, 2006) ix.

[9] UNGA, 'Affirmation of the Principles of International Law Recognized by the Charter of the Nuremberg Tribunal: Report of the Sixth Committee' (11 December 1946) UN Doc A/236, 1144 (also appears as UNGA Res 95(I) (11 December 1946) UN Doc A/64/Add.1, 188).

[10] Documents of the Second Session Including the Report of the Commission to the General Assembly in 'Yearbook of the International Law Commission' vol I (1950) UN Doc A/CN.4.SER.A/1950/Add.I.

In early drafts of the IMT Charter, what came to be called crimes against humanity were referred to as 'atrocities and persecutions and deportations on political, racial or religious grounds'.[11] It was not until relatively late in the negotiations that the words 'crimes against humanity' appeared. A note by Robert Jackson, chief negotiator and later Chief Prosecutor for the United States, indicated that the intention was to make sure that 'we are reaching persecution, etc, of Jews and others in Germany as well as outside of it, and before as well as after commencement of the war'.[12] Sir Hersch Lauterpacht, himself a refugee from the Nazis,[13] had proposed the addition to the text.[14]

As the term 'crimes against humanity' was being inserted into the Nuremberg and Tokyo Charters, another new legal category was also emerging in reaction to the Nazis' targeting of European Jews, namely the crime of genocide. Proposed by another refugee scholar, Rafael Lemkin,[15] 'genocide' criminalised crimes against humanity committed against groups qua groups. Although the term made its way only sparingly into the Nuremberg trial itself,[16] in 1948, this aggravated form of crimes against humanity was made the subject of a new international convention. Subsequently, the Apartheid Convention (1973), and the more recently adopted Convention on Enforced Disappearance (2006) recognised certain offences as crimes against humanity,[17] but enforcement of these treaties has been relatively limited.

---

[11] 'Revised Draft of Agreement and Memorandum Submitted by American Delegation, June 30, 1945', in Report of RH Jackson, US Representative to the International Conference on Military Trials, London 1945 (US Department of State, 1949) 119, 121.

[12] 'Notes on Proposed Definition of "Crimes", Submitted by American Delegation, July 31, 1945', in Jackson, ibid.

[13] P Sands, *East West Street: On the Origins of 'Genocide' and 'Crimes Against Humanity'* (London, Weidenfeld & Nicolson, 2016).

[14] E Lauterparcht, *The Life of Sir Hersch Lauterpacht* (Cambridge, Cambridge University Press, 2010) 272; See also P Sands, 'My Legal Hero: Hersch Lauterpacht' *The Guardian*, 10 November 2010; M Koskenniemi, 'Hersch Lauterpacht and the Development of International Criminal Law' (2004) 2 *Journal of International Criminal Justice* 810, 811; P Sands, 'Twin Peaks: The Hersch Lauterpacht Draft Nuremberg Speeches' (2013) 1 *Cambridge Journal of International and Comparative Law* 37.

[15] In an eerie coincidence revealed recently through the work of Sands, it turns out that Lemkin and Lauterpacht were from and fled the same town in occupied Poland; Sands (n 13).

[16] Sands notes that it was included in the indictment as well as the closing statement of Lord Shawcross (Sands (n 13) 188–90), who led the British prosecution team, using Lemkin's word but holding 'back from embracing the fullness of its meaning' (ibid, 335).

[17] See International Convention on the Suppression and Punishment of the Crime of Apartheid (adopted 30 November 1973, entered into force 18 July 1976) 1015 UNTS 243; International Convention on Enforced Disappearances (adopted 20 December 2006, entered into force 23 December 2010) 2716 UNTS 3 (CED).

II. POST-WAR PROSECUTIONS FOR CRIMES AGAINST HUMANITY

Following the war, crimes against humanity seeped into the legal systems of a handful of countries that had domesticated the crime, including Canada, France, Israel and Poland. Israel prosecuted Adolf Eichmann, for example,[18] which many credit with leading to the German Auschwitz trials.[19] France also conducted a series of trials relying upon the Nuremberg Charter, convicting not only Klaus Barbie, the infamous Butcher of Lyon, but two French participants in the Vichy regime of crimes against humanity.[20] Poland also conducted trials from 1946 to 1948.[21] But these cases were the exception, not the rule, and all involved a link to World War II. (The Polish cases only tried Nazi defendants, for example.)[22]

It was not until the fall of Communism in 1989 and the establishment of the International Criminal Tribunals for the former Yugoslavia and Rwanda by the Security Council[23] that crimes against humanity—and genocide—were once more used in a practical manner to charge individuals who had committed atrocities with crimes under international law.[24] Those tribunals, and their progeny, the Special Court for Sierra Leone, the Extraordinary Chambers in the Courts of Cambodia, and the Special Panels for the Prosecution of Serious Crimes in East Timor, have elaborated a rich jurisprudence defining further the elements of the crime. Unfortunately, however, the statutes of each of the five ad hoc institutions have different definitions of the crime, leading to confusion about its contours and meaning. The International Law Commission continued to work on defining the crime under customary international law in the 1991 and 1996 versions of the Draft Code of Crimes,[25] choosing a course that built upon

---

[18] *Attorney General of Israel v Eichmann* 36 ILR 5 (1961) aff'd 36 ILR 277 (1962).

[19] See generally R Wittmann, *Beyond Justice: The Auschwitz Trial* (Cambridge, MA, Harvard University Press, 2005); DO Pendas, *The Frankfurt Auschwitz Trial, 1963–1965: Genocide, History, and the Limits of the Law* (Cambridge, Cambridge University Press, 2006). See also LN Sadat, 'The Nuremberg Trial, Seventy Years Later' (2016) 15 *Washington University Global Studies Law Review* 575.

[20] See eg LN Sadat, 'The Interpretation of the Nuremberg Principles by the French Court of Cassation: From Touvier to Barbie and Back Again' (1994) 32 *Columbia Journal of Transnational Law* 296 (formerly Wexler); RJ Golsan (ed), *The Papon Affair: Memory and Justice on Trial* (London, Routledge, 2000).

[21] MA Drumbl, 'Stepping Beyond Nuremberg's Halo: The Legacy of the Supreme National Tribunal of Poland' (2015) 13 *Journal of International Criminal Justice 5*, 1.

[22] ibid.

[23] Statute of the International Criminal Tribunal for the Former Yugoslavia (adopted 25 May 1993, as last amended 17 May 2002); Statute of the International Criminal Tribunal for Rwanda (accessed 8 November 1994, as last amended on 13 October 2006).

[24] See eg *The Prosecutor v Jean-Paul Akayesu* (Judgment) ICTR-96-4-T (2 September 1998); *Prosecutor v Tadić* (Judgment) ICTY-94-1-T (7 May 1997).

[25] The ILC took up the question of crimes against humanity as part of its work on 'Draft Code of Crimes Against the Peace and Security of Mankind', which was finalised in 1996, but never adopted. 'Report of the International Law Commission on the Work of its

the Nuremberg and Tokyo Charters, but did not entirely succeed in clarifying the law.[26]

Since the 1990s, jurisprudence on crimes against humanity has developed both in and out of the European context, including in Canada,[27] Latin America,[28] Africa[29] and Asia.[30] But these developments have been sporadic and have been insufficient to prevent the continued commission of mass atrocities during the second half of the twentieth century, and the beginning of the twenty-first.[31] Although full-scale global conflict has thus far been averted, atrocity crimes have mutated and metastasized around the globe. They have emerged in every region of the world—Latin America, Africa, Asia, the Middle East and Europe—and have taken new and previously unimagined forms where they have occurred.[32]

III. THE ROME STATUTE OF THE INTERNATIONAL CRIMINAL COURT

In 1998, building upon the work of the international community in establishing the Yugoslavia and Rwanda Tribunals, a treaty was adopted establishing a new International Criminal Court, the permanent successor of the ad hoc international military tribunals established at Nuremberg.[33]

Forth-Eighth Session' in 'Yearbook of the International Law Commission' (1996) UN Doc A/CN/.4/SER.A/1996/Add.1 (Part 2) 17, 45.

[26] R Rayfuse, 'The Draft Code of Crimes against the Peace and Security of Mankind: Eating Disorders at the International Law Commission' (1997) 8 *Criminal Law Forum* 43.

[27] *R v Finta* (1994) 1 SCR 701.

[28] See eg JM Burt, 'Challenging Impunity in Domestic Courts: Human Rights Prosecutions in Latin America' in F Reátegui (ed), *Transnational Justice: Handbook for Latin America* (Brasilia, Brazilian Amnesty Commission, 2011) 285. For a comprehensive analysis of the codification of crimes against humanity in Latin American states, see RG Falconí, 'The Codification of Crimes Against Humanity in the Domestic Legislation of Latin American States' (2010) 10 *International Criminal Law Review* 453.

[29] *Ministère Public v Hissein Habré* (Judgment) Extraordinary African Chambers (30 May 2016).

[30] K Sellars (ed), *Trials for International Crimes in Asia* (Cambridge, Cambridge University Press, 2015).

[31] One study has suggested that between 1945 and 2008, between 92 and 101 million persons were killed in 313 different conflicts, the majority of whom were civilians. In addition to those killed directly in these events, others died as a consequence, or had their lives shattered in other ways—through the loss of property, victimisation by sexual violence, disappearances, slavery and slavery-related practices, deportations and forced displacements, and torture. MC Bassiouni, 'Assessing Conflict Outcomes: Accountability and Impunity' in MC Bassiouni (ed), *The Pursuit of International Criminal Justice: A World Study on Conflicts, Victimization, and Post-Conflict Justice* (Antwerp, Intersentia, 2010) 6.

[32] W Schabas, *Unimaginable Atrocities: Justice, Politics and Rights at the War Crimes Tribunals* (Oxford, Oxford University Press, 2012). See also M Lattimer and P Sands (eds), *Justice for Crimes Against Humanity* (Oxford, Hart Publishing, 2003).

[33] In 1989, the Cold War ended with the fall of the Berlin Wall. The ICC project was restarted with the introduction of a resolution into the General Assembly by Trinidad and Tobago leading a coalition of sixteen Caribbean nations, and the continuation of work on the

Article 7 of the ICC Statute also included—for the first time in a multilateral convention—a consensus definition of crimes against humanity.[34] The ICC Statute sets forth a list of eleven acts—including murder, extermination, persecutions and torture—that would reach the level of crimes against humanity 'when committed as part of a widespread or systematic attack directed against any civilian population, with knowledge of the attack'.[35] Although some features of Article 7 have been challenged as inconsistent with customary international law, particularly its addition of a 'policy' element to the crime[36] as well as its reference to the word 'civilian', as a limit on the possible victim class,[37] because it is the only definition since Nuremberg to be included in a multilateral treaty, and was the subject of extensive negotiations in Rome, it has had tremendous influence. Indeed, many authorities now consider it to represent customary international law,[38] in spite of the language of the ICC Statute itself, which notes that the definition is '[f]or the purpose of this Statute'.[39]

IV. THE CONTINUED NEED FOR A NEW GLOBAL TREATY ON CRIMES AGAINST HUMANITY

The absence of a comprehensive inter-state treaty on crimes against humanity (other than the ICC Statute) did not mean that international law does not prohibit their commission, as the ICC Statute itself makes clear. However, it makes concrete legal action—either before the ICJ, international criminal tribunals or national jurisdictions—very difficult for a variety of reasons. First, bringing criminal cases under customary international law

Draft Code of Crimes at the International Law Commission. See 'Report of the Commission to the General Assembly on the work of its Forty-Eighth Session' in 'Yearbook of the International Law Commission' (n 25) 15–42; see also LN Sadat, *The International Criminal Court and the Transformation of International Law: Justice for the New Millennium* (Leiden, Brill, 2002).

[34] Rome Statute of the International Criminal Court (adopted 17 July 1998, entered into force 1 July 2002) UN Doc A/CONF 183/9 (ICC Statute), Art 7. The ICC Statute built upon the work done in elaborating the statutes of the International Criminal Tribunals for the former Yugoslavia and Rwanda, each of which included a provision on crimes against humanity.

[35] ibid, Art 7(1).

[36] G Mettraux, 'The Definition of Crimes Against Humanity and the Question of a "Policy" Element' in LN Sadat (ed), *Forging a Convention for Crimes Against Humanity*, 2nd edn (Cambridge, Cambridge University Press, 2013) 142.

[37] K Ambos, 'Crimes Against Humanity and the International Criminal Court' in Sadat (n 36) 279. See also LN Sadat, 'Putting Peacetime First: Crimes Against Humanity and the Civilian Population Requirement' (2017) 31 *Emory International Law Review* 199.

[38] C Kreß, 'On the Outer Limits of Crimes Against Humanity: The Concept of Organization within the Policy Requirement: Some Reflections on the March 2010 ICC Kenya Decision' (2010) 23 *Leiden Journal of International Law* 855; LN Sadat, 'Crimes Against Humanity in the Modern Age' (2013) 107 *American Journal of International Law* 334, 373.

[39] ICC Statute, Art 7(1).

(as opposed to legislation) is problematic in national jurisdictions because of legitimate concerns about fairness to the accused. Second, international tribunal statutes vary considerably in their definitions of crimes against humanity and have very limited, retroactive application to crimes committed only during one specific conflict. Third, as regards state responsibility, the ICJ has no way of asserting jurisdiction in cases involving crimes against humanity (other than genocide or torture) because there is no treaty with a compromissory clause so providing,[40] and states are unlikely to consent to the Court's jurisdiction in a case involving the commission of these crimes. Finally, only a limited number of national jurisdictions have incorporated crimes against humanity into their domestic legislation lack tools for inter-state cooperation in terms of extradition, arrest, prosecution and the gathering of evidence, which make prosecutions very difficult at the national level.[41]

Although the adoption of the ICC Statute represented real progress in defining crimes against humanity, the Statute applies only to those few cases tried before the Court and does not require states to adopt implementing legislation.[42] The ICC represents a vertical mechanism for the prevention and punishment of international crimes, and is a court of limited jurisdiction. It is also a court of last, not first resort, pursuant to the doctrine of complementarity in its Statute. Thus, the ICC takes very few cases. Finally, the ICC Statute provides no vehicle for inter-state cooperation, leaving gaps in mutual legal assistance, extradition and other aspects of the horizontal cooperation needed for the prosecution of atrocity crimes across state borders, which are critically important if states are not to become safe havens for criminal offenders.

Thus the absence of a global treaty on crimes against humanity leads to several categories of difficulties: (i) an impunity gap, in which individuals are unable to be prosecuted or are prosecuted only with difficulty at both the national and international levels; (ii) a state responsibility gap, because the definition of crimes against humanity is uncertain and no compromissory clause exists to permit litigation before the ICJ regarding their commission; (iii) a situation of definitional uncertainty leading to difficult questions regarding whether a particular atrocity was or was not a crime against humanity; and (iv) a downgrading of crimes against humanity and overuse of the Genocide Convention as a legal tool.[43]

---

[40] See eg *Application of the Convention on the Prevention and Punishment of the Crime of Genocide (Bosnia and Herzegovina v Serbia and Montenegro)* (Merits) [2007] ICJ Rep 43.

[41] See eg LM Olson, 'Re-enforcing Enforcement in a Specialized Convention on Crimes Against Humanity' in Sadat (n 36) 323–44.

[42] LN Sadat, 'A Comprehensive History of the Proposed International Convention on the Prevention and Punishment of Crimes Against Humanity' in Sadat (n 36) 323–44.

[43] See GH Stanton, 'Why the World Needs an International Convention on Crimes Against Humanity' in Sadat (n 36) 345.

V. THE CRIMES AGAINST HUMANITY INITIATIVE

Concerned about the problems of continued impunity for the commission of atrocity crimes, in 2008, the Whitney R Harris World Law Institute at Washington University School of Law launched the Crimes Against Humanity Initiative with three primary objectives: (i) to study the current state of the law and sociological reality as regards the commission of crimes against humanity; (ii) to combat the indifference generated by an assessment that a particular crime is 'only' a crime against humanity (rather than a 'genocide'); and (iii) to address the gap in the current law by elaborating the world's first global treaty on crimes against humanity.[44]

The Initiative progressed in phases, each building upon the work of the last. Directed by a Steering Committee of distinguished experts,[45] it commissioned an academic study, and undertook the drafting of a model text of a Proposed International Convention for the Prevention and Punishment of Crimes Against Humanity.[46] In discussing the scholarly work more questions were raised than answered. Would the social harms encompassed by the convention include only atrocities committed by the state, or by non-state actors as well? Would a new legal instrument prove useful in combating atrocity crimes? How would any new instrument interact with the Rome Statute of the ICC? As the initial scholarly work was undertaken, a preliminary draft text of the Convention was circulated to participants at the Initiative's first meeting in April 2009. The draft was prepared by Professor M Cherif Bassiouni, who chaired the Drafting Committee of the Rome Diplomatic Conference establishing the ICC, and who continued to spearhead the drafting effort as the work progressed. During the first three years of the Initiative's work, nearly 250 experts were consulted, many of whom submitted detailed comments (orally or in writing) on the various drafts of the proposed convention circulated, or attended meetings convened by the Initiative in the United States or abroad. Between formal meetings, technical advisory sessions were held during which every comment received—whether in writing or communicated verbally—was discussed as the convention was refined. The Proposed Convention went through seven major revisions (and innumerable minor ones) and was approved by the Steering Committee in August 2010.

---

[44] Sadat (n 42) xxiii–xxiv.

[45] The Steering Committee is composed of Professor MC Bassiouni, Ambassador H Corell, Justice R Goldstone, Professor J Mendez, Professor W Schabas and Judge C Van den Wyngaert.

[46] 'Proposed International Convention on the Prevention and Punishment of Crimes Against Humanity' (Proposed Convention) in Sadat (n 36) 323–44. The Proposed Convention can also be found on p 403 in French and on p 503 in Spanish. These texts, as well as Arabic, Chinese, German and Russian translations, are available at crimesagainsthumanity@wustl.edu.

The Proposed Convention has begun, not ended, the debate. Elaborated by experts without the constraints of government instructions (although deeply cognisant of political realities), it is a platform for discussion by states, the International Law Commission, civil society and academics with a view to the eventual adoption of a United Nations Convention on the Prevention and Punishment of Crimes Against Humanity. The Proposed Convention builds upon and complements the ICC Statute by retaining the ICC's definition of crimes against humanity but has added robust inter-state cooperation, extradition and mutual legal assistance provisions in Annexes 2–6. Universal jurisdiction was retained (but is not mandatory), and the ICC Statute served as a model for several additional provisions, including Articles 4–7 (Responsibility, Official Capacity, and Non-Applicability of Statute of Limitations) and with respect to final clauses. Other provisions draw upon international criminal law and human rights instruments more broadly, such as the recently negotiated Enforced Disappearance Convention, the Terrorist Bombing Convention, the Convention Against Torture, the United Nations Conventions on Corruption and Organized Crime, the European Transfer of Proceedings Convention, and the Inter-American Criminal Sentences Convention, to name a few.[47]

Although the drafting process benefited from the existence of current international criminal law instruments, the creative work of the Initiative was to meld these and our own ideas into a single, coherent model convention that establishes the principle of state responsibility as well as individual criminal responsibility (including the possibility of responsibility for the criminal acts of legal persons) for the commission of crimes against humanity. Article 1 of the Proposed Convention reads:

Article 1

Nature of the Crime

Crimes against humanity, whether committed in time of armed conflict or in time of peace, constitute crimes under international law for which there is individual criminal responsibility. In addition, States may be held responsible for crimes against humanity pursuant to principles of State responsibility for internationally wrongful acts.[48]

The Proposed Convention innovates in many respects by bringing prevention into the instrument in a much more explicit way than predecessor instruments, by including the possibility of responsibility for the criminal

---

[47] A complete list can be found in the table at the back of the Proposed Convention, reproduced in app I and II of Sadat (n 36) 398–401, 445–48.

[48] Proposed Convention (n 46) Art 1. The current draft articles of the International Law Commission make no reference to state responsibility, assuming that this is presumably understood, even without being made explicit in the treaty.

acts of legal persons, by excluding defences of immunities and statutory limitations, by prohibiting reservations, and by establishing a unique institutional mechanism for supervision of the Convention. Echoing its 1907 forebear, it also contains its own 'Martens clause', as follows:

> Declaring that in cases not covered by the present Convention or by other international agreements, the human person remains under the protection and authority of the principles of international law derived from established customs, from the laws of humanity, and from the dictates of the public conscience, and continues to enjoy the fundamental rights that are recognized by international law.[49]

Elaborating the twenty-seven articles and six annexes of the treaty was a daunting challenge, and one that could not have been accomplished without the dedication and enthusiasm of many individuals.[50] The effort has been well rewarded; in 2010, more than seventy-five experts endorsed the objectives of the Initiative in a 2010 Declaration adopted in Washington, DC, as did the Prosecutors of the world's international criminal courts and tribunals.[51] The Proposed Convention has now been translated into Arabic, Chinese, German, Russian and Spanish, and continues to attract discussion and debate.[52]

VI. THE INTERNATIONAL LAW COMMISSION'S CURRENT PROJECT ON CRIMES AGAINST HUMANITY

In 2013, the Initiative began to move from academic drawing board to political reality when the International Law Commission included the topic of crimes against humanity on its long-term work programme in 2013. The Commission's action was in response to a report prepared by Professor Sean Murphy.[53] The report identified four key elements a new convention should have: a definition adopting Article 7 of the ICC Statute; an obligation to criminalise crimes against humanity with national legislation; robust inter-state cooperation procedures; and a clear obligation to prosecute or

---

[49] ibid, Preamble cl 13.

[50] Each member of the Steering Committee brought tremendous energy and expertise to the project, guiding its methodological development and conceptual design, and carefully reading, commenting upon and debating each interim draft of the Proposed Convention extensively. Many also supported—and continue to support—the effort without being on the front pages of it, so to speak. See eg 'Preface and Acknowledgments' in Sadat (n 36) xxvi–xxviii.

[51] 'Declaration on the Need for a Comprehensive Convention on Crimes Against Humanity' reprinted Sadat (n 36) 579; See also 'Kigali Declaration of the Fifth Colloquium of Prosecutors of International Criminal Tribunals' and 'The Fourth Chautauqua Declaration' (ibid, 588, 591).

[52] See *Whitney R Harris World Law Institute*, crimesagainsthumanity.wustl.edu/.

[53] International Law Commission (ILC), 'Report of the Working Group on the Obligation to Extradite or Prosecute (aut dedere aut judicare)' (22 July 2013) UN Doc A/CN.4/L.829.

extradite offenders.[54] The report also emphasised how a new treaty would complement the ICC Statute.[55]

In autumn 2013, states had an opportunity to comment on the Commission's decision at the General Assembly Sixth Committee. Many states commented favourably. Slovenia, for example, stated that 'all efforts should be directed at filling this gap'.[56] Austria, the Czech Republic, Italy, Norway, Peru, Poland and the United States also welcomed the decision.[57] A major focus was the importance of ensuring a new treaty complements the ICC Statute, as the comments of Malaysia and the United Kingdom, for example, made clear.[58] Some states questioned the need for a new treaty. For example, Iran stated that it 'does not seem that … there is a legal loophole to be filled through the adoption of a new international instrument'.[59] Other states questioning the need for a treaty included France, Malaysia, Romania and Russia.[60]

In May 2014, prior to the Commission's July session, the Proposed Convention was the basis of an Experts' Meeting held at the Villa Moynier in Geneva, bringing together international justice experts and members of the International Law Commission. Participants discussed the need for a new convention, its potential content and the process of building support amongst states. These discussions are summarised in a Report published by the Initiative on 17 July 2014.[61] Participants noted the long involvement of the Commission on the subject of crimes against humanity and commented upon the progressive stance of the Commission in delinking crimes against humanity from armed conflict in its formulation of the Nuremberg Principles.[62] It was also observed that the Commission had nearly completed

---

[54] ibid, para 8.

[55] ibid, paras 9–13.

[56] UNGA, 'Statement by Mr B Mahnič' (30 October 2013) 8.

[57] UNGA, 'Statement by G Schusterschitz (28 October 2013) 5; UNGA, 'Statement by Mr P Válek' (29 October 2013) 3; UNGA, 'Statement by Min Plenipotentiary A Tiriticco' (29 October 2013) 5; UNGA, 'Statement on Behalf of the Nordic Countries by Mr RE Fife' (28 October 2013) 3–4; UNGA, 'Intervención de la Misión Permanente del Perú' (29 October 2013) 2; UNGA, 'Statement by Ambassador R Sarkowicz' (30 October 2013) 5; UNGA, 'Statement by the United States' (2013) 4.

[58] UNGA, 'Statement by Ms S Khalilah Abdul Rahman' (30 October 2013) 1, para 3; UNGA, 'Statement by Mr J Clarke' (28–30 October 2013) 5.

[59] UNGA, 'Statement by Prof D Momtaz' (5 November 2013) 7.

[60] UNGA, 'Statement by Mrs E Belliard' (28 October 2013) part I, 2; UNGA, 'Statement by Ms S Khalilah Abdul Rahman' (n 58); UNGA, 'Statement by Mrs A Orosan' (October 2013) 5; UNGA, 'Statement by the Representative of the Russian Federation' (2013) 6.

[61] LN Sadat and DJ Pivnichny, 'Fulfilling the Dictates of Public Conscience: Moving Forward with a Convention on Crimes Against Humanity' (17 July 2014); *World Law Institute* (n 52).

[62] In para 123 of its commentary to 'Principles of International Law Recognized in the Charter of the Nürnberg Tribunal and in the Judgment of the Tribunal', the ILC noted 'that [crimes against humanity] may take place also before a war in connection with crimes against peace'. ILC, 'Report of the International Law Commission on the Work of its Second Session', UN Doc A/1316, para 123 reprinted in 'Yearbook of the International Law Commission' (n 10).

its work on the obligation to extradite or prosecute (*aut dedere aut judi-care*), and was therefore in an excellent position to take up the question of a new convention on crimes against humanity.

On 17 July 2014, the International Law Commission voted to move the topic of a new treaty on crimes against humanity to its active agenda and appointed Professor Murphy as Special Rapporteur.[63] The General Assembly took note of the Commission's decision,[64] and in the Sixth Committee most states commenting on the topic expressed support for the Commission's work.[65]

In 2015, the Special Rapporteur submitted his First Report and proposed two draft articles.[66] After debate and discussion, four Articles emerged from the Drafting Committee, which the Commission then adopted.[67] These Articles (1–4) define the scope of the draft convention, the general obligations of states (to prevent and punish crimes against humanity whether or not committed in time of armed conflict), and define crimes against humanity identically to Article 7 of the ICC Statute, while also including an innovative 'obligation of prevention'. When the Commission's work was again presented to the Sixth Committee, an increased number (twenty-five of the thirty-eight states commenting on the project) reacted positively,[68] while again emphasising the need for the draft articles to be consistent with the ICC Statute.[69] A few states maintained that a Convention on the topic of

[63] ILC, 'Provisional Summary Record of the 3227th Meeting' (29 October 2014) UN Doc A/CN.4/SR.3227. July 17 is an auspicious date as it is now known as day upon which the International Criminal Court Treaty was adopted, and is now known globally as 'International Criminal Justice Day'.

[64] UNGA Res 69/118 (10 December 2014) UN Doc A/Res/69/118, para 7.

[65] See eg UNGA, 'Statement by Ms P Kaukoranta' (27 October 2014) 3; UNGA, 'Statement by Mr P Válek' (27 October 2014) 2; UNGA, 'Statement by Ms P Ridings' (28 October 2014) 3.

[66] S Murphy (Special Rapporteur on Crimes Against Humanity), 'First Report on Crimes Against Humanity' (17 February 2015) UN Doc A/CN.4/680, paras 120, 177.

[67] See ILC, 'Report on the Work of its Sixty-Seventh Session' (2015) UN Doc A/70/10, para 115.

[68] See eg UNGA, 'Statement by Mr A Reinisch' (4 November 2015) 3 ('According to the first draft article, on the scope, the future convention will apply to the prevention and punishment of crimes against humanity. My delegation is in favour of the proposed extension of the scope of the convention also to the prevention of such crimes.'); UNGA, 'Statement by Mr T Hanami' (6 November 2015) 3 ('Japan recognizes that the current work, which will create "horizontal relationships" among states and regulate inter-state cooperation, will lead to strengthening the effort of the international community for preventing those crimes and punishing its perpetrators.'); UNGA, 'Statement by Mr M Mminele' (2 November 2015) 2 ('We support the approach that the draft articles not only apply to after-the-fact punishment of crimes against humanity, but also aims to prevent the commission of these heinous crimes in the first place.').

[69] For an analysis of government reactions, see TL Slater, 'Global Treaty on Crimes Against Humanity and Statements at the UN General Assembly' *Lex Lata Lex Ferenda* (15 December 2015), law.wustl.edu/harris/lexlata/?p=837. See also '70th Session of the UNGA Sixth Committee' in Compilation of Government Reactions to the International Law Commission's Project on Crimes Against Humanity prepared by the WR Harris World Law Institute

crimes against humanity was unnecessary.[70] Others noted that the project was in its infancy and they would continue to develop their views as the Commission progressed in its work.[71]

In May 2016, the Commission considered the Special Rapporteur's Second Report, which proposed six additional draft articles.[72] The Commission also received a memorandum by the Secretariat providing information on treaty-based monitoring mechanisms.[73] After debate, the Commission provisionally adopted draft Articles 5–10 with commentary.[74] These Articles include provisions requiring states to criminalise the offence, provide for command responsibility, eliminate the defence of superior orders, abolish any statute of limitations, impose appropriate penalties, and establish the liability of legal persons over the crime.

The question of liability for legal persons proved somewhat controversial for the Commission, which had to balance a variety of views and a divergence in approaches taken by international legal instruments regarding the responsibility of legal, as opposed to natural, persons. The Commission decided to extend liability to legal persons given their potential to be involved in the commission of crimes against humanity by using language that has been 'widely accepted by States in the context of other crimes' and that allows for considerable flexibility on the part of states in the implementation of their treaty obligation.[75] The draft articles also address jurisdiction, investigation, preliminary measures, *aut dedere aut judicare* and fair treatment of the alleged offender.

The provisional text evinces the careful and thorough work of the Special Rapporteur, as well as the attention devoted to the topic by the Commission. The Drafting Committee clearly took into account the comments of members (particularly with regard to the importance of streamlining the project with pre-existing legal frameworks, such as the ICC Statute), as well as the views of experts and NGOs, and the resulting draft text includes many ideas advanced during these discussions. The reaction of governments

(20 January 2017) law.wustl.edu/harris/cah/docs/6thCommitteeGovernmentalResponses (forpublication).pdf, 11.

[70] Compilation of Government Reactions (n 69). See eg UNGA, 'Statement by Ms M Telalian' (4 November 2015) 5 ('We, therefore, are of the view that the entry into force of the Rome Statute and the establishment of the International Criminal Court has rendered to a large extent unnecessary the elaboration of a Convention on the crimes against humanity.').

[71] Compilation of Government Reactions (n 69). See eg UNGA, 'Statement by Ms R Faden' (6 November 2015) 4 ('To conclude my intervention on this topic, to which Portugal attaches great importance, let me assure Mr Chairman that Portugal will continue to follow with great interest the work of the Commission on this matter.').

[72] S Murphy (Special Rapporteur on Crimes Against Humanity), 'Second Report on Crimes Against Humanity' (21 January 2016) UN Doc A/CN.4/690, Annex II.

[73] ILC, 'Report on the Work of its Sixty-Eighth Session' (2016) UN Doc A/71/10, para 79.

[74] ibid, para 85.

[75] ibid.

to the Commission's 2016 Report was again increasingly positive, with only three states (of thirty-six commenting) proffering negative views,[76] and all others ranging from neutral to strongly positive.[77]

The Third Report of the Special Rapporteur was considered during the sixty-ninth session of the Commission. After extensive debate and discussion, the Commission referred the draft Articles proposed in the Third Report to the Drafting Committee, which, after discussion and debate, sent a draft Preamble, draft Articles 1–15 and a draft Annex to the Commission, which adopted them on first reading.[78] These Articles include provisions on victims and witnesses (12), extradition (13), mutual legal assistance (14), dispute settlement (15), *non-refoulement* (5), and an Annex setting forth detailed processes for mutual legal assistance.[79] The Commission's proposed draft Articles are more modest in scope than the Proposed Convention of the Crimes Against Humanity Initiative; but there are many similarities between the two documents. The draft Articles of the ILC are silent on the question of reservations (although opting out of the dispute settlement mechanism proposed in draft Article 15 is possible), a treaty-monitoring mechanism, and the Preamble contains no 'Martens clause'. States, international organisations and 'others' now have until 1 December 2018 to submit comments and observations to the Secretary General.[80] The responses of governments in the Sixth Committee were overwhelmingly positive, suggesting that political momentum is building—out of fifty-five total interventions, eight were strongly positive, thirty-four were positive, nine were neutral, and only four were negative or strongly negative.[81] The Special Rapporteur has indicated both orally and in earlier reports that he contemplates producing a fourth and final report in 2018,[82] and a revised set of draft Articles may be adopted by the Commission on second reading in Summer 2019. Upon completion of the Commission's work, it can suggest further study, depending upon government reactions, the convening of a diplomatic conference to negotiate a new treaty,[83] or the adoption of the Convention by a General Assembly Resolution.

---

[76] China, Malaysia, and India expressed negative opinions. UNGA, 'Statement by Mr X Hong' (27 October 2016); UNGA, 'Statement by Ms H Ramly' (28 October 2016); UNGA, 'Statement by Dr VD Sharma' (1 November 2016).

[77] See also '71st Session of the UNGA Sixth Committee' in Compilation of Government Reactions (n 69).

[78] ILC, 'Report on the Work of its Sixty-Ninth session' (2017) UN Doc A/72/10, paras 38–44.

[79] ibid.

[80] ibid, para. 43.

[81] '72nd Session of the UNGA Sixth Committee' in Compilation of Government Reactions to the International Law Commission's Project on Crimes Against Humanity prepared by the WR Harris World Law Institute (29 November 2017) law.wustl.edu/harris/cah/docs/6thCommitteeGovernmentalResponses.

[82] Murphy, 'Second Report' (n 72) paras 202–03.

[83] Statute of the International Law Commission (adopted 21 November 1947, as last amended 18 November 1981) UN Doc A/RES/175(II), arts 16, 17.

VII. CONCLUSION

In a world of competing priorities for shrinking global resources, the need for a new global treaty to combat crimes against humanity is sometimes challenged. A new global convention on crimes against humanity is unlikely to have any retroactive effect. It will not right past wrongs; rather, it will protect future, as yet unknown, victims. It is fair to ask why we should protect those who are probably strangers to us, and who are unlikely to be our descendants. There are practical and legal reasons one can evoke in response to this challenge, of increased economic benefits flowing from reductions in international crime, of eliminating the possibility of safe havens for international criminals, as well as benefits that flow from increased global peace and stability. There are also compelling moral arguments.

In a *Theory of Justice*, John Rawls argues that one should evaluate the justness of social rules from behind a 'veil of ignorance'.[84] Put succinctly, the idea is that everyone should choose the rules that apply to them to produce the highest payoff for the least advantaged position, as if they did not know whether or not they would be born weak or strong, poor or rich. From this 'original position', rules that promote social equality are the most desirable as they protect everyone. Extrapolating this to the international legal order, the question is what system is preferable if one cannot know in advance whether one would have been unlucky enough to have been Jewish during the Holocaust, Tutsi during the Rwandan genocide, a wearer of eyeglasses during the Khmer Rouge regime, or a Masalit or Fur tribe member in contemporary Darfur, Sudan. Behind a veil of ignorance, presumably everyone would choose the protection of a strong international justice system capable of restraining and punishing international criminals.[85] This might be even more true today than before, given current patterns of global migration which are disrupting comfortable lives around the world to an extent not seen since the World War II.

If the wars of the twentieth century taught any lessons at all, it was clear that to meet the challenges of a world in which the commission of atrocity crimes is all too common, the international community requires three things: rules, institutions and enforcement. Rules that govern human behaviour, institutions that apply those rules, and institutions that enforce those rules. Although the establishment of the ICC in 1998 was a critically important step forward, without national enforcement of ICC Statute norms, it will not be strong enough to protect potential victims of crimes against

---

[84] J Rawls, *Theory of Justice* (Harvard, Harvard University Press, 2009) 118.

[85] Rawls himself never took this position, I should add. He did pen *The Law of Peoples* which was an effort to move his philosophy to the international arena, but it is not, in my view, as successful as a *Theory of Justice* in explaining why those who are fortunate should help those who are not and frame their social and legal rules accordingly.

humanity or deter—or punish—future offenders. The ICC represents a very powerful idea but is actually a very small and fragile institution, with only eighteen judges, a modest budget and no police force. It represents the hope of millions of victims around the world—but will handle only a fraction of the possible cases that could be brought. The heavy lifting will have to be done by national court systems.

When beginning the Crimes Against Humanity Initiative it was daunting to ask whether it would make a difference, and whether it represented the right step forward. Although concerns remain regarding the content of any new treaty that might be negotiated[86] as well as the relationship of any new convention with the ICC Statute, the absence of a global treaty on crimes against humanity means that our strongest institutions—national governments and courts—are deprived of the tools they need to comprehensively address this terrible crime. The work of the Initiative over the past nine years, combined with the ongoing efforts of the International Law Commission, has demonstrated that the time has come at last to remedy this normative and enforcement gap in international law. In this modern era of increasingly illiberal governments, when echoes of the xenophobia of the past can be heard again on several continents, this effort seems more urgent than ever. In the words of John Donne:

No man is an island,
Entire of itself;
Every man is a piece of the continent,
A part of the main;
…
Any man's death diminishes me,
Because I am involved in mankind.
And therefore never send to know
For whom the bell tolls;
It tolls for thee.

---

[86] Eg, Amnesty International, Conditional Support to the Draft Articles on Crimes Against Humanity Adopted by the International Law Commission in First Reading (October 2017) (expressing general support for the idea of a new convention but stating that the 'Draft Articles, as it is today, may and must be considerably improved by the ILC in 2019').

Bibliography

Abi-Saab, G, 'The Implementation of Humanitarian Law' in Cassese, A (ed), *The New Humanitarian Law of Armed Conflict*, vol I (Napoli, Editoriale scientifica, 1979).

Akande, D, 'Clearing the Fog of War? The ICRC's Interpretive Guidance on Direct Participation in Hostilities' (2010) 59 *ICLQ* 180.

Alvarez, J, 'Torturing the Law' (2006) 37 *Case Western Reserve Journal of International Law* 175.

Andreu-Guzman, F, *Military Jurisdiction and International Law: Military Courts and Gross Human Rights Violations* (International Commission of Jurists, 2004).

Arieli, S and Sfard, M, *The Wall of Folly* (Tel Aviv, Yediot Sfarim, 2008).

Barnidge, RP, Jr, 'A Qualified Defense of American Drone Attacks in Northwest Pakistan under International Humanitarian Law' (2012) 30 *Boston University International Law Journal* 409.

Bassiouni, MC, 'International Crimes: Jus Cogens and Obligatio Erga Omnes' (1996) 59 *Law and Contemporary Problems* 63.

——, 'International Recognition of Victims' Rights' (2006) 6 *Human Rights Law Review* 203.

——, 'Assessing Conflict Outcomes: Accountability and Impunity' in Bassiouni, MC (ed), *The Pursuit of International Criminal Justice: A World Study on Conflicts, Victimization, and Post-Conflict Justice* (Cambridge, Intersentia, 2010).

Bazyler, M and Alford, R (eds), *Holocaust Restitution: Perspectives on the Litigation and its Legacy* (New York, New York University Press, 2006).

Benvenisti, E, 'Judicial Misgivings Regarding the Application of International Norms: An Analysis of Attitudes of National Courts' (1993) 4 *European Journal of International Law* 2.

——, 'Human Dignity in Combat: The Duty to Spare Enemy Civilians' (2006) 39 *Israel Law Review* 81.

——, 'United We Stand: National Courts Reviewing Counterterrorism Measures' in Bianchi, A and Keller, A (eds), *Counterterrorism: Democracy's Challenge* (Oxford, Hart Publishing, 2008).

Best, G, *Humanity in Warfare* (London, Methuen, 1983).

——, *War and Law since 1945* (Oxford, Clarendon Press, 1994).

Bhuta, N, 'The Frontiers of Extraterritoriality—Human Rights as Global Law' in Bhuta, N (ed), *The Frontier of Human Rights* (Oxford, Oxford University Press, 2016).

Bialke, J, 'Al-Qaeda and Taliban Unlawful Combat Detainees, Unlawful Belligerency, and the International Laws of Armed Conflict' (2004) 55 *Air Force Law Review* 1.

Bílková, V, 'Victims of War and Their Right to Reparation for Violations of International Humanitarian Law' (2007) 4 *Miskolc Journal of International Law* 1.

Blank, LR and Farley, BR, 'Characterizing US Operations in Pakistan: Is the United States Engaged in an Armed Conflict?' (2011) 34 *Fordham International Law Journal* 2.

Blum, G and Heymann, P, 'Law and Policy of Targeted Killings' (2010) 1 *Harvard National Security Journal* 145.

Boisson de Chazournes, L and Condorelli, L, 'Common Article 1 of the Geneva Conventions revisited: Protecting Collective Interests' (2000) 837 *Review of the International Red Cross* 67.

Bolton, M, et al, 'The Arms Trade Treaty from a Global Civil Society Perspective: Introducing Global Policy's Special Section' (2014) 5 *Global Policy* 433.

Bothe, M, Partsch HJ and Soft WA, *New Rules for Victims of Armed Conflict: Commentary on the Two 1977 Protocols Additional to the Geneva Conventions of 1949* (The Hague, Martinus Nijhoff Publishers, 1982).

Bothe, M, 'Fact-Finding as a Means of Ensuring Respect for International Humanitarian Law' in Heintschel von Heinegg, W and Epping, V (eds), *International Humanitarian Law Facing New Challenges* (Berlin, Springer, 2007).

Boutruche, T, 'Good Offices, Conciliation and Enquiry' in Clapham, A, Gaeta, P and Sassòli, M (eds), *The 1949 Geneva Conventions: A Commentary* (Geneva/ Oxford, Oxford University Press, 2015).

Brammertz, S and Jarvis, M, *Prosecuting Conflict-Related Sexual Violence at the ICTY* (Oxford, Oxford University Press, 2016).

Breau, S, Aronsson, M and Joyce, R, *Drone Attacks, International Law and the Recording of Civilian Casualties of Armed Conflict* (Oxford, Oxford Research Group, 2011).

Breton-Le Goff, G, 'Ending Sexual Violence in the Democratic Republic of the Congo' (2010) 34 *The Fletcher Forum of World Affairs* 1.

Burt, JM, 'Challenging Impunity in Domestic Courts: Human Rights Prosecutions in Latin America' in Reátegui, F (ed), *Transnational Justice: Handbook for Latin America* (Brasilia, Brazilian Amnesty Commission, 2011).

Carillo, A and Nelson, A, 'Comparative Law Study and Analysis of National Legislation Relating to Crimes against Humanity and Extraterritorial Jurisdiction' (2014) 46 *The George Washington International Law Review* 3.

Caron, DD, 'Towards a Political Theory of International Courts and Tribunals' (2007) 24 *Berkeley Journal of International Law* 401.

Cassese, A, 'Is the Bell Tolling for Universality? A Plea for a Sensible Notion of Universal Jurisdiction' (2003) 1 *Journal of International Criminal Justice* 589.

Chamberlain, M, 'Special Advocate and Procedural Fairness in Closed Proceedings' (2009) 28 *Civil Justice Quarterly* 314.

Chappell, L, *The Politics of Gender Justice at the ICC: Legacies and Legitimacy* (Oxford, Oxford University Press, 2015).

Chinkin, C and Kaldor, M, 'Gender and New Wars' (2013) 67 *Journal of International Affairs* 1.

——, *International Law and New Wars* (Cambridge, Cambridge University Press, 2017).

Clapham, A, 'The Arms Trade Treaty: A Call for an Awakening' (2013) 2 *European Society of International Law Reflections* 5.

——, *Human Rights Obligations of Non-State Actors* (Oxford, Oxford University Press, 2006).

Clapham, A, Casey-Maslen, S, Giacca, G and Parker, S, *The Arms Trade Treaty*: *A Commentary* (Oxford, Oxford University Press, 2016).

Cohen, A, 'The Principle of Proportionality and Operation Cast Lead: Institutional Perspectives' (2009) 35 *Rutgers Law Record* 23.

——, 'Legal Operational Advice in the Israeli Defense Forces: The International Law Department and the Changing Nature of International Humanitarian Law' (2011) 26 *Connecticut Journal of International Law* 367.

—— and Shany, Y, 'Beyond the Grave Breaches Regime: The Duty to Investigate Alleged Violations of International Law Governing Armed Conflict' in Schmitt, MN and Arimatsu, L (eds), *Yearbook of International Humanitarian Law 2011*, vol 14 (The Hague, TMC Asser Press, 2012).

Cohen-Eliya, M, 'The Formal and Substantive Meanings of Proportionality in the Supreme Court's Decision Regarding the Security Fence' (2005) 38 *Israel Law Review* 262.

Condorelli, L, 'The International Humanitarian Fact-Finding Commission: An Obsolete Tool or a Useful Measure to Implement International Humanitarian Law' (2001) 83 *International Review of the Red Cross* 842.

Cook, RJ, and Cusack, S, *Gender Stereotyping: Transnational Legal Perspectives* (Philadelphia University of Pennsylvania Press, 2010).

Cotterrell, R, *The Sociology of Law* (London, Butterworths, 1984).

Craig, A, *International Legitimacy and the Politics of Security: The Strategic Deployment of Lawyers in the Israeli Military* (Lanham, MD, Lexington Books, 2013).

Crawford, E, *The Treatment of Combatants and Insurgents under the Law of Armed Conflict* (Oxford, Oxford University Press, 2010).

Crawford, J, *Brownlie's Principles of Public International Law*, 8th edn (Oxford, Oxford University Press, 2012).

Crawford, NC, *Accountability for Killing: Moral Responsibility for Collateral Damage in America's Post-9/11 Wars* (Oxford, Oxford University Press, 2013).

Da Costa, K, *The Extraterritorial Application of Selected Human Rights Treaties* (Leiden/Boston, Martinus Nijhoff Publishers, 2012).

Dannenbaum, T, 'Translating the Standard of Effective Control into a System of Effective Accountability: How Liability Should be Apportioned for Violations of Human Rights by Member State Troop Contingents Serving as United Nations Peacekeepers' (2010) 51 *Harvard International Law Journal* 1.

Darryl, R, 'How Command Responsibility Got So Complicated: A Culpability Contradiction, its Obfuscation, and a Simple Solution' (2012) 13 *Melbourne Journal of International Law* 1.

David, S, 'Targeted Killing the Israeli Experience' in Ford, CA and Cohen, A (eds), *Rethinking the Law of Armed Conflict in Age of Terrorism* (Plymouth, Lexington Books, 2012).

Dennis, MJ, 'Application of Human Rights Treaties Extraterritorially in Times of Armed Conflict and Military Occupation' (2005) 99 *American Journal of International Law* 119.

Dinstein, Y, 'Article 7 of Additional Protocol I' (2005) 24 *Australian Yearbook of International Law* 65.

——, *Non-International Armed Conflicts in International Law* (Cambridge, Cambridge University Press, 2014).

——, *The Conduct of Hostilities under the Law of International Armed Conflict*, 3rd edn (Cambridge, Cambridge University Press, 2016).

Dolzer, R, 'Settlement of War-Related Claims: Does International Law Recognize a Victim's Private Right of Action—Lessons after 1945' (2002) 20 *Berkeley Journal of International Law* 296.

Dörmann, K, 'War Crimes under the Rome Statute of the International Criminal Court, with a Special Focus on the Negotiations on the Elements of Crimes' (2003) 7 *Max Planck Yearbook of United Nations Law* 341.

—— and Serralvo, J, 'Common Article 1 to the Geneva Convention and the Obligation to Prevent International Humanitarian Law Violations' (2015) 96 *International Review of the Red Cross* 1.

Doswald-Beck, L, 'The Right to Life in Armed Conflict: Does International Humanitarian Law Provide All the Answers?' (2006) 864 *International Review of the Red Cross*, 903.

Drabik, M, 'A Duty to Investigate Incidents Involving Collateral Damage and the United States Military's Practice' (2013) 22 *Minnesota Journal of International Law Online* 15.

Drumbl, MA, 'Stepping Beyond Nuremberg's Halo: The Legacy of the Supreme National Tribunal of Poland' (2015) 13 *Journal of International Criminal Justice* 5.

Falconí, RG, 'The Codification of Crimes against Humanity in the Domestic Legislation of Latin American States' (2010) 10 *International Criminal Law Review* 453.

Feaver, PD, *Armed Servants: Agency, Oversight and Civil–Military Relations* (Cambridge, MA, Harvard University Press, 2005).

Fenrick, WJ, 'The Rule of Proportionality and Protocol I in Conventional Warfare' (1982) 98 *Military Law Review* 91.

——, 'Targeting and Proportionality during the NATO Bombing Campaign against Yugoslavia' (2001) 12 *European Journal of International Law* 489.

Ferraro, T, 'The Applicability of International Humanitarian Law to Multinational Forces' (2014) 95 *International Review of the Red Cross* 891/892.

Ferstman, C and Rosenberg, SP, 'Reparations in Dayton's Bosnia and Herzegovina' in Ferstman, C, et al (eds), *Reparations for Victims of Genocide, War Crimes and Crimes against Humanity: Systems in Place and Systems in the Making* (Leiden, Martinus Nijhoff, 2009).

Franck, TM, *Political Questions/Judicial Answers: Does the Rule of Law Apply to Foreign Affairs?* (Princeton, Princeton University Press, 1992).

Frau, R, 'Unmanned Military Systems and Extraterritorial Application of Human Rights Law' (2013) 1 *Groningen Journal of International Law* 1.

Frulli, M, 'When Are States Liable Towards Individuals for Serious Violations of Humanitarian Law? The *Markovic* Case' (2003) 1 *Journal of International Criminal Justice* 406.

Fux, PY and Zambelli, M, 'Mise en oeuvre de la Quatrième Convention de Genève dans les territoires palestiniens occupés: historique d'un processus multilatéral (1997–2001)' (2002) *Revue internationale de la Croix-Rouge* 661.

Gabriel, RA, *Operation Peace for Galilee: Israeli/Palestine Liberation Organization War in Lebanon* (New York, Hill & Wang, 1985).

Gaeta, P, 'Are Victims of Serious Violations of International Humanitarian Law Entitled to Compensation?' in Ben-Naftali, O (ed), *International Humanitarian Law and International Human Rights Law* (Oxford, Oxford University Press, 2011).

Gaggioli, G and Kolb, R, 'A Right to Life in Armed Conflicts? The Contribution of the European Court of Human Rights' (2007) 37 *Israel Yearbook on Human Rights* 118.

Gaggioli, G, *L'influence mutuelle entre les droits de l'homme et le droit international humanitaire à la lumière du droit à la vie* (Paris, Editions Pedone, 2013).

——, 'Sexual Violence in Armed Conflicts: A Violation of International Humanitarian Law and Human Rights Law' (2014) 96 *International Review of the Red Cross* 894.

——, 'Lethal Force and Drones: The Human Rights Question' in Barela, SJ (ed), *The Legitimacy of Drones* (Burlington, Ashgate Publishing, 2015).

Ganor, B, *Global Alert: The Rationality of Modern Islamist Terrorism and the Challenge to the Liberal Democratic World* (New York, Columbia University Press, 2015).

Garcia, D, *Disarmament Diplomacy and Human Security: Regimes, Norms and Moral Progress in International Relations* (New York, Routledge, 2011).

Gardam, J, 'Proportionality and Force in International Law' (1993) 87 *American Journal of International Law* 391.

——, *Necessity, Proportionality and the Use of Force by States* (Cambridge, Cambridge University Press, 2004).

Garraway, C, 'Interoperability and the Atlantic Divide: A Bridge over Troubled Waters' (2006) 80 *Naval War College International Law Studies*.

Gaudreau, J, 'The Reservations to the Protocols Additional to the Geneva Conventions for the Protection of War Victims' (2003) 849 *International Review of the Red Cross* 143.

Geiss, R, 'The Obligation to Respect and to Ensure Respect for the Convention' in Clapham, A, Gaeta, P and Sassòli, M (eds), *The 1949 Geneva Conventions: A Commentary* (Geneva/Oxford, Oxford University Press, 2015).

Gibson, M, 'International Human Rights Law and the Administration of Justice through Military Tribunals: Preserving Utility while Precluding Impunity' (2008) 4 *Journal of International Law and International Relations* 1.

Gillard, EC, 'Reparation for Violations of International Humanitarian Law' (2003) 85 *International Review of the Red Cross* 532.

Gillespie, A, *A History of the Laws of War*, vol. 2: *The Customs and Laws of War with Regards to Civilians in Times of Conflict* (Oxford, Hart Publishing, 2011).

Goddard, DS, 'Applying the European Convention on Human Rights to the Use of Physical Force: *Al-Saadoon*' (2015) 91 *International Law Studies Series. US Naval War College* 402.

Goldsmith, JL, *Power and Constraint: The Accountable Presidency after 9/11* (New York, Norton and Co, 2012).

Golsan, RJ (ed), *The Papon Affair: Memory and Justice on Trial* (Routledge, 2000).

Gondek, M, 'Extraterritorial Application of the European Convention on Human Rights: Territorial Focus in the Age of Globalization?' (2005) 52 *Netherlands International Law Review* 3.

Green, LC, *The Contemporary Law of Armed Conflict*, 2nd edn (Manchester, Manchester University Press, 2000).

Green, C, et al, 'Gender Based Violence and the Arms Trade Treaty: Reflections from a Campaigning and Legal Perspective' (2013) 21 *Gender and Development* 551.

Grey, R, 'Sexual Violence against Child Soldiers' (2014) 16 *International Feminist Journal of Politics* 4.

Gross, A, 'The Righting of the Law of Occupation' in Bhuta, N (ed), *The Frontier of Human Rights* (Oxford, Oxford University Press, 2016).

Haijer, F and Ryngaert, C, 'Reflections on *Jaloud v the Netherlands*' (2016) 19 *Journal of International Peacekeeping* 1–2.

Hampson, FJ, 'The Geneva Conventions and the Detention of Civilians and Alleged Prisoners of War' [1991] Winter *Public Law*.

Hansen, ST, and Marsh, N, 'Normative Power and Organized Hypocrisy: European Union Member states' Arms Export to Libya' (2015) 24 *European Security* 264.

Harris, WR, *Tyranny on Trial* (Dallas, Southern Methodist University Press, 1999).

Hartmann, J, 'The Copenhagen Process: Principles and Guidelines' (2013) 16 *Yearbook of International Humanitarian Law*.

Hayner, P, *Unspeakable Truths: Transitional Justice and the Challenge of Truth Commissions*, 2nd edn (New York, Routledge 2010).

Henckaerts, JM and Doswald-Beck, L, *Customary International Humanitarian Law*, 2 vols (Cambridge, Cambridge University Press, 2006).

Henkin, L, 'Is There a "Political Question" Doctrine?' (1976) 85 *Yale Law Journal* 5.

Henzelin, M, Heiskanen, V and Mettraux, G, 'Reparations to Victims before the International Criminal Court: Lessons From International Mass Claims Processes' (2006) 17 *Criminal Law Forum* 317.

Hill-Cawthorne, L, *Detention in Non-International Armed Conflict* (Oxford, Oxford University Press, 2016).

Hoffmann, R, 'Reparation for Victims of War and Non-State Actors?' (2007) 32 *South African Year Book of International Law* 291.

Holtzmann, HM and Kristjánsdóttir, E (eds), *International Mass Claims Processes: Legal and Practical Perspectives* (Oxford, Oxford University Press, 2007).

Issacharoff, S and Pildes, RH, 'Drones and the Dilemma of Modern Warfare' in Bergen, PL and Rothenberg, D (eds), *Drone Wars* (Cambridge, Cambridge University Press, 2015).

Jackson, D, 'Reporting and Investigation of Possible, Suspected or Alleged Violations of the Law of War' (2010) 95 *Army Lawyer* 98.

Jackson, M, 'Freeing Soering: The ECHR, State Complicity in Torture, and Jurisdiction' (2016) 27 *European Journal of International Law* 3.

Johnson, JC, 'National Security Law, Lawyers, and Lawyering in the Obama Administration' (2012) 31 *Yale Law & Policy Review* 1.

Jurdi, NN, *The International Criminal Court and National Courts: A Contentious Relationship* (Farnham, Ashgate Publishing, 2011).

Kaldor, M, *New and Old Wars: Organised Violence in a Global Era*, 3rd edn (Cambridge, Polity Press, 2012).

Kalshoven, F, 'State Responsibility for Warlike Acts of the Armed Forces: From Article 3 of Hague Convention IV of 1907 to Article 91 of Additional Protocol I of 1977 and Beyond' (1991) 40 *International and Comparative Law Quarterly* 827.

Kamminga, M, 'Pleidooi voor een claims commissie voor Srebrenica' (2010) 85 *Nederlands Juristenblad* 1111.

Kasher, A and Yadlin, A, 'Military Ethics of Fighting Terror: An Israeli Perspective' (2005) 4 *Journal of Military Ethics* 3.

Kelly, J, 'Re: Civilian Casualty Court Martial: Prosecuting Breaches of International Humanitarian Law Using the Australian Military Justice System' (2013–14) 37 *Melbourne University Law Review* 342.

Kennedy, D, *A Critique of Adjudication* (Cambridge, MA, Harvard University Press, 1997).

Kessing, PV, 'The Extraterritorial Use of Armed Drones and International Human Rights Law: Different Views on Legality in the US and Europe?' in Andersen, EA and Lassen, EM (eds), *Europe and the Americas: Transatlantic Approaches to Human Rights* (The Hague, Brill, 2015).

Kirk-Greene, AHM, *Crisis and Conflict in Nigeria, A Documentary Sourcebook*, vol 1 (Cambridge, Cambridge University Press, 1966–69).

Kleffner, JK and Zegveld, L, 'Establishing an Individual Complaints Procedure for Violations of International Humanitarian Law' (2000) 3 *Year Book of International Humanitarian Law* 384.

Kleffner, JK, 'From "Belligerents" to "Fighters" and Civilians Directly Participating in Hostilities—On the Principle of Distinction in Non-International Armed Conflicts One Hundred Years After the Second Hague Peace Conference' (2007) LIV *Netherlands International Law Review* 315.

——, *Complementarity in the Rome Statute and National Criminal Jurisdictions* (Oxford, Oxford University Press, 2008).

Koh, H, 'Why Do Nations Obey International Law?' (1997) 106 *Yale Law Journal* 2599.

Kolb, R and Hyde, R, *An Introduction to the International Law of Armed Conflicts* (Oxford, Hart Publishing, 2008).

Kolb, R, 'Protecting Powers' in Clapham, A, Gaeta, P and Sassòli, M (eds), *The 1949 Geneva Conventions: A Commentary* (Geneva/Oxford, Oxford University Press, 2015).

Kopel, DB, Gallant, P and Eisen, JE, 'The Arms Trade Treaty: Zimbabwe, the Democratic Republic of the Congo, and the Prospects for Arms Embargoes on Human Rights Violators' (2010) 114 *Penn State Law Review* 101.

Koskenniemi, M, 'Hersch Lauterpacht and the Development of International Criminal Law' (2004) 2 *Journal of international Criminal Justice* 810.

——, *From Apology to Utopia—The Structure of International Legal Argument* (New York, Cambridge University Press, 2005).

Koutroulis, V, 'And Yet It Exists: In Defence of the "Equality of Belligerents" Principle' (2013) 26 *Leiden Journal of International Law* 449.

Krebs, S, Cohen, A and Mimran, T, *'Don't Ask, Don't Tell': Secrecy, Security, and Oversight of Targeted Killing Operations* (Jerusalem, Israel Democracy Institute, 2015).

Kreis, JF, 'Unmanned Aircraft in Israeli Air Operations' (1990) 37 *Air Power History* 4.

Kreß, C, 'On the Outer Limits of Crimes against Humanity: The Concept of Organization within the Policy Requirement: Some Reflections on the March 2010 ICC Kenya Decision' (2010) 23 *Leiden Journal of International Law* 855.

Kretzmer, D, 'Targeted Killing of Suspected Terrorists: Extra-Judicial Executions or Legitimate Means of Defense?' (2005) 16 *European Journal of International Law* 171.

Kristjánsdóttir, E, 'International Mass Claims Processes and the ICC Trust Fund for Victims' in Ferstman, C et al (eds), *Reparations for Victims of Genocide, War Crimes and Crimes against Humanity: Systems in Place and Systems in the Making* (Leiden, Martinus Nijhoff, 2009).

Lattimer, M and Sands, P (eds), *Justice for Crimes against Humanity* (Oxford, Hart Publishing, 2003).

Lauterparcht, E, *The Life of Sir Hersch Lauterpacht* (Cambridge, Cambridge University Press, 2010).

Leiter, B, 'American Legal Realism' in Patterson, DM (ed), *A Companion to Philosophy of Law and Legal Theory*, 2nd edn (Oxford, Blackwell, 2010).

Levrat, N, 'Les consequences de l'engagement pris par les Hautes Parties Contractantes de "faire respecter" les Conventions humanitaires' in Kalshoven, K and Sandoz, Y (eds), *Mise en oeuvre du droit international humanitaire* (Dordrecht, Martinus Nijhoff, 1989).

Lewy, G, *America in Vietnam* (New York, Oxford University Press, 1978).

Liddy, L, 'The Strategic Corporal: Some Requirements in Training and Education' (2013) 11 *Australian Army Journal* 2.

Luban, D, 'Military Necessity and the Cultures of Military Law' (2013) 26 *Leiden Journal of International Law* 315.

Lubell N and Derejko, N, 'A Global Battlefield? Drones and the Geographical Scope of Armed Conflict' (2014) 11 *Journal of International Criminal Justice* 1.

Lustgarten, L, 'The Arms Trade Treaty: Achievements, Failings, Future' (2015) 64 *International and Comparative Law Quarterly* 569.

MacKinnon, C, *Are Women Human? And Other International Dialogues* (Cambridge, MA, Harvard University Press, 2006).

Margalit, A, 'The Duty to Investigate Civilian Casualties During Armed Conflict and Its Implementation in Practice' in Gill, TD, et al (eds), *Yearbook of International Humanitarian Law 2012*, vol 15 (The Hague, TMC Asser Press, 2014).

Margulies, P, 'Networks in Non-International Armed Conflicts: Crossing Borders and Defining 'Organized Armed Group'' (2013) 89 *International Law Studies* 54.

McCormack, T, 'Their Atrocities and Our Misdemeanours: The Reticence of States to Try their Own Nationals for International Crimes' in Lattimer, M and Sands, P (eds), *Justice for Crimes Against Humanity* (Oxford, Hart Publishing, 2003).

McCurley, TM and Maurer, K, *Hunter Killer* (London, Allen & Unwin, 2016).

Melzer, N, 'Interpretive Guidance on the Notion of Direct Participation in Hostilities under International Humanitarian Law' (2008) 90 *International Review of the Red Cross* 991.

——, *Targeted Killings in International Law* (Oxford, Oxford University Press, 2008).

——, 'Keeping the Balance Between Military Necessity and Humanity: A Response to Four Critiques of the ICRC's Interpretive Guidance on the Notion of Direct Participation in Hostilities' (2010) 42 *NYU Journal of International Law and Policy* 831.

——, *International Humanitarian Law: A Comprehensive Introduction* (Geneva, ICRC, 2016).

Meron, T, 'The Humanization of Humanitarian Law' (2000) 94 *American Journal of International Law* 2.

——, *Bloody Constraint: War and Chivalry in Shakespeare* (New York, Oxford University Press, 2001).

Milanovic, M and Papic, T, 'As Bad As It Gets: The European Court of Human Rights' Behrami and Saramati Decision and General International Law' (2009) 58 *International and Comparative Law Quarterly* 2.

Milanovic, M, 'Norm Conflicts, International Humanitarian Law and Human Rights Law' in Ben-Naftali, O (ed), *Human Rights and International Humanitarian Law* (Oxford, Oxford University Press, 2010).

——, *Extraterritorial Application of Human Rights Treaties* (Oxford, Oxford University Press, 2011).

——, 'Extraterritorial Derogations from Human Rights Treaties in Armed Conflict' in Bhuta, N (ed), *The Frontier of Human Rights* (Oxford, Oxford University Press, 2016).

Modirzadeh, NK, 'The Dark Sides of Convergence: A Pro-Civilian Critique of the Extraterritorial Application of Human Rights Law in Armed Conflict' (2010) 86 *US Naval War College International Law Studies* 349.

Morris, M, 'By Force of Arms: Rape, War and Military Culture' (1995–96) 45 *Duke Law Journal* 651.

Morrow, JD, *Order within Anarchy: The Law of War as an International Institution* (Cambridge, Cambridge University Press, 2014).

Munkler, A, 'The Wars of the 21st Century' (2003) *International Review of the Red Cross* 849.

Murphy, R, 'The Legal Framework of United Nations Peacekeeping Forces and the Issue of Command and Control' (1999) 4 *Journal of Armed Conflict Law* 1.

——, 'UN Military Operations and International Humanitarian Law: What Rules Apply to Peacekeepers?' (2003) 14 *Criminal Law Forum—An International Journal* 2.

Murphy, SD, Kidane, W, Snider, TR, *Litigating War: Mass Civil Injury and the Eritrea–Ethiopia Claims Commission* (Oxford, Oxford University Press, 2014).

Murphy, SD, 'New Mechanisms for Punishing Atrocities in Non-International Armed Conflicts' (2015) 16 *Melbourne Journal of International Law* 298.

Murray, D, 'Non-State Armed Groups, Detention Authority in Non-International Armed Conflict, and the Coherence of International Law: Searching for a Way Forward' (2017) 30 *Leiden Journal of International Law* 2.

Murray, RG, 'The Ripple Effect: Guantanamo Bay in the United Kingdom's Courts' (2010) 1 *Pace International Law Review Online Companion* 9.

Nanopoulos, E, 'European Human Rights Law and the Normalisation of the "Closed Material Procedure": Limit or Source?' (2015) 78 *MLR* 913.

The Netherlands Institute for War Documentation (NIOD), *Srebrenica, een 'veilig' gebied: reconstructie, achtergronden, gevolgen en analyses van de val van een Safe Area* (Amsterdam, Boom, 2002).

Newton, M and May, L, *Proportionality in International Law* (Oxford, Oxford University Press, 2014) 241.

Ni Aolain, F, 'Gendered Harms and their Interface with International Criminal Law' (2014) 16 *International Feminist Journal of Politics* 4.

Niebergall, H, 'Overcoming Evidentiary Weaknesses in Reparation Claims Programmes—The Mass Claims Context' in Ferstman, C, et al (eds), *Reparations for Victims of Genocide, War Crimes and Crimes against Humanity: Systems in Place and Systems in the Making* (Leiden, Martinus Nijhoff, 2009).

Nollez-Goldbach, R and Saada, J (eds), *Justice Penal International face aux Crimes de Masse: Approches Critiques* (Paris, Editions Pedone, 2014).

Nollkaemper, A, 'Dual Attribution: Liability of the Netherlands for Conduct of Dutchbat in Srebrenica' (2011) 9 *Journal of International Criminal Justice* 5 1143.

Nystuen, G and Egeland, K, 'The Potential of the Arms Trade Treaty to Reduce Violations of International Humanitarian Law and Human Rights Law' in Bailliet, C and Larsen, K (eds), *Promoting Peace Through International Law* (Oxford, Oxford University Press, 2015).

O'Connell, ME, 'Unlawful Killing with Combat Drones: A Case Study of Pakistan 2004–2009' in Bronitt, S, Gani, M and Hufnagel, S, *Shooting to Kill: Socio-Legal Perspectives on the Use of Lethal Force* (Oxford, Hart Publishing, 2012).

O'Connor, S, 'Up in Arms: A Humanitarian Analysis of the Arms Trade Treaty and its New Zealand Application' (2013) 11 *New Zealand Yearbook of International Law* 73.

O' Rourke, C, Ni Aolain F and Swaine, A, 'Transforming Reparations for Conflict-Related Sexual Violence: Principles and Practice' (2015) 28 *Harvard Human Rights Journal* 97.

Ohlin, JD, 'Targeting Co-Belligerents', in Finkelstein, C, Ohlin, JD, and Altman, A, (eds), *Targeted Killings: Law and Morality in an Asymmetrical World* (Oxford, Oxford University Press, 2012).

Orakhelashvili, A, 'Human Rights Protection During Extra-Territorial Military Operations: Perspectives at International and English Law' in White, N and Henderson, C (eds), *Research Handbook on Conflict and Security Law* (Cheltenham, Edward Elgar, 2012).

Orend, B, *The Morality of War*, 2nd edn (Peterborough, Ont, Broadview Press, 2013).

Oswald, B and Winkler, T, 'Copenhagen Process Principles and Guidelines on the Handling of Detainees in International Military Operations' (2012) 16 *ASIL Insights* 39.

Palwankar, U, 'Applicability of International Humanitarian Law to United Nations Peace-Keeping Forces' (1993) 294 *International Review of the Red Cross* 227.

Parker, S, 'Breaking New Ground? The Arms Trade Treaty' in *Small Arms Survey 2014: Women and Guns* (Cambridge, Cambridge University Press 2014).

Parks, WH, 'Part IX of the ICRC 'Direct Participation in Hostilities' Study: No Mandate, No Expertise, and Legally Incorrect' (2010) 42 *NYU Journal of International Law and Policy* 770.

Paust, JJ, 'Human Rights on the Battlefield' (2016) 47 *George Washington International Law Review* 3.

Pejić, J, 'Procedural Principles and Safeguards for Internment/Administrative Detention in Armed Conflict and Other Situations of Violence' (2005) 87 *International Review of the Red Cross* 375.

——, 'The European Court of Human Rights' *Al-Jedda* Judgment: The Oversight of International Humanitarian Law' (2011) 93 *International Review of the Red Cross* 837.

——, 'The Protective Scope of Common Article 3: More than Meets the Eye' (2011) 93 *International Review of the Red Cross* 881.

——, 'Extraterritorial Targeting by Means of Armed Drones: Some Legal Implications' (2015) 96 *International Review of the Red Cross* 893.

Pendas, DO, *The Frankfurt Auschwitz Trial, 1963–1965: Genocide, History, and the Limits of the Law* (Cambridge, Cambridge University Press, 2006).

Pictet, J, *Commentary on the Geneva Conventions of 12 August 1949* (Geneva, ICRC, 1952–59).

Pilloud, C, et al (eds), *Commentary on the Additional Protocols of 8 June 1977 to the Geneva Conventions of 12 August 1949* (Geneva, ICRC, 1987).

Pitzul, J and Maguire, J, 'A Perspective on Canada's Code of Service Discipline' (2002) 52 *Air Force Law Review* 1.

Plesch, D, Sa'Couto, S and Lasco, C, 'The Relevance of the United Nations War Crimes Commission to the Prosecution of Sexual and Gender-Based Crimes Today' (2014) 25 *Criminal Law Forum* 349.

Poulantzas, NM, *The Right of Hot Pursuit in International Law*, 2nd edn (The Hague, Martinus Nijhoff Publishers, 2002).

Radin, S, 'Global Armed Conflict? The Threshold of Extraterritorial Non-International Armed Conflicts' (2013) 89 *International Law Studies* 696.

Ratner, S, *The Thin Justice of International Law* (Oxford, Oxford University Press, 2015).

Rawls, J, *Theory of Justice* (Cambridge, MA, Harvard University Press, 2009).

Rayfuse, R, 'The Draft Code of Crimes against the Peace and Security of Mankind: Eating Disorders at the International Law Commission' (1997) 8 *Criminal Law Forum* 43.

Ronen, Y, *Transition from Illegal Regimes under International Law* (Cambridge, Cambridge University Press, 2011).

Rowe, P (ed), *The Gulf War 1990–1991 in International and English Law* (London, Routledge, 2005).

——, *The Impact of Human Rights Law on Armed Forces* (Cambridge, Cambridge University Press, 2005).

Ryngaert, C, 'Srebrenica Continued. Dutch District Court Holds the Netherlands Liable for Cooperating with Bosnian Serbs' (2014) 61 *Netherlands International Law Review* 3.

Sadat, LN, 'The Interpretation of the Nuremberg Principles by the French Court of Cassation: From Touvier to Barbie and Back Again' (1994) 32 *Columbia Journal of Transnational Law* 296.

——, *The International Criminal Court and the Transformation of International Law: Justice for the New Millennium* (Leiden, Brill, 2002).

——, 'Crimes Against Humanity in the Modern Age' (2013) 107 *American Journal of International Law* 334.

——, *Forging a Convention for Crimes Against Humanity*, 2nd edn (Cambridge, Cambridge University Press, 2013).

——, 'The Nuremberg Trial, Seventy Years Later' (2016) 15 *Washington University Global Studies Law Review* 575.

——, 'Putting Peacetime First: Crimes Against Humanity and the Civilian Population Requirement' (2017) 31 *Emory International Law Review* 199.

Sandoz, Y, 'Unlawful Damage in Armed Conflicts and Redress under International Humanitarian Law' (1982) 22 *International Review of the Red Cross* 131.

——, Swinarski C and Zimmerman B (eds), *Commentary on the Additional Protocols of 8 June 1977 to the Geneva Conventions of 12 August 1949* (Geneva, ICRC, 1987).

Sands, P, 'The "Political" and the "Legal": Comments of Professor Tushnet's Paper' (2007) 3 *International Journal of Law in Context* 4.

——, 'Twin Peaks: The Hersch Lauterpacht Draft Nuremberg Speeches' (2013) 1 *Cambridge Journal of International and Comparative Law* 37.

——, *East West Street*: *On the Origins of 'Genocide' and 'Crimes Against Humanity'* (London, Weidenfield & Nicolson, 2016).

Sari, A, 'Jurisdiction and International Responsibility in Peace Support Operations: The Behrami and Saramati Cases' (2008) 8 *Human Rights Law Review* 1, 165.

Sassòli, M, 'Mise en oeuvre du droit international humanitaire et du droit international des droits de l'hommes: une comparaison' [1987] *Annuaire suisse de droit international* 59.

——, 'La "guerre contre le terrorisme", le droit international humanitarie et le statut de prisonnier de guerre' (2001) 39 *Annuaire canadien de droit international* 211.

——, 'Transnational Armed Groups and International Humanitarian Law' (2006) 6 *Harvard Program on Humanitarian Policy and Conflict Research* 1.

——, and Olson, LM, 'The Relationship Between International Humanitarian and Human Rights Law where it Matters: Admissible Killing and Internment of Fighters in Non-International Armed Conflicts' (2008) 90 *International Review of the Red Cross* 871.

——, Bouvier, AA and Quintin, A (eds), *How Does Law Protect in War?*, 3rd edn (Geneva, ICRC, 2011).

Savage, C, *Power Wars*: *Inside Obama's Post-9/11 Presidency* (New York, Little Brown and Company, 2015).

Schabas, WA, *Unimaginable Atrocities*: *Justice, Politics and Rights at the War Crimes Tribunals* (Oxford, Oxford University Press, 2012).

——, *An Introduction to the International Criminal Court* (Cambridge, Cambridge University Press, 2014).

Scharf, M, 'Accelerate Formation of Customary International Law' (2014) 20 *ILSA Journal of International & Comparative Law* 305.

Scheffer, D, 'Closing the Impunity Gap in US Law' (2009) 8 *Northwest University Journal of International Human Rights* 30.

Schmitt, MN, Garraway, C and Dinstein, Y (eds), *The San Remo Manual on the Law of Non-International Armed Conflict* (San Remo, 2006).

Schmitt, MN, 'Asymmetrical Warfare and International Humanitarian Law' (2008) 62 *Air Force Law Review* 1.

——, 'Deconstructing Direct Participation in Hostilities: The Constitutive Elements' (2010) 49 *NYU Journal of International Law and Policy* 697.

——, 'Investigating Violations of International Law in Armed Conflict' (2010) 2 *Harvard National Security Journal*.

——, 'Extraterritorial Lethal Targeting: Deconstructing the Logic of International Law' (2013) 52 *Columbia Journal of Transnational Law* 77.

——, *The Tallinn Manual on the International Law Applicable to Cyber Warfare* (New York, Cambridge University Press, 2013).

—— and Merriam, J, 'The Tyranny of Context: Israeli Targeting Practices in Legal Perspectives' (2015) 37 *Pennsylvania Journal of International Law* 53.

Schwager, E and Bank, R, 'Is There a Substantive Right to Compensation for Individual Victims of Armed Conflicts Against a State under International Law?' (2006) 49 *German Year Book of International Law* 367.

Sfard, M, 'The Price of Internal Legal Opposition to Human Rights Abuses' (2009) 1 *Journal of Human Rights Practice* 1.

Shamir, R, 'Landmark Cases and the Reproduction of Legitimacy: The Case of Israel's High Court of Justice' (1990) 24 *Law & Society Review* 3.

Shane, S, *Objective Troy* (New York, Tim Duggan Books, 2015).

Shany, Y, 'A Human Rights Perspective to Battlefield Detention: Time to Reconsider Indefinite Detention' (2017) 93 *International Law Studies* 102.

——, 'The Future of US Detention under International Law: Workshop Report' (2017) 93 *International Law Studies* 272.

Shapiro, M, *Courts: A Comparative and Political Analysis* (Chicago, University of Chicago Press, 1981).

Shaw, MN, *International Law*, 6th edn (Cambridge, Cambridge University Press, 2008).

Singer, P, 'The Five Deadly Flaws of Talking About Emerging Military Technologies and the Need for New Approaches to Law, Ethics, and War' in Bergen, PL and Rothenberg, D (eds), *Drone Wars* (Cambridge, Cambridge University Press, 2015).

Sivakumaran, S, 'Sexual Violence Against Men in Armed Conflict' (2007) 18 *European Journal of International Law* 2.

——, *The Law of Non-International Armed Conflicts*, 1st edn (Oxford, Oxford University Press, 2012).

Smith, R, *The Utility of Force: The Art of War in the Modern World* (New York, Alfred & Knops, 2007).

Solis, G, *The Law of Armed Conflict: International Humanitarian Law in War*, 2nd edn (Cambridge, Cambridge University Press, 2016).

Spaaji, R, 'The Enigma of Lone Wolf Terrorism: An Assessment' (2010) 33 *Studies in Conflict and Terrorism* 9.

Stavrianakis, A, 'Legitimising Liberal Militarism: Politics, Law and War in the Arms Trade Treaty' (2016) 37 *Third World Quarterly* 840.

Stein, Y, 'By Any Name Illegal and Immoral' (2003) 17 *Ethics & International Affairs* 127.

Stewart, J, 'Towards a Single Definition of Armed Conflict in International Humanitarian Law: A Critique of Internationalized Armed Conflict' (2003) 85 *International Review of the Red Cross* 850.

Stigall, DE, 'An Unnecessary Convenience: the Assertion of the Uniform Code of Military Justice ("UCMJ") over Civilians and the Implications of International Human Rights Law' (2009) 17 *Cardozo Journal of International and Comparative Law* 59.

Suter, K, 'An Enquiry into the Meaning of the Phrase "Human Rights in Armed Conflicts"' (1976) 15 *Revue de Droit Penal Militaire et de Droit de la Guerre* 393.

Szpak, A, 'A Change of the US Position Regarding the Extraterritorial Prohibition of Torture—Is it a Breakthrough?' (2015) 17 *International Community Law Review* 496.

Szurek, S, 'Historique: La Formation du droit international pénal' in Ascensio, H, Decaux, E and Pellet, A (eds), *Droit International Pénal*, 2nd edn (Paris, Editions Pedone, 2012).

Teitel, RG, 'Humanity's Law: Rule of Law for the New Global Politics' (2001) 35 *Cornell International Law Journal* 2.

Toharia, JJ, 'Judges' in Wright, JD (ed), *International Encyclopedia of the Social & Behavioral Sciences*, 2nd edn (Amsterdam, Elsevier, 2015).

Tomuschat, C, 'Individual Reparation Claims in Instances of Grave Human Rights Violations: The Position under General International Law' in Randelzhofer, A and Tomuschat, C (eds), *State Responsibility and the Individual—Reparation in Instances of Grave Violations of Human Rights* (The Hague, Kluwer, 1999).

——, 'Reparation for Victims of Grave Human Rights Violations' (2002) 10 *Tulane Journal of International and Comparative Law* 157.

Tsagourias, N, 'The Responsibility of International Organisations for Military Missions' in Odello, M and Piotrowisz, R (eds), *International Military Missions and International Law* (Leiden, Martinus Nijhoff Publishers, 2011).

Tzanakopoulos, A, 'Judicial Dialogue as a Means of Interpretation' in Aust, HP and Nolte, G (eds), *The Interpretation of International Law by Domestic Courts*: *Uniformity, Diversity, Convergence* (Oxford, Oxford University Press, 2016).

Tzevelekos, VP, 'Reconstructing the Effective Control Criterion in Extraterritorial Human Rights Breaches: Direct attribution of Wrongfulness, Due Diligence, and Concurrent Responsibility' (2014) 36 *Michigan Journal of International Law* 129.

Van Schaack, B, 'The United States' Position on the Extraterritorial Application of Human Rights Obligations: Now Is the Time for Change' (2014) 90 *Naval War College International Law Studies* 20.

Vité, S, *Les procédures d'établissement des faits dans la mise en oeuvre du droit international humanitaire* (Brussels, Bruylant, 1999).

——, 'Typology of Armed Conflicts in International Humanitarian Law: Legal Concepts and Actual Situations' (2009) 91 *International Review of the Red Cross* 873.

Watkin, K, 'Opportunity Lost: Organized Armed Groups and the ICRC "Direct Participation in Hostilities" Interpretive Guidance' (2010) 42 *New York University Journal of International Law and Politics* 3.

Weill, S, 'Building Respect for IHL through National Courts' (2014) 96 *International Review of the Red Cross* 895/896.

——, *The Role of National Courts in Applying International Humanitarian Law* (Oxford, Oxford University Press, 2014).

——, 'Reducing the Security Gap through National Courts: Targeted Killings as a Case Study' (2016) 21 *Journal of Conflict and Security Law* 1.

Wilmshurst, E (ed), *International Law and the Classification of Conflicts* (Oxford, Oxford University Press, 2012).

Whittle, R, *Predator: The Secret Origins of the Drone Revolution*, 1st edn (New York, Henry Holt, 2014).

Wiesel, E, *Night* (London, Penguin Books, 2006).

Wilmshurst, E (ed), *International Law and the Classification of Conflicts* (Oxford, Oxford University Press, 2012).

Wittmann, R, *Beyond Justice: The Auschwitz Trial* (Cambridge, MA, Harvard University Press, 2005).

Wolfrum, R and Fleck, D, 'Enforcement of International Humanitarian Law' in Fleck, D (ed), *The Handbook of International Humanitarian Law*, 2nd edn (Oxford, Oxford University Press, 2008).

Wong, S, 'Investigating Civilian Casualties in Armed Conflict: Comparing US Military Investigations with Alternatives under International Humanitarian and Human Rights Law' (2015) 64 *Naval Law Review* 111.

Yates, J and Whitford, A, 'Presidential Power and the US Supreme Court' (1998) 51 *Political Research Quarterly* 2.

Zegveld, L, 'Remedies for Victims of Violations of International Humanitarian Law' (2003) 85 *International Review of the Red Cross* 497.

Ziegler, A and Wehrenberg, S, 'Domestic Implementation' in Clapham, A, Gaeta, P and Sassòli, M (eds), *The 1949 Geneva Conventions: A Commentary* (Geneva/Oxford, Oxford University Press, 2015).

Zongwe, DP, 'The New Sexual Violence Legislation in the Congo: Dressing Indelible Scars on Human Dignity' (2012) 55 *African Studies Review* 2.

Index

Abbreviations used in the index additional to those listed in the table on p xix